The Perennial Philosophy

Series

About this Book

"A highly accurate and encyclopedic compendium of the history of western encounters with eastern religious traditions. One finds herein not just the names of innumerable significant individuals, but a review of their views and their significance. It will long remain a standard reference work."

—**Rama Coomaraswamy**, author of *The Destruction of the Christian Tradition* and *The Invocation of the Name of Jesus: As Practised in the Western Church*

"*Journeys East* is one of the very few intellectual histories of our age, if we take the intellect to be more than the mind or reason. *Journeys East* is an account of the actual philosophers of the recent past rather than of the poseurs and pretenders to that title who in the same breath call themselves empiricists or post-modern."

—**Roger Sworder**, La Trobe University, Bendigo, author of *Mining, Metallurgy, and the Meaning of Life* and *Homer on Immortality: The Journey of Odysseus as a Path to Perfection*

"*Journeys East* is a very comprehensive exposition of the interaction and influence between West and East from Antiquity to the present day: a very valuable book for the reader who desires to be informed of these encounters from the perspective of the *Sophia Perennis*, and a very useful and precious 'textbook' for the teacher who needs to have an historical as well as a logical way of organizing so many complex forms of 'Orientalism.'"

—**Jean-Pierre Lafouge**, Marquette University

World Wisdom
The Library of Perennial Philosophy

The Library of Perennial Philosophy is dedicated to the exposition of the timeless Truth underlying the diverse religions. This Truth, often referred to as the *Sophia Perennis*—or Perennial Wisdom—finds its expression in the revealed Scriptures as well as the writings of the great sages and the artistic creations of the traditional worlds.

The Perennial Philosophy provides the intellectual principles capable of explaining both the formal contradictions and the transcendent unity of the great religions.

Ranging from the writings of the great sages of the past, to the perennialist authors of our time, each series of our Library has a different focus. As a whole, they express the inner unanimity, transforming radiance, and irreplaceable values of the great spiritual traditions.

Journeys East: 20th Century Western Encounters with Eastern Religious Traditions appears as one of our selections in the Perennial Philosophy series.

The Perennial Philosophy Series

In the beginning of the Twentieth Century, a school of thought arose which has focused on the enunciation and explanation of the Perennial Philosophy. Deeply rooted in the sense of the sacred, the writings of its leading exponents establish an indispensable foundation for understanding the timeless Truth and spiritual practices which live in the heart of all religions. Some of these titles are companion volumes to the Treasures of the World's Religions series, which allows a comparison of the writings of the great sages of the past with the perennialist authors of our time.

JOURNEYS EAST

20th Century Western Encounters with Eastern Religious Traditions

by

Harry Oldmeadow

Foreword by
Huston Smith

Journeys East:
20th Century Western Encounters with Eastern Religious Traditions
© 2004 World Wisdom, Inc.

Library of Congress Cataloging-in-Publication Data

Oldmeadow, Harry, 1947-
Journeys East : 20th century Western encounters with Eastern religious traditions /
by Harry Oldmeadow ; foreword by Huston Smith.
   p. cm. – (The library of perennial philosophy)
Includes bibliographical references and index.
ISBN 0-941532-57-7 (pbk. : alk. paper)
1. Religions–Relations. 2. Spirituality–Developed countries–History–20th century. 3.
   Spirituality–Asia–History–20th century. 4. Asia–Religion. 5. East and West. I.
   Title. II. Series.
BL410.O43 2004
201'.5'0904–dc22

                                                                    2004006066

Printed on acid-free paper in Canada.

For information address World Wisdom, Inc.
P.O. Box 2682, Bloomington, Indiana 47402-2682

... the rediscovery of religion is the great intellectual, moral and spiritual adventure of our time.

Bede Griffiths

A mere sensation or a new thrill is of no use to the European mind. We must rather learn to earn in order to possess. What the East has to give us should be merely a help to us in a work which we still have to do. What good is the wisdom of the Upanishads to us, and the insights of Chinese yoga, if we abandon our own foundations like outworn mistakes, to settle thievishly on foreign shores like homeless pirates?

Carl Jung

Poets of the imagination write of the soul, of intellectual beauty, of the living spirit of the world. What does such work communicate to readers who do not believe in the soul, in the spirit of life, or in anything ... which can be called "the beautiful"?

Kathleen Raine

... if you ever really enter this other world ... you may never again be contented with what you think of as "progress" and "civilization" ...

Ananda K. Coomaraswamy

CONTENTS

III. Eastern Influences on Western Thought

Jacobs on Western Psychotherapy and Hindu *Sadhana*—Humanistic and Transpersonal Psychology: Ken Wilber and others—Mystical Experience, Meditation and Biofeedback **C. The Lessons of the East**

IV. Notes on Inter-religious Re-visionings

List of Illustrations

Foreword

Early in the 20th century the great French metaphysician René Guénon argued that the modern West has affirmed the superiority of action over knowledge, whereas the East reversed these modalities. At first glance this may seem too schematic a way of characterizing the halves of the world, but it acquires force when we remember that knowledge in the traditional East amounted to what the West calls wisdom, for it focused on spiritual realities or first principles. Unlike Western philosophy—which since the Renaissance has been primarily empirical and increasingly confined to the academy—the strongest philosophies in the East argue that the goal of human life is to achieve liberation.

The 20th century from which we have recently emerged was the most violent in human history, and in every decade hope and despair bounced off each other like matter and antimatter. Many historical currents went into the making of that century, but the one that has received least attention is precisely the one this book takes up. The world westernized in science, technology, economics, and politics, but the answering wave from Asia has been largely overlooked because it is less tangible. Asia penetrated the West's *mind*, in part actively as philosophers like Vivekananda and Daisetz Suzuki carried Vedanta and Buddhism to the West; but more importantly by simply being available for venturesome minds to explore (such as those of the New England Transcendentalists, notably Emerson, who were a century ahead of their times).

The thoroughness of the research on which the book in hand builds does not obscure the fact that it is really a romance, the *story* of how the Western mind expanded in the 20th century to include Asian wisdom. Its author insures this narrative aspect of the book by keeping its impeccable scholarship in its foundations, so to speak. Everyone knows that worldviews differ, but Harry Oldmeadow calls attention to two commonalities they share. The first of these is the understanding of the physical universe which the proofs of modern science now force everyone to accept; and the second is the metaphysical unity that runs through them all like a golden thread. There is real artistry in the way Oldmeadow describes that thread.

One more virtue should be mentioned. The thoroughness with which the author covers his subject required that his book be long, but general readers should not jump to the conclusion that it is intended exclusively for libraries. To be sure, no major library can now be without it, but its style places it within easy reach of the interested public.

Harry Oldmeadow will be remembered with gratitude for having poured his life into producing this profound and fascinating book that is sure to occupy a durable place in the library of the world's cultural history.

HUSTON SMITH

Preface

Some years ago the splenetic novelist V.S. Naipal, after visiting one of the countries to which he belonged by birth, remarked, "India has been a shock for me, because—you know, you think of India as a very old and very civilized land. One took this idea of an antique civilization for granted and thought that it contained the seed of growth in this century. [But] India has nothing to contribute to the world, is contributing nothing."[1] Consider, too, the reaction of another *litterateur* to India and Japan, Arthur Koestler, who reported his finding in *The Lotus and the Robot* (1960), that both countries were "spiritually sicker, more estranged from a living faith than the West."[2] The present study is motivated by the altogether different conviction that the Eastern religious traditions, even today and despite the ravages of modernization, are custodians of a wisdom of which the West stands in the most urgent need. An attendant notion is that for many in the West the lessons of the East might be mediated and illuminated by the existential engagements of a wide variety of European individuals who have immersed themselves in the spiritual life of the East. Our inquiry focuses on those whose involvements were informed by the sense that, in one way or another, there were intellectual, cultural and spiritual treasures to be discovered in the East.

As nearly everybody knows, there are far too many books in the contemporary world. Why add yet another? One might adduce all manner of justifications but this book's original impetus came from a sense that the West's modern encounter with the East, particularly in the religious domain, was one of the most momentous events of our time and that, despite the many distinguished studies in the field, there was a certain gap which might usefully be filled. This study is less interested in the textual construction of the Orient—a subject which has attracted the most intensive attention in recent years—than in the personal experiences of those individuals who ventured Eastwards to gain immediate experience of the religious cultures of Asia. It directs itself to the 20th century which has hitherto attracted less sustained attention than earlier periods. To make a vast and somewhat unwieldy subject more manageable it is more or less limited to Western encounters with the religious heritage of the five countries which have, at various times, dominated the European imagination and which are also the homelands of the most significant religious traditions of the East: India, Sri Lanka, Tibet, China and Japan. Many of the individuals discussed are already widely known in both the East and the West whilst others are comparatively obscure. I have limited my commentary on those figures who have already generated a significant

---

1 V.S. Naipal quoted in J. Paine, *Father India*, 158.
2 A. Koestler, *The Lotus and the Robot*, 276.

secondary literature (Carl Jung, Thomas Merton and Alan Watts are examples) and have devoted more extended attention to those whose significance has been obscured or neglected (Sister Nivedita, Henri Le Saux and Marco Pallis might represent this group).

Although the Islamic civilizations of the Middle East are often thought of as "oriental" they do *not* come within the compass of this work. There are several reasons for this: Islam properly belongs to the Abrahamic family of Occidental monotheisms rather than to the traditions of the East; secondly, to include the Western encounter with Islam would make an already formidable subject quite unmanageable; thirdly, there already exists a very considerable literature on this fascinating subject.

It might be as well explicitly to disavow certain intentions at the outset. This is not a history of what Edward Said calls the "corporate institution" of orientalism. It is neither a conspectus nor an analysis of Western scholarship though many notable scholars will appear in these pages. Nor is it, at least in the first place, a study of Eastern religious doctrines and practices but rather an exploration of their impact on those individual European figures on whom the book focuses. Although it is impossible to avoid some commentary on massively influential figures such as Swami Vivekananda, Mohandas Gandhi, D.T. Suzuki or the present Dalai Lama, this work is not a study of Eastern gurus and religious leaders although they will, inevitably, appear frequently in the narrative. The book does not in any way address the reception of Western ideas in the East.

The remarks by Naipal and Koestler remind us of that company of European intellectuals, writers and seekers who traveled to the East in search of spiritual and intellectual nutriments but who returned with their hunger unassuaged or, worse, came to the view that the vaunted spiritual treasures of the Orient were a mirage or a fraud perpetrated by tricksters who preyed on Western gullibilities. Shortly after his return from Japan Koestler published an excoriating attack on D.T. Suzuki and his work, accusing Zen in general and Suzuki in particular of being woolly-minded, irrational, amoral, hypocritical and crypto-fascistic, and dismissing Zen as "at best an existentialist hoax, at worst a web of solemn absurdities"[3] and "one of the sick jokes, slightly gangrened, which are always fashionable in ages of anxiety."[4]

The remarks of Naipal and Koestler stand as salutary reminders that not all Western encounters with Eastern spirituality have been rewarded with edifying results. Nor was everyone impressed by those Westerners who became self-styled champions of Eastern spirituality. William Burroughs, for instance, wrote in a letter to Jack Kerouac,

3 A. Koestler, *The Lotus and the Robot*, 233.
4 Passages from Arthur Koestler, "Neither Lotus nor Robot," (*Encounter*, 1960) quoted in L. Fader, "Arthur Koestler's Critique of D.T. Suzuki's Interpretation of Zen," 54 & 56.

I have seen nothing from those California Vedantists but a lot of horse shit, and I denounce them without cavil, as a pack of pathetic frauds. Convinced of their own line to be sure, thereby adding self-deception to their other failings.[5]

We shall pay no more than cursory attention to those Western intellectuals and writers who shared Koestler's view that "to look to Asia for mystic enlightenment and spiritual guidance has become as much of an anachronism as to think of America as the Wild West."[6] Nor need we tarry over claims as absurd as James Hillman's that the meditational practices central to Eastern religions might engender terrorism.[7] Some might, I suppose, take comfort from Carl Jung's observation that "... all mediocre minds in contact with a foreign culture either perish in the blind attempt to deracinate themselves or else they indulge in an uncomprehending and presumptuous passion for criticism."[8] However, it must always be remembered that the European encounter with Eastern religious traditions has for centuries been marked by alternating currents of admiration and repulsion, respect and contempt, by deep ambivalence and contradictory impulses. The flurry of recent studies sparked by Edward Said's *Orientalism* (1978) has excavated some of the evidence of these deep-seated and often obscure tensions.

*

The relentless drive in the Western academic world towards increasing disciplinary specialization has had many regrettable results, one of which is that various intellectual endeavors which should be complementary instead become increasingly hermetic and often quite opaque to non-specialists. This work is deliberately inter-disciplinary and makes every effort to eschew highly specialized disciplinary jargon. In intention and method it perhaps sits most comfortably somewhere between the history of ideas and comparative religion (or, in American terminology, the history of religions). Whilst it covers many of the most important developments of the 20th century it is not a systematic and comprehensive history, nor a work with any sociological pretensions. It is addressed, primarily, to the general reader with an intelligent and sympathetic interest in the West's encounter with the East though I will be pleased if specialist scholars also find something of interest in fields of inquiry contiguous to their own.

The study is structured in four parts. Part I deals with the 19th century background to our subject and takes some account of the fierce debates

---

5 Burroughs to Kerouac, August 18th, 1954, in *The Letters of William S. Burroughs 1945-1959*, 226.

6 A. Koestler, *The Lotus and the Robot*, 276.

7 J. Hillman, *A Blue Fire*, ed. T. Moore, 187.

8 C.G. Jung, "Richard Wilhelm: In Memoriam," *Collected Works* 15, 54.

which have raged around the general subject of "Orientalism" (itself a some-what problematic term). More particularly, it offers some reflections on Edward Said's widely celebrated thesis and suggests some alternative perspectives. Part II, comprising the bulk of the study, examines Western engagements with the East throughout the last century, using a variety of schema to organize the material. Part III surveys several overlapping arenas of Western thought and practice in which Eastern influences have been most creatively assimilated—psychology, philosophy, science, and politics. Part IV essays an inter-religious exegesis of two themes of urgent importance in the contemporary world: the emergence of a cross-cultural religious understanding of the natural order and the ecological crisis, and the metaphysical basis for both the formal diversity and the essential unity of the religious traditions of both East and West.

Many works were important in the genesis of the present study, either by way of provocation or inspiration. Among the studies to which I am most heavily indebted are J.J. Clarke's *Oriental Enlightenment*, Rick Fields' *How the Swans Came to the Lake*, Wilhelm Halbfass' *India and Europe*, and Andrew Rawlinson's *The Book of Enlightened Masters*, all works of considerable distinction. It is a pleasure to acknowledge my debt to these and many other works by scholars such as Carl Jackson and Graham Parkes who have been tilling this field for many years. It goes without saying that there are also those landmark works of scholarship, by authors such as Mircea Eliade, Heinrich Zimmer and Giuseppe Tucci, which no one venturing into the field of East-West inter-religious interactions can afford to ignore. I should also mention the work of traditionalist writers such as René Guénon, Ananda Coomaraswamy and Frithjof Schuon who have had a profound impact on my own intellectual and spiritual journey and who have shaped the outlook which informs the present study.

Finally, at the risk of sounding sentimental, I might add that this work has also been a labor of love and something of a tribute to the many men and women, both European and Asian, who have dedicated their lives to overcoming the barriers of incomprehension and suspicion which have often marked relations between the West and the East. My admiration for many of the figures in these pages will be plain enough. In the present climate, where postmodernist theorists are indulging in the wholesale slaughter of the ancestors and where the hermeneutics of suspicion are the order of the day, I hope that this work might help us to recognize the many noble inter-religious endeavors towards mutual understanding and the development of a world community which cherishes our differences as well as affirming our common humanity.

A Note on Terminology, Quotation and Documentation

- Sanskrit and other Eastern terms have been Anglicized and their spelling made uniform throughout, even within quotations. Apart from those which have by now found a home in English (examples: yoga, Vedanta), such terms are italicized but not accented (*maya*). The titles of Scriptures and other texts are invariably italicized.

- Dates following titles of books in the main body of the text refer to the first publication; dates in footnotes and in the list of Sources refer to the edition consulted in my research.

- Only author's name and titles (sometimes abbreviated) are cited in footnotes: full bibliographical details are provided in the listed Sources.

- Parts of this book have previously appeared in *Sacred Web* (Vancouver), *Esoterica* (electronic journal), *Beyond the Divide* (Bendigo), *The Animist* (electronic journal), the 1995 edition of René Guénon's *The Reign of Quantity* (Ghent: Sophia Perennis et Universalis), *Mircea Eliade and Carl Jung: "Priests without Surplices"?* (Bendigo: La Trobe University, 1995), *Traditionalism: Religion in the light of the Perennial Philosophy* (Colombo: Sri Lanka Institute of Traditional Studies, 2000), and *Seeing God Everywhere*, ed. Barry McDonald (Bloomington: World Wisdom, 2003). I am grateful to the respective editors and publishers for permission to reproduce this material.

- The epigraphs preceding the Contents page come from the following sources:

  Bede Griffiths, *The Golden String*, 13-14.
  Carl Jung, "Richard Wilhelm: In Memoriam," quoted in G. Wehr, *Jung: A Biography*, 462.
  Kathleen Raine, quoted in Huston Smith, *Beyond the Post-Modern Mind*, 82.
  Ananda K. Coomaraswamy, "Philosophy of Mediaeval and Oriental Art" in *Selected Papers 1*, 46-47.

1

Introduction
and
Background

1.

The Debate about "Orientalism"

The West's Encounter with the East since Antiquity—What do we mean by "Orientalism"?—Edward Said and the Critics of Orientalism—Alternative Perspectives—The Traditionalist Outlook

---

The value, efficacy, strength, apparent veracity of a written statement about the Orient therefore relies very little, and cannot instrumentally depend, on the Orient as such. On the contrary, the written statement is a presence to the reader by virtue of its having excluded, displaced, made supererogatory any such real thing as "the Orient" ... that Orientalism makes sense at all depends more on the West than on the Orient, and this sense is directly indebted to various Western techniques of representation. (Edward Said)[1]

Western culture will be in danger of a decline into a sterilizing provincialism if it despises or neglects the dialogue with other cultures ... the West is forced (one might also say: condemned) to this encounter and confrontation with the cultural value of "the others" ... One day the West will have to know and to understand the existential situations and the cultural universes of the non-Western peoples; moreover, the West will come to value them as integral with the history of the human spirit and will no longer regard them as immature episodes or as aberrations from an exemplary History of man—a History conceived, of course, only as that of Western man. (Mircea Eliade)[2]

The West's Encounter with the East since Antiquity

In the early 19th century Hegel remarked that "Without being known too well, [India] has existed for millennia in the imagination of the Europeans as a wonderland. Its fame, which it has always had with regard to its treasures, both its natural ones, and, in particular, its wisdom, has lured men there."[3] Eusebius relates the time-honored anecdote that Socrates himself was visited in Athens by an Indian who asked him about the nature of his philosophizing. When Socrates responded that he was studying the problems of human life, his interlocutor laughed and explained that it was impossible to understand human matters without considering the divine.[4] India is mentioned a

---

1   E. Said, *Orientalism*, 22.
2   M. Eliade, *Myths, Dreams and Mysteries*, 8-9.
3   Hegel quoted in W. Halbfass, *India and Europe*, 2.
4   The anecdote apparently goes back to the Aristotelian Aristoxenes. W. Halbfass, *India and Europe*, 8.

good deal in the classical literature from Herodotus onwards and we know that ancient philosophers and theologians such as Pythagoras, Diogenes, Plotinus and Clement took a close interest in the learning of their Eastern counterparts. Alexander the Great's entourage in his Eastern campaigns included philosophers, historians and writers wishing to learn more about the intellectual and spiritual life of the Eastern barbarians, and we are told that Alexander himself conversed with the gymnosophists, as the Greeks called the naked sages of India.[5]

The Enlightenment *philosophes* had been much attracted to the Chinese civilization. Many aspects of Chinese thought and culture had become well known in Western Europe, largely through the Jesuit missionaries. Writers like Voltaire, Diderot, Helvetius, Leibnitz and David Hume extolled the virtues of many aspects of Chinese civilization, particularly Confucianism which they understood as a rationally-based and humanistic system of social ethics. So widespread was the interest in and enthusiasm for things Chinese that we might speak of a wave of Sinophilia, if not Sinomania, flowing over Western Europe, particularly France, in the first half of the 18th century. However, for reasons which cannot be canvassed here, late in the century the European gaze shifted from China to India.

The beginnings of a serious and informed intellectual interest in the philosophic and religious thought of India can be tied to several specific events in the late 18th century: the founding in the 1780s of the Asiatic Society of Bengal by the remarkable William "Oriental" Jones (1736-1794), lawyer, linguist, poet, scholar, pioneering translator of Hafiz, Rumi, Attar and Kalidasa, and tireless propagandist for Oriental literature; the "discovery" of Sanskrit and the beginnings of serious comparative studies in the over-lapping fields of religion, philosophy and mythology in the journal *Asiatic Researches*; the publication in 1785 of Charles Wilkins' first English translation of the *Bhagavad Gita*, a book "which was to exercise enormous influence on the mind of Europe and America,"[6] followed in 1801 by Anquetil-Duperron's translation from the Persian into Latin of a number of *Upanishads* as *Oupnek'hat*;[7] and the rapid emergence of the first generation of Indologists. The leading lights included not only Jones and Wilkins but also Thomas Henry Colebrook, judge in Calcutta and eminent Sanskritist, and Brian Hodgson, a minor functionary attached to the court of Nepal who

5   W. Halbfass, *India and Europe*, 12. See also Elizabeth Isichei, "Passages to India," 66-67.

6   E. Sharpe, *The Universal Gita*, 10. Warren Hastings, in his Foreword to Wilkins' translation of the *Gita*, hoped that this text would convince his compatriots of the "real character" of the Indian people: "It is not very long since the inhabitants of India were considered by many, as creatures scarce elevated above the degree of savage life; nor, I fear, is that prejudice yet wholly eradicated, though surely abated. Every instance which brings their real character home to observation will impress us with a more generous sense of feeling for their natural rights and teach us to estimate them by the measure of their own"; quoted in R. King, *Orientalism and Religion*, 154.

7   The remarkable story of the translation is told by Stephen Cross in "*Ex Oriente Lux*: How the Upanishads came to Europe." See also W. Halbfass, *India and Europe*, 64-68.

amassed a collection of rare Sanskrit manuscripts.[8] The path-breaking work of such amateur scholars, most of whom pursued legal, administrative and political careers, paved the way for the great orientalist scholars of the 19th century—Eugène Burnouf, Max Müller, Paul Deussen—and for the explosion of interest in Eastern philosophy and metaphysics amongst the German Romantics and the American Transcendentalists. Jones and his collaborators thus inaugurated a tradition of scholarship which has been carried on into our own times.[9]

Sarvepalli Radhakrishnan, the eminent Indian philosopher and first President of India, has written of the West's attraction to "the glamour of the exotic," and has remarked that "The East has ever been a romantic puzzle to the West, the home of adventures like those of the Arabian Nights, the abode of magic, the land of heart's desire ..."[10] Michel Le Bris has characterized the East as it exists in the European imagination as

> That Elsewhere, that yearned for realm where it was supposed that a man might get rid of the burden of self, that land outside time and space, thought of as being at once a place of wandering and a place of homecoming.[11]

But, of course, this is only one facet of a very complex phenomenon. Since the time of the classical historians and playwrights the East has also been depicted not only as exotic, mysterious and alluring but as malignant, dark, threatening. Stephen Batchelor has put the matter in psychological terms:

> In the European imagination Asia came to stand for something both distant and unknown yet also to be feared. As the colonizing powers came to identify themselves with order, reason and power, so the colonized East became perceived as chaotic, irrational and weak. In psychological terms, the East became a cipher for the Western unconscious, the repository of all that is dark, unacknowledged, feminine, sensual, repressed and liable to eruption.[12]

Then too, there is another persistent strain in European attitudes, one which we can mark in the famous and frankly contemptuous remarks by one of the most pompous windbags of the 19th century, the one-time colonial administrator and historian, Thomas Babbington Macaulay. His characterization of Indians as "lesser breeds without the law" has passed into idiomatic currency, even if many are unaware of the provenance of that deeply offensive

---

8 On Jones and the Royal Asiatic Society see R. Fields, *How the Swans Came to the Lake*, Ch 3; R. Schwab, *The Oriental Renaissance*, 33-34; W. Halbfass, *India and Europe*, 62-64.

9 The story of the beginnings of this kind of scholarship with respect to Tibet, China and Japan will be touched on at various points in our narrative, and we will later meet many 20th century heirs of this tradition.

10 S. Radhakrishnan, *Eastern Religions and Western Thought*, 251.

11 Quoted in J.J. Clarke, *Oriental Enlightenment*, 19.

12 S. Batchelor, *The Awakening of the West*, 234.

phrase. Perhaps less well-known, but no less characteristic, was his dismissal of Hinduism[13] as a web of "monstrous superstitions" and of the ancient Sanskrit Scriptures as "less valuable than what may be found in the most paltry abridgments used at preparatory schools in England." He scorned Indian

> medical doctrines which would disgrace an English farrier—astronomy which would move laughter in the girls at an English boarding-school—history, abounding with kings thirty feet long, and reigns thirty thousand years long—and geography made up of seas of treacle and seas of butter. [14]

The history of intellectual and cultural contact between West and East is convoluted, full of ambiguities, enigmas and contradictions. There has been no shortage of attempts to theorize the Western fascination with the East. Most influential of all such theorizations in recent years has been Edward Said's widely-celebrated *Orientalism* in which he argued that the Orient was a "system of ideological fictions" whose purpose was, and is, to legitimize Western cultural and political superiority; furthermore, the Western understanding of the East has grown out of "a relationship of power, of domination, of varying degrees of complex hegemony."[15] Said's argument, it must be said, is addressed primarily to the European encounter with Islam and with the Middle East, although Said himself extends the case to the Orient in general. I believe that a close study of Western engagements in Eastern religion and philosophy in particular exposes certain fundamental weaknesses in Said's analysis, which is not to deny the force and cogency of Said's argument within the Middle Eastern domain with which he is principally concerned. Since Said's landmark work there has been a proliferation of scholars bringing a Foucaldian conceptual apparatus and the intellectual protocols of "post-colonial studies" to an analysis of the loosely defined phenomenon of Orientalism.

What do we mean by "Orientalism"?
In recent times the term "orientalism" has become highly problematic, now carrying several meanings which do not sit together altogether comfortably. Five distinct senses of the word have crystallized over the last two centuries: the *scholarly study* of the languages and texts of the Orient (initially conceived as the Middle East but later encompassing all of Asia); a late 18th-century *policy* of the East India Company favoring the preservation of Indian languages,

---

13 Because of the peculiarities of the Indian tradition the term "Hinduism"—which, in its Western sense, is of 19th century provenance—is even more problematic than its apparent counterparts such as "Buddhism," "Christianity" and the like. See R. King, *Orientalism and Religion*, 100ff. and 143-144. Nonetheless, it is used throughout this work to signify the manifold and profuse doctrines, forms and practices which are encompassed by the tradition issuing from the *Vedas*. For a defense of the term see W. Halbfass, *India and Europe*, 332-3, and S. Radhakrishnan, *The Hindu View of Life*, 13.

14 Macaulay quoted in J.J. Clarke, *Oriental Enlightenment*, 73, and in E. Sharpe, *Universal Gita*, 17.

15 E. Said, *Orientalism*, 321 & 5.

laws and customs; the adoption of an *artistic style and subject matter* associated with East; a *discourse* of power fashioned in the West and deeply implicated in European imperialism; a *corporate institution* harnessed to the maintenance of the ideological and political hegemony of Europe throughout Asia.[16] The second and third senses of the term are peripheral to our present concerns.

From the late 18th to the mid-20th century "orientalism" remained a more or less neutral descriptive term, though not without a cluster of both positive and negative connotations. It referred to the linguistic and philological studies which emerged in the wake of the great maritime voyages and discoveries, the growth of mercantilism and the spread of European colonial power between the 16th and 19th centuries. Although the Western study of Eastern texts and languages had been pursued since ancient times, orientalism is closely associated with the birth in the 1780s of the Indological studies of a group of English civil servants in Bengal, working under the patronage of Governor-General Warren Hastings.

Since the early 1960s "orientalism" has become a much more volatile term. The word has accumulated a new freight of meaning as well as a highly charged ideological nebula through the work of such figures as the Egyptian sociologist Anouar Abdel-Malek, the Syrian historian A.L. Tibawi, the Marxist sociologist Bryan Turner, and, pre-eminently, the Palestinian theorist and writer, Edward Said.[17] Although much of his work was foreshadowed by Tibawi and Abdel-Malek, Said's *Orientalism* marked a watershed in the history of orientalism—both as a term and as an intellectual tradition and scholarly institution. Henceforth in this study I will follow a simple expedient: against the current tide, "orientalism" will continue to be used in a non-pejorative sense to signify an ongoing Western tradition of intellectual inquiry into and existential engagement with the ideas, practices and values of the East, particularly in the religious field, while "Orientalism" will refer, in Said's terms, to an ideologically-motivated "epistemic construction" and a "corporate institution."

Edward Said and the Critics of Orientalism

Said's primary interest lay in the Western perception and subjugation of the Islamic world of the Middle East. Since 1978 his thesis has been extended and extrapolated to cover European interactions (both intellectual and political) with the entire Asian continent. Said's thesis, baldly stated, is that Orientalism was a legatee of a European tradition of "narcissistic" writing, stretching back to Homer and Aeschylus, in which Western intellectuals created an "Orient" that was a fabric of "ideological fictions" whose purpose was

16 See A. Macfie (ed), *Orientalism: A Reader*, 1-2.
17 See A. Macfie (ed), *Orientalism: A Reader*, 1-8; A. Abdel-Malek, "Orientalism in Crisis"; A.L. Tibawi, "English- Speaking Orientalists"; B. Turner, *Marx and the End of Orientalism*; E. Said, *Orientalism*.

to confirm the West's sense of identity and to legitimize Western cultural and political superiority. Orientalism is a "colonizing knowledge" which generates a series of stereotypical dichotomies between a rational, democratic, humanistic, creative, dynamic, progressive and "masculine" "West" and an irrational, despotic, oppressive, backward, passive, stagnant and "feminine" "East." In psychological terms this ideologically charged representation of the East can be seen as the repressed "Other" of the West, "a sort of surrogate or even underground self"[18] associated with the subconscious attraction-repulsion of sexual aberration and corruption, and with a sinister "occultism." In Raymond Schwab's terms, the Orient appears in the Western unconscious as "the unfathomable, the nocturnal figure of the mind."[19] Western intellectuals and writers developed an extensive repertoire of clichés, images and oppositions which derived not from historical realities but from both a troubled fantasy-life and from the imperatives of power. On the material plane Orientalism served the interests of European colonialism by providing an integrated discourse through which the Orient could be filtered into western consciousness. The Orientalist scholar was an accessory, an accomplice, a partner-in-crime, of the politician, merchant, soldier, missionary and colonial administrator.

Ziauddin Sardar has usefully anatomized Said's understanding of Orientalism in seven defining points (the quotations coming directly from Said):

> 1. The classical tradition of studying a region by means of its languages and writings: thus anyone who teaches, researches or writes about the Orient is an orientalist.

> 2. "A way of coming to terms with the Orient that is based on the Orient's special place in European Western experience."

> 3. An overarching style of thought, with a history going back to antiquity, based on an ontological and epistemological distinction made between "the Orient" and "the Occident."

> 4. A "western style for dominating, restructuring and having authority over the Orient."

> 5. "A library or archive of information commonly and, in some of its aspects, unanimously held ... a family of ideas and a unifying set of values ... These ideas explained the behavior of Orientals; they supplied the Orientals with a mentality, a genealogy, an atmosphere; most important, they allowed Europeans to deal with and even to see Orientals as a phenomenon possessing regular characteristics."

> 6. "A system of representations framed by a whole set of forces that brought the Orient into Western learning, Western consciousness, and later, Western empire."

18 E. Said, *Orientalism*, 3.
19 R. Schwab, *Oriental Renaissance*, 484.

7. The western "corporate institution" responsible for dealing with the Orient: describing it, containing it, controlling it, teaching and learning about it, making statements about it, authorizing views of it and ruling over it by these and other means.[20]

Said's thesis, shaped by both Gramscian Marxism and post-modernist French "high theory" (particularly that of Foucault), has provided the magnetic pole around which much of the recent debate about Orientalism has gravitated. Said's argument was not altogether new but the originality and force of *Orientalism* derived, at least in part, from his insistent application of the Foucauldian principle that knowledge can never be "innocent" and is always deeply implicated in the operations of power. Through a wide-ranging analysis of literary texts, travel writing and a mass of European documents, Said uncovered a system of cultural description which was "deeply inscribed with the politics, the considerations, the positions, and the strategies of power."[21]

To understand the general significance of this debate and the sea-change which it signifies we need to understand something of the historical background and of the intellectual changes signaled by the emergence of post-colonial studies. As Maxime Rodinson and others have pointed out, the conditions for a major critique of Orientalism were created by radical changes in the political landscapes of both Europe and Asia in the first half of the century. Amongst the most salient of these changes were the Iranian Revolution of 1906; the Young Turk and Kemalist movements in the years before and after the Great War; the defeat and dismemberment of the German, Austrian, Russian and Ottoman Empires; the rise of Bolshevism; the spread of anti-colonial nationalism in many parts of Asia; and, eventually, decolonization.[22] Such changes made possible a challenge not only to the military and political structures of European imperialism but to the intellectual and theoretical formations which had motivated, rationalized, camouflaged and validated them. Enter Tibawi, Said et al., soon to be joined by various other groups marching behind the banners of anti-Europeanism, anti-colonialism, and anti-elitism.

Since the meteoric appearance of the Saidian critique many other scholars have joined the fray to defend, extend, qualify or repudiate it. It lies outside our present purpose to negotiate this labyrinthine field but we may take note of the work of such scholars as Stuart Schaar, Ronald Inden, Richard King (generally supportive of Said), Bernard Lewis, David Kopf, John Mackenzie and Keith Windshuttle (generally critical), and Aijiz Ahmad, Fred

---

20 Z. Sardar, *Orientalism*, 68.
21 E. Said, "Orientalism Reconsidered," 347.
22 See M. Rodinson, "The Western Image," 55-62.

Halliday and Albert Hourani (somewhere in between).[23] A number of feminist theorists and historians entered the field in the 1990s, either inflect-
ing Said's thesis in new ways or challenging its neglect of a significant body
of orientalist writings by women.[24]

Said's work has been criticized along many different lines. To cite only a
few: *Orientalism* offers us little more than the rehashing of the work of Said's
unacknowledged predecessors in the field (Ziauddin Sardar);[25] it succumbs
to the same homogenizing, essentializing and totalizing tendencies which it
stigmatizes in *Orientalism* (B.J. Moore-Gilbert, Sadik Jalal al 'Azm, Rosane
Rocher);[26] Foucaldian discursive theory (on which Said draws so heavily) is
a remarkably blunt instrument with which to dissect historical particularities
and the "micropractices, irregularities, historical discontinuities and discursive heterogeneity" of Orientalism itself (Ali Behdad);[27] Said's work is motivated by an ideological animus to Zionism and Judaism, and is guilty of "arbitrary rearrangement" and "capricious choice" in its treatment of the historical evidence (Bernard Lewis); his work is "ahistorical," lacking in precision
and subtlety (David Kopf, John Mackenzie); and his analysis is vitiated by the
contradictory epistemological assumptions and methodological procedures
which he variously derives from Gramscian Marxism, Foucaldian theory,
Arnoldian "high culture" and a tradition of secular humanism (James
Clifford, Richard King); *Orientalism* ignores the considerable body of writing
on the East by women (Billie Melman, Lisa Lowe), by such minorities as
Anglo-Indians (B.J. Moore-Gilbert), and the self-representations of the colo-
nized which are passed over in favor of an analysis of canonical Western lit-
erary texts (Ania Loomba);[28] Said's depiction, it is also argued, fails to recog-
nize and account for the significant variations in different national
Orientalist discourses and is unable to account for the fact that German and
Russian orientalism developed independently of Empire (Sheldon Pollock,
C.F. Beckingham, James Clifford).[29]

Whatever assessment one makes of the work of Said and other anti-
Orientalists, it is certainly no longer possible to consider the interactions of

23 In addition to the works cited above, some of the principal works in this debate are: A. Ahmad,
"Between Orientalism and Historicism"; A. Behdad, *Belated Travelers*; C.A. Breckenridge & P. van der
Veer (eds), *Orientalism and the Post-Colonial Predicament*; J. Clifford, *The Predicament of Culture*; F.
Dallmayr, *Beyond Orientalism*; F. Halliday, "Orientalism and Its Critics"; A. Hourani, "The Road to
Morocco"; R. King, *Orientalism and Religion*; D. Kopf, "Hermeneutics versus History"; B. Lewis, *Islam
and the West*; J. Mackenzie, *Orientalism: History, Theory and the Arts*; B.J. Moore-Gilbert, *Postcolonial
Theory: Contexts, Practices, Politics*; K. Windshuttle, *The Killing of History*. Excerpts from many of these
works can be found in A. Macfie (ed), *Orientalism: A Reader*.
24 See Lisa Lowe, *Critical Terrains*, and B. Melman, *Women's Orients*.
25 Z. Sardar, *Orientalism*, 67.
26 B.J. Moore-Gilbert, *Postcolonial Theory*, 53; Sadik Jalal al 'Azm, "Orientalism and Orientalism in
Reverse."
27 A. Macfie, following Ali Behdad, *Orientalism: A Reader*, 7.
28 See A. Loomba, *Colonialism/Postcolonialism*, 49.
29 See S. Pollock, "Indology, Power, and the Case of Germany"; C.F. Beckingham, review of
Orientalism; J. Clifford, *The Predicament of Culture*.

East and West without taking some account of their critiques.[30] There is no gainsaying the brilliance of Edward Said's work; it would be foolish to turn away from his many insights or to ignore the challenges he has posed. Nonetheless, the Saidian thesis has given birth to many lop-sided and reductionistic works in which the hermeneutics of suspicion and malice aforethought have blinded their authors to the many positive aspects of orientalism. Whilst Said and his epigones have dominated the debate within such disciplinary arenas as sociology, political science and post-colonial/subaltern studies their work has exercised a less totalitarian influence in the field of comparative religion and the history of ideas. Here I do not wish to construct any detailed or systematic counter-argument either to Said or to his many successors. I hope that much of the material in this study will enable readers to at least consider some alternative perspectives. However, it is impossible to leave this subject without a few general remarks, the pertinence of which will become clearer as the reader proceeds.

The conceptual apparatus deployed in the contemporary critique of Orientalism has been drawn from a number of sources. Abdel-Malek and Turner drew on Marxist analyses of capitalism and colonialism, Tibawi on post-Enlightenment ideals of scientific detachment and the liberal ideal of inter-cultural respect, and Said on the deconstructionist theories of those monks of negation, the Parisian oracles of post-modernism. All have been influenced by the legacy of the German philosophical tradition, especially the thought of Hegel, Marx and Nietzsche. An obvious irony, which seems to have escaped the attention of some of the more fervent and over-heated critics of Orientalism, is that their assault on the Western fabrication of the Orient is itself a product of the Western intellectual heritage of which they are such strident critics. In Said's case the irony is sharpened by the fact that the "defense" of the Islamic civilization is conducted by a rootless intellectual of Protestant upbringing who is quite unable to conceal his own distaste for the religion that provides the very *raison d'être* of the civilization in question. Moreover, his argument is rooted in ideas and values (secular humanism, high culture) which are irredeemably Western and modernistic, and thus quite out of tune with those values that Muslims themselves hold most dear.

Not only is the theoretical arsenal of the anti-Orientalists drawn almost exclusively from Western sources but, with few exceptions, it is also relentlessly secular, materialist and humanistic in its assumptions, attitudes and values. These critics assert *ad nauseam* that no knowledge can be "apolitical" and "disinterested" but, in terms of their *own* argument, they often seem quite obtuse in understanding the limitations and prejudices which must govern their own outlook. This is especially problematic in the domain of religion.

---

30 A thoughtful, generally sympathetic but balanced consideration of arguments for and against Said's thesis can be found in Richard King's *Orientalism and Religion*, 82-95.

Scholars committed to an essentially modern, Western, areligious world view (which, with respect to religion itself, might be hostile, indifferent or vaguely "tolerant" but which, from a religious viewpoint, will *necessarily* be reductionistic) are thereby disqualified from the deepest understanding of the spiritual impulses which motivate men and women who immerse themselves in the doctrines and practices of alien religious traditions. These critics, for the most part, are locked into Salman Rushdie's facile dichotomy of the "light of secularism" and "darkness of religion."[31] It is all too easy to see the attraction to the East, on the level of the individual, in non-religious terms—the lure of the exotic, the promise of escape, the rebellion against convention and the like. But what of the religious impulse *per se?* For such scholars there is *no* such impulse but only a bogus religiosity which serves as cover for the "real" motivations at work (psychological, political, economic or whatever).

A recent work on Orientalism opens with the following passage:

> The problem of Orientalism, what makes the dissection and display of its skeletal being a tricky matter, is the very fact of its existence. Because Orientalism exists we have a world where reality is differently perceived, expressed and experienced across a great divide of mutual misunderstanding. To discuss Orientalism one has to urge people to go beyond this misunderstanding and see what has been made invisible: to distinguish a different outline in a picture that has been distorted by centuries of myopic vision. There is nothing about Orientalism that is neutral or objective. By definition it is a partial and partisan subject. No one comes to the subject without a background and baggage. The baggage for many consists of the assumption that, given its long history, somewhere within or about this subject there is real knowledge about the Orient; and that this knowledge can be used to develop an understanding of the cultures East of the West. The task of this book is to undermine this assumption ... While Orientalism is real, it is still, nevertheless, an artificial construction. It is entirely distinct and unattached to the East as understood within and by the East. There is no route map, no itinerary locked within the subject to bridge that divide.[32]

Oscar Wilde quipped of *fin-de-siècle* Japanophilia that "In fact the whole of Japan is a pure invention."[33] The witticism has now lost its zest. The kind of passage just cited, asseverating that the Western understanding of the Orient is nothing more than a tissue of mendacious fabrications, is now quite unexceptional—indeed it is standard fare in those fields of study now tyrannized by a peculiar mix of French "high theory," deterministic materialism and psychoanalytic theory. In *Orientalism*, Edward Said cautions that,

> Trouble sets in when the guild tradition of Orientalism takes over the schol-

---

31 See Z. Sardar, *Orientalism*, 75.
32 See Z. Sardar, *Orientalism*, vii.
33 O. Wilde, "The Decay of Lying," 988.

ar who is not vigilant, whose individual consciousness as a scholar is not on guard against *idées reçues* all too easily handed down in the profession.[34]

This passage is not without its unintended ironies, given that for a period of some years almost every nickel-and-dime scholar dealing with the West's encounter with the East took up the Saidian line—*idées reçues* indeed!

Let us return for a moment to the characteristic passage from Ziauddin Sardar cited above. These kinds of claims have become so familiar that we need to take a step back to see what staggering and preposterous claims are being made! Centuries of tireless Western scholarship, of assiduous intellectual explorations, of meticulous translations and painstaking commentaries, not to mention the direct personal testimonies of Europeans living in Asia, all count for nothing more than an "artificial construction" which can only generate "mutual misunderstanding." A melancholy and somewhat ludicrous spectacle! But, wait! After centuries, even millennia of mutual incomprehension, it is now possible, we are told, to erase this monstrous edifice of misunderstanding, to start from zero and to find "*new* bases for *genuine* encounters with the people, places, history, ideas and current existence that is to the East of the West"[35]—as if quite suddenly there is an entirely new dispensation which will allow us to avoid the follies and misdemeanors of the past. The question of quite *how* this is to be done is not specified in anything but the vaguest and most platitudinous terms.

Rather than the fashionable disparaging of the achievements of many orientalists of the past, I incline towards Mircea Eliade's view that

> We have indeed pillaged other cultures. Fortunately, however, there have been other Westerners who have deciphered the languages, preserved the myths, salvaged certain artistic masterpieces. There have always been a few orientalists, a few philosophers, a few poets striving to safeguard the meaning of certain exotic, extra-European spiritual traditions.[36]

Whilst their work was no doubt often contaminated by mixed motives and their work sometimes turned to dubious ends, the scholarly enterprise in itself was a noble one and their heroic labors ought to elicit our admiration and gratitude rather than opprobrium. This is especially the case amongst those writers and researchers who, far from aiding and abetting colonial regimes or reinforcing racist and progressivist ideologies, were inspired by a sense that the East had philosophical, artistic and spiritual riches which could be shared by a Western world which had lost its religious bearings. Prominent amongst such writers were two figures to whom we shall often refer in this study, the Anglo-Ceylonese art historian, Ananda

---

34 E. Said, *Orientalism*, 326.
35 Z. Sardar, *Orientalism*, viii (italics mine).
36 M. Eliade, *Ordeal by Labyrinth*, 68.

Coomaraswamy, and the French metaphysician, René Guénon, each of whom played a decisive role in awakening the West to the profound messages of the Eastern traditions.

Alternative Perspectives

In raising these objections to some aspects of the anti-Orientalist critiques I certainly do not want to retreat into the naïve view of orientalism as an unproblematic domain of "pure" and "disinterested" scholarship. In point of fact the connections between Orientalism and imperialism were exposed long before the current rash of critiques. In 1924, for instance, René Guénon himself was excoriating those European orientalists whose researches had become an instrument in the service of national ambition.[37] It is by no means the case that the recognition of the political and ideological dimensions of Orientalism must derive from the kind of critiques elaborated by Said: Guénon's own outlook could hardly have been further removed from that of Said for whom "traditional," it is all too apparent, is more or less synonymous with backwardness, superstition and ignorance.

Nor should this study be construed in any way as a defense of Western imperialism or a justification of the cultural vandalism which was its inevitable consequence. Nor do I deny the acuity of much of Said's work. My argument is with the blanket condemnation of orientalism as a more or less entirely reprehensible auxiliary of European political and cultural hegemony. The role of orientalism in Western colonialism can hardly be denied but, in Francesco Gabrieli's words, it has been "unjustly exaggerated, generalized and embittered."[38] Furthermore, Said's thesis is found to be quite precarious when we consider Western encounters with the civilizations of India, Tibet, China and Japan (the arenas with which we are primarily concerned). We will see that Western engagements with Eastern thought and spirituality often impelled the most profound and passionate repudiation of the imperial ethos and provided a platform for Western self-criticism of the most searching kind. As J.J. Clarke remarks early in his fine book, *Oriental Enlightenment: The Encounter Between Asian and Western Thought* (1997),

> Orientalism ... cannot simply be identified with the ruling imperialist ideology, for in the Western context it represents a counter-movement, a subversive entelechy, albeit not a unified or consciously organized one, which in various ways has often tended to subvert rather than to confirm the discursive structures of imperial power.[39]

Clarke's study provides us with a model of a much more finely nuanced and judicious account of orientalism, acknowledging those political aspects to

37 R. Guénon, *East and West*, 156.
38 F. Gabrieli, "Apology for Orientalism," 81.
39 J.J. Clarke, *Oriental Enlightenment*, 9.

which Said and the post-colonial critics have brought attention but also affirming the creative, liberating and subversive effects of European engagements with the East. I share Clarke's view that Said's treatment of orientalism, particularly the assertion of the necessary nexus with imperialism, is over-stated and unbalanced. It either ignores or marginalizes the positive motivations and impulses behind many Western encounters with and representations of the Orient and foregrounds those politico-economic and psychological factors which present European engagements in a sinister light. Nor can I accept the notion that orientalists were inevitably chasing mirages, constructing mirror-images and projecting their own fantasies onto an artificial screen called "the East" or "the Orient." Doubtless, this was *part* of the story of Western encounters but there was also *real* understanding of an *actual* Orient.

We are largely concerned in this study with *religious* phenomena which must be treated *sui generis* and not rammed into the theoretical strait-jackets of reductionistic models of religion. As Mircea Eliade has insisted,

> ... a religious phenomenon will only be recognized as such if it is grasped at its own level, that is to say, if it is studied as something religious. To try to grasp the essence of such a phenomenon by means of physiology, psychology, sociology, economics, linguistics, art or any other study is false; it misses the one unique and irreducible element in it—the element of the sacred. Obviously there are no purely religious phenomena ... But it would be hopeless to try and explain religion in terms of any one of these basic functions ... It would be as futile as thinking you could explain *Madame Bovary* by a list of social, economic and political facts; however true, they do not effect it as a work of literature.[40]

The present study takes up the task of considering Western encounters with the Eastern traditions as *religious* phenomena which, in the end, are not amenable to non-religious explanations. As Eliade concedes, "there are no purely religious phenomena," which is to say that any "religious" phenomenon has a history, a social and political context, a location in time and space. This work will not succumb to facile stereotypes about "the mystic East" as a realm outside history and beyond politics; on the other hand, nor will it surrender to the jejune slogan popularized in May 1968, "nothing outside politics." The Western engagement with Asia can be only partially (and quite inadequately) explained by the analytical techniques and conceptual categories of Marxist/Foucauldian/psychoanalytic thought, no matter how sophisticated and refined their application nor how erudite the scholars deploying them.

Mircea Eliade has also argued that

> ... the scholar has not finished his work when he has reconstructed the history of a religious form or brought out its sociological, economic or politi-

---

40 M. Eliade, *Patterns in Comparative Religion*, xiii.

cal contexts. In addition he [or she] must *understand its meaning* ...[41]

It is one of the governing purposes of the present study to disclose, insofar as possible, the *meaning* of Western encounters with Eastern spiritualities *as understood by the European participants themselves*. We shall not restrict our inquiries to such understandings but they will certainly occupy a central place. One of the more insidious effects of much post-modernist theorizing, especially that of Foucault, is to erase the very notion of human agency and to relegate the self-understandings and experiences of human individuals to the sidelines as epiphenomena of little interest; indeed, individuals themselves are reduced to "functions" of the systems within which they operate. Foucault's *The Study of Things*, one of his admirers tells us, "proclaims the eclipse of man as a ground of thought."[42] This is a particularly corrosive form of reductionism, which ultimately leads to the kind of nihilism deplored by the psychologist Victor Frankl:

> The true nihilism of today is reductionism ... Contemporary nihilism no longer brandishes the word nothingness; today nihilism is camouflaged as nothing-but-ness. Human phenomena are thus turned into mere epiphenomena.[43]

The present work is *not* a systematic study of orientalism in any of its senses although it does encompass the scholarly study of Eastern languages and texts. Rather, it is an attempt to survey the *existential and spiritual engagement* of a wide variety of Westerners in Eastern religions, and to do so from a viewpoint sympathetic to all religious traditions but not identified with any particular faith.

The Traditionalist Outlook

In his essay "The Pertinence of Philosophy" Ananda Coomaraswamy suggested that

> ... if we are to consider what may be the most urgent practical task to be resolved by the philosopher, we can only answer that this is ... a control and revision of the principles of comparative religion, the true end of which science ... should be to demonstrate the common metaphysical basis of all religions and that diverse cultures are fundamentally related to one another as being the dialects of a common spiritual and intellectual language ...[44]

This enterprise is high on the agenda of the "traditionalists." The traditionalist perspective was first publicly articulated by René Guénon. Since the time of Guénon's earliest writings, soon after the turn of the last century, a signif-

41 M. Eliade, *The Quest*, 2 (italics mine).
42 J. Merquior, *Foucault*, 55.
43 Victor Frankl, quoted in E.F. Schumacher, *A Guide for the Perplexed*, 15.
44 A.K. Coomaraswamy, *What is Civilization?*, p.18.

icant traditionalist "school" has emerged with Guénon, Ananda Coomaraswamy and Frithjof Schuon acknowledged within the group as its pre-eminent exponents. Later representatives of this school include Titus Burckhardt, Marco Pallis, and Seyyed Hossein Nasr, all of whom have written on Eastern subjects. The present work takes it bearings not from the contemporary debate about Orientalism but from these traditionalist thinkers who have overcome the barriers of Eurocentricism and intellectual provincialism in a much more radical fashion than these latter-day critics. They have done so not by resorting to the currently fashionable theories of deracinated European intellectuals but by their immersion in both the Occidental and Oriental worlds of Tradition, using this term as it is understood in the work of René Guénon. An allegiance to the traditionalist position entails, as a necessary corollary, a rejection of modernism (i.e., the ideas, assumptions and attitudes which inform the prevailing worldview amongst the Western intelligentsia—and increasingly, alas, the Western-educated elites of the East). Chapter 8 of this study is devoted to the role of the traditionalists in the story of East-West encounters but a few introductory remarks here will not be out of place.[45]

The traditionalists, by definition, are committed to the explication of the *philosophia perennis* which lies at the heart of the diverse religions and behind the manifold forms of the world's different traditions. The *philosophia perennis* discloses an axiology, a set of first principles, a "universally intelligible language" and a "common universe of discourse," which provides the basis on which the most meaningful meeting of religious traditions may take place.[46] At the same time—the point is crucial—the traditionalists are dedicated to the preservation and illumination of the traditional forms which give each religious heritage its *raison d'être* and guarantee its formal integrity and, by the same token, ensure its spiritual efficacy. This outlook, based on the wisdom of the ages, is radically at odds with the ethos of modern Western scholarship. The fact that the work of the traditionalists has been largely ignored in Western academia is a sad commentary on a contemporary outlook which prides itself on "open-ness" and "respect for plurality" but which, in fact, is remarkably insular. In the field of study with which we are concerned, how else are we to account for the neglect of works as compelling as Guénon's *East and West* (1924) and *Man and His Becoming According to the Vedanta* (1925) or Frithjof Schuon's *Language of the Self* (1958) and *In the Tracks of Buddhism* (1968)? As Seyyed Hossein Nasr has observed, "One of the remarkable aspects of the intellectual life of this century ... is precisely the neglect of [the

---

45 Readers interested in a much fuller exposition of the traditionalist outlook might consult my *Traditionalism: Religion in the light of the Perennial Philosophy*.
46 A.K. Coomaraswamy, *The Bugbear of Literacy*, 80.

traditional] point of view in circles whose official function is to be concerned with questions of an intellectual order."[47]

Under the view championed by Guénon, Schuon and Nasr (and others), the traditional worlds of East and West have much more in common than either has with the modern West. Traditional civilizations are essentially religious: culture is the outward expression of religion and its application in all aspects of life, is in T.S. Eliot's phrase, the "incarnation of religion."[48] By contrast, modernity defines itself by its irreligious temper and by its attachment to a rationalistic and materialistic science. At the heart of all religious traditions is a metaphysical wisdom which is always the same despite the variegations in its outward vestments whilst the modern worldview is essentially little more than a *negation* of the traditional outlook, fueled by an ignorance of metaphysical principles and by the disavowal of religious forms. The most profound of divisions, therefore, is not between geographically differentiated areas but between traditional societies on one side (all previous cultures, everywhere) and those of modernity on the other (post-medieval Western Europe and its extensions elsewhere in the world). As Coomaraswamy so acutely remarked,

> "East and West" imports a cultural rather than a geographical antithesis: an opposition of the traditional or ordinary way of life that survives in the East to the modern and irregular way of life that now prevails in the West. It is because such an opposition could not have been felt before the Renaissance that we say that the problem is one that presents itself only accidentally in terms of geography; it is one of times much more than places.[49]

In this work we will touch on many issues arising out of the confrontations of tradition and modernity, and consider them in a number of contexts and from a variety of viewpoints. Nonetheless, it would be fraudulent, and no doubt quite futile, to pretend that this work aspires to the chimerical "objectivity" so prized in some academic quarters. Our colors have already been nailed to the mast. In navigating our way through a long and complicated story we shall keep our sights firmly fixed on Guénon's affirmation that

> ... the outstanding difference between the East and West (which really means in this case the modern West), the only difference that is really essential (for all others are derivative), is on the one side the preservation of tradition, with all that this implies, and on the other side the forgetting and loss of this same tradition; on the one side the maintaining of metaphysical

47 S.H. Nasr, *Knowledge and the Sacred*, 67.

48 T.S. Eliot, *Notes Towards the Definition of Culture*, 28.

49 A.K. Coomaraswamy, *The Bugbear of Literacy*, 80. See also, A.K. Coomaraswamy, *Selected Letters*, 69.

knowledge, on the other, complete ignorance of all connected with this realm.[50]

Many of the figures with whom we will be concerned in this study were attracted to the East for reasons which they themselves often barely understood. As often as not, though, we will find some fugitive intuition that the East was capable of imparting to the West, by way of those individuals with eyes to see and ears to hear, an incomparably precious gift—a re-awakened sense of that Ultimate Reality and those perennial verities towards which the genuine religious quest is always directed. In so doing the East enabled those receptive to its message to return to the sources of wisdom within the Western tradition and to uncover those fundamental truths which are ever-present but which "cannot impose themselves on those unwilling to listen."[51]

50 R. Guénon, "Oriental Metaphysics," 55.
51 F. Schuon, "No Activity without Truth," 28.

2.

Ex Oriente Lux: The 19th Century Background

Romanticism and the Orient—The American Transcendentalists—Modernism
and Cultural Crisis—The 1893 World's Parliament of Religions

---

*Whoever has willed or done too much, let him drink from this deep cup a long draught
of life and youth ... Everything is narrow in the West—Greece is small and I stifle;
Judea is dry and I pant. Let me look a little towards lofty Asia, the profound East.*
(Jules Michelet)[1]

*By the middle of the nineteenth century Orientalism was as vast a treasure-house of
learning as one could imagine.* (Edward Said)[2]

The Western engagement with the religious traditions of the East in the
20th century cannot be understood without some reference to developments
in the previous century. Scholars such as Raymond Schwab, Wilhelm
Halbfass, Philip Almond, Thomas Tweed, Arthur Versluis and Carl Jackson,
to name only a few, have provided us with highly detailed works in which
19th century Western encounters with Oriental religions have been depicted
and analyzed from various angles. In this chapter we shall journey rather
quickly through this vast terrain, alighting momentarily, so to speak, to examine four salient markers: the Oriental enthusiasms of the German Romantics
and of the American Transcendentalists, the Eastern imprint on the development of modernism in the literary field, and the event which heralds the
beginning of a new epoch in the popular Western perception of Eastern religions, the World's Parliament of Religions in Chicago in 1893. In later chapters we will, from time to time, return to the 19th century to shade in the
background to the changing European involvements in particular traditions
and locales.

Romanticism and the Orient

Amongst the German Romantics in whom the Eastern Scriptures ignited an
intense if sometimes temporary excitement were Herder, Goethe, Schelling,
Fichte, Schopenhauer, Schleiermacher, Schiller, Novalis, and both
Schlegels—a veritable register of German romanticism. Herder was amongst

---

1   Michelet quoted in J.J. Clarke, *Oriental Enlightenment*, 71.
2   E. Said, *Orientalism*, 51.

the first of the Romantics to "conscript the Orient in pursuit of the goals of Romanticism."[3] His attitude to India is evinced by such comments as "O holy land [India], I salute thee, thou source of all music, thou voice of the heart," and "Behold the East—cradle of the human race, of human emotion, of all religion."[4] Both literally and metaphorically India was the land of the precious metals and stones mentioned by Moses.[5] Many of the German Romantics lauded the Hindu Scriptures, particularly the *Upanishads*: Schelling asserted that the "sacred texts of the Indians" were superior to the *Bible*. In England we can discern various Oriental interests and themes in the work of Southey, Coleridge, Shelley, Byron and De Quincey, though in some cases the interest was once removed, mediated by German Idealism. However, these interests sometimes went quite deep: Shelley's exposition of Vedantic philosophy in *Adonais* might be cited as an example. Edward Said, in somewhat lurid language, refers to "the virtual epidemic of Orientalia affecting almost every major poet, essayist and philosopher of the period."[6]

What was the excitement all about? The East in general and India in particular became a site where several Romantic interests could happily converge: the interest of the early Indologists in the origins of various European and Indian languages, and the claim that these may have had a common genesis, became intertwined with new and burgeoning Romantic conceptions about national and cultural identity, conceptions somewhat paradoxically paralleled by the affirmation of a universal humanity whose lineaments could just as easily be read in the ancient Hindu Scriptures as in the Judeo-Christian heritage or in classical Greece.[7] Several German Romantics believed that the origins of civilization itself were to be found in India. Following Herder, Friedrich Schlegel claimed that, "The primary source of all intellectual development—in a word the whole human culture—is unquestionably to be found in the traditions of the East."[8] Schlegel's linguistic and anthropological speculations traced Germanic culture back to ancient India: this was, in part, a reaction against a classicism "indelibly associated with France."[9] It was Schlegel who minted the term "Oriental Renaissance" to describe the contemporary efflorescence of European interest in matters Eastern, and who was responsible for the second translation of the *Gita* into a European language, in this case Latin.[10] Schlegel also offers us one instance of a recurrent existential pattern, the immersion in Eastern thought and spirituality followed by a return to one's own religious tradition, marked in Schlegel's case by his late conversion to Catholicism. We might

3   J.J. Clarke, *Oriental Enlightenment*, 61.
4   J.J. Clarke, *Oriental Enlightenment*, 61.
5   R. King, *Orientalism and Religion*, 118.
6   E. Said, *Orientalism*, 51.
7   See W. Halbfass, *India and Europe*, Ch 5.
8   J.J. Clarke, *Oriental Enlightenment*, 65.
9   J.J. Clarke, *Oriental Enlightenment*, 65.
10 S. Batchelor, *The Awakening of the West*, 252, and E. Sharpe, *The Universal Gita*, p.18.

also note that the younger Schlegel, August Wilhelm, occupied the first chair in Indology at a German university, in Bonn.[11]

Romantic philosophers found the monistic teachings of the *Upanishads* to be in close harmony with their own idealist beliefs. As J.J. Clarke has remarked,

> ... just as Confucianism had offered the *philosophes* a model for a rationalist, deistic philosophy, so the Hinduism of the Upanishads offered an exalted metaphysical system which resonated with their own idealist assumptions, and which provided a counterblast to the materialistic and mechanistic philosophy that had come to dominate the Enlightenment period.[12]

Indian values and ideas concerning the unity of all life forms and the world-soul could also be seen to validate Romantic ideas about "the transcendental wholeness and fundamentally spiritual essence of the natural world."[13] As Schlegel claimed, "In the Orient we must seek the highest Romanticism."[14] Some of the Romantics, Blake and Novalis among them, nurtured ideas about "a single God for all mankind" and about a universal essence to be found at the heart of all the great mythological and religious traditions, a thesis which later became popular under the rubric of "the perennial philosophy."

Let us look a little more closely at the Eastern interests of one Romantic philosopher, Arthur Schopenhauer (somewhat neglected in the Anglophone world). His principal work *The World as Will and Representation*, first appeared in 1818, before Schopenhauer was exposed to Indian influences. But it was not until its reappearance in two volumes in 1844, now densely textured with Indian references, that it really exerted its influence on European intellectual life. Its impact on Wagner and Nietzsche is well known.[15] Thomas Mann went so far as to call Schopenhauer's book "the great event in Wagner's life ... the deepest consolation, the highest self-confirmation; it meant release of mind and spirit."[16] Schopenhauer had studied under Fichte and Schleiermacher at university in Berlin but the most decisive influence was Kant, whose bust rested on Schopenhauer's desk, rubbing shoulders with a statue of the Buddha.[17]

Schopenhauer, at age twenty-five, was given a copy of Anquetil-Duperron's *Oupnek'hat*. It was a revelation to him: he later praised it as "the most profitable and elevating reading which ... is possible in the world. It has been the solace of my life, and will be the solace of my death."[18] After his introduction to the *Upanishads* Schopenhauer immediately embarked on the

---

11 W. Halbfass, *India and Europe*, 81.
12 J.J. Clarke, *Oriental Enlightenment*, 61.
13 J.J. Clarke, *Oriental Enlightenment*, 62.
14 S. Batchelor, *The Awakening of the West*, 252. See also E. Said, *Orientalism*, 98.
15 W. Halbfass, *India and Europe*, 124.
16 B. Magee, *The Philosophy of Schopenhauer*, 335-336.
17 S. Batchelor, *The Awakening of the West*, 255.
18 J.J. Clarke, *Oriental Enlightenment*, 68.

collection and study of such Asian texts as had been translated into European languages, claiming that "Sanskrit literature will be no less influential for our time than Greek literature was in the 15th century for the Renaissance."[19]

Schopenhauer believed India was "the land of the most ancient and the most pristine wisdom"[20] from whence could be traced many currents within European civilization, Christianity included. He subscribed to the widely held Romantic belief that Christianity "had Indian blood in its veins" and claimed that "Christianity taught only what the whole of Asia knew already long before and even better," for which reason he believed that Christianity would never take root in India: "the ancient wisdom of the human race," he stated, "will not be supplanted by the events in Galilee. On the contrary, Indian wisdom flows back to Europe, and will produce fundamental changes in our knowledge and thought."[21] It is worth remarking here that the dark underside of Schopenhauer's enthusiasm for Indian spirituality was an anti-Semitism, evident in his ideas about Aryan racial purity, the Hindu origins of the *New Testament* (which Schopenhauer wanted to "rescue" from a "Jewish monopoly"), and the "fanatical atrocities" of the Jewish monotheists.[22] Anti-Semitism was one of the forms of an oft-remarked racialism which was always the worm in the rose of German Romanticism.[23]

Anquetil-Duperron was one of the earliest orientalists to promote the perennialist theme, now taken up by Schopenhauer: "The books of Solomon, the Sacred canons of the Chinese, the *Vedas* of the Hindus and the *Zend-Avesta* of the Persians [wrote Schopenhauer] all contained the same basic truth, and had one common parenthood in their origin."[24] "In general," he wrote, "the sages of all times have always said the same."[25] Like many other Romantics, Schopenhauer found in the Eastern Scriptures validation of his own idealist, anti-rationalist agenda but he also discovered in Buddhism resonances with his own particular psychological and ethical interests. The Buddhist ideal of compassion and the metaphysic of emptiness (*sunyata*) struck a deep chord in Schopenhauer who was one of the first to seriously investigate Buddhism as a coherent philosophical system. He can be seen as a transitional figure in the movement of interest away from Hinduism towards Buddhism in the middle of the 19th century. Wilhelm Halbfass has summed up Schopenhauer's encounter with Eastern philosophy this way:

> ... he showed an unprecedented readiness to integrate Indian ideas into his own European thinking and self-understanding, and to utilize them for the

---

19 S. Batchelor, *The Awakening of the West*, 255.
20 J.J. Clarke, *Oriental Enlightenment*, 68.
21 J.J. Clarke, *Oriental Enlightenment*, 69. See also Raymond Schwab, *The Oriental Renaissance*, 427-428, and B. Magee, *The Philosophy of Schopenhauer*, 316-321.
22 See R. Schwab, *The Oriental Renaissance*, 428-431.
23 We will return to this subject in Chapter 14.
24 Schopenhauer quoted in R. King, *Orientalism and Religion*, 120.
25 W. Halbfass, *India and Europe*, 111.

illustration, articulation and clarification of his own teachings and problems. With this, he combined a radical critique of some of the most fundamental presuppositions of the Judaeo-Christian tradition, such as notions of a personal God, the uniqueness of the human individual and the meaning of history, as well as the modern Western belief in the powers of the intellect, rationality, planning and progress.[26]

It is beyond our present scope to fathom either the philosophical depths or the literary attainments of Romanticism but one feels the force of Raymond Schwab's question in his milestone work, *La Renaissance orientale*: " ... was Romanticism itself anything other than an oriental irruption of the intellect?"[27] We can also accede to Edward Said's claim, following Schwab, "Romanticism cannot be understood unless some account is taken of the great textual and linguistic discoveries made about the Orient during the late eighteenth and early nineteenth centuries."[28]

The American Transcendentalists
Soon after the appearance of the revised edition of *The World as Will and Representation*, in the winter of 1846 and on the other side of the Atlantic, Henry David Thoreau watched a group of Irishmen (whom he called "Hyperboreans") carve massive blocks of ice out of Walden pond, ice bound for the southern states and for India. Their labors sparked in Thoreau's imagination another scene:

> Thus it appears that the sweltering inhabitants of Charleston and New Orleans, of Madras and Bombay and Calcutta, drink at my well. In the morning I bathe my intellect in the stupendous and cosmogonal philosophy of the *Bhagavat Geeta*, since whose composition years of the gods have elapsed, and in comparison with which our modern world and its literature seem puny and trivial; and I doubt if that philosophy is not to be referred to a previous state of existence, so remote is its sublimity from our conceptions. I lay down the book and go to my well for water, and lo! there I meet the servant of Bramin, priest of Brahma and Vishnu and Indra, who sits in his temple on the Ganges reading the *Vedas*, or dwells in the root of the tree with his crust and water jug. I meet his servant come to draw water for his master, and our buckets as it were grate together in the same well. The pure Walden water is mingled with the sacred water of the Ganges.[29]

Echoes of Blake's meetings with Old Testament prophets in the back streets of London! Thoreau, like the other American Transcendentalists, met with

26 W. Halbfass, *India and Europe*, 120. For a detailed account of the affinities and discontinuities between Schopenhauer's thought and Buddhism, see Peter Abelsen, "Schopenhauer and Buddhism," 255-278.
27 R. Schwab, *The Oriental Renaissance*, 482.
28 E. Said, *The World, the Text and the Critic*, 140.
29 From Walden, in *The Portable Thoreau*, 538-539.

ancient India in her scriptures and in his own imagination, never traveling far outside his native New England.

Like the German Romantics, the New Englanders derived much of their knowledge of India from the heroic labors of the early Orientalists—Jones, Wilkins, Colebrook, Duperron. William Emerson for instance, liberal Bostonian cleric and father of Ralph Waldo, was an avid reader of *Asiatic Researches* which he covered with extensive annotations.[30] Thoreau's first encounter with an Eastern text was in Emerson's library—Jones' *Laws of Manu* which, said Thoreau, "comes to me with such a volume of sound as if it had been swept unobstructed over the plains of Hindustan."[31] The *Gita*, which Thoreau read under the trees every morning at Walden, had only arrived in Concord in 1843, Wilkins' translation given to Emerson as a gift. Let us glance at the Eastern enthusiasms of the three key imaginative writers in American Transcendentalism: Emerson, Thoreau and Whitman. We might, by way of shorthand, describe their interests as metaphysical, practical and poetic respectively. By way of a context here is J.J. Clarke's useful summation of the Transcendentalist agenda:

> The underlying philosophy of New England transcendentalism ... represent-ed a commitment to ancient and universal ideas concerning the essential unity and ultimately spiritual nature of the cosmos, combined with a belief in the ultimate goodness of man and the supremacy of intuitive over ration-al thought. Its deeply spiritual outlook was one which sought to go beyond creeds and organized religions in favor of a religious experience deemed to be universal. It represented in many ways a continuation and development of ideas of the European Romantic movement, especially those of Goethe, Wordsworth, Coleridge, and Carlyle, and like Romanticism, was inspired by neo-Platonic and mystical traditions. It can also be seen as a reaction against Lockean materialism, utilitarianism, and Calvinistic Christianity ...[32]

For Emerson the Hindu Scriptures were a mine of metaphysical and philosophical insights which corroborated and sharpened his own emergent philosophy, underpinned by the idea of the universal world-soul and the fun-damental unity of God, man and nature for which he found plentiful Indian sanctions. "We lie in the lap of immense intelligence," he wrote, "which makes us organs of its activity and receivers of its truth."[33] Emerson's enthu-siasm for Eastern philosophy and spirituality was more or less restricted to Hinduism and to its primary Scriptures: the *Vedas, Upanishads* and *Gita*. The latter, he confided to his journal, was

---

30 R. Fields, *How the Swans Came to the Lake*, 56.
31 R. Fields, *How the Swans Came to the Lake*, 59.
32 J.J. Clarke, *Oriental Enlightenment*, 84.
33 R. Fields, *How the Swans Came to the Lake*, 58. On Emerson's engagement with Hindu doctrines see S. Nagarajan, "Emerson and *Advaita*: Some Comparisons and Contrasts"; R.B. Goodman, "East-West Philosophy in Nineteenth Century America: Emerson and Hinduism"; G. Ferrando, "Emerson and the East."

the first of books; it was as if an empire spoke to us, nothing small or unworthy, but large, serene, consistent, the voice of an old intelligence which in another age and climate had pondered over and disposed of the same questions which exercise us.[34]

A Hindu imprint is clearly evident in Emerson's poems "Brahma" and "Hamatreya," and in essays such as "Fate," "Plato," "the Over-Soul," "Illusions" and "Immortality." The first four lines of "Brahma," for instance, are almost a paraphrase of Krishna's words to Arjuna in the *Gita*:

> If the red slayer thinks he slays,
> Or if the slain thinks he is slain,
> They know not well the subtle ways
> I keep, and pass, and turn again

Compare with: "He who deems This to be a slayer and he who thinks This to be slain, are alike without discernment; This slays not, neither is it slain."[35]

Emerson's attitude to Buddhism oscillated between the ambivalent and the hostile. In particular, what he understood as the Buddhist idea of *nirvana* was repugnant to him. The idea of annihilation, he wrote, froze him with its "icy light":

> This remorseless Buddhism lies all around, threatening with death and night ... Every thought, every enterprise, every sentiment, has its ruin in this horrid Infinite which circles us and awaits our dropping into it.[36]

In another journal entry the Sage of Concord summarized Buddhism as "Winter. Night. Sleep."[37]

Thoreau, the "Yankee Diogenes," was less interested in metaphysical speculation and more concerned with the practical ideal of a simple, spiritual life. He was much more enthusiastic about Buddhism whilst he shared Emerson's enthusiasm for the *Gita* of which he wrote, "the reader is nowhere raised into and sustained in a higher, purer, or rarer region of thought than in the *Bhagavat-Geeta*."[38] Thoreau adopted as his motto "*Ex Oriente Lux*"— Light comes from the East. In the "Ethical Scriptures" column of *Dial*, the principal organ of the Transcendentalists, Thoreau presented his own translation from Eugène Burnouf's French, of the *Lotus Sutra*, one of the great texts of the Mahayana. The principal lesson Thoreau drew from the Sutra was the necessity for sustained and disciplined meditation, soon to be put

---

34 E. Sharpe, *The Universal Gita*, 24.

35 *Bhagavad Gita* II.19. On "Brahma" see K. Narayana Chandran, "The Pining Gods and Sages in Emerson's 'Brahma,'" 55-57.

36 R. Fields, *How the Swans Came to the Lake*, 60.

37 R. Fields, *How the Swans Came to the Lake*, 60. In recent years there have been several attempts to find some affinities between Emerson's thought and sensibility and Zen Buddhism: see S. Morris, "Beyond Christianity: Transcendentalism and Zen," and J.G. Rudy, "Engaging the Void: Emerson's Essay on Experience and the Zen Experience of Self-Emptying."

38 E. Sharpe, *The Universal Gita*, 27.

into effect during his sojourn at Walden Pond. His temperament was of a much more contemplative turn than Emerson's. Earlier, in 1841 he wrote in his journal that

> one may discover the root of the Hindoo religion in his own private history, when, in the silent intervals of the day or the night, he does sometimes inflict on himself like austerities with a stern satisfaction.[39]

As Rick Fields has remarked, Thoreau was perhaps the first American to explore "the nontheistic mode of contemplation which is the distinguishing mark of Buddhism."[40] His friend Moncure Conway, compared Thoreau with the *sannyasis* and yogis of the Indian forests:

> Like the pious Yogi, so long motionless while gazing on the sun that knotty plants encircled his neck and the cast snake-skin his loins, and the birds built their nests on his shoulders, this poet and naturalist, by equal consecration, became a part of field and forest.[41]

Emerson once famously remarked that Walt Whitman's *Leaves of Grass* was "a mixture of the *Bhagavad-Gita* and the *New York Herald*," the latter a somewhat yellowish rag of the day. Whitman himself said that he had absorbed "the ancient Hindu poems" as well as some of the cardinal texts of the West (Homer, Aeschylus, Sophocles, Dante, Shakespeare) in preparation for his *magnum opus*. Rick Fields describes the poetic process in Whitman as a kind of "ecstatic eclecticism," borne out by passages such as this, from Whitman's "Song of Myself":

> My faith is the greatest of faiths and the least of faiths,
> Enclosing worship ancient and modern and all between ancient and modern,
> Believing I shall come again upon the earth after five thousand years,
> Waiting repose from oracles, honoring the gods, saluting the sun,
> Making a fetish of the first rock or stump, powwowing with the sticks in the circle of obis,
> Helping the lama or Brahmin as he trims the lamps of the idols,
> Dancing through the streets in a phallic procession, rapt and austere
>   in the woods a gymnosophist,
> Drinking mead from the skull-cap, to *Shastras* and *Vedas* admirant
>   minding the *Koran* ...[42]

---

39 E. Sharpe, *The Universal Gita*, 30.
40 R. Fields, *How the Swans Came to the Lake*, 62-63.
41 R. Fields, *How the Swans Came to the Lake*, 64. On the impact of Buddhism on both Thoreau's asceticism and his thought see A.D. Hodder, "'*Ex Oriente Lux*': Thoreau's Ecstasies and Hindu Texts." Although not strictly relevant to our subject we cannot leave Thoreau without recalling his uncommonly sensible remarks on the subject of "news": "I am sure that I never read any memorable news in a newspaper. If we read of one man robbed, or murdered, or killed by accident, or one house burned or one vessel wrecked ... we need never read of another. One is enough. If you are acquainted with the principle, what do you care for myriad instances and applications? To a philosopher, all news, as it is called, is gossip ..."; Thoreau, *Walden*, 347.
42 R. Fields, *How the Swans Came to the Lake*, 66.

More reminiscences of Blake and anticipations of Ginsberg! In one of his later works, *Passage to India*, Whitman traces a journey not "to lands and seas alone" but to "primal thought ... Back, back to wisdom's birth, to innocent intuitions."[43]

Modernism and Cultural Crisis

Before turning our attention to the modernists we must briefly take note of several key developments, between the time of the Transcendentalists and the First World War, which promoted the dissemination of Eastern influences in the intellectual and cultural life of the West. Here we can do no more than catalogue these: the growth of a cluster of Indological disciplines in European universities and the imposing scholarship of figures such as Eugène Burnouf, Max Müller and Paul Deussen; the popularizing of Eastern mythology and teachings by figures such as Edwin Arnold, Paul Carus and Lafcadio Hearn; the proliferation of Eastern texts available in reputable European translations with the *I Ching* and the *Tibetan Book of the Dead* later to become unlikely best-sellers; the rapid growth of the Theosophical Society in four continents and the popularity of "occult" teachings ostensibly derived from Eastern sources—one may mention such formidable figures as Madame Blavatsky, Alexandra David-Neel, W.Y. Evans-Wentz and "the Tiger of Turkestan," the Armenian thaumaturge Georgi Ivanovitch Gurdjieff.

To understand the appeal of Eastern cultural forms and religio-philo-sophical ideas in this period we must take account of the cultural crisis which engulfed the European intelligentsia. The epochal event, of course, was the Great War but the seeds of the crisis go back at least to the mid-19th century when various subterranean fissures in the European psyche were making themselves felt: one need only mention the names of Kierkegaard, Dostoevsky, Baudelaire and Nietzsche who each registered some profound inner disturbances which anticipated the barbarisms of the 20th century.[44] Oriental motifs and images, both visual and literary, abound in the work of the *fin-de-siècle* European avant-garde. As J.J. Clarke has observed,

> Orientalism ... helped to give expression and substance to a deep sense of cultural crisis and to loss of faith in the West's idea of progress through sci-entific rationalism, and to a need for new modes of representation. Responding to the cultural crisis at the turn of the century, modernism meant, in essence, the demand for a new and purified consciousness, one that could replace the discredited tastes and conventions of the Victorian period ...[45]

---

43 R. Fields, *How the Swans Came to the Lake*, 66.
44 On this subject see George Steiner's provocative thesis in *In Bluebeard's Castle*.
45 J.J. Clarke, *Oriental Enlightenment*, 101.

Let us glance at the place of Eastern influences in the work of two modernist poets: Yeats and Eliot.

The influences on Yeats' thought and poetry were many and varied—Celtic mythology, neo-Platonism, Blake, Swedenborg among the more conspicuous. But Yeats also derived nourishment from the East. In 1887 he joined the recently founded Theosophical Society in London, through which he was introduced to *Advaita,* the non-dualistic metaphysical teaching of the Vedanta. He found in Vedanta a corroboration of his own rejection of all forms of philosophical dualism which particularly troubled the poet in its theological forms in the West. In the Hindu Scriptures he found "an alliance between body and soul [which] our theology rejects" as well as the "the mind's direct apprehension of the truth, above all antinomies."[46] He was powerfully attracted by the *Upanishads* and collaborated on a translation with Swami Purohit, one in wide circulation in the counter-culture of the 1960s. Under the influence of Pound he became a fervent admirer of the Japanese Noh plays, and through the writings of D.T. Suzuki an enthusiast of Zen Buddhism which, in its ability to annihilate all intellectual abstractions, he came to regard as the apex of Eastern wisdom.[47] Like Eliot, Yeats was convinced by his studies of Eastern sapiental traditions that Indian wisdom was more accommodating than modern Western philosophy to the "multidimensionality of Truth."[48] Sankaran Ravindran has argued that Yeats' work can be understood as a steady growth in the understanding of the Indian conception of life as a drama played out between the self (the egoic personality) and the Self (*atman*). Other distinctively Indian ideas about *karma,* transmigration, the four stages of life and the interdependence of the inner and outer worlds also find expression, often veiled, in Yeats' poetry and in his later prose works.[49]

Pound, who described Yeats' metaphysical ideas as "very, very, very bughouse,"[50] was more attuned to Chinese aesthetics than Hindu metaphysics. His *Cantos* exhibit strong Oriental influences derived from his study and translation of Chinese poetry and philosophy. Following the work of the American orientalist Ernest Fennellosa, Pound also became entranced by the expressive possibilities of the pictographic Chinese script, charmingly describing his own idiosyncratic poetic exploitation of Chinese characters as "listening to incense."[51] The early Chinese poets, Pound wrote, were

> a treasury to which the next centuries may look for as great a stimulus as the Renaissance had from the Greeks ... The first step of a renaissance, or awakening, is the importation of models for painting, sculpture, writing ... The

46 J.J. Clarke, *Oriental Enlightenment,* 102.
47 J.J. Clarke, *Oriental Enlightenment,* 102.
48 Sankaran Ravindran, *W.B. Yeats and Indian Tradition,* vii.
49 See B.M. Wilson, "'From Mirror to Mirror': Yeats and Eastern Thought," 28-46.
50 See F. Clews, "The Consolation of Theosophy."
51 M. Edwardes, *East-West Passage,* 30.

last century discovered the Middle Ages. It is possible that this century may find a new Greece in China.[52]

In 1911 T.S. Eliot embarked on three years of intensive postgraduate study at Harvard of Sanskrit, Pali, Indian philosophy (particularly logic, ethics and metaphysics, and Patanjali's *Yoga Sutras*), and the religious thought of China and Japan.[53] This three-year immersion in Eastern philosophy, metaphysics and philology at Harvard left a lasting mark, both on his own spiritual development and on his poetic vision and method. Although Eliot summed up the fruit of his Indological studies as "enlightened mystification"[54] the impact was sufficiently serious for him to consider, at the time of composing "The Wasteland," becoming a Buddhist, before committing himself to Anglo-Catholicism.[55] On the evidence of his own testimony it can be argued that Eliot's eventual religious affiliation grew out of his early Indian studies which helped him to escape the intellectual prejudices of his own milieu—a not unfamiliar pattern of spiritual growth.[56]

Eastern themes, motifs and allusions are to be found throughout Eliot's work but particularly in his two poetic masterpieces, "The Wasteland" and *Four Quartets*. The Buddha's "Fire Sermon," the eighth chapter of the *Gita*, and several *Upanishads* figure prominently in these works. Critics have argued about the precise meaning and effectiveness of Eliot's use of Eastern imagery and scriptural allusions but there is little doubt that they contribute significantly to a sharply distinctive method and poetic vision. Eliot himself explicitly acknowledged his poetic debt to "Indian thought and sensibility."[57] The impact of Buddhism is most evident in *Four Quartets* which is pervaded by the premier doctrines of impermanence and suffering, whilst Eliot's treatment of the central theme of time and eternity bears a strong Eastern inflection.[58] We might also note that Eliot's practice of synthesizing themes from Greek, Hindu and Buddhist as well as Christian sources testifies to his belief in a mystical experience which is of neither East nor West and which transcends religious forms—a characteristically though not exclusively Eastern notion.[59] But Eliot was no "New Age" eclectic: his well-known insistence on the intimate relationship of culture and religion, and on the necessity of the

52 Pound quoted in R. Fields, *How the Swans Came to the Lake*, 163.
53 Details of these studies can be found in J. Perl & A. Tuck, "The Hidden Advantage of Tradition: the Significance of T.S. Eliot's Indic Studies," 115ff.
54 Eliot quoted in J. Perl & A. Tuck, "The Hidden Advantage of Tradition: the Significance of T.S. Eliot's Indic Studies," 127.
55 S. Spender, *T.S. Eliot*, 20.
56 See J. Perl & A. Tuck, "The Hidden Advantage of Tradition: the Significance of T.S. Eliot's Indic Studies," 115.
57 From T.S. Eliot, *Christianity and Culture* (1949), quoted in J. Perl & A. Tuck, "The Hidden Advantage of Tradition: the Significance of T.S. Eliot's Indic Studies," 127fn.
58 The most detailed discussion of the impact of the Eastern Scriptures on Eliot's poetry is H.E. McCarthy, "T.S. Eliot and Buddhism," 31-55. See also E. Sharpe, *The Universal Gita*, 132-135.
59 J. Perl & A. Tuck, "The Hidden Advantage of Tradition: the Significance of T.S. Eliot's Indic Studies," 121.

particularities of tradition precluded any sentimental notion of a "distillation" of the "essence" of different religions such as might lead to a new "universal" religion. He also disapproved of those Western appropriations of Eastern religion which ignored or jettisoned "hagiology, rites and customs."[60]

The 1893 World's Parliament of Religions

In 1894 Max Müller compared the World's Parliament of Religions in Chicago with the legendary religious councils of India initiated by the Emperors Asoka (3rd century BC) and Akbar (16th century):

> If the Religious Parliament was not an entirely new idea, it was certainly the first realization of an idea which has lived silently in the hearts of prophets, or has been uttered now and then by poets only, who are free to dream dreams and to see visions.[61]

Anagarika Dharmapala, a delegate from Ceylon, was even more enthusiastic, calling the Parliament "the noblest and proudest achievement in history, and the crowning work of the nineteenth century."[62]

The Parliament was held under the aegis of the Columbian Exposition of 1892. The Rev. Dr John Henry Barrows, chairman of the Parliament, described the glittering exhibition on Lake Michigan's shores as "the most comprehensive and brilliant display of man's material progress which the ages have known." Furthermore, wrote the liberal Presbyterian minister,

> ... since it is as clear as the light that the Religion of Christ has led to many of the chief and noblest developments of our modern civilization, it did not appear that Religion, any more than Education, Art or Electricity should be excluded from the Columbian Exhibition.[63]

The Parliament was the brainchild of a Swedenborgian lawyer, Charles Carroll Bonney, who addressed an opening audience of four thousand, referring to the rising of "the sun of a new era of religious peace and progress ... dispelling the dark clouds of sectarian strife."[64] Barrows traced the origins of the Parliament to the missionary movement which had accompanied the founding of the British Empire in India and harked back to the pioneering work of Sir William Jones and other early orientalists who had initiated the new scholarly field of "comparative theology," leading to "a larger conception of human history, a new and more religious idea of divine providence through all ages and all lands."[65]

---

60 J. Perl & A. Tuck, "The Hidden Advantage of Tradition: the Significance of T.S. Eliot's Indic Studies," 131fn.

61 Max Müller quoted in E.J. Ziolkowski, "The Literary Bearing of Chicago's World's Parliament of Religions," 10-11. The comparison with Asoka's Council was perhaps first made by Dharmapala; see R. Fields, *How the Swans Came to the Lake*, 122.

62 R. Fields, *How the Swans Came to the Lake*, 120.

63 R. Fields, *How the Swans Came to the Lake*, 120.

64 Bonney quoted in J.J. Clarke, *Oriental Enlightenment*, 92.

65 R. Fields, *How the Swans Came to the Lake*, 119.

Christians of nearly all denominations,[66] Buddhists, Hindus, Parsis, Sikhs, Jains, Taoists and Confucianists all rubbed shoulders in the "White City" of the Exposition, listened to lectures and discussed religious issues. Some 150,000 Americans participated in the two-week Parliament.[67] Whilst the climate of the Parliament was intermittently influenced by an over-heated Christian evangelism and by an occasional trumpet-burst of Western triumphalism (religious, political and material), there was on the part of most of the delegates a desire for serious fraternal dialogue and the search for common ground on which a more universalistic understanding of religion might be constructed. Amongst the two hundred-odd delegates from forty-five different religions and denominations were representatives from India, Ceylon, Siam, Japan and China. Three of these were to leave a lasting imprint on the West: the flamboyant and charismatic Swami Vivekananda, disciple of the great sage Ramakrishna and apostle of a new universal religion based on ancient Hindu sources; Anagarika Dharmapala, first of many Theravadin teachers in the West; and the Rinzai Zen master Soyen Shaku who inaugurated a long line of Zen teachers who would have a mesmeric effect on Western seekers.[68] In her autobiography the Chicago poet Harriet Monroe echoes many other observers when she tells us that

> It was Vivekananda, the magnificent, who stole the whole show and captured the town ... the handsome monk in the orange robe gave us in perfect English a masterpiece. His personality, dominant, magnetic; his voice, rich as a bronze bell; the controlled fervor of his feeling; the beauty of his message to the Western world he was facing for the first time—these combined to give us a rare and perfect moment of supreme emotion. It was human eloquence at its highest pitch.[69]

It is a piquant irony that Vivekananda was not an invited delegate but a gate-crasher at the Parliament![70]

Many of the participants seemed to share the ecumenical spirit which moved the chairman to claim that,

> Religion, like the white light of Heaven, has been broken into many colored fragments by the prisms of men. One of the objects of the Parliament has

---

66 A notable exception was the Church of England, the Archbishop of Canterbury having declined to attend because he rejected the implicit premise of the Parliament that the various religions could meet on a footing of equality and parity. There was only one Muslim who was a recent New England convert; the objections of the Sultan of Turkey dissuaded the Muslims from the Middle East from attending. See C.T. Jackson, *The Oriental Religions and American Thought*, 245.

67 D. Eck, *Encountering God*, 23.

68 See E.J. Ziolkowski, "The Literary Bearing of Chicago's World's Parliament of Religions," 10-25.

69 Harriet Monroe quoted in E.J. Ziolkowski, "The Literary Bearing of Chicago's World's Parliament of Religions," 116.

70 R. King, *Orientalism and Religion*, 93. The fascinating figures of Vivekananda, Dharmapala and Soyen Shaku will command more extended attention later in this study.

been to change this many-colored radiance back into the white light of heavenly truth.[71]

Although the Parliament was marred by the missionizing Christian impulse which had been one of the driving motivations of its organizers, by some outbursts of sectarian antagonism and by the intemperate criticisms of many Christian zealots who had refused to participate, the Parliament was undoubtedly a seminal event in the changing Western perception of the religious traditions of the East.[72] Through such articulate and passionate spokesmen as Dharmapala and Vivekananda many Westerners were able to learn something of the Eastern traditions which had previously been shrouded in a fog of ignorance and misunderstanding. The Parliament provided a forum for friendly intercourse between many of the participants, served as a platform for further inter-religious dialogue, and stimulated the scholarly study of Eastern religions in the academies of the West. Larry Fader has provided a colorful summation of the Parliament's significance and an appropriate point at which to draw this chapter to a close:

> The 1893 Chicago World's Parliament of Religions was a significant event in the history of inter-religious dialogue ... As a human spectacle ... consider the curiosity aroused by the appearance of the many delegates espousing strange and little-known beliefs, arriving from distant, mysterious lands, dressed in alien garb, acting in unfamiliar ways and speaking languages rarely heard by Americans ... For those whose vision transcended this superficial level, other flights of imagination predominated. On the coattails of the discovery that there do indeed exist belief systems other than the Judeo-Christian came noble dreams of religious dialogue and expressions of the unanimity of human spiritual purpose. Imagine: the great religions of the world joining hands in mutual respect and admiration—a gallery of scholars and saints in white flowing gowns and saffron robes, resplendent with amulets and bark cloth, beads and trinkets, large braided turbans and feathered headdresses, raising their voices heavenward and proclaiming our collective humanity—kneeling to drink, perhaps at different localities, but from the same thirst-quenching, sweet-water, proverbial lake of truth.[73]

---

71 R. Fields, *How the Swans Came to the Lake*, 121.
72 On the limitations and omissions of the Parliament see D. Eck, *Encountering God*, 27-30.
73 L. Fader, "Zen in the West," 122.

II

Western Engagements
with
Eastern Traditions

3.

Five Bridge-Builders between West and East

Sister Nivedita—Rudolf Otto—Giuseppe Tucci—Gary Snyder—Huston Smith

> *... understanding, at least in realms as inherently noble as the great faiths of mankind, brings respect; and respect prepares the way for a higher power, love—the only power that can quench the flames of fear, suspicion, and prejudice, and provide the means by which the people of this small but precious Earth can become one to one another.* (Huston Smith)[1]

An Anglo-Irish disciple of Vivekananda, a German theologian, an Italian Tibetologist, an American Beat poet, and a scholar who wrote perhaps the century's most widely influential survey of the world's religions—these are the disparate figures, bound together by a fascination with the religious life of the East, to whom we turn in this chapter. We will combine biographical sketches with some general remarks about their significance as bridge-builders between the West and the East, and in so doing adumbrate several themes and problematics which will be elaborated in later chapters.

Sister Nivedita (Margaret Noble)

> You will be in the midst of half-naked men and women with quaint ideas of caste and isolation, shunning the white skin through fear or hatred, and hated by them intensely. On the other hand, you will be looked upon by the whites as a crank, and every one of your moves will be watched with suspicion.[2]

So, in 1898, wrote an Indian swami to a young Anglo-Irish woman who had determined to follow him back to India as his disciple. He was the redoubtable Swami Vivekananda, by now probably the most widely known Indian in the Western world. She was Margaret Noble, thirty years old, daughter of a Congregationalist minister, journalist, headmistress of a progressive school in Wimbledon, agitator for Irish Home Rule, socialist champion of the poor, feminist and something of a firebrand. At Lady Ripon's Sesame Club she had met G.B. Shaw, Huxley and Yeats, and was well established in "a brilliant career" as writer, educationalist, lecturer and champion of "every kind of emancipation."[3]

1 H. Smith, *Religions of Man*, 355.
2 B. Foxe, *Long Journey Home*, 36.
3 B. Foxe, *Long Journey Home*, 17.

Margaret Noble had earlier become disenchanted with the strict Protestant Christianity in which she was raised, and intellectually disturbed by the apparent conflict of religious faith and modern science, particularly Darwinism. For a time she was attracted to Buddhism but it was to be the Hindu tradition which was to become her spiritual home. Initially somewhat skeptical of the charismatic Bengali monk who was exciting such interest on his lecture tours of America and the United Kingdom, Noble found herself deeply attracted to the religious universalism which he had directly inherited from Ramakrishna, one of India's greatest saints and sages. Of Vivekananda's lectures she later wrote,

> The master thought which he continually approached from different points of view, [was] the equal truth of all religions, and the impossibility for us of criticizing any of the divine incarnations, since all were equally forth-shinings of the One.[4]

Another of Vivekanada's central themes also struck a chord: the primacy of spiritual experience over dogmas, creeds, sects, rites and institutions, and the ideal of realization as the supreme end of all religion.

Vivekananda was born Narendra Nath Datta[5] in Calcutta in 1863, into a wealthy family of scholars, philanthropists and monks.[6] At university Narendra had shown prodigious talents—intellectual, musical, theatrical, athletic—exhibiting all the vigor and vitality appropriate to the *Kshatriya* caste to which he belonged. He had an exceptionally intelligent, lively mind and an engaging personality, and seemed poised for a glittering career in law. Instead, answering an inner call which he had felt since childhood, Narendra turned his back on all worldly enticements and ambitions, and became one of the principal disciples of Ramakrishna at Dakshineswar, eventually becoming Swami Vivekananda.

Some years after the death of his master in 1886 Vivekananda, as we have seen, attended the World's Parliament of Religions in Chicago and lectured extensively in America, the UK and Europe. An address to the graduate students in the philosophy department at Harvard generated such enthusiasm that he was forthwith offered a chair in Eastern Philosophy, an offer which his monastic vocation obliged him to decline.[7] His charismatic personality, his spiritual teachings and his nerve-tingling oratory generated a good deal of fervor and it was at this time that he attracted several Westerners who were to be amongst his most devoted and energetic disciples—from England, Captain Sevier and his wife, Josiah J. Goodwin who became the recorder of Vivekananda's lectures, and Margaret Noble. Vivekananda returned to India in a blaze of triumphant publicity and soon turned his considerable energies

---

4   B. Foxe, *Long Journey Home*, 21.
5   "Dutt" in some English renderings.
6   For a brief account of Vivekananda's life and work see W. Halbfass, *India and Europe*, 228-246.
7   B. Foxe, *Long Journey Home*, 19.

to the founding of the Ramakrishna Order, Mission and Math. In *Ramakrishna and His Disciples* Christopher Isherwood has usefully summarized the aims of the Mission:

> The Mission will preach the truths which Ramakrishna preached and demonstrated in his own life. It will help others to put these truths into practice ... It will train men to teach such knowledge or sciences as are conducive to the material and spiritual welfare of the masses. It will establish centers for monastic training and social work in different parts of India. It will also send trained members of the Order to countries outside India, to bring a better relation and a closer understanding between them. Its aims will be purely spiritual and humanitarian; therefore it will have no connection with politics.[8]

By the turn of the century Vivekananda had become closely, and somewhat reluctantly, associated with the cause of Indian nationalism as well as the burgeoning Hindu reform movement.

Margaret Noble arrived in Calcutta in January 1898. Thenceforth, until the early death of Vivekananda in 1902, aged forty, she was to be his closest Western disciple and was referred to by the monks of the order as his "spiritual daughter." Her biographer has described her initial reactions to a land so different from the Victorian drawing-rooms she had left behind:

> ... when, by [Vivekananda's] side she saw Calcutta for the first time—the teeming life of the city, the noise, the color and the peaceful movements of the brown waters of the Ganges—she fell utterly and irrevocably in love—not with Calcutta, but with India. It was a love affair that hit her with immense force because it was so unexpected. She had wanted to help with the work, she had been eager to come, but she had not expected anything like this.[9]

She moved into a small cottage on the banks of the holy river with two of Vivekananda's other Western disciples, Josephine McCleod and Mrs Ole Bull, widow of the Norwegian violinist and friend of Ibsen.

Noble took to heart Vivekananda's injunction:

> You have to set yourself to Hinduize your thoughts, your needs, your conceptions, and your habits. Your life, internal and external, has to become all that an orthodox Hindu Brahmin Brahmacharini's ought to be.[10]

She succeeded remarkably well. She learnt Bengali, visited schools to understand the demands of her chosen field of work, underwent training with Vivekananda and took vows as a novice in the Ramakrishna Order as Sister Nivedita ("the dedicated"). She overcame the initial suspicion, even hostility, of some of the monks of the Order and developed a close relationship with

8 C. Isherwood, *Ramakrishna and His Disciples*, 324.
9 B. Foxe, *Long Journey Home*, 37.
10 B. Foxe, *Long Journey Home*, 92.

the Holy Mother, Sarada Devi (Ramakrishna's wife), with whom she lived for a time. She eventually moved into very humble quarters in one of Calcutta's poorest sectors where she established a school for girls, initially in her own house. (The school, much expanded, survives to this day as the Sister Nivedita School.) Her lifestyle was frugal in the extreme. She also dedicated herself to working with the poor whom she served with indefatigable energy and was much admired by Indians for her heroic efforts during famine, flood and plague epidemics which afflicted Bengal around the turn of the century. She nurtured the education and social emancipation of Indian women, especially widows. Sister Nivedita also became a public speaker of some renown, lecturing on religious and social subjects. One of her early lectures, delivered in Calcutta's Albert Hall to a huge audience, was on the subject of Kali, the terrible goddess to whom Ramakrishna himself had been dedicated, and the controversial practice of Kali worship which she passionately defended against both Western and Indian detractors:

> We are aware [she said] of the many beastly and corrupt rites which have come to be associated with Kali worship. While our regret for them is boundless, we do not see the wisdom of inveighing against Kali worship in wholesale manner ... Destroy the weeds but save the garden![11]

This lecture, to be repeated in many parts of India, earned her acclaim in some quarters, notoriety in others. She later wrote what was to prove one of the most popular of her many books, *Kali the Mother* (much admired by Aurobindo). She accompanied Vivekananda on another tour of America and Britain and became a sought-after lecturer in her own right, using the proceeds to fund her school in Calcutta and her social work amongst the poor. She ignited a storm of controversy in London through her telling criticisms of the ways in which some Christian missionaries so persistently misrepresented Hinduism and the Indian social order. (She was scrupulous in avoiding any criticism of their religious teachings.)[12]

By the time of Vivekananda's death she had left far behind her the naïve British patriotism with which she had arrived in the sub-continent and had become a champion of Indian independence and a fierce critic of the colonial regime—a role for which she was peculiarly well-equipped:

> Her entire nature fitted her for it; all the "fighting Irish" in her was awake; she had already proved that she could rouse large Hindu audiences to enthusiasm; she had the undoubted asset, in India, of being a disciple of their much-loved leader; she was a woman and a nun, and therefore a mother-figure and liable to be treated with respect; she was a member of the ruling nation by birth who had become totally a Hindu in thinking and loyalties ... And she longed to fight for India ...[13]

11 B. Foxe, *Long Journey Home*, 82.
12 See B. Foxe, *Long Journey Home*, 123-124.
13 B. Foxe, *Long Journey Home*, 127-128.

Because of the monastic prohibition on overt political activism she felt she must now sever her formal ties with the Ramakrishna Order but in her heart she remained true to her vows. She also continued her warm friendship with Sarada Devi, with the monks at the Math and with other Western devotees.

As a tireless critic of British rule and advocate of the nationalist cause she befriended such figures as Aurobindo Ghose, Rabindranath Tagore and various other members of that illustrious family, the Congressional leaders G.K. Gokhale and R.C. Dutt, and Mrs Annie Besant, leader of the Indian branch of the Theosophical Movement. She had a fleeting meeting with the young Gandhi, still a somewhat peripheral figure in the independence movement, who later wrote of her in the most respectful terms. In some respects she had anticipated some of the themes central to Gandhi's later campaigns. After meeting the Russian anarchist Prince Kropotkin in London, and reading his work, she had written:

> He knows more than any other man what India needs. What I specially dwell upon is the utter needlessness of governments ... the village system supplies machinery of self-government enough ... We shall one day peacefully wait upon the Viceroy and inform him, smiling, that his services are no longer required. The great means of doing it will be elaborated by degrees as we come to have what Mr Geddes calls "a theory of the Pacific Life."[14]

She spoke on political themes in many parts of India and published in a wide variety of newspapers and journals, for a time editing Aurobindo's *Karma Yogin*. Nivedita left her Calcutta school in the capable hands of her friend Sister Christine,[15] and in 1902, 1904, and again in 1907, spoke at venues all over the sub-continent on both religious and political subjects. She was an eloquent advocate for the *swadeshi* movement (the boycott of British-made goods) and an equally forceful opponent of Bengali partition, imposed by Curzon in 1905. As Gandhi was to do, she enjoined Muslims and Hindus to stand side-by-side as Indians:

> What then was the duty of the Indian Mussalman? It was not to relate himself to Arabia ... he had no need of that; it had been accomplished for him by the faith and patient labor of his forefathers. No; his duty was to relate himself to India—his home by blood or by adoption and hospitality ...[16]

Nor did she have any patience with one of the constant themes of imperialist propaganda—that "India" enjoyed no unity beyond that "given" to her by her benevolent colonizers:

14 B. Foxe, *Long Journey Home*, 125. This last reference is to Professor Patrick Geddes, the British sociologist and participant in the Paris Congress of the History of Religions in 1900. Nivedita briefly assisted him with his work.

15 Christine Greenstidel, German by birth, American by citizenship and another of Vivekananda's Western disciples; see her "Memories of Swami Vivekananda" in *Vedanta for the Western World*, 156-175.

16 B. Foxe, *Long Journey Home*, 166.

There is a religious idea that may be called Indian, but it is of no single sect; ... there is a social idea, which is the property of no caste or group; ... there is a historic evolution, in which we are all united; ... it is the thing within all these which alone is called "India."[17]

Furthermore, she claimed, "the presence of a foreign bureaucracy adds immensely to the evil characteristics of the modern epoch."[18]

Her friend H.W. Nevinson has left us a vivid pen-portrait of Sister Nivedita at this time:

It is as vain to describe Sister Nivedita in two pages as to reduce fire to a formula and call it knowledge ... Like fire, and like Shiva, Kali and other Indian powers of the spirit, she was at once destructive and creative, terrible and beneficent. There was no dull tolerance about her, and I suppose no one ever called her gentle ...[19]

In fact, she was capable of great sensitivity and gentleness, evident in her loving nursing of Gopaler-Ma, an elderly disciple of Ramakrishna who survived him by many years and for whom Nivedita always showed the most tender solicitude, as for Sarada Devi. But this was not the public face she exposed in pursuing the Indian cause.

Sister Nivedita published a good many books in her lifetime, some of the better-known being *Kali the Mother*, *The Web of Indian Life*, *Footfalls of Indian History*, *Cradle Tales of Hinduism* (for children) and her hagiography of Vivekananda, *The Master as I Saw Him*. Of these only the last retains much interest for the modern reader. Nonetheless, in their day they did much to dispel some of the prejudices and misconceptions about Hinduism and India which were rampant in the West, and helped to awaken in Indians a renewed sense of pride in their own religious and cultural heritage. In her later years she became deeply interested in traditional Indian art and a ferocious critic, in both the Indian and English press, of the then widely held "Hellenic theory" which postulated the Greek origins of Indian art—recall the episode in Kipling's *Kim* in the Lahore Museum where the lama "in open-mouthed wonder" beholds "the Greco-Buddhist sculptures done, savants know how long since, by forgotten workmen whose hands were feeling ... for the mysteriously transmitted Grecian touch."[20] It was left to Nivedita's friend Ananda Coomaraswamy finally to demolish the Hellenic theory in 1927, after pointing out in the course of his argument that

... this [Hellenic] view was put forward, as M. Fouchet [one of its principal exponents] himself admits, in a manner best calculated to flatter the prejudices of European students and to offend the susceptibilities of Indians: the creative genius of Greece had provided a model which had later been bar-

17 B. Foxe, *Long Journey Home*, 173.
18 B. Foxe, *Long Journey Home*, 183.
19 B. Foxe, *Long Journey Home*, 166.
20 R. Kipling, *Kim*, 8.

barized and degraded by races devoid of true artistic instincts, to whom nothing deserving the name fine art could be credited.[21]

In the domain of the arts and crafts Sister Nivedita sought to reanimate traditional Indian ideals and in this campaign too she fought under the same banner as Coomaraswamy:

> ... we would remind all students of art that their true function is the revelation of the beautiful, the true, the good. It is not the fugitive moments of personal experience, but the eternal and universal, that best comes to the world through them.[22]

Her last years were marked by illness and the apparent defeat of her most cherished projects: the partition of Bengal had taken place; nationalist activities had been repressed and there was a hiatus in the independence movement, many of its leaders in prison, hiding or exile; her school was foundering; attempts to establish the Ramakrishna Mission in England had thus far met with meager success. She was not to know that all these vicissitudes were temporary and that she had sown many seeds which were to germinate in the following decades. She would have been surprised to know that in 1967, on the centenary of her birth, an Indian stamp was issued in her honor. However, she seemed to have reached the inner quietude of the authentic *karma yogi*, attaining that detachment from the fruits of one's work which is so exalted in the *Bhagavad Gita*. She died in Darjeeling in 1911 after contracting a fatal strain of dysentery. The epitaph on her tomb reads, "Here repose the ashes of Sister Nivedita, who gave her all for India."[23]

Rudolf Otto

In Europe 1917 marked a year of war, revolution, widespread dislocation, a mood of confusion, anxiety and nihilism. It was the year in which Rudolf Otto's book *Das Heilege* appeared. It was to become one of the century's most influential books on the nature of religious experience, in some ways a descendant of William James' *The Varieties of Religious Experience* (1902). Soon translated into all the major European languages it was immensely popular in the decade after its publication. As Eric Sharpe wittily observed, it is a book that nearly every comparative religionist imagines she/he has read.[24]

The Idea of the Holy (its English title) was an attempt to establish a category under which religious experience could be understood in its own right, free of any theoretical schema imported from outside. It was also an attempt

---

21 Coomaraswamy quoted in S.K. Abe, "Inside the Wonder House," 81. For Coomaraswamy's final and decisive demolition of this theory see "Origins of the Buddha Image." See also "The Influence of Greek on Indian Art."

22 B. Foxe, *Long Journey Home*, 200.

23 B. Foxe, *Long Journey Home*, 225.

24 E. Sharpe, *Comparative Religion*, 161.

to valorize the non-rational (as distinct from irrational) elements of religion. Otto's work was attuned to the spirit of Pascal's maxim,

> ... if one subjects everything to reason our religion will lose its mystery and its supernatural character. If one offends the principles of reason our religion will be absurd and ridiculous ... These are two equally dangerous extremes, to shut reason out and to let nothing else in.[25]

In 1913 Otto's friend, the Swedish theologian Nathan Söderblom, had written, "Holiness is the great word in religion; it is even more essential than the notion of God."[26] Otto's purpose was to recuperate the full meaning of the word "holy" and to take hold of the religious experience to which this word points. Otto believed the word had become contaminated by moral associations which were quite secondary to its fundamental meaning and turned to an old Latin word "*numen*" to signal the realm of the most profound religious experience. The holy, he wrote, "is a category peculiar to religion ... [it] is perfectly *sui generis* and irreducible to any other; and therefore, like every absolutely primary and elementary datum, while it admits of being discussed, it cannot be defined"[27] but only evoked on the basis of experience. To experience the numinous is to encounter the *mysterium trememdum* which is marked by an overpowering sense of otherness, of awefulness, majesty and energy but which is also *fascinans*—beautiful, alluring, captivating. This real presence, neither a phantom nor a projection of the sub-conscious but, in Christian terms, the "living God," calls up "creaturely feeling" and appears "in a form ennobled beyond measure where the soul held speechless, trembles inwardly to the furthest fiber of its being."[28] In an Appendix Otto reproduces the thrilling passage from the *Bhagavad Gita* where Arjuna "smitten with amazement" beholds the manifold forms of Krishna, more dazzling than "the light of a thousand suns."[29]

Part of the book's appeal, for both general reader and for the student of religion, was Otto's understanding of religion primarily in experiential rather than creedal terms. At a time when "religion" was often conceived to hinge on belief and morality Otto turned attention to the religious experience, not to offer any reductionistic "scientific" explanation but to affirm its mystery and power, and its centrality in religion. Comparative religionists were later to take up Otto's interest in the holy (now more often than not termed "the sacred") as one of the structuring principles of their inquiries. Unhappily, the very popularity of this germinative work has somewhat obscured Otto's many other achievements, not least in the field of Indological studies and in the promotion of global inter-religious understanding.

25 See John Harvey's Translator's Preface to the second edition of *The Idea of the Holy*, xix.
26 N. Söderblom, "Holiness" in J. Hastings (ed), *Encyclopedia of Religion and Ethics*, V6, 731.
27 R. Otto, *The Idea of the Holy*, 7.
28 R. Otto, *The Idea of the Holy*, 17.
29 R. Otto, *The Idea of the Holy*, Appendix 2.

Otto was born in 1869 in Northern Germany, into a strict Lutheran family, the twelfth of thirteen children.[30] He studied theology, languages, music and art at the universities of Erlangen and Göttingen. The young theologian was disenchanted with the "ossified intellectualism" of the prevailing rationalistic theology and was strongly attracted to Martin Luther's insistence that the knowledge of God had little to do with the rational faculties.[31] Indeed, Otto's dissertation for his licentiate in theology was on Luther's view of the Holy Spirit and he repeatedly returned to the Pauline maxim that "the letter killeth but the spirit giveth life." Otto was also much influenced in his early years by Kant, Schleiermacher, Fries, Albrecht Ritschl and Ernest Troeltsch, each of whom provided a strong antidote to the reigning theological orthodoxies of the period. Otto was swimming against the tide of the regnant theologians of the day, Rudolf Bultmann, Karl Barth and Emil Brunner, which "overwhelmed Otto at the pinnacle of his career, and resulted in a widespread rejection of his work among theologians."[32] Nearly half a century later Karl Barth recalled this uncongenial climate:

> Everything that even from afar smelt of mysticism and morals, of pietism and romanticism or even idealism, how suspect it was and how strictly prohibited or confined in the straitjacket of restrictions.[33]

Otto trained for the Lutheran ministry and after two years in a theological seminary he traveled to the Middle East. In Cairo he was profoundly influenced by the Coptic liturgy, by some Jewish rites in Jerusalem and by a Dervish ceremony which he described as "unspeakable." After these experiences, formative in his intellectual and spiritual development, he returned to Germany via the great monastic center at Mt Athos where he spent ten days. This trip provided the catalyst for his great intellectual enterprise—the construction of "a methodology of religious feeling."

Otto was neither Indologist nor comparative religionist: his professional life, apart from brief stints in the Lutheran ministry and as a member of the Prussian Parliament, was as an academic systematic theologian. He was appointed to a position at Göttingen University in 1898 where he worked before moving as a full professor to Breslau in 1915, and three years later to Marburg where he succeeded the illustrious Wilhelm Herrmann. He wrote on a wide range of religious subjects and lectured at many universities on both sides of the Atlantic. Joachim Wach has left us a vivid pen portrait of Otto in his later years:

> Rudolf Otto was an imposing figure. He held himself straight and upright. His movements were measured. The sharply cut countenance kept a grave

---

30 For biographical sketches of Otto see H. Turner & P. Mackenzie, *Commentary on 'The Idea of the Holy'*; Gregory D. Alles in R. Otto, *Autobiographical and Social Essays*; P. Almond, *Rudolf Otto*.
31 J. Wach, *Types of Religious Experience*, 213.
32 G. Alles in R. Otto, *Autobiographical and Social Essays*, 9.
33 G. Alles in R. Otto, *Autobiographical and Social Essays*, 9.

expression which did not change much even when jesting. The color of his skin was yellowish-white and betrayed past illness. Otto had contracted a tropical disease in India which forced him ever after to husband his strength strictly. His hair was white and clipped ... A small white moustache covered his upper lip. His most fascinating features were his steel-blue eyes. There was a rigidity in his glance, and one had the impression that he was "seeing" something, as he spoke, to which his interlocutor had no access ... An air of genuine mystery surrounded Otto. Familiarity was the last thing which a visitor would have expected of the great scholar or he himself would have encouraged. The students who followed his lectures tensely and with awe called him the Saint ... neither before nor since my meeting Otto have I known a person who impressed one more genuinely as a true mystic. There was something about him of the solitude into which an intimate communion with the Divine has frequently led those who were favored in this way.[34]

Nine of Otto's books appeared in English in the interwar years but many of his essays have only recently appeared in English, thanks largely to the enterprise of Gregory Alles. He was throughout his adult life engaged in a range of extra-academic activities—the movement for liturgical and ecclesiastical reform (including the creation of ministries for women), electoral change and efforts to establish an international Religious League. Ill health forced Otto's early retirement in 1929. He died of pneumonia in 1937, shortly after suffering an almost fatal sixty-foot fall from a tower which he had climbed in Staufenberg. The last years of his life were marred by severe illness, morphine addiction, depression and possibly more severe psychiatric disturbance; it is possible that Otto's "fall" was a suicide attempt.[35] The inscription on Otto's tomb in Marburg is "Heilig, Heilig, Heilig, ist der Herr Zaboath," the *sanctus* which had taken on a particular resonance in his life and work.

Otto's work falls quite neatly into two distinct periods: the early years of his professional life in which he was engrossed in teaching and writing about Protestant theology; and the later years in which his attention often turned Eastwards and towards more universal religious problems and themes. *The Idea of the Holy* is a kind of fulcrum between these two periods. In the present context it is Otto's engagement with the East which is our primary concern.

In 1911 Otto traveled extensively in North Africa, the Middle East and India: his experiences were to be decisive in the gestation of *The Idea of the Holy*. In a now-famous passage in letter to a German church weekly he described the effect of hearing the *Trisagion* of Isaiah in the synagogue in Moroccan Mogador:

It is Sabbath, and already in the dark and inconceivably grimy passage of the house we hear that sing-song of prayers and reading of scripture, that nasal half-singing half-speaking which Church and Mosque have taken over from the Synagogue. The sound is pleasant, one can soon distinguish modulations and cadences that follow one another at regular intervals, like

34 J. Wach, *Types of Religious Experience*, 210-211.

Leitmotive. The ear tries to grasp individual words but it is scarcely possible ... when suddenly out of the babel of voices, causing a thrill of fear, there it begins, unified, clear and unmistakable: *Kadosh Kadosh Kadosh Elohim Adonai Zebaoth Male'u hashamayim wahaarets kebodo!* (Holy, holy, holy, Lord of hosts, the heavens and the earth are full of thy glory.) I have heard the *Sanctus Sanctus Sanctus* of the cardinals in St Peters, the *Swiat Swiat Swiat* in the Cathedral of the Kremlin and the Holy Holy Holy of the Patriarch in Jcrusalcm. In whatever language they resound, these most exalted words that have ever come from human lips always grip one in the depths of the soul, with a mighty shudder exciting and calling into play the mystery of the other world latent therein. And this more than anywhere else here in this modest place, where they resound in the same tongue in which Isaiah first received them and from the lips of the people whose first inheritance they were.[36]

The Asian leg of his journey also left an abiding impression on Otto. Soon after arriving in Karachi he was astonished when a newly-met young Hindu launched into an eloquent discourse on the philosophy of Kant. Otto sailed up the Indus river to Lahore and thence to Calcutta and Orissa where he was lavishly entertained by a Maharajah in whom he found an attractive blend of European learning and Hindu piety. In India he had sympathetic encounters with Muslims, Sikhs, Hindus and Parsees. From India Otto traveled to Burma where he was much impressed by the vitality of Theravadin Buddhism. In Japan he visited universities, temples and monasteries and may have been the first Westerner to address a large gathering of Zen monks. He went on to China where he stayed for two months before returning to Europe through Siberia, accompanied by a collection of priceless religious artifacts which he deposited in the Museum of World Religions which he established in Marburg.

Despite poor health Otto returned to India in 1927. He was by now an accomplished Sanskritist, had translated several early Vedic texts and had published his most important contribution to Western understanding of the Hindu tradition, *Mysticism East and West* in which he continued Schopenhauer's association of Vedantic metaphysics and Meister Eckhart's apophatic theology. Whilst not unaware of "manifold singularities," Otto found in the mystics of both East and West "an astonishing conformity in the deepest impulses of human spiritual experience," independent of "race, clime and age."[37] As Richard King has noted, Otto's enterprise is colored by his apparent intention to rehabilitate Eckhart's standing within German Protestantism through the comparison with Sankara—an example of "the projection of Christian theological debates ... onto an Indian canvas."[38]

35 See P. Almond, *Rudolf Otto*, 24-25.
36 From H. Turner & P. Mackenzie, *Commentary on 'The Idea of the Holy,'* 4. For another translation of this passage see R. Otto, *Autobiographical and Social Essays*, 80.
37 R. Otto, *Mysticism East and West*, v.
38 R. King, *Orientalism and Religion*, 126.

Nonetheless, Otto's work remains a pioneering work of remarkable acuity in the field of comparative mysticism.

A visit to Elephanta Island (near Bombay), like his earlier experiences in the Middle East, left a profound impression on him. His description (often cited):

> One climbs halfway up the mountainside on magnificent stone steps until a wide gate opens on the right, in the volcanic rocks. This leads into one of the mightiest of early Indian rock temples. Heavy pillars hewn out of the rock support the roof. The eye slowly accustoms itself to the semi-darkness, gradually distinguishes awesome representations—carved into the wall—of the religious epics of India, until it reaches the imposing central recess. Here an image rises up out of the rock which I can only compare with the great representations of Christ in early Byzantine churches. It is a three-headed form, carved only as far as the breast, in threefold human size ... Still and powerful the central head looks down, with both the others in profile. Over the image rests a perfect peace and majesty ... Nowhere else have I found the secret of the transcendent world, the other world more grandly and perfectly expressed than in these three heads ... To see this place were alone worth a journey to India, while from the spirit of religion which has lived here, one may experience more in a single hour of contemplation than from all the books.[39]

After this second trip to India Otto wrote a good many scholarly works on the Vaishnavite tradition, translated several texts, including those of Ramanuja, the *Katha Upanishad* and the *Bhagavad Gita* with which he originally felt little sympathy but on which he was to write with considerable discernment.[40] Otto also wrote another comparison of his own tradition and Hinduism, *India's Religion of Grace and Christianity* (1928). Amongst his most interesting and penetrating essays was one on Gandhi whom Otto recognized as a distinctly Indian type.[41] He also discerned in Gandhi the beneficent influence of the various religions to which he had been exposed and to whose ethical teachings he was peculiarly receptive—Jainism, Islam and Christianity, as well as his own Vaishnavite tradition.[42]

Although Otto was most strongly attracted to Hinduism, especially its medieval expressions, he also wrote sympathetically about Buddhism of both the Theravadin and Mahayana traditions and a percipient essay (1924) on

39 Quoted in P. Almond, *Rudolf Otto*, 23-24. Alternative translation in R. Otto, *Autobiographical and Social Essays*, 94-95. For a similar epiphany experienced by a Western Christian in the face of traditional sculptures see Thomas Merton's moving account of his encounter with the Buddha figures of Polonnaruwa, in Sri Lanka, quoted in Chapter 9. See also Henri Le Saux's description of his experience at Elephanta which left him "thunderstruck," in O. Baumer-Despeigne, "The Spiritual Journey of Henri Le Saux-Abhishiktananda," 322. See also Bede Griffiths' account of a very similar experience at Elephanta in *The Marriage of East and West*, 10-11.

40 See H. Rollmann, "Rudolf Otto and India." See Otto's remarks on Gandhi's devotion to the *Gita* in *Autobiographical and Social Essays*, 204.

41 See passage from Otto on Gandhi cited in Chapter 14.

42 R. Otto, *Autobiographical and Social Essays*, 203.

Zen Buddhism at a time when it was virtually unknown in the West. Unlike many of his predecessors and contemporaries he did not find Buddhism either "nihilistic" or "pessimistic" and in Zen discerned a radical mystical method, "almost torn away from all rational schemata," aimed at a direct encounter with the numinous, the "wholly other."[43] In 1925 Otto wrote the preface to the first book on Zen in German, a collection of classical texts translated by Ohasama Shuei, entitled *Zen—Living Buddhism in Japan*. His later essay "Numinous Experience in Zen" has also been heralded as an important work.[44]

As early as 1913 Otto had conceived the idea of a Religiöser Menschheitbund (Inter-religious League) which would bring together representatives of all the world's religions to work towards international peace, social justice and moral progress. In the sorry aftermath of World War I Otto pleaded eloquently and passionately for the RMB:

> I hope that the misery which all nations suffer today will finally teach them what religion and ethics should have taught them a long time ago: that they do not walk alone. People of every land and nation must constantly bear in mind that they face great collective tasks, and that to accomplish these tasks they need brotherly collaboration and cooperation. By themselves, political associations cannot do what is needed ... Will [the League of Nations] become anything more than a "limited liability corporation" that actively pursues the special interests of whatever groups temporarily find themselves in power ... In and of themselves, institutions, laws, decrees, and negotiations are powerless. They require the continual support of an awakened collective conscience ...

After commending the efforts of his friend, Swedish Archbishop Nathan Söderblom, to initiate a more lively and fertile Christian ecumenicism (eventually leading to the formation of the World Council of Churches in 1948), Otto went on:

> But Christianity hardly encompasses all of humanity ... What would it mean if perhaps every three years those who represent the consciences of individual nations—the most influential leaders and emissaries of all churches all over the world—assembled publicly to discuss issues of universal concern, to display personally their common feeling for all of humanity, and then to take home a heightened will to create a global community? In time this assembly would develop into a forum that would be completely independent of the struggles and limitations of diplomacy. It could discuss the great issues of the day.

Otto's identification of those problems strikes a very contemporary note:

> ... issues of public and international morality, social and cultural issues that all nations share, unavoidable clashes between different nations and how to

43 See P. Almond, "Rudolf Otto and Buddhism" and R. Otto, "Professor Rudolf Otto on Zen."
44 See H. Dumoulin, *Zen Buddhism in the 20th Century*, 5. (This essay is apparently not yet in English translation.)

alleviate them, issues of class, gender, and race ... The same body would also provide a natural court of appeals for oppressed minorities, classes, and nations.[45]

Under Otto's leadership the RMB actually flourished for a time in the 1920s and attracted participants from Asia and North America as well as many European countries. Otto's trip to the subcontinent in 1928-29 was principally to gain support for the RMB, efforts which met with considerable success. It was dissolved in 1933 but was revived by Friedrich Heiler and Karl Küssner in 1956 and thereafter became the German branch of the World Congress of Faiths which had been founded early in the century by Sir Francis Younghusband.

Although Otto's work has been strangely neglected in the Western world over the last fifty years there is no doubting his influence on both theologians and comparative religionists. For many years Paul Tillich alone amongst German theologians really carried Otto's banner but the climate today, in which "theologians now inhabit a world of religious pluralism, uncertain truth claims, and inter-religious dialogue" may well make Otto's ideas congenial once again.[46] Amongst comparative religionists his legacy was perhaps most evident in the work of his compatriot Joachim Wach but Otto also palpably influenced figures such as Mircea Eliade, Friedrich Heiler, Gerardus van der Leeuw and Ugo Bianchi. As early as 1912 he had struck a prophetic note with these words:

> We in the West now realize that we have no monopoly of religious truth. We must in honesty change our attitude towards other faiths, for our watchword must be "Loyalty to truth." This changed attitude, however, does not weaken, but rather, instead, reinforces one's faith in God, for He is seen to be not a small or partial being but the Great God who is working throughout all times and places and faiths.[47]

The ideals for which Otto strived and the values he upheld, both within the Church and in the wider world, have lost none of their pertinence or urgency.

Giuseppe Tucci

Shortly after the death of Giuseppe Tucci, in 1984, Mircea Eliade wrote of the Italian Tibetologist:

> Giuseppe Tucci was one those rare scholars whose biographies cannot be reduced to their bibliographies. His learning was vast and profound, his linguistic and historiographical erudition reminds us of such giants as Paul

45 R. Otto, *Autobiographical and Social Essays*, 145.
46 G. Alles in R. Otto, *Autobiographical and Social Essays*, 11.
47 R. Otto, "Parallelisms in the Development of Religion East and West," *Transactions of the Asiatic Society of Japan*, 40, 1912, 158, quoted in P. Almond "Rudolf Otto and Buddhism," 69.

Pelliot or Berthold Laufer, and his writings (some sixty volumes and more than two hundred articles) are of an amazing variety of contents and literary styles. But Giuseppe Tucci was also a prodigious traveler and an indefatigable explorer.[48]

Unlike many contemporaneous Tibetologists, Tucci actually made extended visits to Tibet: between 1927 and 1948 he visited Tibet and the contiguous Himalayan kingdoms no less than eight times. Edward Conze tells us that Tucci believed that the friendly reception he was accorded in Tibet derived from the fact that in a previous life he had been a Tibetan who decided to be reborn in the West in order to help his people.[49] He had earlier spent five years in India (1925-30), and later, in the 50s, directed two expeditions to Nepal.[50] He combined in himself the qualities of the explorer, naturalist, linguist and scholar. Tucci was one of the last links in a very long chain of Italian exploration of the Tibeto-Himalayan region, stretching back to Marco Polo and running through such figures as the Jesuit missionary and scholar Father Ippolito Desideri and the celebrated mountaineer, the Duke of Abruzzi. *In Tibet, Land of Snows* (1967) Tucci describes his impressions of both the landscape and the culture in rhapsodic prose:

> Only those who have been in Tibet know the fascination of its huge landscapes, its diaphanous air that scarfs the icy peaks with turquoise, its vast silence that at once humbles man and uplifts him.[51]

Elsewhere we find him writing this:

> In Tibet, a land I know well and have often visited, I have always dwelt under the impression that I found myself in a place not only remote in space, but above all remote in time, as if by betaking myself there, I had by a work of magic gone backwards in the path of centuries, or evoked ... a society, such as it would have been around the year one thousand of our era: the same intenseness of spiritual life, the same religious bent, the same want of distinctness, even lack of boundaries between reality and imagination ...[52]

The trope of Tibet as "medieval survival," a "timeless reliquary," was a popular one in many European writings of the time and was given perhaps its most extended and poignant expression in *Secret Tibet* (1952), by Fosco Mariani, Tucci's photographer on his last Tibetan expedition.[53]

Tucci recounted his experiences on the 1948 expedition in *To Lhasa and Beyond*. He visited Western Tibet and joined pilgrimages to Mt Kailas and

---

48 M. Eliade, "Giuseppe Tucci," 57. On Eliade's relationship with Tucci see Gherado Gnoli's obituary, "Mircea Eliade."

49 E. Conze, *Memoirs of a Modern Gnostic* 2, 51; for reflections on Tucci see 47-53.

50 For a brief account of Tucci's career see L. Petech, "Giuseppe Tucci."

51 G. Tucci, *Tibet, Land of Snows*, 13-14.

52 G. Tucci, "A Propos East and West," 346.

53 For some discussion of the medieval theme in Mariani and others see P. Bishop, *The Myth of Shangri-La*.

Lake Manasarovar. "Those places," he wrote, "deserve to be sacred, if for nothing else, for the natural beauty God lavished on them in the luckiest days of His creation."[54] He also visited Tibet's ancient Western capital, Sakya, where he explored its temples and libraries while the 1948 expedition included researches in Shigatse, Gyantse and the Yarlung Valley as well as Lhasa and the great monasteries of Drepung, Sera and Ganden. He was accompanied on part of this expedition by Sherpa Tenzing, soon to ascend Mt Everest with Edmund Hilary.[55] Tenzing recalls his meeting with Tucci:

> Professor Tucci was a strange man: indeed, one of the most remarkable I have ever met. He was very serious and absolutely devoted to his work. But, unlike the mountaineers I had known, who were mostly quiet men, he was terrifically excitable and temperamental, and everything had to be just so, or there was a great explosion ... But in time I grew to like Professor Tucci as well as any man I have ever known ... he was a great scholar, knowing much more about the country than the people who lived there. And I have never been able to count how many languages he knew. Often his conversations to me would begin in one, change suddenly to another, and end up in a third ... From him I learned all sorts of things.[56]

To Lhasa and Beyond includes a fascinating account of Tucci's highly formal audience with the fourteen-year old Dalai Lama who, more than three decades later, was warmly to commend a new edition of the book, writing, "Tucci's description of the timeless civilization of the Tibetan people is as perceptive and relevant today as it was when he wrote the book thirty years ago."[57]

Tucci was born in 1894 in Macerata (Adriatic Italy), the birthplace of the 18th century Capuchin Tibetologist, Cassiano Beligatti. His intellectual development was precocious and he rapidly mastered Greek and Latin, his first published article being on some Latin inscriptions found near his home town. He graduated from the University of Rome and turned firstly to Chinese subjects, translating Mencius and producing a history of early Chinese philosophy. By the mid-20s his interests were concentrated on India, in particular Mahayana Buddhism. Tucci spent five fertile years in India, lecturing at the universities of Shantiniketan and Calcutta, developing many friendships with Indian pandits and writers, including Rabindranath Tagore, and laying the foundations for "a series of accurate and philologically impeccable" editions of Mahayana texts.[58] It was also in Calcutta that Tucci first met Mircea Eliade with whom he was to have a long association.[59] Soon after his return to Italy he was appointed to the Chair of Chinese at the Oriental

---

54 G. Tucci, *To Lhasa and Beyond*, 8.
55 For Tucci's comments on Tenzing see *Tibet, Land of Snows*, 13.
56 T. Norgay, *Man of Everest*, 112-114.
57 Preface to *To Lhasa and Beyond*, 1983 ed., 5.
58 L. Petech, "Giuseppe Tucci," 138.
59 Mircea Eliade dedicated *Occultism, Witchcraft and Cultural Fashions* to Tucci "in memory of our discussions in Calcutta, 1929-1931."

Institute in Naples before moving on to the University of Rome as Professor of Religions and Philosophies of India and the Far East. Tucci remained in this position until his retirement in 1969. Tucci's scholarly work was by no means restricted to the realm of Tibetan Buddhism. Indeed, by the time he turned to Tibetan studies, in the early 30s, he was already an authority on a staggeringly diverse range of Oriental subjects. A recent bibliography of Tucci's work, probably incomplete, runs to some 360 items.[60]

The Tibetan phase of Tucci's career lasted from the early 30s until about 1950 by which time the Chinese invasion had put a stop to the field trips which Tucci had undertaken so often in the previous two decades. Nonetheless, Tibet had left a deep spiritual imprint on him: he kept a shrine in his home and regarded himself as a practitioner of the Kargyu school.[61] In his later years Tucci carried out archaeological work in Nepal, in the region of the Afghani-Pakistan border, and in Iran, also writing extensively on related subjects. During the 30s Tucci founded the Italian Institute for the Middle and Far East (IsMEO), a center for research and cultural exchanges, and the publisher of two important periodicals, *Asiatica* and *East and West*. It was largely through his role at IsMEO that Tucci became entangled in fascist politics. Gustavo Benavides has examined the linkages between Tucci's ideological leanings—overtly fascist in the pre-World War II period—and his representation of "the East," particularly Tibet. The collusion of Orientalism and fascism is an important but hazardous territory into which we will venture only later in this study. Here we shall be concerned principally with Tucci's contribution to 20th century Tibetology.

Tucci was always warmly welcomed in Tibet where he impressed his hosts by his ability to engage in lively philosophical disputations with Tibetan lamas in their own language. They were often astonished to discover that Tucci knew more about the texts and sacred objects in the many monasteries that he visited than did their custodians.[62] His expertise in the Vajrayana extended through Tantra, iconography, philosophy and metaphysics, folk music, and the study of royal tombs. Much of his scholarly work from this period is found in the massive seven-volume series *Indo-Tibetica* (1932-1941) whilst his Tibetan masterwork was *Tibetan Painted Scrolls* (1959)—"a real summa of the art, literature, religion and history of Tibet,"[63] "a prodigious, learned and original contribution" to the study of Vajrayana.[64] (So lavishly produced is this volume that it is infrequently seen outside the rare book collections of a few select universities.)[65] The bent of Tucci's most significant work was archaeological, historical and philological rather than comparative

---

60 See J. Nattier, "Buddhist Studies in the Post-Colonial Era," 476.
61 S. Batchelor, *The Awakening of the West*, 317.
62 See T. Norgay, *Man of Everest*, 119-120.
63 L. Petech, "Giuseppe Tucci," 139.
64 M. Eliade, "Giuseppe Tucci," 158fn.
65 See D. Lopez, *Prisoners of Shangri-La*, 353fn.

and phenomenological. He also produced travel books and widely read works of a more popular nature, including *The Theory and Practice of the Mandala* (1949) and *The Religions of Tibet* (1970), and produced an important Italian translation of *The Tibetan Book of the Dead* (1949). In his monograph on the mandala, at that time still only sketchily understood in the West, Tucci alludes positively to the pioneering work of Carl Jung in this field, but then goes on to articulate a principle which was to become one of the corner-stones of the so-called phenomenological method of comparative religious studies:

> My desire has been to discuss the mandala in such a way that I shall not mis-represent the opinions of the Indian Masters. In other words, I have been at pains not to lend to the ideas they express anything which might render those ideas incomprehensible to the men who formulated them.[66]

Tucci's critics, particularly those anatomizing some of the ideological fault lines in European Orientalism, have made much of the oppositions (e.g. the historical, time-burdened, "progressive" West vs. the "mystical" and "timeless" East) which are doubtless to be found in his work. Nonetheless, in this context, it is interesting to come across a passage such as the following, written in 1958. Of the East-West divide, an ever-present theme in the Orientalist literature, Tucci had this to say:

> There is again much talk of the means of attaining a better reciprocal under-standing between East and West. Having stated the problem in this way, it is plain to everyone that an antithesis is implicitly involved ... between Asia on one side, and Europe and its American extension on the other ... but ... Europe and Asia have since the dawn of history been closely joined and intercommunicating through migrations, invasions, conquests, trade, pil-grimages and interchanges of the arts and ideas, so that not one single event of any significance has ever occurred in one part without its [reaction] on the other, thus establishing the just claim to a common history, a history, that is, of the Euro-Asian continent. At any rate, to revert to our argument, men of culture who, if they be really so, have always been messengers of spir-itual understanding, have never believed in any such differences between East and West.[67]

Gary Snyder

In his autobiography Alan Watts describes Gary Snyder as

> a wiry sage with high cheek-bones, twinkling eyes, and a thin beard, and the recipe for his character requires a mixture of Oregon woodsman, seaman,

---

66 G. Tucci, *The Theory and Practice of the Mandala*, viii.
67 G. Tucci, "A Propos East and West," 343-4. (Tucci goes on to argue that the difference between Latins and Anglo-Saxons might be as significant as that between Latins and Asians.)

Amerindian shaman, oriental scholar, San Francisco hippie, and swinging monk, who takes tough discipline with a light heart.[68]

Jack Kerouac had already conferred a kind of immortality on Snyder through the character of Japhy Ryder in *The Dharma Bums.* Snyder, born in California in 1930, was raised on small farms in Washington and Oregon. As a young man he worked as logger, seaman, fire-look-out and trail crew worker for the US Forest Service. Snyder had been interested in Asian cultures since being impressed as a boy by Chinese landscape paintings in the Seattle Art Museum. At Reed College Snyder studied anthropology, linguistics, literature and American Indian culture. While still a student, and with his friend Philip Whalen, Snyder began a systematic and disciplined study of Buddhism after reading translations of the Chinese classics by Pound and Waley in the late 40s, and R.H. Blyth's four-volume translation, *Haiku* (1949-1952)—also being read by his friends Kenneth Rexroth, Jack Kerouac and Allen Ginsberg.[69] In 1951 D.T. Suzuki's *Essays in Zen Buddhism* provided Snyder's first introduction to Zen, and helped him to understand some of the connections between Hinduism, Buddhism and Taoism. Snyder also developed an abiding interest in Chinese and Japanese poetry, and undertook translations of works such as the poems of Han Shan ("Cold Mountain"). In an interview in the mid-50s he characterized the Beat movement this way:

> In a way the Beat Generation is a gathering together of all the available models and myths of freedom in America that had existed before, namely: Whitman, John Muir, Thoreau, and the American bum. We put them together and opened them out again, and it becomes a literary motif, and then we added some Buddhism to it.[70]

His interest in Buddhism ran so deep that in May 1956, aided by Alan Watts and Ruth Fuller Sasaki, he left America to spend much of the next ten years in study in Japan, becoming a disciple of Rinzai Zen master Oda Sesso Roshi, Abbot of Daitoku-ji in Kyoto, and eventually taking lay monastic vows.[71] (Snyder is but one of a wave of westerners who have found their way into Japanese monasteries since Rudolf Otto's visit in 1912: in the last five decades one may mention such figures as Ruth Fuller Sasaki, Philip Kapleau, Robert Aitken, Irmgard Schloegl, Jan van der Wetering, Harold Stewart, Karlfried Graf Dürckheim, Elsie Mitchell, Richard Baker, Jiyu Kennett, Gerta Ital, Peter Matthiessen.) Snyder returned briefly to America in 1958 and was one of the contributors to a special "Zen" issue of the *Chicago Review*, a sign-

---

68 A. Watts, *In My Own Way*, 439.

69 See P. B. Chowka, "The *East West* Interview" (April 1977), reproduced in G. Snyder, *The Real Work*, 92-137. (Of the many interviews Snyder has given over the years the *East West* one with Barry Chowka remains one of the most illuminating.)

70 Snyder quoted in C. Tonkinson (ed), *Big Sky Mind*, 172.

71 For some comments by Snyder on the Roshi see P.B. Chowka, "The *East West* Interview," 97-98. Other Western students of the Roshi included Janwillem van der Wetering and Irmgard Schloegl—see "Some Further Angles" in *The Real Work*, 178.

post to the mushrooming American interest in Zen. The issue included Snyder's essay "Spring Sesshin at Sokoku-ji," Alan Watts' "Beat Zen, Square Zen, and Zen," translations of Chinese and Japanese spiritual classics by D.T. Suzuki and Ruth Fuller Sasaki, and poems by Kerouac and Whalen.[72] Snyder also traveled throughout India in 1962 with Joanne Kyger and Allen Ginsberg, recounting experiences which "deepened, widened and saddened" his mind in *Passage Through India*.[73] They visited Bodhgaya and the Deer Park of Sarnath and had an audience with the Dalai Lama: the main subject of their questionings seems to have been drug-induced experiences (one of the staples of both the Beat and hippie movements in which Snyder and Ginsberg were leading lights).[74] In a more recent Foreword to that book Snyder highlights his understanding of India this way:

> I honor India for many things: those neolithic cattle breeders who sang daily love songs to God and Cow, as a family, and whose singing is echoed even today in the recitation of the Vedas and the sutra chanting of Los Angeles and Japan. The finest love poetry and love sculpture on earth. Exhaustive meditations on mind and evocations of all the archetypes and images. Peerless music and dance. But most, the spectacle of a high civilization and accomplished art, literature and ceremony without imposing a narrow version of itself on every tribe and village. Civilization without centralization or monoculture ... no culture but India prior to modern times imagined such a scale of being—light years vast universes, light year size leaps of time. Dramas of millions of lifetimes reborn. How did they do it? Soma? Visitors from Outer Space? Nah. I think just Big Mind drank in with Himalayan snow-melt rivers and seeing Elephant's ponderous daintiness, and keeping ancient shamanistic sages and forest hermits fed on scraps of food, to hear and respect their solid yoga studies. The Buddha Shakyamuni, one of those, was loved, and listened to by cowgirls, traders, and courtesans.[75]

After his return from Japan Snyder plunged into the late 60s counter-culture which was "eclectic, visionary, polytheistic, ecstatic and defiantly devotional."[76] More distinctively, he "attempted to work out an alternative ethic which drew on both Buddhist and native American ideals, as well as American natural rights ideology,"[77] an ethic which he expressed in his poetry, his talks and essays (which reveal considerable though lightly-worn learning and a mind of great suppleness), and through social and ecological activism. His capsule summary of Buddhist teachings: "impermanence, noself, the inevitability of suffering and connectedness, emptiness, the vastness

---

72 R. Fields, *How the Swans Came to the Lake*, 220-221.

73 It is interesting to compare Ginsberg and Snyder's respective accounts of their trip in *Indian Journals March 1962-May 1963* and *Passage Through India*.

74 R. Fields, *How the Swans Came to the Lake*, 294-295.

75 G. Snyder, *Passage Through India*, x.

76 R. Fields, *How the Swans Came to the Lake*, 248.

77 J.J. Clarke, *Oriental Enlightenment*, 104.

of mind, and a way to realization."[78] Taking his cue from Blake's "Energy is Eternal Delight," in *Turtle Island* Snyder wrote this:

> Delight is the innocent joy arising
> with the perception and realization of
> the wonderful, empty, intricate,
> inter-penetrating,
> mutually-embracing, shining
> single world beyond all discriminations
> or opposites.

In a nutshell, Buddhist metaphysic as the basis for ecological awareness. Throughout his life Snyder has been deeply concerned with "our ethical obligations to the nonhuman world," a notion, he says, which "rattles the foundations of occidental thought."[79] Thanks to the sustained efforts of poets and writers like Snyder, Wendell Berry, and Wes Jackson (amongst many others) the idea now has a much wider currency. Also among Snyder's most notable achievements has been his sensitive and intelligent receptivity to the traditions of the American Indians.[80]

Snyder has also been one of a stream of writers who have drawn on Eastern spirituality and philosophy in their attempts to fashion a new aesthetic and fresh expressive modes—poetic, in Snyder's case. As one commentator noted,

> All of Snyder's study and work has been directed toward a poetry that would approach phenomena with a disciplined clarity and that would then use the "archaic" and "primitive" as models to once again see this poetry as woven through all parts of our lives.[81]

Snyder has published several collections of essays and some fifteen-odd volumes of poetry—one of which, *Turtle Island* (1974) was awarded the Pulitzer Prize. A useful compendium of four decades of essays on culture, nature and poetics is *A Place in Space: Ethics, Aesthetics, and Watersheds* (1996). He has often been interviewed in the organs of counter-cultural America, has pounded the "alternative" lecture circuit visiting, he says, "practically every university in the United States"[82] and has been an energetic advocate of many progressive and ecological causes—the "unofficial poet laureate of the environmentalist movement." Along with Robert Aitken, Joanna Macy, and Richard Baker he was a founder, in 1978, of the Buddhist Peace Fellowship, a sign of the increasing interest amongst Western dharma practitioners in

---

78 C. Trevor, "The Wild Mind of Gary Snyder," *Shambhala Sun* (website).
79 G. Snyder, *A Place in Space*, 246.
80 For Snyder's recent ruminations on the Beats, poetry, Zen, Amerindian tradition, ecology and aesthetics, see *A Place in Space*. (We will return to some of these issues in a later chapter.)
81 S. McLean, Introduction to G. Snyder, *The Real Work*, xiii.
82 C. Trevor, "The Wild Mind of Gary Snyder," *Shambhala Sun* (website).

welding together Eastern spiritual practice and Western forms of social and political activism; "engaged Buddhism" became one of the labels by which such concerns came to be identified. This vein of "spiritual politics" has many antecedents in American Romanticism and Transcendentalism; as someone recently remarked, "If Ginsberg is the Beat movement's Walt Whitman, Gary Snyder is the Henry David Thoreau."[83] In recent years Snyder has evinced more interest in a non-adversarial political agenda, has become more open to *bhaktic* forms of religious practice, and has been increasingly influenced by the great 13th century master Dogen Zenji.[84] He still practices *zazen*. Let us leave Snyder with the words of Jim Dodge:

> Having achieved the "mythopoetic interface of society, ecology, and language" that he chose as his fields of inquiry, his point of multiple attention, Gary Snyder is justly honored as an elder in the environmental movement, a revolutionary social critic, an excellent translator, a Buddhist scholar and eminent practitioner, and, of course, a premier poet. He is also a nature writer of surpassing lucidity ... one of the great synthesizing intellects of our age ... [and] a Warrior of the Imagination ...[85]

Huston Smith

If Otto's *The Idea of the Holy* was one of the most widely read books on religion of the inter-war period, Huston Smith's *The Religions of Man* must surely be the most popular of the second half of the century. First published in 1958 it has been in print ever since, selling millions of copies and now re-titled as *The World's Religions: Our Great Wisdom Traditions*.[86] The hallmarks of Smith's approach to the comparative study of the world's religions were evident from the outset: the conviction that each religion was the custodian of timeless truths and values; the attempt to understand the forms and practices of any particular tradition from the viewpoint of its adherents; an intuitive sympathy which enabled Smith to "tune into" a wide diversity of spiritual modalities; an understanding that the hyper-rationalism of much modern philosophy and the pseudo-scientific methodologies of the so-called social sciences were inadequate tools with which to grasp human realities; a style of exposition free of the specialized jargon of the disciplines on which Smith drew (most notably philosophy, theology, comparative religion) and one immediately accessible to the intelligent general reader. One might say that Smith's mode turned on a kind of natural courtesy and respect for the traditions he was exploring. He also situated the study of religion within an existential context:

83 I came across this quote on a website that has since disappeared.
84 C. Trevor, "The Wild Mind of Gary Snyder," *Shambhala Sun* (website).
85 J. Dodge, Foreword to G. Snyder, *The Gary Snyder Reader*, xix.
86 The change of title and the addition of the sub-title are both suggestive, as is the insertion of a new segment on primal traditions.

Religion alive confronts the individual with the most momentous option this world can present. It calls the soul to the highest adventure it can undertake, a proposed journey across the jungles, peaks and deserts of the human spirit. The call is to confront reality, to master the self. Those who dare to hear and follow this secret call soon learn the dangers and difficulties of its lonely journey.[87]

Since 1958 Smith's understanding of both the inner unity and the formal diversity of the world's integral religious traditions has been both deepened and sharpened by his encounter with the traditionalist perspective exemplified in the works of such figures as René Guénon, Ananda Coomaraswamy and Frithjof Schuon. Within the academic world he has been a passionate and eloquent spokesman for the traditionalist school, and has engaged many of the deepest problems and issues arising out of the contemporary collision of the forces of tradition and modernity. His essential vocation has been as an *educator*.

Smith was born in 1919 in Soochow, China.[88] His parents were missionaries and he was to spend the first seventeen years of his life in China. One of his former students, Philip Novak, writes:

If you would know Huston Smith, start with China ... Beholding him, one wonders whether fantastic tales about Chinese magic are not true after all. There is something distantly—and yet distinctly—Asian in his physiognomy. China paused on his skin, it seemed, before proceeding to his marrow ... Open the pages of the *Analects* to Confucius's description of the *chun-tzu* (ideal gentleman) and you touch Huston's fiber. Chun-tzu ... one who possesses a truly human heart, who cherishes the arts of learning and teaching, and who is as concerned to teach by moral example as by intellectual knack.[89]

After his schooling at the Shanghai American School Smith studied at the Central Methodist College in Fayette, Missouri, where his intellectual engagements were primarily theological and philosophical. Thereafter he pursued further studies at the prestigious Divinity School at the University of Chicago and at the University of California at Berkeley during which time, partly under the influence of the "Californian Vedantins" (Gerald Heard and Aldous Huxley amongst them) he became more deeply engaged in the study of mysticism. A series of teaching appointments followed at the universities of Denver and Colorado, Washington University in St Louis, the Massachusetts Institute of Technology (1958-1973) and Syracuse University (1973-1983). Early in his career Smith also served as a chaplain and associate minister in the Methodist Church, improbably combining these duties with

87 H. Smith, *Religions of Man*, 11.

88 For biographical details see "Biographical Sketch" in A. Sharma (ed), *Fragments of Infinity*, xi-xii; M.D. Bryant in H. Smith, *Essays on World Religion*; H. Smith, *Why Religion Matters*, xiii-xiv; H. Smith & D.R. Griffin, *Primordial Truth and Postmodern Theology*.

89 P. Novak, "The Chun-Tzu," 8.

the presidency of the St Louis Vedanta Society! In later years Smith has been one of the prime movers in the establishment of the Foundation of Traditional Studies, based in Washington D.C. and of which he is the Vice-President.[90] As the editor of a *festschrift* in his honor remarked,

> Professor Smith's teaching career has been devoted to bridging intellectual gulfs: between East and West, between science and the humanities, and between the formal education of the classroom and informal education via films and television.[91]

His films and television programs have focused on Hinduism, Buddhism, Sufism and Tibetan music. In 1996 Bill Moyers hosted a five-part PBS television series, *The Wisdom of Faith with Huston Smith.*

From Smith's wide-ranging scholarly oeuvre we may select three works of signal importance: *The World's Religions* (1991), a masterly and engaging conspectus of the world's major religious traditions; *Forgotten Truth: the Primordial Tradition* (1977) in which he expounds the perennial wisdom which lies at the heart of manifold sapiential doctrines and religious forms; and *Beyond the Post-Modern Mind* (1982) which elaborates a critique of the intellectual habits and prejudices of the prevailing contemporary worldview, particularly as it finds expression in the Western academic ethos and in the highly reductive disciplinary specializations which purport to "explain" religious phenomena. As well as these three major landmarks we should note a recent anthology of some of Smith's most important articles, *Essays on World Religion* (1992) which includes many pieces on Asian subjects—a sample of titles indicates the range of Smith's interests: "Transcendence in Traditional China," "Tao Now: An Ecological Statement," "A Note on Shinto," "Spiritual Discipline in Zen," "India and the Infinite," "Vedic Religion and the Soma Experience," "The Importance of the Buddha," "Tibetan Chant: Inducing the Spirit."

The most decisive shift in Smith's outlook occurred as a consequence of reading the works of Frithjof Schuon, the master expositor of the *religio perennis* in modern times. Smith had been introduced to the works of Guénon, Schuon and other traditionalists by Seyyed Hossein Nasr during his time at MIT. Smith:

> I discovered that [Schuon] situated the world's religious traditions in a framework that enabled me to honor their significant differences unreservedly while at the same time seeing them as expressions of a truth, that because it was single, I could affirm. In a single stroke I was handed a way of honoring the world's diversity without falling prey to relativism, a resolution I had been seeking for more than thirty years.[92]

One of the penalties of fame is the exposure to endless invitations to

---

90 See S.H. Nasr, "Homage to Huston Smith."
91 Arvind Sharma in A. Sharma (ed), *Fragments of Infinity*, xi-xii.
92 Huston Smith in H.Smith & D.R. Griffin, *Primordial Truth and Postmodern Theology*, 13.

write Prefaces, Forewords, Introductions and the like. It is a measure of both his international standing and his generosity of spirit to note some of the books which Smith has helped introduce to a wider audience, many of which have become classics of their kind: Philip Kapleau's *The Three Pillars of Zen* (1967), Dwight Goddard's *A Buddhist Bible* (1970), *Zen Mind, Beginner's Mind* (1970) by Shunryu Suzuki, S.H. Nasr's *Ideals and Realities of Islam* (1972), Frithjof Schuon's *The Transcendent Unity of Religions* (1975), Swami Prabhavananda's *The Spiritual Heritage of India* (1979), *On Having No Head* (1986) by D.E. Harding, *A Treasury of Traditional Wisdom* (1986) edited by Whitall Perry, W.T. Stace's *Mysticism and Philosophy* (1987), *The Wheel of Life* (1988) by John Blofeld, and a new edition of *The Way of a Pilgrim and the Pilgrim Continues His Way* (1991).[93]

Whilst the Judeo-Christian tradition in which he was raised has provided Smith with a firm spiritual anchorage his life and work alike testify to his willingness to immerse himself in the religious forms and practices of other traditions, not by way of any kind of sycretism or "universal" religion, but in the search for understanding and for "the light that is of neither East nor West."[94] Religious *experience* has been a watchword in his writings and amongst his own spiritual encounters we may note his boyhood exposure to a Confucian master, his spell as a Methodist minister, weekly sessions with a Vedantin swami, the practice of yoga and an intensive reading of the *Upanishads* and other Hindu Scriptures in the 1950s, a summer of meditation and *koan*-training in a Myoshinji monastery in Kyoto in the 60s (where he developed a close friendship with D.T. Suzuki, doyen of modern Zen scholars, and practiced Zen with dharma-brother Gary Snyder), his inquiries into the possible links between drug-induced experiences and mysticism, his close association with traditionalist Sufis in Iran and the USA. He has been a sympathetic and no doubt exemplary guest in many Houses of the Spirit. As well as moving freely through the corridors of academia (where, it must be said, his ideas encountered some suspicion and skepticism as well as acclaim) he has met countless rabbis, clerics, swamis, Zen masters, lamas, mystics and the like; by all reports such meetings are marked by that rapport which arises out of the spontaneous and mutual recognition of the radiant spiritual maturity which marks those who have traveled a goodly distance on the path.

In the conclusion to the most recent edition of *The World's Religions* the author observes that we have just survived "the bloodiest of centuries; but if its ordeals are to be birth pangs rather than death throes, the century's scientific advances must be matched by comparable advances in human relations." Such advances depend on our ability to listen to voices from all over

93 For details of these and other works see M. Darrol Bryant's Bibliography in H. Smith, *Essays on World Religion*, 286-287.
94 A *Newsweek* reviewer of "The Wisdom of Faith with Huston Smith" trivialized Smith as a "spiritual surfer," just as his more academic critics have mistakenly accused him of "eclecticism" and "syncretism." See S. Glazer, *The Heart of Learning*, 228, and S.H. Nasr, "Homage to Huston Smith," 7.

the planet and to nurture a peace

> built not on ecclesiastical or political hegemonies but on understanding and
> mutual concern. For understanding, at least in realms as inherently noble as
> the great faiths of mankind, brings respect; and respect prepares the way for
> a higher power, love—the only power that can quench the flames of fear,
> suspicion, and prejudice, and provide the means by which the people of this
> small but precious Earth can become one to one another.[95]

Huston Smith: scholar, minister, teacher, culture critic, pilgrim, bridge-
builder; in each of these roles he has served the cause of inter-religious
understanding with great distinction and, in the words of one of his students,
with "honesty of person, penetrating sensitivity ... and flowing kindness."[96]

95 H. Smith, *The World's Religions*, 390.
96 M. Gustin, "Tribute to Huston Smith," 13.

4.

Theosophy and Western Seekers in the Sub-continent, 1900-1950

Theosophy and the "White Buddhists"—Annie Besant and Krishnamurti—A Miscellany of Early Western "Converts" to Hinduism—Fictional Passages to India—Californian Proselytes and the Appeal of Vedanta—A Note on Ramakrishna and Vivekananda—Theravadin Buddhism and White Buddhists in Ochre Robes—Christmas Humphreys

---

To form the nucleus of a Universal brotherhood of Humanity, without distinction of race, creed, sex, caste or color; to study the ancient and modern religions, philosophies and sciences ... ; and to investigate the unexplained laws of Nature and the psychical powers latent in man. (Aims of the Theosophical Society)[1]

Earlier we noted something of those changes in the intellectual and spiritual climate of the West which germinated new interests in all things Eastern, and of those moments and movements where these interests came into sharpest focus. The founding of the Ramakrishna Order in America and England in the 1890s and of the Buddhist Societies in England (1903) and Germany (1906) were a sign of the spiritual hunger of the times. J.J. Clarke has usefully summarized the cultural climate in *fin-de-siècle* Europe which

> ... witnessed a growing sense of disenchantment amongst educated Europeans with the rationalist ideals of the Enlightenment and the Victorian faith in progress, accompanied by a fascination with ideas of degeneration and decadence, and a willingness to explore strange new seas of thought. The very speed of progress, the rapid transformation from traditional to modern social and economic formations, the growth of science-inspired materialist philosophies, and the ever-slackening hold of ancient religious beliefs and rituals, all of these combined to create a mood of discontent with the comforts and promises of western civilization, and to encourage a search for more satisfying and meaningful alternatives.[2]

Clarke also reminds us of the significance of European imperial expansion which provides a backdrop against which the growth of interest in the East must be understood. The full cultural impact of imperial expansion on the European mind, he argues, did not make itself felt until the 20th century and is manifested in two developments: the engendering of a sense of "oth-

---

1   S. Batchelor, *The Awakening of the West*, 268.
2   J.J. Clarke, *Oriental Enlightenment*, 96.

erness," and of a cultural divide more keenly understood, "confirming for some the superiority of Western civilization, and for others the need to draw from the ancient traditions of the East qualities which the West conspicuously lacked";[3] and, secondly, amongst the intelligentsia at least, "a sense of anxiety tinged with guilt" which helped to fertilize ideas about religious dialogue.

In this chapter we shall meet a sample of Westerners who submerged themselves in the spiritual life of the East, sometimes becoming citizens of the homeland of their adopted tradition. Each affiliated with some branch of Hinduism in India or Theravadin Buddhism in Sri Lanka or South East Asia. However, we shall start with a figure who represents one of the most popular and influential trans-religious movements of the late 19th century and which laid claim to a timeless esoteric wisdom and a universal religious vision which might unite adherents from all faiths; the movement is Theosophy, the individual Annie Besant.

Theosophy and the "White Buddhists"
Perhaps it was Porphyry, the 4th century philosopher who coined the term "theosophy" to denote a "divine wisdom" whose origins lay in Pythagoreanism, Platonism, gnosticism, and hermeticism. The term has a long and tangled pedigree but was appropriated in the late 19th century by the founders of the Theosophical Society, the German-Russian occultist Madame Blavatsky and American lawyer, Colonel Henry Olcott, who claimed this ancient lineage for their own movement. The Society, founded in 1875, proclaimed a primordial wisdom tradition which underpinned divergent religions and which found expression in enlightened individuals. The stated aims of the Society were

> To form the nucleus of a Universal brotherhood of Humanity, without distinction of race, creed, sex, caste or color; to study the ancient and modern religions, philosophies and sciences ... ; and to investigate the unexplained laws of Nature and the psychical powers latent in man.[4]

The theoretical scaffolding of Theosophy (as we shall call this movement, in contradistinction to earlier forms of theosophy) was, in the first place, an admixture of heterogeneous elements drawn from the subterranean streams of Western esotericism (hermeticism, Rosicrucianism, freemasonry, Boehme, Paracelsus, Swedenborg), 19th century evolutionism, Victorian spiritualism and psychism (telepathy, mesmerism, and the like), to which were eventually added a scramble of Eastern elements drawn principally from Buddhism and *Advaita* Vedanta.[5] The Oriental ingredients were dram-

---

3   J.J. Clarke, *Oriental Enlightenment*, 97.
4   S. Batchelor, *The Awakening of the West*, 268.
5   For a well-informed account of the evolution of Blavatskyism see J. Godwin, *The Theosophical Enlightenment*, 277-331.

atized by the highly publicized visit of Blavatsky and Olcott to the sub-continent in the late 70s where they became enthusiastic apostles of Buddhism. Buddhism, proclaimed Blavatsky, "even in its dead letter," is "incomparably higher, more noble, more philosophical and more scientific than the teaching of any other church or religion."[6] On arrival in Ceylon Olcott had confided to his journal that

> Our Buddhism was that of the Master-Adept Gautama Buddha which was identically the Wisdom Religion of the Aryan *Upanishads*, and the soul of all ancient world faiths. Our Buddhism was, in a word, not a creed but a philosophy.[7]

At a temple in Galle, on May 25, 1880, both Blavatsky and Olcott formally took refuge through the five vows (*pansil*) before a *bhikkhu*, thus earning the sobriquet "the White Buddhists." As Edward Conze has noted,

> Rather suddenly and unexpectedly [a] few members of the dominant race, white men and women from Russia, America and England, Theosophists, appeared among Hindus and Ceylonese to proclaim their admiration for the ancient wisdom of the East.[8]

In 1882 the headquarters of the Society were moved from New York to Adyar, near Madras.

Present at the Galle ceremony was David Hewivittarne, a youth who was to leave his own imprint on the history of Buddhism in the West under the name he assumed when committing himself to both Buddhism and Theosophy, Anagarika Dharmapala. He had been stirred by a public letter Olcott and Blavatsky had earlier written, offering their help to the Buddhists of Ceylon. "My heart warmed towards these two strangers, so far away and yet so sympathetic, and I made up my mind that, when they came to Ceylon, I would join them."[9] For the next twenty years he worked closely with Olcott in their joint task of creating a universal Buddhism to which end Dharmapala created the Maha Bodhi Society in 1891, subsequently establishing branches in the USA and in several European countries. Dharmapala is most widely remembered for his role at the World's Parliament of Religions where he was often mistaken for a Theravadin monk. He spent the rest of his life working towards the re-awakening of Buddhism in India and the development of a Western *sangha* (monastic community), a task in which he was succeeded by one of his biographers, the Venerable Sangharakshita.[10] Dharmapala has also been heralded as a forerunner of the "engaged Buddhism" of recent decades.

We are not presently concerned with the authenticity of the teachings promulgated by Blavatsky and Olcott, and by other Theosophical luminaries

6   S. Batchelor, *The Awakening of the West*, 269.
7   Olcott quoted in R. Fields, *How the Swans Came to the Lake*, 97.
8   E. Conze, *Buddhism: Essence and Development*, 211.
9   Dharmapala quoted in T. Tweed, *The American Encounter with Buddhism*, 52.

such as the Anglo-Indian A.P. Sinnett (author of *Esoteric Buddhism*, 1883) and the notorious English cleric C.W. Leadbetter, or their latter day successors such as Alice Bailey. Nor shall we trace the lurid melodrama of the various feuds, factions, schisms, scandals and ostracisms which overtook the movement early in the new century.[11] Here we need only note that, whatever the provenance of Theosophical ideas and whatever the motivations of its leading exponents, the movement had a significant impact in both East and West: by the turn of the century it boasted some four hundred branches in America, Europe, India and Australia, and by 1920 claimed 45,000 members and some 1500 lodges, probably marking its zenith. It sponsored a vigorous publishing program and ran libraries, shops and institutes in many Western cities. As J.J. Clarke has observed,

> Theosophical teachings, with their openness to a variety of paths to the truth, and their emphasis on the underlying congruence of the great religious traditions, represented in many ways a radical challenge to orthodox religious ideas, and, in their attempt to construct a philosophy which reconciled recent scientific discoveries with ancient wisdom traditions appealed widely to educated Westerners and Indians alike.[12]

The Theosophical movement played no small part in the Theravadin revival in Sri Lanka and South-East Asia and also gave some impetus to the Hindu reform movements of the late 19th century. In the pages of this book we shall meet many Europeans who were, at least for a time, influenced by Theosophical ideas, these sometimes being an avenue to less adulterated Eastern religious forms. Consider, for starters: W.B. Yeats, Ananda Metteya, Krishna Prem, W.Y. Evans-Wentz, René Guénon, Christmas Humphreys, Nyanatiloka Thera, Miriam Salanave. In its heyday Theosophy also had a considerable impact on the artistic life of Western Europe. Baudelaire, Verlaine and Rimbaud had all evinced interest in occultist ideas, as did post-surrealist writers such as René Daumal whilst Schoenberg, Mondrian, Klee and Kandinsky were all Theosophists to some degree. Theosophy also played a role in the Irish literary renaissance through Yeats, George Russell and Charles Johnston.[13] Then, too, there are those not insignificant Asian figures who came within the Theosophical orbit: to Dharmapala we can add Krishnamurti and Gandhi, to mention three with whom we shall have some dealings. Of course there were also those European commentators who found the scientistic bent of theosophy quite repugnant to the religious impulse. Thus, for instance, Rudolf Otto:

10 See A. Rawlinson, *The Book of Enlightened Masters*, 243-245.
11 On the early history of the Theosophical movement see J. Godwin, *The Theosophical Enlightenment*, and W. Quinn, *The Only Tradition*.
12 J.J. Clarke, *Oriental Enlightenment*, 90.
13 See Mircea Eliade's essay "The Occult and the Modern World" in *Occultism, Witchcraft and Cultural Fashions*, and E.B. Sellon & R. Weber, "Theosophy and the Theosophical Society."

... the characteristic mark of theosophy is just this: having confounded analogical and figurative ways of expressing feeling with rational concepts, it
then systematizes them, and out of them spins, like a monstrous web, a science of God, which is and remains something monstrous.[14]

Annie Besant and Krishnamurti

On a warm summer's night in 1891, in the London Hall of Sciences, Mrs
Annie Besant, hitherto an exemplary rationalist, political radical, journalist
and notorious advocate of birth control, addressed an assembly of agnostics,
rationalists, materialists and atheists at London's Secular Society. She told
her astonished audience that she too had received communications from the
"Mahatmas," out-of-body oracular sages who ethereally resided in the furthest reaches of Tibet and who had been the inspiration of Madame
Blavatsky's *The Secret Doctrine* (1888). To say that her talk caused a sensation
would be to understate the case. Of "the calamity" of Mrs Besant's conversion
to Theosophy G.B. Shaw said that it was "as if some one had blown up Niagra
(sic) or an earthquake had swallowed a cathedral."[15]

Annie Besant was born in 1847 into the Victorian middle class and, like
Margaret Noble, raised in a repressive atmosphere of Protestant piety.[16] An
unfortunate marriage to a gloomy young cleric ended in a divorce which precipitated Annie into a science degree and the Free Thought movement, a
secular religion for which she now became a passionate evangelical. After the
scandal at the London Hall of Sciences Shaw took some comfort in the fact
that this was just the latest in a long succession of conversions:

> She was successively a Puseyite Evangelical, an Atheist Bible-smasher, a
> Darwinian secularist, a Fabian Socialist, a Strike Leader, and finally a
> Theosophist, exactly as Mrs. Siddons was Lady Macbeth, Lady Randolph,
> Beatrice, Rosalind and Volumnia.[17]

Shaw could hardly have foreseen how seriously Annie (with whom he had
had an affair) was to take her new "role": by 1893 she had completed a lecture tour of America propagating Theosophy, and had expatriated to India
where she was to translate the *Bhagavad Gita* (a translation much admired by
Gandhi), establish the Hindu Central College in Benares as well as several
schools, spread the *sanatana-dharma* textbooks throughout India,[18] be a
prime mover in the India Home Rule League, edit the nationalist newspaper
New India, be interned by the colonial administration, and become President
of the Indian National Congress. She was also the adoptive mother of

14 R. Otto, *The Idea of the Holy*, 107-108.
15 G.B. Shaw quoted in J. Paine, *Father India*, 61.
16 Annie Besant's life story has been told in R. Dinnage, *Annie Besant*.
17 G.B. Shaw quoted in R. Dinnage, *Annie Besant*, 78.
18 On the *sanatana-dharma* textbooks see W. Halbfass, *India and Europe*, 345.

Krishnamurti. She also assumed the Presidency of the Theosophical Society on Olcott's death in 1907 and moved her residence from Benares to Adyar.

Annie Besant's sojourn in India was to be permanent. In many ways her Indian "career" has parallels with Sister Nivedita's: a spiritual conversion, "going native" (i.e., adopting the Indian lifestyle), an involvement in education and social reform, a concern for the rights of women, and eventually, despite a previous disavowal of politics, a serious commitment to the nationalist movement. On the other hand, Margaret Noble observed the disciplines and enjoyed the fellowship of Vivekananda's monastic community: it was from her allegiances to Hinduism that much of her other work sprung. If we are to believe Jeffery Paine, Annie Besant's Theosophical enthusiasms, while not necessarily insincere, were perhaps somewhat opportunistic and superficial. The crusade for social and political reform remained the driving force in her personality and work; Theosophy provided the vehicle, so to speak.[19] In this context we should note that Besant made little contribution to the "intellectual" or "theoretical" aspect of Theosophy, this role being taken up by the charlatan, pedophile and fraudulent "mystic," the Rev. C.W. Leadbetter (1847-1934), whom Annie had befriended and with whom she co-authored such books as *Occult Chemistry*. Their association survived Leadbetter's expulsion from the Theosophical Society for his sexual misadventures with Indian boys. (One of his defenses before the Theosophical "court" was that he had been a Greek in a previous lifetime!)[20]

Indeed, it was Leadbetter who in 1909 was to conjure up Jiddu Krishnamurti, a ragged Telegu schoolboy who, under their tutelage, would emerge as the new "World Teacher" and transform Theosophy into a global religion. In 1925 Annie announced, at the completion of Krishnamurti's apprenticeship in England, that a new *avatar* had arrived: "The Divine Spirit has descended once more on a man. The World Teacher is here."[21] The flamboyant career of the new Messiah need not detain us here, save to note that he very soon disavowed Theosophy and set up as an independent, iconoclastic and highly successful "guru" (or "anti-guru" as his "anti-disciples" prefer) in both East and West.[22] One can only endorse Marco Pallis' observation that

> If Krishnamurti showed good sense in breaking loose from the grotesquely inflated role for which he was being briefed by his Theosophist sponsors ... one may yet wonder whether, after that, he might not have done better to retire quietly into the fold of his ancestral Hinduism where his remarkable talents could then have ripened in the normal way, and who can say how far this course might subsequently have taken him?[23]

19 See J. Paine, *Father India*, 78-79.
20 J. Paine, *Father India*, 84.
21 J. Paine, *Father India*, 86.
22 On Krishnamurti's life and career as a guru see M. Lutyens, *The Life and Death of Krishnamurti*.
23 M. Pallis, review of J. Needleman's *The New Religions*, 189.

The defection of Krishnamurti was a disabling if not quite fatal blow, both to Besant personally and to Theosophy. However, the Theosophical movement pulled through the crisis and despite several secessions and schisms has survived down to the present day in three different organizations: the Theosophical Society (headquarters still at Adyar), the Theosophical Society International (Pasadena) and the United Lodge of Theosophists.[24] It might also be argued that some of the impulses which were manifested in late 19th century Theosophy are alive and well in the contemporary West but have been deflected into New Age-ism.[25]

In 1917, through a concatenation of circumstances, Annie Besant became president of the Indian National Congress, founded by another Theosophist, A. O. Hume.[26] It was perhaps her greatest political triumph but also marked the decline of her reputation and influence. As Jeffery Paine has observed

> Now that she was president, her statements frequently took the form of fiat. To the British she might sound like a ventriloquist, as though India were speaking through her, but Indians detected in her pronouncements the commanding diction of the memshahib. Her affront to authority, her radical moral rhetoric, had not changed since she mounted soapbox and platform in England ... [but she] spoke in India for people, causes and ideas that were not her own.[27]

Besant continued her frenetic involvement in politics over the last decades of her life, but her moment in the sun had passed. Her views about Home Rule became increasingly disfavored by emerging nationalist leaders such as Tilak and Gandhi and she slowly faded to the periphery. She continued to live at Adyar until her death in 1933.

A Miscellany of Early Western "Converts" to Hinduism

We turn now to a small sample of Westerners who went to India as spiritual searchers in the first half of the century and who ended up somewhere in the Hindu fold. Of the many candidates for this brief survey I have chosen an English Theosophist-turned-Vaishnavite renunciate, a Dutch-American who became a swami in the Ramakrishna Order, a "beguiling charlatan"[28] who became a pop-guru in the West, and a cosmopolitan French scholar and musician who became a pandit in Benares and an authority on the Saivite branch of the Hindu tradition. Each represents certain psychological, intellectual and spiritual impulses found amongst many Western seekers in the

24 The United Lodge of Theosophists appears to be a network of independent organizations without any central headquarters. (The ULT has a high internet profile.)

25 On this subject see W. Hanegraaff, *New Age Religion and Western Culture*; D. Cush, "British Buddhism and the New Age"; P. Almond, "Towards an Understanding of the New Age."

26 See R. Dinnage, *Annie Besant*, 112-114.

27 J. Paine, *Father India*, 88-89.

28 J. Paine, *Father India*, 217.

sub-continent. We should also note in passing that the term "Hindu converts," used from time to time in our discussion, is problematic. From a strictly orthodox Hindu viewpoint, one cannot "convert" to Hinduism as membership of one of the castes, integral to the whole Hindu system, is attained only by birthright.

Sri Krishna Prem (Ronald Nixon)

Ronald Nixon was born in Cheltenham in 1898, raised as a Christian Scientist, served in the War as a pilot and studied at Cambridge where he became interested in philosophy, Theosophy and Buddhism, and took up the study of Pali. Through the Cambridge branch of the Theosophical Society he met Christmas Humphreys, at that time probably the best known Western Buddhist in England.[29] After graduation Nixon went to India in search of a guru, and soon found a job through the Vice-Chancellor of the University of Lucknow, Dr G.N. Chakravati, himself a Theosophist and friend of both Blavatsky and Besant. The doctor's wife, Monika Devi, was an adherent of Gaudiya Vaishnavism, into which she initiated Nixon, and after a mystical vision herself became a *vairagi* (a renunciate within the Gaudiya sect) and guru. Nixon took renunciate vows from Srimati Yashoda Mai, as Monika had now become, and assumed the name Sri Krishna Prem. After a couple of itinerant years the two set up the Radha-Krishna temple near Almora, established an ashram, attracted many disciples (mainly Indians but with a fair sprinkling of Westerners), and spent the rest of their lives there until their respective demises in 1944 and 1965.[30] One of Prem's few departures from the ashram was to visit Ramana Maharshi in 1948, also meeting Aurobindo and the Mother.[31]

Krishna Prem is interesting for several reasons: he spoke Hindi and Bengali fluently, achieved some competency in Sanskrit and wrote several commentaries, in strictly orthodox vein, on the *Upanishads* and the *Gita*; he rigorously adhered to his renunciate vows and lived a highly disciplined life; as Ramana is reported to have observed, he seemed to combine the insights of the *jnanin* with the devotional fervor of a *bhakta*; like Ramakrishna, he had the gift of "seeing God everywhere"; he typifies a certain trajectory through Theosophy towards more authentic traditional religious forms; he was loved, even adored, by many Indians. When the Beatles went to India to sit at the feet of the Maharishi Mahesh Yogi they were following an oft-trod path: Indians sitting at the feet of a Western guru preaching orthodox Hinduism was a much rarer event. A measure of the respect in which Sri Krishna Prem

29 See A. Watts, *In My Own Way*, 89. (Watts mis-names Nixon as "Nicholson.")
30 For a brief account of the life of Nixon/Prem see A. Rawlinson, *The Book of Enlightened Masters*, 380-381.
31 For a traditionalist critique of Aurobindo see Rama P. Coomaraswamy, "The Desacralization of Hinduism for Western Consumption," 199-203.

was held is that he was the first Westerner allowed entry to one of the temples at Vrindaban.[32] It is also worth noting that Nixon dedicated himself to the bhaktic cult of Krishna rather than to the highly intellectualized forms of Buddhism or *Advaita* Vedanta which, in the early decades of the century, attracted so many from the West. He insisted on the scrupulous observance of the forms and rites laid down by tradition. When goaded by a modernized Indian about "all this ritualistic procedure" and "orthodox restrictions" Prem replied:

> ... this happens to be the path laid down by those who have gone before me and reached the goal. Who am I, just entering on the path, to say "I will do this and not that, accept this discipline but not that?" I accept the whole.[33]

It was appropriate, perhaps, that his obituary in the principal organ of Indian Theosophy, *The Aryan Path*, should be written by Gertrude Emerson Sen,[34] the grand-daughter of the great American transcendentalist:

> Having imbibed the spiritual teaching of the great risis and saints, handed down in this country for thousands of years, and having lived the life, he has awakened in [Indians] the awareness of their own spiritual heritage. That he chose to renounce the West for India touched their hearts, but they have honored, respected and loved him because he dedicated his life to their ancient ideal of realizing his oneness with the Eternal and the Imperishable. They have lighted their torches at his flame.[35]

Swami Atulananda (Cornelius Heijblom)

Cornelius Heijblom (or HeŚblom) was a Dutch-American born in Amsterdam in 1870, the son of a Protestant tea merchant, who migrated to New York after graduation. Like many of those attracted to the teachings of Vivekananda (whom he met in 1900), Heijblom reacted against the cramped Protestant ethos in which he was raised and found in Vedanta, as taught by Swami Abhedananda, a spiritual liberation: "It was as though a new revelation opened up. I knew at once that it was the Truth."[36] He joined the Ramakrishna Order in America around 1899 and spent several years in Swami Turiyananda's Shanti Ashrama in the San Antonio Valley of California. Now known as Gurudas Maharaj, he moved in 1906 to India where he took up the life of the *sannyasi*, but returned to America defeated by ill health after two years, only to return in 1911, and repeating the pattern

---

32 D.L. Haberman, "The Transformation of Ronald Nixon," 217.
33 Prem quoted in D.L. Haberman, "The Transformation of Ronald Nixon," 221.
34 Gertrude Emerson married an Indian botanist, Boshi Sen, lived in Almora and was closely associated with the Radha-Krishna ashram. See D.L. Haberman, "The Transformation of Ronald Nixon," 225fn.
35 Sen quoted in A. Rawlinson, *The Book of Enlightened Masters*, 384.
36 Swami Vidyatmananda, "A Holy Man of Europe," 36.

in 1917, until again returning in 1922, eventually settling in the Ramakrishna Mission in Kankhal, near Rishikesh. He was now known as Swami Atulananda. For the last thirty years of his life he lived as a hermit. He wrote an account of his early involvement in the order and of the work of Indian teachers in the West, *With the Swamis in America and India*, not published until 1989, well after his own death at the age of ninety-six in 1966. He also wrote *Atman Alone Abides*. Another Western member of the Ramakrishna Order, Swami Vidyatmananda, writes that Atulananda is of interest to us today for three reasons: he was intimate with several of Ramakrishna's direct disciples (including Swamis Brahmananda and Shivananda), and received their grace; he played a role in the beginnings of the Ramakrishna movement in the West; he was "a man of real spiritual development."[37]

Paul Brunton

Raphael Hurst (1898-1981) launched a long writing career with *A Search in Secret India*, published in 1934 and an immediate success due, doubtless, to the combination of an accessible journalistic style and an exotic subject. The Foreword was written by Sir Francis Younghusband. Hurst assumed the pseudonym Paul Brunton and retained it thereafter; likewise a self-bestowed doctorate.[38] The book tells of Brunton's meetings with various sages, fakirs and yogis on his travels through India, including Ramana and Meher Baba. His account of his first meeting with Ramana is worth recalling, as it describes an experience shared by many others:

> There is something in this man which holds my attention as steel filings are held by a magnet. I cannot turn my gaze away from him. My initial bewilderment, my perplexity at being totally ignored, slowly fade away as this strange fascination begins to grip me more firmly ... I become aware of a silent, resistless change which is taking place within my mind. One by one, the questions which I have prepared in the train with such meticulous accuracy drop away. For it does not now seem to matter whether I solve the problems which have hitherto troubled me. I know only that a steady river of quietness seems to be flowing near me, that a great peace is penetrating the inner reaches of my being, and that my thought-tortured brain is beginning to arrive at some rest.[39]

The Sage of Arunachala's many other Western visitors included Arthur Osborne, Somerset Maugham, Lanzo del Vasto, Henri Le Saux, Jules Monchanin and Marco Pallis.

Brunton's second book came hard on the heels of the first: *The Secret Path: A Technique of Self-Discovery* (1935), introduced by Alice Bailey, was both an exposition of Ramana's teachings and a practical manual of meditation,

---

37 Swami Vidyatmananda, "A Holy Man of Europe," 35.
38 See A. Storr, *Feet of Clay*, 164.
39 P. Brunton, *A Search in Secret India*, 141.

and resorted to the full repertoire of romantic clichés about the "mystic East," on display in this passage early in the book:

> I hoped to wander through the yellow deserts of Egypt and among the wisest sheikhs of Syria; to mingle with the vanishing fakirs of remote Iraq villages; to question the old Sufi mystics of Persia in mosques with graceful bulbous domes and tapering minarets; to witness the marvels performed by the Yogi magicians under the purple shadows of Indian temples; to confer with the wonder-working lamas of Nepal and the Tibetan border; to sit in the Buddhistic monasteries of Burma and Ceylon, and to engage in silent telepathic conversation with century-old yellow sages in the Chinese hinterland and the Gobi desert.[40]

Within two years Brunton had also published *A Message from Arunachala* (1936) in which he sketched a critique of Western civilization before providing more lessons about the path to full "soul consciousness." Brunton went on to produce a flurry of books until the early 1950s. A few titles suggest the nature of the oeuvre: *A Search in Secret Egypt* (1936), *A Hermit in the Himalayas* (1936), *The Quest of the Overself* (1937), *The Hidden Teaching beyond Yoga* (1941).

Brunton traveled in the East in the two decades following his first trip and became a kind of *de facto* guru, known to some of his disciples as Philo S. Opher.[41] He eventually settled in Switzerland and devoted much time in his later years to his Notebooks in which he elaborated an agenda for universal salvation—some 7000 pages, published posthumously in 16 volumes, a veritable cornucopia of "spiritual" writings flavored with pop-Vedanta, astrology, Theosophy and various other mysterious ingredients. And still selling well! The Paul Brunton Philosophical Foundation in New York continues to spread the message.

Many extravagant claims have been made on Brunton's behalf: his son, for instance, asserts that Brunton "introduced the terms yoga and meditation to the Western world," as if Blavatsky, Vivekananda *et al.* had never been.[42] His editors do not hesitate to compare the *Notebooks* with the *Upanishads*.[43] What are we to make of this somewhat ambiguous figure? Clearly he had a lively and receptive intelligence, a fertile imagination, an engaging literary style, considerable personal charm. By most accounts he was a kindly, sensitive and gentle man who did not seek the limelight and who did not cultivate a following of disciples. He was not a hoaxer of the Lobsang Rampa type; nor did he have the "overweening arrogance, sexual predation, murderous activities, ruthless greed, and insatiable appetite for luxury"[44] (to use Jeffrey

40 P. Brunton, *The Secret Path*, 14.
41 See P. French, *Younghusband, the Last Great Imperial Adventurer*, 350.
42 See Introduction to *A Search in Secret India* by Brunton's son Kenneth Thurston Hurst, 8.
43 See A. Rawlinson, *The Book of Enlightened Masters*, 198.
44 J. Masson, *My Father's Guru*, xv. In this book Jeffrey Masson gives us a personal account, often sharply critical but not altogether unsympathetic, of Paul Brunton and the spell he exercised over Masson's father.

Masson's catalogue) which so often marks the counterfeit gurus of our own day—Bhagwan Rajneesh being an exemplary case.[45] He impressed many thoughtful and knowledgeable people. On the other hand it can be said that Brunton's understanding of Vedanta was never more than rudimentary, that his understanding of Indian history, culture and language was, at best, exiguous, that his message became increasingly distant from the Vedantic teachings which he claimed to be the bedrock of his own philosophy. His ideas in his later years, as we have them in the *Notebooks*, are almost self-parodic, quirky, sometimes preposterous, and anticipate some of the wilder shores of the later New Age movements.

Alain Daniélou

In 1987 Ravi Shankar, the internationally renowned Indian sitarist, wrote of Alain Daniélou:

> Having covered the entire length and breadth of our great heritage during his long span, so deep were his feelings for the Motherland that he embraced Hinduism and took the name of "Shiv Sharan." Thus began the incessant flow of his glorious writings on Indian culture especially covering music, philosophy and religion. To this day his continuous contribution to the promotion of India's cultural heritage abroad through his works has no parallel in modern history. His unflinching devotion to our culture and, above all, love for Mother India, defy all expression.[46]

Outside a small coterie of European scholars and musicologists Alain Daniélou is not as well known as might be expected for a man of his accomplishments—as scholar, translator, artist, musician, philosopher, pandit. It is worth looking at his life and work in some detail.

Daniélou was born into a distinguished aristocratic family in Paris in 1907. His mother, an ardent Catholic, founded a religious order as well as the famous "Sainte Marie" teaching establishments. His brother, Jean, was to become a noted Catholic theologian and cardinal. Daniélou exhibited many talents as a boy, particularly in painting, singing, classical dancing and sports. Jacques Cloarec, an intimate associate, tells us that

> He was quite an agitator. He refused all limitations on his personal liberties and on his thought. He was very much anti-establishment—most of the time—although he came forth out of very conservative elements. He broke away from his family at a very tender age and became quite a wild person in the artistic milieu.[47]

In 1932, together with the Swiss photographer Raymond Burnier, this adventurous youth departed for the East, finally arriving in India in 1935. In 1937,

45 On Rajneesh see A. Storr, *Feet of Clay*, 45-63.
46 R. Mathur, "Shiv Sharan" (website).
47 R. Mathur, "Shiv Sharan" (website).

after a period at Tagore's Shantiniketan academy, Daniélou settled in Benares where he undertook a lengthy period of study and spiritual practice. There he found a traditional world of writers, scholars, brahmins and monks who were completely indifferent to modern trends of thought. They preserved the traditional ideas, sciences, rites and philosophic systems of ancient India. Daniélou made an intensive study of Sanskrit and Hindi, classical Indian music and philosophy. He was initiated into the tradition of the Saiva Agamas and given the name "Shiv Sharan." He followed a traditional Hindu lifestyle including strict vegetarianism and daily bathing in the Ganges.

In 1949, Sharan was appointed professor at the Hindu University of Benares and director of the College of Indian Music. He was also deeply interested in Hindu architecture and sculpture, making lengthy visits to Khajuraho, Bhuvaneshvar and Konarak, as well as many other sites. In 1954, he became the director of the Adyar Library of Sanskrit manuscripts and editions at Madras. In 1956, he was made a member of the Institut Française d'Indologie at Pondicherry, and subsequently of the Ecole Française d'Extreme Orient.

After leaving India in the early 60s Daniélou lived in various European cities, mingling with a cosmopolitan intelligentsia—amongst his friends and acquaintances were Stravinsky, Jean Genet, Andre Malraux, Yehudi Menuhin, Nicholas Nabokov, Jean Renoir, Henry Corbin and others in the Eranos cabal. He settled in the Italian village of Zagarolo and devoted himself to many scholarly works which include *Hindu Polytheism* (1964), *Shiva and Dionysius* (1979) and several works on Indian music. He also wrote a fascinating memoir, *The Way to the Labyrinth: Memories of East and West* (1981), one of the more distinguished examples of the genre. In Europe he is best known not for his scholarly works but for his promotion of the classical music of India. In 1963 he created the International Institute for Comparative Music Studies in Berlin and Venice. Through concerts featuring Asian artists and the publication of recorded collections of traditional music under the aegis of UNESCO, he played a distinguished part in the rediscovery of Asian art and music in the West. It was for this work that he was awarded the Légion d'Honneur and the UNESCO/CIM prize for music. He died in 1994 and was cremated in Lausanne.

There are many aspects of Daniélou's thought and work which deserve much wider attention. In the present context we can do no more than sketch out a few of these. In both his own spiritual journey and in his scholarly work Daniélou affirms a form of Saivite mysticism which celebrates the sacramental and theophanic forms of the natural world. This is an important antidote to the mistaken view, widespread in the West (and sometimes sponsored by "Vedantins"), that the Hindu tradition "rejects" the material world, regarding it as chimerical, illusory, unreal.[48] Daniélou also represents a spiritual

---

48 See H. Oldmeadow, "Sankara's Doctrine of Maya."

type whose insight is triggered by an aesthetic perception and intuition. Further, Daniélou was a spokesman for the traditional Hindu world which he contrasted with a modernized (and thus corrupted) India. He believed that the tradition itself, and Indian society which was its expression, had been compromised by the foreign occupations of both Muslims and British. It was always to the *traditional* sources and values, untouched by imperialism and by the forces of modernity, that he returned, and it was in the traditional milieu of Benares that he submerged himself:

> I found myself immersed in a society whose conceptions of the nature of man and the divine, of morality, love and wisdom were so different from those I had learned in childhood that I had to make a clean sweep of every-thing I believed I knew, all my habits, all my patterns of thought. This system of values could not have been more unfamiliar to me if I had suddenly found myself transported into Egypt during the reign of Ramses II.[49]

Daniélou treated with suspicion Anglicized Indians whose Western edu-cation, he believed, disqualified them from a proper appreciation of their own traditions. On this basis he had little time for either Nehru or Tagore and wrote,

> Men like Nehru and Tagore knew nothing about Hindu culture except through British authors ... I soon discovered that I had nothing to learn from English-speaking Indians—not even from such well-known philoso-phers as Vivekananda, Radhakrishnan, Aurobindo or Bhagwan Das. Tagore himself had learned Hindu philosophy through British authors and was very much opposed to the rigors of the traditional society ...[50]

Unlike many Western seekers who evince an enthusiasm for India's spir-itual treasures but who wish to "reform" its social order, Daniélou under-stood and respected traditional institutions which were so often the target of Anglicized Indians and Westerners alike—arranged marriages and the caste system, to mention just two.[51] In this respect, as in many others, he exhibits a thoroughly traditional outlook, one shared by his compatriot and corre-spondent, René Guénon, one of the century's most authoritative Western expositors of traditional Hindu doctrines. Daniélou also thoroughly disap-proved of the neo-Hindu "reform" movements such as the Arya-Samaj of Swami Dayananda Saraswati and Raja Ram Mohan Roy's Brahmo-Samaj. He chided figures like Devendranath Tagore, Madame Blavatsky, Annie Besant, Vivekananda, Radhakrishnan, Aurobindo and Gandhi himself for creating an "English language version" of Hinduism which pandered to "the religious, moral and social ideas of Anglican Protestantism" and which provided a

49 A. Daniélou, *The Way to the Labyrinth*, 136.
50 A. Daniélou, *The Way to the Labyrinth*, 134.
51 A. Daniélou, *The Way to the Labyrinth*, 316-322, 179-185.

pseudo-religious rationale for the Indian National Movement and the Congress. The nationalist leaders, he wrote

> ... had two countries and two allegiances, and were constantly faced with the dilemma of betraying the one for the other. This explains the strange mixture of love and hatred, admiration and hostility towards England that characterized the Nationalist Movement and the politics of India after independence was won. The profound influence of British education on the Indian intelligentsia created men who literally had two countries: the land of their birth, with its vast heritage, first imposed on them and then disowned, and that faraway ideal, England ... although it always kept them at a distance and treated them like second-class citizens, neither quite accepted nor rejected.[52]

The general case may be illustrated with reference to Vivekananda. Although he was not educated in England, as many of the other reformers were, and not a nationalist leader in the narrow political sense, there is no doubt that he was the spearhead of the nationalist movement in the years around the turn of the century. During his college education in Calcutta he studied Western philosophy and European and British history, and was for a time a great enthusiast of the ideas of John Stuart Mill and Herbert Spencer: thus was laid a deposit of ideas which even Ramakrishna himself was not able to entirely neutralize.[53]

In later years Daniélou also expressed a sharp skepticism about "pseudomystical adventurers"[54] posing as Vedantins who were exploiting the credulousness of Westerners.

> True Hinduism has very little to do with those mindless ramblings that seem so much more congenial to people in search of a vague form of Orientalism which, like fashionable yoga, does not disturb their habits and is ultimately only a means of escaping reality.[55]

As we started this survey of Western engagements with the Theosophical Movement and with Mrs Annie Besant we may close it with Daniélou's harsh assessment of the Adyar ashram at Madras, which he had seen at close quarters:

> This was the first of the "ashrams," organizations that are created to gather together (and exploit) dropouts from society, people vaguely interested in spiritism, "the Orient," vegetarianism, ghosts, and other such nonsense. The Society has branches in every country in the world, and is very, very rich.[56]

*

52 A. Daniélou, *The Way to the Labyrinth*, 217.
53 See C. Isherwood, *Ramakrishna and His Disciples*, 191-192.
54 A. Daniélou, *The Way to the Labyrinth*, 328. Some readers will be interested in Daniélou's gayness, about which he writes in this memoir, 322-325.
55 A. Daniélou, *The Way to the Labyrinth*, 236. See also 214.
56 A. Daniélou, *The Way to the Labyrinth*, 199.

There were many other Westerners who, in the first half of the century, became Hindu disciples/*sannyasis*/gurus: others included the Mother (b. Mira Alfassa, Paris, 1878), perhaps the first Westerner to become a guru in India;[57] Swami Abhayananda (b. Marie Louise) one of only three Westerners whom Vivekananda, in 1895, initiated as *sannyasis*—the other two being Leon Landsberg/Swami Kripananda and Dr Street/Swami Yogananda; Sister Devamata (b. Laura Glenn, Ohio, 1867), a disciple of Swami Pramananda. Then too there were quaint characters like Sri Mahendrananth (b. Lawrence Miles, London, 1911) who lived as a *sadhu* in India for thirty years but also claimed initiation in the Vajrayana in Bhutan as well as ordination as a Taoist priest in Malaya and as a Theravadin monk in Sri Lanka, eventually settling in Gujurat where he founded the Merlin Oracle Lab! The somewhat eccentric Dane Alfred Sorenson (b.1890-1984) went to India at the behest of Rabindranath Tagore and eventually became "Sunyabhai" or "Shunyata," a *sannyasi* of sorts, in the Almora district. At one time he was gardener for the Nehru family who had a house in the district. During his fifty years in India Sunyabhai also met Krishna Prem, Evans-Wentz, Lama Govinda, Anandamayi Ma and Neem Karoli Baba. He visited Arunachala in the mid-30s where he met Paul Brunton as well as receiving Ramana's *darsan* (spiritual radiance).[58]

We should also note the role of figures such as Sir John Woodroffe (1865-1936) (a.k.a. Arthur Avalon), and William Warren Atkinson (1862-1932) in introducing Hindu doctrines and practices to the West. Woodroffe was a one-time High Court judge in India who translated esoteric texts and explored the tantric tradition (at that time still an unknown world in Europe) in works such as *Tantra of the Great Liberation* (1913), *Shakti and Shakta* (1918) and *The Serpent Power* (1919). In the 20s a series of Atkinson's works on yoga appeared in English and German under the authorial name of Ramachakra. Atkinson was a lawyer from Chicago who abandoned his practice to study in India.[59]

Fictional Passages to India

Let us momentarily return to England to take a cursory glance at some literary representations of India in the first half of the century. Among the literary creations of English novelists of the Raj two texts stand out: Rudyard Kipling's *Kim* (1901) and *Passage to India* (1924) by E.M. Forster. Kipling spent several years of his childhood in India where his father was a teacher, returning for another seven years as a young man. Although Kipling is forever associated with the unhappy lines, "Oh, East is East, and West is West, and

57 See A. Rawlinson, *The Book of Enlightened Masters*, 442-448.

58 Some information on these figures can be found in A. Rawlinson, *The Book of Enlightened Masters*: on Mira Alfassa/the Mother, see 442-448; on Swamis Abhayananda, Kripananda and Yogananda, 145-146; on Sister Devamata, 238-239; on Miles, 433-34; on Sorensen, 528-530. There are also a few passing references to Sunyabhai in K. Winkler, *A Thousand Journeys*. On Aurobindo, Auroville and the Mother see also A. Daniélou, *The Way to the Labyrinth*, 210-211.

59 See G. Feuerstein, *Sacred Paths*, 32.

never the twain shall meet," his novel *Kim* represents a feat of some imaginative sympathy in its attempt to overcome the "tripled-ringed uninterest of the creed that lumps together nine-tenths of the world under the title of 'heathen'."[60] As Richard Cronin has recently observed, *Kim* comes to embody India itself by being variously "a low-caste Hindu, a Muslim Pathan, a Buddhist novice, and a young white Christian."[61] The Tibetan Lama is perhaps the most sympathetic of the many characters jostling their way through Kipling's narrative, a figure in whom Kipling embodies all those characteristics of Eastern religious life which he found most congenial: tolerance, gentleness, equanimity, the pursuit of wisdom. However, it is also the case that Kipling is less interested in religion as such than in "local color ... exotic detail, and the all-enclosing realities of the Great Game."[62] Doubtless Kipling's fiction is underpinned by an imperialist discourse (sustained in the novel primarily through the "Great Game" plot, and girded by the assumption of the necessity of British rule) but this should not obscure his genuine if limited interest in and sympathy for the many expressions of Indian spirituality which he encountered in his time in the sub-continent and which he imaginatively recreates in his fiction.[63]

E.M. Forster's *A Passage to India* is the best known of all English novels of the Raj. It deals with the encounter between Indians and the English colonialists ("well-developed bodies, fairly developed minds, and undeveloped hearts"), and with the "resistances to empire" dramatized by the liberal Englishman Fielding, the Muslim nationalist Aziz, and, Godbole, "the almost surrealistic Hindu."[64] As Edward Said has remarked,

> ... in *A Passage to India*, it is Forster's great achievement to show with remarkable precision (and discomfort) how the moral drama of contemporary Indian mysticism and nationalism—Godbole and Aziz—unfolds against the older clash between the British and Mogul empires.[65]

Forster explores a "complex bewilderment" about man's social and spiritual identity through a searching examination of "the areas of relationship and dissonance between the ancient and enduring patterns of Indian civilization" and those of the modern West.[66]

A work which achieved some popularity in the post-war years was Somerset Maugham's *The Razor's Edge* (1944) which takes its title from the *Katha Upanishad* and whose protagonist, Larry Darrell, turns his back on the

---

60 R. Kipling, *Kim*, 124.
61 R. Cronin, "The Indian English Novel," 205-206.
62 E. Said, *Culture and Imperialism*, 139.
63 For an incisive but not unsympathetic account of Kipling's implication in the discourse of empire see E. Said, *Culture and Imperialism*, 132-162.
64 E. Said, *Culture and Imperialism*, 201.
65 E. Said, *Culture and Imperialism*, 189.
66 B. Parry, "Passage to More than India," 160. See also K.J. Phillips, "Hindu Avatars, Moslem Martyrs, and Primitive Dying Gods in E.M. Forster's *A Passage to India*," and "The Experience of OM in Hesse's *Siddhartha* and Forster's *A Passage to India*."

decadent West, enters an ashram in India and aspires to "non-attachment";
he is an early prototype of the "drop-out" figure. It is a novel riddled with
many of the familiar East-West stereotypes and is characterized by "moral
confusions and simplifications, lapses in taste and overall implausibility."[67] In
Jeffery Paine's words, it "is a wooden work, full of shopworn hocus-pocus and
wordy raptures about nirvana."[68] It has none of the complexities and creative
ambiguities of Forster's work: Maugham was very much out of his depth once
he moved outside the seedy colonial milieu which he depicted so vividly in
many of his short stories. *The Razor's Edge* has twice been filmed, but neither
is a work of any distinction. Much more interesting is Maugham's account of
his sojourn in India in 1936, taken partly under the influence of Aldous
Huxley and Gerald Heard, two of the foremost "Californian Vedantists."
Maugham's sympathetic portrait of Ramana Maharshi, whom he visited in
Tiruvannamalai, is not without interest.[69] Christopher Isherwood's *A Meeting
by the River* (1967) belonged to the same sub-genre as Maugham's novel
(alienated young Western seeker in the East) but was much less popular.

Californian Proselytes and the Appeal of Vedanta
The branch of the Hindu tradition which has been most attractive to
Westerners is undoubtedly Vedanta, especially the *Advaitan* (non-dualistic)
school associated with the great eighth-century South Indian sage and metaphysician, Sankara. This monistic school, with its elevated metaphysics, its
hospitality to other schools and sects which it is able to subsume, its universalism and its systematic philosophical discourses, has attracted a range of
Western intellectuals, many of whom first came to Vedanta through the
Ramakrishna movement. Many of the spokesmen for Hinduism who have
had the most impact in the West taught some form of Vedanta, albeit one
often contaminated by Western influences—Vivekananda, Tagore,
Aurobindo, Radhakrishnan—as did some of the most influential Western
popularizers. Many Western enthusiasts of Vedanta have echoed
Radhakrishnan's claim (itself influenced by Vivekananda and by earlier orientalist scholarship) that "The Vedanta is not a religion, but religion itself in
its most universal and deepest significance."[70] All this should alert us to the
dangers implicit in the "Vedantic" bias of many neo-Hindu and Western constructions of Hinduism, both popular and scholarly.

Vedanta's strongest footholds in the West were in New York, and in
California where a constellation of writers gravitated around the Vedanta
Center: the principal figures here are Aldous Huxley and Christopher
Isherwood whilst the bit players include Romain Rolland and Gerald Heard.
These writers are primarily of interest in their attempts to propagate the

67 M. Willy, "Somerset Maugham," 825.
68 J. Paine, *Father India*, 218.
69 See "The Saint" in S. Maugham, *Points of View*, 56-95.
70 S. Radhakrishnan, *The Hindu View of Life*, 18. See also R. King, *Orientalism and Religion*, 135ff.

"perennial philosophy," the foundations of which they believed were most easily and clearly discerned in the Vedanta. They were all influenced, one way or another, by the universalist strain in the neo-Hindu movements.

Huxley is best known in the West for the dystopian *Brave New World* but the novel which bears the heaviest Eastern impress is the later Utopian novel, *Island*. From an early age Huxley was deeply interested in Eastern religion and philosophy. He made a close study of the work of such orientalists as Edward Conze, Heinrich Zimmer and D.T. Suzuki as well as of the great scriptures and spiritual classics of the East. Although not primarily a scholar Huxley was a man of wide learning. In mid-life, in the late 1930s, Huxley moved to California where he became closely associated with the Vedanta Center and, with Isherwood and Heard, edited the magazine *Vedanta and the West*. These writers were convinced that many of the ills of the modern West could be remedied by Eastern values and ideas, most particularly the Vedanta which Vivekananda had so eloquently championed at the World's Parliament of Religions. Their ideas, along with those of various Hindu gurus with whom they were associated, are most readily met with in two anthologies, edited by Isherwood, which first appeared in the 1940s and have remained in print ever since: *Vedanta for Modern Man* (1945) and *Vedanta for the Western World* (1948).

The most significant work to emerge from the coterie of "Californian Vedanta" was Huxley's *The Perennial Philosophy* which appeared in 1946. The work was an anthology of quotations drawn from the world's sacred texts, strung together by Huxley's commentary which attempts to identify what he rather clumsily calls "the Highest Common Factor" to be found in the world's religions. Whilst not questioning the intelligence, learning and good will which Huxley bought to this undertaking I must say that his vision of the perennial philosophy is seriously marred by all manner of disabling modern prejudices and assumptions. To give but two examples: Huxley fell prey to the sentimental notion that the perennial philosophy could issue in a new universal religion, a kind of religious Esperanto—with, we might say, about the same prospects for success; and secondly, for all his disquiet about the scientistic ideology of the modern West Huxley himself succumbs to it over and over again. We shall return to this subject in more detail in Chapter 10. However, at this juncture we must sharply distinguish Huxley from the traditionalist writers (Guénon, Coomaraswamy, Schuon) to whom we can turn for a much more authoritative explication of the *sophia perennis*.

Christopher Isherwood's reputation as a novelist is in well-deserved decline although interest in him as a "personality" does not seem to have abated—note the widespread interest in his interminable and self-important diaries! However Isherwood did perform one very honorable service for which he deserves our lasting gratitude: I refer to his biography of the remarkable *Paramahamsa*, Ramakrishna, one of the few indubitable Indian saints and sages amidst the veritable plague of so-called swamis, gurus, "enlightened masters," maharishis, "bhagvans" and the like of recent times. Isherwood's *Ramakrishna and His Disciples* (1965), whilst clearly written by an adherent, is informative, judicious and sensible as well as being finely attuned to the spiritual modalities in which Ramakrishna's religious genius expressed itself. An earlier biographer of Ramakrishna was the French writer Romain Rolland whose *Life of Ramakrishna* (1929)[71] introduced the Bengali saint to a wider Western European audience. Rolland also produced one of the early Western appreciations of Mahatma Gandhi.[72] The author of the celebrated *Jean-Christophe* (1906-1912) and winner of the 1916 Nobel prize for Literature, was also a fervent admirer of Vivekananda whom he esteemed as an "heroic genius" comparable to Beethoven, Michelangelo and Tolstoy, on each of whom Rolland had written earlier studies.[73]

Christopher Isherwood's Introduction to *Vedanta for the Western World* (1948) provides us with a fair sample of the way in which Vedanta was understood by many Western intellectuals and writers:

> Vedanta is the philosophy of the *Vedas* ... In India today ... there are hundreds of sects. Vedanta Philosophy is the basis of them all. Indeed, in its simplest form, it may be regarded as a statement of the *Philosophia Perennis* ... Reduced to its elements, Vedanta Philosophy consists of three propositions. First, that Man's real nature is divine. Second, that the aim of human life is to realize the divine nature. Third, that all religions are essentially in agreement.[74]

In a lecture in London in 1896, Vivekananda (who almost single-handedly constructed the vocabulary in which Vedanta was discussed in the West) claimed that

> The salvation of Europe depends on a rationalistic religion, and Advaita non-duality, the Oneness, the idea of the Impersonal God—is the only religion that can have any hold on intellectual people.[75]

Many Western Vedantins shared the view that the Vedanta, the seedbed of all Hinduism (so they asserted), could provide the foundation for a new world religion in the West, replacing the "outmoded" cosmologies and value systems of the Judeo-Christian tradition. Gerald Heard, also writing in the late 40s, provides us with a representative specimen of this theme:

> ... we may say that the appearance of Vedanta in the West as a living religion ... is inevitable just because the religious heredity of the West has now out-

---

71 In its first English translation it was titled *Ramakrishna the Man-God and the Universal Gospel of Vivekananda* (Calcutta 1979). For some unsympathetic remarks about Rolland see A. Daniélou, *The Way to the Labyrinth*, 99.

72 R. Rolland, *Mahatma Gandhi: The Man who became One with Universal Being* (1924).

73 See E. Ziolkowski, "The Literary Bearing of the World's Parliament of Religions," 20.

74 C. Isherwood, *Vedanta for the Western World*, 9.

75 Vivekananda, "The Absolute and Manifestation," lecture in London 1896, quoted in R. King, *Orientalism and Religion*, 141.

grown the tight Hebrew pot of cosmology ... for people really interested in the spiritual world, really desirous of growing in spirituality and filled with a real longing to know and love God, such doctrines were, far from being any help, a terrible obstacle. Catholicism has become increasingly dogmatic, Protestantism increasingly secular and humanist. Where were men to find a religion that was intense but not cruelly narrow, wide but not vague, loose but not tepid? ... the very breadth of Vedanta, combined with its force, is bound to embrace and develop much that is now lying latent in our Western thought and spirit.[76]

The disenchantment with a pinched and moralistic form of Protestantism was also a persistent theme in the spiritual autobiographies of many Western would-be Vedantins. Take this, from Isherwood:

When I looked at Christians around me (I knew hardly any serious ones, and none of them intimately) I willfully saw them as a collection of dreary, canting hypocrites, missionaries of reaction and ignorance, who opposed all social reform lest it should endanger the status and privileges of their Church, and all personal freedom lest people should discover for themselves that the "don'ts" were unnecessary. I disliked their stiff Sunday clothes, their sickly humility, their lack of humor, their special tone when speaking of God, their selfish prayers for rain, health, and national victory in war.[77]

It is worth noting that Isherwood also recognized, in his later years, that his hostility to Christianity was, in some measure, pathological and irrational.[78] In fact, his commitment to Vedanta allowed him, eventually, better to understand Christianity and to appreciate its mystical tradition. This pattern was not uncommon.

On the basis of a sociological and psychological examination of the empirical evidence available about the Ramakrishna movement, and on the testimony of its adherents, historian Carl Jackson has identified several factors which explain the popularity of the Ramakrishna movement in America around the turn of the century. The wider appeal of Vedanta on both sides of the Atlantic can be at least partially explained in much the same terms: a tolerant universalism which is perceived to be in sharp contrast to Christian exclusivism; the sense that Vedanta could provide a spiritual vision and a path that was attuned to the times (as opposed to "out-dated," and "bankrupt" Western religious forms); its apparent rationality and the fact that it could be reconciled with the findings of modern science; its practical, experiential emphasis; its therapeutic efficacy, through meditation, yoga and the

---

76 G. Heard, *Vedanta for Western Man*, 18.
77 C. Isherwood, "What Vedanta Means to Me," 127.
78 See C. Isherwood, "What Vedanta Means to Me," 127, and C.T. Jackson, *Vedanta for the West*, 101.

like, in relieving or annihilating psychological disturbances.[79] No doubt the charismatic personalities of Vivekananda, Prabhavananda and others also played a part. Its appeal in recent times may also be partly explained by its association with the most universally acclaimed Indian saint of the 20th century, Ramana Maharshi.[80]

A Note on Ramakrishna and Vivekananda

Later in this study we shall turn to the traditionalists to provide us with a framework within which the somewhat effusive writings of many so-called Western Vedantins can properly be assessed. However, it is worth pausing momentarily to register what Frithjof Schuon has had to say about Vivekananda and his relationship with Ramakrishna. Of the *Paramahamsa* and his mission Schuon writes this:

> In Ramakrishna there is something which seems to defy every category: he was like the living symbol of the inner unity of religions; he was, in fact, the first saint to wish to penetrate foreign spiritual forms, and in this consisted his exceptional and in a sense universal mission ... In our times of confusion, disarray and doubt he was the saint called to "verify" forms and "reveal," if one can so express it, their single truth ... His spiritual plasticity was of a miraculous order.[81]

While leaving no doubt as to Ramakrishna's sanctity and the spiritual radiance which emanated from his person, Schuon notes several vulnerabilities in his position *vis-à-vis* an emergent neo-Hinduism: a *jnana* (spiritual knowledge) extrinsically ill-supported because of his almost exclusive faith in the spiritual omnipotence of love, whence "an inadequate integration of the mind in his perspective"; a universalism "too facile because purely bhaktic"; an absence of safeguards against the dissolving influences of a modernism which left the saint himself untouched but which pervaded the milieu in which he found himself and which, in a sense, took a posthumous revenge through the influence of Vivekananda.[82] Ramakrishna, although instinctively suspicious of movements like the Brahmo-Samaj, was not altogether cognizant of the dangers posed by modernism. Furthermore, he attributed to his disciple Narendra "a genius for ontological and plastic realization which he neither had nor could have,"[83] Narendra being a person in the grip of certain "dynamic" mental tendencies which precluded any kind of realization comparable to that of the Master himself.[84]

---

79 C.T. Jackson, *Vedanta for the West*, 101-102.

80 It is with some astonishment that one finds this sage described by Alain Daniélou, usually an insightful commentator, as "in insignificant man, extremely fat, [who] allowed himself to be worshipped like a Buddha." See *The Way to the Labyrinth*, 211-212.

81 F. Schuon, *Spiritual Perspectives*, 115 & 119.

82 F. Schuon, *Spiritual Perspectives*, 116-118.

83 F. Schuon, *Spiritual Perspectives*, 119.

84 The kinds of absurdities to which Vivekananda sometimes surrendered are suggested by such

In a traditional framework which was "entire, closed and without fissures" the potentialities for heterodoxy which lurked in Vivekananda's make-up might well have been "rectified, neutralized and compensated." However, as it was, Vivekananda's development was shaped not only by the *Paramahamsa* but an "Occidentalism which was unknown and incomprehensible to Ramakrishna but which stimulated in the disciple exactly those tendencies the development of which had at times been feared by the master."[85] One such development, of which Ramakrishna had some premonition, was the founding of a sect or order, a function which he explicitly rejected as being outside Vivekananda's proper vocation.[86] It might also be noted that Ramakrishna could not have foreseen the consequences of causes which he himself had not conceived—the fact, for instance, that Vivekananda's interpretation of Vedanta was to be filtered through a screen of misconceptions and prejudices which derived not only from his own disposition but from modernist influences, of which evolutionism was perhaps the most subversive.

Schuon concedes that the enigma of Vivekananda can perhaps be explained in terms of the fact that Hindu-Indian nationalism was inevitable and that the Swami was its predestined champion. In order to fulfill such a role Vivekananda had need of a certain anti-traditional mental dynamism and of some of the ideological premises of the modern West:

> In "modernizing" Hinduism Vivekananda did at the same time "Hinduize" modernism, if one may so put it, and by that means neutralized some of its destructive impetus ... if it was inevitable that India should become a "nation" it was preferable that it should become so in some way under the distant auspices of Ramakrishna rather than under the sign of a modernism that brutally denied all that had given India its reason to live for thousands of years past.[87]

Theravadin Buddhism and White Buddhists in Ochre Robes

The 19th Century Background
Just as the story of the West's encounter with Hinduism has been played out in two locales—India on one hand, and Europe and its extensions on the

---

preposterous claims as: "The visions of Moses are more likely to be false than our own because we have more knowledge at our disposal and are less subject to illusion" (from *Inspired Talks*), and "The Buddhas and Christs we know are heroes of the second grade compared with those greater ones of which the world knows nothing" (from *Karma Yoga*). See F. Schuon, *Spiritual Perspectives*, 124-125.

85 F. Schuon, *Spiritual Perspectives*, 118.

86 See Swami Vireswarananda's *Life of Shri Ramakrishna* cited in F. Schuon, *Spiritual Perspectives*, 119fn. Incidentally, Schuon does point out that "there are contemplatives of the line of Ramakrishna whose spirituality is impeccable" and who transmit "a perfectly regular doctrine ... whatever may be their feelings on the subject of Vivekananda." Swami Brahmananda is one such. See 120fn. On Vivekananda and Ramakrishna see also W. Halbfass, *India and Europe*, 228-242.

87 F. Schuon, *Spiritual Perspectives*, 121.

other—so too with Theravadin Buddhism. We shall focus on Westerners in the bastions of Theravadin Buddhism: Ceylon (as it then was) and S.E. Asian countries such as Thailand, Burma and Indo-China.[88] After a glance at several European incursions into the *sangha* we shall use the early life and work of Christmas Humphreys (who later became a popularizer of Zen Buddhism) to illustrate the spiritual, intellectual and cultural intercourse between Theravadin Buddhism and the West in the first half of the century. However, let us first recall a few of the key figures in the gradual awakening of European sensibilities to Buddhism, particularly in its Theravadin form. Several figures of the late 19th century deserve passing mention.

Orientalist scholars such as Max Müller (editor of the *Sacred Books of the East* series) and Rhys Davids (who had founded the Pali Text Society in England in 1881) were promoting a more firmly-based understanding of various key concepts and doctrines of the Buddhist tradition. This was possible thanks to the pioneering work of philological orientalists such as the French savant Eugène Burnouf (1801-1852) who had translated many foundational texts for the first time. It is worth noting that scholarly European interest in Buddhism, especially in Britain, was at this time firmly fixed on the Theravadin rather than the Mahayana branch of Buddhism. There were several reasons for this: British colonialism had exposed many Westerners to the Theravadin cultures of Ceylon and Burma whilst countries such as Tibet and Japan were still comparatively remote; the Theravadin tradition was perceived to be the "original" and thus "purest" form of Buddhism, free of the "corruptions" of the Mahayana, and well suited to the obsessive scholarly pursuit of origins; perhaps most important of all was the appeal of Theravadin Buddhism as "rational," "scientific," "empirical"—a "philosophy of life" which could be reconciled with modern science and with humanistic aspirations. We should also note that, in the present-day climate of postcolonial theory, some scholars have recently stigmatized a "Pali Text mentality," associated with orientalists such as Rhys Davids, which "essentialized Buddhism in terms of its 'pristine' teachings."[89] Whatever force this sort of critique carries, we should not lose sight of the very substantial achievements of Rhys Davids and others like him. As Charles Hallisey points out, not only are there his scholarly achievements to be taken into account but also the establishment of the School of Oriental and African Studies, "from which all students of Buddhism still benefit."[90]

---

88 The story of Buddhism's arrival in the West has already been told in some detail. See works such as R. Fields, *How the Swans Came to the Lake*; S. Batchelor, *The Awakening of the West*; I. Oliver, *Buddhism in Britain*; P. Croucher, *Buddhism in Australia*.

89 Readers interested in Rhys Davids particularly or more generally in the orientalist constructions of Buddhism in the late 19th century should see C. Hallisey, "Roads Not Taken." He argues that a kind of "intercultural mimesis" was taking place between orientalist scholars and those representatives of Theravada with whom they came into contact, various influences and projections working in both directions.

90 C. Hallisey, "Roads Not Taken," 34.

On the popular front there were signs of a growing interest in Buddhism on both sides of the Atlantic. The epic poem by the English journalist and poet Edwin Arnold, *The Light of Asia* (1879), became a permanent fixture on the best-seller lists, going through some eighty editions. Rick Fields suggests that it was from this book more than any other that Americans first learned of the Buddha's life and teachings.[91] In the Preface Arnold had affirmed that Buddhism embraced "the eternity of a universal hope, the immortality of a boundless love, an indestructible element of faith in final good, and the proudest assertion ever made of human freedom"[92]—a catalogue of ideals well able to stir the hearts and minds of progressive and educated Victorians. Paul Carus (1852-1919) was a German-born American polymath whose *Gospel of Buddha* (1894) and *Buddhism and Its Christian Critics* (1897) present- ed Buddhism in a sympathetic light to a large popular audience and helped to dispel, at least amongst some readers, the tenacious belief that Buddhism was "nihilistic" and "pessimistic."[93] We have already made mention of the emergence of the Theosophical Society and of the embrace of Buddhism by its two founding figures, Blavatsky and Olcott. Olcott's *Buddhist Catechism* (1881) was another book which went through many editions. By century's end Buddhist monks and teachers, such as Anagarika Dharmapala and Abbot Soyen Shaku, had made a considerable impression at the World's Parliament of Religions and on subsequent lecture tours, even if they could not generate the electrifying effects of Vivekananda. By the early years of the new century Buddhist Societies, promoting the dissemination of Buddhist values and practices, were beginning to appear in the West.

Nyanatiloka Thera and the Island Hermitage

German orientalists had developed a strong Buddho-logical/Indological tra- dition since the Romantic eruption of interest in the late 18th century: one may mention such scholars as Ernst von Hartmann, Karl Eugen Neumann, Hermann Oldenberg, Max Müller, and Paul Deussen as well as figures such as Karl Seidenstücker, founder of one of the earliest German Buddhist Societies, and Paul Dahlke, a Berlin physician and homeopath, active in the translation and publication of Buddhist texts, and the founder of *Das Buddhistische Haus*, a Buddhist meditation center in Berlin. A German branch of Dharmapala's Maha Bodhi Society had been established in 1891.[94] It is perhaps not surprising that some of the earliest Westerners who entered the Theravadin *sangha* should come from the land of Schopenhauer. Among

---

91 R. Fields, *How the Swans Came to the Lake*, 69. (The full title of Arnold's book was *The Light of Asia, or the Great Renunciation, Being the Life and Teachings of Gautama, Prince of India and Founder of Buddhism.*)

92 Arnold quoted in T. Tweed, *The American Encounter with Buddhism*, 148.

93 On Carus see C.T. Jackson, "The Meeting of East and West: the Case of Paul Carus," and M.J. Verhoeven, "Americanizing the Buddha."

94 See E. Benz, "Buddhism in the Western World," 318-319, and S. Batchelor, *The Awakening of the West*, 314-315.

these was Anton Gueth, born in Weisbaden in 1878, brought up as a Catholic, and deeply influenced by Romanticism as well as Plato, Descartes and Kant. As a young man Gueth exhibited some ascetic tendencies, a gift for languages and music, a love of solitude. His interest in Buddhism was fired at a Theosophical lecture and after some research which deepened his aspirations to become a Buddhist monk, he headed eastwards—Bombay, Ceylon, and, in 1904, Burma where he took full ordination and was named Nyanatiloka ("knower of the three worlds"). He returned to Ceylon and by 1906 had produced a massive compendium of extracts from the Pali canon, *Das Wort des Buddha*, soon translated into many European and sub-continental languages. Over the next few years he took on several European students of Buddhism, some of them would-be monks and in 1911 founded the Island Hermitage on Polgasduwa, the first Buddhist monastery in Asia for European *sangha*, mostly from Germany.

The monks lived by the traditional precepts and the rules of the *Vinaya* but inevitably had to make some accommodations. Andrew Rawlinson suggests (not unkindly) that the Island Hermitage "could fairly be described as a rural retreat with a library."[95] Nyanatiloka spent the best part of five decades in Ceylon, traveling in the Far East during the first War (Germans being regarded in both India and Ceylon as "undesirable aliens"), spending six years (1920-26) in Japan as a professor at Komazawa University, and occasionally returning to Europe where he ordained several Europeans as monks, perhaps the first such ordinations in a non-Buddhist country. Nyanatiloka was an impressive linguistic and philological scholar and produced a formidable array of anthologies, translations, commentaries and grammars, including the translation into German of the immense *Anguttara-nikaya*.

Among the Island Hermitage *sangha* were: Ernst Hoffman who later committed himself to the Tibetan form of Buddhism and, as Lama Anagarika Govinda, became well-known in the West;[96] Siegmund Feniger, a German Jew, who fled Nazi Germany in 1935 and was ordained in 1937 as Nyanaponika Thera, the author of *The Heart of Buddhist Meditation* (1956), founder of the Forest Hermitage near Kandy, and mainstay of the Buddhist Publication Society until his death in 1966;[97] Nanaloka Thera, Nyanatiloka's successor as abbot of the Island Hermitage in 1957; Nanavira Thera (b. Harold Musson, 1920, Aldershot), who eventually left the hermitage in 1954 to spend eleven years in seclusion, and whose writings on Buddhism include attempts to synthesize traditional teachings with the insights of writers such as Kierkegaard, Nietzsche, Dostoevsky, Kafka and the French Existentialists;[98] Osbert Moore, another Englishman who joined the *sangha* as Nanmoli. Else

95 A. Rawlinson, *The Book of Enlightened Masters*, 460.
96 On Lama Govinda see Chapter 6. See also, A. Govinda, *The Way of the White Clouds*, 73.
97 On Nyanaponika Thera see A. Rawlinson, *The Book of Enlightened Masters*, 460-461fn, and S. Batchelor, *The Awakening of the West*, 319.
98 See *Clearing the Path: Writings of Nanavira Thera.*

Buchholz (1888-1982) accompanied Nyanatiloka back to Ceylon after his visit to Germany in 1920, became a kind of lay nun and spent the rest of her life there, eventually devoting herself to reclusive and intensive meditation in a hermitage near Kandy. This Island Hermitage group, both through their example and through their writings, have played a central role in making Theravadin Buddhism more accessible to the West. As Andrew Rawlinson remarks, a full-scale study of the history and influence of the Island Hermitage would be welcome.[99]

Ananda Metteya (Alan Bennett)

One of the avenues through which Europeans often came to Eastern traditions in the early years of the century was esoteric occultism. Some, like René Guénon, eventually repudiated occultism completely in favor of orthodox doctrines and methods while others sought some sort of synthesis of Western esotericism and Eastern spirituality. Theosophists were particularly prone to this latter enterprise. Of the various Eastward-turning Europeans whose formative influences included Theosophy and occultism we may take Alan Bennett as a representative case.[100]

Bennett's occultist credentials included his membership of both the Esoteric Section and the Golden Dawn of the Theosophical Society, and of the British Circle of the Universal Bond, drug-induced "mystical" experiences (heroin, cocaine, mescalin, peyote), and his role as Aleister Crowley's teacher in the "magical arts." In the midst of these enthusiasms Bennett read *The Light of Asia* which, in turn, led him to the study of recently-translated texts of this "pure and rational Faith."[101] In 1898, at the age of about twenty-five, Bennett headed for Ceylon to study yoga and Buddhism close-up. He was financially sponsored by Crowley who had extracted funds from the woman with whom he was having an affair at that particular moment. Bennett underwent some training under one Sri Parananda who, on Crowley's testimony, taught Bennett Patanjali's *ashtanga-yoga*, resulting in the development of wondrous psychic powers, including *buchari siddhi*—"the power of jumping like a frog"! Bennett moved to Burma, where ordination could be achieved rather more easily, and took on the monastic name Ananda Metteya (sometimes "Maitreya").[102] Most of the next decade he spent in Burma. He soon produced a pamphlet entitled *The Foundation of the Sangha of the West* and in 1903 set up the Buddhasasana Samagama/International Buddhist Society, an English branch being established in 1907 under the Presidency of no less impressive a personage than

99   A. Rawlinson, *The Book of Enlightened Masters*, 461.

100   On Bennett see also I. Oliver, *Buddhism in Britain*, 43-45; S. Batchelor, *The Awakening of the West*, 40-42; J. Godwin, *The Theosophical Enlightenment*, 369-375.

101   Bennett quoted in J. Godwin, *The Theosophical Enlightenment*, 369.

102   Bennett should not be confused with Ananda Maitreya Maha Nayaka Thera, a contemporaneous Ceylonese monk and scholar. See I. Oliver, *Buddhism in Britain*, 77.

T.W. Rhys Davids. Ananda Metteya and several Burmese supporters spent six months in England galvanizing the new organization. He eventually returned to Britain permanently, abandoned his robes and resumed life as Alan Bennett until his death in 1923, the year in which his most substantial work, *The Wisdom of the Aryas*, was published. In that work he suggests that

> ... surely the Western world, amidst this present darkness ... may well find in this ancient Truth [Buddhism] some answers to its deepest problems; some solace for the sorrows and nescience of life.[103]

Bennett worked energetically for the establishment of international organizations and forums where Buddhists of all kinds could find common cause. Amongst these efforts was the establishment of the International Buddhist Union which showed only sporadic signs of life before being revived in 1950 by Dr. G.P. Malalaskera as the World Fellowship of Buddhists.[104]

Andrew Rawlinson points out that Bennett was the first fully ordained Theravadin monk to visit the West (remembering that Anagarika Dharmapala was not a monk). He envisaged the creation of a Western *sangha* but his efforts actually produced a raft of Buddhist societies and organizations, some of them still flourishing. Rawlinson also suggests that the failure of the indigenous Theravadin *sangha* to establish any sort of organizational foothold in Western countries meant that early Western forms of this tradition were usually admixed with Western elements, more often than not being drawn from Theosophy, occultism, "magic" and the like.[105]

*

Before turning to another Englishman who significantly influenced the evolution of Buddhist societies in the West brief mention should be made of some other Europeans who became Buddhist monks or who in some other way became closely associated with Theravada in the first half of the century. Gordon Douglas was the first Briton, perhaps the first Westerner, to be ordained as a Buddhist monk, in Thailand in about 1899. Details of his life as Bhikku Ashoka are hazy but he died in Burma in 1905.[106] Salvatore Cioffi (1897-1966) was an Italian, educated at Columbia University in New York and employed in research by the Rockefeller Institute before going to Burma in 1925 to become Lokanatha Thera. He spent most of his life in Burma but also traveled in the West after World War II.[107] W.Y. Evans-Wentz, later to become famous as the purported translator of *The Tibetan Book of the Dead*,

103 Bennett quoted in K. Mullen, "Ananda Metteya," 94.
104 See C. Humphreys, *Exploring Buddhism*, 123. Later in this study we will consider the more successful efforts of another English *bhikkhu*, Sangharakshita, to form an international, non-denominational Buddhist organization, the FWBO (see Chapter 11).
105 See A. Rawlinson, *The Book of Enlightened Masters*, 161-162.
106 See S. Batchelor, *The Awakening of the West*, 40-41.
107 On Lokanatha Thera see A. Rawlinson, *The Book of Enlightened Masters*, 615-616.

spent a year in Ceylon in 1897 where he researched the ancient history, customs and religious folklore of the country and gathered an invaluable collection of Pali manuscripts, later donated to his *alma mater*, Stanford University. Like several other Theosophists in the sub-continent, Evans-Wentz became embroiled in a slanging match with Christian missionaries in Ceylon, criticizing their over-zealous evangelizing and their ignorance about the spiritual traditions they were seeking to displace.[108] Frederick Fletcher's ecumenical commitments were echoed in his Pali-Tibetan-Sanskrit name, Bhikkhu Dorje Prajnananda! Inspired by *The Light of Asia* he spent time in Ceylon in the 1890s and there met Anagarika Dharmapala. He returned to England, fought in the First World War, joined an expedition to Tibet and was received by the Panchen Lama at Shigatse where he was subsequently ordained as a novice. In 1924 he returned to Ceylon where he took the higher ordination as a *bhikkhu*.[109] Bhikkhu Kapilavaddho was born William Purfurst in England, 1906. As a young man he joined the Buddhist Society and became a lecturer of some repute at many Society events. He was ordained in London in 1952 by the Burmese master U Thittila, and again ordained in Thailand some years later. He disrobed in 1957 and died in 1971. He recounted his spiritual experience in *Life as a Siamese Monk*, written under the pseudonym Richard Randall and published posthumously.[110]

Christmas Humphreys

The intersections of Theosophy, occultism and Theravadin Buddhism are nicely personified in Christmas Humphreys. He was born in 1901 into a family of distinguished lawyers, his father being Sir Travers Humphreys, and was educated at Malvern School and Trinity, Cambridge. In his teens he was a sincere Christian but was much affected by his brother's death in World War I in Belgium. This led to a questioning of his belief in a benevolent deity: "from that hour I began a journey and it has not ended yet, a search for the purpose of the universe, assuming it has one, and the nature of the process by which it came into being."[111] He continued attending services in Anglican, Catholic and Quaker churches but was soon drawn into Theosophy as well as Buddhism.[112] With his wife Puck he devoted himself to the task of making the teachings of Theosophy and Buddhism better known in the West, especially in England: "... we never found anything more important to do than that, to do completely and utterly, and with the whole soul's will ... Such was our great adventure ..."[113]

108   On Evans-Wentz see Chapter 6.
109   On Fletcher see S. Batchelor, *The Awakening of the West*, 316-317.
110   On Purfurst/Kapilavaddho see A. Rawlinson, *The Book of Enlightened Masters*, 350; I. Oliver, *Buddhism in Britain*, 100; S. Batchelor, *The Awakening of the West*, 41-42.
111   C. Humphreys, *Both Sides of the Circle*, 32.
112   C. Humphreys, *Both Sides of the Circle*, 38-39.
113   C. Humphreys, *Both Sides of the Circle*, 55. For something of the Theosophical-Buddhist milieu

Amongst the early influences on Humphreys' intellectual and spiritual development were Ananda Coomaraswamy's *Buddha and the Gospel of Buddhism* (1916) after reading which he declared, "If that is Buddhism then whatever else I am I am a Buddhist."[114] He was attracted by the Buddhist notion of an "unborn, unoriginated, unformed" Absolute which "appealed to me as a great improvement on God" and was also impressed by Buddhism's "Middle Way" and its pacific and tolerant outlook.[115] He discovered Theosophy at Cambridge. He was somewhat disenchanted by various "limpet organizations" such as the Liberal Catholics, Co-Masonry and the Star of the East which he believed obscured the teachings of Blavatsky in whom Humphreys retained blind faith for the rest of his life. Of *The Secret Doctrine*, for instance, he wrote in his autobiography:

> ... this volume is unique ... no other ... sets forth the vast process of cosmogenesis and anthropogenesis, not as a pastiche of a doctrine found in one form or another in the religions of the world, but as their common source. Not all their scriptures combined describe with the clarity and totality of *The Secret Doctrine* the Wisdom of which each is a partial and generally mangled expression.[116]

He was interested in paranormal phenomena and believed himself to have psychic powers, and was stirred by Annie Besant whom he heard lecturing in London in the 1920s. He was also greatly impressed by *The Mahatma Letters to A.P. Sinnett* (published early 20s), and later edited this massive work, a task on which he was engaged for five years. He also did a major abridgement of *The Secret Doctrine*. The confluence of Buddhism and Theosophy may be seen clearly in Humphreys' catalogue of the seven loci of the search for knowledge, all of which he finds in Buddhism: science, sociology, spiritualism & ESP, psychology, religion, spiritual teachers, meditation.[117] Like many other Theosophists, Humphreys was also sanguine about the ways in which Buddhism and the findings of modern science might be harmonized. In *Buddhism* (1951) he was to write, in typical vein,

> The Buddhist attitude to all phenomena and to all teaching about it has ever been that of the modern scientist, let all things be examined dispassionately, objectively, assuming nothing, testing all, for such was the Buddha's injunction to his followers.[118]

Another decisive influence was D.T. Suzuki whose first series of *Essays in Zen Buddhism* appeared in 1927. Humphreys described Suzuki as "the greatest, in

---

in Britain, and some remarks on Humphreys and his wife Puck, see A. Watts, *In My Own Way*, Ch 3.
114 C. Humphreys, *Both Sides of the Circle*, 32. See also C. Humphreys, "The Buddhist Society: A Brief History," 8.
115 C. Humphreys, *Both Sides of the Circle*, 35-36.
116 C. Humphreys, *Both Sides of the Circle*, 42-43.
117 C. Humphreys, *Exploring Buddhism*, 128-129.
118 C. Humphreys, *Buddhism*, 223.

the sense of the most spiritually developed, man that I have known and dared to call my friend."[119] He was instrumental in having many of Suzuki's subsequent works published in Britain, acting as an informal literary agent and publicist. Through Suzuki's influence Humphreys was taken beyond the confines of the Theravada and into the Mahayana, particularly the Rinzai tradition of Zen.

Humphreys had a distinguished career as a barrister and judge but he clearly saw the popularizing of Buddhism and Theosophy as his real vocation, an impression reinforced by his autobiography, *Both Sides of the Circle* (1978), which portrays a liberal-minded, tolerant and affable personality, perhaps somewhat lacking in both the self-critical faculty and real intellectual discernment, but totally committed to his appointed task in which he was assisted by his no less enthusiastic wife. In 1924 he founded the Buddhist Lodge within the Theosophical Society, a successor to the Buddhist Society (founded in 1907 by Alan Bennett), which had dissolved during the war. The institutional link with the Theosophical Society was broken in 1926 when the Lodge transmuted back into an independent Buddhist Society.[120] Humphreys soon developed connections with many different Buddhist teachers and leaders in Britain and in Asia. He met Alan Watts in the early 30s and was enthused by his *The Spirit of Zen* (1935) which Watts had penned at the age of nineteen. He was also much impressed by his meeting with Carl Jung, "one of the really great minds of this century."[121] Over the years he met many people involved in the Western dissemination of Eastern religion, including Sir Francis Younghusband, Father Heinrich Dumoulin, Ruth Sasaki, Alexandra David-Neel, John Blofeld and Edward Conze, as well as Eastern religious leaders such as the Dalai Lama, Meher Baba, the Karmapa, Dudjom Rinpoche and the ubiquitous Krishnamurti.

Humphreys was an indefatigable lay Buddhist as a speaker, publicist, writer and organizer. He contributed to and/or edited *The Buddhist Lodge Monthly Bulletin, Buddhism in England, The Middle Way* and *The Theosophical Review.* He spoke on Buddhism at the World Congress of Faiths in 1935 where he shared the platform with speakers such as Radhakrishnan, D.T. Suzuki and Younghusband. After the Second World War he worked on the War Trials in Tokyo and met many eminent Buddhists in Japan, including Suzuki whom he visited in his modest home at Kamakura. He was "confirmed," as he puts it, in the Zen tradition, at the large temple at Sojiji, near Yokohama. He developed an interest in matters both Japanese and Chinese, especially artistic:

> I developed the thesis that the Japanese personality is delicate, chaste and refined, while the inner individuality is the cult of the sword and a longing

---

119 C. Humphreys, *Both Sides of the Circle*, 57.

120 On the mutations and transformations of various Buddhist organizations in England see I. Oliver, *Buddhism in Britain*, 49-64.

121 C. Humphreys, *Both Sides of the Circle*, 87.

for conquest. The Chinese, on the other hand, are as a nation inwardly female, gentle, introvert, absorbing alien nations, and, as someone put it, "spitting them out when done with." But the individual Chinese personality is cheerfully extrovert, noisy, loving bright colors and far from delicate or refined.[122]

He became a popular apostle of Zen, a mission in which his main qualification was enthusiasm rather than training or discrimination. Nonetheless, as Rawlinson points out, "graduates" from his classes on Zen included Irmgard Schloegl and Jiyu Kennett—for which, given their later attainments, he deserves some credit. In the post-war years Humphreys also visited Hong Kong, China, Thailand, Burma, India and Ceylon. His Asian travels gave "a wider vision," a deeper understanding of Eastern spirituality, religious forms and their value to the West. His Asian experiences are recounted in *Via Tokyo* (1948).

In an attempt to bolster efforts at securing international Buddhist cooperation he articulated the Twelve Principles of Buddhism which he submitted to several Buddhist authorities and organizations in Japan, Thailand, and Burma (where he met some resistance from the Burmese *sangha* who thought the purity of the Theravada had been compromised and demanded to know, for example, where "the doctrine of the unity of life" was to be found in the Pali Canon).[123] He visited Calcutta, Bodhgaya, Bombay, and the Theosophical headquarters at Adyar. He perceived "Indians as a whole to be the most spiritually minded race on earth."[124] He was the English delegate to World Fellowship of Buddhists in Katmandu in 1956, and the Buddha Jayanti in India, and subsequent World Fellowships in Rome and Sarnath. Through his connections with figures such as Indian Prime Minister Nehru and the royal families of Bhutan and Sikkim, Humphreys was also helpful in arrangements for the work of the Dalai Lama in exile.

Humphreys wrote some twenty-five books, most of them accessible and "common sense" books about the elementary doctrines and practices of Buddhism. He also wrote some fiction, plays and travelogues, scores of articles and his autobiography. Amongst his most popular books can be counted *What is Buddhism?* (1928), *Zen Buddhism* (1949), *Buddhism* (1951), *A Western Approach to Zen* (1971) and *Exploring Buddhism* (1974). As a writer Humphreys evinced a genial broadmindedness and liberal outlook; his books exhibit all the strengths and weaknesses which such a description implies. He addressed his work to the sympathetic general reader. In the words of one his introductions, his intention was not to write "clever books" for "clever people" but "helpful" ones for "ordinary people."[125]

122 C. Humphreys, *Both Sides of the Circle*, 131.
123 C. Humphreys, *Both Sides of the Circle*, 142.
124 C. Humphreys, *Both Sides of the Circle*, 144.
125 C. Humphreys, *A Western Approach to Zen*, 15.

5.

Eranos and the Comparative Mythographers

Myth and Depth Psychology—Carl Jung and the East—Eranos—Heinrich Zimmer—
Joseph Campbell—Mircea Eliade—Reflections on Jung and Eliade

Symbols not only disclose a structure of the real or even a dimension of existence, at the same time they carry a significance for human existence. This is why even symbols bearing on ultimate reality conjointly constitute some existential revelations for the man who deciphers their message. (Mircea Eliade)[1]

Myth and Depth Psychology

The word "myth" has a pedigree stretching back to the Greek *mythos* which, in its earliest phase, referred to an utterance, as opposed to *ergon*, deed. This is the Homeric sense but over time *mythos* came to be distinguished from other forms of speech. As one historian encapsulates its Greek development,

> ... *mythos* became the word as the most ancient, the original account of the origins of the world, in divine revelation or sacred tradition, of gods and demigods and the genesis of the cosmos, cosmogony; and it came to be sharply contrasted with *epos*, the word as human narration, and—from the Sophists on—with *logos*, the word as rational construction.[2]

In popular parlance in our own time "myth" has come to carry a negative meaning—a fanciful story or fabrication in which only credulous and ignorant people might believe. Within religious studies and related fields the term has undergone many revalorizations from the German Romantics onwards. Certainly few scholars of comparative religion would now take seriously the widely-held Victorian belief, articulated by figures such as E.B. Tylor, Herbert Spencer and Andrew Lang, that religious myths are "a product of the childhood of the human race, arising out of the minds of a creature that has not yet learned to think in terms of strict cause and effect."[3] Less tyrannized, perhaps, than the Victorians by the chimera of scientific objectivity, less captive to evolutionist assumptions, less complacent about our cultural "superiority," we are now much more likely to understand Ananda Coomaraswamy's claim that

1   M. Eliade, *Symbolism, the Sacred and the Arts*, 5.
2   Eric Kahler, quoted in W. Paden, *Religious Worlds*, 70. See also M. Eliade, *Myth and Reality*, 1-2.
3   E. Sharpe, *Comparative Religion*, 61.

95

myth is the penultimate truth, of which all experience is the temporal reflection. The mythical narrative is of timeless and placeless validity, true nowhere and everywhere ... Myth embodies the nearest approach to absolute truth that can be stated in words ...[4]

In Mircea Eliade's words, "Myth expresses in action and drama what metaphysics and theology define dialectically."[5] Theories about myth still abound but most comparative religionists accept the sacred and paradigmatic place of myths within any religiously based culture.

Myths from the various spiritual universes of India and the Far East have long since engaged scholarly attention. The 20th century saw an efflorescence of serious comparative studies of oriental mythologies; a good deal of this interest was prompted, at least partially, by the emergence of a depth psychology which posited the close correspondence between dreams and myths, the existence of a more or less universal symbolic vocabulary in which they found expression, and the belief that myths could disclose some of the deepest secrets of the human psyche, and thus carry a timeless message to the modern West in which existential anxiety, alienation and soullessness were the order of the day. The most influential of what we might call the myth-dream theorists was the Swiss psychiatrist-psychologist and one-time disciple of Freud, Carl Jung. Mircea Eliade compared his ground-breaking explorations of the unconscious to the maritime discoveries of the Renaissance, the invention of the telescope and the discoveries of oceanographers and speleologists—each leading to a "breakthrough in plane" and the opening up of new worlds the existence of which had hitherto been only dimly suspected.[6]

Jung had an extraordinarily wide range of interests and his theories encompassed all manner of psychic, spiritual and social phenomena. His collected works run to eighteen substantial volumes; this literature in turn has attracted endlessly proliferating commentaries. The Jungian corpus is dense, abstruse, gnomic, sometimes opaque, and certainly neither systematic nor consistent. His life and personality have also generated many stormy controversies among his biographers and he has been painted in various colors— latter-day magus, Tiresias-like seer, anti-Christ, obscurantist, philanderer, crypto-fascist. There is no denying that his influence on contemporary thought has been manifold.

Of the great foundational psychological theorists of the century Jung certainly evinced the most serious and sustained interest in the myths, doctrines and spiritual techniques of the Eastern traditions. Jung's pioneering work in stimulating a dialogue between modern Western psychology and Eastern

4 A.K. Coomaraswamy, *Hinduism and Buddhism*, 6 & 33fn21.
5 Eliade quoted in E. Wasserstrom, *Religion after Religion*, 103.
6 Mircea Eliade, "Encounters at Ascona," xviii-xix.

spirituality has by now engendered a substantial body of scholarly mono-graphs: the most comprehensive and incisive of these is J.J. Clarke's *Jung and Eastern Thought* (1994) but other more narrowly focused works, such as Radmilla Moacanin's *Jung's Psychology and Tibetan Buddhism* (1986), continue to uncover interesting and suggestive parallelisms between Jung's governing ideas and those of Eastern philosophies and psycho-spiritual techniques. Other scholars such as Luis O. Gómez have analyzed Jung's complicity in a camouflaged form of colonialist Orientalism.[7] Here we shall restrict our dis-cussion to some general remarks about Jung and the East before turning to a group of scholars who took some of their inspiration from Jung's ideas, par-ticularly Heinrich Zimmer, Joseph Campbell and Mircea Eliade. None of these were psychologists and cannot properly be called disciples of Jung, nor "Jungians" in anything but the loosest sense: each had a distinctive contribu-tion to make to the study of Eastern traditions and each moved away from Jungian readings of the religious phenomena they were studying. It can also be argued that each actually surpassed Jung in their penetration and under-standing of mythological materials. By way of an aside it should also be point-ed out that Zimmer and Eliade made highly significant contributions to the study of religion in many fields other than comparative mythography, as did Jung himself. We should also note that Jungian psychotherapists such as Marie-Louise von Franz, Károly Kerényi, Erich Neumann, and Helen Luke have written provocative works on both Occidental and Oriental myths—but these highly specialized and often technical works lie beyond the reach of this study as does the work of other scholars who have inflected an essential-ly Jungian understanding of myths in new ways.[8] We will return to Jung later in the chapter which concludes with some comparative reflections on his work and that of Mircea Eliade.

Carl Jung and the East

Taoism, Tibetan Buddhism, Zen and Indian yoga all left an imprint on Jung's work, though some of his more scientistic followers have sought to obscure these influences which they see as antagonistic to a scientific objectivity. Indeed, Jung himself was often troubled by the tensions created by the com-mitment of Western psychology to the modern scientific paradigm and his own explorations. His interest in Oriental doctrines can be traced back to his teenage years when he was much influenced by his reading of Schopenhauer who, as we have seen, believed that India was "the land of the most ancient and the most pristine wisdom" from whence could be traced many currents

---

7   See L. Gómez, "Oriental Wisdom and the Cure of Souls."
8   Wendy Doniger O'Flaherty's book *Women, Androgynes and Other Mythical Beasts* (1980) is one such re-working of Jungian perspectives on mythology.

within European civilization.[9] One senses in Jung's somewhat ambivalent attraction to the East something of these Schopenhauerian motifs.

Jung launched his inquiries into Eastern religions in 1909 when he turned to a cross-cultural study of religious mythology and symbolism. It was out of these researches that Jung fashioned the cardinal idea of the collective unconscious—one which helped rupture his relationship with Freud. We can find more than a few traces of Eastern thought in such early works as *Psychology of the Unconscious* (1912) and *Psychological Types* (1921). However, it was only in the 1920s that Jung's interest in Eastern psychology came into sharp focus, largely through his encounters with the German missionary and Sinologist Richard Wilhelm and the German Indologist Heinrich Zimmer, leading to a series of short but potent works. These included his foreword to D.T. Suzuki's *Introduction to Zen Buddhism* (1927) and his commentaries on *The Secret of the Golden Flower* (1929), the *I Ching* (1950) and *The Tibetan Book of the Dead* (1954).[10]

In his commentary on *The Secret of the Golden Flower* Jung avowed that he wanted to build "a bridge of psychological understanding between East and West":[11]

> he claimed to discover in this ancient text an unexpected "agreement between the psychic states and symbolisms of East and West" which not only helped to provide confirmation for his theory of the collective unconscious, but also indicated that the goal of becoming a conscious and fully realized person "unites the most diverse cultures in a common task."[12]

From *The Tibetan Book of the Great Liberation* Jung derived the lesson of the fundamental reality of mind, or consciousness, insisting that the text "bases itself upon psychic reality, that is upon the psyche as the main and unique condition of existence."[13] Of *The Tibetan Book of the Dead*, some time after its appearance in English, Jung wrote that it

> has been my constant companion, and to it I owe not only many stimulating ideas and discoveries, but also many fundamental insights ... Its philosophy

---

9 Schopenhauer quoted in J.J. Clarke, *Oriental Enlightenment*, 68-69. See also R. Schwab, *The Oriental Renaissance*, 427-428.

10 Most of Jung's writings on Eastern subjects (though not including his commentary on *The Secret of the Golden Flower*) can be found in Volume 11, *Psychology and Religion: West and East*, of *The Collected Works of Carl Jung*, London: Routledge, 1969 (second edition). The dates given in the text refer to the first English translations. There has been a recent surge of interest in Jung's understanding of Eastern doctrines and on his role in disseminating them in the West. For a sample of this literature see J.J. Clarke, *Jung and Eastern Thought: A Dialogue with the Orient*; H. Coward, *Jung and Eastern Thought*; R. Moacanin, *Jung's Psychology and Tibetan Buddhism*; P. Novak, "C.G. Jung in the Light of Asian Psychology"; H. Oldmeadow, *Mircea Eliade and Carl Jung: 'Priests without Surplices'*. On Jung's role in the recent history of Western esotericism see A. Faivre, *Access to Western Esotericism*; G. Wehr, "C.G. Jung in the Context of Christian Esotericism and Cultural History"; W.J. Hanegraaff, *New Age Religion and Western Culture*, 496-513.

11 C. Jung, *Collected Works*, V13, 55.

12 J.J. Clarke, *Oriental Enlightenment*, 154.

13 C.G. Jung, "Commentary on *The Tibetan Book of the Great Liberation*," *Collected Works*, V11, 481.

contains the quintessence of Buddhist psychological criticism; and as such, one can truly say that it is of unexampled superiority ...[14]

His interest in Tibetan doctrines helped to strengthen the tenuous connections between the Vajrayana in the East and both psychotherapy and esotericism in the West.

Jung's Oriental interests culminated in a somewhat unsatisfactory trip, in 1938, to India and Ceylon of which he wrote:

> I had felt the impact of the dreamlike world of India ... My own world of European consciousness had become peculiarly thin, like a network of telegraph wires high above the ground, stretching in straight lines all over the surface of an earth looking treacherously like a geographic globe.[15]

He was profoundly disturbed by the thought that the world of Indian spirituality might be the real world and that the European lived in "a madhouse of abstractions."[16] His ambivalence is captured in the autobiographical *Memories, Dreams, Reflections* (1963):

> By that time I had read a great deal about Indian philosophy and religious history, and was deeply convinced of the value of Oriental wisdom. But I had to travel in order to form my own conclusions, and *remained within myself* like a homunculus in a retort. India affected me like a dream ...[17]

We might also observe that Jung's jest, "I got dysentery because I could not digest India," might be more suggestive than he realized.[18]

In general terms we can say that Jung's project was to reanimate an understanding of the inner psychological world which had been neglected by the Western preoccupation with a mastery of the physical world. He believed that Eastern myths and doctrines could play a vital role in counterbalancing a Western science engrossed in the physical properties and processes of the external material world. J.J. Clarke has identified six aspects of Jung's thought which show a close affinity with "Eastern" themes:

> (1) The emphasis in Jung's writings on the primacy of inner experience and the reality of the psychic world. (2) His insistence that a certain kind of numinous experience, rather than creeds or faith, is the essence of religion. (3) The quest for an amplified notion of selfhood which goes beyond the narrow confines of the conscious ego. (4) The belief in the possibility of self-transformation by one's own efforts. (5) His endeavor to overcome the intransigent opposition of matter and mind ... (6) Above all, the quest for wholeness based on creative interaction between complementary opposites within the psyche.[19]

14 C.G. Jung, "Psychological Commentary" in *The Tibetan Book of the Dead*, xxxvi-xxxvii.
15 Jung quoted by G. Wehr, *Jung: A Biography*, 283.
16 C.G. Jung, "The Dreamlike World of India" in *Collected Works*, V10, 518, cited in G. Wehr, *Jung: A Biography*, 283.
17 C.G. Jung, *Memories, Dreams, Reflections*, 304 (italics mine).
18 Jung quoted in J. Paine, *Father India*, 106.
19 J.J. Clarke, *Jung and Eastern Thought*, 5-6.

Nonetheless, Jung had grave misgivings about the direct European application of Eastern spiritual techniques. He was also careful to distinguish between the metaphysical and religious dimensions of the Eastern texts, and their psychological significance.[20] Despite the fact that Jung saw considerable overlap between his own therapeutic practices to enhance individuation and the techniques of Indian yoga, he wrote of the latter: "... yoga in Mayfair or Fifth Avenue, or in any other place which is on the telephone, is a spiritual fake."[21] Likewise, "Study yoga, you will learn an infinite amount from it—but do not try to apply it." Here we may read "yoga" as signifying all Eastern psycho-spiritual techniques, be they Indian, Tibetan or Chinese. Eastern techniques of spiritual transformation, he believed, had over millennia grown in a climate very different from that of the West whose development "had been along entirely different lines."[22] As Jung had insisted to Frau Fröbe, and as he wrote in the Eranos *Jahrbuch* of 1934, "The Western road to health must be built upon Western groundwork with Western symbols, and be formed from Western material."[23]

In many respects Jung's work marks an attempt at the kind of synthesis of oriental and occidental ideas which had been one of the principal aims of Keyserling's School of Wisdom, founded in Darmstadt in 1920—and with which Jung had some contact in its early years. Count Hermann Keyserling (1880-1946) traveled extensively in Ceylon, India, China and Japan early in the 20th century, and subsequently wrote *The Travel Diary of a Philosopher* (1919), an influential book in the inter-war period in which he argued for an internationalist outlook which could accommodate the best of Eastern and Western thought. More recently Keyserling is of interest as one of the primary influences on Roberto Assagioli and his system of "Psychosynthesis" which, it might be remarked, also owed a good deal to Eastern mystical traditions.[24]

Eranos

Jung played a pivotal role in the development of the Eranos conferences which took place annually at Ascona on Lake Maggiore from 1933 to 1969 under the patronage of Frau Olga Fröbe-Kapteyn. *Eranos*: a banquet to which each participant brings a contribution. In Joseph Campbell's words, "a spiri-

---

20 "I quite deliberately bring everything that purports to be metaphysical into the daylight of psychological understanding ... [and] strip things of their metaphysical wrappings in order to make them objects of psychology."; from *Psychology and the East*, quoted in J.J. Clarke, *Oriental Enlightenment*, 154-155.

21 C.G. Jung, "Psychological Commentary" on *The Tibetan Book of the Great Liberation* (1939), *Collected Works*, V11, 500.

22 C.G. Jung, *Psychology and the East*, 82.

23 Jung quoted in G. Wehr, *Jung: A Biography*, 268.

24 On Keyserling see M.G. Parks, *Introduction to Keyserling: An Account of the Man and his Work*, esp. Ch. 3. For some commentary on Keyserling's influence on Assagioli see J. Hardy, *A Psychology with Soul: Psychosynthesis in Evolutionary Context*.

tual feast."[25] The name was suggested by Rudolf Otto.[26] Olga Fröbe, a wealthy Dutch widow who had been imbued with the ideals of the Anglo-Indian Theosophical movement, described the initial intention in these words:

> The Eranos Conferences have set themselves the goal of mediating between East and West. The task of this mediation ... [has] become ever clearer. The question of a fruitful confrontation of East and West is above all a psychological one. The clear-cut questions posed by Western people in matters of religion and psychology can undoubtedly find added, meaningful fructification in the wisdom of the Orient. It is not the emulation of Eastern methods and teachings that is important, nor the neglecting or replacing of Western knowledge about these things, but the fact that Eastern wisdom, symbolism and methods can help us to discover the spiritual values that are most distinctly our own.[27]

The Eranos lectures and seminars were directed towards the task of "encompassing and assimilating the world's wealth of poetic and religious visions, modes and dreams of life and readings of the mystery of death."[28] This agenda entailed an arcane hermeneutics of symbolism; as R.J. Zwi Werblowsky tersely observed, "Eranos is, as it were, a gigantic symposium on symbolism."[29] Gershom Scholem, one of the century's most eminent Judaists and an Eranos luminary, wrote of

> ... the attempt to discover the hidden life beneath the external shapes of reality and to make visible that abyss in which the symbolic nature of all that exists reveals itself: this attempt is as important for us today as it was for those ancient mystics.[30]

In much the same vein Eliade later wrote that

> If the discovery of the unconscious has compelled Western man to confront his own individual, secret and larval "history," the encounter with non-Western cultures will oblige him to delve very profoundly into the history of the human spirit, and will perhaps persuade him to admit that history as an integral part of his own being.[31]

One of the guiding aims of the Eranos program was to uncover common ground between the religious and spiritual traditions of both West and East, and indeed, of archaic and "primitive" cultures. It brought together distinguished scholars from different fields of study concerned with "the deepest experiences of the human psyche and their cultural expressions"—psychology, philosophy, theology, orientalism, ethnology and comparative religious

---

25 J. Campbell, *Spiritual Disciplines*, xv.
26 E. Wasserstrom, *Religion after Religion*, 36.
27 Olga Fröbe quoted in G. Wehr, *Jung: A Biography*, 263.
28 J. Campbell, *Spiritual Disciplines*, xv.
29 E. Wasserstrom, *Religion after Religion*, 85.
30 G. Scholem, *Major Trends in Jewish Mysticism*, 38.
31 M. Eliade, *Myths, Dreams, and Mysteries*, 12.

studies—in the hope that their combined researches might bring closer "an integral knowledge of man."[32] Furthermore, as the biologist Adolf Portman put it, "accepting the mystery of the spirit with reverence; saying what can be said and knowing that the unutterable is present: this is the spirit of the work of Eranos."[33]

While Eranos was not restricted to a Jungian agenda or methodology Jung was its single most influential member and it was at the Eranos seminars that Jung launched some of his most arresting theories about alchemy, archetypes and synchronicity.[34] But Eranos attracted a shimmering array of scholars and thinkers, many of whom played a critical role in the development of comparative religious studies. Mention might be made of such figures as Giuseppe Tucci, Henry Corbin, Jean Daniélou, Friedrich Heiler, Raffael Pettazzoni, Louis Massignon, Laurens van der Post, Gershom Scholem, Martin Buber, Paul Tillich, Caroline Rhys Davids and D.T. Suzuki, as well as Zimmer, Campbell and Eliade—an honor roll of comparative religionists in the mid-20th century, as Eric Sharpe noted in his history of the discipline.[35] Closely associated with the Eranos Conferences, and guided by the same ethos, was the Bollingen Foundation, sponsored by the American philanthropist Mary Mellen, which published the *Eranos Jahrbuchs*, the six volumes of *Papers from the Eranos Yearbooks* as well as many major scholarly works by those who had gathered on the shores of Lake Maggiore to discuss "the efficacy of their methods, the value of their discoveries, and the meaning of their cultural adventures."[36] It was not without reason that Erich Neumann had described Eranos as "a navel of the world"[37]—although we must also take account of the testimony of participants such as Alain Daniélou who found the Eranos seminars "boring and pretentious, with psycho-mystical tendencies far removed from human reality."[38] Steven Wasserstrom has summed up the Eranos enterprise this way:

> These [participants] provided not merely moral support but also models of engaged scholarship, unstinting infusions of passion, world-class literary aspirations, and myriad particular means ... for sustaining a career at the very top of the intellectual world. Most especially they provided a view of religion ... determined to exhibit the treasures of spiritual history in their own terms, and not in the "reductionistic" terms current in the social sciences. And they all understood this common work in the History of Religions furthermore to be a religious task of a certain sort: a paradoxically unconventional kind, one often verging on the visionary and the ecstatic while not belonging to contemporary churches, synagogues, or mosques. Their guiding task ... was to forge another spiritual intelligence collectively,

32 M. Eliade, "Encounters at Ascona," xvii, x.
33 Portman quoted in G. Wehr, "C.G. Jung and Christian Esotericism," 396.
34 See J.J. Clarke, *Jung and Eastern Thought*, 61.
35 E. Sharpe, *Comparative Religion*, 211.
36 M. Eliade, "Encounters at Ascona," xix.
37 Neumann quoted in G. Wehr, *Jung: A Biography*, 277.
38 A. Daniélou, *The Way to the Labyrinth*, 248-249.

a soteriologically vibrant conversation of like-minded intellectuals, a transcultural circle of intensively learned but entirely nonpracticing believers, an invisible congregation of the very few, a quiet scattered commonweal, perhaps, for all that, a religion after religion.[39]

Heinrich Zimmer

The very first person whom Olga Fröbe invited to speak at an Eranos gathering was Heinrich Zimmer, professor of Indology at Berlin University: his subject was Indian tantric yoga, at the time a very exotic subject indeed![40] Heinrich Zimmer was born in 1890, the son of a scholar in Celtic mythology and Indian studies, Sanskritist and author of a distinguished work on Vedic culture. Zimmer's studies in German and comparative philology in Berlin were interrupted by four years of military service in the First World War. Among Zimmer's intellectual progenitors were Hegel, Schopenhauer and Nietzsche, and from the German Romantics he inherited the image of an idealized India.[41] After further studies Zimmer was appointed as a professor in Indian philology at the University of Heidelberg, a post he held until he was dismissed by the Nazis in 1938 because of his criticism of the regime and his wife's Jewish ancestry. After taking up an honorary appointment at Oxford Zimmer and his family moved to America where he developed a close association with Columbia University. Among the many well-known American scholars and psychologists who came within Zimmer's orbit were Mircea Eliade, Ananda Coomaraswamy, Swami Nikhilananda, Stella Kramrisch, Joseph Kitagawa, Esther Harding, and, most portentously, Joseph Campbell. In 1943 Zimmer died rather suddenly of pneumonia.

Zimmer identified three major influences on his thinking: the Indian Tantric texts edited and published by Sir John Woodroffe (Arthur Avalon) early in the century; the *Puranas* (compendia of Indian mythological and folkloric materials); and Jung's *Psychology of the Unconscious*.[42] Zimmer and Jung met in 1932: "When I first met him [Zimmer later wrote] he struck me as the most accomplished embodiment of the big medicine man, of the perfect wizard, the master of Zen initiations."[43] During the ensuing years Zimmer was a regular participant in the Eranos Conferences.[44] Writing of his early interactions with Jung, Zimmer observed

> Here, I felt, a new sort of collaboration between modern psychology on the one hand, and Oriental philology and ethnology on the other hand, had been inaugurated, and I was delighted by the privilege to join in.[45]

---

39 E. Wasserstrom, *Religion after Religion*, 248.
40 See W. McGuire, "Zimmer and the Mellens," 22. (The lecture can be found in J. Campbell (ed), *Spiritual Disciplines*, 3-58.)
41 See M. Kapstein, "Schopenhauer's *Shakti*."
42 M.F. Linda, "Zimmer and Coomaraswamy," 131.
43 H. Zimmer, "The Impress of Dr. Jung," 45.
44 See G. Chapple, "Heinrich Zimmer and Henry R. Zimmer," 71-73.

In an address to the Analytical Psychology Club of New York, in 1942, Heinrich Zimmer observed that much contemporary orientalist scholarship restricted itself to dry philological inquiry and dealt with mythological materials in "a purely positivistic unimaginative way with no sense for its secret meanings," an approach he contrasted with that of Carl Jung:

> By the analysis of dreams [Jung] had got down to the very core of inner depth, from which at all times the visions and images of mythology, the pictorial script of its figures and epics, have welled up. He had descended to their source in the deeper layers of the human psyche which have remained relatively unaltered through the changes of civilization and environment affecting the surface of man's conscious behavior. I felt it was a master key, unlocking many treasures—in fact, the whole range of variegated mythology and ethnology with rituals and institutions, customs and superstitions of peoples bygone and present.[46]

Whilst Jung's psychological theories, particularly the homologizing of dreams and myths, had a decisive effect on the orientation of Zimmer's best known work, remember that Zimmer was already an Indologist and comparative mythologist of considerable standing before the meeting with Jung. He had already found in the work of another Swiss "solitary master," Johann Jacob Bachofen, a deeper approach to Indian mythology than that followed by most academic philologists.[47] Well before encountering Jung, Zimmer had penetrated deep into what, at the time, was still very arcane territory for most European scholars—Vedic magic, tantric yoga, Vedantic metaphysics, the ritual uses of sacred art, the symbolism of archaic myths, traditional Indian medicine. As early as 1928 a contemporary German orientalist was lauding Zimmer in these terms:

> ... Heinrich Zimmer is surely the most profound and gifted interpreter of the Indian mind today ... he knows how to grasp the enormously remote and foreign world of India with such lucidity of vision and precision of conceptualization—while placing it before our very eyes with artistic power—that he stands in the front rank of living oriental scholars.[48]

Zimmer remained alert to the dangers of a psychologistic reductionism and was always at pains to respect the integrity of the Indian myths and symbols

45 H. Zimmer, "The Impress of Dr. Jung," 45.
46 H. Zimmer, "The Impress of Dr. Jung," 44-45.
47 H. Zimmer, "The Impress of Dr. Jung," 45. Bachofen also influenced Joseph Campbell, particularly through his postulation of an archaic matriarchal order. See R. Segal, "Joseph Campbell on Jews and Judaism," 166. On Bachofen see J. Waardenburg (ed), *Classical Approaches to the Study of Religion*, 117-125. Bachofen was also a central figure in the *Konservative Revolution* of reactionary Romanticism and significantly influenced the orientalist and fascist ideologue, Julius Evola, to whom we shall turn in Chapter 14. See F. Farraresi, "Julius Evola: tradition, reaction, and the radical right," 109-111.
48 Hans Heinrich Schrader in a letter to Hugo von Hoffmannsthal in June 1928, soon after the poet became Zimmer's father-in-law. See G. Chapple, "Heinrich Zimmer and Henry R. Zimmer," 68-69.

which he sought to interpret:[49] the reproach that Zimmer's work "became hostage to Jung's depth psychology" is injudicious.[50] Nor should it be forgotten that the intellectual traffic between Zimmer and Jung went in both directions. Jung himself acknowledged that Zimmer had given him

> invaluable insights into the Oriental psyche, not only through his immense technical knowledge, but above all through his brilliant grasp of the meaning and content of Indian mythology ... [he] overcame the limitations of the specialist and, turning towards humanity, bestowed upon it the joyous gift of "immortal fruit."[51]

Zimmer is best known in the English-speaking world as the author of four substantial scholarly works exploring the sacred art, mythology and philosophy of India: *Myths and Symbols in Indian Art and Civilization* (1946), *The King and the Corpse* (1948), *Philosophies of India* (1951), and *The Art of Indian Asia* (1955). Each of these was published posthumously in the Bollingen Series, under the editorial hand of Zimmer's protégé, Joseph Campbell.[52] In these books Zimmer analyzed, compared and illuminated a vast array of Indian myths and expounded the symbolic vocabulary in which they were cast. In this work he often followed the lead of Ananda Coomaraswamy to whom he wrote, in a letter,

> I need not say how much it means to me to have met you personally. Your inspiring way of dealing with Hindu art and religion has, since I became a student, been one of the main elements of my initiation into this revelation of truth.[53]

Through his translations and commentaries he directed attention to many unknown or neglected texts in the Hindu corpus, particularly the later *Puranas*. He disavowed the positivistic, reductionist and pseudo-scientific methodology of contemporary philology and anticipated later developments in the discipline of comparative religion through his insistence on the use of inter-disciplinary perspectives and *sympathetic* hermeneutics (themes to be elaborated in the work of Mircea Eliade). He also honored the role of intuition and vision in any creative interpretation. As two scholars have noted,

> There is a certain Orphic cast to Zimmer's reading of Hindu or European material. He is a seeker after wisdom, an adept in his own scholarly way of Shiva, the Master yogi, or a reader of runes or symbols. He may be called, indeed, a comparative esotericist.[54]

49 See H. Nette, "An Epitaph for Heinrich Zimmer," 27.
50 See M. Case, *Heinrich Zimmer*, 4-5.
51 C.G. Jung, "The Holy Men of India," 576-577.
52 Wendy Doniger has explored the question of the intellectual influences which flowed in both directions, and more particularly, the contribution Campbell made to the Zimmer volumes in the Bollingen series. See W. Doniger, "The King and the Corpse," 48-49.
53 R. Lipsey, *Coomaraswamy: His Life and Work*, 212.
54 F. Sandler & D. Reeck, "The Masks of Joseph Campbell," 3.

The traumatic experiences of the war had convinced Zimmer that scholarship with no apparent relationship to real life was barren. Discussing Western perceptions of Indian thought and spirituality Zimmer referred to "the sterilizing anatomy and dehydration of the merely intellectual approach of sheer scientist-philologists." Recalling his student days Zimmer wrote,

> My teacher in Sanskrit, Heinrich Lueders, was an arch-craftsman in philology, in deciphering manuscripts, inscriptions, a skilled super-mechanic, one of the past masters of philological craft in the field of Indic studies. But he was not interested in Indian thought, a plain liberal citizen from the republic of Luebeck, anti-philosophic, indifferent to mysticism, and with a meager sense for artistic qualities and implications. I was bought up on a wholesome diet of stones instead of bread.[55]

It was Zimmer's purpose to bring the spiritual treasures of India to life for Western readers and seekers—in short, to offer bread rather than stones, an enterprise always viewed with suspicion in many academic quarters. Doubtless Zimmer would have endorsed Mircea Eliade's claim that "Creative hermeneutics changes man; it is more than mere instruction, it is a spiritual technique susceptible of modifying the quality of existence itself."[56] It was with good cause that Zimmer asserted that "The current representation of India lacked color, intensity, consistency, life."[57] As a recent commentator has noted,

> Zimmer found Western scholars of India deficient on two grounds: pedants by nature or training, they failed to relate philological findings to human questions; and, faced with ideas and images they did not understand, they dismissed them as worthless on the basis of their own cultural assumptions.[58]

Zimmer's work can be understood as a corrective to both of these deficiencies and the product of a real existential engagement with the Indian tradition, despite the fact that his several attempts to visit the sub-continent were, unhappily, frustrated. As he wrote of his first book, *Artistic Form and Yoga in the Sacred Images of India* (1926), "I did not write it for professionals, nor as a contribution to specialized studies. I had to write it, to realize my self and to come into my own."[59] Zimmer's understanding of Indian art and spirituality was less circumscribed by the narrow Eurocentric assumptions shared by many contemporary orientalists and was informed by the conviction that the Indian heritage was as rich as that of Europe:

> I had faith. Not the faith ever to understand or to decipher the characters of that strange other script. But the faith that they contained as much truth,

55 M. Kapstein, "Schopenhauer's *Shakti*," 110.
56 M. Eliade, *The Quest*, 62.
57 M. Case, *Heinrich Zimmer*, 5.
58 M. Case, *Heinrich Zimmer*, 5.
59 M. Case, *Heinrich Zimmer*, 6. (This work was not published in English translation until 1984.)

no more and no less, than the familiar script in which I was brought up and which was taken for the script of knowledge and reality all around me.[60]

Zimmer had the gift of bringing "that strange other script" to life as a living and transformative philosophy. As Joseph Campbell wrote in his obituary,

> Zimmer's chief endowment was a genius for language, in the service of extraordinary insight: an ability not only to translate with deceptive ease the profoundest concepts of the Orient, but also to capture in a word the secret of a personality, the quality of a work of art, or the feeling of a landscape.[61]

Zimmer's insight was by no means restricted to the somewhat hermetic world of orientalist scholarship. Many of his insights strike an uncannily contemporary chord. Take, for example, a prescient and poetic discussion in one of his Eranos lectures of Hamlet as the prototype of modern man:

> This world no longer possesses a sheltering womb where one could be perfectly safe ... in Wittenberg, Europe everywhere, a new breed of man has been concocted, the womb of Holy Mother Church is breached, the umbilical cord that bound him to her is cut, and that oriental/Roman mother was the ultimate, spiritualized form of Mother Earth. Mother Isis, the World Mother. Now man will tear to pieces the body of his mother, Nature, and will quarry her for new and different forms of power and resources: her body, gagged and bound, no longer sacrosanct, must yield up its energy in ever-changing forms to satisfy those human demands—however destructive, however excessive they may be—that man's capriciousness or mutual distrust might spawn.[62]

The work of this "scholar of Indian philosophy, religion and art ... philologist, mythologist, psychologist, translator and fabulator *extraordinaire*"[63] has recently been more widely recognized and celebrated, as evidenced by the appearance in 1994 of a fascinating volume of biographical and critical essays, *Heinrich Zimmer: Coming Into His Own*. The editor hailed Zimmer's originality as a scholar and affirmed his

> ... rightful place in that small group of great scholars—which includes Ananda Coomaraswamy and Stella Kramrisch—who were part of the first generation to confront the end of European empires in India and the rest of Asia. They were among the first to try to decolonize the European mind.[64]

Perhaps this resurgence of interest will remedy the unhappy fact that Zimmer's work has been overshadowed by two figures—Jung and

---

60 M. Case, *Heinrich Zimmer*, 8-9.

61 Campbell quoted in G. Chapple, "Heinrich Zimmer and Henry R. Zimmer," 81.

62 Zimmer quoted in G. Chapple, "Heinrich Zimmer and Henry R. Zimmer," 84. (This lecture is still unavailable in English translation.)

63 G. Chapple, "Heinrich Zimmer and Henry R. Zimmer," 61.

64 M. Case, *Heinrich Zimmer*, 13. Coomaraswamy was to assist Campbell in the editing of the four Bollingen volumes.

Campbell—whose understanding of the Indian tradition could certainly not match his own.

Joseph Campbell

In 1924 Joseph Campbell traveled by ocean liner to Europe. During the voyage the twenty-year old Columbia student met and was much impressed by an aristocratic Indian man whom he knew only as "Krishna" and who was given to philosophical discoursing, surrounded by a small group of votaries. One of these gave Campbell a book which, he later declared, changed his life forever. The Indian was none other than Jiddu Krishnamurti, the anointed Messiah of the Theosophical movement. The book was Edwin Arnold's *The Light of Asia.*[65] Thus began Campbell's long romance with the East, one which eventually soured.[66] (Campbell maintained contact with Krishnamurti whose identity he only later discovered: it was after hearing one of the Indian iconoclast's lectures, in 1927, that he repudiated his affiliation to the Catholic tradition in which he had been raised.)

Campbell was born into a well-to-do New York family in 1904. As a young boy he was taken to Madison Square Garden to see Buffalo Bill's Wild West Show—the beginning of a lifelong interest in Native American culture. Campbell studied biology and mathematics before plunging into the humanities. During the 1920s, at Columbia, the Sorbonne and Munich University, he pursued intensive studies in European languages, medieval literature, German Romantic philosophy, Sanskrit and psychology. In 1934 Campbell was appointed to the faculty of Comparative Literature at Sarah Lawrence College in Bronxville, a position he was to fill for nearly forty years. His intellectual interests were still largely literary, philosophical and Occidental: Kant, Schopenhauer, Oswald Spengler, Thomas Mann, James Joyce, Sir James Frazer, Freud, Jung. In 1940 Campbell's dormant Oriental interests were reawakened when Swami Nikhilananda (one of the leading lights of the New York Jungian circle), impressed by both his knowledge of Sanskrit and his literary abilities, persuaded Campbell to help him complete a book on Ramakrishna. Through the Swami Campbell was soon to meet the man who exercised the most decisive influence on his intellectual development and subsequent career as a writer: Heinrich Zimmer. As Campbell later recalled, "If I do have a guru ... it would be Zimmer—the one who really gave me the courage to interpret myths out of what I knew of their common symbols."[67] The meeting with Zimmer kindled what was to become Campbell's lifelong project thenceforth: a somewhat Frazerian comparative study of myths within a framework fashioned by German Romanticism and Jungian psychology,

65 See J. Campbell & M. Toms, *An Open Life*, 120.
66 For Campbell's experiences in India see J. Campbell, *Baksheesh and Brahman.*
67 See J. Campbell & M. Toms, *An Open Life*, 123.

and motivated by the conviction, inherited from Zimmer, that myths enshrined "messages that were valid for life."[68]

Soon after Zimmer's abrupt death Campbell was approached by Zimmer's widow, Christiane, to edit the formidable mass of work-in-progress which had been left behind. As we have seen, the result of a heroic labor on Campbell's part saw the publication of the four books which have secured Zimmer's reputation in the Anglo-American world. Campbell's absorption in Zimmer's work also acted as a trigger for his long-standing desire to visit India. As for Jung, but for rather different reasons, Campbell's visit to India in 1954-55 was, on the whole, a disillusioning experience, summed up in his remark, "I came to India to hear of Brahman, and all I have heard so far is politics and patriotism."[69] Like many both before and after him Campbell was not altogether able to cope with the many perplexities and conundrums which this ancient land so often presents to Westerners. His equivocal response to the social realities of India are signaled by the title of his posthumously published journal of his Indian trip, *Baksheesh and Brahman.*[70]

Campbell produced his own first major work in 1949, a book which has assumed a canonical position in the popular literature of comparative mythology and which promoted the Eranos outlook,[71] *The Hero with a Thousand Faces.* In this work Campbell reconstructs a single structure of meaning which, he argues, is woven through apparently diverse mythical narratives from all parts of the world—in Campbell's terms, the "monomyth" of the archetypal hero's journey. This was to be a pervasive theme in all of Campbell's work, including his reflections on contemporary popular culture: the hero's journey is a narrative template as easily discerned in *Star Wars* as it is in the *Odyssey.*[72] In the early 50s Campbell became increasingly closely associated with Jungian circles in both America and Switzerland, meeting Jung himself, Eliade and D.T. Suzuki at Ascona and becoming, in 1953, the editor of the Eranos Yearbooks.[73] In 1958 he produced the first of the four volumes in his *magnum opus, The Masks of God.* Over the next three decades Campbell continued to write copiously and became something of a talk-show star on the American television circuit. He was, for a time, much in vogue in counter-cultural circles in the late 60s and, not surprisingly, lectured frequently at the Esalen Institute in California. His public exposure reached its zenith in the mid-80s through the six-hour PBS television series with Bill

68 Campbell quoted in H. Coward, "Joseph Campbell and Eastern Religions," 48.
69 Campbell quoted in Editor's Foreword to J. Campbell, *Baksheesh and Brahman*, x.
70 Whilst on this sabbatical Campbell also visited Sri Lanka, Thailand, Burma, Hong Kong and Japan. His account of these experiences was slated for publication as *Journey to the Sun's Door* but, at the time of writing, has not yet appeared.
71 See S. Wasserstrom, *Religion after Religion*, 140.
72 See J. Campbell, *The Power of Myth*, 177-179.
73 For some account of how Campbell's work diverges from Jung's see Robert Segal in R. Segal (ed), *Hero Myths*, 16ff.

Moyers, *Joseph Campbell and the Power of Myth* (later published in book form). Interest in his work has burgeoned since his death in 1987.

Campbell's metaphysical position can be discerned in the following passage from *The Hero with a Thousand Faces*:

> ... the universal doctrine teaches that all the visible structures of the world—all things and beings—are the effects of a ubiquitous power out of which they rise, which supports and fills them during the period of their manifestation, and back into which they must ultimately dissolve. This is the power known to science as energy, to the Melanesians as *mana*, to the Sioux Indians as *wakonda*, the Hindus as *shakti*, and the Christians as the power of God. Its manifestation in the psyche is termed, by the psychoanalysts, *libido*. And its manifestation in the cosmos is the structure and flux of the universe itself.[74]

In a memorable phrase on the opening page of the same book he had characterized myth as "the secret opening through which the inexhaustible energies of the cosmos pour into human cultural manifestation."[75] For Campbell, as for many of the psychological mythographers, the discernment of universal mythological structures, themes and motifs was impelled by the belief that they carried a fundamental message for the modern world: "Myths are clues to the spiritual potentialities of the human life."[76] Furthermore, it was psychoanalysis which was most adequately equipped, in the contemporary world, to unlock the mysteries of the world's myths. It was Campbell's purpose

> To uncover some of the truths disguised for us under the figures of religion and mythology ... But first we must learn the grammar of the symbols, and as a key to this mystery I know no better tool than psychoanalysis. Without regarding this as the last word on the subject, one can nevertheless permit it to serve as an approach.[77]

Like Jung, Campbell was much interested in the relationship of dream to myth and of their common "archetypal" origins. In *The Mythic Image* (1974), a work which many scholars regard as his finest, Campbell recalled a telling image from one of his intellectual ancestors, Arthur Schopenhauer: everything in the universe is "a vast dream, dreamed by a single being, in such a way that all the dream characters dream too."[78]

Steven Wasserstrom has reflected on the role of Campbell and other Eranos figures in preparing the soil for what has come to be known as New Age Religion:

> It is not an accident that a certain sort of post-Christianity, so-called New Age Religion, emerged during the Cold War. Religious intellectuals like the

74 J. Campbell, *The Hero with a Thousand Faces*, 257-258.
75 J. Campbell, *The Hero with a Thousand Faces*, 3.
76 J. Campbell, *The Power of Myth*, 5
77 J. Campbell, *The Hero with a Thousand Faces*, vii.
78 J. Campbell, *The Mythic Image*, 497, quoted in C. Long, "The Dreams of Joseph Campbell," 168.

Historians of Religion [Eliade, Gershom Scholem, Henry Corbin] spear-headed a notion of religion that seemed to transcend denominational boundaries even as it presumed some kind of transcendent unity to world religions. The geopolitical antagonism of the Cold War, seemingly so consti-tutive of the age, stimulated at the same time what seemed like a planetary ecumenicism. This Eranos kind of public gnosis, popularized by Jung, Campbell, and Eliade, could espouse its identity, seriatim, with alchemy, shamanism, yoga, Templarism. Such a secularized esoterism, of course, is now familiar in its subsequent popularized forms as (tellingly) New Age Religion. Their characteristically promiscuous application of correspon-dences, often claimed as a Hermetic principle, underwrote a riot of analo-gies.[79]

There is much in Campbell's work which is unattractive: a deep-seated animus towards and dismissal of the great Occidental monotheisms and more generally a hostility to institutionalized religion which is often treated in simplistic terms and in strident tone; a facile and tedious diffusionism often asserted with little or no scholarly support; a tendency to surrender to glib dichotomies which did little to mask his own prejudices; an inability to understand the ways in which his own American background limited his intellectual horizons; a sometimes sentimental and psychologistic reading of Vedantic monism (a common failing amongst self-styled American Vedantins!); an appropriation of mythic materials which, from one vantage point, might be seen as a form of cultural imperialism;[80] an oscillation between the extremes of Orientalist romanticism and a recoil into Western prejudices (most clearly evidenced in his wildly fluctuating perceptions of Indian society—his stereotypical misunderstanding of the caste system, for instance);[81] the reduction of metaphysics to a purely psychic realm (a reduc-tion more severe and more facile than we find in Jung, Zimmer or Eliade);[82] a covert strain of anti-Semitism (more openly expressed in his personal life).[83] One can see something of Campbell's simultaneous insight and myopia in a characteristic claim such as "religion is a misinterpretation of mythology."[84] Then, too, there is something offensive in Campbell's collu-sion in the popular perception of him as a *jnanin*—and here one is remind-ed of another highly talented popularizer who was all too often mistaken for a sage, Alan Watts. Campbell's work has attracted a good deal of scholarly criticism, some of it no doubt deriving from the intellectual snobbery of more highly specialized academic scholars but much of it cogent.[85] His work,

79 E. Wasserstrom, *Religion after Religion*, 142.

80 See F. Sandler & D. Reeck, "The Masks of Joseph Campbell," 9.

81 See F. Sandler & D. Reeck, "The Masks of Joseph Campbell," 15.

82 See J. Campbell, *The Hero with a Thousand Faces*, 259, where Campbell states quite baldly, with-out qualification or equivocation, that "the metaphysical realm = the unconscious."

83 See R. Segal, "Joseph Campbell on Jews and Judaism."

84 J. Campbell & M. Toms, *An Open Life*, 78.

85 See especially M. Manganaro, *Myth, Rhetoric and the Voice of Authority*, 151-185; R. Ellwood, *The Politics of Myth*, 127-170; E. Wasserstrom, *Religion after Religion*; W. Doniger's review in D. Noel (ed), *Paths to the Power of Myth*, 181-186.

whilst often dazzling, lacks the subtlety and depth of Zimmer's. It must also be said that the appeal of Campbell's treatment of Eastern mythological and scriptural materials owes much to his literary prowess and little to any groundbreaking scholarship. Nonetheless, there is no gainsaying Campbell's prodigious talents, his encyclopedic grasp of myths from all over the globe and his appeal for the general reader whom he engaged by "his extraordinary fluency and enthusiasm, his erudition especially in out-of-the-way material, his provocative cross-cultural juxtapositions and his intellectual range and generosity of spirit." Furthermore,

> From the viewpoint of religious studies, the significance of Campbell's work is that he formulates for a large general audience outside the discipline the challenge of the present era: he insists that the study of mythology and religion must take into account all human culture, and he emphasizes ... that the enterprise must find its central point of coherence in the interrelationship of East and West.[86]

Nor should we doubt that his work, considered as a whole, was motivated by a noble end which was articulated in his first major work:

> ... a comparative elucidation [of myths] may contribute to the perhaps not-quite-desperate cause of those forces that are working in the present world for unification, not in the name of some ecclesiastical or political empire, but in the sense of mutual human understanding. As we are told in the *Vedas*: "Truth is one, the sages speak of it by many names."[87]

Mircea Eliade

It is not too much to assert that the academic study of religion over the last half-century has been more influenced by Mircea Eliade than any other single figure. His scholarly oeuvre is formidable indeed, ranging from highly specialized monographs to his magisterial *A History of Religious Ideas*, written in three volumes over the last decade of his life. His last major project was editing the sixteen-volume *The Encyclopedia of Religion*, published posthumously and the first enterprise of this kind, on this sort of scale, since the Hastings *Encyclopedia of Religion and Ethics* published in 1913. As Editor-in-Chief Eliade addressed the following remarks to the fourteen hundred contributors commissioned to write the 2750 articles which comprise the *Encyclopedia*:

> In the last half century new methodological approaches and more adequate hermeneutics have enhanced our knowledge of the existential value, the social function and the cultural creativity of religions throughout history ... impressive advances in information and understanding helped to eradicate the clichés, highly popular in the nineteenth century, concerning the men-

---

86 F. Sandler & D. Reeck, "The Masks of Joseph Campbell," 1.
87 J. Campbell, *The Hero with a Thousand Faces*, viii.

tal capacity of "primitive" man and the poverty and provinciality of non-Western cultures ... Perhaps for the first time in history we recognize today not only the unity of the human races but also the spiritual values and cultural significance of their religious creations.[88]

No one contributed more to the changes to which Eliade refers than did he himself. As well as his prodigious scholarly work in the history of religions (as Eliade himself styled the discipline of comparative religion) he wrote several novels, short stories, literary essays, journals and an autobiography. He was the author of some fifty-odd books and myriad articles. He was recognized throughout the world, elected to many different Academies, showered with honors.[89]

Eliade was born in Romania in 1907 and died in Chicago in 1986. His Romanian nationality was a decisive factor in his life and work; from an early age he felt he had one foot in the Occident, the other in the Orient, reflected in the title of the first volume of his autobiography *Journey East, Journey West* (1981). He developed an early interest in folklore, mythology and religion, and learnt English in order to read Max Müller and J.G. Frazer. At university he mastered Hebrew, Persian and Italian and embarked on a postgraduate study of the influence of Hermeticism and the Kabbalah on Italian Renaissance philosophy.

Whilst visiting Italy he read Dasgupta's famous work, *The History of Indian Philosophy*. So deeply affected was he by this work that he soon left for Calcutta to study Indian philosophy and spirituality under Dasgupta. In Calcutta he immersed himself in Sanskrit, classical Indian philosophy, and Tibetan, and developed an interest in the psycho-spiritual disciplines of yoga and tantra. He spent six months at the holy city of Rishikesh, at the foot of the Himalayas, under the guidance of Swami Shivananda. Later he developed a close friendship with Rabindranath Tagore, and it was also in India that Eliade first met the scholar whom, in some respects, he regarded as his Master: Giuseppe Tucci.[90] In his fascinating conversations with Claude-Henri Rocquet, many years later, Eliade includes amongst the highlights of his Indian experiences his initiation into yogic disciplines in Rishikesh, his visit to the Ajanta caves and his encounter with the pre-Aryan Santali aborigines of central India. These might be seen to correspond with the three "decisive lessons" of his Indian experiences: firstly, the discovery of the psycho-physical techniques of *Samkhya*-Yoga and Tantra (which had foreshadowed some of the "discoveries" of psychoanalysis) and the realization that there existed "an Indian philosophy, or rather a spiritual dimension, that was neither that of classical India—let us say, that of the *Upanishads* and the Vedanta, of the monist philosophy, in short—nor that of religious devotion or *bhakti*"; sec-

---

88 From the Contributor's Manual, quoted by G. Gnoli, "Mircea Eliade," 291.
89 For an Eliade Bibliography see M. Eliade, *Ordeal by Labyrinth*, 213-225.
90 See G. Gnoli, "Mircea Eliade."

ondly, "the discovery of the importance of religious symbolism in traditional cultures"; and thirdly, and perhaps more surprisingly, "the discovery of Neolithic man" and of "cosmic religious feeling" through his encounter with the Santali.[91]

After more than three years in the sub-continent he returned to Romania where he took up teaching and writing. Apart from a shadowy interlude during the war when he carried out diplomatic work in Lisbon, Eliade devoted the rest of his life to writing and teaching about religious phenomena. After the Soviet seizure of Romania he settled in Paris where Georges Dumézil introduced him to the Ecole Pratique des Hautes Etudes. Over the next decade he moved from one temporary post to another, living a rather precarious existence between lecturing stints at universities in Rome, Lund, Marburg, Munich, Frankfurt, Padua and Strasbourg. The Communist takeover of Romania left him in an exile that was to be permanent. His work was denounced in Romania itself as being "obscurantist," "mystic" and "fascist." Decoded these words might signify an interest in the past and in religion, and a hostility to Communist totalitarianism. In the 1970s he resisted inducements from the Romanian government to return, refusing to make any compromise with the communist dictatorship.[92] (Eliade was, in fact, somewhat fascistic in his political sympathies: this will be taken up in our discussion of orientalism and fascism in Chapter 14.)

In 1956 Eliade was invited to the University of Chicago as a visiting professor. He was to remain there for the rest of his life. When he took up a chair in the History of Religions at Chicago it was one of very few such chairs; within fifteen years there were at least twenty-five chairs in the major American universities, nearly all of them occupied by his former students.[93]

Eliade defined his "essential problems" as "sacred space and time, the structure and function of myth, and the morphology of divine figures."[94] In the late 40s and early 50s he produced several works which quickly established his international reputation: *Patterns in Comparative Religion* (1949), *The Myth of the Eternal Return* (1949), *Shamanism: Archaic Techniques of Ecstasy* (1951). Two of Eliade's most scholarly and specialized works are devoted to Indian subjects: *Yoga: Immortality and Freedom* (1954) and *Patanjali and Yoga* (1962), but much of his writing is densely textured with reference to Eastern traditions. Eliade, something of a *littérateur* as well as a student of religion and a painter, also wrote several novels, two with Indian settings: *Midnight in Serampore* and *Bengal Night*.

For Eliade, as for Jung, Zimmer and Campbell, the study of foreign religious forms could throw light on the cultural crisis of the modern West:

91 See M. Eliade, *Ordeal by Labyrinth*, 54-56.
92 M. Eliade, *Autobiography 2*, xiv-xv.
93 See M. Eliade, *Autobiography 2*, 208-9.
94 M. Eliade, *Autobiography 2*, 174.

The history of religious forms can play an extremely important role in the crisis we are living through. The crises of modern man are to a large extent religious ones, insofar as they are an awakening of his awareness to an absence of meaning. When one feels that one has lost the key to the meaning of existence ... that is undoubtedly a religious problem, since religion is precisely a reply to fundamental questions ... that is why I think that this "total discipline" can have a sovereign function.[95]

His work has been both applauded and criticized from many different angles.[96] Rather than offering yet another conspectus of Eliade's work I will instead turn to some comparative reflections about the work of Eliade and Jung, perhaps the two most influential mythographers of the 20th century.

Reflections on Jung and Eliade
Like Zimmer and Campbell, Eliade was deeply influenced by the work of Carl Jung. Eliade was first invited to the annual Eranos Conferences in 1950 and attended annually until 1962, the year of Olga Fröbe's death, delivering lectures at most conferences. In his journal Eliade recounts his first meeting with Jung at a dinner in an Ascona restaurant:

> ... he is a captivating old gentleman, utterly without conceit, who is as happy to talk as he is to listen. What could I write down here first of this long conversation? Perhaps his bitter reproaches of "official science"? In university circles he is not taken seriously. "Scholars have no curiosity," he says with Anatole France. "Professors are satisfied with recapitulating what they learned in their youth and what does not cause any trouble ..."[97]

In an interview late in his life he again recalled his first meeting with Jung, speaking this time in terms reminiscent of Zimmer's first impressions:

> After half an hour's conversation I felt I was listening to a Chinese sage or an east European peasant, still rooted in the Earth Mother yet close to Heaven at the same time. I was enthralled by the wonderful simplicity of his presence ... [98]

In 1952 Eliade conducted a lengthy interview with Jung for the Parisian magazine *Combat*, at a time when Jung's recently published *Answer to Job* was provoking a fierce controversy.[99] (Recall Gershom Scholem's only half-jesting remark that Jung had tried to psychoanalyze Yahweh.)[100] In the same

95 M. Eliade, *Ordeal by Labyrinth*, 48-49.
96 See especially R. Ellwood, *The Politics of Myth* and E. Wasserstrom, *Religion after Religion*.
97 *Journal 1*, August 23, 1950, quoted in G. Wehr, *Jung, A Biography*, 273-274. In his autobiography Eliade again refers to Jung's "bitter comments" about "official science." See *Autobiography 2*, 147.
98 M. Eliade, *Ordeal by Labyrinth*, 162-3.
99 An edited version of this interview can be found in *C. G. Jung Speaking, Interviews and Encounters*, 225-234. Unfortunately Eliade's introductory comments and his interpolations have been severely abridged in this edition.
100 M. Eliade, *Autobiography 2*, 162.

year, Jung read Eliade's massive work on shamanism and the two had a long and intense conversation about it. They met several times over the next few years, the last occasion being at Kusnacht in 1959 where they had a lengthy conversation in the garden, primarily about the nature of mystical experience. Eliade's rather fragmentary remarks about this last encounter are not without interest. He tells us that Jung no longer had any interest in therapies and case studies, nor in contemporary theology, but that he retained his appetite for patristic theology. He also notes again Jung's disenchantment with the scientific establishment:

> ... now and then it seemed to me that I detected a trace of bitterness. Speaking about the structures of mystical experiences, he declared the medical doctors and psychologists are "too stupid or too uncultivated" to understand such phenomena.[101]

Eliade's connections with the Jungian establishment were institutional as well as personal. In the early 50s he was awarded a special grant by the Bollingen Foundation which enabled him and his wife to escape "the nightmare of poverty."[102] Several of Eliade's major works appeared in the Bollingen Series. In 1953 Eliade gave five two-hour lectures at the Jung Institute in Zurich.

There are a great many subjects which commanded the attention of both Jung and Eliade: mythological symbolisms; esoteric spiritual disciplines such as alchemy; the mystical literature of the East; dreams and the structures of the unconscious; the pathologies of modern civilization, to name a few. One is constantly struck by parallels. For instance, Jung's work on alchemy and Eliade's on shamanism both provided a unified view of reality in which physical and psychic energy are two aspects, or dimensions, of a single reality (hence the possibility of paranormal powers and the like).[103] In their approach to these subjects both showed a sympathetic receptivity to the spiritual messages of the documents they were studying. There are also obvious parallels in their biographies: academic resistance to their discoveries; the hostility of particular disciplinary coteries (the Freudians in Jung's case, the anthropologists in Eliade's); the importance of Eranos as a forum where ideas could be ventilated and hypotheses tested amongst kindred spirits; the trips to India, Africa and America; the intrepid exploration of what Eliade calls "foreign spiritual universes." Consider this passage from Eliade's *Journal*, written in 1959:

> These thirty years, and more, that I've spent among exotic, barbaric, indomitable gods and goddesses, nourished on myths, obsessed by symbols, nursed and bewitched by so many images which have come down to me from those submerged worlds, today seem to me to be the stages of a long initiation. Each one of these divine figures, each of these myths or symbols,

101 M. Eliade, *Autobiography 2*, 205. See also *No Souvenirs* June 6, 1959, 41-2.
102 M. Eliade, *Autobiography 2*, 149.
103 See G. Wehr, *Jung: A Biography*, 254-5.

is connected to a danger that was confronted and overcome. How many times I was almost lost, gone astray in this labyrinth where I risked being killed ... These were not only bits of knowledge acquired slowly and leisurely in books, but so many encounters, confrontations, and temptations. I realize perfectly well now all the dangers I skirted during this long quest, and, in the first place, the risk of forgetting that I had a goal ... that I wanted to reach a "center."[104]

With a few words changed how easily this could have come from Jung! Like Jung, Eliade seems to have understood his own role in somewhat prophetic terms. From his *Journal*: "I feel as though I am a precursor; I am aware of being somewhere in the *avant-garde* of the humanity of tomorrow or after."[105]
In his autobiography Eliade says this:

... the re-entry of Asia into history and the discovery of the spirituality of archaic societies cannot be without consequence ... The camouflage or even occultation of the sacred and of spiritual meanings in general characterizes all crepuscular eras. It is a matter of the larval survival of the original meaning, which in this way becomes unrecognizable. Hence the importance I ascribe to images, symbols and narratives, or more precisely to the hermeneutical analysis which describes their meanings and identifies their original functions.[106]

There are many parallels here with Jung's work. For the moment, however, we can note an interesting divergence in their work. For all his sympathetic inquiries into primal mythologies and Eastern spirituality, and despite the importance of his excursions into other cultures, Jung remained resolutely European in his orientation: his intellectual anchorage, so to speak, was always in the West. This is nicely illustrated by his extraordinary reluctance to visit the sage of Arunachala, Ramana Maharshi, possibly as if he felt somewhat threatened by the spiritual force to which such a visit would expose him.[107] One cannot help but feel that Jung did not fully confront or assimilate this experience, that he turned his back on India in a self-defensive reflex, so to speak.[108] One senses no such inhibition in Eliade's immersion in Indian spirituality: his work ratifies his claim that his three years in India were "the essential ones in my life. India was my education."[109] However, it is interesting to note that both Jung and Eliade's enthusiasm for Eastern subjects

104 M. Eliade, *No Souvenirs* November 10, 1959, 74-5.
105 Eliade, quoted by R. P. Coomaraswamy, review of M. Eliade, *No Souvenirs*, 123.
106 M. Eliade, *Autobiography 2*, 153.
107 See C.G. Jung, *Memories, Dreams, Reflections*, 305. Ramana Maharshi is not mentioned by name but is clearly one of the "holy men" in question. See also Titus Burckhardt's comment on this episode in "Cosmology and Modern Science," 178. On Jung's experiences of India generally see an excellent account in J.J. Clarke, *Jung and Eastern Thought*, 61-63.
108 Jung has similarly been criticized for his limited understanding of Chinese spirituality. One is reminded of the somewhat unkind joke, "What is Chinese philosophy? Well, there is *yin* and *yang*, and then there is Jung."
109 M. Eliade, *Ordeal by Labyrinth*, 54. See Eliade's remarks about his Indian experience, 54-64.

waned in their later work, Jung turning more to aspects of Western esotericism and Eliade to primal non-literate cultures.[110]

Jung's insights into archaic mythologies and cosmologies were undoubtedly of decisive importance in Eliade's intellectual development, particularly Jung's stress on a "universal parallelism" of analogous symbolisms and motifs in mythologies from all over the world.[111] Eliade repeatedly acknowledges the debt. At points Jung concedes the metaphysical status of myths:

> No science will ever replace myth, and a myth cannot be made out of any science. For it is not that "God" is a myth, but that myth is the revelation of a divine life in man. It is not we who invent myth, rather it speaks to us as a Word of God.[112]

But one finds in Jung the more or less constant attempt to bring archaic cosmology and metaphysics back into the psychic domain while Eliade is prepared to go beyond it. This can be seen in the different senses in which Jung and Eliade use the term "archetypes": for Jung the archetypes are "structures of the collective unconscious" while Eliade uses the term in its neo-Platonic sense of exemplary and "transhistorical" paradigms.[113] Jung also tended to homologize dreams and myths. In this context, Eliade's differentiation of the two is suggestive:

> The resemblances between dreams and myths are obvious, but the difference between them is an essential one: there is the same gulf between the two as between an act of adultery and *Madame Bovary*; that is, between a simple experience and a creation of the human spirit.[114]

Likewise, Jung's interest in the qualitative determinations of time, most notably in his ideas about synchronicity and psychosynthesis,[115] remains within the psychic arena while for Eliade sacred time is itself an irreducible category and one altogether indispensable to an understanding of the archaic and mythological modes.[116] Jung evinced much less interest in the question of sacred space which has been pivotal in Eliade's work.

The bringing of other spiritual universes within the ambit of the West was an important but subsidiary task in Jung's lifework; it has been the motive force in Eliade's. The following passage from *Myths, Dreams and Mysteries* might well stand as an epigraph for Eliade's work over half a century:

---

110 Eliade somewhere remarked that there was something dangerous in his fascination with India which might distract him from his more universal vocation as a student of religious phenomena. See G. Gnoli, "Mircea Eliade," 283.

111 See A. Jaffé, *The Myth of Meaning*, 15.

112 C.G. Jung, *Memories, Dreams, Reflections*, 373.

113 M. Eliade, *Autobiography 2*, 162.

114 M. Eliade, *Ordeal by Labyrinth*, 162. (Clearly this formulation, a characteristic one, is open to the charge that it reduces myths to no more than cultural creations.)

115 See C.G. Jung, *Memories, Dreams, Reflections*, 160, and G. Wehr, *Jung: A Biography*, 111.

116 Eliade's most accessible treatment of this theme is to be found in *The Sacred and the Profane*.

> ... the "exotic" and "primitive" peoples have now come within the orbit of
> history, so that Western man is obliged to enquire into their systems of val-
> ues if he is to be able to establish and maintain communication with them
> ... We have to approach the symbols, myths and rites of the Oceanians or the
> Africans ... with the same respect and the same desire to learn that we have
> devoted to Western cultural creations, even when those rites and myths
> reveal "strange," terrible or aberrant aspects.[117]

Clearly, for Eliade this was not simply a grandiose academic project but one
driven by certain existential imperatives—a common motif in the life and
work of all the comparative mythographers. Consider this, for instance, from
Eliade's *Journal*:

> ... it is not some kind of infatuation with the past that makes me want to go
> back to the world of the Australian aborigines or the Eskimos. *I want to rec-
> ognize myself—in the philosophical sense—in my fellow men.*[118]

Our encounters with other spiritual worlds are urgently necessary for our
own spiritual health. We must no longer regard them "as immature episodes
or as aberrations from some exemplary history of man—a history conceived,
of course, only as that of Western man."[119]

For Freud psychoanalysis was a rigorously scientific discipline which must
remain uncontaminated by all those modes of understanding which he herd-
ed together under the pejorative label of "occultism." Freud's views on religion are well known and need not be rehearsed here; as Jung noted in
Memories Freud saw any expression of spirituality as a function of repressed
sexuality.[120] Suffice it to say that Freud surrendered to a severely reductionist view altogether characteristic of the late 19th century intellectual alienated from religious tradition.[121] Eliade himself wrote of Freud's major work on
religion, *Totem and Taboo*, in appropriately scathing terms:

> Of course the genius of Freud and the merits of psychoanalysis ought not to
> be judged by the horror-stories presented as objective historical fact in *Totem
> and Taboo*. But it is highly significant that such frantic hypotheses could be
> acclaimed as sound scientific theory in spite of all the criticisms marshaled
> by the major anthropologists of the century ... after 1920 the Freudian ide-
> ology was rather taken for granted in its entirety. A fascinating book could
> be written about this *roman noir frénétique*, *Totem and Taboo*. Using the very
> tools and methods of modern psychoanalysis, we can lay open some of the

---

117 M. Eliade, *Myths, Dreams and Mysteries*, 9, 10, 12.
118 M. Eliade, *Ordeal by Labyrinth*, 137 (italics mine).
119 M. Eliade, *Australian Religions*, xix.
120 C.G. Jung, *Memories, Dreams, Reflections*, 172.
121 For a brief but useful account of Freud's views on religion see D.W.D. Shaw, *The Dissuaders*.
In his journal Eliade dismisses Freud's extraordinary lucubrations on this subject thus: his "explanations of religious experiences and other spiritual activities are purely and simply inept"; *Journal 1*,
April 23, 1953, quoted in G. Steiner, "Ecstasies, not arguments," 1015. For an interesting account of
the effects of Freud's alienation from his Judaic heritage, see "The Revolt Against Moses, A New Look
at Psychoanalysis," in W. Perry, *Challenges to a Secular Society*, 17-38.

tragic secrets of the modern Western intellectual: for example, his profound dissatisfaction with the worn-out forms of historical Christianity, and his desire violently to rid himself of his forefathers' faith, accompanied by a strange sense of guilt, as if he himself had killed a God in whom he could not believe but whose absence he could not bear.[122]

For Jung the problem of religion was much more complex. He rejected the narrow dogmatism and stifling moralism which characterized his father's faith but affirmed the richness, potency and psychologically liberating elements within Christianity and in esoteric Western traditions such as gnosticism, hermeticism and alchemy.

> ... all religions [wrote Jung], down to the forms of magical religion of primitives, are psychotherapies, which treat and heal the sufferings of the soul, and those of the body that come from the soul.[123]

On the other side, Jung rejected the rampant materialism of a profane science whilst retaining his faith in an empirical mode of inquiry. The appeal of psychiatry, he tells us, was precisely that it was a meeting ground for the biological and the spiritual:

> Here was the empirical field common to biological and spiritual facts, which I had everywhere sought and nowhere found. Here at last was the place where the collision of nature and spirit became a reality.[124]

This, of course, anticipates the great Jungian theme of the *coincidentia oppositorum*.

In Eliade's work, the opposites present themselves not as the "biological" and the "spiritual" but rather in terms of a set of dichotomies which structure the whole of his agenda: the sacred and the profane; the archaic and the modern; the mythological and the historical; the poetic and the scientific. Eliade's work as a whole can be seen as a project to recuperate the former mode of each of these pairings. For Eliade the problem of scientific materialism exerted itself largely through the reductionist models of the anthropologists. Eliade's task was to revalorize manifestations of the sacred, to restore to them their experiential and ontological meanings and to resist the "audacious and irrelevant interpretations" of reductionists of every ilk—Marxist, Freudian, Durkheimian, or whatever.[125]

> Such a demystifying attitude [he wrote] ought to be arraigned in its turn, on charges of ethnocentrism, of Western "provincialism," and so, ultimately, be demystified itself.[126]

---

122 M. Eliade, "Cultural Fashions and the History of Religions," 25.
123 A 1935 paper on psychotherapy, quoted in G. Wehr, *Jung: A Biography*, 293.
124 C.G. Jung, *Memories, Dreams, Reflections*, 130.
125 M. Eliade, *The Quest*, 5.
126 M. Eliade, *Ordeal by Labyrinth*, 137.

Eliade also challenged his own colleagues:

> ... the majority of the historians of religion defend themselves against the messages with which their documents are filled. This caution is understandable. One does not live with impunity in intimacy with "foreign" religious forms ... But many historians of religion end by no longer taking seriously the spiritual worlds they study; they fall back on their personal religious faith, or they take refuge in a materialism or behaviorism impervious to every spiritual shock.[127]

One of Eliade's most important contributions to the discipline of religious studies was his insistence on explanatory categories which are *sui generis*, peculiar to religious phenomena, which are autonomous, so to speak. Here Eliade is much closer to the great German theologian, Rudolf Otto:

> ... a religious phenomenon will only be recognized as such if it is grasped at its own level, that is to say, if it is studied as something religious. To try to grasp the essence of such a phenomenon by means of physiology, psychology, sociology, economics, linguistics, art or any other study is false; it misses the one unique and irreducible element in it—the element of the sacred. Obviously there are no purely religious phenomena ... But it would be hopeless to try and explain religion in terms of any one of these basic functions ... It would be as futile as thinking you could explain *Madame Bovary* by a list of social, economic and political facts; however true, they do not effect it as a work of literature.[128]

One cannot help noticing in the autobiographical writings of both Jung and Eliade a certain reticence about their own religious beliefs and affiliations. Eliade remarked, in an interview late in his life, "I made the decision long ago to maintain a kind of discreet silence as to what I personally believe or don't believe."[129] One obvious possibility is that both felt that too open an affirmation of such beliefs might compromise their academic standing in a milieu which privileged the ideal of a scientific objectivity and detachment, to such an extent, indeed, that one can speak here of a kind of pseudo-cult. Professional pressures and expectations sometimes "diluted [Jung's] most potent observations in deference to a more conventional audience."[130] As Jung himself observed in a frequently cited passage, "Today the voice of one crying in the wilderness must necessarily strike a scientific tone if the ear of the multitude is to be reached."[131] Another possibility is that both struggled with the problems of religious faith without ever resolving the many difficult questions which were latent in Nietzsche's famous pronouncement of "the death of God." Emil Cioran referred to himself and his friend Eliade as "would-have-been believers: we are all religious spirits without religion."[132]

127 M. Eliade, *The Quest*, 62.
128 M. Eliade, *Patterns in Comparative Religion*, xiii.
129 M. Eliade, *Ordeal by Labyrinth*, 132.
130 P. Novak, "C.G. Jung in the Light of Asian Psychology," 66-7.
131 Jung quoted in W. Smith, *Cosmos and Transcendence*, 127.
132 Cioran quoted in E. Wasserstrom, *Religion after Religion*, 247.

On theological questions Mircea Eliade often retreats into a post-Nietzschean kind of *credo*. In 1965, for example, he wrote this;

> In a "world" composed of billions of galaxies ... all the classical arguments for or against the existence of God seem to me naïve and even childish. I do not think that, for the moment, we have the right to argue philosophically. The problem itself should be left in suspension as it is. We must content ourselves with personal certitudes, with wagers based on dreams, with divinations, ecstasies, aesthetic emotion. That also is a mode of knowing, but without arguments ...[133]

Eliade only reveals something of his personal religious beliefs in informal mode in his autobiographical writings, almost, one feels, when he is caught off guard. Like Jung he was often prepared to state things more directly face to face than he was in more professional contexts. In an interview with Claude-Henri Rocquet, Eliade put the matter quite unequivocally:

> If God doesn't exist, then everything is dust and ashes. If there is no absolute to give meaning and value to our existence, then that means that existence has no meaning. I know there are philosophers who do think precisely that; but for me, that would be not just pure despair but also a kind of betrayal. Because it isn't true, and I know that it isn't true.[134]

However, Eliade's apparent lack of any personal commitment to a religious tradition and his failure to understand the full implications of the many scriptures and sacred writings which he explicated have been trenchantly criticized by traditionalists. Alain Daniélou, while deeply respecting Eliade's scholarship, contrasts him with another great scholar, Henry Corbin who was also a Sufi: "this was not the case with Mircea Eliade, the famous prophet of religious history whose superb work always struck me as being based on exterior knowledge rather than actual experience."[135] David Lake thus: "One has the impression of an uprooted and genial academic busily drifting from article to article, without inward center or the intellectual discrimination to master his prodigious mental fertility."[136] Rama Coomaraswamy is even harsher: "The man is a dilettante, a mere scholar, and in outlook, a totally profane person. When I say he is a dilettante, I refer to the spiritual realm."[137] Both reviewers accuse Eliade of a kind of psychologism but take no account of Eliade's own exposure of psychological relativism. In *No Souvenirs*, for instance (the book under review by both Coomaraswamy and Lake) Eliade has this to say:

> Psychoanalysis justifies its importance by asserting that it forces you to look to and accept reality. But what sort of reality? A reality conditioned by the

133 *Journal* quoted in G. Steiner, "Ecstasies, not arguments," 1015.
134 M. Eliade, *Ordeal by Labyrinth*, 67.
135 A. Daniélou, *The Way to the Labyrinth*, 248.
136 D. Lake, review of *No Souvenirs*, 244.
137 R.P. Coomaraswamy, review of *No Souvenirs*, 123.

materialistic and scientific ideology of psychoanalysis, that is, a historical product ... [138]

In this context it is also worth recalling René Guénon's not unsympathetic remarks about Eliade's work. In a letter of September 1949, Guénon wrote of the Romanian:

> I have reviewed several of his works ... You will note that I treat him rather carefully and that I try above all to refer to that which is good ... he is basically very nearly in agreement with traditional ideas, but he does not dare to show it in his writing, since he fears colliding with officially admitted opinions; this produces a rather unfortunate mix ... we hope, however, that some encouragement will help to make him a little less timid.[139]

*

Considered from the traditionalist perspective Jung and his fellow mythographers can be accused of a kind of "humanism" with quasi-religious trappings; from this point of view they are implicated in the destruction of religion begun by the materialistic and humanistic sciences of the Renaissance and more or less completed by Darwinian evolutionism and Freudian psychoanalysis. As Ananda Coomaraswamy so neatly put it, "While 19th century materialism closed the mind of man to what is above him, 20th century psychology opened it to what is below him."[140] Certainly I cannot accept either Jung or Eliade as sages or prophets: they both exemplify some of the confusions of the age in their life and work. I am not much impressed by the "prophetic" tone which each sometimes strikes in writing of their own work. Our age has not been much blessed by either sages or prophets, and it is perhaps not surprising that both Jung and Eliade have sometimes been mistaken for such. The fact that they cannot live up to the claims of their more excitable acolytes is no reason to dismiss or ignore their work which has a richness and depth not often found amongst the self-styled savants of our times. Both Jung and Eliade were profoundly concerned with man's position in a world in which science had stripped the cosmos of meaning, apparently eroded the pillars of religious faith, and robbed man of his spiritual dignity. Whatever our views on some of the questions I have been canvassing, we should be grateful to both Jung and Eliade for rescuing their respective disciplines from the clutches of the materialists and their accomplices, and for their attempts to bridge the apparent chasm between traditional religion and modern science, and between East and West. They each have a great deal to say to us. Nevertheless, if we are to draw what is valuable from their work we need to maintain a sense of proportion and to apply a discernment which, in

---

138 M. Eliade, *No Souvenirs*, October 7th, 1965, 269.

139 Guénon quoted in E. Wasserstrom, *Religion after Religion*, 46.

140 A. K. Coomaraswamy, quoted in W. Perry, "Drug-Induced Mysticism," 196. (Coomaraswamy was paraphrasing René Guénon.)

my view, can only be drawn from the treasuries of metaphysical and spiritual teachings found within the integral religious traditions. As for Jung, I cannot improve on Philip Novak's carefully considered judgment:

> Of Jung's enduring value, however, there can be no doubt. For modern psychotherapy and the religious quest alike, he dug a seed-bed from which much life-giving and soul-invigorating insight has sprung ... But Jung yearned for absoluteness and for Truth—he so wanted to bring a saving message to man—and the clash of this yearning with his avowed vocation, that of empirical scientist and physician, created a lifelong battle of forces within his breast. These tensions spilled over to the printed page, not least when Jung had there to confront the Asian systems which adumbrated the spiritual completion of psychological man that he sought, but with doctrines and methods he could not accept.[141]

The more crucial general point towards which Novak's assessment points is one which many people are determined to ignore. It has been precisely stated by Frithjof Schuon:

> Outside tradition there can assuredly be found some relative truths or views of partial realities, but outside tradition there does not exist a doctrine that catalyzes absolute truth and transmits liberating notions concerning total reality.[142]

141 P. Novak, "C.G. Jung in the Light of Asian Psychology," 84. We will return to the traditionalist critique of Jung and of psychologism in Chapter 12.
142 F. Schuon, "No Activity Without Truth," 36.

6.

The Western Quest for "Secret Tibet"

A. Pathfinders and Mythologizers: Desideri, de Koros, Waddell, Taylor **B. In Search of "Secret Tibet":** Madame Blavatsky—Alexandra David-Neel—W.Y. Evans-Wentz—Heinrich Harrer—Marco Pallis—Anagarika Govinda **C. Tibet and the West in the Contemporary Era:** Later Travelers and Seekers in Tibet—Counterfeit Tibetan Esotericism: the Lobsang Rampa Case—Tibet, Western Esotericism and New Age Orientalism

---

Only those who have been in Tibet know the fascination of its huge landscapes, its diaphanous air that scarfs the icy peaks with turquoise, its vast silence that at once humbles man and uplifts him. Flights of mountain ranges flow on endlessly like the elaborations of a single musical theme in some oriental melody ... Bountiful hospitality, constant *good humor, attentiveness to the stranger, sincerity of religious beliefs yet sensible tolerance ... life in Tibet was lived on another plane, a kind of miraculous mediaeval survival behind the sheltering, isolating mountain-belt.* (Giuseppe Tucci)[1]

As recently as 1962 an eminent Western Buddhist wrote, "Nowhere save in Tibet is there so much sorcery and 'black' magic, such degradation of the mind to selfish, evil ends."[2] Another European practitioner, writing a few years later, asserted that the Vajrayana "is the ultimate flowering of the Mahayana doctrine."[3] Yet another argued that, "The importance of Tibetan tradition for our time and for the spiritual development of humanity lies in the fact that Tibet is the last living link that connects us with the civilizations of a distant past."[4] These were familiar motifs in the Western literature on Tibet which has often evoked deeply ambivalent European reactions—fear and contempt on one side, romantic idealizations on the other. At one moment Tibet is seen as a "feudal" and "Oriental" despotism pervaded by a degenerate "Lamaism" in which base superstition, "devil-dances and butter statues," "mummery" and "black magic" (exerting its own sinister fascination) are the order of the day; at the next Tibet appears as the last surviving treasure-house of a primordial wisdom, as the crown-jewel of the Mahayana, as an idyllic land hermetically sealed against all the contaminations and pathologies of modernity. In the period since the earliest European incursions in the 17th century Tibet has become a "focus of European desire and

---

1   G. Tucci, *Tibet, Land of Snows,* 13-14.
2   C. Humphreys, *Buddhism,* 189.
3   J. Blofeld, *The Tantric Mysticism of Tibet,* 35.
4   A. Govinda, *Foundations of Tibetan Mysticism,* 13.

fantasy."[5] As Donald Lopez has observed, the whole corpus of Western writing on Tibet is shot through with a series of oppositions by which the religious-cultural heritage is variously perceived as pristine and polluted, authentic and derivative, holy and demonic.[6] In recent times the positive aspects have been foregrounded. "Shangri-La," "Shambhala," "the Forbidden City," "Potala"—these words have long since acquired a talismanic charge in the Western imagination.

"Tibet," the realm created by Western imaginings, has also become a kind of sacred space within the desecrated wastes of the modern West. As Peter Bishop has observed,

> Sacred space has been defined in terms of its separation from the profane world, by the limited access accorded to it, by a sense of dread or fascination, as well as by a sense of order and power combined with ambiguity and paradox.[7]

Tibet has been amenable to all of these characterizations. Bishop has also noted how "Tibet" has been constructed in three European imaginative contexts: those of European imperialism, of adventure and exploration, and of comparative religion and mysticism. Moreover, "Tibet also lay at the intersection of three discourses, namely those concerning the relationship of the West (1) to nature ...; (2) to non-European cultures; and (3) to ideas of personal experience."[8] Western writings often reveal "contradictions, tensions and paradoxes" in the European understanding of this alluring land.

Both in its historical actuality and as an imaginary European construct, Tibet has played a significant but somewhat neglected role in the development of Western esotericism. In this context it might be remarked that the attraction of Tibet for occultists and esotericists of various kinds, like the appeal of the Orient generally, can be read in *both* negative and positive terms: as an "escape," a romantic flight, as a kind of hallucination, *and* as a means of confronting and challenging the tyranny of scientific rationalism in the West. These impulses are distinct but often inseparable and can be clearly discerned in figures as diverse as Madame Blavatsky, Carl Jung and Hermann Keyserling, to mention three who have played a significant role in the recent history of Western esotericism. This chapter offers a brief sketch of European presences since the arrival of the first missionaries, an account of the Tibetan engagements of several key figures in the 20th century, and reflections on the significance of Tibet in the recent psychological and spiritual history of the West.

5   D. Lopez, "Foreigners at the Lama's Feet," 252.
6   D. Lopez, "New Age Orientalism: The Case of Tibet," 38.
7   P. Bishop, *Tibet in Its Place*, 3.
8   P, Bishop, *Tibet in Its Place*, 5.

A. Pathfinders and Mythologizers

Desideri, de Koros, Waddell, Taylor

Donald Lopez has analyzed three "moments of urgency" in the Occidental encounter with Tibet, dramatized in the experiences of an Italian missionary, a Hungarian philologist and a British colonial functionary.[9] These moments can serve as convenient points of departure for our present inquiry. The first European missionary to enter Tibet was probably Father Antonio d'Andrade, a Portuguese Jesuit who established a small mission at Tsaparang in Western Tibet in 1624. Throughout the 17th century there was an intermittent missionary presence in Western Tibet and in the Himalayan borderlands. In 1707 two Capuchin missionaries, Fathers François de Tours and Giuseppe d'Ascoli, were the first to reach Lhasa but the earliest sustained visit was by the Jesuit Ippolito Desideri who walked from Delhi to Ladakh and across western Tibet to Lhasa. He remained in Tibet for five years (1716-1721) before a Vatican directive forced him to leave in favor of a rival Capuchin mission.[10]

Desideri was a man of considerable intellectual means; his was the first systematic attempt by a European to explain the doctrines and practices of the Tibetan Buddhists.[11] One of Desideri's successors in the long line of Italian Tibetologists, Luciano Petech, describes Desideri's writings on Tibetan religion as "A stupendous description of lamaist religion, penetratingly and profoundly understood in its essential nature as few European scholars have been able to do in the following two centuries."[12] Desideri's time in Tibet included a lengthy stay at the great monastery of Sera where his researches included a study of the *Kangyur* and *Tengyur* and a translation of Tsong-kha-pa's *Lam rim chen mo*. Desideri's study was motivated by missionary zeal. His initial encounters with Buddhism persuaded him that in order to convert the Tibetans he must first understand the cardinal doctrine of emptiness (*sunyata*). As Lopez notes, Desideri's "pressing agenda" could not be implemented without the aid of his "perceived opponents."[13] The ambivalence of the European before the lama was to become a familiar thread in the Western fascination with Tibet.

Two years after Desideri's reluctant departure from Tibet, Csoma de Koros, a member of the Magyar nobility in search of the provenance of the Hungarian language, somewhat unexpectedly found himself in Ladakh.[14]

---

9 D. Lopez, "Foreigners at the Lama's Feet," 251-295.

10 See D. Snellgrove & H. Richardson, *A Cultural History of Tibet*, 202, 220-224.

11 See R. Sherburne, "A Christian-Buddhist Dialog? Some Notes on Desideri's Tibetan Manuscripts," 295-305.

12 Petech quoted in J.W. De Jong, *A Brief History of Buddhist Studies in Europe and America*, 13.

13 D. Lopez, "Foreigners at the Lama's Feet," 254.

14 Material on de Koros is taken mainly from D. Lopez, "Foreigners at the Lama's Feet," 256-259.

His agenda was philological and nationalistic, rather than evangelical, and anticipates the 19th century obsession with origins (of nations, cultures, languages, religions). After travels in Afghanistan, the Punjab and Kashmir, all preparatory to an expedition to Bokhara where he hoped to discover "the obscure origins" of his homeland amongst the Hungars of Mongolia, de Koros encountered Dr William Moorcroft, East India Co. representative, veterinarian, explorer and spy. Moorcroft persuaded de Koros that a knowledge of Tibetan was crucial to his linguistic researches. De Koros was to spend the next seven years in Ladakh and southwestern Tibet, studying under several lamas and producing a Tibetan-English dictionary, a grammar, and a translation of a compendium of Buddhist terminology. After leaving Tibet de Koros published these works and a series of articles in the *Journal of the Asiatic Society of Bengal*, earning him the posthumous title of "the Father of Tibetology." He was one of the first to turn the attention of European Buddhologists away from the Pali texts to those of the Vajrayana, asserting that, "The principal seat of Buddhism is in Tibet."[15] His ultimate destination of the Tarim Basin was never attained: de Koros died of malaria in Darjeeling in 1842.

L. Austine Waddell filled a minor colonial post in Sikkim between 1885 and 1895 during which time he made a close study of "Lamaism"—the religious beliefs and practices of a distinctively Tibetan variant of Buddhism mixed with the potent remnants of the shamanistic Bönpo indigenous to the Tibeto-Himalayan regions. The monks of Sikkim apparently believed that Waddell was an incarnation of the Buddha Amitabha whose coming was prophesied in their Scriptures. "This recurrent trope of the colonial conqueror, reminiscent of Cortés and Captain Cook, allowed Waddell a double claim to superiority: on the one hand, he was an emanation of the Buddha of Infinite light; on the other, he understood, better than the credulous monks and lamas, that he was not."[16] This, says Lopez, allowed Waddell "a posture of control over and contempt for his informants" which characterized many Victorian Orientalists.

Waddell unsuccessfully adopted the time-honored stratagem of trying to enter forbidden Tibetan territory in the disguise of a pilgrim but finally reached Lhasa as a medical officer on the Younghusband expeditionary force of 1904, sent to secure a trading agreement between Britain and Tibet. Waddell's account of the expedition in *Lhasa and Its Mysteries* (1905) captures something of the romantic mystique which had accumulated around Tibet and exposes an ideologically-governed mythology of imperial conquest.

> Wreathed in the romance of centuries, Lhasa, the secret citadel of the "undying" Grand Lama, has stood shrouded in impenetrable mystery on the Roof-of-the-World, alluring yet defying our most adventurous travelers to enter her closed gates. With all the fascination of an unsolved enigma, this

15 R. Fields, *How the Swans Came to the Lake*, 285.
16 D. Lopez, "Foreigners at the Lama's Feet," 259.

mysterious city has held the imagination captive, as one of the last secret places of the earth, as the Mecca of East Asia, the sacerdotal city where the "Living Buddha," enthroned as a god, reigns eternally over his empire of tonsured monks, weaving ropes of sand like the schoolmen of old, or placidly twirling their prayer-wheels, droning their mystic spells and exorcising devils in the intervals of their dreamy meditations. But now ... the fairy Prince of "Civilization" has roused her from her slumbers, her closed doors are broken down, her dark veil of mystery is lifted up, and the long-sealed shrine, with its grotesque cults and its idolized Grand Lama, shorn of his sham nimbus, have yielded up their secrets and lie disenchanted before our Western eyes.[17]

The Viceroy of India, also referring to the Younghusband expedition, apologized to the thwarted Swedish explorer Sven Hedin: "I am almost ashamed of having destroyed the virginity of the bride to whom you aspired, viz. Lhasa."[18] The sexual imagery of penetration and conquest, and its association with a civilizing mission, attest to some of the highly charged, subterranean currents in the Orientalist discourse of the era.

Although Waddell's major work, *The Buddhism of Tibet or Lamaism* (1895), contained a good deal of information hitherto unknown, his understanding was severely limited by his Protestant prejudices and by his animus to what he took to be alien elements in Tibetan Buddhism, evident in his dismissal of much of Tibetan Buddhism as "contemptible mummery and posturing"[19] (a view which persisted amongst some Tibetologists for many years). Waddell reinforced the Orientalist myth of the Tibetan tradition as deviant and degenerate:

> ... the Lamaist cults comprise much deep-rooted devil-worship ... For Lamaism is only thinly and imperfectly varnished over with Buddhist symbolism, beneath which the sinister growth of poly-demonist superstition darkly appears.[20]

Interestingly, Francis Younghusband himself seems to have experienced a revelatory awakening as he departed Lhasa after his bloody and ultimately futile campaign in which hundreds of Tibetans were needlessly slain.[21] Surveying the mountainous vista Younghusband felt an exhilaration which "thrilled through me with overpowering intensity. Never again could I think evil, or ever be at enmity with any man. All nature and all humanity were bathed in a rosy glowing radiancy."[22] "That single hour on leaving Lhasa," he

---

17 D. Lopez, "Foreigners at the Lama's Feet," 263. See also Lopez's comments on this passage, 292, fn27.

18 P. Bishop, *Tibet in Its Place*, 10.

19 R. Fields, *How the Swans Came to the Lake*, 285.

20 D. Lopez, "New Age Orientalism," 38.

21 For an account of this campaign see P. French, *Younghusband: The Last Great Imperial Adventurer*, Chs 14-16. See also Younghusband's own *India and Tibet* (1910).

22 Younghusband, quoted in Pico Iyer, "Lost Horizons," *The New York Review of Books*, January 15th, 1998 (internet website).

wrote, "was worth all the rest of a lifetime."[23] The experience, in the words of his biographer, was an "epiphanic marker from which the second half of his life could be charted."[24] On his return to London he founded the World Congress of Faiths, dedicated to the promotion of inter-faith understanding.

Annie Taylor presents us with another type altogether.[25] An English missionary with the China Inland Mission, she had arrived in the Orient in 1884. She soon determined to spread the Good News to the Tibetan heathens. For eight years she tried to enter Tibet through India to the south and China to the east, only to be repeatedly frustrated although she did visit the great Tibetan monastery at Kumbum in 1887. But she was nothing if not determined and in September 1892 she finally left the Chinese city of Tauchau, her sights firmly set on Lhasa which had not been visited by Europeans since 1846 when the French Jesuits Abbés Huc and Gabet had been evicted and the doors of Tibet closed to missionaries. Taylor was accompanied by a Chinese guide and four Tibetans on a spectacularly ill-prepared expedition but, through indefatigable will-power and a measure of luck, the diminishing party survived illness, robbery, accident and the many hazards of a brutally inhospitable environment to get within three day's walk of Lhasa, only to be captured and turned back by Tibetan officials. By the time she arrived back in China Annie Taylor had walked some 1300 miles in seven months. Although she made no significant observations—scientific, anthropological or religious—her heroic but largely forgotten trek deserves at least a footnote in the chronicles of late Victorian travelers in the trans-Himalaya. Alexandra David-Neel's exploits have somewhat overshadowed other women explorers in the Tibetan region in the Victorian and Edwardian periods. These included Nina Mazuchelli, Isabelle Bird Bishop, Fanny Bullock Workman and Jane Duncan.[26]

B. In Search of "Secret Tibet"

Madame Blavatsky

The role of the redoubtable Madame Helena Petrovna Blavatsky in popularizing "Eastern" doctrines remains hotly contested. However, it is now clear that, despite the legend which she and her hagiographers propagated, Blavatsky never stepped on Tibetan soil.[27] Her claims that her later writings derived from Himalayan Mahatmas, forming a kind of Atlantean brother-

---

23 Quoted in P. Bishop, *Tibet in Its Place*, 4.

24 P. French, *Younghusband: The Last Great Imperial Adventurer*, 251. See also Jeremy Bernstein, "The Road to Lhasa."

25 Material on Annie Taylor taken from L. Miller, *On Top of the World: Five Women Explorers in Tibet*, 47-69. See also P. French, *Younghusband: The Last Great Imperial Adventurer*, 205-206, for her later Tibetan encounter with Younghusband.

26 The first three are portrayed in L. Miller, *On Top of the World: Five Women Explorers in Tibet.*

hood residing in secrecy in a remote region of Tibet and with access to long-hidden, antediluvian sources of esoteric wisdom, need not be treated seriously. Nonetheless, she contributed to the association of Tibet with a mystique of occultism and arcane doctrines originating in a primordial wisdom associated with hermeticism, gnosticism, the Kabbalah, and alchemy. Whilst *Isis Unveiled* (1877) was based on heterogeneous Occidental sources, her second major work, *The Secret Doctrine* (1888), includes elements that clearly derive from the Vajrayana, often conflated with Vedantic ideas. Wouter Hanegraaff observes that any "attempt to reduce Blavatsky's later synthesis of western occultism and 'Oriental wisdom' to specific sources is likely to suffer shipwreck on the capacity of her 'omnivorous mind' to assimilate whatever she found useful."[28] Nonetheless, Lama Kazi Dawa-Samdup was sufficiently confident of Blavatsky's account of the *Bardo* to endorse her claim that she had been initiated into "the higher lamaistic teachings"[29] whilst no less an authority than D.T. Suzuki was prepared to say that her explication of Buddhist teachings in *The Voice of Silence* (1869) testified to an initiation into "the deeper side of Mahayana doctrine."[30] On the other hand her many blistering critics have included Max Müller, René Guénon and Carl Jung, while Agehananda Bharati dismissed *The Secret Doctrine* as "a melee of horrendous hogwash and of fertile inventions of inane esoterica."[31] In *Ulysses* Joyce refers to *Isis Unveiled* as "Yogibogeybox" while Eliot satirized Blavatsky as Madame Sosostris in "The Waste Land." Mircea Eliade has pointed out that

> Mme Blavatsky presented a theory of indefinite spiritual evolution through metempsychosis and progressive initiation ... But I must interrupt at this point to observe that if there is anything characteristic of all Eastern traditions, it is precisely an anti-evolutionistic conception of the spiritual life.[32]

Whatever might be said about the pedigree of Blavatsky's ideas—and a great deal *has* been said: a recent count of books directly about Blavatsky and her teachings numbered no less than six hundred![33]—there is no question that Blavatsky played a significant role in wedding Western esotericism and

27 Even today it is still often asserted that Blavatsky spent time in Tibet, despite the absence of a particle of evidence to support such a claim. See, for example, E. Campbell & J.H. Brennan, *Dictionary of Mind, Body and Spirit*, 55, or E.B. Sellon & R. Weber, "Theosophy and the Theosophical Society," 312.

28 W.J. Hanegraaff, *New Age Religion and Western Culture*, 454. (The same problem arises with a good many "occultists" and "esotericists" in the modern world: precisely the same observation might have been made, for instance, about Gurdjieff.)

29 W.Y. Evans-Wentz (ed), *The Tibetan Book of the Dead*, 7fn.

30 A. Rawlinson, *The Book of Enlightened Masters*, 195, fn3.

31 A. Bharati, "Fictitious Tibet: The Origins and Persistence of Rampaism."

32 M. Eliade, *The Quest*, 43.

33 For a review of the recent and ever-proliferating literature on Blavatsky see S. Prothero, "Theosophy's Sinner/Saint: Recent Books on Madame Blavatsky," 256-262. See also F. Clews, "The Consolation of Theosophy." For a brief, dispassionate and well-informed discussion of Blavatsky's influence on Western occultism and esotericism see W.J. Hanegraaff, *New Age Religion and Western Culture*, 448-455.

Eastern religious traditions and in popularizing concepts such as *maya*, *karma*, and meditation.[34] Indeed, it has recently been argued that perhaps the signal achievement of the Theosophical movement, of which Blavatsky remains the presiding deity, has been its role in generating interest in and respect for Eastern religious conceptions.[35] However, it should also be noted that Blavatsky's purported shift from a "Hermetic" to an "Oriental" perspective has been greatly exaggerated. Hanegraaff, drawing on the work of Helmuth von Glasenapp and Jörg Wichmann, persuasively argues that this shift is "more apparent than real" and that Theosophy as a whole, despite its popularization of some Indian doctrines, "is not only rooted in Western esotericism, but has remained an essentially Western movement."[36]

Alexandra David-Neel

After a flamboyant career in France as student anarchist, opera singer, journalist, feminist, and adventurer, Alexandra David-Neel (b.1868) was introduced to Buddhism through her studies at the Sorbonne in the first decade of the century. Her teachers included the eminent orientalists, Sylvain Levi and Edouard Foucaux, the latter providing her introduction to Tibetan Buddhist texts. She had made her first trip to the East in 1891, to Ceylon and India, where she received some training in the Vedanta. She also visited Hanoi as part of a touring opera company. After producing a well received book on Buddhism (*The Buddhism of the Buddha and Buddhist Modernism*), in 1911 David-Neel set out again for India, with serious intent:

> There are great men at the Sorbonne, who know all the roots of the words and the historical dates, but I wish to live philosophy on the spot and undergo physical and spiritual training, not just read about them.[37]

She was one of the earliest in a long line of seekers for whom bookish learning was only a prelude to a more direct engagement with Eastern spirituality. This sojourn in Asia was to last fourteen years. We cannot here retrace David-Neel's many peregrinations through ashrams, temples, monasteries, shrines and centers of learning in the subcontinent, in the Tibeto-Himalayan regions, Southeast Asia and China—but she had adventures aplenty. She interviewed the thirteenth Dalai Lama, was befriended by the Crown Prince of Sikkim, studied Tibetan doctrines with Lama Kazi Dawa-Samdup, adopted a novice Kargyu monk in Sikkim (Yongden, who was to remain her constant companion until his death in 1955), spent a harsh Tibetan winter in a cave under the tutelage of a reclusive *gomchen*, became highly fluent in Tibetan, spent three years in the monastic citadel of Kumbum and undertook enthu-

---

34 J.J. Clarke, *Oriental Enlightenment*, 89. See also M. Bevir, "The West Turns Eastward: Madame Blavatsky and the Transformation of the Occult Tradition," 747-765.

35 E.B. Sellon & R. Weber, "Theosophy and the Theosophical Society," 325-326.

36 W.J. Hanegraaff, *New Age Religion and Western Culture*, 455.

37 David-Neel quoted in L. Miller, *On Top of the World*, 145.

siastic studies of Vajrayana texts and practices. During her travels she also encountered figures such as Nyanatiloka Thera, Anagarika Govinda, and D.T. Suzuki.

In her fifty-fifth year, disguised as a Tibetan beggar-woman and accompanied by Yongden, she embarked on her most famous expedition, the journey to Lhasa, 2000 miles on foot, achieving a goal that had defied many intrepid travelers throughout the 19th century. In fact, the French priests Huc and Gabet and the eccentric Englishman Thomas Manning were the only European visitors to Lhasa during the whole of the 19th century. Amongst those who had failed to reach the Tibetan capital were the Russian explorer Prejevalsky in 1879 and the Swede Sven Hedin in 1898, as well as several American and English travelers.[38] David-Neel's account of this journey and of her two months in Lhasa (described in distinctly anti-romantic terms) has recently been challenged as a fabrication but the case against her is flimsy in the extreme.[39] No doubt David-Neel herself played a significant part in creating her own legend—her biographers have had the devil's own job in separating fact and fiction in her multifarious writings[40]—but she was certainly neither a fraud nor a credulous sentimentalist.

After her return to Europe David-Neel was showered with honors, and became a popular lecturer and prolific writer on Eastern subjects. In 1936 she returned to the Orient, via Siberia, for what was to be another long stay, extended by the vicissitudes of war, after which she returned to her home in Digne, France. Befitting such an indomitable explorer, David-Neel lived on until 1969, her one hundred and first year.

David-Neel's most significant works on Tibetan subjects are *My Journey to Lhasa* (1927), *Magic and Mystery in Tibet* (1931), *Initiates and Initiations in Tibet* (1931) and *The Secret Oral Teachings in Tibetan Buddhist Sects* (1967), the last of which was first published in English by the Beat poet and bookseller Lawrence Ferlinghetti. As one scholar has recently observed, "The representation of Tibetan Buddhism historically has been and continues to be situated in a domain where the scholarly and the popular commingle, a domain that is neither exclusively one or the other."[41] Alexandra David-Neel's writings illustrate the point, occupying a position somewhere between those of the popular Theosophists/occultists on one flank and the more sober (though often misinformed) works of orientalist scholars on the other. David-Neel herself is often relegated to the ranks of "women adventurers"—

38 See P. Bishop, *Tibet in Its Place*, 1. Sven Hedin spent several hazardous years in southern Tibet where he conducted valuable scientific and surveying work.

39 See B. & M. Foster, *The Secret Lives of Alexandra David-Neel*, 225-234. (Fraudulent travel accounts comprise a distinct sub-genre of the Victorian literature: its Tibetan branch is perhaps best represented by Henry Savage Landor's *In the Forbidden Land*.)

40 The two most recent biographies are those by the Fosters (already cited) and Ruth Middleton's *Alexandra David-Neel: Portrait of an Adventurer*. (Although the Fosters have a taste for the lurid and the sensational their biography is rather more robust than Middleton's.)

41 D. Lopez, *Prisoners of Shangri-La*, 110.

this despite the production of some forty-odd books, several of which have wielded an extraordinary influence. Her absence from the annals of orientalist scholarship is to be explained, perhaps, by the fact that her writings are an idiosyncratic admixture of autobiography, travelogue, scholarship and, at least according to her detractors, fantasy.[42] Her books have been disparaged by both practitioners and scholars. John Blofeld, for instance, wrote that, "David-Neel was so deeply concerned with her public image that her most widely read books are limited to Tibetan Buddhism's popular aspects. Little is said about its spiritually or philosophically profound aspects."[43] The occultists and esotericists, for their part, are often out of sympathy with the rational and skeptical aspects of David-Neel's sensibility.[44]

Whatever one might make of the contradictory claims made about David-Neel, the tangible achievements remain, and many have found intellectual and spiritual nourishment in her work and inspiration in her example—Alan Watts, Lama Govinda, Peter Matthiessen among them. Not without reason did Lawrence Durrell call her "the most astonishing woman of our time."[45] Unlike most of her predecessors she believed that the only way to understand the spiritual economy of the Tibetans was to live amongst the common people as one of them.[46] Her close familiarity with ordinary folk in the Tibeto-Himalayan regions, her mastery of Tibetan, her lengthy studies under authentic teachers, her austerities and sustained meditational practice, and her residence in several great monasteries all qualified her to speak and write about the mysteries of the religious heritage. Her now well-known accounts of such alien practices as divination or *lung-gom-pa* gather more weight when we remember that David-Neel thought of herself as an orthodox Buddhist who abhorred superstition of any kind. Nonetheless, she was able to approach strange religious practices with an open mind and a sympathetic receptivity. One of her contemporaries, Professor A. d'Arsonval, wrote of the Frenchwoman:

> This Easterner, this complete Tibetan, has remained a Westerner, a disciple of Descartes and of Claude Bernard, practicing the philosophical skepticism of the former which, according to the latter, should be the constant ally of the scientific observer. Madame David-Neel has observed everything in Tibet in a free and impartial spirit.[47]

The claim may be naïve but certainly David-Neel cannot be dismissed as either gullible or simple-minded. Her accounts of Tibetan doctrines and practices, and of the culture at large, need to be treated with some caution;

---

42 For instance, there is no mention of her in recent works by J.J. Clarke and Donald Lopez although she is clearly more significant than many of the figures they do discuss.

43 Blofeld cited in B. & M. Foster, *Secret Lives*, 299 (source uncited).

44 For bibliographical information on books by and about David-Neel see B. & M. Foster, *Secret Lives*, 310-319.

45 B. & M. Foster, *Secret Lives*, xxi.

46 See L. Miller, *On Top of the World*, 171-172.

47 Quoted in L. Miller, *On Top of the World*, 186.

nevertheless, they retain much that is lively and illuminating, and we would be the poorer without them.

W.Y. Evans-Wentz

"In this book I am seeking—so far as possible—to suppress my own views and to act simply as the mouthpiece of a Tibetan sage, of whom I was the recognized disciple." So wrote W.Y. Evans-Wentz in his Preface to *The Tibetan Book of the Dead*, published for the first time in English in 1927, and later to become a canonical text amongst Westerners turning to Tibetan teachings.[48] The credentials of the "Tibetan sage" (Lama Kazi Dawa-Samdup), the nature of the "discipleship," and Evans-Wentz's scholarly qualifications (which did not include fluency in Tibetan) have all come under scrutiny in recent years.[49] Nonetheless, the publication of this text remains a portentous moment in the Western encounter with Tibet. Evans-Wentz was subsequently instrumental in the translation and publication of three other texts seminal in the rapidly growing field of Tibetology: *Tibet's Great Yogi, Milarepa* (1928), *Tibetan Yoga and Secret Doctrines* (1935) and *The Tibetan Book of the Great Liberation* (1967).[50]

Walter Yeeling Evans-Wentz was born in 1878 into a wealthy American business family of one-time Baptists who had turned to spiritualism and Theosophy.[51] From an early age Evans-Wentz was disenchanted with conventional Christianity and interested in psychic phenomena, coming under the spell of Madame Blavatsky's writings. He retained an interest in Theosophy throughout his life and wrote in his unpublished autobiography, "As I have held myself formally with no one country or race, so I have not allied myself formally with any of the world's religions. I have embraced them all."[52]

Evans-Wentz studied religion, philosophy and history at Stanford where he was little impressed by his teachers but much affected by two visitors to the university, William James and W.B. Yeats. His subsequent studies at Oxford produced his first major work, *The Fairy Faith in Celtic Countries* (1911), in wide circulation to this day. At Oxford Evans-Wentz met T.E. Lawrence with whom, he later somewhat implausibly claimed, he fought atop camels in the Middle East. Lawrence encouraged him to visit the Orient.

48 W.Y. Evans-Wentz, *The Tibetan Book of the Dead*, ix.

49 For some merciless criticism of the Evans-Wentz/Dawa-Samdup translations see J. Reynolds, trans & ed., *Self-Liberation through Seeing with Naked Awareness*. This is a new translation of what Evans-Wentz published as *The Tibetan Book of the Great Liberation*. See also D. Lopez, *Prisoners of Shangri-La*, Ch 2.

50 In each case the translation work was done primarily by Dawa-Samdup, Evans-Wentz being a compiler, editor and commentator.

51 Most of the biographical material which follows is taken from K. Winkler, *Pilgrim of the Clear Light: The Biography of Dr. Walter Y. Evans-Wentz*. A short sketch can also be found in R. Fields, *How the Swans Came to the Lake*, 285-287.

52 W.Y. Evans-Wentz, "Some Notes for an Autobiography," quoted in K. Winkler, *Pilgrim of the Clear Light*, 8-9.

After a year in Egypt, Evans-Wentz boarded a ship in Port Said for Colombo, and so launched a journey which was to last three decades and which he later described as "wandering from the palm-wreathed shores of Ceylon, and thence through the wonder-land of the Hindus, to the glacier-clad heights of the Himalayan Ranges, seeking out the Wise Men of the East. Sometimes I lived with city-dwellers, sometimes in jungle and mountain solitude among yogis, sometimes in monasteries with monks; sometimes I went on pilgrimages as one of the salvation-seeking multitude."[53]

Evans-Wentz initially devoted himself to studying the ancient history, customs and religious tradition of Ceylon, amassing a collection of valuable Pali manuscripts which he later donated to Stanford. In 1918 he set off on pilgrimage to virtually every major religious site in India—Madurai, Madras, Amritsar, Simla, Badrinath, Rishikesh, Benares, Bodhgaya, Calcutta, Darjeeling among them. He interviewed Annie Besant in Madras (where he briefly became entangled in Theosophical Society machinations), developed close relationships with Swamis Satyananda and Syamananda, and later in his Indian travels met Krishnamurti, Paul Brunton, Ramana Maharshi, Swami Yogananda, Sri Krishna Prem, and Sunyabhai. The most providential of these meetings proved to be with Lama Kazi Dawa-Samdup in Sikkim. The lama, who had already acted as a translator for Alexandra David-Neel, was at this time the headmaster of a boys' school in Gangtok. He had earlier been Tibetan Plenipotentiary in India and on the staff of the thirteenth Dalai Lama during his Indian exile in 1910.

The lama was a colorful character, fond of the drink and given to wandering off for days at a time to the neglect of his pedagogical duties. Alexandra David-Neel, in a charming portrait of the lama in *Magic and Mystery in Tibet*, tells us that

> His passion for reading literally tyrannized the man. Wherever he went he carried a book with him and, absorbed in it, he lost himself in a kind of ecstasy. For hours he would forget where he was. His learned translations, long conversations with lamas and the celebrating of occult rites constantly distracted him from attending school. Indeed, he often seemed to forget of its very existence.[54]

His foibles should not obscure the fact that the lama was also a man of considerable learning, spiritual discernment, humility and good humor, and the compiler of an English-Tibetan dictionary. It was he who translated the *Bardo Thodol*, using Evans-Wentz as his "living English dictionary." Evans-Wentz's references to himself as a disciple of the lama seem to have been rather loose, this kind of relationship never being confirmed by the lama himself nor by anybody else. Kazi Dawa-Samdup was appointed as a lecturer at the University of Calcutta in 1919 and died three years later. It was not until 1927

---

53 Preface to the first edition of *The Tibetan Book of the Dead*, xix-xx in the 3rd edition.
54 A. David-Neel, *Magic and Mystery in Tibet*, 17.

that Evans-Wentz was able to publish the translation which owed so much to the efforts of the lama.

The later life of Evans-Wentz, this eccentric and insular "gypsy-scholar" (so dubbed by one of his Oxford professors, Dr Marrett) is not without many intriguing aspects—his friendship with Lama Govinda, his encounters with figures such as Carl Jung and Dwight Goddard, his work on sacred geography, culminating in his last publication, *Cuchama and Sacred Mountains* (1981) (a work which foreshadows the contemporary interest in a resacralized nature), and his defense of the spiritual heritage of the American Indians. He was a highly principled, somewhat puritanical and isolated man who, despite considerable wealth, lived the last twenty-five years of his life in a down-'n-outers motel in San Diego. He spurned public life and never took on the role of spiritual teacher. Of his life he wrote—and the evidence supports the claim—that he had "striven to love all mankind of all nations and races and faiths ... dwelt in the solitude of deserts, of the jungles, of the mountain tops ... sought neither worldly goods nor worldly honors ... relinquished those things men struggle for most."[55]

In our present context his work on the religious literature of Tibet is of primary interest. In considering Evans-Wentz's significance for Tibetology it needs to be remembered that the central Tantric texts of the Vajrayana were at that time completely unknown in the West. Those few scholars who knew something about Tibetan tantra, such as Sir John Woodroffe, tended to dismiss it as a degraded form of Hinduism. It is not surprising that the collaborative efforts of Evans-Wentz and Dawa-Samdup produced translations which subsequent scholarship has shown to contain a good many errors.[56] It must also be said that Evans-Wentz understood Tibetan Buddhism through spectacles tinged by Theosophy and by his intent to find in the Himalayas a worldwide "wisdom religion" of whose existence he had been persuaded by his inquiries into Gnosticism, the Egyptian and Greek Mysteries, and Hinduism.[57]

Although Evans-Wentz only spent one day of his life on Tibetan soil, and notwithstanding the various criticisms to which his work has been subjected, nor forgetting the contribution of Lama Kazi Dawa-Samdup, there can be no doubt that he performed a valiant labor in bringing the Tibetan texts to a Western audience. He was also successful in spreading the view, earlier treat-

55 "Some Notes for an Autobiography," quoted in K. Winkler, *Pilgrim of the Clear Light*, 1.
56 See comments by Lama Govinda in K. Winkler, *Pilgrim of the Clear Light*, vi. In defense of Evans-Wentz it must be said that he was always ready to be apprised of errors and inadvertencies: after World War II, for instance, his friend Lama Govinda (at this time living on Evans-Wentz's modest "estate" at Kasar Devi, near Almora) came across an authorized Tibetan block print of the *Bardo Thodol* with which he closely compared the Evans-Wentz translation. Govinda's corrections appeared in subsequent editions of the text. See Evans-Wentz's Preface to third edition. Details of Evans-Wentz's friendship with Govinda and his wife, Li Gotami, can be found in K. Winkler, *A Thousand Journeys*, Ch 12.
57 See R. Fields, *How the Swans Came to the Lake*, 286.

ed with scholarly derision, that the Vajrayana was neither a degeneration of Theravadin Buddhism nor incompatible with it, but the highest expression of Buddhist esotericism, related to orthodox Buddhism as "higher mathematics to lower."[58] In introducing *The Tibetan Book of the Dead* he voiced his hope that the translation would "serve as one more spiritual strand in an unbreakable bond of good will and universal peace, binding East and West together in mutual respect and understanding, and in love such as overleaps every barrier of creed and caste and race."[59] It was a noble if grandiose hope; who is to say that it has not been at least partially realized?

Heinrich Harrer

In 1939, after climbing the north face ("Murder Wall") of the Eiger in Switzerland, Heinrich Harrer joined a mountaineering expedition in the Himalayas.[60] The outbreak of war saw the Austrian captured by the British, his fellow-internees including Nyanatiloka Thera and Lama Govinda. In 1943 Harrer and a companion, Peter Aufschnaiter, escaped and trekked from the Indian foothills, over some of the most dangerous passes in the Himalayas, across the Tibetan border, eventually arriving in Lhasa nearly two years later after covering almost two and a half thousand kilometres without benefit of maps, guides or equipment. Harrer spent the next five years in Tibet, acting for a time as a tutor to the young Dalai Lama who was aged eleven when they first met in 1946. The Chinese invasion of 1950 prompted Harrer's departure from Tibet.

Harrer's *Seven Years in Tibet* (English edition, 1953) offered colorful and engaging, if not very deep, accounts of various Tibetan rites and customs, and undoubtedly served for many Westerners as their first introduction to Tibetan culture. It was also through this book that many first became aware of the institution and the person of the Dalai Lama. It became an immediate best-seller, and was eventually translated into nearly fifty languages; it still sells well today.

The recent film of the same name, starring Brad Pitt as Harrer, prompted an Austrian reporter to delve into Harrer's life in the 30s, leading to the disclosure of Harrer's involvement in both the SA and the SS, and his continuing links with underground Nazi groups. The ensuing publicity was something of an embarrassment for the Hollywood producers who thought they had a sure-fire winner on their hands with a film about the now-*chic* subject of ante-Chinese Tibet.[61]

58 Evans-Wentz quoted in R. Fields, *How the Swans Came to the Lake*, 287.
59 W.Y. Evans-Wentz, *The Tibetan Book of the Dead*, xxi in 3rd edition.
60 Aficionados of mountaineering literature will be familiar with Harrer's magnificent history of attempts on the Eiger North Face, *The White Spider* (first published 1959).
61 See W. Cash, "The Nazi who Climbed a Mountain and Came Down a Hollywood Film Star," *The Age* (Melbourne), October 18, 1997, News Extra 8. The Harrer case also raises again the painful

Marco Pallis

Marco Pallis was born of Greek parents in Liverpool in 1895, educated at Harrow and Liverpool University, and served in the British army during the Great War.[62] Later he studied music with Arnold Dolmetsch, and was much influenced by the writings of two great perennialists, Ananda Coomaraswamy and René Guénon, whom he visited in Cairo and two of whose books he translated with his friend Richard Nicholson. In 1923 Pallis visited southern Tibet on a mountaineering trip. He returned to the area in 1933 and 1936, consumed by an interest in its traditional culture, and stayed in monasteries in Sikkim and Ladakh. He returned for a more extended visit after World War II. After visiting Ceylon and South India, and receiving the *darsan* of Ramana Maharshi at Tiruvannamalai, he studied under Tibetan lamas near Shigatse and was initiated, with the Tibetan name of Thubden Tendzin, into one of the lineages.[63] Pallis returned to England in 1950 and with Richard Nicholson and some other musicians formed the English Consort of Viols, a group dedicated to the preservation of early English music. Pallis made several concert tours with this group. On one such tour to the USA he visited the Abbey of Gethsemani (Kentucky) where he met Thomas Merton, with whom he had already opened a correspondence.[64]

Marco Pallis wrote two books deriving from his experiences in Tibet: *Peaks and Lamas* (1939) which was reprinted several times and became something of a bestseller, and *The Way and the Mountain* (1960). They are a unique blend of travelogue, botanical lore, discursive essays on Tibetan civilization, and metaphysical expositions. In the former Pallis allows the reader to become familiar with the landscape, with its inhabitants and with the values which govern their lives without obtruding Western "interpretations" on his subjects. The second of his books, written in the light of a fully matured understanding of the Vajrayana, includes several peerless essays on such subjects as the "presiding idea" of Tibetan Buddhism, the institution of the Dalai Lama (on which any amount of nonsense had hitherto appeared), and Buddhism in Sikkim. Pallis' oeuvre is unhampered by any assumptions about the superiority of the West; indeed, his books derive much of their insight from his adamantine opposition to the modern spirit and his receptivity to the lessons of tradition in one of its last strongholds. During his trips he enhanced his fluency in the Tibetan language, wore Tibetan clothes and mixed freely not only with learned lamas and geshes but with ordinary folk.[65]

problem of the possible collusions between Orientalism, Western exponents of Eastern practices and fascism, which will be discussed in Chapter 14.

62 Information on Pallis taken from his own books, from his article "A Fateful Meeting of Minds: A.K. Coomaraswamy and René Guénon," 175-188, and from T. Merton, *The Asian Journal of Thomas Merton*, 71-72. I am also indebted to Paul Goble for some personal reminiscences of Marco Pallis and his companion Richard Nicholson.

63 A. Desjardins, *The Message of the Tibetans*, 20.

64 See M. Pallis, "Thomas Merton, 1915-1968," 138-146.

65 See R.W.J. Austin, review of a later edition of M. Pallis, *Peaks and Lamas*, 253-254.

He achieved momentary public attention for his role in the exposure of Lobsang Rampa (about whom more presently). Pallis wrote many articles for *Studies in Comparative Religion,* some of which are included in his last publication, *A Buddhist Spectrum* (1980). Marco Pallis died in 1990. One can only concur with Huston Smith's judgment: "For insight, and the beauty insight requires if it is to be effective, I find no writer on Buddhism surpassing him."[66]

Lama Anagarika Govinda

To strike a personal note: in the early 1970s I returned to Australia from post-graduate studies in England. Although I had a vague but sympathetic interest in matters religious and spiritual my worldview was largely shaped by a constellation of humanistic and radical European thinkers to whom I had been exposed in my undergraduate studies. During my absence my brother Peter had become deeply interested in Buddhism, particularly the Vajrayana, and was much impressed by the works of one Lama Anagarika Govinda. His efforts to persuade me to read this author met with some resistance and it was not until I was on a visit to India and Nepal in 1974 that I finally, and somewhat reluctantly, picked up a copy of *Foundations of Tibetan Mysticism* (1960). It proved to be an astonishing experience and helped to alter my own spiritual and intellectual trajectory. Soon after, on the slopes of the Himalayas and in sight of Mt Annapurna, I read the autobiographical *The Way of the White Clouds* which—though I would scarcely have thought it possible—made an even more profound impact than *Foundations.* A whole new world opened up before me. I was amazed by the density and color of Tibetan iconography, by the profundity of the doctrines explicated in these books, by the spiritual richness of the traditional Tibetan culture, and by the acute intelligence and noble character of the author. Although I never became a Buddhist Govinda's works were decisive in my eventual return to the fold of the tradition to which I belonged by both birth and upbringing, and in my intellectual commitment to the field of comparative religion. My experience was not uncommon: one could find copies of Govinda's works anywhere on the "hippie trail" of the time—Amsterdam, Marrakesh, Istanbul, Kabul, Katmandu, Bali, San Francisco. By this time Govinda's works were not only well known amongst counter-cultural aspirants but were also infiltrating academia (though they continued to be regarded with suspicion in some academic quarters).

Lama Govinda was born Ernst Hoffman in Saxony in 1898, the son of a German father and a Bolivian mother. After being invalided out of the war with tuberculosis he studied architecture and philosophy at Freiburg

---

66 Huston Smith, review of Marco Pallis, *A Buddhist Spectrum,* 145. (The work of Marco Pallis fulfils a vital function in the traditionalist school in which Buddhism has received comparatively little attention.)

University, and soon became interested in Buddhism, particularly Buddhist philosophy and meditation, on which he published two books. In 1928 he determined to join the *sangha* by way of a small community of German Buddhist monks in Ceylon, headed by Nyanatiloka Thera. Govinda took vows and found time in his monastic schedule, after mastering Pali, to make a close study of the *Abhidharma*, leading to the publication of another work under the name Brahmachari Govinda.

In 1931 Govinda attended a Buddhist conference in Darjeeling, intending to affirm the purity of the Theravadin tradition against the Mahayana which, in his view, had degenerated into "a system of demon-worship and weird beliefs."[67] He little realized that the trip was to alter his life. There he met his Tibetan guru, Tomo Geshe Rinpoche, under whose influence he "converted" and by whom he was initiated into the Gelugpa sect. He spent the next thirty years in northern India and Sikkim, made several visits to Tibet, most notably in 1933 and 1948-49, and was initiated into the Kargyu and Nyingma lineages. He was interned by the British during World War II, and after his release married the Indian artist Li Gotami, Govinda himself being an accomplished painter. During the 60s and 70s Govinda lectured widely in Europe and America and spent his later years in California where he died in 1985.

In 1933 Govinda founded the Order of the Arya Maitreya Mandala, dedicated to the preservation and dissemination of the Tibetan religious heritage, and by the 50s had accumulated a small circle of Western "disciples." The German branch of the Order (still in existence) enjoys the distinction of opening the first center in the West devoted entirely to the study and propagation of Tibetan Buddhism.[68] In recent decades Govinda's Order has been somewhat overtaken by the presence in the West of significant numbers of Tibetan teachers of whom Chögyam Trungpa, Tarthang Tulku, Namkhai Norbu, Lama Yeshe, Lama Zopa, Sogyal Rinpoche, and the Dalai Lama himself have been amongst the most influential.

Govinda's Tibetan experiences are recounted in his luminous *The Way of the White Clouds* which includes elements from several genres—spiritual journal, adventure narrative, anthropological field report, philosophical commentary. To my mind it is one of the century's classic spiritual autobiographies. As well as the works already mentioned Govinda also published *Psycho-Cosmic Symbolism of the Buddhist Stupa* (1940), *The Psychological Attitude of Early Buddhist Philosophy* (1969), *Creative Meditation and Multi-Dimensional Consciousness* (1976) and *The Inner Structure of the I Ching, the Book of Transformation* (1981). Some of his lectures and talks were collected by his students in two posthumous anthologies, *A Living Buddhism for the West* (1990) and *Insights of a Himalayan Pilgrim* (1991).

67 A. Govinda, *The Way of the White Clouds*, 13.
68 A. Rawlinson, *The Book of Enlightened Masters*, 276.

Lama Govinda's credentials as an expositor of Tibetan Buddhism and a spokesman for Tibetan culture have been queried by Donald Lopez in *Prisoners of Shangri-La*.[69] Lopez makes a great deal of several apparently damaging "facts" about Govinda's "career" as a spokesman for Tibetan Buddhism. He is skeptical about Govinda's various initiations, emphasizes his reliance on secondary Western sources, and charges Govinda with "psychologizing" various Tibetan texts and doctrines. He also derides Govinda's "extravagant commentary" in *Foundations of Tibetan Buddhism*. These criticisms certainly have some force. On the other hand, very little is made in Lopez's account of the fact that Govinda spent seventy years immersed in the intensive study and sincere practice of Buddhism, that those who knew the lama personally were almost invariably impressed by his scholarship, his integrity, his commitment to the Dharma and his wisdom, that his works have been applauded by all manner of commentators, Buddhist and non-Buddhist alike, as providing deep spiritual and intellectual sustenance. He was described by another Western Buddhist, John Blofeld, as "that golden eagle amongst adepts," one "who possesses that rare and indescribable quality by which a man of transcendent spiritual attainment is instantly recognized."[70]

C. Tibet and the West in the Contemporary Era

Later Travelers and Seekers in Tibet

Western writings on Tibet have rapidly proliferated in recent times. "Secret Tibet" and "the Forbidden City" have continued to draw a steady stream of Westerners—mountaineers and explorers, adventurers, pilgrims, anthropologists, missionaries, monks, occultists, travel writers, scholars, artists. One may here mention such figures as Nicholas Roerich,[71] Spencer Chapman, André Guibaut, André Migot, George Patterson, Geoffrey Bull, Han Suyin, John Blofeld, Sorrell Wilby and Robert Thurman.[72] Similarly, large numbers of Westerners with a variety of motives visited and resided in the Tibetan bor-

---

69 See D. Lopez, *Prisoners of Shangri-La*, 59-62, 125-126.

70 J. Blofeld, *The Wheel of Life*, 236-237.

71 Roerich (1874-1947) was a Russian aristocrat, Theosophist, painter and "channeler" who, after the Revolution, fled Russia through Mongolia to Tibet where he lived for some years and painted an arresting series of landscapes. His account of his Tibetan experiences can be found in *Altai-Himalaya* (1929). He spent his later years at Nagga, in the Himalayas. His wife Helena was well known in European occultist circles as something of a seer and exponent of "Agni Yoga." See A. Daniélou, *The Way to the Labyrinth*, 188. There are several websites where one can view examples of Roerich's art. A reproduction of one of his paintings appears on the front cover of this book.

72 Amongst the many works by such authors, as well as works cited elsewhere in this chapter, the following are amongst the better-known: Spencer Chapman, *Lhasa, The Holy City* (1940); André Guibaut, *Tibetan Venture* (1949); André Migot, *Tibetan Marches* (1955); George Patterson, *Tibetan Journey* (1956); Geoffrey T. Bull, *When Iron Gates Yield* (1955); Han Suyin, *Lhasa, the Open City* (1976) (an apologia for the Chinese occupation); Sorrell Wilby, *Tibet, a Woman's Lone Trek across a Mysterious Land* (1988), and Robert Thurman & Tad Wise, *Circling the Sacred Mountain* (2000).

der regions and the Himalayas of India and Nepal. Among the more well known were Paul Brunton, David Snellgrove, Arnaud Desjardins, Lizelle Raymond, Thomas Merton, John Snelling, Andrew Harvey and Peter Matthiessen.[73] Here we can only cast a quick glance over a few works which elucidate aspects of the Tibeto-Himalayan religious heritage.

One of the more authoritative historical accounts appeared in 1968, *A Cultural History of Tibet*, by David Snellgrove and Hugh Richardson. Richardson had spent nine years in Lhasa as the Head of the British Mission, arriving in Tibet in 1936.[74] Almost at the moment the first great wave of Tibetan refugees were leaving their homeland, David Snellgrove published a scholarly edition of *Hevajra Tantra*, the first complete tantra to be published in English, soon to be followed by Herbert Guenther's translation of Gampopa's *Jewel Ornament of Liberation* (both 1959). Snellgrove had made a seven-month journey in northwestern Nepal in 1956, recounting his experiences in *Himalayan Pilgrimage*, one of the best books in the genre. Both Snellgrove and Richardson published important scholarly works on Tibetan religion and together founded the Institute of Tibetan Studies at Tring.

In the Preface to their book the authors wrote this:

> We have taken upon ourselves to write this book at this time because the civilization of the Tibetan people is disappearing before our very eyes, and apart from a few gentle protests here and there the rest of the world lets it go without comment and without regret ... If we succeed in awakening the interest of readers in this tragic drama, which affects us so closely in the human problems involved, the task of writing this book will have been well repaid.[75]

This echoed some of the themes of the Foreword to Lama Govinda's *The Way of the White Clouds* which had appeared in the year previous. Another book which appeared at the same time, and with similar sentiments expressed in the Foreword, was *The Tantric Mysticism of Tibet* (1968) by John Blofeld. It deserves mention as one of the earliest of the books by Western Buddhists which, in its attempt to explain meditational techniques, was directed not towards scholarship but practice.

Four later books by Western seekers of different kinds, all written in the period of the Tibetan exile, deserve particular mention as distinguished works. Arnaud Desjardins' *The Message of the Tibetans* (1969) offers a clear, sensible and accessible account of some of the distinctive aspects of the Tibetan tradition, based on Desjardins' interviews with Tibetan lamas in exile in India. *The Asian Journal of Thomas Merton* (1975) records the deep impressions made on the Trappist by his meetings with the Dalai Lama and

73 As well as works already cited elsewhere see Paul Brunton, *A Hermit in the Himalayas* (1937), John Snelling, *The Sacred Mountain* (1983), and Lizelle Raymond, *To Live Within* (1973).

74 For a biographical sketch and a brief assessment of Richardson's scholarly work, see the tribute by his collaborator, David Snellgrove, "An Appreciation of Hugh Richardson."

75 D. Snellgrove & H. Richardson, *Cultural History*, 13.

with several Nyingma monks in Dharamsala and Darjeeling, shortly before his death in Bangkok.[76] *The Snow Leopard* (1979) by the novelist and Zen practitioner Peter Matthiessen (later to become a Zen roshi), vividly recounts a journey in the Nepalese Himalayas with the naturalist George Schaller. The book blends travel narrative and spiritual journal, and offers a recent specimen of what Bishop has called "mountain mysticism."[77] Andrew Harvey's *A Journey to Ladakh* (1983) also belongs to the time-honored genre in which the physical adventure is paralleled by a spiritual odyssey. These books by Matthiessen and Harvey were widely, and properly, celebrated in the Western press. However, neither can match those by Pallis and Govinda which are less self-preoccupied, and written by men much more deeply immersed in the Tibetan tradition.

Counterfeit Tibetan Esotericism: the Lobsang Rampa Case

The best selling books on Tibet in the 20th century have been T. Lobsang Rampa's "autobiographical" trilogy: *The Third Eye* (1956), *Doctor from Lhasa* (1959), and *The Rampa Story* (1960). Donald Lopez has given us a detailed anatomy of the whole Rampa case in *Prisoners of Shangri-La* on which the skeletal account which follows draws heavily. This trilogy purports to tell the life story of Tuesday Lobsang Rampa, born into an aristocratic Lhasa family closely associated with the thirteenth Dalai Lama. The boy was identified at an early age as having an extraordinary and providential role to play in the spread of Tibetan esotericism "among strange people." As well as undertaking intensive training under the most eminent lamas of the day, at the age of eight Rampa was given a surgical procedure to create "the third eye," thus releasing various clairvoyant powers and the ability to discern auras.[78] The Dalai Lama himself, we are told, commissioned Rampa to undertake his great work in preserving the wisdom of Tibet. After all manner of astounding trials and tribulations in Tibet itself—the most strenuous training and asceticism, perilous journeyings far and wide, horrific initiation rites, and some spectacular astral journeys—the Dalai Lama instructs Rampa to leave Tibet for China where there is a profound ignorance of "the Science of the Overself."

In the second volume our protagonist enrols in a medical college in China, registering as "Tuesday Lobsang Rampa, Lama of Tibet. Priest-Surgeon Chakpori Lamasery. Recognized Incarnation. Abbot Designate. Pupil of Lama Mingyar Dondup." Here he complements his occult Tibetan

<hr/>

76 Excerpts from Merton's *Asian Journal* concerning aspects of Eastern spirituality have recently been published as *Thoughts on the East.* The passages concerning Tibetan Buddhism can be found on pages 70-81.

77 P. Bishop, *Tibet in Its Place,* 6.

78 The doctrine of the "third eye" has a long and honorable pedigree in many religious traditions: as is the case with much of Rampa's "esoterica," what we get in these books is often a parody of authentic doctrines.

medical and psychological knowledge with training in both Chinese and western healing disciplines. After teaching himself to fly he is recruited into Chiang Kai-Shek's army as a medical airman. Following a return to Lhasa to participate in the funeral ceremonies for the Dalai Lama, Rampa serves in flying ambulances in China. During the war with Japan he is shot down, taken prisoner, survives brutal tortures and interrogations, escapes, is recaptured and incarcerated, and eventually transferred to a camp for recalcitrant prisoners near Hiroshima. He escapes on the very day the bomb is dropped on Hiroshima and drifts into the Japan Sea in a stolen fishing boat.

The third volume opens fifteen years later by which time Rampa is living in Windsor in Canada but is in constant telepathic communication with lamas in Tibet who, in the face of the Chinese invasion, are hoarding a collection of Tibet's most precious religious texts and artifacts in an underground labyrinth in a remote part of the country. High Tibetan lamas telepathically instruct Rampa to write his third book which recounts events of the intervening years—Rampa's experiences as a dog trainer in the Russian army, torture in Lubyanka, deportation to Poland, involvement in Czechoslovakian smuggling operations, crossing the Atlantic as a merchant seaman, a spell as a radio announcer in Schenectady, various escapades in America before returning by sea to India and thence to Tibet. He tells of an earlier astral journey with his guru to another planet where he received instructions on his mission from extra-terrestrials. Most extraordinary, however, is an astral meeting in "the Land of the Golden Light" with the late Dalai Lama who tells him that he is to take over the body of a man in England, but also warning him that if Rampa agrees to return to earth he will "return to hardship, misunderstanding, disbelief, and actual hatred, for there is a force of evil which tries to prevent all that is good in connection with human evolution."[79] After his clandestine return to Tibet he undertakes another astral journey to the Akashic Record where he familiarizes himself with the past of the man whose body he is soon to inhabit and in which incarnation he would write his trilogy, thus fulfilling his task of bringing the treasures of "Lamaism" (which he distinguishes from Buddhism) to a Western audience at a time when the Tibetan heritage was threatened with extirpation. As well as tracing the life-story of Rampa, the trilogy offers commentaries on all kinds of recondite doctrines and techniques—astral travel, psychic healing, Egyptian death practices, clairvoyance, breath control—as well as an account of the earth's prehistory.

The story of the controversial publication and reception of Rampa's books in the West, and the exposure of "Lobsang Rampa" as Cyril Hoskin, a surgical goods maker and part-time photographer who had apparently never left Britain, has been analyzed in some detail by Lopez. Here we shall only touch on a few aspects of this curious case. When the first manuscript of *The*

---

79 Quoted in D. Lopez, *Prisoners of Shangri-La*, 93.

Third Eye was sent by a potential publisher to Hugh Richardson he immediately adjudged the book a "fake built from published works and embellished by a fertile imagination."[80] His assessment was endorsed by David Snellgrove, Agehananda Bharati (who later called the book "these cretinistic confabulations"), Heinrich Harrer and Marco Pallis, amongst others. Nonetheless, Secker & Warburg published *The Third Eye* in 1956. Despite the most damaging reviews by various Tibetologists the book was a runaway hit and was quickly translated into French and German. Marco Pallis was so appalled by this "libel on both Tibet and its religion" that, in 1958 and on behalf of a group of Tibet experts, he hired a private detective to investigate the identity of "Lobsang Rampa." This led to Rampa's subsequent exposure in the press, one which did not prevent him from publishing many more books before his death in Canada in 1981. (One of his later works was *My Trip to Venus* the royalties of which were donated to one of Rampa's pet causes, the Save a Cat League of New York.)

On one level the Rampa case seems to be nothing more than a somewhat lurid instance of the literary hoax in which, as Lopez nicely remarks, the ghostwriter turns into a ghost! At this level the Rampa books

> are the works of an unemployed surgical fitter, the son of a plumber, seeking to support himself as a ghostwriter. The first book ... could have been drawn from various English language sources ... supplemented with an admixture of garden variety spiritualism and Theosophy ... providing an exotic route through Tibet back to the familiar themes of Victorian and Edwardian spiritualism ...[81]

However, as Lopez remarks, it also raises interesting questions about who has authority to speak and write about Tibet/"Tibet." Reflecting on the career of Rampa, Lopez writes,

> The confluence of the scholarly and the popular is strikingly evident in *The Third Eye*, where Rampa draws on the accounts of travelers and amateur scholars ... and combines them with standard occult themes ... into a work that is neither wholly fact nor wholly fiction ... he was able to represent the Tibet of Western fantasies ...[82]

The Rampa books furnish further proof—if any be needed!—that there remains an insatiable public appetite for "occultist" fantasies in which one often finds a warmed-over stew of traditional esoteric doctrines, Blavatskyisms, science fiction, psychoanalysis and pop-existentialism. Layfayette Ronald Hubbard, Eric von Danniken, and Georgi Ivanovitch Gurdjieff furnish us with variations on the theme. Rampa's success also attests to the anti-scholasticism of all millenarian movements, another canopy under which the Rampa trilogy might also be situated. There remain

80 Quoted in D. Lopez, *Prisoners of Shangri-La*, 98.
81 D. Lopez, *Prisoners of Shangri-La*, 105.
82 D. Lopez, *Prisoners of Shangri-La*, 112.

all manner of baffling aspects to this particular case and we need not sub-scribe to the view that Hoskin's "Lobsang Rampa" was a completely fraudu-lent creation. As Whitall Perry has remarked,

> ... since not just anyone could pull the stunt and everything has its explana-tion, one can admit the hypothesis that Hoskins [sic] might somewhat improbably be the beneficiary of certain errant psychic residues emanating from Tibet, his distortions approximating those monitored by spiritist medi-ums contacting the residues or "psychic cadavers" of the dead—with a large serving of imagination to embellish the fragments.[83]

Tibet, Western Esotericism and New Age Orientalism

One chapter in Western engagements in Tibet which remains largely unex-plored is the impact of Tibetan mysticism on Western esotericism. One finds frequent reference and allusion to esoteric Tibetan doctrines and practices in the works of Theosophists, Anthroposophists, Gurdjieffians, traditional-ists, and occultists of various stripe. In recent decades there is no doubt that books such as *The Tibetan Book of the Dead* and Govinda's *Foundations of Tibetan Mysticism* as well as the deluge of recent books on Tibetan tantra by both exiled Tibetan lamas and their Western disciples, have generated interest in the esoteric traditions not only of Tibet but of the West. As yet this territory remains largely uncharted. Note, for instance, that in the two most compre-hensive and scholarly histories of Western esotericism and of "New Age Religion," by Antoine Faivre and Wouter Hanegraaff respectively, we find no mention of Tibet.[84]

A fertile line of inquiry might take up the model of Western esoteric thought proposed by Faivre to see how well it characterizes Western under-standings of Tibetan mysticism.[85] Faivre posits six "fundamental characteris-tics" of Western esoteric thought (the first four indispensable and the latter two "relative"): 1. the principle of symbolic and real *correspondences* among all parts of the universe, often underpinned in traditional esotericisms by the doctrine of macrocosm and microcosm and recently evinced in more popu-lar ideas about "interdependence"; 2. the idea of *Living Nature*—the cosmos as complex, plural, hierarchical and vital, a linch-pin of many forms of Western "magic" and integral to alchemy and all forms of *magia naturalis*; 3. the visionary uses of the *imagination* in "meditations" and explorations of a "mesocosm"; 4. *the experience of transmutation* afforded by gnosis; 5. *the praxis of concordance* which embraces the *philosophia perennis* in its several variations; 6. an emphasis on *transmission* which affirms the need for authentic lineages

83 W. Perry, review of Christopher Evans, *Cults of Unreason*, 185.

84 A. Faivre, *Access to Western Esotericism* and W.J. Hanegraaff, *New Age Religion and Western Culture: Esotericism in the Mirror of Secular Thought*.

85 See A. Faivre, *Access to Western Esotericism*, 10-15. (I thank Arthur Versluis for alerting me to this passage.)

of esoteric wisdom such as can issue in genuine initiation. A detailed exploration of this model with reference to Western writings on Tibetan esotericism would take us beyond the compass of the present work. However, it can be stated with some confidence that each of these marks of Western esoteric thought is to be found in abundance in Western renderings of the Vajrayana. The most problematic component, at first sight, might appear to be the concept of "Living Nature" which, Faivre suggests, might be undermined by Oriental forms of "monist spiritualism." My own view is that it is quite mistaken to understand various metaphysical monisms, such as those of *Advaita* Vedanta and Mahayana Buddhism, most fully elaborated by Sankara and Nagarjuna respectively, as being "world-denying" or implacably antithetical to ideas about "Living Nature" as Faivre articulates them. Such pivotal metaphysical concepts as *maya* and *sunyata* have all too often been understood only in their negative applications—but this is a theme which cannot be pursued here.[86] However, we can perhaps pause to take note of a representative sample of quotations from *Creative Meditation and Multi-Dimensional Consciousness* by Lama Anagarika Govinda to suggest that Faivre's six marks of Western esoteric thought can easily be found in Western writings on some of the more arcane and occult teachings of the Tibetans. (This particular book has been chosen because of its widespread popularity amongst the more serious-minded Western seekers tapping into the sources of Tibet's wisdom tradition. However, the exercise could easily be repeated with any number of books written by Westerners and dealing with Tibetan esotericism.) Here I can do no more than simply list these quotations, randomly chosen, by way of suggestive illustration:

1. *Correspondences & Interdependence*
Even the simplest form or color is a symbol revealing the nature of the primordial reality of the universe and the structure of the human psyche in which this universal reality is mirrored. In fact, if the structure of our consciousness did not correspond to that of the universe and its laws, we should not be aware of either the universe or the laws that govern it. (162)

2. *Living Nature*
The Tantric Buddhist does not believe in an independent or separately existing external world. The inner and outer worlds are the warp and woof of the same fabric in which the threads of all forces and of all events, of all forms of consciousness and of their objects, are woven into an inseparable net of endless, mutually conditioned relations ... (40)

3. *Imagination*
This power of the creative imagination is not merely content with observing the world as it is, accepting a given reality, but is capable of creating a new reality by transforming the inner as well as the outer world. This is the very

---

86 For some commentary related to this general issue see my articles "Sankara's Doctrine of Maya" and "'The Translucence of the Eternal': Religious Understandings of the Natural Order." See also S.H. Nasr, *Religion and the Order of Nature*, 46-48.

heart of the Tantric teaching and experience ... a spiritual discipline or meditational practice which shuns the power of imagination deprives itself of the
most effective and vital means of transforming human nature as it is into
what it could be ... (42-43)

4. *Transmutation*
Liberation is not escapism, but consists in the conscious transformation of
the elements that constitute our world and our existence. This is the great
secret of the Tantras and of the mystics of all times ... It is an act of resurrection, in which the ultimate transformation takes place ... in which all things
become transparent, and all that has been experienced, whether in joy or in
suffering, enters into a state of transfiguration ... (288-289)

5. *Concordance*
... even before the advent of the Buddha, great saints and sages had gained
the highest realization ... The awe before all that is great is the root of all
that is great in ourselves ... he who possesses this awe, this profound reverence ... has at the same time respect for the living form and the inherent law
of each spiritual way and the symbols in which they are expressed ... (196)

6. *Transmission*
... the Guru is the living representative, the mouthpiece of the Buddha, the
transmitter and the embodiment of the Buddha's teaching, who kindles the
flame of faith in the disciple and inspires him to follow in the footsteps of
those who have realized the Sacred Teaching ... Thus the term "Guru" comprises the complete chain of spiritual teachers who passed on the living tradition through millennia from generation to generation ... (140)

Whilst these passages may not all mesh precisely with Faivre's six criteria, they
do so sufficiently closely to warrant further investigation of the possible parallels and interactions between Western and Eastern esotericism. No doubt
we should be cautious in constructing facile "correspondences" of our own
and we must be attentive to the many conspicuous differences between the
esoteric traditions of East and West. Nonetheless, Faivre's "intrinsic elements" of Western esotericism are also readily apparent in European understandings of the Vajrayana. Furthermore, I suggest, the whole field of possible convergences between scholarly inquiries into and experiential encounters with Western esotericism on the one hand, and Western engagements
with esoteric Eastern spirituality on the other, awaits much more detailed
exploration.

*

The popular success of books such as James Hilton's exotic novel *Lost
Horizons* (1933) (in which we find a variant of the "white brotherhood" myth
perpetrated by the Theosophists), Harrer's *Seven Years in Tibet*, the Rampa
trilogy, and recent films such as *Seven Years in Tibet* and *Kundun*, testify to the
continuing potency of Tibet in the Western imagination.[87] The presence of

87 For a thoughtful review of the films *Seven Years in Tibet* and *Kundun* see Pico Iyer, "Lost
Horizons."

a growing number of Tibetan teachers in the West, the proliferation of monasteries, institutes and centers of learning devoted to Tibetan religion, the tireless work of the Dalai Lama in bringing the attention of the world to the plight of his compatriots, the disillusionment with communist China amongst the radical/liberal intelligentsia (and thereby their greater willingness to denounce the imperial barbarities of the Chinese occupation) and the recruitment of Western media celebrities such as Richard Gere and political figures such as the late Petra Kelly to the Tibetan cause, have all conspired to make Westerners much better informed about Tibetan realities.[88] Nonetheless, a certain mystical aura still surrounds the very name of Tibet, deriving in part from those persistent myths which writers like Peter Bishop and Donald Lopez have so rigorously dissected. No doubt the image of Tibet in the West has as much, or more, to do with deep-seated fears and fantasies in the European psyche, as with the realities of Tibetan history and culture. As Ursula Bernis has put it,

> Tibet evoked a longing for purity of spirit and perfection. Images of Tibet answered our need for otherness to speak to us in terms of spiritual authenticity. Tibet became ours in a very profound way. We internalized the vast, forbidding, inaccessible, mysterious spaces of Tibet described by early travelers. They became the hidden domain of a collective spiritual depth-dimension filled with our soul's innermost yearnings. Always withdrawing from ordinary gaze, Tibet's uniqueness today serves the basic human craving for meaning on levels other than the material.[89]

Tibet has variously been constructed as a dark realm of superstition, sorcery and decadent Buddhism, and as a never-never land peopled by childlike peasants of simple piety and by monks of fabulous psychic powers. Sometimes the two streams of European fantasy commingle in the same site, producing those peculiar ambivalences which mark much of the Western literature, especially in the 19th century. Doubtless, too, a sentimental romanticism has obscured the material particularities of Tibetan history. The processes of mythologizing can indeed often be accommodated in recent models of Orientalism, such as that intimated by Gustavo Benavides when he writes,

> Orientalism could ... serve as a conduit through which Western elites could replenish their ideological arsenal by employing representations that because of their spatial, temporal, and even ontological otherness could function as utopian horizons.[90]

Furthermore, we may in some measure agree with Lopez when he argues that the Western romance of "Tibet" may actually be harmful to the current Tibetan cause:

88 Many of these developments are discussed in the most recent edition of R. Fields, *How the Swans Came to the Lake.*

89 U. Bernis, "Tibet in the Shadow of Our Imagination," 84.

90 G. Benavides, "Giuseppe Tucci, or Buddhology in the Age of Fascism," 181.

Fantasies of Tibet have in the past three decades inspired much support for the cause of Tibetan independence. But those fantasies are ultimately a threat to the realization of that goal. It is not simply that learning that Tibet was not the place we dreamed it to be might result in some "disillusionment." It is rather that to allow Tibet to circulate as a constituent in a system of fantastic oppositions ... is to deny Tibet its history, to exclude Tibet from the real world of which it has always been a part, and to deny Tibetans their role as agents participating in the creation of a contested quotidian reality.[91]

These observations notwithstanding, the fact remains that the most fundamental significance of Tibet in the modern world is as a living refutation of all those values and ideas which define modernity. In the Preface of *The Way of the White Clouds* Govinda makes an eloquent plea for the preservation of Tibetan culture, one which has only taken on a deeper poignancy in the light of subsequent events. It is worth quoting at some length as it beautifully articulates the case for a unique religious and cultural heritage whose extinction would remove one of the last fully traditional cultures to survive the onslaughts of modernity:

> Why is it that the fate of Tibet has found such a deep echo in the world? ... Tibet has become the symbol of all that present-day humanity is longing for ... the stability of a tradition, which has its roots not only in a historical or cultural past, but within the innermost being of man, in whose depth this past is enshrined as an ever-present source of inspiration. But more than that: what is happening in Tibet is symbolical for the fate of humanity. As on a gigantically raised stage we witness the struggle between two worlds, which may be interpreted, according to the standpoint of the spectator, either as the struggle between the past and the future, between backwardness and progress, belief and science, superstition and knowledge—or as the struggle between spiritual freedom and material power, between the wisdom of the heart and the knowledge of the brain, between the dignity of the human individual and the herd-instinct of the mass, between the faith in the higher destiny of man through inner development and the belief in material prosperity through an ever-increasing production of goods. We witness the tragedy of a peaceful people without political ambitions and with the sole desire to be left alone, being deprived of its freedom and trampled underfoot by a powerful neighbor in the name of "progress," which as ever must serve as a cover for all the brutalities of the human race.[92]

Lopez cites part of this passage as an instance of the post-diaspora tendency to idealize Tibetan culture "as if it were itself another artifact of Shangri-La from an eternal classical age, set high in a Himalayan keep outside time and history."[93] Lopez's interrogation and debunking of the perpe-

91 D. Lopez, "New Age Orientalism," 43. See also Lopez's comments on what he calls "the demonization of China" which he sees as "yet a further manifestation of the continuing orientalist romance of Tibet," in *Curators of the Buddha*, 292-293, fn32.
92 A. Govinda, *The Way of the White Clouds*, xi.
93 D. Lopez, *Prisoners of Shangri-La*, 7

trators of a "mystical" romance of Tibet is often well directed and some of the shocks he administers are no doubt therapeutic. But one cannot help feeling that at times he succumbs to the postmodernist climate of suspicion in which anything and everything must be subjected to a corrosive irony. Lopez is all too ready to speak glibly about "fantasies of lost wisdom," as if it were reprehensible to acknowledge a sapiential tradition, or to recognize a culture as authentically traditional, or to regret its extinction. There *is* a kind of experiential understanding of the Tibetan wisdom which far outstrips anything "scholarship" might have to say on the subject, an understanding which is not restricted, either in principle or in practice, to Tibetans. To my mind we find just such an understanding pre-eminently in the work of Lama Govinda and Marco Pallis (about whom Lopez has remarkably little to say, given the attention he devotes to far less significant figures in the Western encounter with Tibet). In *Peaks and Lamas* Marco Pallis wrote this:

> Sheltered behind the rampart of the Himalaya, Tibet has looked on, almost unscathed, while some of the greatest [religious] traditions of the world have reeled under the attacks of the all-devouring monster of modernism.[94]

Lopez adduces this claim as evidence of the "volatility of the mythologizing and mystification of Tibetan culture."[95] One might retort that Lopez's treatment of figures like Pallis and Govinda betokens his own apparent surrender to a postmodernist relativism which is suspicious of *all* values and commitments, particularly religious ones. The past becomes a shifting sand which can never be understood for what it was but only as a kind of mirage viewed through ideologically-tinted spectacles. Lopez does us a useful service in dismantling and qualifying some of the more persistent popular stereotypes about Tibet—as a "timeless" culture, as an Edenic paradise, as a static polity—but in so doing he all too often seems to surrender to a danger of which he is intermittently aware, that of reducing Tibet to a vacuum filled by nothing more than the "ideological fictions" of the West. On the other hand, for Marco Pallis, as for Govinda, the significance of Tibet is to be found in the word *traditional*, which is to say that the separation between religion and culture is non-existent, the whole social order being shaped and governed by that distinctive form of Buddhism which had developed over centuries and which kept alive a sense of the sacred in every aspect of Tibetan life.

In *The New Religions* Jacob Needleman suggested that "a land like Tibet perhaps stands to the whole world like ... a teacher stands to ordinary men."[96] One cannot, of course, expect those in the West who are unaware of their own spiritual impoverishment and thus oblivious to their need for teachers of any kind, to understand this kind of claim. It must also be said that the lim-

---

94 Pallis quoted in D. Lopez, *Prisoners of Shangri-La*, 8.
95 D. Lopez, *Prisoners of Shangri-La*, 8.
96 J. Needleman, *The New Religions*, 168.

itations of the modern (i.e., profane) outlook are all too evident in the work of many scholars seeking to explain the significance of Tibet *exclusively* in terms of Western "fantasies" and "mythologies," Orientalist "constructions" and "nostalgic meta-narratives" which are only, apparently, to be understood within the Freudian/Foucaldian/Saidian categories—"fantasy," "projection," "discourse," "hegemony," "Otherness," "ideologizations" and the like. Indeed, it might be observed that the ostensible critique of Orientalism by such scholars is, as often as not, an inverted form of the very phenomena which they themselves so robustly castigate—which is to say that the post-colonial scholarly apparatus constitutes yet another imposition of essentially alien ideas, values and categories onto phenomena which actually surpass their reach. One is also reminded of Govinda's remark about our absurd modern attitude whereby

> a scholar is regarded as being all the more competent ("scholarly") the less he believes in the teachings he has undertaken to interpret. The sorry results are only too apparent, especially in the realm of Tibetology, which such scholars have approached with an air of their own superiority, thus defeating the very purpose of their endeavors.[97]

However starry-eyed many Western understandings of Tibet may be, and no matter what psychic and political motivations may be at play, the fact remains that this culture represented one of the very last living expressions of Tradition (in the Guénonian sense) in the modern world. Most Western observers, even those whom we might reasonably have expected to be more or less impervious, registered something of the spiritual radiance issuing from this condition even if they were ill-equipped to understand it. Let us give the last word not to a febrile "occultist," not to a library-bound orientalist, nor to a parricidal post-colonial skeptic. Instead, let us ponder the words of a self-effacing Englishman who knew Tibet and the Tibetans better than most, who loved and committed his life to the Dharma whilst respecting the claims of all integral traditions, and who had no axe to grind beyond a sincere wish to help preserve and make more widely known the spiritual treasures of the Tibeto-Himalayan region. No one has stated the fundamental significance of Tibet, beyond all immediate and expedient considerations, more profoundly than Marco Pallis, with whose words we bring this chapter to its conclusion:

> One can truly say that this remote land behind the snowy rampart of the Himalaya had become like the chosen sanctuary for all those things whereof the historical discarding had caused our present profane civilization, the first of its kind on record, to come into being ... the violation of this sanctu-

97 A. Govinda, "Introductory Foreword" to *The Tibetan Book of the Dead*, lxiii. Arnaud Desjardins recalls showing some passages from the works of "certain celebrated Western scholars" to Tibetan lamas in India, passages which "caused them considerable astonishment"—to which one can only say, "no doubt!" See *The Message of the Tibetans*, 132.

ary and the dissipation of the sacred influences hitherto concentrated there becomes an event of properly cosmic significance, of which the ulterior consequences for a world that tacitly condoned the outrage or, in many cases, openly countenanced it on the plea that it brought "progress" to a reluctant people, have yet to ripen.[98]

98 M. Pallis, review of Jacob Needleman, *The New Religions*, 189-190.

7.

The "Floating Worlds" of China and Japan

A. China: European Perceptions—Arthur Waley—Richard Wilhelm and Carl Jung— John Blofeld—René Guénon—Joseph Needham **B. Japan:** Ernest Fennellosa and the Late 19th Century—D.T. Suzuki and Western Zen in the Inter-war Years— Europeans in Japan—A Note on Shin and Other Japanese Traditions

It may well be that the publication of D.T. Suzuki's Essays in Zen Buddhism *in 1927 will seem in future generations as great an intellectual event as William of Moerbeke's translations of Aristotle in the thirteenth century or Marsiglio Ficino's of Plato in the fifteenth.* (Lynn White)[1]

A. China

European Perceptions

The European enthusiasm for Asian ideas, expressive modes and spiritual practices has flowed in successive waves. The height of Occidental Sinophilia was reached in England in the 17th century and in Western Europe in the 18th, only to be massively overtaken by India-mania during the Romantic period. In France many Enlightenment *philosophes* saw in Confucianism a rational and humanistic understanding of human nature and of the social order. At a time when chinoiserie was fashionable in many French salons, Voltaire, whilst conceding a Chinese deficiency in physics and mechanics, stated that "they have perfected morality, which is the first of the sciences." He lauded Confucius for teaching the virtues, indulging in no mysteries and teaching through "pure maxims in which you find nothing trivial and no ridiculous allegory."[2] In such a model, Enlightenment thinkers found inspiration for their own efforts to detach morality from the clutches of religious superstition. As Zhang Longzi has written, Enlightenment thinkers

> suddenly discovered, to their astonishment, that in great antiquity in China—a country whose material products had won the admiration of the ... people in the market—Confucius had taught the philosophy of a state built on the basis of ethical and political *bon sens*, and that the Chinese civilization

1 L. White, *Frontiers of Knowledge in the Study of Man* (1956), quoted in H. Smith, "D.T. Suzuki: Some Memories," 152.
2 Zhang Longzi, "The Myth of the Other," 118.

had developed on principles different from, yet in many respects superior to, those of the West.[3]

Thus Confucius became a distant but benign "patron saint" (if a somewhat secularized one!) of the French Enlightenment whilst this reassuring figure took up permanent residence in the repertory of European images of China. Montaigne, Malebranche, Leibnitz, Christian Wolff, Voltaire, Diderot, Montesquieu, Bayle, Adam Smith and Oliver Goldsmith were amongst the many 18th century intellectuals who took a serious and sustained interest in China, though it should be noted that they almost universally dismissed Taoism as a popular superstition of no interest to refined Europeans.[4] In both England and the continent the zeal for matters Chinese was evident throughout the 18th century although for each positive representation we can always find its shadow. In the second part of Defoe's famous novel, Robinson Crusoe travels through China which he finds, in contrast to the achievements, riches and powers of Europe, "a barbarous nation of pagans, little better than savages ... a contemptible herd or crowd of ignorant, sordid slaves, subjected to a government qualified only to rule such a state," their Confucian philosophy being no more than "refined paganism" and their government "an absolute tyranny." Dr Johnson was wary of the "boundless panegyricks (sic) which have been lavished upon the Chinese learning, policy and the arts."[5] As we have been more acutely aware since Edward Said's *Orientalism*, "China, India, Africa and the Islamic Orient have all served as foils to the West at one time or another, either as idealized utopias, alluring and exotic dreamlands, or lands of eternal stagnation, spiritual purblindness, and ignorance."[6]

The encounter of the Enlightenment thinkers with Chinese thought developed against the historical backdrop of the European voyages of discovery and conquest in the 15th and 16th centuries, and the rapid growth in trade and missionary enterprise which came in their wake. The missionaries were to play a critical role in awakening Western understandings of foreign religious doctrines and practices. The first missionaries to penetrate deep into Asia—in India, Tibet and Japan as well as China—were the Jesuits, "the shock troops of the Catholic Counter-Reformation."[7] We remember Fr Ippolito Desideri's remarkable incursion into the alien spiritual universe of the Tibetan Vajrayana. His counterpart in China was Fr Matteo Ricci (1552-1610). The Jesuit missionaries, generally "highly educated and cultured men who had absorbed the mind-broadening ideals of Renaissance humanism,"[8] developed a high regard for Chinese civilization and its cultural manifesta-

3   Zhang Longzi, "The Myth of the Other," 118.
4   See J.J. Clarke, *Oriental Enlightenment*, 99.
5   Defoe and Johnson quoted in Zhang Longzi, "The Myth of the Other," 121 & 122.
6   Zhang Longzi, "The Myth of the Other," 127.
7   J.J. Clarke, *Oriental Enlightenment*, 40.
8   J.J. Clarke, *Oriental Enlightenment*, 40.

tions concerning which they sent back to Europe well-informed reports, translations and commentaries.

By the end of the 18th century Sinophilia, for reasons which need not be rehearsed here, was somewhat on the wane, being replaced by another orientalist enthusiasm which was to reach more dizzying heights—the Romantic ardor for India. China was never to regain its centrality in the European imagination. (The contemporary interest in China arising out of the *Realpolitik* of the late 20th century is, of course, a phenomenon of a quite different kind.) If Voltaire's enthusiasm was characteristic of the 18th century then Emerson's view might represent a commonly held view in the 19th:

> In the grave and never-ending series of sandaled Emperors whose lives were all alike, and whose deaths were all alike, and who ruled over myriads of animals hardly more distinguishable from each other, in the eye of an European, than so many sheeps' faces—there is not one interesting event, no bold revolutions, no changeful variety of manners and character. Rulers and ruled, age and age, present the same doleful monotony, and are as flat and uninteresting as their own porcelain ware.[9]

When we turn to Westerners in search of some kind of spiritual vision in the traditions of the East their comparative lack of enthusiasm for the religious forms of China is quite striking. Certainly there has always been a scholarly interest in Chinese religion but one does not find countless Europeans sitting at the feet of Taoist mystics or Confucian masters. True, there has recently been a growing interest in Taoism and in the contribution it might make to eco-philosophy, a move which we shall pick up later in the study. As J.J. Clarke has remarked, "Chinese Taoism represents the last major wave of Eastern philosophy to break over the Western mind."[10] The principal Chinese legacy to Western seekers is to be found not in China itself but in Japan where Zen Buddhism has exercised a powerful allure for Westerners. Nonetheless, we must give some account of a few representative Westerners who did immerse themselves in Chinese religion and intellectual life. Five figures will briefly command our attention before we cross the Japan Sea: a translator, a missionary-Sinologist, a pilgrim, a metaphysician, and a scientist.

Arthur Waley

An anthology of appreciative essays about the somewhat eccentric Arthur Waley was aptly entitled "Madly Singing in the Mountains." Waley was prone to conversational gambits such as "The verb 'to say' in the *Tao te ching* is never used transitively."[11] He supplies us with an example of a sub-species of orientalist—those whose whole adult life and work is dominated by a country in which they never set foot, in this case China. (Another such case is the

9 Emerson quoted in C.T. Jackson, *The Oriental Religions and American Thought*, 48.
10 J.J. Clarke, *Oriental Enlightenment*, 99.
11 C. Blacker, "Intent of Courtesy," 24.

Mahayanist Buddhologist, Edward Conze, who claimed that meeting living flesh-and-blood Buddhists might turn him off his subject!)[12] Perhaps, as Raymond Mortimer suggested, Waley "felt so much at home in T'ang China and Heian Japan that he could not face the modern ugliness amid which one has to seek out the many intact remains of beauty."[13] Waley also declined many invitations to travel to American universities, explaining in a reply to Columbia University that he was "invincibly set against *déplacements* of any kind."[14]

Waley was born in 1889 in Tunbridge Wells, and educated at Rugby and King's College, Cambridge where he took the Classical tripos. In 1913 he was appointed to the Oriental Sub-department of Prints and Drawings at the British Museum where he worked with Laurence Binyon. He was a formidable linguist and autodidact, and became a fluent reader in Greek, Latin, Italian, Dutch, Portuguese, French, German, Spanish, Ainu, Chinese, and Japanese. Because of his knowledge of Japanese he worked as a censor in the Ministry of Information during World War II following which he was elected Honorary Fellow of King's College and, in 1948, Honorary Lecturer in Chinese Poetry at the School of Oriental Studies. Various honors were bestowed on him by the British and Japanese governments.[15]

Waley published a vast array of translations from the Chinese and Japanese, and wrote several popular and influential commentaries on Eastern art, poetry, and drama. The appearance of *A Hundred and Seventy Chinese Poems* in 1918 was followed by translations of *The No Plays of Japan* (1923), the medieval Japanese *The Tale of Genji* in six volumes (1923-33), *The Pillow Book of Sei Shonagon* (1928), *The Analects of Confucius* (1938) and *Monkey* (1942), as well as a series of commentaries on Chinese painting, Taoist and Confucian philosophy and Chinese shamanism. As a translator Waley always used a "creative" mode of translation rather than a literal and technical word-by-word translation, a technique which attracted some academic flak.[16] His most prodigious feat of translation was of the enormous 10th century Japanese novel, *The Tale of Genji*.

> It must have come as a revelation to many people that a work challenging comparison with Proust in its subtle treatment of time and of mental association, and displaying a quite "modern" development of character, should have appeared some six centuries before the first crude beginnings of the novel in Europe. The sheer application required to translate a work of this size at all (and medieval Japanese is an extremely difficult language to translate from) is staggering. But to have translated with delicacy and tact, and sustained these qualities throughout the book's whole length, so that the

12 E. Conze, *Memoirs of a Modern Gnostic 2*, 30-31.
13 I. Morris, "The Genius of Arthur Waley," 80.
14 I. Morris, "The Genius of Arthur Waley," 81.
15 On Waley's personal life see Alison Waley's *A Half of Two Lives*.
16 See J.M. Cohen, "Dr Waley's Translations," 29-36.

novel emerged in English dress as the great and important work of art it is—this was a work of genius.[17]

Concerning the religio-philosophical tradition of China, Waley's most popular work was probably *Three Ways of Thought in Ancient China* (1939), a book which has been through many printings. We should also note that in 1923, four years before the appearance in the West of D.T. Suzuki's *Essays in Zen Buddhism* and a year before Rudolf Otto's article, Waley produced a substantial essay on Zen Buddhism.[18]

Richard Wilhelm and Carl Jung

Richard Wilhelm's place in the annals of East-West encounters is assured by two singular contributions: the first European translation of the *I Ching* and his role in introducing Carl Jung to Chinese alchemy through *The Secret of the Golden Flower*. Wilhelm had gone to China as a young missionary and was soon engrossed in a study of the Chinese tradition, particularly its most ancient texts. It was through his friendship with a Chinese sage, Lau Nai Süan, that he came to an intensive study of the *I Ching*. Wilhelm and Jung met at Count Keyserling's School of Wisdom at Darmstadt in the early 20s. Jung had already read the *I Ching* (*Book of Changes*) on which Wilhelm was lecturing; it was through this oracular text that the Swiss psychologist developed some of his most arresting ideas about synchronicity. Jung had found corroboration for his own readings of this enigmatic text in Wilhelm's commentary and considered the translation "the greatest of [Wilhelm's] achievements."[19] The two subsequently collaborated on a translation and commentary of the alchemical and mystical text *The Secret of the Golden Flower*, a work which was later described as "one of the cornerstones of the Jungian edifice."[20] It also had a decisive effect on the studies of Heinrich Zimmer even though he was initially so infuriated by Jung's commentary that he "threw the book at the wall."[21] In his autobiography Jung wrote of the missionary and Sinologist,

> Wilhelm was a truly religious spirit ... He had the gift of being able to listen without bias to the revelations of a foreign mentality, and to accomplish that miracle of empathy which enabled him to make the intellectual treasures of China accessible to Europe. He was deeply influenced by Chinese culture, and once said to me, "It is a great satisfaction to me that I never baptized a single Chinese!"[22]

17 D. Hawkes, "From the Chinese," 49.
18 A. Waley, "Zen Buddhism and Its Relation to Art," 1923.
19 C.G. Jung, "Richard Wilhelm: In Memoriam," *Collected Works*, V15, 54.
20 E. Sharpe, *Comparative Religion*, 207. See Jung's "Commentary on *The Secret of the Golden Flower,*" *Collected Works*, V13, 1-55.
21 M. Case, *Heinrich Zimmer*, 7.
22 C.G. Jung, *Memories, Dreams, Reflections*, 407.

Wilhelm eventually took up an appointment at the China Institute in Frankfurt. Jung believed that through a "passive assimilation" he was gradually overwhelmed by the European and Christian milieu in which he now found himself, his "Chinese" personality, as it were, returning to the sub-conscious. Jung:

> Wilhelm's problem might also be regarded as a conflict between consciousness and unconsciousness, which in his case took the form of a clash between West and East ... I understood his situation, since I myself had the same problem ...[23]

Interesting!

John Blofeld

In 1959 the Englishman John Blofeld published *The Wheel of Life: The Autobiography of a Western Buddhist* in which he recalls his many years of travel through China, Southeast Asia, Japan, India and the Himalayan kingdoms. The book belongs to that popular genre, dating back to Homer, which intertwines travel narrative with a spiritual quest. The distinction of this simple but charming book lies in the picture it gives us of pre-Communist southern China and the forms of Buddhism practiced there in pre-revolutionary years. Blofeld (b.1913) spent some seventeen years in China itself, having gone there soon after his conversion to Buddhism and his graduation from Cambridge. He later lived and traveled in Mongolia, Burma, Thailand, Japan and India, working at one time for the United Nations. Although a great admirer of Chinese and Japanese forms of Buddhism it was to the Vajrayana that he gave his deepest commitment. *The Tantric Mysticism of Tibet* (1970) was one of a rush of books in the 60s and 70s introducing Western readers to Tibet's religious heritage.

As well as being a regular contributor to *The Middle Way* Blofeld also wrote a good many useful introductory books on both Chinese Buddhism and Taoism: *The Secret and the Sublime: Taoist Mysteries and Magic* (1973), *Beyond the Gods: Taoist and Buddhist Mysticism* (1974), *Bodhisattva of Compassion: The Mystical Tradition of Kuan Yin* (1977), and *Taoism: the Road to Immortality* (1981). Most of these good-humored books draw heavily on Blofeld's own experiences. He is also the author of several translations of Chinese classics, and books about Bangkok and Peking. His works on Taoism usefully fill a niche between the standard scholarly books about Chinese religious philosophy (Legge *et al.*) and, on the other side, sentimental New-Age appropriations of Taoism. The mainstream non-Chinese religious traditions of the East have all by now generated a vast popular literature by Western writers. Works of this kind on Taoism or Confucianism are comparatively scarce. Blofeld's works can take their place alongside such works as Jean

---

23 C.G. Jung, *Memories, Dreams, Reflections*, 408.

Cooper's more authoritative *Taoism: the Way of the Mystic* (1972) and *Yin and Yang* (1981),[24] Raymond Dawson's *Confucius* (1981), Thomas Merton's engaging and very free rendering of *The Way of Chuang Tzu* (1965) and Alan Watts' *Tao the Watercourse Way* (1975), as books for the intelligent, serious-minded Western lay reader who is often seeking spiritual sustenance rather than the often indigestible fare of the academic scholars. However, to discover the most remarkable of Western writings on the Chinese tradition—neither scholarly nor popular—we must turn to the French metaphysician René Guénon.

René Guénon

The next chapter provides a sustained look at a school of thinkers amongst whom René Guénon was pre-eminent. Guénon's writings on Eastern subjects will be situated in the context of his life and work as a whole. However, it is here worth briefly noting something of his contribution to the study of the Chinese tradition. Guénon's earliest encounters with Taoism came by way of the Ecole Hermétique and the Eglise Gnostique Universelle, two of the principal organs of French esotericism. Through his participation in these organizations Guénon met Albert de Pouvourville. Pouvourville (known in French esoteric circles by his Chinese name, Matgioi) had been a colonial functionary in Tonkin and had received a Taoist initiation whilst in China, going on to publish a translation of the *Tao Te Ching*. The son of Pouvourville's Taoist master visited France to assist with the translation, at this time meeting Guénon. Jean Borella tells us that it is likely that Guénon himself received a Taoist initiation.[25] What is beyond doubt is that Guénon later demonstrated a profound understanding of the mystical and philosophical tradition of China (as opposed to the magico-popular variants).

It was one of Guénon's signal contributions to show that the sharp distinction between Confucianism and Taoism as two separate "systems" was spurious and that they were, respectively, the exoteric and esoteric dimensions of a single tradition which pre-dated them:

> Both Confucianism and Taoism are, each in their own way, merely "re-adaptations" necessitated by conditions which had led to the tradition in its original form no longer being understood in its entirety.[26]

The whole tradition, Guénon insisted, was embryonically present in the trigrams, whose origins are lost in primordial time. The various Chinese "schools," and the apparently divergent Taoist and Confucian branches of the tradition, have only arisen by way of a multitude of contingent applica-

24 Jean Cooper was born in Chefoo in North China and schooled at Kuling. Before her recent death she lived and taught in England.

25 See J. Borella, "René Guénon and the Traditionalist School," and P. Chacornac, *The Simple Life of René Guénon*, 23.

26 R. Guénon, *The Great Triad*, 9.

tions of principles which are in themselves timeless and which bind the tradition as a whole together.[27] (One might draw parallels with the six schools of traditional Indian philosophy, each remaining orthodox and integral to the tradition as a whole while presenting a certain "point of view" [*darsana*]—which is to say that the schools were complementary rather than competitive and mutually exclusive.)

Guénon's ability to fathom ancient metaphysical and cosmological doctrines arose, in large measure, from his penetration of traditional symbolism. It was in this domain that Guénon "opened up" the Chinese tradition in a way quite incomprehensible to those who did not share his grasp of the cosmological and metaphysical principles on which are based all traditional doctrines and techniques—in China as everywhere else. Of Guénon's many magisterial works, the most significant in our present context is *The Great Triad* (the last to be published before his death in 1951) and the essay "Taoism and Confucianism" which first appeared in English in the journal *Tomorrow*. *The Great Triad* explores traditional cosmological and metaphysical doctrines within the framework of the great Taoist ternary Heaven-Man-Earth (*T'ien-Ti-Jen*).

In his essay on Taoism and Confucianism Guénon quotes the *Chuang Tzu* on the perfect sage. The accounts of Guénon in his later years in Cairo (whence he had moved in 1929) testify to the fact that Guénon himself embodied just such an ideal:

> He hath attained such perfect impassibility; for him life and death are alike indifferent, and the upheaval of the world would move him not at all. By penetration he hath reached the Immutable Truth, the Knowledge of the One Universal Principle. He letteth all beings roll on according to their destinies ... The outer sign of his inner state is imperturbability, not that of the warrior who for love of glory swoopeth down upon an army ranged in battle, but that of the spirit, superior to Heaven, to Earth and, to all beings, who dwelleth in a body for which he careth not, taking no account of the images perceived by the senses and knowing all, in his immobile unity, by a knowledge all-embracing.[28]

Joseph Needham

Joseph Needham (1900-1995), biochemist, Master of Gonville and Caius College (Cambridge) and Fellow of the Royal Society, first became interested in the Far East when several young Chinese scientists came to study with him at Cambridge. During World War II Needham led a mission of scientific and technological liaison to China, developing an abiding interest in the history of science in China—the subject of his massive and most distinguished work *Science and Civilization in China*, which Alan Watts described as

27 R. Guénon, "Taoism and Confucianism," 239-241.
28 R. Guénon, "Taoism and Confucianism," 244.

"the most marvelous historical enterprise of this century."[29] Also pertinent to our concerns is a selection of talks and papers, *Within the Four Seas: The Dialogue of East and West* (1969). As a Marxist Needham was sympathetic to the Communist revolution and visited China several times in the 50s and 60s.[30]

In his 1955 presidential addresses to the Britain-China Friendship Association, Needham made the following remarks:

> For three thousand years a dialogue has been going on between the two ends of the Old World. Greatly have they influenced each other ... Many people in Western Europe and European America suffer from what may be called spiritual pride ... In deep ignorance of the intellectual and social conceptions and traditions of other peoples, they think it quite natural to impose upon them their own ideas and customary practices, whether of law, of democratic society, or of political institutions ... Europeans [have] an almost unconscious psychology of domination ... We need to free ourselves from what Claude Roy has so well called "the iron curtain of false enigmas" ...[31]

In the same address, Needham deplored the ignorance that many Westerners still exhibited with regard to all matters Oriental and forcefully dismantled a series of popular misconceptions about China. He also reminds his audience of the great Chinese creations and inventions in many different fields—physics, technology, the arts of government, jurisprudence, philosophy. European civilization has benefited enormously from many Chinese achievements but more often than not Europeans have forgotten the origin of these ideas and discoveries, often claiming them as their own.

Needham also played a part in the sea-change evident in the philosophy of science marked by the growth of the "new physics" and the erosion of the atomistic and mechanistic paradigms of the Galilean-Newtonian picture of the universe. He brought to Western attention various aspects of Taoism which, he said, had been

> much misunderstood if not ignored by Western translators and writers. Taoist religion has been neglected, Taoist magic written off wholesale as nothing more than superstition, and Taoist philosophy interpreted purely as religious mysticism and poetry. The scientific side of Taoism has been largely overlooked.[32]

Needham foregrounded several Taoist themes which he believed could serve as an antidote to the rigid and mechanical determinism of Western science, particularly the understanding of nature as an organic unity, held together

29 A. Watts, *Tao, the Watercourse Way*, xv.

30 His life story has been retold in the rather uncritical *Joseph Needham: 20th Century Renaissance Man* by Maurice Goldsmith. For some fragmentary reminiscences of Needham see E. Conze, *Memoirs of a Modern Gnostic 2*, 57-60.

31 J. Needham, *Within the Four Seas*, 11, 12, 30.

32 J. Needham, *The Shorter Science and Civilization in China*, Vol. 1, 86, quoted in J.J. Clarke, *Oriental Enlightenment*, 169.

in a pattern of inter-relations and processes which could not be understood in simplistic cause-and-effect terms. The affinities of Eastern thought and new scientific paradigms in the West were to become popularized later by writers such as Frithjof Capra and to be often deployed in environmental debates.

Needham's *Science and Civilization in China* has been mobilized as a case-study from which to repudiate some aspects of Foucault's anti-hermeneutics and his theorizing about "the discourses of power," and to question Said's critique of Orientalism. Deploying the work of Alasdair MacIntyre, Arran Gare has persuasively argued that Needham's work, "far from being complicit in Western imperialism, has contributed at least in a small way to the liberation of China from Western domination."[33]

The juxtapositioning of Guénon and Needham suggests several issues which must here, at the least, be touched on. In his address at Richard Wilhelm's memorial service in Munich (May, 1930) Carl Jung recalled an incident when

> The then president of the British Anthropological Society asked me how it was that so highly intelligent a people as the Chinese had produced no science. I replied that this must be an optical illusion, since the Chinese did have a science whose standard textbook was the *I Ching*, but that the principle of this science, like so much else in China, was altogether different from the principle of our science. The science of the *I Ching* is based not on the causality principle but on one which—hitherto unnamed because not familiar to us—I have tentatively called the synchronistic principle.[34]

It was Needham's achievement to annihilate the "optical illusion" but it is also true that his *magnum opus* is marred by certain modernistic and humanistic assumptions which disqualify him from the deepest understanding of many of China's traditional sciences. He fails to grasp what Guénon explicates so forcefully in many of his works—that the modern sciences (which Needham so admires) mark no "advance" on traditional sciences of which they are actually no more than a materialized residue, stripped of all principial understanding (i.e., divorced from the ultimate science of metaphysics). Not surprisingly, given his training as a biochemist, Needham is captive to the scientistic assumptions which are so pervasive in the modern West—evolutionism of both a biological and cultural kind, a materialistic understanding of time and space and of the phenomenal world, a belief that the modern sciences (profane, quantitative, horizontal) are superior to the *sacra scientia* of traditional societies. It is also the case, Needham's intellectual humility and openness notwithstanding, that his understanding of the traditional civilization of China is colored by his own humanistic values. (On the evidence of works other than *Science and Civilization* it is possible to re-construct

33 A. Gare, "Understanding Oriental Cultures," 324.
34 C.G. Jung, "Richard Wilhelm: In Memoriam," 56-57.

Needham's personal philosophy as an idiosyncratic blend of Marxist human-ism, Taoist metaphysics and Christian ethics.)[35] To consolidate the point one might compare Needham's work with that of another contemporary scholar, Seyyed Hossein Nasr, also a historian of science but one thoroughly conver-sant with the traditional outlook which informed all sciences until those of the recent European past.[36]

B. Japan

Ernest Fennellosa and the Late 19th Century

In 1884 the American Japanophile Ernest Fennellosa was completing a search for sacred art works in remote Japanese temples. He wrote to a friend:

> ... I cannot see why my work this summer was not just as important at bot-tom as much of that which the world's archaeologists are doing in Greece and Turkey ... I expect the time will come when it will be considered as nec-essary for a liberally educated man to know the names and deeds of man's great benefactors in the East, and the steps of advance in their culture, as it is now to know Greek and Latin dates and the flavor of their production.[37]

Fennellosa had arrived in Japan in the late 1870s, recruited to teach political economy and philosophy at the Imperial University of Tokyo. Fennellosa was born in Salem in 1853, his father a musician and Spanish immigrant, his mother from a distinguished New England family.[38] Fennellosa studied phi-losophy and divinity at Harvard before taking up drawing, painting and art history at the Boston Museum of Fine Arts. Once in Japan he embarked on an enthusiastic study of traditional sculptures and religious paintings (some-what neglected in Japan itself where many educated people regarded them as feudal relics). Fennellosa did invaluable work in uncovering many neglect-ed masterworks of the Japanese Buddhist tradition. He accumulated a vast collection of Japanese artifacts which was eventually deposited in the Boston Museum. By 1917 the Boston Museum of Fine Arts Far Eastern art collection included five thousand paintings, sixty thousand prints, seven thousand ceramics, eight hundred Noh costumes.[39] The issue of the expatriation of indigenous art treasures from Asian countries is not a subject into which we can enter here but even at this time there was considerable disquiet in both Japan and America about such Western treasure hunts.[40]

---

35 See J. Needham, "Femininity in Chinese Thought and Christian Theology."
36 See S.H. Nasr, *Islamic Science: An Illustrated History*. See also P.L. Wilson, review of *Science and Civilization*, V5.
37 Fennellosa quoted in C.T. Jackson, *Oriental Religions and American Thought*, 202.
38 On Fennellosa's life and his Japanese experiences, see C.T. Jackson, *Oriental Religions and American Thought*, 215-218.
39 See R. Lipsey, *Coomaraswamy: His Life and Work*, 131-132.
40 See R. Fields, *How the Swans Came to the Lake*, 151.

Fennellosa also felt the spiritual attraction of Japan and in 1885 took the precepts (*san-ki-kai*) of Tendai Buddhism.[41] He returned to America where he became involved, with Arthur Wesley Dow, in elaborating a new system of art education. He later crossed swords with the great Buddhologist Rhys Davids, arguing against his view that the Mahayana was a corrupt and degraded form of the "pure" Buddhism of the ancient Theravada. Fennellosa was also a stern critic of the Theosophical brand of "Buddhism" and of the popular notion that Buddhism was "selfish," concerned only with the liberation of the individual.[42]

Following a scandalous divorce and remarriage, Fennellosa returned to Japan and settled in Kyoto where he expanded his Oriental interests to include Noh drama and the Chinese classic, the *I Ching*. He returned finally to America in 1900. On the occasion of his death in 1908 the Japanese government dispatched a warship to collect his ashes for burial in the temple grounds at Miidera.[43] His major work, *Epochs of Chinese and Japanese Art*, completed by his wife Mary, was published in 1912. It was whilst in England to arrange publication that she met the young American poet, Ezra Pound, who was to make creative use of some of Fennellosa's insights into the expressive forms of China and Japan.[44]

Another ground-breaker in the late 19th century awakening of Western interest, was Fennellosa's friend Lafcadio Hearn (1850-1904)—born in Greece, raised in Ireland, educated in France, journalist and novelist in America.[45] Early in life he became disenchanted with the American ethic of competition and success and dedicated himself to "the worship of the Odd, the Queer, the Strange, the Exotic, the Monstrous," cultivating interests in ancient Greek philosophy, Hinduism, Finnish mythology, Arabic and Jewish folklore. His interest in Buddhism was triggered by Arnold's *The Light of Asia*: "It has enchanted me,—perfumed my mind with the incense of a strangely new and beautiful religion."[46] In 1890, he was sent on assignment to Japan by Harper's, never to return. He had found his spiritual domicile and underwent a more or less complete assimilation, formally converting to Buddhism, becoming a Japanese citizen, adopting the kimono, marrying a Japanese woman. Soon after his arrival he wrote in a letter:

> I feel indescribably towards Japan ... What I love in Japan is the Japanese,—
> the poor simple humanity of the country ... There is nothing in the world
> approaching the naïve natural charm of them ... their art is as far in advance

41 C.T. Jackson, *Oriental Religions and American Thought*, 216.
42 R. Fields, *How the Swans Came to the Lake*, 156-158.
43 M. Edwardes, *East West Passage*, 129.
44 R. Fields, *How the Swans Came to the Lake*, 163.
45 On Hearn's life see C.T. Jackson, *Oriental Religions and American Thought*, 223-241, and R. Fields, *How the Swans Came to the Lake*, 159-160.
46 C.T. Jackson, *Oriental Religions and American Thought*, 225.

of our art as old Greek art was superior to that of the earliest European art-gropings ... We are the barbarians. I do not merely think these things: I am as sure of them as of death.[47]

He was the author of *Glimpses of Unfamiliar Japan* (1894) and *Gleanings in a Buddhist Field* (1897), books which inspired a youthful Alan Watts' earliest interest in Buddhism while Edward Conze was another who first came to Buddhism through *Gleanings*.[48] Hearn's impressionistic writings on many aspects of Japanese religion and culture are distinguished by his appreciative accounts of Shintoism, at that time understood hardly at all in the West.[49]

Other late 19th century Americans to take a serious interest in Japanese culture included Edward Morse, a New Englander connected to the Imperial University in Tokyo and author of a classic article, "Latrines of the East," William Sturgis Bigelow, a convert to Buddhism and trustee of the Boston Museum of Fine Arts, the orientalist Percival Lowell and author of *The Soul of the Far East* (1888) (acclaimed by Hearn as "incomparably the greatest of all books on Japan, and the deepest"),[50] the eccentric writer John la Farge and Henry Adams.[51] Given the later Western explosion of interest in Zen it is interesting, and perhaps salutary, to note the absence of any significant mention of this tradition in the works of these European observers.[52]

*

The first Europeans to set foot on Japanese soil were Portuguese sailors, ship-wrecked off a southern Japanese island in 1542. Within three years the Portuguese had commenced trading with Japan while Frances Xavier arrived soon after, the first of a wave of Jesuit missionaries over the next century. Following the *Kirishitan* uprising at Shimbira in 1637-38, the Tokugawa regime issued an edict of national exclusion: foreigners were to remain excluded from Japan for over two centuries until Commodore Perry's gun-boats penetrated Tokyo Bay in 1853. It was not long thereafter that the arts of Japan were exciting a good deal of enthusiasm amongst Western intellectuals and artists, especially in France. A flood of Japonaiserie swept over the country, leaving its mark on the development of Impressionism, *art nouveau* and other artistic movements. Claude Monet acquired his first Japanese prints in 1857 and the Goncourt brothers were launched on their immense collection of Japonaiserie. The enthusiasm soon rippled out from France to other Western capitals. The Japanese craze is evident in the work of the American-born painter James McNeill Whistler who had studied in Paris and

47 C.T. Jackson, *Oriental Religions and American Thought*, 228.
48 A. Watts, *In My Own Way*, 81, 84; E. Conze, "A Personal Tribute," 84.
49 See C.T. Jackson, *Oriental Religions and American Thought*, 232-233.
50 Hearn quoted in C.T. Jackson, *Oriental Religions and American Thought*, 207.
51 On Bigelow see R. Lipsey, *Coomaraswamy: His Life and Work*, 130, and Elsie Mitchell, *Sun Buddhas, Moon Buddhas*, 131-139. On the Boston Buddhists generally see C.T. Jackson, *Oriental Religions and American Thought*, Ch 11.
52 This point is made in R. Sharf, "The Zen of Japanese Nationalism," 146fn3.

settled in England. "The story of the beautiful," he claimed, "is already complete—hewn in the marbles of the Parthenon—and embroidered, with the birds, upon the fans of Hokusai—at the foot of Fusayama."[53] Japanese prints, gardens, lampshades, furniture, lacquered artifacts of every kind, porcelain vases, fans, bamboo fretwork—all these, and much more, found their way into the homes of the English well-to-do. The popularity of Gilbert and Sullivan's *The Mikado* (1885) and Puccini's *Madame Butterfly* (1904) were signs of the times. Rudyard Kipling caught the essentially *aesthetic* appreciation of Japan in the West when he wrote,

> Japan is a great people. Her masons play with stone, her carpenters with wood, her smiths with iron, and her artists with life, death, and all the eye can take in. Mercifully she has been denied the least touch of firmness in her character which would enable her to play with the whole round world. We possess that—We, the nation of the glass flower-shade, the pink worsted mat, the red and green china puppy-dog, and the poisonous Brussels carpet. It is our compensation.[54]

However, it was to be the best part of half a century before Japanese religious forms were to follow Japanese art into the cafés, salons and drawing rooms of the West.

D.T. Suzuki and Western Zen in the Inter-war Years

D.T. Suzuki

A measure of Daisetz Teitaro Suzuki's peculiar standing, as a bridge builder between the two hemispheres, as the most influential expositor of Zen in the modern era, and simply as a man, is to be found in the heartfelt and often moving tributes which were occasioned by his death in 1966. Even an attenuated list of those who expressed the most profound admiration, their deepest respect, often their love, for this gentle and humble Japanese scholar, and who acknowledged debts of a kind that cannot be repaid, reads like an honor roll of East-West cultural and spiritual dialogue. Restricting our list to those Westerners whom we will meet elsewhere in these pages: Robert Aitken, Ernest Benz, Edward Conze, Heinrich Dumoulin, Erich Fromm, Christmas Humphreys, Philip Kapleau, Joseph Kitagawa, Richard De Martino, Thomas Merton, Charles A. Moore, Huston Smith, Gary Snyder, Alan Watts. To these we can add some further well-known names who have testified to the impact of Suzuki's teachings: Carl Jung, Karen Horney, Martin Heidegger, Aldous Huxley, R.H. Blyth, Arnold Toynbee, Allen Ginsberg, Aelred Graham, Gerta Ital, John Cage. Consider: "about the most gentle and enlightened person I have ever known" (Alan Watts);[55] "the 'True Man of No Title,' and a figure

---

53 M. Edwardes, *East West Passage*, 124.
54 Kipling quoted in M. Edwardes, *East West Passage*, 128-129.
55 A. Watts, *In My Own Way*, 89.

whom we may compare with Einstein and Gandhi as a symbol of the century" (Thomas Merton);[56] "a religious leader of genius" (Edward Conze);[57] "an authority purely by his being" (Erich Fromm);[58] "probably the most comprehensive and thoroughgoing scholar in the entire history of Zen" (Charles Moore);[59] "the greatest Buddhist mind of [the] century" (Christmas Humphreys);[60] "a genuine sage" and "the principal spokesman for the epochal breakthrough of Zen in the West" (Heinrich Dumoulin);[61] "the first patriarch of American Zen" (Rick Fields).[62] Reading through these tributes today one is struck by several persistent themes: firstly, Suzuki's saintly qualities as a person—simplicity, humor, generosity, humility, his freedom from egoism, from selfish desires and ambitions, his lightly-worn wisdom which was undoubtedly the flower of his own *satori* (of which he very rarely spoke); secondly, his sense of vocation as an expositor of Zen Buddhism and as a mediator between the East and West, his commitment to this mission being evident in his indefatigable labors and his unstinting generosity in contributing to myriad different efforts at building a global community; thirdly, the radical significance of his contribution to the Western understanding of Zen.

Let us recount the bare facts of his life before highlighting a few aspects of his achievements and touching on some controversies which have accumulated around "the Zen of Japanese Nationalism." Suzuki was born in Kanazawa in 1870.[63] He was a fellow-student and close friend of Nishida Kitara, by many reckonings "the foremost philosopher in modern Japan."[64] Suzuki studied at Tokyo Semmon Gakko (later Waseda University) and at Tokyo Imperial University where his subjects included English Literature, Emerson being the Western writer who made the deepest impress (perhaps rivaled by William James). For four years he practiced the disciplines of Rinzai Zen, including *koan* study, under the tutelage of Imakita Kosen and Soyen Shaku, the "Zen prodigy of the day."[65]

In 1893 Soyen made his landmark appearance in Chicago at the World's Parliament of Religions in Chicago. Whilst the Japanese abbot personally made a less immediate impression than either Vivekananda or Dharmapala, his visit nonetheless sowed a good many seeds that would later grow into the first shoots of a Zen movement within North America. Not the least important fruit of Soyen's visit was the appearance on the American scene of D.T.

56 Thomas Merton, "The Man and His Work," 3.
57 E. Conze, "A Personal Tribute," 84-85.
58 E. Fromm, "Memories of Dr. D.T. Suzuki," 87.
59 C. Moore, "Suzuki: the Man and the Scholar," 17.
60 C. Humphreys, "The Buddhist Society: A Brief History," 11.
61 H. Dumoulin, *Zen Buddhism in the 20th Century*, 5 & 7.
62 R. Fields, *How the Swans Came to the Lake.*
63 The biographical facts which follow are taken primarily from Joseph Kitagawa's obituary, "Daisetz Teitaro Suzuki" and from R. Fields, *How the Swans Came to the Lake*, 136-140, 186-188, 195-197.
64 J. Kitagawa, "Daisetz Teitaro Suzuki," 265.
65 P. Besserman & M. Steger, *Crazy Clouds*, 142.

Suzuki in 1897. Through Soyen Shaku, Suzuki developed an abiding friendship with Dr Paul Carus, translating *The Gospel of Buddha* into Japanese, and living with Dr Carus for over a decade (1897-1909) in La Salle, Illinois, where he worked with the Open Court Publishing Company, of which Carus was the editor.[66] Among his less mundane duties were the translation of the *Tao Te Ching* and Ashvagosha's *The Awakening of Faith in the Mahayana*. It was in this period that Suzuki launched his own long and fertile scholarly career. Robert Sharf has argued that Carus' influence on Suzuki in these years has been willfully neglected by Suzuki's "hagiographers" who lay much more stress on his early Zen training with Soyen Shaku: "we may assume that [Suzuki] continued to imbibe Carus' philosophical monism, his belief in the essential unity of all religions, and his view of pure Buddhism as basically rational, empirical, and scientific"—an understanding which Sharf dismisses as an "ethnographically, historically and philosophically naïve characterization of Buddhism."[67]

In 1908 and 1911 Suzuki visited Europe, each time at the invitation of the Swedenborg Society, Suzuki in this period being under the spell of the Magus of Stockholm. In 1910 Suzuki took up a chair in English Literature at the Peers' School in Tokyo and two years later married an American Theosophist, Beatrice Lane, his constant companion and co-worker until her death in 1939, and herself the author of *Mahayana Buddhism* (1938). In the years before the war his interests expanded to embrace the Pure Land schools of Buddhism and Chinese philosophy. In 1921 he accepted a chair at Otani University where he remained until his "retirement" to Kamakura in 1945. He founded and edited *The Eastern Buddhist* and in the inter-war years traveled extensively in Korea, Manchuria, China, Europe and America. In 1949 he spent a year teaching in Hawaii (a significant locus of the Western encounter with Buddhism) and subsequently spent most of the 50s in America, lecturing on Zen at Columbia University, and continuing his vast output of scholarly and popular books. He was a regular participant in the Philosophy East and West Conferences in Hawaii. After a visit to India in 1960 he returned to Japan where he remained remarkably active and alert to the end of his long life.

Suzuki's scholarly output is far too formidable to catalogue in anything but abbreviated form. (The Japanese *Collected Works* run to some thirty-two volumes.) Amongst his most influential books were a translation of Soyen Shaku's *Sermons of a Buddhist Abbot* (1906), *Outlines of Mahayana Buddhism* (1907), *A Brief History of Chinese Philosophy* (1914), *Essays in Zen Buddhism* (three series, 1927, 1933, 1934), *Studies in the Lankavatara Sutra* (1930), *The Training of the Zen Buddhist Monk* (1934), *Japanese Buddhism* (1938), *The Zen Doctrine of No-Mind* (1949), *Mysticism: Christian and Buddhist* (1957), *Zen and*

66 See L. Fader, "Zen in the West."
67 R. Sharf, "The Zen of Japanese Nationalism," 121.

Japanese Culture (1959), and, with Erich Fromm and Richard De Martino, *Zen Buddhism and Psychoanalysis* (1960). These books have introduced legion Western readers to Zen Buddhism, including many serious practitioners. Assuredly it is no accident that Suzuki's landmark work, *Essays in Zen Buddhism* (1927), was the catalyst of many Western engagements with Zen. However, it is often forgotten that this work did not mark the first European-language appearance of any serious writing on Zen; at the very least we can point to earlier, and important, essays by Arthur Waley and Rudolf Otto in the early 1920s.

Of the many encomiums that have been written to Suzuki's writings, one of the more interesting comes from Thomas Merton (who knew Suzuki personally):

> ... he has left us a whole library of Zen in English ... without question the most complete and authentic presentation of an Asian tradition and experience by any one man in terms accessible to the West.

In his many books on Zen, Merton remarks, Suzuki

> ... says very much the same thing, tells the same wonderful Zen stories perhaps in slightly different words, and ends with the same conclusion: Zero equals infinity. Yet there is no monotony in his works ... because in fact each book is brand new. Each book is a whole new experience. Pseudo-Dionysius says that the wisdom of the contemplative moves in a *motus orbicularis*—a circling and hovering motion like that of the eagle above some invisible quarry, or the turning of a planet around an invisible sun. The work of Dr Suzuki bears witness of a silent orbiting of *prajna* ... one of the unique spiritual and intellectual achievements of our time.[68]

Some of the persistent themes in the writings of this "Zen word magician"[69] include the following: Buddhism is a dynamic tradition, and the opposition between "pure" Theravadin and "corrupt" Mahayana is factitious; the end of Zen practice is *satori* in the light of which all Zen teachings are to be understood; the enlightenment experience to which Zen disciplines gives access is not essentially different from the mystical experiences of adepts of other traditions; indeed, there is an underlying unity of all religions; there is no fundamental discord between Buddhism and science. Suzuki's understanding of Zen grew out of the Rinzai tradition, with its emphasis on *satori*; the Soto tradition is somewhat marginal in his work. Dumoulin has remarked that "This neglect is not merely a superficial deficiency; it profoundly affects the character of what has been called 'Suzuki Zen,' leading to an excessive emphasis on the paradoxical and irrational."[70]

68 T. Merton, "The Man and His Work," 6, 8.
69 H. Tworkov, *Zen in America*, 6.
70 H. Dumoulin, *Zen Buddhism in the 20th Century*, 5.

Robert Sharf's Critique of Suzuki's Zen

Robert Sharf, one of a clutch of post-Saidian theorizers who have turned their attention to the interactions of Orientalism and Buddhism, has argued that Suzuki's construction of Zen bears the imprint of unorthodox, modern (post-Meiji) developments within Japan, of Japanese cultural chauvinism, and of Occidental values and assumptions such as those Suzuki absorbed from Paul Carus and other Western intellectuals. He also seeks to explain the appeal of Zen in the West in these terms:

> Philosophers and scholars of religion were attracted to Zen for the same rea-
> son that they were attracted to the mysticism of James, Otto and Underhill:
> it offered a solution to the seemingly intractable problem of relativism
> engendered in the confrontation with cultural difference. The discovery of
> cultural diversity, coupled with the repudiation of imperialist and racist
> strategies for managing cultural difference, threatened to result in "the
> principle of arbitrariness" ... In mysticism intellectuals found a refuge from
> the distressing verities of historical contingency and cultural pluralism.[71]

He returns to the theme of "intercultural mimesis" which we met with in Charles Hallisey's analysis of the 19th century constructions of Theravadin Buddhism:

> The irony ... is that the "Zen" that so captured the imagination of the West
> was in fact a product of the New Buddhism of the Meiji. Moreover, those
> aspects of Zen most attractive to the Occident—the emphasis on spiritual
> experience and the devaluation of institutional forms—were derived in
> large part from Occidental sources. Like Narcissus, Western enthusiasts
> failed to recognize their own reflection in the mirror being held out to
> them.[72]

This, says Sharf, prevented both sides from "recognizing the historical mischief entailed in the radical decontextualization of the Zen tradition."[73]

Sharf has performed a useful service in demystifying some of the sentimental aura which has gathered around Zen and in locating the work of Suzuki, and Western responses to it, in a firm historical context. Granted, too, that we need to be wary of those "representatives" of Eastern traditions who have diluted or compromised traditional teachings, adapting them to appeal to the Western prejudices and fashions of the moment, not to mention the further distortions often brought about by their epigones. In an earlier chapter precisely this kind of criticism was pressed against some of the neo-Hindu reformers. Doubtless, too, Sharf's specific criticisms of some aspects of Suzuki's work are cogent: we need not hide from the fact that Suzuki's work did indeed exhibit certain "ideological and rhetorical dimensions."[74] No problem here. But the effect of Sharf's essay as a whole, only par-

71 R. Sharf, "The Zen of Japanese Nationalism," 139.
72 R. Sharf, "The Zen of Japanese Nationalism," 140.
73 R. Sharf, "The Zen of Japanese Nationalism," 140.
74 R. Sharf, "The Zen of Japanese Nationalism," 145.

tially mitigated by a later postscript, is dismissive and condescending. Furthermore, his asseverations and judgments should be treated with the same kind of critical rigor on which such critics pride themselves. A lengthy critique of Sharf's thesis would be out of place here, so a few simple observations must suffice to indicate the possible lines along which it might be advanced. Firstly, there is nothing reprehensible about recognizing that there is a way out of the *cul-de-sac* of relativism—not everyone believes that *everything* can be explained in terms of "the distressing verities of historical contingency and cultural pluralism"; nor is it necessary to reproach "philosophers and scholars of religion" for finding a "refuge" from a corrosive relativism, any more than one would reproach a man for fleeing an angry tiger. A "radical decontextualization of the Zen tradition" might, actually, represent a healthy escape from a historicism which has oppressed the Western mind for some centuries now.[75] In discerning an esoteric and changeless core in Zen Buddhism we may be liberating ourselves from an Occidental prejudice which these Saidian critics, good secularists that they are, are utterly unable to recognize and which immunizes them against the very wisdom which Suzuki wishes to affirm. Empirical historicism and its unlikely accomplice, the over-valuation of Theory, can, after all, only take us so far! The key to Sharf's own commitments and, dare one say, prejudices, lies near the end of his article where, after again tediously disparaging "romanticized notions of true or essential religion" he claims that the "complex dialogue" of orientalism, comparative religion and Asian intellectuals and spiritual leaders "raises serious questions as to the very foundation of the secular study of comparative religion in the West"—as if this was self-evidently a Bad Thing! Many believe, as I do, that the "secular study of comparative religion" is precisely what *does* need to be questioned, especially if we decode this phrase to expose its true meaning—the study of comparative religion on the basis of a rootless humanism which is committed to nothing more than "the distressing verities of historical contingency and cultural pluralism." Perhaps this is what explains Sharf's animus towards Suzuki, the very fact that he was, through the vehicle of scholarship, a *religious teacher*. ("Apologetics" is a very grubby word in the Sharfian lexicon!) And one more thing: what point is there in laboring the fact that Suzuki was neither monk nor Master? He never pretended to be either.

The Growth of Zen in America

In the inter-war years a good many Japanese Zen masters traveled to Europe and the USA. Zen halls appeared in San Francisco in 1928, and in Los Angeles the following year; the Buddhist Society of America, which later became the First Zen Institute for America, was established in 1931. As Dumoulin observes,

---

75 This issue is touched on in the well-known controversy between the Chinese historian Hu Shih and Suzuki himself in 1953. See T.H. Barrett, "Arthur Waley, D.T. Suzuki and Hu Shih."

A great variety of Zen forms were propagated—those of traditional Buddhist schools and lineages, with variants introduced by individual masters, and also secularized forms, which tended to dissolve the religiously Buddhist character of Zen. Whether Zen was bound to be denatured by this transportation became a serious question ...[76]

... and has remained so ever since.

Amongst the seminal figures in the emergence of American Zen we must first mention Nyogen Senzaki (1876-1958), a monk and another of Soyen Shaku's disciples (although, like Suzuki, not a "lineage holder").[77] Another early arrival was the Japanese monk Sokei-an who, nearly three decades later was to be the prime mover in establishing the Buddhist Society in New York. Senzaki was the first Japanese Zen teacher to take up permanent residence in the USA. Found by a traveling Soto monk as an orphaned baby in Siberia, Senzaki was schooled in Soto Zen, Shingon and the Chinese classics before moving to the Engaku Temple to study with Soyen Shaku. As well as undergoing five years of Rinzai Zen training Senzaki studied Western philosophy and was significantly influenced by the German thinker Friedrich Froebel. He proved to be something of a maverick within the Zen establishment and strained relations with his master by denouncing the nationalistic fervor that embroiled Japan in the Russo-Japanese War of 1905, enthusiastically supported in most Zen monasteries.[78] Senzaki accompanied Soyen on his visit to the West Coast in 1905, and remained there after being instructed not to teach for twenty years, an interdiction which Senzaki observed, working for two decades as a domestic, dish washer, elevator operator, laundryman, clerk and, briefly, hotel owner. In 1922 he started renting halls ("floating zendos") and giving public talks on Zen. By the early 30s he had gathered together a small band of American followers dedicated to at least rudimentary Zen training. Like most other Japanese in America he was interned during World War II. Among his many students after the war was Robert Aitken, who had been interned in Japan. After a long residence in America Nyogen Senzaki identified eight aspects of the national life and character which made the country receptive to Zen: American philosophy is practical; Americans do not cling to formality; the majority are optimists; Americans love nature; they are capable of simple living; universal brotherhood is one of their highest ideals; the American conception of morality is rooted in the individual; Americans are rational thinkers.[79] Hmm! Senzaki died in 1958. Of American Zen he wrote,

> America has had Zen students in the past, has them in the present, and will have many of them in the future. They mingle easily with so-called

76 H. Dumoulin, *Zen Buddhism in the 20th Century,* 9.

77 On Senzaki see R. Fields, *How the Swans Came to the Lake* (see index); C. Besserman & M. Steger, *Crazy Clouds,* 138-157; R. Aitken, *Original Dwelling Place,* 7-14; J. Coleman, *The New Buddhism,* 59.

78 See B. Victoria, *Zen at War.*

79 See C. Besserman & M. Steger, *Crazy Clouds,* 155.

worldlings. They play with children, respect kings and beggars, and handle gold and silver as pebbles and stones.[80]

It was through Senzaki's efforts that another influential Japanese teacher appeared in America in 1949, the Rinzai teacher Nakagawa Soen (1907-1984).[81] In turn Soen was instrumental in the arrival in 1962 of Haku'un Yasutani (1885-1973), student of Dai'un Harada (1871-1961) in the Soto tradition originating in Eihie Dogen Zenji (1200-1253). Harada was "long considered the regenerative force of Soto Zen in this century."[82] Soen and Yasutani were each to leave an indelible mark on American Zen, through their teaching and example, and through their American disciples and dharma-heirs. These Zen teachers from Japan were soon to be joined by several more who have become iconic figures in American Zen, among them Taizan Maezumi (b. 1931) and Shunryu Suzuki (1904-1971). We shall not here attempt to unravel the tangled skein of Rinzai and Soto lineages and transmissions: interested readers can find these detailed elsewhere.[83] Nor need we dwell on the differences between the Rinzai and Soto traditions except to say that the former is distinguished by its orientation towards *satori* and by the use of *koans* whilst the latter emphasizes *zazen* ("just sitting") without undue concern for any results. Several of the Zen teachers in the West have tended to blur these differences and to eschew the more divisive aspects of Japanese monastic sectarianism.

Helen Tworkov has argued that "From the 1930s to the 1950s, Zen traveled a fairly narrow channel in the United States from a recognizable intelligentsia to the avant-garde underground [i.e. the Beats]."[84] Prominent in the "recognizable intelligentsia" were the wealthy Californian Japanophiles, Mr and Mrs Alexander Russell, Senzaki's first hosts. Ruth Fuller Everett spent some months in a Japanese monastery, became a leading light in the Buddhist Society of America, and later married Sokei-an, taking his family name of Sasaki.[85] Alan Watts, youthful author of *The Spirit of Zen* (1935) and Ruth Fuller Everett's son-in-law, was destined to become one of Zen's most successful popularizers.[86] Dwight Goddard, an engineer, one-time Congregationalist missionary in China and in later life a Zen practitioner, attempted to found an American monastic order but his real success was as the editor of *ZEN, a Magazine of Self-Realization* first published in 1930, later

---

80 Senzaki quoted in R. Aitken, *Original Dwelling Place*, 14.

81 On Soen see Aitken's fascinating essay "Remembering Soen Roshi" in *Original Dwelling Place*, 15-22.

82 H. Tworkov, *Zen in America*, 12.

83 See A. Rawlinson, *The Book of Enlightened Masters*, 316-317, 534; H. Tworkov, *Zen in America*, 253. See also Chapter 11.

84 H. Tworkov, *Zen in America*, 7.

85 On Ruth Fuller Everett/Sasaki see R. Fields, *How the Swans Came to the Lake*, 187-192. For a miniature portrait see I. Schloegl, "My Memory of Ruth Fuller Sasaki."

86 On Watts see Chapter 10.

to become *A Buddhist Magazine*, and as the author of *A Buddhist Bible* (1932), a popular anthology of Buddhist Scriptures.[87] Nancy Wilson Ross was a journalist, traveler, novelist and author of *Three Ways of Asian Wisdom*, *The World of Zen* and *Buddhism: A Way of Life and Thought*. Elsie Mitchell, a post-war pilgrim to Japan, underwent a *tokudo* (ordination) ceremony in the Soto tradition, founded the Cambridge Buddhist Association, and was the author of *Sun Buddhas, Moon Buddhas* (1973). She was also interested in Christian-Buddhist dialogue and friendly with Dom Aelred Graham.[88] Tworkov's "avant-garde underground" of the 50s will command our attention in a later chapter, as will the emergence of a whole generation of American Zen teachers, both within and outside the traditional lineages. But now we turn to some rapid snap-shots of sundry European figures who also felt the enticements of Zen, most of them spending some time in the zendos of Japan.

Europeans in Japan

Eugen Herrigel, Karlfried Graf Dürckheim, Gerta Ital, Irmgard Schloegl

Eugen Herrigel was born near Heidelberg in 1884. He studied theology and philosophy at university, and was much influenced by neo-Kantianism as well as developing a serious interest in Eckhartian mysticism. From 1924 to 1929 he taught philosophy at Tokyo University and for six years devoted himself to Zen training and to the ancient art of archery (*kyujutsu*) on which subject he produced a small volume, *Zen in the Art of Archery* (1953), highly popular in the 60s not only in the West but also in Japan.[89] Herrigel returned to Germany to take up a position at Erlangen University where he remained until his retirement in 1951. Herrigel also wrote an introduction to Zen practices, *The Method of Zen* (1960), which was arranged from his notes after his death in 1955. His wife, Gustie, produced a companion volume to the monograph on archery, *Zen in the Art of Flower Arrangement* (1958). Both books were introduced by D.T. Suzuki with whom the Herrigels were friendly.[90]

Count Karlfried Graf Dürckheim was another German drawn to Japan in the inter-war years.[91] He was born in Munich in 1896, served in World War I, studied philosophy and psychology at Munich and Kiel, taking academic

87 See R. Aitken, "The Christian-Buddhist Life of Dwight Goddard."
88 On Nancy Wilson Ross and Elsie Mitchell see S. Boucher, Turning the Wheel, 184-191. On Aelred Graham, see Chapter 16.
89 Herrigel's account of archery and of his own experiences under his teacher, Awa Kenzo, have recently come under sustained critical scrutiny, Yamada Shoji arguing that Herrigel was a "credulous enthusiast" and a principal contributor to a contemporary Western mythology of "Japanese-ness." See Yamada Shoji, "The Myth of Zen in the Art of Archery."
90 Information on the Herrigels taken from their own books and from Yamada Shoji, "The Myth of Zen in the Art of Archery."
91 His full name was Karl Friedrich Alfred Heinrich Ferdinand Maria Graf von Dürckheim! Biographical information taken from A. Rawlinson, *The Book of Enlightened Masters*, 251-254; G. Wehr, "C.G. Jung and Christian Esotericism," 395-396; G. Wehr, "The Life and Work of Karlfried Graf Dürckheim" at website: http://tedn.hypermart.net/trans3.htm.

appointments in Leipzig, Breslau and Kiel. During the 30s Dürckheim did informal diplomatic work for the National Socialists before being sent to Japan where he remained until the end of the war. He had been deeply affected by the *Tao Te Ching* soon after the Great War, particularly by this verse:

> Thirty spokes converge upon a single hub, It is on the hole in the center that the use of the cart hinges, We make a vessel from a lump of clay, It is the empty space within the vessel that makes it useful. We make the doors and windows for a room; but it is these empty spaces that make the room livable. Thus, while the tangible has advantages, it is the intangible that makes it useful.

Dürckheim described a powerful experience triggered by this passage:

> And suddenly it happened! I was listening and lightning went through me. The veil was torn asunder, I was awake! I had just experienced "It." Everything existed and nothing existed. Another Reality had broken through this world. I myself existed and did not exist ... I was seized, enchanted, someplace else and yet here, happy and deprived of feeling, far away and at the same time deeply rooted in things. The reality which surrounded me was suddenly shaped by two poles: one which was the immediately visible and the other an invisible which was the essence of that which I was seeing. I truly saw Being.[92]

In Japan he inevitably encountered D.T. Suzuki, practiced *zazen* with a number of Masters, trained in archery after reading an article by Herrigel, and became interested in the tea ceremony, martial arts and T'ai Ch'i. He was arrested at war's end by the Americans and spent sixteen months in prison where he did a good deal of meditating. After returning to Europe he developed a distinctive form of "initiation therapy" which drew heavily on Zen, Eckhartian mysticism and the analytical psychology of Carl Jung (an intersection of interests which we also find in Suzuki's work). Dürckheim's approach was marked by a willingness to use the insights of Jungian psychology while at the same time avoiding the pitfalls of a psychologistic reductionism in the spiritual and religious domain.[93] His most widely known works in the English-speaking world are *Hara: the Vital Center of Man* (1956), *The Japanese Cult of Tranquility* (1960), *The Way of Self-Transformation* (1974) and *The Grace of Zen* (1977). Dürckheim died in 1988. Both Eugen Herrigel and Dürckheim (as well as Giuseppe Tucci and Heinrich Harrer) have been inculpated in the linkages between European fascism and orientalism.[94]

---

92 Dürckheim and *Tao Te Ching* quoted in G. Wehr, "The Life and Work of Karlfried Graf Dürckheim."
93 See G. Wehr, "C.G. Jung and Christian Esotericism," 395-396.
94 Rawlinson suggests that Herrigel was actually much more sympathetic to Nazism than Dürckheim but does not adduce any evidence for the claim (which I have no reason to disbelieve). A. Rawlinson, *The Book of Enlightened Masters*, 252.

Gerta Ital was an acclaimed actress from a sophisticated European background when she became a student of Eugen Herrigel, by then back in Germany.[95] In 1962 she entered monastic training in Japan, living in a temple for two extended stays during the 60s and becoming a disciple of the lay Zen Master, Roshi Mumon Yamada. Her experiences are recounted in two memoirs, *The Master, Monks and I* (1962) and its sequel *On the Way to Satori* (1971). In her later years she was interested in inter-religious dialogue but somewhat frustrated by the recalcitrant exclusivism of the Catholic hierarchy, despite the real advances made on this front at Vatican II.[96] Like Dürckheim she took a critical interest in the work of Jung. Ital died in 1988.

Irmgard Schloegl (Myokyo-ni) was born and educated in Austria where she completed a doctorate in natural sciences.[97] She moved to England in 1950 to become a lecturer in geology at the University of London. Her interest in Zen was sparked in one of Christmas Humphreys' classes, leading to twelve years of Rinzai training in Kyoto (1962-74) under Oda Sesso Roshi and Soko Morinaga Roshi (each of these being students of Goto Zuigan Roshi). Schloegl eventually returned to London, becoming the librarian of the Buddhist Society, a translator, writer and teacher. In 1984 she became a fully ordained Rinzai priest, one of very few fully credentialed women Rinzai Zen teachers in the West (others are Maurine Stewart and Jiyu Kennett). She has published an anthology of Zen stories and aphorisms, *Wisdom of the Zen Masters* (1975), *The Zen Way* (1977), and translated *Zen Teaching of Rinzai* (1976), and *Gentling the Bull* (1987); her writings on Zen are concise and thoroughly traditional in outlook, making little concession to Western prejudices.

R.H. Blyth, Harold Stewart and Adrian Snodgrass

Shojun Bando recalls his days as a young student at Tokyo University where he attended classes on English Literature, given by a foreigner who frequently referred in his lectures to haikus which

> left a strong impression in the minds of us young students; for they helped in turning our attentions inwards rather than outwards, to things Oriental or traditionally Japanese, to which we had become completely insensitive.[98]

The man in front of the class was Reginald Horace Blyth, English tutor to the Crown Prince. Blyth was born into a working class family in London in 1898.[99] He left England after three years of hard labor to which he was sentenced for his conscientious objection to the war. After a period in India, where he was repelled by the colonialist attitudes of his compatriots, he

95 See G. Ital, *On the Way to Satori*.
96 See Ital's postscript in *On the Way to Satori*.
97 See A. Rawlinson, *The Book of Enlightened Masters*, 515.
98 Shojun Bando, "In Memory of Professor Blyth," 134.

moved to Korea where he taught English at Seoul University and first became interested in Zen, spending some time in a Rinzai temple. He arrived in Japan in 1940 where, with the outbreak of war, he found himself interned as an enemy national. He made good use of four years of incarceration, writing *Zen in English Literature and Oriental Classics* (1942) "a grand cultural leap"[100] through which he examined both the English literary canon and Zen in the light each threw on the other. He also started work on the four-volume work *Haikus* (1949) which was to be devoured by the Beat poets in the following decade.[101] Another internee in Japan at the time was a young Robert Aitken who read Blyth's first book at least ten times, eventually meeting the author himself when their separate camps were consolidated.[102] Blyth returned to teaching after the war, married a Japanese woman with whom he had two daughters and spent the rest of his life in Japan, passing away in 1964.

Blyth became known in the West as the author of over a dozen books on various aspects of the Zen tradition, particularly its poetry and the haiku form. His first love was always poetry, on which he wrote with great warmth:

> What is the standard by which we judge all things, judge Zen itself, which is the essence of Christianity, the essence of Buddhism? It is not morality, or aesthetics, or science: it is "poetry," a faculty by which we know the living truth ... Poetry transmutes everything into itself, but poetry is a kind of pain, whose depth reconciles us to it.[103]

He was also a lover of nature, an iconoclast and a vinegary wit ("All teaching must be more or less malicious"), and something of a misogynist.[104] His books have been described as "wry, ironic, common-sensical, pessimistic and rigorously non-metaphysical."[105] Amongst his most widely-read works, along with those already mentioned, were *Japanese Humor* (1957), *Zen and the Classics* (1960-64)[106] and *A History of Haiku* in two volumes (1963-64). Each and every book Blyth published is dedicated to his friend D.T. Suzuki. Some of Blyth's most popular writings were assembled in *Games Zen Masters Play: Writings of R.H. Blyth* (1976).

Given Blyth's association with haiku, mention might also be made at this juncture of two Australians who spent many years in Japan. The Australian poet Harold Stewart (1916-1995)[107] achieved some renown in his own country as one of the principal perpetrators of a celebrated literary hoax, the

99 On Blyth's life and work see D. T. Suzuki, "Reginald Horace Blyth (1898-1964)" and "Ancestors: R.H. Blyth" in *Tricycle* (website).

100 R. Fields, *How the Swans Came to the Lake*, 201.

101 See R. Fields, *How the Swans Came to the Lake*, 212.

102 R. Fields, *How the Swans Came to the Lake*, 210.

103 R.H. Blyth, *Zen and Zen Classics*, quoted by Shojun Bando, "In Memory of Professor Blyth," 136.

104 See R. Aitken, *Original Dwelling Place*, 26.

105 T. Ferris, "Past Present" (website).

106 By the time of Blyth's death only three of the eight volumes he envisaged were complete.

107 Information on Harold Stewart taken from Peter Kelly, *Buddha in a Bookshop*.

"Ern Malley" affair. Stewart was associated with a group of Australian writers and artists interested in the traditionalist writings of René Guénon and Ananda Coomaraswamy. In 1966 he settled in Kyoto where he spent the last three decades of his life, devoted to the study of Shin and haiku, as well as to his own poetry. Stewart was a close friend of Shojun Bando with whom he worked on a translation of the Shin classic, *Tannisho*. Although of somewhat reclusive temperament Stewart became a well-known identity in Kyoto. He is best remembered for two major poetic works, *A Net of Fireflies: Japanese Haiku and Haiku Paintings* and *By the Walls of Kyoto: A Year's Cycle of Landscape Poems and Prose Commentaries*. The latter is a four hundred and sixty page narrative poem diffused with the spirit of Shin Buddhism; the second half of the book is made up of discursive essays on many different aspects of Japanese culture.

Adrian Snodgrass also became interested in Oriental art and architecture through the works of Ananda Coomaraswamy. After training and practicing as an architect he left Sydney at the age of twenty-five to study Sanskrit and Indian art. After five years in India he moved to Japan where he mastered Buddhist hybrid Sanskrit, Chinese and Japanese, and trained in both Shingon and Jodo-shin. Further travels throughout Southeast Asia were followed by a seven-year stay in Japan. He returned to Sydney in 1974 to take up a position at Sydney University.[108] He is the author of three imposing scholarly works, *The Symbolism of the Stupa* (1985), *Architecture, Time and Eternity* (2 vols.) (1990) and *The Matrix and Diamond World Mandalas in Shingon Buddhism* (2 vols.) (1992).

Three Writers in Japan

Nikos Kazantzakis, the distinguished Greek poet and novelist, visited both China and Japan in the mid-30s, leaving us an account of his experiences in *Travels in China and Japan*. Whilst there is little sustained description of religion as such the book is adorned with many sharp insights and poetic passages. Here, for instance, is a passage on Mt. Fuji and its place in the Japanese psyche:

> Sky-high, pure white, snow-clad from the foot to the summit, disciplined in the simplest curves, full of grace and power, airy, tranquil and silent, the holy mountain of Japan is silhouetted on the sapphire sky ... The Japanese see Fuji with pure eyes. Surely, looking at it, their souls take in its silhouette, austere, restrained, full of grace. This mountain is the true ancestor god, who created in his own image the Japanese. Legends, gods, fairy tales, phantoms, all the play of the Japanese imagination, were also created in his own image ... Fuji subjugated the Japanese hands into its own rhythm, and in the smallest thing, carved in wood, stone or ivory, you will discern the nobility of Fuji's form, the decisive flow without vain unnecessary curves. The heart of Japan is not, as the Japanese song goes, the cherry blossom; the heart of

108 Information on Adrian Snodgrass based on personal communication.

Japan is Fuji: an indomitable fire, covered, in a disciplined way, with untrodden snows.[109]

A reviewer in *The Middle Way* described Janwillem van der Wetering's *The Empty Mirror* (1973) as "a delightful record of a young man stumbling into a Japanese Zen monastery."[110] The operative words here are "delightful" and "stumbling." It is an often amusing and candid story of a confused, sometimes weak-willed but likeable Dutchman struggling to come to terms with the demands of monastic life. This book was followed by his account of a stay in an unidentified American Zen community, *A Glimpse of Nothingness* (1974).[111] Van der Wetering's books are down-to-earth antidotes to some of the more rarified accounts of Zen practice. Van der Wetering was born in Rotterdam in 1931, lived and worked in the textile business in Amsterdam, and is the author of a series of detective novels.

Peter Matthiessen is a well-known novelist, naturalist and explorer. In the previous chapter mention was made of his best-selling account of a journey through Western Nepal, *The Snow Leopard*. Less well known is the fact that Matthiessen is a fully ordained Zen roshi, trained under Soen Nakagawa Roshi, Shimano Eido Roshi, Taizan Maezumi Roshi and Tetsugen Glassman-sensei. *Nine-Headed Dragon River* (1986) is a fine book which intersperses an account of Matthiessen's personal journey with a history of Japanese Zen, and much intelligent commentary on Zen in America.

A Note on Shin and Other Japanese Traditions

In this rapid survey of the modern Western fascination with Japan we have concentrated on Zen, undoubtedly the most influential of Japanese religious forms in Europe and America. However, it should not be forgotten that Buddhism constitutes only one strand in the religious heritage and spiritual life of Japan, and within Buddhism itself the Pure Land, Shingon and Nicheren schools each have more adherents than does Zen. We might also note in passing that the Zen tradition is not restricted to Japan, and that Vietnamese Zen Buddhists such as Thich Nhat Hanh and Thich Thien-An have also played a role in its Western dissemination. Archaic shamanism (still practiced), Shintoism, Japanese Confucianism and Jodo/Shin Buddhism have also attracted the interest and the spiritual commitment of a significant (though comparatively small) number of Westerners. Some milestone works on these traditions include Joseph Kitagawa's *Religion in Japanese History* (1966), Carmen Blacker's *The Catalpa Bow: A Study of Shamanistic Practices in Japan* (1975), and D.T. Suzuki's *Shin Buddhism*.[112] Joseph Kitagawa (b. 1915,

109 N. Kazantzakis, *Travels in China and Japan*, 166-167.
110 Quoted on the cover of J. van der Wetering, *A Glimpse of Nothingness*.
111 The community in question was actually the Moonspring Hermitage, founded by Roshi Walter Nowick in 1969. Nowick was a professional pianist who first came to Zen through Sokei-an's First Zen Institute in New York before training at Daitokuji with Zuigan Goto Roshi, becoming the first Western Dharma-heir in the Rinzai tradition. See A. Rawlinson, *The Book of Enlightened Masters*, 458-459.
112 Suzuki's book has recently been reprinted under the new title *The Buddha of Infinite Light*.

Osaka), a Japanese-American has been a leading member of the "Chicago school" of comparative religionists. His father was a Confucianist-turned-Christian minister in Kashiwara City where Kitagawa grew up. Kitagawa joined the University of Chicago in 1951, was Dean of the Divinity School for some years, a close associate of Mircea Eliade and a frequent visitor to the land of his birth.[113] He is a recognized authority on the Japanese religious tradition as a whole. Some of his most important essays have been gathered together in *On Understanding Japanese Religion* (1987). Carmen Blacker lectured in Japanese at Cambridge University and did some Zen training in Japan in the early 50s, well before Zen practice became, in her words, "the modish and silly form of exhibitionism which we heard so much about in the late 50s and 60s."[114]

The handful of Westerners who became Shin Buddhists in the pre-World War II years include M.T. Kirby who went to Japan in 1913, practiced Shin before transferring to Rinzai and was possibly the first Westerner to become a sensei (teacher); Ernest Hunt (1878-1967), an Englishman who became a Shin Buddhist in Hawaii in 1924 before later ordination in the Soto tradition, and who may well have been the first Westerner to attain the rank of "Osho"; and Robert Clifton (1903-1963), who was ordained as a Shin priest in San Francisco in 1933 and later came under the influence of Sokei-an Sasaki in New York, subsequently becoming a novitiate at the Soto Temple of Tsurumi.[115] Shin Buddhism is sometimes disparaged by Western Zen enthusiasts as a "Christian" and/or "superstitious" form of Buddhism. In this context it is worth recalling D.T. Suzuki's remark that many more Buddhists have been liberated through the heartfelt devotions of Shin than through all the insights of Zen and Ch'an put together.[116]

*

No doubt there is still a good deal of truth in the observation made by George Sansom in 1953: "Few countries have been more copiously described than Japan, and perhaps few have been less thoroughly understood."[117] Nevertheless, in the five decades since Sansom's remark, Zen Buddhism has become better understood and a remarkably pervasive influence in Western culture, especially in America. Later in this study we shall inquire into several other aspects of the Western assimilation of Zen Buddhism. As well as portraying some of the principal Western Zen teachers in the contemporary world we shall return to Zen Buddhism in relation to fascism and orientalism, existentialist philosophy, psychotherapy, aesthetics and expressive forms, inter-religious dialogue and Christian renewal, eco-sophy and the environmental movement, and the "feminization" of Buddhism.

113 See Notes on Contributors in J. Kitagawa & M. Eliade (eds), *The History of Religions: Essays on Methodology*, 162, and J. Kitagawa, *On Understanding Japanese Religion*, ix-x.
114 C. Blacker, "Some Reminiscences of Zen Training in Japan," 107.
115 On Kirby, Hunt and Clifton see A. Rawlinson, *The Book of Enlightened Masters*, 613, 612, 211-212.
116 See J. Kornfield, "Buddhism in America," xxvi.
117 Sansom quoted in J. Kitagawa, *On Understanding Japanese Religion*, 286.

8.

Traditionalism and the *Sophia Perennis*

Introduction—René Guénon, Tradition and Oriental Metaphysics—Ananda Coomaraswamy, Scholar and Dharma-Warrior—Frithjof Schuon and the *Religio Perennis* in East and West—Other Traditionalists

---

> ... there are those whose vocation it is to provide the keys with which the treasury of wisdom of other traditions can be unlocked, revealing to those who are destined to receive this wisdom the essential unity and universality and at the same the formal diversity of tradition and revelation. (Seyyed Hossein Nasr)[1]

Introduction

We have already met with Ananda Coomaraswamy's claim that

> ... if we are to consider what may be the most urgent practical task to be resolved by the philosopher, we can only answer that this is ... a control and revision of the principles of comparative religion, the true end of which science ... should be to demonstrate the common metaphysical basis of all religions ... [2]

This, precisely, is one of the central tasks of a group of thinkers who can be gathered together under the term "traditionalists." It was the French writer René Guénon who was the first to articulate the traditionalist perspective in modern times. Since the time of Guénon's earliest writings, early in the 20th century, a significant traditionalist "school" has emerged with Guénon, Coomaraswamy and Frithjof Schuon recognized as its most authoritative exponents. The traditionalists are committed to the explication of the timeless wisdom which lies at the heart of the diverse religions and behind their manifold forms. But, unlike many so-called perennialists, they are also dedicated to the preservation and illumination of the divinely-appointed forms which give each religious heritage its *raison d'être,* providing its formal integrity and ensuring its spiritual efficacy.[3] The traditionalists stand implacably opposed to the prevailing modern

---

1 S.H. Nasr, *Sufi Essays*, 126.
2 A.K. Coomaraswamy, *What is Civilization? and Other Essays*, 18.
3 The traditionalists are still conflated with other so-called "perennialists," despite this fundamental divergence. J.J. Clarke, for instance, lumps together Huxley and Guénon: *Oriental Enlightenment*, 207.

worldview (secular, humanistic and scientific) which originated in the Renaissance and which has been strengthening its tyrannical grip on the modern mentality ever since. We have already had occasion to refer to the works of several traditionalists but in this chapter we will take a sustained look at the lives and work of the "great triumvirate," touching on the principles and themes which govern their work as a whole but highlighting their role in opening the spiritual treasures of the East to the West without thereby corrupting or compromising the traditional teachings.

René Guénon, Tradition and Oriental Metaphysics
Ananda Coomaraswamy wrote that

> ... the least important thing about Guénon is his personality or biography ... The fact is he has the invisibility that is proper to the complete philosopher: our teleology can only be fulfilled when we really become no one.[4]

The American traditionalist, Whitall Perry, who knew Guénon personally, speaks of his "outer anonymity" and of this "austere yet benevolent figure ... ungraspable and remote."[5] There is indeed something elusive and enigmatic about René Guénon the man. He left an extensive legacy of writings which testify to his achievements as a metaphysician but his personal life remains shrouded in obscurity.

René Guénon was born in Blois in 1886. He grew up in a strict Catholic environment and was schooled by Jesuits. As a young man he moved to Paris to take up studies in mathematics. However, his energies were soon diverted from academic studies and in 1905 he abandoned his preparation for *Grandes Écoles*. For the next few years, seized by what Anatole France called "the vertigo of the invisible," Guénon submerged himself in *fin-de-siècle* French occultism.[6] He became a leading member in several secret societies—Theosophical, spiritualistic, Masonic and "gnostic." From the vantage point of his later work it was a murky period in his life, one of which he apparently did not care to be reminded. Nevertheless, Guénon learned a good deal in this period and indeed, he was eventually to become one of the most unsparing critics of these occultist movements.

In its sociological dimension occultism provided, as doubtless it still does, a framework for the repudiation of the bourgeois ideologies and institutions of the day. Most of the occult groups turned to the archaic past in search of authentic spiritual values against which modern civilization was measured and found wanting. As Mircea Eliade has observed,

---

4 Letter to Kurt Leidecker, November 1941, A.K. Coomaraswamy, *Selected Letters*, 49-50.
5 W. Perry, "Coomaraswamy: the Man, Myth and History," 160, and "The Man and the Witness," 6.
6 France's phrase is cited in M. Eliade, *Occultism, Witchcraft and Cultural Fashions*, 51.

... involvement with the occult represented for the French literary and artistic avant-garde one of the most efficient criticisms and rejections of the religious and cultural values of the West—efficient because it was considered to
be based on historical facts.[7]

Although Guénon was to disown the philosophical and historical assumptions on which such movements were built and to contrast their "counterfeit
spirituality" with what he came to see as genuine expressions of esotericism,
as a traditionalist he remained steadfastly opposed to contemporary
European civilization.

Some of these occult movements stimulated a study of ancient esoteric
traditions in Egypt, Persia, India and China, and directed attention towards
the sacred writings of the East. Precisely how Guénon came to a serious study
of Taoism, Hinduism and Islam remains unclear. Whitall Perry has suggested that the "catalyzing element" was Guénon's contact in Paris with some
Indians of the *Advaita* school.[8] Guénon's life also entered a new phase in
1912, one marked by his marriage to a devout Catholic. He emerged from
the rather subterranean world of the occultists and now moved freely in an
intensely Catholic milieu, leading a busy social and intellectual life. The next
fifteen years were the most public of Guénon's life. He attended lectures at
the Sorbonne, wrote and published widely, gave public lectures himself and
maintained many social and intellectual contacts. He published his first
books in the 1920s and soon became well known for his work on philosophical and metaphysical subjects.

The years 1927 to 1930 mark another transition in Guénon's life, culminating in his move to Cairo in 1930 and his open commitment to Islam. In
January 1928 Guénon's wife died rather abruptly. Following a series of fortu-
itous circumstances Guénon left on a three-month visit to Cairo.[9] He was to
remain there until his death in 1951. In Cairo Guénon was initiated into the
Sufic order of Shadilites and invested with the name Abdel Wahed Yahya. He
married again and lived a modest and retiring existence.

... such was his anonymity that an admirer of his writings was dumbfounded
to discover that the venerable next door neighbor whom she had known for
years as Sheikh Abdel Wahed Yahya was in reality René Guénon.[10]

A good deal of Guénon's energies were directed in the 1930s to a massive
correspondence he carried on with his readers in Europe. Most of Guénon's
published work after his move to Cairo appeared in *Études Traditionnelles*
(until 1937 *Le Voile d'Isis*), a formerly Theosophical journal which under
Guénon's influence was transformed into the principal European forum for
traditionalist thought. It was only the war which provided Guénon with

7   M. Eliade, *Occultism, Witchcraft and Cultural Fashions*, 53.
8   W. Perry, "The Revival of Interest in Tradition," 8-9.
9   J.P. Laurant, "Le problème de René Guénon," 60.
10 W. Perry, "Coomaraswamy: the Man, Myth and History," 160.

enough respite from his correspondence to devote himself to the writing of some of his major works, including *The Reign of Quantity* (1945).

The relationship between Guénon's life and his work has engaged the attention of several scholars. Jean-Pierre Laurant has suggested that his intellectual, spiritual and ritual life only achieved a harmonious resolution after his move to Cairo and within the protective embrace of Islam.[11] P.L. Reynolds has charted the influence of his French and Catholic background on his work.[12] Others, especially those committed to traditionalism, have argued that Guénon's whole adult life represents a witness to an unchanging vision of the truth and that his participation in occultism was part of this function.[13] Each of these kinds of claims carries some legitimacy.

Guénon was a prolific writer. He published seventeen books during his lifetime, and at least ten posthumous collections and compilations have since appeared. Here we shall only take an overview of his work. The *oeuvre* exhibits certain recurrent motifs and preoccupations and is, in a sense, all of a piece. Guénon's understanding of tradition is the key to his work. As early as 1909 we find Guénon writing of "... the Primordial Tradition which, in reality, is the same everywhere, regardless of the different shapes it takes in order to be fit for every race and every historical period."[14] As the English traditionalist Gai Eaton has observed, Guénon

> believes that there exists a Universal Tradition, revealed to humanity at the beginning of the present cycle of time, but partially lost ... his primary concern is less with the detailed forms of this Tradition and the history of its decline than with its kernel, the pure and changeless knowledge which is still accessible to man through the channels provided by traditional doctrine ... [15]

The existence of a Primordial Tradition embodying a set of immutable metaphysical and cosmological principles from which derive a succession of traditions each expressing these principles in forms determined by a given

---

11 J.P. Laurant, "Le problème de René Guénon," 66-69.
12 P.L. Reynolds, "René Guénon." These influences, Reynolds argues, account for various imbalances and inadvertencies in Guénon's work.
13 Such commentators suggest that his thought does not "evolve" but only shifts ground as Guénon responds to changing circumstances. Thus Michel Valsan, a collaborator on *Ètudes Traditionnelles*, writes: "It is useful to clarify in the present case that the special privilege that belongs to this work of playing the role of truth, regularity, and traditional plenitude in the face of Western civilization derives from the sacred and non-individual character that clothed the function of René Guénon. The man who had to accomplish this function would certainly have been prepared from long ago, rather than improvising [his role]. The matrices of Wisdom had predisposed and formed his being according to a precise economy, and his career fulfilled itself in time by a constant correlation between his possibilities and the exterior cyclic conditions [of the age]." Quoted in the Special Issue of *Ètudes Traditionnelles: Le Sort de l'Occident*, November, 1951 (Translated by Pamela Oldmeadow).
14 R. Guénon, "La Demiurge" *La Gnose* , 1909, quoted in M. Bastriocchi, "The Last Pillars of Wisdom," 351.
15 G. Eaton, *The Richest Vein*, 188-189.

Revelation and by the exigencies of the particular situation, is axiomatic in Guénon's work.[16] It is a first principle which admits of no argument; nor does it require any kind of "proof" or "demonstration," historical or otherwise.

Guénon's work, from his earliest writings in 1909 onwards, can be seen as an attempt to give a new expression and application to the timeless principles which inform all traditional doctrines. In his writings he ranges over a vast terrain—Vedanta, the Chinese tradition, Christianity, Sufism, mythology from all over the world, the secret traditions of gnosticism, alchemy, the Kabbalah, and so on, always intent on excavating their underlying principles and showing them to be formal manifestations of the one Primordial Tradition. Certain key themes run through all of his writings and one meets again and again such notions as these: the concept of metaphysics transcending all other doctrinal orders; the identification of metaphysics and the "formalization," so to speak, of gnosis (*jnana* if one prefers); the distinction between the exoteric and esoteric domains; the hierarchic superiority and infallibility of intellective knowledge; the contrast of the modern Occident with the traditional Orient; the spiritual bankruptcy of modern European civilization; a cyclical view of Time, based largely on the Hindu doctrine of cosmic cycles; a contra-evolutionary view of history. Guénon gathered together doctrines and principles from diverse times and places but emphasized that the enterprise was a synthetic one which envisaged formally divergent elements in their principial unity rather than a syncretic one which press-ganged incongruous forms into an artificial fabrication. This distinction is crucial not only in Guénon's work but in traditionalism as a whole.[17]

Guénon repeatedly turned to oriental wisdoms, believing that it was only in the East that various sapiential traditions remained more or less intact. It is important not to confuse this Eastward-looking stance with the kind of sentimental exoticism nowadays so much in vogue. As Coomaraswamy noted,

> If Guénon wants the West to turn to Eastern metaphysics, it is not because they are Eastern but because this is metaphysics. If "Eastern" metaphysics differed from a "Western" metaphysics—one or the other would not be metaphysics.[18]

One of Guénon's translators made the same point in suggesting that if Guénon turns so often to the East it is because the West is in the position of the

> foolish virgins who, through the wandering of their attention in other directions, had allowed their lamps to go out; in order to rekindle the sacred fire,

16 The relationship between the Primordial Tradition and the various traditions needs clarification in that while each tradition in fact derives its overall form and principal characteristics from a particular Revelation, it nevertheless carries over (in many of its aspects) certain essential features of the tradition which precedes it.

17 See R. Guénon, *The Symbolism of the Cross*, x-xi, and *Crisis of the Modern World*, 9 & 108ff.

18 A.K. Coomaraswamy, *The Bugbear of Literacy*, 72-73.

which in its essence is always the same wherever it may be burning, they must have recourse to the lamps still kept alight.[19]

The contrast between the riches of traditional civilizations and the spiritual impoverishment of modern Europe sounds like a refrain through Guénon's writings. In all his work

> Guénon's mission was twofold: to reveal the metaphysical roots of the "crisis of the modern world" and to explain the ideas behind the authentic and esoteric teachings that still remained alive ... in the East.[20]

Guénon's attempts to visit India were thwarted by the refusal of a visa. Alain Daniélou has speculated on two possible reasons: the British government frowned on any praise of Hinduism lest it fan Indian nationalism; secondly, Guénon's denunciation of the Theosophical Movement may have prompted Annie Besant's intervention against him.[21] (Daniélou adduces no evidence for these suggestions but they are both plausible.)

By way of an expedient we can divide Guénon's writings into five categories, each corresponding roughly with a particular period in his life: the occultist periodical writings of the pre-1912 period; the reaction against and critique of occultism, especially spiritualism and Theosophy; writings on Oriental metaphysics; on aspects of the European tradition and on initiation; and, fifthly, the critique of modern civilization as a whole.

Guénon's earliest writings appeared, as we have seen, in the organs of French occultism. In the light of his later work some of this periodical literature must be considered somewhat ephemeral. Nonetheless the seeds of most of Guénon's work can be found in articles from this period. The most significant, perhaps, were five essays which appeared in *La Gnose* between September 1911 and February 1912, under the title "La constitution de l'être humain et son évolution selon le Védânta"; these became the opening chapters of one of his most influential studies, *Man and His Becoming According to the Vedanta*, not published until 1925. Other writings from this period on such subjects as mathematics and the science of numbers, prayer and incantation, and initiation, all presage later work.

As early as 1909 we find him attacking what he saw as the misconceptions and confusions abroad in the spiritualist movements.[22] Whilst his misgivings about many of the occultist groups were growing in the 1909-1912 period it was not until the publication of two of his earliest books that he mounted a full-scale critique: *Le théosophisme, histoire d'une pseudo religion* (1921) and *L'erreur spirite* (1923). The titles are suggestive: these were lacerating attacks not only on theosophy and spiritualism but also on the "Gnostic" groups and

19 G. Eaton, *The Richest Vein*, 199.
20 J. Needleman, *Foreword to The Sword of Gnosis*, 11-12.
21 A. Daniélou, *The Way to the Labyrinth*, 145.
22 R. Guénon, "La Gnose et les Ecoles Spiritualistes," *La Gnose*, December, 1909.

on movements such as Rosicrucianism. Only the Masons escaped relatively unscathed. As Mircea Eliade has noted:

> The most erudite and devastating critique of all these so-called occult groups was presented not by a rationalist outside observer, but by an author from the inner circle, duly initiated into some of their secret orders and well acquainted with their occult doctrines; furthermore, that critique was directed, not from a skeptical or positivistic perspective, but from what he called "traditional esotericism." This learned and intransigent critic was René Guénon.[23]

The most fundamental part of Guénon's indictment was that such movements, far from preserving traditional esotericisms, were made up of a syncretic mish-mash of distorted and heterogeneous elements forced into a false unity, devoid of any authentic metaphysical framework. Thus they were vulnerable to the scientistic ideologies of the day and inevitably fell prey to the intellectual confusions rampant in Europe. One of the most characteristic confusions of such groups, to cite but one example, was the mistaking of the psychic for the spiritual. Occultism as a whole he now saw as one of the "signs of the times," a symptom of the spiritual malaise in modern civilization. Guénon took up some of these charges again in later works, especially *The Reign of Quantity*.

Guénon's interest in Eastern metaphysical traditions had been awakened some time around 1909 and some of his early articles in *La Gnose* are devoted to Vedantic metaphysics. His first book, *Introduction générale à l'étude des doctrines hindoues* (1921) marked Guénon as a commentator of rare authority. It also served notice of Guénon's role as a redoubtable critic of contemporary civilization. Of this book Seyyed Hossein Nasr has written,

> It was like a sudden burst of lightning, an abrupt intrusion into the modern world of a body of knowledge and a perspective utterly alien to the prevalent climate and world view and completely opposed to all that characterizes the modern mentality.[24]

However, Guénon's axial work on Vedanta was published in 1925, *L'homme et son devenir selon le Védânta*. Other significant works in the field of oriental traditions include *La métaphysique orientale*, delivered as a lecture at the Sorbonne in 1925 but not published until 1939, *La Grande Triade*, based on Taoist doctrine, and many articles on such subjects as Hindu mythology, Taoism and Confucianism, and doctrines concerning reincarnation. Interestingly, Guénon remained more or less ignorant of the Buddhist tradition for many years, regarding it as no more than a "heterodox development" within Hinduism and without integrity as a formal religious tradition. It was only through the intervention of Marco Pallis, one of his translators,

23 M. Eliade, *Occultism, Witchcraft and Cultural Fashions*, 51.
24 S.H. Nasr, *Knowledge and the Sacred*, 101.

and Ananda Coomaraswamy, that Guénon revised his attitude to Buddhism. Of Guénon's works on the Hindu tradition, Alain Daniélou said this:

> When I first became interested in the religion and philosophy of India, the only works I found useful were those of René Guénon. *L'Introduction aux doctrines hindoues* remains one of the few works of scholarship that give a true picture of the philosophic and cosmological foundations of Indian civilization.[25]

The quintessential Guénon is to be found in two works which tied together some of his central themes: *La crise du monde moderne* (1927) and his masterpiece, *Le règne de la quantité et les signes des temps* (1945). The themes of these two books had been rehearsed in an earlier work, *Orient et Occident* (1924). They mounted an elaborate and merciless attack on the foundations of the contemporary European worldview.

The Reign of Quantity is a magisterial summation of Guénon's work. It is, characteristically, a difficult work. He was quite unconcerned with reaching a wide audience and addressed the book to those few capable of understanding it "without any concern for the inevitable incomprehension of the others." He set out to challenge nearly all of the intellectual assumptions current in Europe at the time. The book, he writes, is directed to

> ... the understanding of some of the darkest enigmas of the modern world, enigmas which the world itself denies because it is incapable of perceiving them although it carries them within itself, and because this denial is an indispensable condition for the maintenance of the special mentality whereby it exists.[26]

At first sight the book ranges over a bewildering variety of subjects: the nature of time, space and matter as conceived in traditional and modern science; the philosophical foundations of such typically modern modes of thought as rationalism, materialism and empiricism; the significance of ancient crafts such as metallurgy; the nature of shamanism and sorcery; the "illusion of statistics"; the "misdeeds of psychoanalysis"; the "pseudo-initiatic" pretensions of spiritualism, Theosophy and other "counterfeit" forms of spirituality; tradition and anti-tradition; the unfolding of cosmic and terrestrial cycles. Some study of the book reveals that these apparently disparate strands have been woven into a work of subtle design and dense texture. *The Reign of Quantity* is a chilling indictment of modern civilization as a whole. It has less polemical heat and moral indignation than some of his earlier works but is none the less effective for that. The book is a controlled and dispassionate but devastating razing of the assumptions and values of modern science. At the same time it is an affirmation of the metaphysical and cosmological principles given expression in traditional cultures and religions.

25 A. Daniélou, *The Way to the Labyrinth*, 145. (Daniélou is writing in 1981.)
26 R. Guénon, *The Reign of Quantity*, 11.

Guénon unfolds a startling thesis about the present terrestrial situation in the light of the doctrine of cosmic cycles. His vision is rooted in the Hindu conception of the *Kali-Yuga* but is not restricted to the purely Indian expression of this doctrine. There is a dark apocalyptic strain in the book which some readers are tempted to dismiss as the rantings of another doom-sayer. For Guénon the dire circumstances in which the modern world finds itself are largely to be explained through an elucidation of the cyclic doctrine whereby humankind is seen to be degenerating into an increasingly solidified and materialized state, more and more impervious to spiritual influences. Inversely, the world becomes increasingly susceptible to infernal forces of various kinds. The forced convergence of different civilizations is the spatial correlate of the temporal unfolding of the present terrestrial cycle, moving towards an inexorable cataclysm.

Closely related to the doctrine of cycles is Guénon's profoundly challenging thesis about the nature of time, space and matter, one based on traditional cosmologies. Contrary to the claims of modern science, says Guénon, time and space do not constitute a uniform continuum in the matrix of which events and material phenomena manifest themselves. Rather, time-and-space is a field of *qualitative* determinations and differences. In other words, the nature of time and space is not a constant, fixed datum but is subject to both quantitative and qualitative change. Any exclusively quantitative and materialistic science such as now tyrannizes the European mind cannot accommodate this principle. It strives rather to reduce qualitatively determined phenomena to the barren and mechanistic formulae of a profane and materialistic science. (One might add that some of the "discoveries" of physicists since Guénon's time have done nothing to disprove his thesis and indeed, to some minds, give it more credibility. Guénon himself would have argued that metaphysical and cosmological principles such as he was applying could in no way be affected by empirical considerations.)[27]

Guénon's critique of scientism—the ideology of modern science—is something quite other than just another attack on scientific reductionism, although that surely is part of his case. Nor is it a catalogue of the inadequacies of this or that scientific theory. Rather, it is a radical and disturbing challenge to almost every postulate of modern European science. The critique hinges on the contrast between sacred, traditional sciences on the one hand, and a profane, materialistic science on the other. In an earlier work Guénon had elaborated the basis of this contrast in uncompromising terms:

> Never until the present epoch had the study of the sensible world been regarded as self-sufficient; never would the science of this ephemeral and changing multiplicity have been judged truly worthy of the name of knowledge ... According to the ancient conception ... a science was less esteemed for itself than for the degree in which it expressed after its own fashion ... a reflection of the higher immutable truth of which everything of any reality

---

27 See also Chapter 13.

necessarily partakes ... all science appeared as an extension of the traditional doctrine itself, as one of its applications, secondary and contingent no
doubt ... but still a veritable knowledge none the less ... [28]

For Guénon and the other traditionalists, the notion of a self-sufficient, self-
validating, autonomous material science is a contradiction, an incongruity,
for all sciences must have recourse to higher and immutable principles and
truths. Science must be pursued in a metaphysical and cosmological framework which it cannot construct out of itself. In another work Guénon wrote
that modern science,

> in disavowing the principles [of traditional metaphysics and cosmology] and
> in refusing to re-attach itself to them, robs itself both of the highest guaran-
> tee and the surest direction it could have; there is no longer anything valid
> in it except knowledge of details, and as soon as it seeks to rise one degree
> higher, it becomes dubious and vacillating.[29]

The Reign of Quantity also seeks to demonstrate the intimate connections
between traditional metaphysics and the arts, crafts and sciences which are
found in any traditional culture, and to show how many modern and profane
sciences are really a kind of degenerated caricature of traditional sciences.[30]
Such a demonstration turns largely on Guénon's explanation of the nature
of symbolism and of the initiatic character of many traditional sciences.

There is in Guénon's work an adamantine quality, an austerity and inflexibility, and a combative tone as well as his "icy brilliance."[31] He was not one
to coax, cajole or seduce his readers. Something of Guénon's unyielding posture is evinced in the following passage (remember that he is writing in the
1920s):

> ... hitherto, so far as we are aware, no one else beside ourselves has consis-
> tently expounded authentic Oriental ideas in the West; and we have done so
> ... without the slightest wish to propagandize or to popularize, and exclusive-
> ly for the benefit of those who are able to understand the doctrines just as
> they stand, and not after they have been denatured on the plea of making
> them more readily acceptable ... [32]

Guénon's "inflexibility" is nothing other than an expression of his fierce
commitment to the truth and it is precisely his refusal to compromise first
principles which gives his work its power and integrity

It is worth noting that, long before Edward Said, Guénon was scathing
about "orientalism," if by this term we mean the Western study of Eastern

---

28 This passage is quoted in G. Eaton, *The Richest Vein*, 196; the source is not given but for a more
extended discussion of precisely this contrast see R. Guénon, *Crisis of the Modern World*, 37-50.

29 Quoted in W.T. Chan, "The Unity of East and West" in W.R. Inge et al, *Radhakrishnan:
Comparative Studies in Philosophy Presented in Honor of His Sixtieth Birthday*, 107-108. (This passage is
from *East and West*).

30 See R. Guénon, *The Reign of Quantity*, 14.

31 G. Eaton, *The Richest Vein*, 183.

32 R. Guénon, *The Reign of Quantity*, 103.

texts and doctrines using historicist and philological methods, driven by scholarly or antiquarian motives. In *East and West* he recognized that orientalism could become "an instrument in the service of national ambition," and reproached those scholars who were driven not by any intention of learning from the peoples of the East but rather by the (unacknowledged, perhaps unconscious) intent, "by brutal or insidious means, to convert them to [the West's] own way of thinking, and to preach to them."[33] But this was not the nub of the case:

> ... most orientalists are not and do not wish to be anything but scholars; so long as they confine themselves to historical or philological works it does not matter very much; ... their only real danger is the one which is common to all abuses of scholarship, and which consists in the spread of the "intellectual short-sightedness" that limits all knowledge to research after details ... But much more serious in our eyes is the influence exerted by those orientalists who profess to understand and to interpret the doctrines, and who make the most incredible travesty of them, while asserting sometimes that they understand them better than the Orientals themselves do ... and without ever dreaming of accepting the opinion of the authorized representatives of the civilizations they seek to study.[34]

After lambasting the European over-valuation of the Greco-Roman civilization and the way in which Eastern conceptions are often forced into classical moulds, Guénon takes aim at the German school of orientalists: Schopenhauer, Deussen, Oldenberg and Müller all come under heavy fire for their role in perpetrating Western misconceptions about Eastern traditions. However, Guénon reserves his most withering scorn for the "dreams and vagaries of the Theosophists, which are nothing but a tissue of gross errors, made still worse by methods of the lowest charlatanism."[35]

Like other traditionalists, Guénon did not perceive his work as any kind of essay in creativity or personal "originality," repeatedly emphasizing that in the metaphysical domain there was no room for "individualist considerations" of any kind. In a letter to a friend he wrote, "I have no other merit than to have expressed to the best of my ability some traditional ideas."[36] In the same spirit Coomaraswamy wrote,

> I am not a reformer or propagandist. I don't think for myself ... I am not putting forward any new or private doctrines or interpretations ... For me there are certain axioms, principles or values beyond question; my interest is not in thinking up new ones, but in the application of these that are.[37]

33 R. Guénon, *East and West*, 135, 156.
34 R. Guénon, *East and West*, 151-152.
35 R. Guénon, *East and West*, 157.
36 W. Perry, "The Man and His Witness," 7.
37 Letter to Herman Goetz, January 1947, *Selected Letters*, 33. See also his remarks in "The Seventieth Birthday Address," in *Selected Papers* 2, 434: "... the greatest thing I have learned is never to think for myself ... what I have sought is to understand what has been said, while taking no account of the 'inferior philosophers'."

For the traditionalists Guénon is the "providential interpreter of this age."[38] It was his role to remind a forgetful world, "'in a way that can be ignored but not refuted,' of first principles and to restore a lost sense of the Absolute."[39]

Ananda Coomaraswamy, Scholar and Dharma-Warrior

Ananda Coomaraswamy was a much more public figure than René Guénon. By the end of his life Coomaraswamy was thoroughly versed in the scriptures, mythology, doctrines and arts of many different cultures and traditions. He was an astonishingly erudite scholar, a recondite thinker and a distinguished linguist. He was a prolific writer, a full bibliography running to upwards of a thousand items on geological studies, art theory and history, linguistics and philology, social theory, psychology, mythology, folklore, religion and metaphysics.[40] He lived in three continents and maintained many contacts, both personal and professional, with scholars, antiquarians, artists, theologians and spiritual practitioners from all over the globe. The contributors to a memorial volume—some one hundred and fifty of them—included eminent scholars like A.L. Basham, Joseph Campbell, Heinrich Zimmer and V.S. Naravarne, writers such as T.S. Eliot and Aldous Huxley, art historians like Herman Goetz and Richard Ettinghausen, the distinguished Sanskritist Dr V. Raghavan—the list might go on.[41] Coomaraswamy was a widely known and influential figure. The contrast with Guénon is a marked one.

We can discern in Coomaraswamy's life and work three focal points which shaped his ideas and writings: a concern with social and political questions connected with the conditions of daily life and work, and with the problematic relationship of the present to the past and of the "East" to the "West"; a fascination with traditional arts and crafts which impelled an immense and ambitious scholarly enterprise; and thirdly, an ever-deeper preoccupation with religious and metaphysical questions which was resolved in a "unique balance of metaphysical conviction and scholarly erudition."[42] His early concerns took on a different character when, following his encounter with the work of Guénon, Coomaraswamy arrived at a thoroughly traditionalist understanding.

Born in Ceylon in 1877 of a Tamil father and an English mother, Coomaraswamy was brought up in England following the early death of his father. He was educated at Wycliffe College and at London University where he studied botany and geology. As part of his doctoral work Coomaraswamy carried out a scientific survey of the mineralogy of Ceylon and seemed poised for an academic career as a geologist. However, under pressure from

---

38 F. Schuon, "L'Oeuvre," quoted by M. Bastriocchi, "The Last Pillars of Wisdom," 359.

39 W. Perry, "Coomaraswamy: the Man, Myth and History," 163.

40 The definitive bibliography is J. Crouch, *A Bibliography of Ananda Kentish Coomaraswamy* (2001).

41 See list of contributors in S.D.R. Singam, *Ananda Coomaraswamy, Remembering and Remembering Again and Again*, vii.

42 Roger Lipsey quoted in W. Perry, "Coomaraswamy: the Man, Myth and History," 206.

his experiences while engaged in his fieldwork, he became absorbed in a study of the traditional arts and crafts of Ceylon and of the social conditions under which they had been produced. In turn he became increasingly distressed by the corrosive effects of British colonialism.

In 1906 Coomaraswamy founded the Ceylon Social Reform Society of which he was the inaugural President and moving force. The Society addressed itself to the preservation and revival not only of traditional arts and crafts but also of the social values and customs which had helped to shape them. The Society also dedicated itself, in the words of its Manifesto, to discouraging "the thoughtless imitation of unsuitable European habits and custom."[43] Coomaraswamy called for a re-awakened pride in Ceylon's past and in her cultural heritage. The fact that he was half-English in no way blinkered his view of the impoverishment of national life brought by the British presence in both Ceylon and India. In both tone and substance the following passage is characteristic of Coomaraswamy in this early period:

> How different it might be if we Ceylonese were bolder and more independent, not afraid to stand on our own legs, and not ashamed of our nationalities. Why do we not meet the wave of European civilization on equal terms? ... Our Eastern civilization was here 2000 years ago; shall its spirit be broken utterly before the new commercialism of the West? Sometimes I think the Eastern spirit is not dead, but sleeping, and may yet play a greater part in the world's spiritual life.[44]

Prescient words indeed in 1905!

In the years between 1900 and 1913 Coomaraswamy moved backwards and forwards between Ceylon, India and England. In India he formed close relationships with the Tagore family and was involved in both the literary renaissance and the *swadeshi* movement.[45] All the while in the subcontinent he was researching the past, investigating arts and crafts, uncovering forgotten and neglected schools of religious and court art, writing scholarly and popular works, lecturing, and organizing bodies such as the Ceylon Social Reform Society and, in England, the India Society. If Guénon's disillusionment with contemporary civilization was first fashioned by French occultism, Coomaraswamy's was impelled by the contrast between the traditional and the modern industrial cultures of the two countries to which he belonged by birth.

In England he found his own social ideas anticipated in the work of William Blake, John Ruskin and William Morris, three of the foremost representatives of a fiercely eloquent and morally impassioned current of anti-industrialism.[46] Such figures had elaborated a biting critique of the ugliest

---

43 *Manifesto of the Ceylon Reform Society*, almost certainly written by Coomaraswamy, quoted in R. Lipsey, *Coomaraswamy: His Life and Work*, 22.

44 A.K. Coomaraswamy, *Borrowed Plumes*, 1905, quoted in R. Lipsey, *Coomaraswamy: His Life and Work*, 18.

45 R. Lipsey, *Coomaraswamy: His Life and Work*, 75ff.

and most dehumanizing aspects of the industrial revolution and of the acquisitive commercialism which increasingly polluted both public and private life. They believed the new values and patterns of urbanization and industrialization were disfiguring the human spirit. These writers and others like Thomas Carlyle, Charles Dickens and Matthew Arnold, protested vehemently against the conditions in which many were forced to carry out their daily work and living. Ruskin and Morris, in particular, were appalled by the debasing of standards of craftsmanship and of public taste. Coomaraswamy picked up a catch-phrase of Ruskin's which he was to mobilize again and again in his own writings: "industry without art is brutality."[47] This was more than a glib slogan and signals one of the key themes in Coomaraswamy's work. For many years he was to remain preoccupied with questions about the reciprocal relationships between the conditions of daily life and work, the art of a period, and the social and spiritual values which governed the civilization in question. The Arts and Crafts Movement of the Edwardian era was, in large measure, stimulated by the ideas of William Morris, the artist, designer, poet, medievalist and social theorist. Morris' work influenced Coomaraswamy decisively in this period and he involved himself with others in England who were trying to put some of Morris' ideas into practice. The Guild and School of Handicraft, with which Coomaraswamy had some connections, was a case in point.[48]

We can catch resonances from the work of the anti-industrialists in a passage such as this, written by Coomaraswamy in 1915:

> If the advocates of compulsory education were sincere, and by education meant education, they would be well aware that the first result of any real education would be to rear a race who would refuse point-blank the greater part of the activities offered by present day civilized existence ... life under Modern Western culture is not worth living, except for those strong enough and well enough equipped to maintain a perpetual guerilla warfare against all the purposes and idols of that civilization with a view to its utter transformation.[49]

This voices a concern with the purposes of education which was to remain with Coomaraswamy all his life. The tone of this passage is typical of Coomaraswamy's writings on social subjects in this period.

46 For a chronological account of Coomaraswamy's involvement in English social reform movements and of the development of his own ideas under English intellectual influences see R. Lipsey, *Coomaraswamy: His Life and Work*, 105ff.

47 R. Lipsey, *Coomaraswamy: His Life and Work*, 114. For a penetrating analysis of the anti-industrial movement in England see R. Williams, *Culture and Society*.

48 Lipsey offers a persuasive discussion of the influence of Morris. For other material on this phase of Coomaraswamy's life and his involvement in the Arts and Crafts Movement see W. Shewring, "Ananda Coomaraswamy and Eric Gill," and A. Crawford, "Ananda Coomaraswamy and C.R. Ashbee."

49 A.K. Coomaraswamy, "Love and Art," 1915, quoted in R. Lipsey, *Coomaraswamy: His Life and Work*, 105.

Later in life Coomaraswamy turned less often to explicitly social and political questions. By then he had become aware that "politics and economics, although they cannot be ignored, are the most external and least part of our problem."[50] However, he never surrendered the conviction that an urbanized and highly industrialized society controlled by materialistic values was profoundly inimical to human development. He was always ready to pull a barbed shaft from his literary quiver when provoked. As late as 1943 we find him writing to *The New English Weekly*, again on the subject of education, in terms no less caustic than those of 1915:

> We cannot pretend to culture until by the phrase "standard of living" we come to mean a qualitative standard ... Modern education is designed to fit us to take our place in the counting-house and at the chain-belt; a real culture breeds a race of men able to ask, What kind of work is worth doing?[51]

Coomaraswamy's significance as a social commentator is not fully revealed until his later work when the political and social insights from the early period in his life found their proper place within an all-embracing framework which allowed him to elaborate what Juan Adolpho Vasquez has called "a metaphysics of culture."[52] In the years before he moved to America he was more significant as a propagandist and educator than as a theorist. Ultimately Coomaraswamy's most important function as a social commentator lay in his insistence on relating social and political questions back to underlying religious and metaphysical principles.

The second refrain which sounds through Coomaraswamy's life is closely related to his interest in social questions and became the dominant theme of his public career—his work as an art historian. From the outset Coomaraswamy's interest in art was controlled by much more than either antiquarian or "aesthetic" considerations. For him the most humble folk art and the loftiest religious creations alike were an outward expression not only of the sensibilities of those who created them but of the whole civilization in which they were nurtured. There was nothing of the *art nouveau* slogan of "art for art's sake" in Coomaraswamy's outlook. His interest in traditional arts and crafts, from a humble pot to a Hindu temple, was always governed by the conviction that something immeasurably precious and vitally important was disappearing under the onslaught of modernism in its many different guises. As his biographer remarks, "... history of art was never for him either a light question—one that had only to do with pleasures—or a question of scholarship for its own sake, but rather a question of setting right what had gone amiss partly through ignorance of the past."[53] Coomaraswamy's achievement as an art historian can perhaps best be understood in respect of

---

50 A.K. Coomaraswamy quoted in D. Riepe, *Indian Philosophy and Its Impact on American Thought*, 126.
51 Letter to *The New English Weekly*, April 1943, *Selected Letters*, 293.
52 See Juan Adolpho Vasquez, "A Metaphysics of Culture."
53 R. Lipsey, *Coomaraswamy: His Life and Work*, 20.

three of the major tasks which he undertook: the "rehabilitation" of Asian art in the eyes of Europeans and Asians alike; the massive work of scholarship which he pursued as curator of the Indian Section of the Boston Museum of Fine Arts; the penetration and explanation of traditional views of art and their relationship to philosophy, religion and metaphysics.

In assessing Coomaraswamy's achievement it needs to be remembered that the conventional attitude of the Edwardian era towards the art of Asia was, at best, condescending, and at worst, frankly contemptuous. Asian art was often dismissed as "barbarous," "second-rate" and "inferior" and there was a good deal of foolish talk about "eight-armed monsters" and the like.[54] In short, there was, in England at least, an almost total ignorance of the sacred iconographies of the East. Such an artistic illiteracy was coupled with a similar incomprehension of traditional philosophy and religion, and buttressed by all manner of Eurocentric assumptions. Worse still was the fact that such attitudes had infected the Indian intelligentsia, exposed as it was to Western education and influences.

Following the early days of his fieldwork in Ceylon, Coomaraswamy set about dismantling these prejudices through an affirmation of the beauty, integrity and spiritual density of traditional art in Ceylon and India and, later, in other parts of Asia. He was bent on the task of demonstrating the existence of an artistic heritage at least the equal of Europe's. He not only wrote and spoke and organized tirelessly to educate the British but he scourged the Indian intelligentsia for being duped by assumptions of European cultural superiority. In studies like *Medieval Sinhalese Art* (1908), *The Arts and Crafts of India and Ceylon* (1913), and his earliest collection of essays, *The Dance of Shiva* (1918), Coomaraswamy combated the prejudices of the age and reaffirmed traditional understandings of Indian art. He revolutionized several specific fields of art history, radically changed others. His work on Sinhalese arts and crafts and on Rajput painting, though they can now be seen as formative in the light of his later work on Buddhist iconography and on Indian, Platonic and Christian theories of art, were nevertheless early signs of a stupendous scholarship. His influence was not only felt in the somewhat rarefied domain of art scholarship but percolated into other scholarly fields and eventually must have had some influence on popular attitudes in Ceylon, India, England and America.[55] As Meyer Schapiro observed,

He was one of the luminaries of scholarship from whom we have all learned. And by the immense range of his studies and his persistent questioning of

---

54 R. Lipsey, *Coomaraswamy: His Life and Work*, 60-61, and W. Perry, "The Bollingen Coomaraswamy," 214.

55 See the following essays in S.D.R. Singam, *Ananda Coomaraswamy, Remembering and Remembering Again and Again*: B. Heiman, "Indian Art and Its Transcendence," 24-26; K.C. Kamaliah, "Ananda Coomaraswamy's Assessment of Dravidian Civilization and Culture," 43-52; A. Ranganathan, "Ananda Coomaraswamy: Confluence of East and West," 53-58; B.N. Goswamy, "Ananda Coomaraswamy as a Historian of Rajput Painting," 75-83; M.S. Randhava, "Rediscovery of Kangra Painting," 201-204.

the accepted values, he gave us an example of intellectual seriousness, rare among scholars today.[56]

As a Curator at the Boston Museum Coomaraswamy performed a mighty labor in classifying, cataloguing and explaining thousands of items of oriental art. Through his professional work, his writings, lectures and personal associations Coomaraswamy left an indelible imprint on the work of many American galleries and museums and influenced a wide range of curators, art historians, orientalists and critics—Stella Kramrisch, Walter Andrae, and Heinrich Zimmer to name a few of the more well-known.[57] Zimmer wrote of Coomaraswamy: "the only man in my field who, whenever I read a paper of his, gives me a genuine inferiority complex."[58]

Traditional art, in Coomaraswamy's view, was always directed towards a twin purpose: a daily utility, towards what he was fond of calling "the satisfaction of present needs," and to the preservation and transmission of moral values and spiritual teachings derived from the tradition in which it appeared. A Tibetan *tanka*, a medieval cathedral, a Red Indian utensil, a Javanese puppet, a Hindu deity image—in such artifacts and creations Coomaraswamy sought a symbolic vocabulary. The intelligibility of traditional arts and crafts, he insisted, does not depend on a more or less precarious *recognition*, as does modern art, but on *legibility*. Traditional art does not deal in the private vision of the artist but in a symbolic language.[59] By contrast modern art, which from a traditionalist perspective includes Renaissance and, generally speaking, all post-Renaissance art, is divorced from higher values, tyrannized by the mania for "originality," controlled by aesthetic and sentimental considerations, and drawn from the subjective resources of the individual artist rather than from the well-springs of tradition. The comparison, needless to say, does not reflect well on modern art! An example:

> Our artists are "emancipated" from any obligation to eternal verities, and have abandoned to tradesmen the satisfaction of present needs. Our abstract art is not an iconography of transcendental forms but the realistic picture of a disintegrated mentality.[60]

During the late 1920s Coomaraswamy's life and work somewhat altered their trajectory. The collapse of his third marriage, ill-health and a growing awareness of death, an impatience with the constrictions of purely academic scholarship, and the influence of René Guénon all cooperated to deepen

---

56 Letter to Doña Luisa Coomaraswamy, 12th September 1947, quoted in R. Lipsey, *Coomaraswamy: His Life and Work*, 246.

57 See R. Lipsey, *Coomaraswamy: His Life and Work*, 206-231, and A. Ripley Hall, "The Keeper of the Indian Collection," 106-124. This article includes a bibliography of Coomaraswamy's writings for the bulletin of the Museum.

58 Zimmer quoted in W. McGuire, "Zimmer and the Mellens," 38.

59 See A.K. Coomaraswamy, *Christian and Oriental Philosophy of Art*.

60 A.K. Coomaraswamy, "Symptom, Diagnosis and Regimen" in *Selected Papers 1*, 316-317.

Coomaraswamy's interest in spiritual and metaphysical questions.[61] He became more austere in his personal lifestyle, partially withdrew from the academic and social worlds in which he had moved freely over the last decade, and addressed himself to the understanding and explication of traditional metaphysics, especially those of classical India and pre-Renaissance Europe. Coomaraswamy remarked in one of his letters that "my indoctrination with the *Philosophia Perennis* is primarily Oriental, secondarily Mediaeval, and thirdly classic."[62] His later work is densely textured with references to Plato and Plotinus, Augustine and Aquinas, Eckhart and the Rhineland mystics, to Sankara and Lao-tse and Nagarjuna. He also explored folklore and mythology since these too carried profound teachings. Coomaraswamy remained the consummate scholar but his work took on a more urgent nature after 1932. He spoke of his "vocation"—he was not one to use such words lightly—as "research in the field of the significance of the universal symbols of the *Philosophia Perennis*" rather than as "one of apology for or polemic on behalf of doctrines."[63]

The influence of Guénon was decisive. Coomaraswamy discovered Guénon's writings through Heinrich Zimmer some time in the late 20s and, a few years later, wrote,

> ... no living writer in modern Europe is more significant than René Guénon, whose task it has been to expound the universal metaphysical tradition that has been the essential foundation of every past culture, and which represents the indispensable basis for any civilization deserving to be so-called.[64]

Coomaraswamy told one of his friends that he and Guénon were "entirely in agreement on metaphysical principles" which, of course, did not preclude some divergences of opinion over the applications of these principles on the phenomenal plane.[65]

The vintage Coomaraswamy of the later years is to be found in his masterly works on Vedanta and on the Catholic scholastics and mystics. Some of his work is labyrinthine and not easy of access. It is often laden with a mass of technical detail and with linguistic and philological subtleties which test the patience of some readers. Of his own methodology as an exponent of metaphysics Coomaraswamy wrote,

> We write from a strictly orthodox point of view ... endeavoring to speak with mathematical precision, but never employing words of our own, or making any affirmation for which authority could not be cited by chapter and verse; in this way making our technique characteristically Indian.[66]

61 See R. Lipsey, *Coomaraswamy: His Life and Work*, 161-175. On Coomaraswamy's move from "descriptive iconography" towards metaphysics see his letter to Herman Goetz, June 1939, *Selected Letters*, 26-27.
62 Letter to Artemus Packard, May 1941, *Selected Letters*, 299.
63 A.K. Coomaraswamy, "The Bugbear of Democracy, Freedom and Equality," 134.
64 Quoted in R. Lipsey, *Coomaraswamy: His Life and Work*, 170.
65 W. Perry, "The Man and the Witness," 5.
66 Quoted in V.S. Naravarne, "Ananda Coomaraswamy: A Critical Appreciation," 206.

Sometimes one wishes the chapter and verse documentation was not quite so overwhelming! Coomaraswamy was much more scrupulous than Guénon in this respect, the latter sometimes ignoring scholarly protocols at the cost of exposing some of his claims to academic criticism.

Coomaraswamy's later writings demand close attention from anyone seriously interested in the subjects about which he wrote. There is no finer exegesis of traditional Indian metaphysics than is to be found in Coomaraswamy's later works. His work on the Platonic, Christian and Indian conceptions of sacred art is also unrivalled. Roger Lipsey has performed an invaluable service in bringing some of Coomaraswamy's finest essays on these subjects together in *Coomaraswamy, Vol II: Selected Papers, Metaphysics*. Special mention should be made of "The Vedanta and Western Tradition," "Sri Ramakrishna and Religious Tolerance," "Recollection, Indian and Platonic," "On the One and Only Transmigrant" and "On the Indian and Traditional Psychology, or Rather Pneumatology." But it hardly matters what one picks up from the later period: all his mature work is stamped with rare scholarship, elegant expression and a depth of understanding which makes most of the other scholarly work on the same subjects look vapid and superficial. Of his later books three in particular deserve much wider attention: *Christian and Oriental Philosophy of Art* (1939), *Hinduism and Buddhism* (1943) and *Time and Eternity* (1947). *The Bugbear of Literacy* (1979) (first published in 1943 as *Am I my Brother's Keeper?*) and two posthumous collections of some of his most interesting and more accessible essays, *Sources of Wisdom* (1981) and *What is Civilization?* (1989), offer splendid starting-points for uninitiated readers.

From this brief sketch it will be clear enough that Coomaraswamy was a man of wide interests and achievements. From a traditionalist point of view and in the context of our present study we can unhesitatingly ratify Coomaraswamy's own words: "I have little doubt that my later work, developed out of and necessitated by my earlier works on the arts and dealing with Indian philosophy and Vedic exegesis, is really the most mature and most important part of my work."[67] Furthermore, this work was not fuelled by a sterile academic ideal but by a real existential engagement. As Coomaraswamy remarked,

> The passionless reason of ... "objective" scholarship, applied to the study of "what men have believed," is only a sort of frivolity, in which the real problem, that of knowing what should be believed, is evaded.[68]

A tribute from his friend Eric Gill, the English designer and writer, will leave us at an appropriate point to conclude this introduction:

---

67 Coomaraswamy quoted in R. Lipsey, *Coomaraswamy: His Life and Work*, 248.
68 A.K. Coomaraswamy, *The Bugbear of Literacy*, 22.

Others have written the truth about life and religion and man's work. Others have written good clear English. Others have had the gift of witty exposition. Others have understood the metaphysics of Christianity and others have understood the metaphysics of Hinduism and Buddhism. Others have understood the true significance of erotic drawings and sculptures. Others have seen the relationships of the true and the good and the beautiful. Others have had apparently unlimited learning. Others have loved; others have been kind and generous. But I know of no one else in whom all these gifts and all these powers have been combined ... I believe that no other living writer has written the truth in matters of art and life and religion and piety with such wisdom and understanding.[69]

We can hardly doubt that the life and work of this "warrior for dharma"[70] was a precious gift to all those interested in the ways of the spirit.

Frithjof Schuon and the *Religio Perennis* in East and West

With the person of Frithjof Schuon we move back into the shadows of a deliberate anonymity.[71] Schuon was born of German parents in Basle in 1907. He was schooled in both French and German but left school at sixteen to work as a textile designer in Paris. From an early age he devoted himself to a study of philosophy, religion and metaphysics, reading the classical and modern works of European philosophy, and the sacred literatures of the East. Amongst the Western sources Plato and Eckhart left a profound impression while the *Bhagavad Gita* was his favorite Eastern reading.[72] Even before moving to Paris Schuon came into contact with the writings of René Guénon "which served to confirm his own intellectual rejection of the modern civilization while at the same time bringing into sharper focus his spontaneous understanding of metaphysical principles and their traditional applications."[73]

From his earliest years Schuon was also fascinated by traditional art, especially that of Japan and the Far East. In an unusual personal reference in one of his works he tells us of a Buddha figure in an ethnographical museum. It was a traditional representation in gilded wood and flanked by two statues of the Bodhisattvas Seishi and Kwannon. The encounter with this "overwhelming embodiment of an infinite victory of the Spirit" Schuon sums up in the phrase *"veni, vidi, victus sum."*[74] One commentator has drawn attention to the

---

69 E. Gill, *Autobiography*, 174.
70 M. Pallis, "A Fateful Meeting of Minds," 187.
71 See B. Perry, *Frithjof Schuon, Metaphysician and Artist.* Fragmentary information can also be found in *The Essential Writings of Frithjof Schuon* and in S.H. Nasr, "The Biography of Frithjof Schuon," 1-6.
72 B. Perry, *Frithjof Schuon, Metaphysician and Artist,* 2.
73 B. Perry, *Frithjof Schuon, Metaphysician and Artist,* 2. See also W. Perry, "The Revival of Interest in Tradition," 14-16.
74 F. Schuon, *In the Tracks of Buddhism,* 121. See also B. Perry, *Frithjof Schuon, Metaphysician and Artist,* 2.

importance of aesthetic intuition in accounting for Schuon's extraordinary understanding of traditional religious and social forms: "It suffices for him to see ... an object from a traditional civilization, to be able to perceive, through a sort of 'chain-reaction,' a whole ensemble of intellectual, spiritual and psychological ideas."[75] This may seem an extravagant claim but those who have read Schuon's work will not doubt the gift to which it testifies.

After working for a time in Mulhouse, in Alsace, Schuon underwent a year and a half of military service before returning to his design work in Paris. There, in 1930, his interest in Islam led him to a close study of Arabic, first with a Syrian Jew and afterwards at the Paris mosque, and to his formal commitment to Islam.[76] In the 30s Schuon several times visited North Africa, spending time in Algeria, Morocco and Egypt where he met René Guénon, with whom he had been corresponding for some years. In many respects Schuon's work was to be an elaboration of principles first given public expression by Guénon. Schuon's direct master was not Guénon, who never took on the role of spiritual teacher, but Shaikh Ahmad Al-'Alawi, the Algerian Sufi sage and founder of the 'Alawi order.[77] Schuon has written of this modern saint:

> ... someone who represents in himself ... the idea which for hundreds of years has been the life-blood of that civilization [the Islamic]. To meet such a one is like coming face to face, in mid-20th century, with a medieval Saint or a Semitic Patriarch.[78]

The contemplative climate of India also held a strong attraction for Schuon but a visit to the subcontinent was cut short by the outbreak of World War II which obliged him to return to Europe. Schuon served for some months in the French army before being captured by the Germans. His father had been a native of southern Germany while his mother had come from German-Alsatian stock. Such a background ensured some measure of freedom for Schuon but when the Nazis threatened to forcibly enlist Alsatians in the German army he seized an opportunity to escape to Switzerland. He was briefly imprisoned before being granted asylum. He settled in Lausanne and, some years later, took out Swiss nationality.[79]

---

75 B. Perry, *Frithjof Schuon, Metaphysician and Artist*, 1.

76 B. Perry, *Frithjof Schuon, Metaphysician and Artist*, 3.

77 See M. Lings *A Sufi Saint of the Twentieth Century*, and M. Valsan, "Notes on the Shaikh al-'Alawi, 1869-1934." It has been wrongly suggested that Schuon was a "disciple" of Guénon and/or Coomaraswamy. See, for instance, E.J. Sharpe, *Comparative Religion*, 262, and R.C. Zaehner, *At Sundry Times*, 36, fn2. Further, it needs to be remembered that "To follow Guénon is not to follow the man, but to follow the light of traditional truth ..."; B. Kelly, "Notes on the Light of the Eastern Religions," 160-161.

78 F. Schuon, "Rahimahu Llah," *Cahiers du Sud*, August-September 1935, quoted in M. Lings, *A Sufi Saint of the Twentieth Century*, 116. (There is a moving portrait of the Shaikh by Schuon, facing page 160.)

79 B. Perry, *Frithjof Schuon, Metaphysician and Artist*, 3.

In 1949 Schuon married Catherine Feer, the daughter of a Swiss diplomat. It was she who introduced him to the beauties of the Swiss Alps. Schuon's love of nature, which runs through his work like a haunting melody, was further deepened during two periods which he and his wife spent with the Plains Indians of North America. "For Schuon, virgin nature carries a message of eternal truth and primordial reality, and to plunge oneself therein is to rediscover a dimension of the soul which in modern man has become atrophied."[80] The Schuons had previously developed friendly contacts with visiting Indians in Paris and Brussels in the 1950s. During their first visit to North America in 1959, the Schuons were officially adopted into the Red Cloud family of the Lakota tribe, that branch of the Sioux nation from which came the revered "medicine-man" Black Elk.[81] As well as making visits to America Schuon traveled in North Africa and the Middle East, maintaining on-going friendships with representatives of all the great religious traditions. Earlier he lived in reclusive circumstances in Switzerland but spent his later years in America until his death in May, 1998.

Schuon's published work forms an imposing corpus and covers a staggering range of religious and metaphysical subjects without any of the superficialities and simplifications which we normally expect from someone covering such a boundless terrain. His works on specific religious traditions have commanded respect from scholars and practitioners within the traditions in question. As well as publishing over twenty books he was a prolific contributor to journals such as *Études Traditionnelles, Islamic Quarterly, Tomorrow, Studies in Comparative Religion* and *Sophia Perennis*. Almost his entire oeuvre is now available in English translation.[82]

Schuon's works are all governed by an unchanging set of metaphysical principles. They exhibit nothing of a "development" or "evolution" but are, rather, re-statements of the same principles from different vantage points and brought to bear on divergent phenomena. More so than with either Guénon or Coomaraswamy, one feels that Schuon's vision was complete from the outset. The term "erudition" is not quite appropriate: Schuon not only knows "about" an encyclopedic range of religious manifestations and sapiential traditions but seems to understand them in a way which, for want of a better word, we can only call intuitive. Seyyed Hossein Nasr puts the matter this way:

> If Guénon was the master expositor of metaphysical doctrines and Coomaraswamy the peerless scholar and connoisseur of Oriental art who began his exposition of metaphysics through recourse to the language of

---

80 B. Perry, *Frithjof Schuon, Metaphysician and Artist*, 6.

81 For some account of the Schuons' personal experiences with the Plains Indians see F. Schuon, *The Feathered Sun*, Parts 2 & 3. Schuon, Coomaraswamy and Joseph Epes Brown, and the artist Paul Goble, have all been at the forefront of efforts to preserve the precious spiritual heritage of the Plains Indians. See R. Lipsey, *Coomaraswamy: His Life and Work*, 227-228.

82 For a full bibliography of Schuon's writings up to 1990 see *Religion of the Heart*, ed. S.H. Nasr & W. Stoddart, 299-327.

artistic forms, Schuon seems like the cosmic intellect itself impregnated by the energy of divine grace surveying the whole of the reality surrounding man and elucidating all the concerns of human existence in the light of sacred knowledge.[83]

Several of Schuon's books are devoted to the Islamic and Christian traditions. Nasr, himself an eminent Islamicist, wrote of *Understanding Islam*, "I believe his work to be the most outstanding ever written in a European language on why Muslims believe in Islam and why Islam offers to man all that he needs religiously and spiritually."[84] Nasr has been no less generous in commending later works.[85] Whilst all of Schuon's works have a Sufic fragrance his work has by no means been restricted to the Islamic heritage. Two major works focus on Hinduism and Buddhism: *Language of the Self* (1959) and *In the Tracks of Buddhism* (1969).[86] He also refers frequently to Red Indian spirituality, to the Chinese tradition and to Judaism. His writings on the spiritual heritage of the Plains Indians have been collected, together with reproductions of some of his paintings, in *The Feathered Sun: Plains Indians in Art and Philosophy* (1990).

All of Schuon's work is concerned with a re-affirmation of traditional metaphysical principles, with an explication of the esoteric dimensions of religion, with the penetration of mythological and religious forms, and with the critique of a modernism which is indifferent to the principles which inform all traditional wisdoms. His general position was defined in his first work to appear in English, *The Transcendent Unity of Religions* (1953), a work of which T.S. Eliot remarked, "I have met with no more impressive work on the comparative study of Oriental and Occidental religion."[87] *Spiritual Perspectives and Human Facts* (1954) is a collection of aphoristic essays including studies of Vedanta and sacred art, and a meditation on the spiritual virtues. *Gnosis: Divine Wisdom* (1959), *Logic and Transcendence* (1976) and *Esoterism as Principle and as Way* (1981) are largely given over to extended and explicit discussions of metaphysical principles. Schuon suggested some years ago that *Logic and Transcendence* was his most representative and inclusive work. That distinction is perhaps now shared with *Esoterism as Principle and as Way* which includes Schuon's most deliberate explanation of the nature of esotericism,[88] and with *Survey of Metaphysics and Esoterism* (1986) which is a masterly work of metaphysical synthesis.

Stations of Wisdom (1961) is directed mainly towards an exploration of certain religious and spiritual modalities but includes "Orthodoxy and

83 S.H. Nasr, *Knowledge and the Sacred*, 107.
84 See S.H. Nasr, *Ideals and Realities of Islam*, 10.
85 See his Prefaces to F. Schuon, *Dimensions of Islam* and *Islam and the Perennial Philosophy*.
86 A revised and enlarged version of the latter was published by World Wisdom Books in 1993 as *Treasures of Buddhism*.
87 Cover of Harper & Row edition of 1975.
88 Schuon's translators often use the word "esoterism"; I have preferred "esotericism." Schuon's comment about *Logic and Transcendence* is recorded in Whitall Perry's review of *Logic and Transcendence*, 250.

Intellectuality," an essay of paramount importance in understanding the traditionalist position. *Light on the Ancient Worlds* (1965) includes a range of essays on such subjects as the Hellenist-Christian "dialogue," shamanism, monasticism and the *religio perennis*. Schuon's most recent works are *To Have a Center* (1990), *Roots of the Human Condition* (1991), *The Play of Masks* (1992) and *The Transfiguration of Man* (1995).

The two Schuon books most directly addressed to themes which bear on our present study are *Language of the Self*, concentrating on aspects of the Indian spiritual heritage, and *In the Tracks of Buddhism* which, leaving aside the works of Marco Pallis, is the only extended traditionalist work on Buddhism. Dr. V. Raghavan wrote the Foreword to the former:

> It is a matter of singular satisfaction to the present writer to be associated with this book, the first publication in India of a class of writings which ... has contributed in a unique way to the true understanding of Hinduism in the West ... writings different from [those] of the Orientalists ... but [which] may be considered the consummation of the work which these "orientalists" had done since the discovery of Sanskrit or the East by editing and translating Eastern classics and tracing the development of the different branches of Oriental thought. To adopt the language of the *Mundaka*, all that they have done may be called the *apara vidya*, while the class of writings dealt with here may be deemed the *para vidya* ... Nothing is more significant or has climaxed this effort in a more befitting manner than the fact that His Holiness Sri Sankaracarya, Jagadguru on the Kanci Kamakoti Pitha, has been pleased to accept the dedication of this book to him; *the authenticity and orthodoxy of Schuon's exposition stand in need of no further testimony.*[89]

The book includes essays on the principles of Hindu orthodoxy, the Vedanta, yoga, the originality of Buddhism, and sacred art. Schuon also explicates the doctrines and principles which inform the Indian caste system in what is, along with Coomaraswamy's essay "The Bugbear of Democracy, Freedom and Equality,"[90] undoubtedly its most authoritative defense by a Western writer. "Self-Knowledge and the Western Seeker" is an essay of special interest in our current context. Here we shall limit ourselves to quoting a few highly suggestive passages. Firstly, concerning the disenchantment with Christianity amongst many who are thereby attracted to the wisdom traditions of the East:

> ... one has to face the fact that many people of European and therefore Christian ancestry have been caused to react strongly, for reasons with which one can often sympathize, against the sentimentality and unintelligence that have increasingly invaded their own traditional home during recent centuries. Those who have not let themselves succumb, without more ado, to the prevailing religious indifference, have almost inevitably been drawn to

89 Dr. V. Raghavan, Foreword to F. Schuon, *Language of the Self*, ix-x (italics mine).
90 This is one of Coomaraswamy's late essays, written sometime between 1944 and his death, and was not published until it appeared in the revised and expanded *The Bugbear of Literacy* (1979).

look in an easterly direction for a corrective to the ills they deplore, with a strong bias in favor of the sapiential doctrines rather than those which, having a bhaktic character, reminded them too obviously of Christian modes of expression now grown suspect in their eyes, often mistakenly so ... these seekers have moreover awakened to the fact, familiar to every true Hindu, that Knowledge is not merely a matter of right theory ... but is something to be "actualized" with the help of a method running parallel to the doctrine and requiring for its effective communication, the presence of a guru ...[91]

Such aspirants are often impatient (a sign of the very ignorance which they are seeking to remedy) and insufficiently aware of the need to integrate certain "psychic and physical elements" before any real spiritual growth can proceed. This is matched by a certain lack of prudence on the part of Eastern teachers who in other respects might be thoroughly orthodox in their teachings. This circumstance is exacerbated by the fact that modern modes of communication (printing presses, mass media, the internet) facilitate the publicizing of the teacher and the teachings in ways which all too easily lead to the personal adulation of the teacher and the "distortion or dilution" of the doctrines. All too often the end result is a kind of "spiritual demagoguery." Furthermore, a purely mental acceptance of the teachings, unaccompanied by any deeper transformations, will often lead the Westerner to "... an intellectual automatism and all sorts of vices, such as pride, pretentiousness, obstinacy, mental petrifaction, dialectical monomania and a lack of a sense of the sacred."[92] Who can have failed to meet the type of Western "seeker" to which Schuon here refers? Schuon goes on to write of the dangers arising out of the different spiritual climates of India and the West, and the divergent spiritual temperaments to which the religious traditions are addressed:

> We do not say that a Jew or a Christian can never follow a Hindu *sadhana*; we say that, if they follow it, they must ... take account of their own mental make-up. They are neither Hindus nor Brahmins [this state being only accessible by birthright]; *jnana* is more dangerous for them than for the men belonging to the elite of India. Being Europeans, they think too much, which gives them an appearance of intelligence; in reality their thought, more often than not, is basically passionate and has no contemplative serenity whatsoever ...[93]

Herein we have at least a partial explanation of the well-attested phenomena of well-educated, articulate and clever Western intellectuals who have, apparently, a thorough *mental* grasp of the most profound teachings but who, whatever their pretensions, have undergone none of that alchemical transmuta-

91 F. Schuon, *Language of the Self*, 48.
92 F. Schuon, *Language of the Self*, 51.
93 F. Schuon, *Language of the Self*, 55.

tion of the soul which leads to wisdom and saintliness. Western seekers cannot too often be reminded that

> If metaphysics is a sacred thing, that means it could not be ... limited to the framework of the play of the mind. It is illogical and dangerous to talk of metaphysics without being preoccupied with the moral concomitances it requires, the criteria of which are, for man, his behavior in relation to God and to his neighbor.[94]

*

Guénon, Coomaraswamy and Schuon have played different but complementary roles in the development of traditionalism, each fulfilling a function corresponding to their distinct sensibilities and gifts. Guénon occupies a special position by virtue of being the first to articulate the fundamental metaphysical and cosmological principles through which the *sophia perennis* might be rediscovered and expressed anew in the West. We have already noted Schuon's recognition of Guénon as a "providential interpreter, at least on the doctrinal level" for the modern West. In a like sense Laurant refers to Guénon's "hieratic role."[95] Guénon's critique of the "reign of quantity" also provides the platform from which more detailed criticisms might be made by later traditionalists. His reaction to modernism was integral to his role and constitutes a kind of clearing of the ground.

Coomaraswamy brought to the study of traditional metaphysics, sacred art and religious culture an aesthetic sense and a scholarly aptitude not found in Guénon. The Frenchman had, as Reynolds observes, "no great sensitivity for human cultures."[96] Coomaraswamy, in a sense, brings the principles about which Guénon wrote, down to a more human level. His work exhibits much more of a sense of history, and a feel for the diverse and concrete circumstances of human experience. There is also a sense of personal presence in Coomaraswamy's writings which is absent in Guénon's work which, to some readers at least, must appear somewhat abstract and rarefied. As Gai Eaton put it, to move from Guénon's work to Coomaraswamy's is to "... descend into a far kindlier climate, while remaining in the same country ... The icy glitter is replaced by a warmer glow, the attitude of calm disdain towards all things modern by a more human indignation."[97] Whitall Perry contrasts their roles through a metaphor which each would have appreciated:

> Guénon was like the vertical axis of a cross, fixed with mathematical precision on immutable realities and their immediate applications in the domain of cosmological sciences; whereas Coomaraswamy was the horizontal complement, expanding these truths over the vast field of arts, cultures,

94 F. Schuon, *Spiritual Perspectives and Human Facts*, 173.
95 J.P. Laurant: "Le problème de René Guénon," 63.
96 P.L. Reynolds, "René Guénon," 6.
97 G. Eaton, *The Richest Vein*, 199.

mythologies and symbolisms: metaphysical truth on the one hand, universal beauty on the other.[98]

Schuon combined in himself something of the qualities of both Guénon and Coomaraswamy. His work includes psychic, moral and aesthetic dimensions which are missing from Guénon's writings. As Jean Tourniac has remarked

> Another writer, M. Frithjof Schuon, for his part, had to develop the spiritual exegesis of traditional forms in a series of works of a different kind to those of Guénon, works of high color—this word is not excessive, for beauty and color play a distinctive role in the work of F. Schuon—more "Christly" than those of Guénon which essentially hold themselves to defining the mechanisms of invariable principles.[99]

Schuon's work has a symmetry and an inclusive quality not found in the work of his precursors; there is a balance and fullness which give his writings something of the quality of a spiritual therapy. In this sense Schuon does not simply write about the perennial philosophy but gives it a direct and fresh expression proportioned to the needs of the age.

The contrast with Guénon can be clearly seen in the style and tone of language. If Guénon's expositions can be called "mathematical," Schuon's might be described as "musical," this, of course, not implying any deficiency in precision but rather the addition of a dimension of Beauty. As S.H. Nasr has observed, "His authoritative tone, clarity of expression and an 'alchemy' which transmutes human language to enable it to present the profoundest truths, make of it a unique expression of the *sophia perennis* ..."[100] Marco Pallis refers to what he rather loosely calls "the gift of tongues": "the ability, that is to say, both to speak and to understand the various dialects through which the Spirit has chosen to communicate itself ..."[101]

Writing of the work of Guénon and Coomaraswamy, Whitall Perry suggested that

> The complement and copestone of this witness remained to be realized in the message of Schuon, coming freshly from the sphere of the *Religio Perennis*, in contradistinction to the *Philosophia Perennis* which was the legacy of the other two. His was the third pole, needed to complete the triangle and integrate the work on an operative basis.[102]

There is a nobility of spirit in Schuon's work which makes it something much more than a challenging and arresting body of ideas: it is a profoundly moving *theoria* which reverberates in the deepest recesses of one's being. He is

98 W. Perry, "The Man and the Witness," 7.
99 J. Tourniac, *Propos sur René Guénon*, 16, quoted in P.L. Reynolds, "Rene Guénon," 13 (Translation by Pamela Oldmeadow).
100 S.H. Nasr, Preface to F. Schuon, *Islam and the Perennial Philosophy*, viii.
101 M. Pallis, *The Way and the Mountain*, 78.
102 W. Perry, "The Man and the Witness," 7.

the most sublime metaphysician of the age. It is not without reason that Whitall Perry has recently compared Schuon's work to that of Plato and Sankara.[103] In Schuon's work we find the richest, the most authoritative and the most resonant expression of the *sophia perennis* in modern times. One might borrow the following words, applied to Meister Eckhart but equally true of Schuon:

> Being wholly traditional in the truest sense, and therefore perennial, the doctrine he expounds will never cease to be contemporary and always accessible to those who, naturally unsatisfied with mere living, desire to know how to live, regardless of time or place.[104]

Other Traditionalists

Titus Burckhardt (1908-1984)

In the previous chapter we made some note of the work of another leading traditionalist, Marco Pallis. We will bring this one to its conclusions with some brief notes on the other principal figures. In recent times the most distinguished exponent of traditional thought, after Schuon, was Titus Burckhardt.[105] Born in Florence in 1908, he was the son of the Swiss sculptor Carl Burckhardt, and a member of a patrician family of Basle. His friendship with Frithjof Schuon went back to their school days together. Although Burckhardt first followed in his father's footsteps as a sculptor and illustrator, he was from childhood attracted to medieval and Oriental art. This early interest led Burckhardt to a theoretical study of medieval and Eastern doctrines and awoke in him a realization of the metaphysical or intellectual principles that govern all traditional forms. For Burckhardt, the relationship between art and metaphysics finds perfect expression in the words of Plato: "Beauty is the Splendor of Truth." In the same vein a medieval artist had declared *"ars sine scientia nihil"* ("art without science is nothing").[106] Following the same line of thought Burckhardt has shown how, in a traditional society, every art is a science, and every science an art. Given that the contemplation of God is the "art of arts" and the "science of sciences," one can see from the foregoing how intellectuality and spirituality are but two sides of the same coin, and how each is wholly indispensable. Without true intellectuality there can only be heresy; and without true spirituality there can only be hypocrisy. This, in a nutshell, is the doctrine which Burckhardt exemplified in his life's work. He died in Lausanne in 1984.

103 W. Perry, "The Revival of Interest in Tradition," 15.
104 C.F. Kelley, *Meister Eckhart on Divine Knowledge*, xv.
105 For biographical information on Burckhardt see W. Stoddart: "Right Hand of Truth" and M. Lings, "Titus Burckhardt," both in the Titus Burckhardt Memorial Issue of *Studies in Comparative Religion*, 16:1 & 2, 1984.
106 See A.K. Coomaraswamy, *"Ars Sine Scientia Nihil"* in *Selected Papers 1*, 229.

Burckhardt's most significant writings on Eastern subjects appear in *Sacred Art in East and West* (1967) and in his collected essays, *Mirror of the Intellect* (1987), edited by William Stoddart. Burckhardt's work is in one sense a prolongation of that of Frithjof Schuon, but at every turn it also bears witness to his own spiritual originality and imposing gifts. Primarily a metaphysician, his works on sacred art and alchemy also testify to his gift for elucidating the cosmological principles that inform traditional arts and sciences.

Martin Lings (b. 1909)

The English traditionalist, Martin Lings, was born in Burnage, Lancashire, in 1909.[107] After studying English at Oxford he was appointed Lecturer in Anglo-Saxon at the University of Kaunas. As with many of his fellow-traditionalists, an interest in Islam took him traveling to the Middle East and North Africa. A trip to Egypt in 1939 brought an appointment as Lecturer in Shakespeare at Cairo University. He spent many years in Cairo where he had a close association with Guénon. In 1952 Lings returned to England to take out a doctorate in Arabic (in which he was already fluent) at London University. He worked for many years at the British Museum where he was Keeper of Oriental Manuscripts and Printed Books. He is an authority on Koranic manuscripts and calligraphy. As well as his expertise in the field of Islamic studies Lings brings to traditionalism a cultivated English sensibility and a gift for expressing complex truths in simple language.

Whitall Perry (b. 1920)

The most authoritative traditionalist of American background is Whitall Perry.[108] He was born near Boston in 1920. His early intellectual interests included Platonism and Vedanta. He traveled in the Middle and Far East both before and after World War II with a brief interlude of study at Harvard University. He was one of several Harvard students who came under Coomaraswamy's influence in the 1940s, Joseph Epes Brown being another. Between 1946 and 1952 Perry and his wife lived in Egypt, at which time he developed close ties with René Guénon, after whose death he moved with his family to Switzerland. He was already a close associate of Frithjof Schuon with whom he returned to the United States in 1980.

Coomaraswamy once expressed the view that the time was ripe for someone well versed in the world's great religious traditions and fluent in several languages to compile an encyclopedic anthology drawing together the spiritual wisdom of the ages in a single volume. This task was to be accomplished by Whitall Perry whose seventeen-year labor bore fruit in *A Treasury of*

---

107 Information on Lings taken from his own publications.
108 Material on Perry drawn from his own publications, especially "The Man and the Witness" and Marco Pallis' Foreword to W. Perry, *Treasury of Traditional Wisdom*, 7-11.

Traditional Wisdom (1971). This is a work of singular importance. In his Introduction Perry invites the reader

> to enter upon a spiritual journey. In this book he will encounter the heritage he shares in common with all humanity, in what is essentially timeless and enduring and pertinent to his final ends. Out of this myriad mosaic of material emerges a pattern of the human personality in the cosmos that is unerringly consistent, clear and struck through with a resonance infallible in its ever renewed reverberations of the one same Reality.[109]

Thousands of quotations have been woven into an immense tapestry whose threads have been drawn from all the major religious and esoteric traditions. Each section of the book is introduced with a concise and acute commentary, usually referring to the works of Guénon, Coomaraswamy and Schuon to whom Perry acknowledges a debt of "profound gratitude" and "whose several roles," Perry tells us, "have been altogether indispensable in the formation of this work." While performing a valuable service in bringing the work of "the great triumvirate" to the attention of a wider audience Perry has himself discharged an awesome labor in pulling together the many strands of traditional wisdom between the covers of a single volume in which the concrete reality of the *sophia perennis,* axiomatic in traditionalism, is revealed and documented. It would, of course, be impossible to uncover every manifestation of the Primordial Wisdom in all its plenitude but Perry has surely come close to such an ideal. It is a monumental and profoundly impressive achievement in the light of which the only remotely comparable book, Aldous Huxley's *The Perennial Philosophy* (1945), pales into insignificance.[110]

Seyyed Hossein Nasr (b. 1933)

An eminent Islamicist and of the living traditionalists the most widely known in academic circles, Seyyed Hossein Nasr, was born in Tehran.[111] As a young man he studied physics and the history of science at the Massachusetts Institute of Technology and at Harvard University. He rapidly established himself as an authority on Islamic philosophy and science, and on Sufism. In 1958 he became Professor of Science and Philosophy at Tehran University and in 1964-65 occupied the first Aga Khan Chair of Islamic Studies at the American University at Beirut. Nasr became Chancellor of Aryamehr University in 1972 and was also the Founder President of the Imperial

---

109 W. Perry, *Treasury of Traditional Wisdom,* 19.

110 We shall have more to say about Huxley's idiosyncratic view of the perennial philosophy in Chapter 10.

111 Information about Nasr taken from notes accompanying his own publications, from Notes on Contributors in Y. Ibish & P.L. Wilson, *Traditional Modes of Contemplation and Action,* 472, and from Notes on Contributors in several journals. A useful biographical sketch can be found in W. Chittick (ed), *The Works of Seyyed Hossein Nasr Through His Fortieth Birthday.* See also William Stoddart's Introduction to T. Burckhardt, *Mirror of the Intellect,* 3-9.

Iranian Academy of Philosophy which published the traditionalist journal *Sophia Perennis*.

Since the political changes in Iran Nasr has lived in the U.S.A. and after some years in the Religious Studies Department at Temple University is now the University Professor of Islamic Studies at George Washington University. Nasr has lectured extensively not only in the U.S.A. but in Europe, the Middle East, Pakistan, India, Japan and Australia. He has published widely, being the author of some two dozen books and a frequent contributor to Islamic and traditionalist journals,

The hallmarks of Nasr's work are his rigorous scholarly methodology, his encyclopedic erudition about all matters Islamic, a robustness of critical thought, and a sustained clarity of expression. His most important works fall into three groups: those concerned with Islamic science and philosophy which include *An Introduction to Islamic Cosmological Doctrines* (1964), *Science and Civilization in Islam* (1968), and *Islamic Science: An Illustrated History* (1976); works dealing with Islam more generally or with the mystical traditions of Sufism; and thirdly, books in which specifically modern problems are investigated in the light of traditional metaphysics: *The Encounter of Man and Nature* (1968), *Islam and the Plight of Modern Man* (1976), and *Religion and the Order of Nature* (1996). His Gifford Lectures of 1981 were subsequently published under the title *Knowledge and the Sacred*. Nasr has been the foremost traditionalist thinker bringing the wisdom of the ages to bear on the contemporary environmental crisis.

*

Other traditionalists include Lord Northbourne, Leo Schaya, Philip Sherrard, Joseph Epes Brown, Gai Eaton, Rama Coomaraswamy, William Stoddart and Ranjit Fernando (of whom the first four are no longer living). There are, apart from the traditionalists themselves, several scholars and thinkers whose work exhibits, in varying degree, a strong traditionalist influence. Mention should be made of Huston Smith, Elémire Zolla, Toshihiko Izutsu, Kathleen Raine, Brian Keeble, William Chittick, James Cutsinger, Wolfgang Smith, Shojun Bando, Adrian Snodgrass, E.F. Schumacher and Julius Evola (about whom more later).[112] The names of other traditionalists can be found in the pages of journals such as *Studies in Comparative Religion*, *Sophia Perennis*, *Études Traditionnelles*, *Sophia*, *Temenos*[113] and *Sacred Web* (though it must be remembered that many contributors to these journals are in no way traditionalist). Discussing the work of contemporary traditionalists, Gai Eaton observed that

112 For information on some of these figures see Notes on Contributors in Y. Ibish & P.L. Wilson, *Traditional Modes of Contemplation and Action*, 469-477.

113 There are two journals published under this name, one in Scandinavia, the other in London. It is to the latter that we here refer. This journal was succeeded by *Temenos Academy Review*.

These books and articles present variety in unity, very different voices speaking from a single standpoint. Few readers respond to them in a neutral or tepid fashion. For some they open up new horizons, often with a sense of shock, discovery and delight, while others, who cannot bear to have their ingrained habits of thought and all the cherished assumptions of the age so ruthlessly challenged, are angered and outraged. They provoke ... a polarization of perspectives which serves to clarify thought and to define the demarcation line between the basic tendencies of our time, the traditional and the modernist ...[114]

114 G. Eaton, *King of the Castle*, 219.

9.

Christian Missionaries, Monks and Mystics in India

Christian Missionaries and Monks in India—Jules Monchanin—Henri le Saux—
Bede Griffiths—A Note on the Christian Ashram Movement—Thomas Merton and
Eastern Spirituality—Jottings on other Christian Missionaries—A Closing Reflection
on Monasticism

Let the athlete of the spirit ever integrate himself
Standing in a place apart,
alone, his thoughts and self restrained,
Devoid of earthly hope, possessing nothing.
(Bhagavad Gita 6.10)

It is no secret that over the last century Christian missionaries have had a
bad press. The Theosophists, the neo-Hindu reformers, Western Vedantins,
fictionalists such as Somerset Maugham, historians, the post-colonial critics,
have all slipped the boot into the whole missionary enterprise. Its auxiliary
role in the spread of European imperialism and in the extirpation of traditional cultures has, quite properly, come under heavy fire. On the other
hand, it must be recognized that the enemies of Christianity (and often of
religion in general) are ever ready to portray its representatives in the worst
possible light, to attribute to them the most sinister of motives and to sheet
home to them all manner of ills. Certainly there is no hiding from the dismal
fact that an arrogant and intolerant Christian exclusivism has sometimes
been an accomplice in rapacious empire building—a sad and sorry chapter
in the history of Christianity. At the same time, it is as well to remember that
missionaries often resisted and condemned the exploitative aspects of imperialism. Recent scholarship has only confirmed "the great variety of missionary relationships to and attitudes toward imperialism, so that no generaliza-
tion, save that of variety, can be maintained."[1]

We have already encountered several figures whose life and work suggest
that we should not be too hasty in a blanket condemnation of missionaries.
Recall the pioneering work of the Jesuits in India, Tibet, China and Japan in
dispelling European ignorance about Asian religions and the cultures which
were their outward expression: the legacy of men such as Fathers Nobili,
Desideri, Matteo Ricci and Francis Xavier in promoting a genuine dialogue

---

1   C.W. Forman, "The Growth of the Study of the Expansion of Christianity," 32. See also S.
Lund, "The Christian Mission and Colonialism."

between West and East and in opening European eyes to the spiritual riches of the East is not one that can be easily waved away. Think, too, of the role of missionaries who have, in some sense, become advocates of Asian religious and philosophical traditions *against* the European values and assumptions which they themselves ostensibly represent: one thinks of figures such as Dwight Goddard, Richard Wilhelm and, more recently, the comparative religionist Klaus Klostermaier and the missionary-sinologist, D.H. Smith. In recent times missionaries have often been in the vanguard of movements for national liberation and the achievement of human rights and social justice. So, the story of missionary activity is a complex one. We shall not here essay any attempt at a history of Western missions in the East; rather, without gainsaying the sometimes disastrous effects of Christian missionizing, we shall turn to some of its more positive outcomes.

In this chapter, after a quick survey of some of the landmarks of Christian missionizing in India, we shall direct the spotlight onto a group of Benedictine monks whose experiences in south India comprise an interesting strand in the larger story of East-West religious encounters. We will then turn to a Trappist who is perhaps the best known of all the Christian religious who have turned Eastwards, Father Thomas Merton.

Christian Missionaries and Monks in India

Vasco da Gama arrived in the south Indian port of Calicut in 1498, and Pedro Cabral in Cochin two years later. The search for spices was soon joined by the quest for souls. The earliest European missionaries in India were Franciscans and Dominicans, soon to be followed by the redoubtable Jesuits. By the middle of the 16th century the Jesuits were entrenched in Goa and its hinterland, and well advanced on their first major task—the mastery of the principal languages of the region. In 1579 the British Jesuit Thomas Stephens arrived in Goa and was soon able to produce several works in Indian languages, culminating in his 11,000-verse *Christian Purana*, "the unsurpassed masterpiece of Christian missionary literature in an Indian vernacular."[2] But it was Father Roberto Nobili (1577-1656) who "led the missionary effort to an entirely new level of theoretical and hermeneutic awareness" and who best exemplifies "the problematic nature of the encounter between Christianity and Hinduism."[3] His efforts to find some sort of doctrinal rapprochement between the two traditions inevitably overstepped the ecclesiastical bounds of orthodoxy. Nobili found in the *Upanishads* a pristine monotheism and even intimations of the "recondite mystery of the most sacred trinity," discerned the "natural light" of reason in Brahminical sciences and philosophy, and argued against their dismissal by Europeans as superstitious, "as if the heathen sages were not also bringing forth valuable teachings which could likewise be of use to Christians."[4] Nobili found some

2   W. Halbfass, *India and Europe*, 37-38.
3   W. Halbfass, *India and Europe*, 38.
4   W. Halbfass, *India and Europe*, 40.

precedent for his approach to Hinduism in the reception of Greek thought by the early Fathers. Nobili in turn was to serve as an inspiration for Father Bede Griffiths, an English Benedictine monk in India three centuries later. Nor was Nobili playing a lone hand. Heinrich Roth (1620-1668) produced the first European Sanskrit grammar, philosophical commentaries and translations. Father J.F. Pons, another Jesuit, was probably the author of a grammar of Sanskrit in Latin in about 1733. Then, too, there were the Protestant missionary scholars such as the Dutch Calvinists Abraham Roger and Philippus Baldaeus who published Indological works in the 17th century, and the Moravian Bartholomäus Ziegenbalg who wrote substantial hermeneutical works on the customs and beliefs of the Hindus.

In his remarkable study of the encounter between India and Europe Wilhelm Halbfass has pointed out that the work of the missionaries of the 17th and 18th centuries laid the foundations of Indological research well before the appearance of the Asiatic Society of Bengal in 1784 and the pioneering scholarship of Jones, Wilkins and Colebrooke, the first British orientalists-proper. The legacy of the Jesuits was to be found not only in their texts—grammars, dictionaries, translations, commentaries and the like—but in the collection of manuscripts and their development of methods of collaboration with native Indian scholars.[5]

By the mid-19th century the missionary ethos was increasingly influenced by the idea of fulfillment, foreshadowed in some of Nobili's writings and embryonic in the ideas of Max Müller and Monier Monier-Williams. The missionary and Indologist J.N. Farquhar was perhaps its most influential exponent. Thus, following T.E. Slater's claim that "All religions wait for their fulfillment in Christianity," Farquhar could argue that

> The Vedanta is not Christianity, and never will be—simply as the Vedanta: but a very definite preparation for it ... It is our belief that the living Christ will sanctify and make complete the religious thought of India. For centuries ... her saints have been longing for him, and her thinkers, not least the thinkers of the Vedanta have been thinking his thought.[6]

Furthermore, he added,

> This is the attitude of Jesus to all other religions also. Each contains a partial revelation of God's will, but each is incomplete; and He comes to fulfill them all. In each case Christianity seeks not to destroy but to take all that is right and raise it to perfection.[7]

This idea was later to find an ironic echo in the neo-Hindu and Vedantin claim that all other religions and creeds are subsumed by Vedanta.

---

5 W. Halbfass, *India and Europe*, 45.
6 Farquhar quoted in W. Halbfass, *India and Europe*, 51.
7 Farquhar quoted in E. Sharpe, *Not to Destroy But to Fulfill*, 260.

During the 20th century many missionary societies and individual missionaries have had to come to terms with the palpable historical fact that, in India at least (and indeed most other Asian countries, the Philippines and to a lesser extent Korea, being the notable exceptions), Christian triumphalism was quite misplaced, that the rates of conversion are pitifully small, that while most Hindus are perfectly willing to accept the divinity of Christ as one *avatar* among many, they remain quite impervious to the fulfillment theory and its many variants. So much for the kind of thinking behind Macaulay's boast in 1836 that English education would see to it that thirty years hence "there will not be a single idolater [Hindu] among the respectable classes in Bengal."[8] The general failure of Christian missionaries to win a significant number of converts eventually moved the accent of mission work onto ideals of witness, service and dialogue rather than conversion.[9] However, it would be a mistake to measure the validity of the missionary enterprise purely in terms of conversion rates. As Frithjof Schuon has remarked,

> [Christian] missionaries—although they have profited from abnormal circumstances inasmuch as Western expansion at the expense of other civilizations is due solely to a crushing material superiority arising out of the modern deviation—follow a way that possesses, at least in principle, a sacrificial aspect; consequently the subjective reality of this way will always retain its mystic meaning.[10]

Surveying over three centuries of European missionizing in India, Wilhelm Halbfass concludes:

> ... the missionary efforts in this country can hardly be described as having been successful, and dogmatism and intolerance have frequently played a dominating role ... This notwithstanding, the achievements of the missionaries comprise a very important chapter in the Western encounter with Indian thought, a chapter that is exemplary from a hermeneutic standpoint and which, moreover, has had historical consequences. The missionaries have performed pioneering, detailed work in several areas. *But primarily, in spite of or perhaps precisely because of their "prejudice" and dogmatic limitations, they have also helped to define and clarify the central problems involved in approaching and understanding that which is alien* ... their outstanding exponents embody a desire to understand whose singular power and problematic nature arise from their deep and uncompromising *desire to be understood.* [11]

The "problematic nature" of missionizing is dramatically personified in the lives and work of three Benedictine monks, each of whom wished to reconcile Hinduism and Christianity: Jules Monchanin, Henri Le Saux and Bede Griffiths. Certain themes and issues circulate through the experiences and

---

8 *Life and Letters of Lord Macaulay*, 455.

9 For one recent and personal understanding of missionary work, quite at odds with the notion of missionizing as a form of imperialism, see Nicholas Colasuonno, "The Pilgrim Missionary."

10 F. Schuon, *Transcendent Unity of Religions*, 81.

11 W. Halbfass, *India and Europe*, 53 (italics mine except for the last phrase).

writings of each: the so-called "problem" of religious pluralism, the proper role of Christianity in India, the renewal of Christian monasticism and the revival of its contemplative and mystical heritage, the doctrinal reconciliation of a non-dualistic Vedanta with a Trinitarian Christianity, the existential problem of living out a spirituality which drew on both Eastern and Western sources. Rather than any kind of exhaustive treatment of these concerns with respect to each of these men we shall simply foreground one or two of them in each case.

Jules Monchanin (Swami Arubianandam)

The first forty years of Jules Monchanin's life were quite unexceptional for a provincial French priest.[12] He was born near Lyons in 1895, decided at an early age to enter the priesthood and completed his theological training in 1922. Despite his intellectual distinction he did not complete his doctoral studies but instead asked to be sent to a miners' parish in a poor suburb of Lyons. He served in three parishes before serious illness led to less demanding appointments as a chaplain, first in an orphanage and then at a boys' boarding school. Throughout these years he continued to move in a university milieu and applied himself to a range of studies. Since boyhood he had felt an attraction to India which now steered him towards Sanskrit, and Indological and comparative religious studies. From the early 30s Monchanin was exploring the possibility of living some sort of Christian monastic life in India, no easy task for someone bound to Mother Church. It took many years of negotiations before Monchanin finally received the approval of the Bishop of Tiruchirapalli to work amongst the scattered Indian Christians in the region evangelized centuries before by both Francis Xavier and Roberto Nobili. Monchanin left Marseilles for India in May 1939.

For the next decade Monchanin was immersed in pastoral work in India. These were years of social deprivation, physical hardship, and acute loneliness, preparatory to the contemplative life for which he yearned. At last, in 1950, he was able to establish a monastic hermitage on the banks of the Kavery River, a Christian ashram which he and his fellow Benedictine and compatriot, Henri le Saux, called "Saccidananda." Le Saux articulated their agenda:

> Our goal: to form the first nucleus of a monastery (or rather a laura, a grouping of neighboring anchorites like the ancient laura of Saint Sabas in Palestine) which buttresses the Rule of Saint Benedict—a primitive, sober, discrete rule. Only one purpose: to seek God. And the monastery will be Indian style. We would like to crystallize and transubstantiate the search of the Hindu *sannyasi.* Advaita and the praise of the Trinity are our only aim. This means we must grasp the authentic Hindu search for God in order to Christianize it, starting with ourselves first of all, from within.[13]

12 Most of the biographical information following is taken from J.G. Weber, *In Quest of the Absolute: the Life and Work of Jules Monchanin.*
13 Le Saux quoted in J.G. Weber, *In Quest of the Absolute,* 73.

Vedantic philosophy, Christian theology, Indian lifestyle. The hope was that "what is deepest in Christianity may be grafted on to what is deepest in India."[14] This was not a syncretic exercise which would issue forth some kind of religious hybrid but an attempt to fathom the depths of Christianity with the aid of the traditional wisdom of India which, in the monks' view, was to be found in Vedanta and the spiritual disciplines of the renunciate. The lifestyle was to be thoroughly Indian: meditation, prayer, study of the Scriptures of both traditions, a simple vegetarian diet, the most spartan of amenities. Each donned the ochre cloth of the *sannyasi*, Monchanin (informally) becoming Swami Arubianandam and le Saux Swami Abhishiktananda.

Monchanin had alluded earlier to the case of Dom Joliet, a French naval officer in China who became a Benedictine in 1897 and waited thirty years to realize his dream of founding a Christian monastery in the Far East. Monchanin had written, "Will I someday know the same joy, that in India too—from its soil and spirit—there will come a [Christian] monastic life dedicated to contemplation?"[15] The dream was not to be fully realized in Monchanin's own lifetime. On the face of it, the efforts of the French monks were less than successful: it was a constant struggle to keep the ashram afloat; there was little enthusiasm from either European or Indian quarters; there were endless difficulties and hardships; not a solitary Indian monk became a permanent member of the ashram. By the time of Monchanin's death in 1957 there seemed little to show for the hard years behind them. Monchanin was not even able to realize his desire to die in India as he had been sent to Paris for medical treatment. But the seeds had been sown. A decade after Monchanin's death Father Bede Griffiths and two Indian monks left their own ashram and committed themselves to Saccidananda ashram. There were to be many difficult years still ahead but Monchanin's dream finally came to fruition under the husbandry of Bede Griffiths who later wrote of Monchanin's mission:

> The ashram which he founded remains as a witness to the ideal of a contemplative life which he had set before him, and his life and writings remain to inspire others with the vision of a Christian contemplation which shall have assimilated the wisdom of India, and a theology in which the genius of India shall find expression in Christian terms.[16]

In Monchanin we find a formidable intellect, considerable erudition, a refined sensibility with an appreciation of Europe's cultural heritage; he might easily have fashioned a splendid academic or ecclesiastical career. We

14 Bede Griffiths quoted in J.G. Weber, *In Quest of the Absolute*, 2.
15 J.G. Weber, *In Quest of the Absolute*, 21-22.
16 Bede Griffiths quoted in J.G. Weber, *In Quest of the Absolute*, 3.

Lama Anagarika Govinda (1898-1985)

Alexandra David-Neel (1868-1969)

Walter Y. Evans-Wentz (1878-1965) with Lama Kazi Dawa-Samdup

Sister Nivedita (1867-1911)

Mircea Eliade (1907-1986)

Rudolf Otto (1869-1937)

René Guénon (1886-1951)

Ananda K. Coomaraswamy (1877-1947)

Frithjof Schuon (1907-1998)

Marco Pallis (1895-1990)

Daisetz Teitaro Suzuki (1870-1966)

Thomas Merton (1915-1968)

Heinrich Zimmer (1890-1943)

Huston Smith (1919-)

Bede Griffiths (1906-1993)

Gary Snyder (1930-)

have the testimony of some of the leading French Indologists of the day to this effect.[17] His closest associate, Henri Le Saux, said of him,

> He was one of the most brilliant intellects among the French clergy, a remarkable conversationalist, at home on every subject, a brilliant lecturer and a theologian who opened before his hearers marvelous and ever new horizons.[18]

Instead, all is surrendered to plunge himself into the materially impoverished life of the Indian villager and the eremitic life of the monk, the Christian *sannyasi*. In 1941 he had written in his journal, "May India take me and bury me within itself—in God."[19] It was a noble ideal.

The annals of Christian missionizing are replete with stories of heroic self-sacrifice, of dedication to tireless, often thankless work in arid fields, an exacting and lonely life in the service of Christian ideals—precisely, the pursuit of a vocation. Monchanin, however, is a fascinating case because in him the missionary dilemma, if one may so express it, becomes fully and acutely self-conscious. The poignancy and tragedy of Monchanin's life in India is that he was unable to find his way out of the dilemma. Here is a telling passage from Alain Daniélou's autobiography:

> Then there was the curious little ashram of Père Montchanin (sic). This priest ... had been deeply influenced by Hinduism and wanted to combine the two religions. He wore the draped orange cloth of Hindu monks, but obviously did not perform the ritual ablutions ... he lived in a hermitage with a few followers and exerted a great influence on that special brand of foreigner who, while acknowledging the spiritual, philosophical, and moral superiority of Hinduism, still insists on Christian supremacy ... Instead of mellowing through Hinduism, Montchanin and his devotees remained frustrated, neurotic, ill at ease, and, on the whole, rather disagreeable people ... The word *ashram*, which is literally "a place of rest" has come to mean "a pseudo-spiritual gathering place for maladjusted Westerners with a craving for exoticism."[20]

This passage is itself somewhat "disagreeable," lacking in charity, tainted with that condescension which is often the mark of the Western Vedantin and apparently immune to Monchanin's saintly qualities (which any number of people, Hindus and Christians alike, have attested). Nonetheless, it is insightful. It is perfectly clear from Monchanin's own writings that he intuitively understood "the limits of religious expansionism" (to borrow a phrase from Schuon). He was intelligent enough to see that insofar as Christians were bent on converting Indians, the enterprise was doomed to failure (the odd individual convert being the exception that proves the rule). He rightly

17 J.G. Weber, *In Quest of the Absolute*, 16.
18 Le Saux quoted in E. Vattakuzhy, *Indian Christian Sannyasa and Swami Abhishiktananda*, 67.
19 J.G. Weber, *In Quest of the Absolute*, 56.
20 A. Daniélou, *The Way to the Labyrinth*, 213.

sensed that devout Hindus found the idea of conversion abhorrent—"a betrayal, cowardice."[21] Shortly before his death he wrote,

> The root of the matter is that Hindus are not spiritually uneasy. They believe they possess supreme wisdom and thus how could they attach any importance to the fluctuations or investigations of those who possess lesser wisdom. Christ is one among avataras. Christianity in their eyes is a perfect moral doctrine, but a metaphysics which stops on the threshold of the ultimate metamorphosis.[22]

He was also, as Daniélou intimates, well equipped to appreciate the vast storehouse of Indian spirituality. But throughout he felt bound to the conventional Christian belief in the ultimate superiority of his own faith, a position to which he was theologically committed by the weight of the centuries. His friend Père Henri de Lubac had characterized Monchanin's task this way: "to rethink everything in the light of theology, and to rethink theology through mysticism."[23] The problem was that the theology and the mysticism were pulling in opposite directions, the tension arising out of a dogmatic literalism and an ossified exotericism in the Catholic Church which insisted on the *exclusive* truths of Christianity and, *ipso facto*, on its *superiority* to other faiths. During a near-fatal illness in 1932 Monchanin had vowed that, if he were to recover, he would devote himself to the salvation of India:[24] his years in India taught him, at least sub-consciously, that India (insofar as it still cleaved to Hindu orthodoxy) was in no need of salvation! Consider a sample of quotes from Monchanin's writings:

> India has stood for three millennia, if not longer, as the seat of one of the principal civilizations of mankind, equal to if not greater than that of Europe and China ...

> India has received from the Almighty an uncommon gift, an unquenchable thirst for whatever is spiritual. Since the time of the *Vedas* and the *Upanishads*, countless numbers of its sons have been great seekers of God.

> Century after century there rose up seers and poets singing the joys and sorrows of a soul in quest of the One, and philosophers reminding every man of the supremacy of contemplation ...

Cheek by jowl with lofty passages such as these we find quite contradictory ones:

> Unfortunately Indian wisdom is tainted with erroneous tendencies ... Outside the unique revelation and the unique Church man is always and everywhere incapable of sifting truth from falsehood and good from evil.

21 J.G. Weber, *In Quest of the Absolute*, 96.
22 J.G. Weber, *In Quest of the Absolute*, 97.
23 J.G. Weber, *In Quest of the Absolute*, 25.
24 J.G. Weber, *In Quest of the Absolute*, 16.

> So also, confident in the indefectible guidance of the Church, we hope that India, once baptized into the fullness of its body and soul and into the depth of its age-long quest for Brahma, will reject its pantheistic tendencies and, discovering in the splendors of the Holy Spirit the true mysticism and finding at last the vainly longed-for philosophical and theological equilibrium between antagonistic trends of thought, will bring forth for the good of humanity and the Church and ultimately for the glory of God unparalleled galaxies of saints and doctors.

> ... we cannot hide [Hinduism's] fundamental error and its essential divergence in terms of Christianity. Hinduism must reject its *atman-Brahman* equation, if it is to enter into Christ.[25]

How much easier Monchanin's life would have been had the Vatican II renovation of Catholic attitudes to other religions taken place half a century earlier. (Vatican II was, in common parlance, a "a very mixed bag" but the mitigation of centuries of rigid Christian exclusivism was a significant step in the right direction.) How much agonizing he might also have been spared by recourse to the works of traditionalists such as his fellow countryman, René Guénon, or Frithjof Schuon. Seyyed Hossein Nasr has stated the problem in a nutshell:

> The essential problem that the study of religion poses is how to preserve religious truth, traditional orthodoxy, the dogmatic theological structures of one's own tradition, and yet gain knowledge of other traditions and accept them as spiritually valid ways and roads to God.[26]

This was the problem which Monchanin could never quite overcome. His successor, Bede Griffiths, was able to at least partially resolve the dilemma by discerning that the task at hand was not to "Christianize" Hinduism—an undertaking to which the Indians themselves remained, for the most part, supremely indifferent—but to "Hinduize" Christianity, that is, to recover the mystical and contemplative dimension of the Christian tradition, and its metaphysical underpinnings, by recourse to a sapiential wisdom and a more or less intact spiritual methodology still comparatively untouched by the ravages of modernity.

Henri Le Saux (Swami Abhishiktananda)

Henri Le Saux arrived in India in 1948 to join Monchanin in the monastic venture at Shantivanam. He was never to leave the shores of his adopted country. Le Saux was born in Brittany in 1910 and entered a Benedictine monastery in 1929. Like Monchanin he felt the call of India as a young man but he too had to endure a lengthy wait before achieving "his most ardent

---

25 All passages cited in J.G. Weber, *In Quest of the Absolute*, 77-78, 82, 126. (Weber himself, writing in somewhat hagiographic mode, seems impervious to the flagrant contradictions found in these and in many other passages in Monchanin's writings.)

26 S.H. Nasr, *Sufi Essays*, 127.

desire," and embarking for the sub-continent.[27] Soon after setting up the modest ashram the two French Benedictines traveled to Arunachala to visit Ramana Maharshi who made the most profound impression on Le Saux:

> Even before my mind was able to recognize the fact, and still less to express it, the invisible halo of this Sage had been perceived by something in me deeper than any words. Unknown harmonies awoke in my heart ... In the Sage of Arunachala of our time I discerned the Unique Sage of the eternal India, the unbroken succession of her sages, her ascetics, her seers; it was as if the very soul of India penetrated to the very depths of my own soul and held mysterious communion with it. It was a call which pierced through everything, rent it in pieces and opened a mighty abyss ...[28]

It is interesting to compare this with a strikingly similar account of the Maharshi's nature and significance by Schuon:

> In Sri Ramana Maharshi one meets again ancient and eternal India. The Vedantic truth—the truth of the *Upanishads*—is brought back to its simplest expression but without any kind of betrayal. It is the simplicity inherent in the Real, not the denial of that complexity which it likewise contains ... That spiritual function which can be described as "activity of presence" found in the Maharshi its most rigorous expression. Sri Ramana was as it were the incarnation, in these latter days and in the face of modern activist fever, of what is primordial and incorruptible in India. He manifested the nobility of contemplative "non-action" in the face of an ethic of utilitarian agitation and he showed the implacable beauty of pure truth in the face of passions, weaknesses and betrayals.[29]

In the years following Ramana's death Le Saux spent two extended periods as a hermit in one of the holy mountain's many caves. He wrote of an overwhelming mystical experience while in retreat at Arunachala and stated that he was "truly reborn at Arunachala under the guidance of the Maharishi,"[30] understanding "what is beyond silence: *sunyata.*" "Ramana's *Advaita* is my birthplace. Against that all rationalization is shattered."[31] He also became a disciple of Sri Gnanananda Giri of Tiruykoyilur, giving an account of this in *Guru and Disciple* (1967) and *The Secret of Arunachala* (1974).[32] Interestingly, he remarks that upon meeting Gnanananda he *automatically* yielded his alle-

---

27 O. Baumer-Despeigne, "The Spiritual Journey of Henri Le Saux-Abhishiktananda," 312.

28 Abhishiktananda, *The Secret of Arunachala*, quoted in O. Baumer-Despeigne, "The Spiritual Journey of Henri Le Saux-Abhishiktananda," 313.

29 F. Schuon, *Language of the Self*, 44.

30 Abhishiktananda, *Diary*, quoted in J.M.D. Stuart, "Sri Ramana Maharshi and Abhishiktananda," 170.

31 Abhishiktananda, *Diary*, quoted in O. Baumer-Despeigne, "The Spiritual Journey of Henri Le Saux-Abhishiktananda," 316.

32 See also O. Baumer-Despeigne, "The Spiritual Journey of Henri Le Saux-Abhishiktananda," 314.

giance to him, something which he had never previously done.[33]

Over the next few years Abhishiktananda gradually loosened his connections with the ashram at Shantivanam (though he continued to visit right up to the time of his death) and spent much of his time as a wandering *sannyasi* in the Himalayas. It was his impregnable conviction that the life of renunciation was the meeting point of Christianity and Hinduism:

> Believe me, it is above all in the mystery of *sannyasa* that India and the Church will meet, will discover themselves in the most secret and hidden parts of their hearts, in the place where they are each most truly themselves, in the mystery of their origin in which every outward manifestation is rooted and from which time unfolds itself.[34]

He formalized his Indian citizenship in 1960 (he had long been a spiritual citizen), and founded a small hermitage on the banks of the Ganges at Uttarkashi in the Himalayas. Here he plunged ever deeper into the *Upanishads*, realizing more and more the Church's need of India's timeless message. He also consolidated his grasp of Sanskrit, Tamil and English, and often participated in retreats, conferences and inter-faith gatherings. It was appropriate that most of his books were written here, near the source of the Ganges. In his last two years he gathered a small group of disciples, including Marc Chaduc (Swami Ajatananda).[35] Abhishiktananda crossed to the further shore in 1973. In his final illness he had experienced again "an inner apocalypse," "an awakening beyond all myths and symbols,"[36] returning him to one of his favorite Upanishadic verses:

> I know him, that great Purusha
> Of the color of the sun,
> Beyond all darkness.
> He who has known him
> Goes beyond death.
> There is no other way.
> (*Svetasvatara Upanishad*, III.8.)

He wrote in one of his last letters, "the quest is fulfilled."[37]

Abhishiktananda seems to have had a more natural affinity for the actual practices of Hindu spirituality than did Monchanin and was less troubled by the doctrinal tensions between the two traditions which he was seeking to bridge. It is surely significant that it was Abhishiktananda who was able to surrender to the extraordinary *darsan* of Ramana. It is also suggestive that of the three Benedictines with whom we are presently concerned only Le Saux

33 J.E. Royster, "Abhishiktananda: Hindu-Christian Monk," 311.
34 Abhishiktananda, *Guru and Disciple*, 162.
35 See A. Rawlinson, *The Book of Enlightened Masters*, 146-150, and JMDS in "Editor's Note" in Abhishiktananda, *Saccidananda* (JMDS must be J.M.D. Stuart).
36 O. Baumer-Despeigne, "The Spiritual Journey of Henri Le Saux-Abhishiktananda," 327-328.
37 Letter to Odette Baumer-Despeigne, October 1973, quoted in O. Baumer-Despeigne, "The Spiritual Journey of Henri Le Saux-Abhishiktananda," 329.

became universally known under his Indian name. Unlike Monchanin, he became the *chela* of a Hindu guru, and was at home in the pilgrimage sites, the maths and ashrams of India, mixing freely with swamis and sadhus the length and breadth of the subcontinent. One also gets the impression, in reading the writings of the two men (including their more intimate letters and journals), that Abhishiktananda suffers little of Monchanin's angst about their missionizing. Indeed, he affirms quite explicitly that the true monk has no essential function but to be.[38] In a tribute to Monchanin he wrote that

> The monk is a man who lives in the solitude (Greek: *monos*) of God, alone in the very aloneness of the Alone ... He does not become a monk in order to do social work or intellectual work or missionary work or to save the world. The monk simply consecrates himself to God.[39]

Abhishiktananda makes an interesting contrast with Monchanin insofar as he gave primacy to his own mystical realization over the theological doctrines to which he was formally committed as a Christian. As he somewhere remarked, "Truth has to be taken from wherever it comes; that Truth possesses us—we do not possess Truth." On the basis of his own testimony and that of those who knew him in later years we can say of Abhishiktananda that through the penetration of religious forms he became a fully realized *sannyasi*—which is to say, neither Hindu nor Christian, or, if one prefers, both Christian and Hindu, this only being possible at a mystical and esoteric level where the relative forms are universalized. As he wrote in *The Further Shore*, "The call to complete renunciation cuts across all dharmas and disregards all frontiers ... it is anterior to every religious formulation."[40] One of his disciples referred to his "glorious transfiguration" and "the transparence of his whole being to the inner Mystery, the divine Presence."[41] (The fact that this kind of language is used indiscriminately about all manner of dubious "gurus" should not blind us to the fact that, in some cases—and this is one— such language is perfectly appropriate.) In his diary he wrote of himself as "at once so deeply Christian and so deeply Hindu, at a depth where Christian and Hindu in their social and mental structures are blown to pieces, and are yet found again ineffably at the heart of each other."[42] As Frithjof Schuon has remarked,

---

38 Abhishiktananda, *The Further Shore*, 13.

39 From Abhishiktananda, "Le Père Monchanin," quoted in A. Rawlinson, *The Book of Enlightened Masters*, 148. See also "Sannyasa" in *The Further Shore*, 1-56.

40 Abhishiktananda, *The Further Shore*, 27.

41 O. Baumer-Despeigne, "The Spiritual Journey of Henri Le Saux-Abhishiktananda," 327.

42 Abhishiktananda, *Diary*, June 30th, 1964, quoted in J.M.D. Stuart, "Sri Ramana Maharshi and Abhishiktananda," 173.

When a man seeks to escape from "dogmatic narrowness" it is essential that it should be "upwards" and not "downwards": dogmatic form is transcended by fathoming its depths and contemplating its universal content, and not by denying it in the name of a pretentious and iconoclastic "ideal" of "pure truth."[43]

Abhishiktananda never denied or repudiated the doctrines or practices of either Christianity or Hinduism, nor did he cease to observe the Christian forms of worship and to celebrate the sacraments; rather, he came to understand their limitations as religious *forms*, a form necessarily being limited by definition. His own "statements" on doctrinal matters, he said, were to be regarded as "no more than working hypotheses" and as "vectors of free inquiry."[44] Religious structures (doctrines, rituals, laws, techniques etc.) were *signposts* to the Absolute but could not be invested with any absolute value themselves.[45] In this insight he again echoes Schuon who writes:

> Exotericism consists in identifying transcendent realities with the dogmatic forms, and if need be, with the historical facts of a given Revelation, whereas esotericism refers in a more or less direct manner to these same realities.[46]

It is true that Abhishiktananda many times referred to the tensions arising out of the simultaneous "presence of the *Upanishads* and the Gospel in a single heart"[47] and that he occasionally used the language of fulfillment when addressing Christians but this would seem to have been a case of *upaya*, "skilful means" as the Buddhists have it, or what Schuon calls "saving mirages."[48] As Schuon also observes, "In religious exoterisms, efficacy at times takes the place of truth, and rightly so, given the nature of the men to whom they are addressed."[49] In Abhishiktananda's case we can trace through his writings a move away from all notions of Christian exclusivism and triumphalism, *towards* the *sophia perennis*. All the evidence suggests that Abhishiktananda did indeed undergo the plenary experience and see that Light that, in Koranic terms, is "neither of the East nor of the West." In communicating that experience, and the knowledge that it delivers, Abhishiktananda felt comfortable resorting to the spiritual vocabulary of both theistic Christianity and monistic Hinduism. Take, for instance, passages such as these:

43 F. Schuon, *Stations of Wisdom*, 16.
44 O. Baumer-Despeigne, "The Spiritual Journey of Henri Le Saux-Abhishiktananda," 320.
45 Abhishiktananda, *The Secret of Arunachala*, 47.
46 F. Schuon, *Logic and Transcendence*, 144.
47 Letter to Odette Baumer-Despeigne, January 1969, quoted in "The Spiritual Journey of Henri Le Saux-Abhishiktananda," 310.
48 F. Schuon, *Survey of Metaphysics and Esoterism*, 185, fn2.
49 F. Schuon, *The Transfiguration of Man*, 8.

The knowledge (*vidya*) of Christ is identical with what the *Upanishads* call divine knowledge (*brahmavidya*) ... It comprises the whole of God's self-manifestation in time, and is one with his eternal self-manifestation.[50]

Step by step I descended into what seemed to me to be successive depths of my true self—my being (*sat*), my awareness of being (*cit*), and my joy in being (*ananda*). Finally nothing was left but he himself, the Only One, infinitely alone, Being, Awareness and Bliss, *Saccidananda*.[51]

In 1971, in his Introduction to the English edition of *Saccidananda*, Abhishiktananda had this to say:

Dialogue may begin simply with relations of mutual sympathy. It only becomes worthwhile when it is accompanied by full openness ... not merely at the intellectual level, but with regard to [the] inner life of the Spirit. Dialogue about doctrines will be more fruitful when it is rooted in a real spiritual experience at depth and when each one understands that *diversity does not mean disunity, once the Center of all has been reached.*[52]

One measure of Abhishiktananda's mystical extinction in Advaitic non-dualism, and the problems this posed for some of his Christian contemporaries (and for all rigidly theistic theologies), is evident in the manuscript of a talk he prepared in the last months of his life:

In this annihilating experience [of *Advaita*] one is no longer able to project in front of oneself anything whatsoever, to recognize any other "pole" to which to refer oneself and to give the name of God. Once one has reached that innermost center, one is so forcibly seized by the mystery that one can no longer utter a "Thou" or an "I." Engulfed in the abyss, we disappear to our own eyes, to our own consciousness. The proximity of that mystery which the prophetic traditions name "God" burns us so completely that there is no longer any question of discovering it in the depths of oneself or oneself in the depths of it. In the very engulfing, the gulf has vanished. If a cry was still possible—at the moment perhaps of disappearing into the abyss—it would be paradoxically: "but there is no abyss, no gulf, no distance!" There is no face-to-face, for there is only That-Which-Is, and no other to name it.[53]

This passage, reminiscent of Eckhart, can take its place amongst the most exalted of mystical commentaries; it also dispels any doubts as to the validity and fullness of Abhishiktananda's own mystical annihilation, called by whatever name.

The last decade of Abhishiktananda's life saw the publication of a series of books bearing the fragrance of his long years of prayer, meditation, study and spiritual awakening. The English-language versions of these books are:

50 Abhishiktananda, *Guru and Disciple*, xi.
51 Abhishiktananda, *Saccidananda*, 172.
52 Abhishiktananda, *Saccidananda*, xiii (italics mine).
53 Abhishiktananda quoted in W. Teasdale, "Bede Griffiths as a Visionary Guide," 14.

The Mountain of the Lord (1966), an account of his pilgrimage to Gangotri, the sacred source of the Ganges, *Prayer* (1967), *Hindu-Christian Meeting Point* (1969), *The Church in India* (1969), *Towards the Renewal of the Indian Church* (1970), *Saccidananda: A Christian Experience of Advaita* (1974), probably his most mature theological work, *Guru and Disciple* (1974) and *The Secret of Arunachala* (1974), in which he recalls his experiences with Ramana and with Gnanananda, and *The Further Shore* (1975), his deepest meditation on the *Upanishads* and the ideal of *sannyasa*. A collection of several of his essays appeared posthumously as *The Eyes of Light* (1979).

There can be no doubt that, in the words of his friend Raimundo Pannikar, Abhishiktananda was "one of the most authentic witnesses of our times of the encounter in depth between Christian and Eastern spiritualities."[54] But his significance goes well beyond this. In his last work, *The Further Shore*, Abhishiktananda writes movingly and wisely of the ideal of the *sannyasi*:

> *Sannyasa* confronts us with a sign of that which is essentially beyond all signs-indeed, in its sheer transparency [to the Absolute] it proclaims its own death as a sign ... However the *sannyasi* lives in the world of signs, of the divine manifestation, and this world of manifestation needs him, "the one beyond signs," so that it may realize the impossible possibility of a bridge between the two worlds ... It needs to know that they are there [i.e. in the forest and the hermitages], so that it may preserve a reminder of transcendence in the midst of a transient world ... The sign of *sannyasa* ... stands then on the very frontier, the unattainable frontier. Between two worlds, the world of manifestation and the world of the unmanifest Absolute. It is the mystery of the sacred lived with the greatest possible interiority. It is a powerful means of grace—that grace which is nothing else than the Presence of the Absolute, the Eternal, the Unborn, existing at the heart of the realm of becoming, of time, of death and life; and a grace which is at the same time the irresistible drawing of the entire universe and its fullness towards the ultimate fullness of the Awakening to the Absolute, to the *Atman* ... Finally, it is even the *taraka*, the actual one who himself carries men across to the other shore, the one and only "ferryman," manifested in manifold ways in the form of all those rishis, mahatmas, gurus and buddhas, who throughout history have themselves been woken and in turn awaken their brother-men.[55]

Abhishiktananda himself came to embody and to live this ideal. No man could have a more sublime epitaph.

Bede Griffiths (Swami Dayananda)

Of the several Benedictine monks associated with the Saccidananda Ashram of Shantivanam by far the best known in the West is Father Bede Griffiths. It

54 Pannikar quoted in J.E. Royster, "Abhishiktananda: Hindu-Christian Monk," 308.
55 Abhishiktananda, *The Further Shore*, 42-43.

was under his guidance that the ashram really came to life and, at least in part, came to realize the ideals which had inspired Monchanin and Le Saux many years before.

Alan Griffiths was born into a middle-class Anglican family in 1906.[56] He exhibited a keen intellect at school and went on to studies at Oxford where he belonged to the "aesthetes" rather than the "athletes," developing a life-long enthusiasm for Wordsworth and Coleridge, and for Romantic nature-mysticism. As a seventeen-year old he experienced an epiphany while walk-ing near his school's playing fields. He had suddenly felt himself to be in "the Garden of Paradise," and was overcome by a sense of awe: "I hardly dared look on the face of the sky, because it seemed as though it was but a veil before the face of God."[57] Nevertheless, he left Oxford with a vague agnosti-cism and, disenchanted with the modern world, went to live in severe sim-plicity with two friends in a small cottage in the Cotswolds. Through his stud-ies there, his friendship with C.S. Lewis (who dedicated *Surprised by Joy* to Griffiths) and other "Inklings" such as Owen Barfield, and through several other formative experiences, his religious faith was awakened, leading him into the fold of the Roman Catholic Church and his eventual commitment to a monastic vocation. He was now convinced that "the rediscovery of reli-gion is the great intellectual, moral and spiritual adventure of our time."[58] In 1933 he entered the Benedictine Prinknash Abbey in Gloucester and was ordained to the priesthood in 1940. He served in various monastic roles. The story of Griffiths' early life and his conversion to Catholicism is told in one of the most captivating spiritual autobiographies of the century, *The Golden String* (1954).

One of Carl Jung's earliest followers, Toni Sussman, had escaped from Germany with her Jewish husband and settled in London where she opened a yoga and meditation center. It was partly under Sussman's influence that Griffiths' interest in the East was quickened in the early 40s, leading to inten-sive study of Eastern Scriptures from the Hindu, Buddhist and Chinese tra-ditions.[59] Griffiths left for India in 1955, "to seek for the other half of my soul."[60] He had received an invitation from an Indian Benedictine to estab-lish a monastery in the Bangalore region, an enterprise which was never real-ized but which led to an encounter with Father Francis Mahieu. Mahieu was

56 Biographical material taken primarily from B. Griffiths, *The Golden String* and W. Teasdale, "Bede Griffiths as a Visionary Guide." The fullest biography of Griffiths is Shirley du Boulay, *Beyond the Darkness: A Biography of Bede Griffiths* (1998); there is also a good deal of biographical material in Judson Trapnell's *Bede Griffiths: A Life in Dialogue*. An earlier biography by Katherine Spink, *A Sense of the Sacred: A Biography of Bede Griffiths* (1988), is a comparatively flimsy affair.
57 B. Griffiths, *The Golden String*, 9.
58 B. Griffiths, *The Golden String*, 13-14.
59 H. Luke, "Bede Griffiths at Apple Farm," 39.
60 W. Teasdale, "Bede Griffiths as a Visionary Guide," 7.

a Belgian Cistercian, a few years younger than Griffiths, who had arrived in India a few months after the Englishman, with similar aspirations. The two fathers established a Cistercian ashram ("Kurishumala") at Kottayam in Kerala. They followed the Syrian liturgy which was deeply rooted in Kerala, tracing its origins back to the arrival of St Thomas the Apostle on the Malabar coast in 52AD. Kerala has long been the most Christian of the Indian states, something in the order of a third of its population being of this faith. Here Griffiths remained for ten years, serving as the novice master. In 1968 he was invited to take charge of Saccidananda ashram. Monchanin was long since dead and Abhishiktananda had retired to his Himalayan hermitage. The latter's commitment to the ashram had always been somewhat ambivalent, the life of the solitary *sannyasi* always beckoning after his experiences at Arunachala. Griffiths' arrival was to give the ashram a new lease of life; his presence was the key factor in attracting Indian monks of whom some fifteen were in permanent residence by the early 90s. The ashram also became a vibrant center for spiritual seekers from all over the globe, many attracted by the *darsan* of Griffiths himself. He has sometimes been called "charismatic" which, indeed he was, but not in the now colloquial sense of someone with flashy oratorical skills, a highly extrovert personality and the like: the qualities which struck many visitors, this author included, were his sweetness, gentleness and natural courtesy combined with strength and fearlessness, as well as that sense of humor which is so often one of the marks of the sage.

The achievement was not without considerable personal cost to Griffiths himself: physical hardship, loneliness, illness, some personal tensions with Abhishiktananda, vitriolic attacks from evangelical fundamentalists, hostility from some Hindu quarters, difficulties with ecclesiastical authorities (some of whom were angered by Griffiths' bold calls for sweeping reforms within the church and his stinging criticisms of Cardinal Ratzinger and other ecclesiastical heavyweights).[61] In his later years Griffiths became increasingly convinced that the authoritarian, highly bureaucratized, legalistic structures of the Church and its over-rationalized and masculinist doctrinal edifice must give way to a renewed mystical tradition. He remarked to Matthew Fox, "If Christianity cannot recover its mystical tradition and teach it, it should simply fold up and go out of business—it has nothing to offer."[62] He also observed, with characteristic insouciance, "Don't worry about the Vatican. It will all come tumbling down overnight someday, just like the Berlin Wall."[63]

61 Recounted in S. du Boulay, *Beyond the Darkness*.

62 M. Fox & B. Griffiths, "Spirituality for a New Era," 315. Compare Griffiths' remark with Karl Rahner: "The Christian of the future will be a mystic or he or she will not exist at all."; from *The Practice of Faith* (1985), quoted in S. du Boulay, *Beyond the Darkness*, 269.

63 M. Fox, *Confessions*, 214.

In 1980 Father Bede formally joined the Camoldolese Order under whose auspices the ashram thereafter operated. In his last years two strokes seem to have ignited further mystical illumination, much as Abhishiktananda's heart attack shortly before his death presaged "an extraordinary spiritual adventure."[64] We have the testimony of many of those who knew him in the last months of his life that he was filled, in St Benedict's phrase, with "the inexpressible sweetness of love."[65] Griffiths died in 1993 and was succeeded as prior by the Indian Brother Martin John Kuvarupu. By the time of his death he was widely known in the West and tributes were forthcoming from figures such as Cardinal Hume, the Dalai Lama, Andrew Harvey, Helen Luke, Yehudi Menuhin, Raimundo Pannikar, Matthew Fox, Odette Baumer-Despeigne, and many others. Griffiths' life story has been recounted in an intelligent, sympathetic and unsentimental biography by Shirley du Boulay, *Beyond the Darkness: A Biography of Bede Griffiths* (1998).

The last two decades of Griffiths' life saw him travel widely in Europe, America, Asia and Australia, lecturing, participating in conferences and retreats, meeting religious leaders such as the Dalai Lama. He was an indefatigable scholar and writer, producing some three hundred articles. His ten books found a responsive audience in the West and many were translated into other languages. Along with *The Golden String*, the most important were *Return to the Center* (1976), *The Marriage of East and West* (1982), *The Cosmic Revelation: The Hindu Way to God* (1983) and *A New Vision of Reality: Western Science, Eastern Mysticism, and Christian Faith* (1989). Unlike Abhishiktananda, Griffiths took a close interest in intellectual and cultural developments in the West and, for better or worse, was more attuned to the contemporary spirit. In his later years, for instance, he avidly read the works of contemporary thinkers like Ken Wilber, Frithjof Capra, David Bohm, Matthew Fox and Rupert Sheldrake. Depending on one's point of view one might either regret or applaud Griffiths' efforts to stay abreast of the latest developments in Western theology, philosophy, psychology and physics, which, in his last book, he sought to synthesize with traditional Christian and Hindu doctrines and with the teachings of the mystics.

Wayne Teasdale has argued that Griffiths' life is best understood as a search for Wholeness, a goal to be reached through a synthesis of the values and modes of both East and West. In his pre-India days he had taken a close interest in the work of Jung and often returned to the great Jungian theme of the reconciliation of the opposites, particularly the masculine and the feminine. Like many pilgrims to the East, Griffiths was a resolute critic of those aspects of Western life which stifled spirituality—a hyper-rational and over-masculinized intellectual ethos which privileged conceptualization and analytical reason over intuition and direct experience, a lifestyle riddled with

---

64 B. Griffiths, *Diary*, quoted in S. du Boulay, *Beyond the Darkness*, 328.
65 L. Freeman, "Bede Griffiths," 282.

materialism and consumerism, the absence of any living sense of the sacred, the brutal desecration of Nature herself, the ossification of religious forms, the authoritarianism and legalism of ecclesiastical institutions, the blind technological frenzy. He was not insensible to the achievements of Western culture and science, nor did he reject the Judeo-Christian moral heritage. Rather, he found in Indian spirituality and in the values and customs of traditional village life an antidote to many of the ills that beset the West whilst always believing that the West had its own gifts to share with the East.

The "problem" of religious pluralism was less acute for Bede Griffiths than for his predecessors, largely because of the more hospitable climate engendered by Vatican II and by the conciliar document *Nostra Aetate* which radically modified both the exclusivism and the triumphalism of the Catholic Church in relation to other religions. We can trace in his writings a very clear trajectory from an early variant of fulfillment theology, through a period of uncertainty about the relationship of the world's major religions, arriving finally at a theology of religious diversity which is substantially the same as that of the perennialists and of neo-Hinduism, what has sometimes been called the complementarity theory—in brief, the seemingly divergent religions are different paths to the same summit.[66] Certainly, Father Bede believed that Christianity had a unique contribution to make to the world's spiritual treasury and his own commitment to Christ never wavered. On the other hand he was victim to neither "fulfillment" nor "inclusivist" theology, each of which saw other religious traditions as somehow preparatory to Christianity. In the light of Griffiths' maturing understanding of the perennial philosophy the problem of religious pluralism simply dissolved. As early as 1956 Griffiths had spoken and written of the timeless wisdom of which the religions are but particular expressions which have been corrupted but which are "*divine in their origin*": " ... they are all in their different ways forms of the one true religion, which has been made known to man from the beginning of the world"[67]—words which could easily have come from the pen of René Guénon.[68] In *The Marriage of East and West* Griffiths had written,

> It is no longer possible for one religion to live in isolation from other religions. For many this presents a real problem. Each religion has been taught to regard itself as the one true religion ... We begin to realize that truth is one, but that it has many faces, and each religion is, as it were, a face of the one Truth, which manifests itself under different signs and symbols in the different historical traditions.[69]

66 This trajectory has been traced by Joel Smith in "Religious Diversity, Hindu-Christian Dialogue and Bede Griffiths."

67 B. Griffiths, "Symbolism and Cult" (1956), quoted in S. du Boulay, *Beyond the Darkness*, 117 (italics mine).

68 It is highly unlikely that Griffiths had actually read Guénon at this point though he certainly did later in life. He also read the works of several other traditionalists and acclaimed Seyyed Hossein Nasr's *Knowledge and the Sacred* as the most authoritative exposition of the perennial philosophy he had encountered. See S. du Boulay, *Beyond the Darkness*, 197.

69 B. Griffiths, *The Marriage of East and West*, 24-25.

As we saw in the last chapter, this is precisely one of the central principles of the traditionalist understanding of the *sophia perennis*. Echoing Abhishiktananda, Griffiths spoke of the renunciate's vocation to penetrate the world of religious forms in order to reach their formless essence:

> ... the *Sannyasi* is called to go beyond all religion, beyond every human institution, beyond every scripture and creed, till he comes to that which every religion and scripture and ritual signifies but can never name.

But the call to go "beyond all religion" could never mean the rejection of religion: "To go beyond the sign is not to reject the sign, but to reach the thing signified."[70] Griffiths remained alert to the dangers of both syncretism—the assembling of heterogeneous elements from different religions into a spurious unity—and a sentimental "universalism," a kind of religious "Esperanto" as Coomaraswamy called it, based on the absurd notion that the particular forms of each religion were now "out-dated."[71] Doubtless he would have endorsed Frithjof Schuon's remark,

> ... as for an exhausting of the religions, one might speak of this if all men had by now become saints or Buddhas. In that case only could it be admitted that the religions were exhausted, at least as regards their forms.[72]

Bede Griffiths has attracted some caustic criticism from traditionalists. Rama Coomaraswamy, for example, has lamented the influence on Griffiths' thought of Aurobindo and of Marxist and evolutionist ideas and situates Griffiths, along with Mahesh Yogi, Aurobindo and Bhagavan Rajneesh, in a movement of "the desacralization of Hinduism for Western consumption."[73] There is no denying that Griffiths sometimes fell prey to modernistic and evolutionistic ideas. Nonetheless, in my view, Rama Coomaraswamy's judgment is harsh and fails to take into account the very considerable common ground which Griffiths shares with the traditionalists.

A Note on the Christian Ashram Movement
There are today something like fifty Christian ashrams in India, owing much to the pioneering efforts of Fathers Monchanin, Mahieu, Le Saux and Griffiths. Many of these ashrams are peopled entirely by Indian Christians who continue the task of seeking out and living a distinctively Indian form of Christianity. Amongst the most enduring of these ashrams, along with Saccidananda and Kurisumala, are Christukula, established by two Anglican missionaries in the early 1930s, Christa Prema Seva Ashram, founded by John Winslow in 1927 in Shivajinagar (Mumbai region), Jyotiniketan in Bereilly,

---

70 B. Griffiths, *The Marriage of East and West*, 42-43.
71 See J.B. Trapnell, "Bede Griffiths, Mystical Knowing, and the Unity of Religions."
72 F. Schuon: "No Activity Without Truth," 29. See also F. Schuon, *Stations of Wisdom*, 11.
73 See Rama P. Coomaraswamy, "The Desacralization of Hinduism for Western Consumption," esp. 203.

and the Christi Panti Ashram in Varanasi. This movement still awaits a thorough phenomenological analysis.[74] The Christian ashram movement in general and the "Trinity from Tannirpalli" (Monchanin, Le Saux and Griffiths) in particular, have come under vituperative attack from some Hindu quarters. This ugly and unhappy controversy (which included a series of letters exchanged between Bede Griffiths and Swami Devananda, leading the Hindu charge) can be viewed from the side of the Hindu partisans in Sita Ram Goel's acidic *Catholic Ashrams: Adopting and Adapting Hindu Dharma* (1988).

Thomas Merton and Eastern Spirituality

Thomas Merton must surely be the best-known Christian monk of the century. His spiritual autobiography *The Seven Storey Mountain* (1948)[75] covering his early life, his conversion to Catholicism and his decision to become a monk, has been a perennial favorite and is regarded by many as one of the exemplary spiritual documents of our times.[76] Merton himself seems to have been addicted to writing, producing a massive corpus of books (historical, theological, autobiographical, devotional, exegetical), articles, reviews, letters, journals, stories, manuals, memoirs, poetry, meditations—an almost exhaustive repertoire of literary genres. In turn he has generated a veritable Merton industry, excavating his life and work in almost stupefying detail—one which shows no sign of flagging. Here we shall only offer a skeletal account of his life and then isolate some of his concerns which relate most closely to our present study.

Merton was born in France in 1915, his mother a cultured and sensitive woman from a well-to-do American family, his father an artist from New Zealand.[77] Thomas' mother died when he was six, his father when he was fifteen. The boy lived a somewhat peripatetic existence in the USA, England and France, attending boarding schools on either side of the English Channel. Religion was a somewhat marginal affair in family life though his father, Owen, was a nature mystic of sorts whilst the principal characteristic of the somewhat anodyne Christianity of his American relatives seems to have been a mild anti-Catholicism. Merton early revealed a gift for writing, producing two novels by the age of twelve, contributing poetry, stories and

74 For some material on the Christian ashram movement see Helen Ralston, *Christian Ashrams: A New Religious Movement in Contemporary India* (1987); Sister Vandana Mataji, *Gurus, Ashrams and Christians* (1978), and "Spiritual Formation in Ashrams in Contemporary India" (1990); Sister Vandana Mataji (ed), *Christian Ashrams: A Movement with a Future?* (1993); E. Vattakuzhy, *Indian Christian Sannyasa and Swami Abhishiktananda* (1981); Philipos Thomas, "Christian Ashrams and Evangelization of India," *Indian Church History Review*, 11, 1977.
75 In England it appeared, after editing by Evelyn Waugh, as *Elected Silence*.
76 *The Seven Storey Mountain*, for all its freshness, is, on Merton's own admission, a somewhat gauche work and slightly marred by the sentimental excesses of a recent convert.
77 Biographical material taken primarily from Thomas Merton, *The Seven Storey Mountain*, and Monica Furlong, *Merton: A Biography*.

reviews to school and university magazines. He was weak in mathematics and took an early dislike to Plato and Socrates, matched by an enthusiasm for Blake (on whom he wrote his Masters thesis at Columbia University). His first significant spiritual experience was at the age of about sixteen when he was

> overwhelmed with a sudden and profound insight into the misery and corruption of my own soul ... and my soul desired escape and liberation and freedom from all this with an intensity and an urgency unlike anything I had ever known before ... for the first time in my life I really began to pray ...[78]

Merton studied at Cambridge and before leaving England had a brief affair which resulted in the birth of a child; it troubled his conscience for many years thereafter. (Both mother and child were killed in a bombing raid during the war.) As a student at Columbia Merton hurled himself into a bohemian lifestyle, becoming a habitué of coffee shops, wine bars and jazz cellars in Greenwich Village as well as taking an active part in university literary circles and student politics. His political interests were sharpened by a visit to Cuba where he felt a close identification with the poor.

Whilst at Columbia Merton met a Hindu *sannyasi* who urged him to read St Augustine's *Confessions*. Other way stations on the path to the monastery included Etienne Gilson's *The Spirit of Medieval Philosophy* and Huxley's *The Perennial Philosophy*, the works of Jacques Maritain, the poetry of Blake and Hopkins, and a visit to France where he was ravished by the beauty of the medieval churches. In 1938 he was baptized and within two years had decided to enter the priesthood:

> Now I had entered into the everlasting movement of that gravitation which is the very life and spirit of God: God's own gravitation towards the depth of His own infinite nature, His goodness without end. And God, that center Who is everywhere, and whose circumference is nowhere, finding me ... And He called out to me from His own immense depths.[79]

On an Easter retreat in 1941 he thrilled with the discovery of the world of the Trappists, Carthusians and Camaldolese. He had discovered the Catholic expression of the ancient ideal of renunciation:

> What wonderful happiness there was, then, in the world! There were still men on this miserable, noisy, cruel earth, who tasted the marvelous joy of silence and solitude, who dwelt in forgotten mountain cells, in secluded monasteries ... They were poor, they had nothing, and therefore they were free and possessed everything, and everything they touched struck off something of the fire of divinity ...[80]

The road to the monastery gates turned out to be full of hazards and obsta-

78 T. Merton, *The Seven Storey Mountain*, 111.
79 T. Merton, *The Seven Storey Mountain*, 225.
80 T. Merton, *The Seven Storey Mountain*, 316.

cles but finally, in 1948, Merton was accepted as a novice at Gethsemani, a Trappist monastery in Kentucky.

The story of Merton's twenty years in the monastery has been told, in intricate detail, in Michael Mott's door-stopper, *The Seven Mountains of Thomas Merton*, the most complete biography we have. Some of the recurring motifs: Merton's love of the ancient rhythms of both the natural and the liturgical seasons; his devotion to the monastic ideal; his urgent advocacy of ecclesiastical and monastic reform coupled to his commitment to ecumenical and inter-religious dialogue; his often prickly relationship with his superiors (complicated by Merton's rapidly growing celebrity as an author); his extraordinary fecundity as a writer and his torrential correspondence with artists, intellectuals, musicians, activists, spiritual leaders; his yearning for a more radical solitude married to his passionate engagement with the political and social issues of the day (race relations, Latin American politics, the Cold War, the nuclear threat, the brutalities of totalitarian regimes of both "left" and "right," Vietnam, the pervasive violence of modern life, the environmental crisis). Despite his enclaustration, Merton maintained warm relationships with many intellectuals and spiritual leaders—Mark van Doren, Thich Nhat Hanh (who wrote a poem entitled "Thomas Merton is My Brother"), Daniel Berrigan, Rosemary Radford Ruether, Czeslaw Milosz, Marco Pallis, D.T. Suzuki, to name but a few.

By the early 60s Merton had immersed himself not only in the "waters of silence" but in the mystical literature of Taoism, Tibetan and Zen Buddhism, Hinduism and Sufism. In the decade before his death he produced a series of strikingly fresh, often poetic, beautiful and profound works. In 1968, after years of conflict with his abbot, Merton was finally allowed to go on a long-desired trip to Asia, principally to participate in an inter-religious monastic conference in Bangkok but also to make a pilgrimage to the sacred sites of India and South-East Asia and to meet representatives of the Eastern traditions. Merton's sojourn in Asia was abruptly ended when, apparently, he was fatally electrocuted by a faulty appliance in his room in Bangkok.[81]

Merton's writings have been a delight to readers all over the world. The early works are confined within the sometimes claustrophobic walls of mid-century Catholic piety but Merton's understanding of the spiritual life, of the centrality of mystical experience and of the inter-relations of the great religious patrimonies of both East and West gradually matured into one of the most profound spiritual visions of the century. Both in his person and in his work he came to represent some of the deepest spiritual currents of our times. Before turning to Merton's encounter with the East mention must be made of a few of his more singular and enduring works on Christian and

---

81 Some, such as Matthew Fox, have speculated on the possibility that Merton was actually assassinated by the CIA. See M. Fox, *Confessions*, 73-74.

Western themes: *The Waters of Siloe* (1949), a monastic history, *The Silent Life* (1957), a limpid account of the monastic ideal, *New Seeds of Contemplation* (1961), the most beautiful of Merton's meditations on Christian spirituality, *Conjectures of a Guilty Bystander* (1966), an arresting collection of fragments on contemporary political issues, *Raids on the Unspeakable* (1966), which includes some of Merton's most lively and imaginative literary work. His literary essays, poems, letters and journals (in six volumes) have been posthumously published as well as countless anthologies. When T.S. Eliot was asked his view of Merton's poetry he sternly replied that he wrote too much and should be more careful.[82] Marco Pallis makes the same reproach about Merton's output as a whole;[83] coming from a writer who himself took the most scrupulous care to treat the religious subjects about which he wrote with both the precision and the formality which he thought their due, one is not entirely unsympathetic to the observation. But perhaps this is to misunderstand the nature of Merton's peculiar gifts as a writer: his deficiencies are, in a sense, the very token of his virtues as a writer—immediacy, spontaneity, fluidity, the sense of a real presence, often humorous, sometimes acerbic, very rarely dull.

Throughout his last journey Merton kept a haphazard collection of notes and jottings which were compiled after his death and published as *The Asian Journal of Thomas Merton*. The book gives a very immediate and intimate sense of Merton's exhilaration as he meets his fellow-monks in India, Ceylon and Thailand, visits sacred sites, returns to the ancient scriptures, ponders the art and architecture of India, meets with spiritual leaders. He also refers to the reading matter in his kit-bag for his various journeyings—Sankara, Milarepa, Ramanuja, Masao Abe, Aelred Graham, Evans-Wentz, Tucci, Herman Hesse, Abhishiktananda, Dasgupta, T.R.V. Murti, Marco Pallis, Edward Conze, and many more—a veritable East-West library! Despite its fragmentary nature *The Asian Journal* is at once charming, piercingly insightful, often moving. All of it testifies to Merton's extraordinary receptivity to the spiritual messages emanating from the people, the temples, shrines and stupas, the artworks, the landscape itself. Here, for instance, is the passage describing his experience before the Buddha figures of Polonnaruwa, (somewhat reminiscent of Otto's encounter with the *mysterium tremendum* in the statues of Elephanta):[84]

> The path dips down to Gal Vihara: a wide, quiet, hollow, surrounded by trees. A low outcrop of rock, with a cave cut into it, and beside the cave a big seated Buddha on the left, a reclining Buddha on the right, and Ananda, I guess, standing by the head of the reclining Buddha. In the cave, another seated Buddha. The vicar general [Merton's host], shying away from "paganism," hangs back and sits under a tree reading the guidebook. I am able to approach the Buddha barefoot and undisturbed, my feet in wet grass, wet

82 See M. Furlong, *Merton: A Biography*, 215.
83 See M. Pallis, "Thomas Merton."
84 See Chapter 3.

sand. Then the silence of the extraordinary faces. The great smiles. Huge and yet subtle. Filled with every possibility, questioning nothing, knowing everything, rejecting nothing, the peace not of emotional resignation but of *Madhyamika*, of *sunyata*, that has seen through every question without trying to discredit anyone or anything—without refutation—without establishing some other argument. For the doctrinaire, the mind that needs well-established positions, such peace, such silence, can be frightening. I was knocked over with a rush of relief and thankfulness at the obvious clarity of the figures, the clarity and fluidity of shape and line, the design of the monumental bodies composed into the rock shape and landscape, figure, rock and tree ... Looking at these figures I was suddenly, almost forcibly, jerked clean out of the habitual, half-tied vision of things, and an inner clearness, clarity, as if exploding from the rocks themselves, became evident and obvious. The queer evidence of the reclining figure, the smile, the sad smile of Ananda standing with his arms folded (much more "imperative" than Da Vinci's *Mona Lisa* because completely simple and straightforward). The thing about all this is that there is no puzzle, no problem, and really no "mystery." All problems are resolved and everything is clear, simply because what matters is clear. The rock, all matter, all life, is charged with *Dharmakaya* ... everything is emptiness and everything is compassion. I don't know when in my life I have ever had such a sense of beauty and spiritual validity running together in one aesthetic illumination. Surely, with Mahabalipuram and Polonnaruwa my Asian pilgrimage has come clear and purified itself. I mean, I know and have seen what I was obscurely looking for. I don't know what else remains but I have now seen and have pierced through the surface and have got beyond the shadow and the disguise. This is Asia in its purity, not covered over with garbage, Asian or European or American, and it is clear, pure, complete. It says everything; it needs nothing. And because it needs nothing it can afford to be silent, unnoticed, undiscovered. It does not need to be discovered. It is we, Asians included, who need to discover it.[85]

On this trip Merton had three cordial meetings with the Dalai Lama, who, when some time later was asked whether he believed in God replied, "It depends what you mean by 'God': if you mean by 'God' what Thomas Merton means, then yes, I do." He also had fruitful encounters with many other monks of the Tibetan diaspora including Chögyam Trungpa, Kalu Rinpoche and Chatral Rinpoche, with Theravadins such as Nyanaponika Thera, the English Bikkhu Phra Khantipalo, and with scholars and writers such as Lobsang Lhalungpa and Dr Raghavan.

Most of Merton's writings on the Eastern traditions can be found in his introductions to *The Way of Chuang Tzu* (1965) (the "translation" of which he described as the most enjoyable project of his life) and *Gandhi on Non-Violence* (1965), and two collections of essays on Eastern subjects, *Mystics and Zen Masters* (1967) and *Zen and the Birds of Appetite* (1968). We have already encountered Merton's eloquent tribute to D.T. Suzuki. Here we might recall

85 T. Merton, *Asian Journal*, 33-36.

that Suzuki believed Merton to be one of very few Westerners who fully understood Zen.[86] Certainly Merton's several essays on Zen match anything of comparable intent written by a Westerner.[87]

As intimated earlier, there is now a Merton publishing industry: the rivers of ink continue to flow freely. Here we may mention just a few works of interest. Of the several biographies of Merton the most exhaustive is Mott's aforementioned *The Seven Mountains of Thomas Merton* (1984) while two sympathetic but not uncritical biographies of more modest proportions are Monica Furlong's well-known *Merton: A Biography* (1980) and a book which deserves a much wider audience, William Shannon's *Silent Lamp: The Thomas Merton Story* (1992), in many respects the most penetrating of the three. A collection of photos and reminiscences by his friend John Howard Griffin, *A Hidden Wholeness*, presents an intimate portrait of Merton and his life at Gethsemani. (Griffin was a writer, photographer, and author of the remarkable *Black Like Me.*) Among the more percipient commentators on Merton's work are William Shannon, Patrick Hart, Marco Pallis, Henri Nouwen, Thérèse Lentfoehr, Walter Capps, Bonnie Thurston, Peter Francis and George Woodcock.[88]

In the present context it is quite impossible to do justice to Merton's immense contribution to the intellectual and spiritual life of our times. Nor can we here measure his impact on the development of more open and creative communication between the religions of Occident and Orient. However, we can take note of some of the persistent Mertonian themes which mark his writings on inter-religious subjects: the indispensability to spiritual vitality of contemplation, meditation, prayer; the inadequacy of language to express spiritual experience, and the dangers of the Western preoccupation with definition, measurement, conceptualization and analysis; the role of solitude in nurturing an understanding of the illusory nature of the egoic self; the universality of the monastic ideal (even where it is not institutionalized, as in Islam); the rejection of the rationalist-masculinist-instrumentalist paradigm of Western modernity; the notion that creative dialogue springs from a commitment to and knowledge of one's own tradition, and from an open heart; the West's need for much more *wu wei*—the "creative quietude"[89] of Chuang Tzu and the Taoist masters; the reconciliation of the opposites; the relevance to the West of the Gandhian ideals of *ahimsa* (noninjuriousness), *satyagraha* ("truth-force") and *brahmacharya* (self-control, renunciation), all informed by the *Gita's* teaching of non-attachment to the fruits of one's action; the spiritual potentialities of expressive modes such as painting, music and poetry; the critique of the anti-mystical, exclusivist and legalistic posture of some ecclesiastical institutions and authorities; the liberating power of love and compassion; the impermanence and "emptiness" of

86 See Patrick Hart in T. Merton, *Asian Journal,* xxvii.
87 See Irmgard Schloegl's Introduction to *Thomas Merton on Zen,* vii-x.
88 Works by most of these authors will be found in the List of Sources at the end of this work.

all phenomena. By way of a conclusion we shall make do with a sample of passages from several of Merton's writings, each suggestive of the themes and preoccupations which concerned him most deeply.

A Miscellany of Fragments from Father Louis (Thomas Merton)

• Let us face the fact that the monastic vocation tends to present itself to the modern world as a problem and as a scandal. In a basically religious culture, like that of India, or of Japan, the monk is more or less taken for granted.[90]

• The monastery is neither a museum nor an asylum. The monk remains in the world from which he has fled, and he remains a potent, though hidden, force in that world ... the monk acts on the world simply by being a monk ... in the loneliness of his detachment he has a far higher vocation to charity than anyone else ... [91]

• The vocation to solitude is ... to become fully awake ... [92]

• Contemplation is the highest expression of man's intellectual and spiritual life. It is that life itself, fully awake, fully active, fully aware ...[93]

• God cannot be understood except by Himself.[94]

• One of the most widespread errors of our time is a superficial "personalism" which identifies the "person" with the external self, the empirical ego, and devotes itself solemnly to the cultivation of this ego. But this is a cult of pure illusion, the illusion of what is popularly imagined to be "personality" or worse still "dynamic" and "successful" personality. When this error is taken over into religion it leads to the worst kind of nonsense, a cult of psychologism and self-expression which vitiates our whole cultural and spiritual self.[95]

• That which is oldest is most young and most new. There is nothing so ancient and so dead as human novelty. The "latest" is always stillborn. What is really new is what was there all the time.[96]

• I believe that by openness to Buddhism, to Hinduism, and to these great Asian traditions, we stand a wonderful chance of learning more about the potentiality of our own traditions ... [97]

• The monk is a man who, in one way or another, pushes to the frontiers of

89 Huston Smith's phrase in *The Religions of Man*, 204.
90 T. Merton, *The Silent Life*, viii.
91 T. Merton, *The Silent Life*, 172.
92 T. Merton, *The Power and Meaning of Love*, 50.
93 T. Merton, *New Seeds of Contemplation*, 1.
94 T. Merton, *New Seeds of Contemplation*, 132.
95 T. Merton, *New Seeds of Contemplation*, 281.
96 T. Merton, *New Seeds of Contemplation*, 107.
97 T. Merton, *Asian Journal*, 343.

human experience and strives to go beyond, to find out what transcends the ordinary level of existence.[98]

• It was the spiritual consciousness of a people that was awakened in the spirit of one person [Mahatma Gandhi]. But the message of the Indian spirit, of Indian wisdom, was not for India alone. It was for the entire world.[99]

• Such men (true solitaries), out of pity for the universe, out of loyalty to mankind, and without a spirit of bitterness or resentment, withdraw into the healing silence of the wilderness, or of poverty, or of obscurity, not in order to preach to others but to heal in themselves the wounds of the whole world.[100]

• It is absolutely essential to introduce into our study of the humanities a dimension of wisdom oriented to contemplation as well as wise action. For this, it is no longer sufficient merely to go back over the Christian and European cultural tradition. The horizons of the world are no longer confined to Europe and America. We have to gain new spiritual perspectives, and on this our spiritual, and even our physical survival may depend.[101]

Jottings on other Christian Missionaries
In this chapter we have restricted our view to a handful of Catholic monks in India. It hardly needs pointing out that they represent only a small part of the overall story of Christian witness in Asia. A comprehensive inquiry would demand an examination not only of the involvement of other Catholic orders but the many successive waves of Protestant missionaries. In a later chapter we will pay some attention to the role of figures like Heinrich Dumoulin, William Johnston, Hugo Enomiya-Lasalle and Aelred Graham in inter-religious dialogue, and to the contribution of lay Christians such as Diana Eck. Before leaving the phenomena of Christian missionizing in Asia we should make mention of at least a small sample of those who have left their mark on the East-West encounter of the 20th century.

In the realm of missionaries-scholars the name of Klaus Klostermaier comes quickly into the foreground. He followed the path traced earlier by J.N. Farquhar and Richard Wilhelm: years of missionary endeavor in Asia were followed by an academic career in the West, in comparative religion or a related field. During his decade in India, Klostermaier spent two years in Vrindaban, the center of the Krishna cult, about which he later wrote a delightful account, *In the Paradise of Krishna*. Klostermaier eventually took up an appointment at the University of Manitoba. He is recognized as an author-

98 T. Merton, "Renewal and Discipline," quoted by Tarcisus Conner, "Monk of Renewal" in P. Hart, *Thomas Merton, Monk*, 183.
99 T. Merton, *Gandhi on Non-Violence*, 5.
100 T. Merton. I have been unable to trace this quote which I have copied into a notebook—but it is so eloquent, and so Mertonian, that I have included it anyway.
101 T. Merton, *Mystics and Zen Masters*, 80.

ity on Hinduism and has been a lively contributor to the many disciplinary debates within comparative religion. He is the author of *A Survey of Hinduism.*[102] Similarly, D.H. Smith's many years of missionary activity in China, brought to an end by the Communist Revolution, were followed by an appointment as a lecturer in comparative religion at the University of Manchester. His *Chinese Religions* appeared in 1968. Two of the most distinguished of Anglican missionaries in the subcontinent were Lesslie Newbegin and Stephen Neil. The former was intimately involved in the creation of the United Church of South India, in which he became a bishop. He also worked for many years for the World Council of Churches. Newbegin's autobiography, *Unfinished Agenda* (1985), is largely concerned with his experiences in Pakistan and India. Stephen Neil spent twenty years as a missionary in India, eventually serving as the Anglican Bishop of Tinnevelly, a diocese of some 120,000 Indian Anglicans. He too was instrumental in the creation of the new Indian church. Forced by ill health to return to England in 1944 he became an authority on the history of missions as well as frequently writing on Indian Christianity. For a time he was Professor of Missions and Ecumenical Theology at the University of Hamburg. Among his many works are *A History of Christian Missions* (1964) and *Bhakti: Hindu and Christian* (1974).

There is a vast literature recounting the experiences of Christian missionaries in Asia. We can do more than mention a few remarkable cases in India alone. Amy Carmichael's route into missionary work was through the Keswick Conventions (an evangelical movement in England in the late 19th century). She went to India for the Zenana Missionary Society in 1892 and remained there for the rest of her very active life which included the production of over thirty books on the practical demands of mission work. She died in 1948.[103] Contemporary with Carmichael was the Danish Lutheran, Lars Peter Larsen, who served in India for over forty years, being one of the moving forces behind the establishment of the United Theological College of Bangalore.[104] John Copley Winslow went as an Anglican missionary to India in 1914. He met and was much influenced by Narayam Vaman Tilak, and subsequently became involved in the Indian independence movement, the "indigenization" of the Indian church, and the emergence of Christian ashrams.[105] Murray T. Titus, an American Methodist, was an evangelical missionary in India, devoting most of his efforts to work amongst Indian

---

102 For some fragmentary biographical material on Klostermaier see his article "All Religions are Incomplete."

103 See E. Sharpe, "The Legacy of Amy Carmichael" and F. Houghton, *Amy Carmichael of Dohnavur.*

104 See E. Sharpe, "The Legacy of Lars Peter Larsen."

105 See W.W. Emilsen, "The Legacy of John Copley Winslow."

Muslims. After forty years in India he became Professor of Missions and World Religions at the Westminster Theological Seminary in Maryland.[106] Among his many books are *Indian Islam* (1930) and *Islam in India and Pakistan* (1959).

A Closing Reflection on Monasticism

Given that our focus has been on monks, and remembering that men like Monchanin, Abhishiktananda, Griffiths and Merton all saw the monastic ideal as a vital link between Eastern and Western spirituality, it is perhaps appropriate to finish this chapter with a few reflections about monasticism and its place in the modern world. We can do no better than turn once again to the writings of Frithjof Schuon:

> When anyone reproaches a hermit or a monk for "running away from" the world, he commits a double error: firstly, he loses sight of the fact that contemplative isolation has an intrinsic value that is independent of the existence of a surrounding "world"; secondly, he pretends to forget that there are escapes that are perfectly honorable and that, if it is neither absurd nor shameful to run away from an avalanche, it is no more so to run away from the temptations or even the distractions of the world ... In our days people are very ready to say that to escape the world is to shirk "responsibilities," a completely hypocritical euphemism that dissimulates behind "altruistic" or "social" notions a spiritual laziness and a hatred of the absolute; people are happy to ignore the fact that the gift of oneself for God is always a gift of oneself for all. It is metaphysically impossible to give oneself to God in such a way that good does not ensue to the environment: to give oneself to God, though it were hidden from all men, is to give oneself to man, for this gift of self has a sacrificial value of an incalculable radiance.[107]

No one in the East still attuned to their own religious tradition could conceive of the reproaches to which Schuon alludes, let alone take them seriously. It is a measure of the spiritually sterile climate in which many Westerners live that such prejudices can be harbored by so many. The monks and nuns of Christianity and Buddhism, the Hindu *sannyasi* and *parivraj*, the Taoist recluse, the Zen master, the Tibetan *naldjorpa*, the Sufi contemplative, remind a forgetful world, as their predecessors have done through the ages, of the highest spiritual ideals by living as a "sign beyond signs," showing us a bridge not just between the East and West but between the manifest and the Absolute. There is no higher vocation.

---

106 C. Pickering, "Murray T. Titus: Missionary and Islamic Scholar."
107 F. Schuon, *Light on the Ancient Worlds*, 120-121.

10.

Dharma Bums: Beats, Hippies, and the Counter-culture

A. The Beats and Hippies Turn East: Jack Kerouac—The San Francisco Be-In and the "Armies of the Night" at the Pentagon **B. To a Buddhist Beat:** Allen Ginsberg on Politics, Poetics and Spirituality—Politics, Poetics and the Western Encounter with Eastern Spirituality **C. "Pop Gurus," "New Consciousness" and Drugs:** Ram Dass—Alan Watts—"New Consciousness," New Universalism?—A Note on Drugs, Mysticism and Spirituality—Closing Reflections

---

> ... a great rucksack revolution, thousands or even millions of young Americans ... all of 'em Zen lunatics who go about writing poems that happen to appear in their heads for no reason ... wild gangs of holy men getting together to drink and talk and pray. (Jack Kerouac)[1]

A. The Beats and Hippies Turn East

The American Beats of the 50s were, in many respects, the direct descendants of the New England Transcendentalists: in each movement we find a sovereign concern with the nature of consciousness, a rejection of conventional Christianity, the repudiation of the "Enlightenment Project," and a turn to the East for more authentic modes of experience, thought and expression. However, the Transcendentalist agendas of Emerson and Thoreau were always the preserve of a small coterie: the Beats and their progeny in the counter-culture, on the other hand, triggered a revolution in popular consciousness, first amongst American youth but by now with reverberations throughout the Western world. As Carole Tonkinson puts it,

> Not only did the Beats adapt the wisdom teachings of the East to a new, peculiarly American terrain, they also articulated this teaching in the vernacular, jazzy rhythms of the street, opening up what had been the domain of stuffy academics and stiff translators to a mainstream audience ... the voices of American poets recounted the teachings of the Buddha to the general public for the first time.[2]

The Beat movement drew on many different cultural streams: Blake and the Romantic poets, American Transcendentalism, black musical idioms, European existentialism. Among their Eastern sources Japanese Zen was pre-

---

1   Jack Kerouac, *The Dharma Bums*, 1959, 78 quoted in J.J. Clarke, *Oriental Enlightenment*, 104.
2   C. Tonkinson (ed), *Big Sky Mind*, viii.

eminent but the Beats also showed a serious interest in aspects of Buddhism at large, Hinduism and Taoism. The movement was eclectic and ecumenical. Kerouac in 1959: " ... for the crucifix I speak out, for the Star of Israel I speak out ... for sweet Mohammed I speak out, for Buddha I speak out, for Lao-tse and Chuang-tse I speak out, for D.T. Suzuki I speak out..."[3] Ginsberg, echoing Blake and Whitman, also captured this spirit in "Wichita Vortex Sutra" when he invoked

> million-faced Tathagata gone past suffering
> Preserver Harekrishna returning in the age of pain
> Sacred Heart my Christ acceptable
> Allah the Compassionate One
> Yahweh Righteous One
> all Knowledge-Princes of Earth-man, all
> ancient Seraphim of heavenly Desire, Devas, yogis
> & holyman I chant to

But it was to Buddhism that the Beats were most often attracted.

By the early 60s when the Beat movement was apparently strangled by media hype and before the hippies had appeared, there were also signs of a budding interest in some of the more arcane aspects of Eastern traditions, perhaps most notably the convergence of psychedelic experimentation and the *Tibetan Book of the Dead*.[4] Aldous Huxley's earlier experiences with mescalin anticipated the counter-cultural preoccupation with consciousness-altering drugs such as LSD and "magic mushrooms": *The Doors of Perception* ranked highly on the hippie curriculum along with the *I Ching*, Hesse's *Siddhartha* and various books of dubious provenance, perhaps most notably Carlos Casteneda's "Don Juan" series.

The outlandish and iconoclastic aspects of the Beats have, until recently, rather obscured what was in many instances a radical encounter with Eastern spirituality. Orgiastic sexual escapades, monster drug binges, disreputable life-styles, Ginsberg's "Howl," alcoholism, Burroughs' bizarre killing of his wife, strange happenings of all manner and kind, fear and loathing in the suburbs—these are some of the motifs foregrounded in the public perception of the Beats. The organs of American conservatism variously painted the Beats as drug-crazed misfits, shiftless lay-abouts, primitivists and pagans, "nay-sayers." Norman Podhoretz's over-heated indictment of Kerouac's *On the Road* (1957) in *Partisan Review* showed that the Beats had indeed touched some raw nerves in the American psyche. Podhoretz denounced Beat bohemianism as "hostile to civilization: it worships primitivism, instinct, energy, 'blood' ... This is the revolt of the spiritually under-privileged and the crip-

---

3   Jack Kerouac, "The Origins of Generation," *Playboy*, June 1959, quoted in C. Tonkinson, *Big Sky Mind*, 71.
4   See T. Schwartz, *What Really Matters*, Ch 1, and T. Roszak, *The Making of a Counter-culture*, Ch's 4 & 5.

pled of soul."[5] But there was always serious intent amongst the Beats. Allen Ginsberg recently summed up their agenda this way:

> What we were proposing was some new sense of spiritual consciousness. We were interested in non-violence, sexual freedom, the exploration of psyche-delic drugs and sensitivity. We were aware that the entire government ... was corrupt. We were interested in Eastern thought and meditation. We had quite an open heart and open mind ...[6]

We need not look very deeply into the Beat movement to find plentiful evidence of a deep-seated interest in and, in several cases, sustained commit-ment to Eastern religious teachings and practices. A few examples. Philip Whalen was perhaps the first of the Beat poets to develop a serious interest in Buddhism which he discovered, along with the Theosophical writings of A.P. Sinnett and Madame Blavatsky, in the Portland Public Library in the early 1940s. He was eventually ordained as a Zen monk in 1972 and became the head monk at the Zen Mountain Center in Tassajara Springs, California. As we noted earlier, Gary Snyder spent the best part of a decade in a Zen monastery in Japan. Over a period of several years Jack Kerouac made an intensive study of Eastern religious texts, translated Buddhist Scriptures from French into English, attempted to live like a Buddhist monk and wrote an unpublished biography of the Buddha. Kenneth Rexroth translated Japanese and Chinese poetry. Over the last twenty-five years of his life Allen Ginsberg devoted much of his exuberant energy to dharma work. Here too we find, perhaps for the first time, a significant engagement with Buddhism by women writers, amongst whom we may mention Diane di Prima and Joanne Kyger, both students of Shunryu Suzuki at the San Francisco Zen Center, Lenore Kandel, influenced by Hindu and Buddhist tantra, LeRoi Jones (Amiri Baraka) and Anne Waldman who, with Ginsberg and by invita-tion from Chögyam Trungpa, established the Jack Kerouac School of Disembodied Poetics at the Naropa Institute, a Mecca for all manner of counter-cultural types in the 70s and beyond. Many of the Beats as well as counter-cultural figures such as Alan Watts made pilgrimages to the East—to visit holy sites, to take teachings, to live the monastic life. It was not without reason that Jack Kerouac asserted that "the Beat Generation is basically a reli-gious generation."[7]

The hippie "flower power" movement and the emergent counter-culture of the late 60s was in many ways, "the apotheosis of the beat movement." J.J. Clarke has characterized it as a reaction against "the competitive materialism of conventional culture," a "radical critique of scientific rationalism," and religiously, "a search for new routes to spiritual enlightenment through the

5 Podhoretz quoted in S. Prothero, "Introduction" to C. Tonkinson (ed), *Big Sky Mind*, 8.
6 Interview with Henry Tischler, "Allen Ginsberg—Journals Mid-Fifties: 1954-1958," (website).
7 Jack Kerouac quoted in S. Prothero, "Introduction" to C. Tonkinson, *Big Sky Mind*, 6.

use of mind-expanding techniques and drugs."[8] In many cases a spiritual agenda was wedded to a politics of liberation. In this chapter we shall glance at the involvement in Eastern spirituality of Jack Kerouac, the quintessential Beat writer, take a snapshot of the counterculture in 1967, and examine the spiritual trajectory of Allen Ginsberg. Then follow notes on the careers of Ram Dass and Alan Watts, and a brief discussion of the hyperventilated subject of drugs, spirituality and mysticism.

Jack Kerouac

In *The Dharma Bums* (1959) Jack Kerouac mythologized "a great rucksack revolution, thousands or even millions of young Americans ... all of 'em Zen lunatics who go about writing poems ... wild gangs of holy men getting together to drink and talk and pray."[9] Kerouac's own interest in Eastern spirituality was quickened, in the winter of '53-54, by Thoreau's *Walden*, particularly those passages dealing with the *Bhagavad Gita*. Dwight Goddard's *A Buddhist Bible* (1932) provided another stimulus to a wide-ranging program of reading which included the *Vedas*, Patanjali, Lao Tse, Confucius, and the Buddhist sutras, which became his favorite Eastern texts.[10] Kerouac was particularly attracted by the First Noble Truth, and by the Mahayana, suspended as it is between the twin poles of suffering and compassion; he found in its teachings a direct confrontation with pain and suffering, and a spiritual economy not incompatible with his own lingering Catholicism (to which he recommitted himself in his later years—to the disgust of some of his fellow-Beats, Burroughs and Snyder particularly, who harbored some animus towards Christianity).[11]

Kerouac's interest in Buddhism went beyond the merely theoretical and textual. For some years in the mid-50s he meditated daily, chanted sutras, and practiced various monkish austerities. In a letter to Ginsberg (July 14, 1955) Kerouac wrote of *The Diamond Sutra*,

> By living with this greatest of sutras, you become immersed in the Truth that it is all One Undifferentiated Purity, creation and the phenomena, and become free from such conceptions as self, other selves, many selves, One Self ...[12]

As well as a daily recitation of the Sutra, Kerouac rendered it into his own much imitated "bop prosody." He also translated Buddhist texts from French into English, gathering them together with some commentaries, musings,

---

8 J.J. Clarke, *Oriental Enlightenment*, 104.
9 Jack Kerouac, *The Dharma Bums*, 1959, 78, quoted in J.J. Clarke, *Oriental Enlightenment*, 104.
10 See R. Fields, *How the Swans Came to the Lake*, 210-211.
11 See Prothero, "Introduction" to C. Tonkinson (ed), *Big Sky Mind*, 17. (Snyder's view of Christianity seems to have mellowed in recent years.)
12 Jack Kerouac quoted in C. Tonkinson (ed), *Big Sky Mind*, 47.

haikus and aphorisms in *Some of the Dharma*, and wrote a life of the Buddha, *Wake Up*: both remain unpublished. Buddhist motifs are most strongly evident in *The Dharma Bums, Mexico City Blues* (1959), *The Scripture of the Golden Eternity* (1960), and *Desolation Angels* (1965). Rick Fields has applauded *The Scripture of the Golden Eternity* as "one of the most successful attempts yet to catch emptiness, nonattainment and egolessness in the net of American poetic language," a work which "might have been written by a lyrical American Nagarjuna."[13] Well, perhaps.

The San Francisco Be-In and the "Armies of the Night" at the Pentagon

January 19th, 1967, Golden Gate Park, San Francisco: the Human Be-In which, the organizers promised, would be "the joyful face-to-face beginning of a new epoch." Allen Ginsberg, one of the Organizing Committee, anticipated a "gathering together of younger people aware of the planetary fate ... imbued with a new consciousness and desiring of a new kind of society involving prayer, music and spiritual life together rather than competition, acquisition and war."[14] During 1966 San Francisco had already witnessed the Tripps Festival (conceived by Ken Kesey and organized by Bill Graham), a Love Pageant Rally and Now Day. Thirty thousand people assembled for the "Gathering of the Tribes." Gary Snyder, just returned from Japan, was there, along with fellow-poets Ginsberg, Lawrence Ferlinghetti, Lenore Kandel and Michael McClure. Also present on the stage, Richard Alpert and Tim Leary, apostles of the new psychedelics, and anti-war activist Jerry Rubin. Shunryu Suzuki briefly turned up, holding a single flower. Mantras were chanted, poems read, the *Prajnaparamita* recited by Ginsberg. Leary urged the festive crowd to "turn on, tune in, drop out." The Grateful Dead, Jefferson Airplane and Quicksilver Messenger Service played acid rock while the Hell's Angels provided security. The Diggers, a local alternative community, distributed free sandwiches garnished with LSD. Amongst the many banners and posters were to be seen exotic images of Krishna and the Buddha. Ginsberg compared the Be-In, which included purificatory circumambulations of the park, to the traditional Hindu *mela*.[15]

In October of the same year, fifty thousand protesters besieged the Pentagon. Norman Mailer was in the midst of "the armies of the night." *The East Village Other* reported that as well as quite ordinary folk also in attendance were companies of "witches, warlocks, holy men, seers, prophets, mystics, shamans, troubadours, minstrels, bards, roadmen, and madmen," all on hand to participate in a "mystic revolution." As well as the usual fare—marches, pickets, rousing speeches, sit-downs and the like—there was an "exor-

---

13 R. Fields, *How the Swans Came to the Lake*, 216.
14 Allen Ginsberg quoted in M. Schumacher, *Dharma Lion*, 480.
15 See R. Fields, *How the Swans Came to the Lake*, 248-249; B. Miles, *Ginsberg: A Biography*, 394-395; M. Schumacher, *Dharma Lion*, 480-481.

cism" of the Pentagon by "warlocks" who "cast mighty words of white light against the demon-controlled structure."[16]

Many of the ingredients of the counter-culture were on display on both occasions: the anti-war protest; "New Left" liberatory political activism (often growing out of the Civil Rights movement of the 50s and early 60s) combined with hybrid forms of Eastern spirituality; psychedelics and consciousness-changing drugs of varied kind, as well as a new "anti-psychiatry" discourse; eclectic forms of cultural expression—in poetry, music, clothes, life-style. Theodore Roszak was soon to write in his pioneering study, *The Making of a Counter-culture* (1969),

> ... the interests of our college-age and adolescent young in the psychology of alienation, oriental mysticism, psychedelic drugs, and communitarian experiments comprise a cultural constellation that radically diverges from values and assumptions that have been in the mainstream of our society at least since the Scientific Revolution of the seventeenth century.[17]

The continuities between the Beat movement of the 50s and the hippies of the late 60s and early 70s were also plain enough. Journalist Jane Kramer nominated Ginsberg as "guru and *paterfamilias*" of the Flower Power movement:

> Preaching and colonizing a brave new never-never world of bearded, beaded, marijuana-smoking, mantra-chanting euphoria, Ginsberg set the style for the Be-Ins, Love-Ins, Kiss-Ins, Chant-Ins, sacred orgies, and demon dispelling circumambulations of local draft boards, all of which began with the San Francisco Gathering of the Tribes.[18]

B. To a Buddhist Beat

Allen Ginsberg on Politics, Poetics and Spirituality

On May 6, 1972, Allen Ginsberg took the Three Refuges of Buddhism. At a ceremony in the Dharmadhatu Meditation Center in Boulder, Colorado, Ginsberg—disaffected Jew, Beat poet, counter-culture eminence, gay spokesman, teacher, itinerant bard, political dissident, prankster—pledged to take refuge in the Buddha, the Dharma (Buddhist teachings) and the *sangha* (the Buddhist community). In addition he took the Bodhisattva vows which committed him, in the face of inexhaustible obstacles, to work ceaselessly for the liberation of all sentient beings. As part of the ceremony Ginsberg accepted his refuge name of "Dharma Lion," bestowed by his

---

16 From *The East Village Other*, quoted in T. Roszak, *The Making of a Counter-culture*, 124.
17 T. Roszak, *The Making of a Counter-culture*, xii.
18 Jane Kramer quoted in M. Schumacher, *Dharma Lion*, 481.

Tibetan guru, Chögyam Trungpa.[19] This consummated an interest in Buddhism going back to the early 50s. Until his death in April 1997 Ginsberg remained committed to the Buddhist path. For many years he sat in meditation for at least an hour a day and did many extended retreats in which he underwent advanced training in various Buddhist disciplines. He worked enthusiastically on behalf of several Buddhist organizations, particularly the Naropa Institute in Boulder and, in his later years, the Jewel Heart Center in Ann Arbor, Michigan.

Ginsberg's death occasioned much comment on his role in American letters and in the cultural disturbances of the last four decades but, outside the organs of the American Buddhist community, surprisingly little notice was directed to Ginsberg's engagement with Eastern forms of spirituality. Ginsberg's public career and private life (a somewhat slippery distinction in this case!) have been documented in detail by two recent biographers. There is no point in rehearsing that story here; rather, we might reflect on his encounter with Asian religious forms. Ginsberg's life and work may be seen as an exemplary site on which various convergences and syntheses take place. Most notably perhaps, we can discern a creative fusion of various polarities and categorizations—East and West, the sacred and profane, the religious and the political, the intellectual and the sensual, the spiritual and the aesthetic.

In retracing his own spiritual growth Ginsberg invariably referred to a pivotal experience in the summer of 1948. At the time he was an undergraduate at Columbia, studying under Lionel Trilling and Mark van Doren, and living in East Harlem. He had already met both William Burroughs and Jack Kerouac with whom he spent a good deal of time discussing "new consciousness," smoking dope, and experimenting with literary forms which might best capture "the texture of consciousness" (one of Ginsberg's favorite phrases). He had also embarked on a wide-ranging exploration of the mystical literature of the West, particularly Plotinus, St John of the Cross, St Teresa of Avila, Marvell and Blake. Here is one of Ginsberg's many accounts of the experience:

> ... on the sixth floor of a Harlem tenement on 121st Street looking out at the roofs while reading Blake, back and forth, [I] suddenly had an auditory hallucination, hearing Blake—what I thought was his voice, very deep, earthen tone, not very far from my own mature tone of voice ... reciting a poem called "The Sunflower," which I thought expressed some kind of universal longing for union with some infinite nature ... I looked out the window and began to notice the extraordinary detail of the intelligent labor that had gone into the making of the rooftop cornices ... And I suddenly realized that the world was, in a sense, not dead matter, but an increment or deposit of living intelligence and action and activity that finally took form ... And as I

19 See B. Miles, *Ginsberg*, 446.

looked at the sky I wondered what kind of intelligence had made that vastness, or what was the nature of the intelligence that I was glimpsing, and felt
a sense of vastness and of coming home to a space I hadn't realized was
there before but which seemed old and infinite, like the Ancient of Days, so
to speak.[20]

In a much earlier account Ginsberg described the voice in these terms: "The
peculiar quality of the voice was something unforgettable because it was like
God had a human voice, with all the infinite tenderness and mortal gravity
of a living Creator speaking to his son."[21] Elsewhere he called the experience
a "beatific illumination" in which he "saw the universe unfold in my brain."[22]

Several other intense experiences, each linked to one of Blake's poems,
ensued in the following weeks. All the while Ginsberg was experimenting
with drugs—marijuana, peyote, mescalin, later LSD—though no drug-
induced experience left as deep an imprint as "The Sunflower" episode. In
his researches into Zen Buddhism in the early 50s Ginsberg was struck by the
apparent affinities between his own experience and *satori* as described by
D.T. Suzuki and others. In fact, Ginsberg remained preoccupied with recre-
ating this experience for the next fifteen years, only snapping out of what he
described as a kind of stupefaction during a meeting in India with Dudjom
Rinpoche, head of the Nyingma branch of Tibetan Buddhism. The
Rinpoche's adjuration to forego clinging to experiences, whether pleasant or
unpleasant, struck home.[23]

In the early 50s Kerouac introduced Ginsberg to several Buddhist texts,
singing passages from Sanskrit sutras *à la* Frank Sinatra.[24] Ginsberg's initial
reactions to the rudimentary teachings of the Buddha are interesting:

> as an ex-Communist Jewish intellectual, I thought his pronouncement of the
> First Noble Truth, that existence was suffering, was some sort of insult to my
> left-wing background, since I was a progressive looking forward to the univer-
> sal improvement of matters ... [25]

Ginsberg tells us that it took him two years to accept Kerouac's insistence that
the First Noble Truth was "a very simple fact." Also crucial to Ginsberg's initiation into the world of Eastern spirituality was his discovery of Chinese
painting in the Fine Arts Room of the New York Public Library, an interest
in Tibetan iconography (particularly the terrific "deities") and the *Book of the
Dead*. This triggered a lot of "new mind and eyeball kicks" and stimulated a

20 A. Ginsberg, "The Vomit of a Mad Tyger," *Shambhala Sun,* July 1995 (website).
21 B. Miles, *Ginsberg,* 99. The most detailed account of this experience is to be found in
Ginsberg's interview with Tom Clark in *Paris Review,* 37, Spring 1966.
22 Ginsberg, quoted in T. Roszak, *The Making of a Counter-culture,* 127.
23 B. Miles, *Ginsberg,* 104.
24 Allen Ginsberg, excerpt from *Disembodied Poetics: Annals of the Jack Kerouac School,*
http://www.naropa.edu/ginsbuddhist2.html. Kerouac himself had first turned to these texts in reaction against Neal Cassady's preoccupation with Edgar Cayce—whom Ginsberg later described as a
"crackpot."
25 Ginsberg, "The Vomit of a Mad Tyger."

massive reading program which included Suzuki's *Introduction to Zen Buddhism* (1934).[26]

By 1962 Ginsberg, now probably the best-known and certainly the most controversial poet in America, felt the need for a spiritual teacher sufficiently acutely to go on an extended visit to India with his friend and fellow poet Gary Snyder. Although he visited many holy sites and met a range of distinguished spiritual leaders and teachers (including Swami Shivananda, Dudjom Rinpoche, the Gyalwa Karmapa, and the Dalai Lama) Ginsberg did not attach himself to any particular guru nor commit himself to any specific spiritual method. An eclectic mixture of the Hindu and the Buddhist, haphazard meditation of one kind and another, mantra chanting and more drugs remained the order of the day. It was not until 1970 that Swami Muktananda introduced Ginsberg to a systematic meditation practice. However, it was to be Chögyam Trungpa, met briefly in India in 1962, who was to become Ginsberg's guru.

Trungpa was a highly charismatic and controversial figure in American Buddhism. Born in Tibet in 1939, he was identified as a *tulku* (reincarnation of an enlightened teacher) at thirteen months and underwent the intensive Tibetan training culminating in full ordination in the Kargyu sect at the age of eighteen. After a highly dramatic escape from Tibet following the Chinese invasion, and a period in India, Trungpa had gone to Oxford to study philosophy, comparative religion and fine art before setting up the Samye-Ling Meditation Center in Scotland. Some years later he moved to America and was the prime mover in establishing the Naropa Institute in Boulder, Colorado.[27] He was to have a profound impact on Ginsberg—so much so that Ginsberg was later to say that, "he left such an imprint on my consciousness that I in a sense see through his eyes or see through the same eyes of those occasions where he pointed direction to me."[28]

After an apparently chance encounter in a New York street in 1970, Trungpa and Ginsberg developed a close and complex relationship—guru and *chela*, philosophical sparring partners, drinking buddies, fellow poets, tricksters, kindred spirits. Under the Tibetan's invitation Ginsberg, with Anne Waldman, set up the Jack Kerouac School of Disembodied Poetics within the Naropa Institute. For many years Ginsberg taught a summer school there which explored the connections between meditation and poetry:

26 B. Miles, *Ginsberg*, 153.

27 For a detailed narrative of Trungpa's part in the spread of Buddhism in America see R. Fields, *How the Swans Came to the Lake*. For Trungpa's own story of his early life see *Born in Tibet* (1966). See also Chapter 11.

28 Canadian Broadcasting Corporation, "Interview with Allen Ginsberg" (website).

... the life of meditation and the life of art are both based on a similar conception of spontaneous mind. They both share renunciation as a way of avoiding a conditioned art work, or trite art, or repetition of other people's ideas.[29]

Under Trungpa's guidance, he also developed his own meditational practice and deepened his understanding of the Vajrayana tradition in particular (though he retained an interest in Zen Buddhism and Hinduism, as well as later turning back to the Judaism which was his patrimony). It was Trungpa who persuaded Ginsberg to perform improvisational poetry.

From the early 70s onwards Ginsberg could properly be described as a serious Buddhist practitioner: as one observer noted in 1976, "classical Buddhist practice has become the core of Ginsberg's life."[30] Three years after Trungpa's death in 1986 Philip Glass introduced Ginsberg to another Tibetan master with whom he also developed a close relationship—Kyabje Gelek Rinpoche of the Gelugpa sect, based at the Jewel Heart Center in Ann Arbor, Michigan. Ginsberg himself has noted how the intense devotion and desire which he had previously directed to his literary heroes, friends and multifarious lovers—often to no very good effect—was now largely transferred to the dharma and the guru.[31]

Some of the attractions of Buddhism for one of Ginsberg's temperament and experience are plain enough. Buddhism offered a spiritual therapy which could address his deep psychic wounds. Buddhist teachings and meditational practice certainly helped Ginsberg to at least partially heal some of the deep-seated confusions and anxieties, "elements of resentment, aggression and dead-end anger" which were the legacy of a painful and traumatic childhood. He never lost his sharp sense of life's absurdities but increasingly understood the pain and pathos of the condition to which the Buddha's First Noble Truth alerts us. The form of Buddhism espoused by Trungpa was pragmatic and experiential in method, doctrinally "open," and free of any disabling associations with either conservative politics or puritanical moralism. Buddhism's non-theistic metaphysic appealed to Ginsberg's anti-authoritarian personality ("there is no Central Intelligence Agency in the universe") and provided a vocabulary in which he could better understand the hierophanies of his student days.[32]

By way of an aside we might note that Ginsberg's various involvements with Tibetan Buddhist organizations in the 70s and 80s, and the controversies and tensions in which he often found himself involved—most notably the "Naropa Poetry Wars"[33]—illuminate several aspects of the "Americanizing" of

---

29 A. Ginsberg, "Meditation and Poetics" in *Spiritual Quests: The Art and Craft of Religious Writing,* ed. W. Zinsser, 163.

30 P.B. Chowka, "This is Allen Ginsberg?", the 1976 *New Age Interview* (website).

31 A. Ginsberg, "Allen Ginsberg: Anxious Dreams of Eliot," *The Boston Book Review,* Interview with Harvey Blume, 1995 (website).

32 See A. Ginsberg, "The Vomit of a Mad Tyger."

33 See B. Miles, *Ginsberg,* 466-482.

the Vajrayana. Jack Kornfield has identified democratization (the disassembling of patriarchal and authoritarian power structures, and the move from a monastic to a lay orientation), feminization (the inclusion of women at all levels of practice and leadership), and integration (the adaptation of Buddhist practice to the exigencies of everyday lay life in late 20th century America) as the three key changes in this process.[34] Another conspicuous motif in the development of American Buddhism is the rapid emergence of what has come to be called "engaged Buddhism," one dynamically concerned with the most pressing socio-political issues of the day.[35]

Of the many ceremonies that marked Allen Ginsberg's death the Jewel Heart Memorial Service at Ann Arbor was especially poignant. The religious service included both Tibetan and Jewish chants and prayers, and was followed by a concert of poetry and music, read or sung by Anne Waldman, Bob Rosenthal (Ginsberg's personal secretary), Natalie Merchant and Patti Smith, and including works by Ginsberg, Kerouac and Bob Dylan. The San Francisco ceremony at the Temple Emmanuel included tributes from Snyder, Diane Di Prima, Lawrence Ferlinghetti, Robert Hass, Joanne Kyger and Andrew Schelling.[36]

Politics, Poetics and the Western Encounter with Eastern Spirituality

Several questions arise. As the old song has it, "What's it all about Alfie?" How did this encounter with Buddhism impact on Ginsberg's politics, his aesthetics and his worldview generally? In the context of American cultural transformations what might Ginsberg's experience exemplify? Ginsberg's *persona* and his place in American cultural life probably has as much to do with his role as a political gadfly and poet—and indeed he would not have separated the two. From the early Columbia days right down to his death Ginsberg was a burr under the saddle of conservative America, constantly mocking bourgeois values and scandalizing the burghers, puncturing uncomfortable hypocrisies and exposing corruption in the body politic. With his own inimitable mixture of insouciance, *outré* charm, moral gravity and impassioned eloquence he championed causes such as the protection of free expression, gay rights, the ending of the Vietnam War, ecological awareness, the unmasking of American imperialism. All of this is quite unexceptional. What is interesting in this context is the way in which Ginsberg's career fuses spiritual and political values, and creates a style and vocabulary of political critique which owes much more to the prophets of ancient Israel, Blake, and Thoreau than to, say, Marx or Bakunin—or indeed to Mill, or the Webbs. He had little time for the confrontationist and angry slogans of the SDS and the Weathermen

---

34 See J. Kornfield, "American Buddhism" in D. Morreale (ed), *The Complete Guide to Buddhist America.*

35 See F. Eppsteiner (ed), *The Path of Compassion: Writings on Socially Engaged Buddhism.*

36 For information about tributes, ceremonies, remembrances and the like, see: http://www.tricycle.com/ginsberg.html.

and believed that the rather facile politicization of youth much in evidence in the 60s had somewhat undermined the Beat impulses towards spiritual liberation.[37]

Interviewer: Kenneth Rexroth deemed you "a poet of revolt" ... are you still?

Ginsberg: I never have been a poet of revolt, never never never. That's saying you want to become wiser by becoming dumber, you want to become more peaceful by getting angry ... *My interest is in alteration in consciousness, in new vision* ... [this] goes back to 1945 conversations with Kerouac. Revolt of consciousness, ok.

Interviewer: How have you been active in fighting for gay rights?

Ginsberg: I don't believe in fighting.[38]

European radicalism since the 18th century has been, in the main, fiercely secular and militantly atheistic. Institutional religion has been seen, more often than not, as an oppressive and reactionary force and notions of the "spiritual" and "mystical" have been variously stigmatized as superstition, obscurantism, alienation, escapism, selfishness and neurosis. It is no surprise that Ginsberg should align himself, emotionally and intellectually, with the one significant group of political radicals who did not accept the materialistic, positivistic and progressivist assumptions of the Enlightenment, namely the Romantic poets. Nor is it an accident that Romantic values should have figured so largely, though often in caricature, in the counter-culture of the 60s. What the counter-culture offered was, in Theodore Roszak's words, "a defection from the long-standing tradition of skeptical, secular intellectuality which has served as the prime vehicle for three hundred years of scientific and technical work in the West."[39] Ginsberg's principal role as counter-cultural figure was as a "vagabond proselytizer" of a this-worldly mysticism, "an ecstasy of the body and the earth that somehow embraces and transforms mortality ... a joy that includes ... the commonplace obscenities of our existence."[40]

Ginsberg's "beatific illuminations" and his subsequent involvements in Indian, Tibetan and Japanese spirituality gave him a perspective and a metaphysic which certainly did not blunt his political radicalism but which provided a certain distance, a sense of proportion, and a scale of values which moved him past an adolescent rage at the cultural wasteland of Ike and Dale Carnegie and Lassie, and the Single Vision of a materialistic gospel of progress, and beyond the narrow, antagonistic dichotomies of Marxist rhetoric and the easy sentimentalities of Utopianism in its manifold guises. Increasingly his political stance, and indeed his poetry, seemed to derive less

37 See S. Goddard, "The Beats and Boom: A Conversation with Allen Ginsberg" (website).
38 "Allen Ginsberg interviewed by Jeffrey Goldsmith" (website) (italics mine).
39 T. Roszak, *The Making of a Counter-culture*, 141.
40 T. Roszak, *The Making of a Counter-culture*, 129.

from the impulse to mockery, from hatred and alienation, and more from a sense of compassion—remembering that in the Buddhist context compassion (*karuna*) is inseparable from wisdom (*prajna*) of which it is actually the dynamic aspect. In his later interviews Ginsberg repeatedly affirms the non-combative and compassionate values which lie at the heart of the Buddhist tradition.

In a larger context we might ponder the significance of the changes whereby the iconic figures of the secular left (say, Lenin, Emma Goldman, Trotsky, Che Guevara) have lost a good deal of their luster whilst those whose radicalism is governed by a "politics of eternity" (say, Gandhi, Martin Luther King, the Dalai Lama) take on a new aura. This answers to something much deeper than the whimsies of political fashion. It is tempting to believe that a new paradigm of socio-political transformation is still being fashioned, one drawing on the European post-Enlightenment, radical mainstream but discarding its one-dimensional materialism and utilitarian rationality (and the scientistic ideologies from which they derive), and much more receptive to the spiritual messages of both our own largely-forgotten tradition and of non-Western cultures alike.

Mark Linenthal has claimed, persuasively enough, that Ginsberg, "more than any other writer changed what a whole generation thought a poem should or could be."[41] Our interest here is not so much in the literary upheaval unleashed by the first public reading of "Howl" (1955)—the "most widely sold, read, and discussed poem of the decade"[42]—but rather in the inter-relations of aesthetics, politics and metaphysics in Ginsberg's life and work. Clearly the "alteration in consciousness" of which he so often spoke encompasses all of these dimensions. Ginsberg once defined classical poetry as "a 'process,' or experiment—a probe into the nature of reality and the nature of the mind."[43] How easily the definition fits Buddhism itself. Ginsberg repeatedly talks of "new consciousness" as providing the emergent Beat writers with their focal point and as impelling their interest in writers such as Blake, Rimbaud, Baudelaire, and Yeats ("our great grandfathers among hermetic poets and philosophers").[44] Of course, since time immemorial poetry has been the medium in which the religious sensibility most readily and fully expresses itself—think of Homer, the Psalms, the rhapsodies of the Vedic rishis.[45] "Poet is Priest," as Ginsberg puts it in the first line of "Death to Van Gogh's Ear."

The Beats' search for new consciousness and for new poetic forms, their rejection of the General Motors/Walt Disney version of the American

---

41 "San Francisco Says Goodbye to a Bard," *San Francisco Chronicle*, Monday April 21, 1997, A1.

42 D. Hoffman (ed), *Harvard Guide to Contemporary American Writing*, 519.

43 A. Ginsberg, "Meditation and Poetics," 145. Cf. Philip Whalen: "My Writing is a Picture of the Mind Moving"; quoted in C. Tonkinson (ed), *Big Sky Mind*, 135.

44 A. Ginsberg, "Meditation and Poetics," 148.

45 On this subject see B. Griffiths, *The Marriage of East and West*, 47ff.

Dream, their impulse to escape the grip of Urizen (Blake's mythical person-ification of "Single Vision"—instrumentalist rationality, the Human Imagination petrified, Newton's Pantocrator) were all of a piece:

> We didn't have what you would call a philosophy. I would say there was an ethos, that there were ideas, themes, preoccupations ... *the primary thing was a move towards spiritual liberation*, not merely from Bourgeois, 50s quietism, or Silent Generation, but from the last centuries of mechanization and homog-enization of cultures, the mechanical assault on human nature and all nature culminating in the bomb ... the search for new consciousness ... I don't think we had it clearly defined, but we were looking for something ... as a kind of breakthrough from the sort of hyper-rationalistic, hyper-scientif-ic, hyper-rationalizing of the post-war era.[46]

As Michael McClure put it in his memoir *Scratching the Beat Surface*, "None of us wanted to go back to the gray, chill, militaristic silence, to the intellective void—to the land without poetry—to the spiritual drabness. We wanted to make it new ... We wanted voice and we wanted vision."[47] Here indeed were "angel headed hipsters burning for ancient heavenly connection"! In this context it is no surprise that a good many of the Beat circle developed a seri-ous and sustained interest in aspects of Eastern religion, art and philosophy.

The whole literary experiment of the Beats, at least for Ginsberg (and certainly for Kerouac and Snyder) was impelled by a spiritual rather than an aesthetic aspiration. Or, to put it differently, the new literary forms emerged out of the explorations of consciousness rather than out of any coherent aes-thetic theory, and certainly not out of any blind iconoclasm. As is so often the case with avant-garde movements in whatever domain, theory *followed* prac-tice. As Ginsberg himself succinctly characterized the Beat movement: "a spiritual revolution that took form in the changes in the literary method ..."[48] Or again, to put the point differently, poetry, for Ginsberg, became a form of spiritual practice—and one nicely attuned to the spiritual economy of Buddhism with its pervasive concern with "the texture of consciousness," underpinned by a metaphysic of "voidness" which, far from constituting a nihilistic negation, provided the basis for what Ginsberg called "continuous generous activity, exuberant activity," without hope or fear, non-attached and compassionate—in short, for *karuna*.[49] Ginsberg repeatedly foregrounds the intersections of meditational practice and the writing of poetry: in each case it is a matter of "noticing my thoughts, noticing that I'm noticing it, observ-ing what's there, then realizing what is really there ... being a stenographer of your own mind ... scanning your mind and observing your thoughts, and

---

46 S. Goddard, "The Beats and Boom: A Conversation with Allen Ginsberg" (italics mine) (web-site). See also "Allen Ginsberg interviewed by Jeffrey Goldsmith" where Ginsberg says, "My own idea is that the origins of beat writings were in some kind of spiritual revolution."
47 S. Silberman, "How Beat Happened" (website).
48 S. Goddard, "The Beats and Boom: A Conversation with Allen Ginsberg."
49 S. Goddard, "The Beats and Boom: A Conversation with Allen Ginsberg."

what forms arise and flourish."[50] Thus, "there's a natural affinity between non-theistic practice and up to date modern and post-modern American poetic practice."[51]

C. "Pop Gurus," "New Consciousness" and Drugs

There was another figure at the San Francisco Be-In whose influence probably extended even further than that of the "Buddhist Jew" (as Ginsberg often described himself): Alan Watts. Watts might have found his place in this study in several different chapters—as a popularizer of Eastern doctrines, as an early practitioner of Buddhism, as a bridge-builder between Western psychology and Eastern spirituality. However it was as a "guru" of the counter-culture that he reached the zenith of his influence. We will turn presently to an overview of Watts' whole career but first it is worth tracing another "passage to India" by one of the other figures on the stage in Golden Park in the summer of 1967.

Ram Dass (Richard Alpert)

One of the more appealing counter-cultural celebrities/teachers to emerge in the 60s was Ram Dass. As Richard Alpert he achieved notoriety as one of the Harvard LSD "researchers" who produced *The Psychedelic Experience*, an adaptation of *The Tibetan Book of the Dead* for the guidance of trippers (the other two "authors" were Timothy Leary and Ralph Metzner). Alpert came from a wealthy New England family. After studying at Tufts University and completing a doctorate in psychology at Stanford, he joined the faculty at Harvard (which had earlier rejected his application for admission), where he befriended Timothy Leary. Their work with psychedelic drugs (including extensive personal experimentation) and their growing interest in Eastern spirituality provoked the chairman of their department to remark in a memo to the faculty:

> It is probably no accident that the society which has most consistently encouraged the use of these substances, India, produced one of the sickest social orders ever created by mankind, in which thinking men spent their time lost in the Buddha position under the influence of drugs exploring consciousness, while poverty, disease, social discrimination and superstition reached their highest and most organized form in all history.[52]

We will not here unpack the manifold prejudices which lurk in this passage— but it does tell us something about attitudes to both consciousness-altering

---

50 Jim Moore, "Public Heart: An Interview with Allen Ginsberg" (website).
51 Canadian Broadcasting Corporation, "Interview with Allen Ginsberg."
52 Quoted in T. Schwartz, *What Really Matters*, 37. (In fairness it should also be pointed out that the chairman protected Leary and Alpert for as long as he reasonably could.)

drugs and Eastern religions. By May 1963 both Leary and Alpert had been dismissed from Harvard but continued their experimentation and their pros-elytizing for drug-induced experiences. A flyer for their journal *The Psychedelic Review* began,

> Mescalin! Consciousness! Phantastical Transcendence! Hashish! Visionary Botany! Ololiuqui! Physiology of Religion! Internal Freedom! Morning Glory! Politics of the Nervous System![53]

We shall return presently to the controversies which still surround the rela-tionship between mysticism and drug-induced experiences.

Alpert's burgeoning interest in Eastern mysticism led to a trip to India in the late 60s where he met his guru, "Maharajji" (Neem Karoli Baba), who gave him the name "Ram Dass" ("servant of God") and about whom he later wrote *Miracle of Love* (1979). Ram Dass spent a year under his guru, return-ing to India for a longer stay in the early 70s. Ram Dass' enduring signifi-cance has been as popularizer of a Hindu-based but rather eclectic mélange of Eastern doctrines, values, and practices. He has also been a "servant of God" whose spiritual practice has been harnessed to steadfast social service with the dying and with prisoners. More recently he has worked with the blind in India and Nepal, and with development projects in Guatemala. He has been the driving force in the establishment of various non-profit organi-zations such as the Hanuman Foundation, the Seva Foundation and the Shanti Project.

Ram Dass' *Be Here Now*, published in 1972 by the Lama Foundation (ded-icated to "watering the spiritual garden around the world"), became some-thing of a hippie manual on techniques of meditation, breath control, yoga, and chanting. It was replete with stories, aphorisms, and practical advice. But it was a series of books written after his transformative experiences in India which marked him as one of the more engaging guides to a rather free-wheeling spirituality based primarily on the Hindu ideals of *bhakti* and *karma-yoga*: *The Only Dance There Is* (1973), *Grist for the Mill* (1977), written with Stephen Levine, and *Journey of Awakening* (1979). Amongst Ram Dass' many endearing qualities are his manifest sincerity and compassion, his openness about his own limitations and failings, his eschewing of any grandiose claims about his own spiritual experience, a refusal to elevate himself to guru status, and an accommodating attitude to doctrines and practices from different religious traditions (including a rediscovery of the Judaism into which he was born). As Tony Schwartz has written,

> Among all the seekers who emerged from the counterculture ferment of the 1960s, perhaps no one more than Richard Alpert so dramatically turned his back on a traditional American success story, embraced such a radically dif-

---

53 Quoted in W. O'Neill, *Coming Apart: An Informal History of America in the Sixties*, 239.
54 T. Schwartz, *What Really Matters*, 24.

ferent path, and still managed to make his perspective seem both accessible and appealing.[54]

Ram Dass would not himself claim to be a scholar, an expositor of orthodox doctrines, or an "enlightened being." He would be the first to admit that he is no saint. But his influence, through his writings and his social service, has been widespread, lasting and benign. Andrew Rawlinson, a scholar of wide experience and erudition who has constructed a massive study of Western dharma teachers, reckons Ram Dass one of the four foremost popularizers of Eastern spirituality this century, the other three being D.T. Suzuki, Alan Watts and Chögyam Trungpa.[55]

Alan Watts

Alan Watts was an Englishman who moved to America in 1938 (about the same time as his famous compatriot Aldous Huxley), in flight from the impending war. Watts had already made a mark in England as something of a *wunderkind*—a mover and shaker in the Buddhist Society, close associate of Christmas Humphreys, at the age of nineteen author of *The Spirit of Zen* (1935) (dedicated to Humphreys), editor of *Buddhism in England* (later *The Middle Way*) and a public speaker of some renown. His interest in the East had been triggered by a number of Japanese scrolls, Chinese embroideries and various other Asian artifacts which adorned the family home at Chislehurst, Kent.[56] The writings of Lafcadio Hearn, particularly *Gleanings in Buddha-Fields*, and the Fu Manchu novels of Sax Rohmer also played a part.[57]

As a fifteen-year old schoolboy Watts prepared a paper on Japanese painting, the first of an apparently endless stream of writings to flow from his pen. From the start Watts was an eloquent, witty and highly attractive writer and speaker. As one of his friends has observed, "Alan Watts' way with words was one of the primary facts of his existence."[58] As a person Watts has been described as "energetic, friendly, charismatic, full of ideas, alcoholic, egotistical, lonely"[59]—intimating some of the contradictions which were to run through his life. Although he rebelled against a rather grim fundamentalist upbringing he never lost his interest in the mystical aspects of Christianity and in its earlier myths, symbols and liturgies:

> However much we may imagine ourselves to have cut adrift from the Church's symbols, they return to us under many forms in our dreams and phantasies, when the intellect sleeps and the mind has liberty to break from the rational order which it demands.[60]

55 A. Rawlinson, *The Book of Enlightened Masters*, 620.
56 M. Furlong, *Genuine Fake*, 13-15.
57 See M. Furlong, *Genuine Fake*, 36, and A. Watts, *The Early Writings of Alan Watts*, 7.
58 A.W. Sadler, "The Vintage Alan Watts," 144.
59 Review of Furlong's *Genuine Fake*, http://socrates.cs.man.ac.uk/reviews/watts-amiss.html.
60 A. Watts, *The Legacy of Asia and Western Man*, 1937, quoted in M. Furlong, *Genuine Fake*, 61.

Indeed, Watts spent several troubled years in the 40s as an Episcopalian priest and university chaplain.[61] After this turbulent interlude Watts spent most of the rest of his life, in Tim Leary's words, as "a wandering, independent sage,"[62] a free-lance lecturer and writer, disseminating "Eastern" teachings but also trying to work out a synthesis of medieval Christianity, Eastern mysticism and modern psychology (of a more or less Jungian kind).

The early 50s found Watts in dire straits: self-exiled from the church, shunned by much of the religious establishment, recently divorced and no longer with access to the patronage of his former wife's family, unemployed, and with a new wife to support. The timely intervention of Joseph Campbell secured him a grant from the Bollingen Foundation and allowed him to continue his investigations into Oriental and Christian philosophy, mythology, and Jungian psychology, and to write *The Wisdom of Insecurity* (1951). Soon after Watts moved to San Francisco to join the American Academy of Asian Studies, set up to cater for a blossoming American interest in all things Asian and which Watts hoped could be instrumental in "the practical transformation of human consciousness."[63] It provided a congenial milieu for Watts. Among the students at the Academy were Gary Snyder, Michael Murphy and Richard Price (who later founded Esalen), and the artist Jean Varda. Watts was actually instrumental in the scholarship grant which allowed Snyder to go to Japan in 1956.[64] Through Snyder Watts came to know most of the writers, artists and intellectuals who comprised the Beat generation. Watts himself appears in *The Dharma Bums*, thinly disguised as Arthur Whane, director of the Buddhist Association. Watts maintained some informal links with both the churches and the academy—but his attitude towards all institutions was wary. One of his friends characterized Watts' own "theology" as "a curious but amicable blend of the Hindu *lila* doctrine, Taoist philosophy, medieval Christian myth, and Zen humor,"[65] to which we might add contemporary Western psychology—each of these elements being foregrounded at different times.

It would be a mistake to think of Watts as no more than a popularizer. Several of his books are based on genuine scholarship and on rigorous intellectual inquiry: one may cite *The Way of Zen* (1957), *Psychotherapy East and West* (1961), *Myth and Ritual in Christianity* (1968) and the posthumous *Tao, the Watercourse Way* (1975) as works of some substance, though not bereft of the charm and humor which imbues most of his work. At the same time it must be admitted that many of Watts' books are marred by the self-indulgent prejudices of the day—not of the Establishment but of the counter-culture, but

---

61 For Watts' theological position and his existential anxieties in this period see *Behold the Spirit*, 1947.
62 Leary quoted in M. Furlong, *Genuine Fake*, 146.
63 Watts quoted in M. Furlong, *Genuine Fake*, 118.
64 M. Furlong, *Genuine Fake*, 124.
65 A.W. Sadler, "The Vintage Alan Watts," 147.

prejudices nonetheless! One might mention, by way of an example, Watts' frequent and absurd assertions—also often made by the likes of Aldous Huxley and Krishnamurti—that "Eastern" religious life had little to do with "beliefs" or "ethics" or "rites"! Here was a "spirituality" cut to measure for the hipster. Sentimentality and foggy thinking are perhaps most apparent in one of Watts' most popular and most muddled books, *The Book on the Taboo Against Knowing Who You Are* (1966).

In his rather scurrilous memoirs Edward Conze had this to say of Alan Watts:

> Most of my American students first became interested in Buddhism through Alan Watts. It is true that they had to unlearn most of what they had learnt. It is equally true that he put out the net which caught them in the first place.[66]

The editor of *The Middle Way*, in a memorial article written ten years after Watts' death, called him

> a kind of spiritual fifth columnist who infiltrated advance information about the Eastern religions into the Western consciousness. We owe him a great debt for this—and for doing it so lucidly, elegantly and entertainingly. But perhaps we owe him an equal debt for his mistakes ...[67]

His biographer pronounces him as a "genuine fake," and concedes that many of his students became much more assiduous students of Buddhism than he was.[68] Douglas Harding refers to "the more-or-less ramshackle human vehicle" who conveyed many "eternal verities" to his readers.[69] One unkind academic called Watts "the Norman Vincent Peale of Zen"[70] while a recent reviewer refers to him as "a genial huckster."[71] These somewhat ambivalent tributes touch on Watts' gifts and limitations, both conspicuous. Watts himself was well aware of both. In a candid moment in his autobiography, *In My Own Way*, he wrote

> ... as I look back I could be inclined to think that I have lived a sloppy, inconsiderate, wasteful, cowardly and undisciplined life, only getting away with it by having a certain charm and a big gift of the gab.[72]

Whatever might be said about the excesses of a somewhat profligate personal life and the trail of human havoc which Watts left behind him, there is no doubt that from the appearance in 1935 of *The Spirit of Zen* until his death in 1973 Alan Watts was the most influential of all Western popularizers of

---

66 E. Conze, *The Memoirs of a Modern Gnostic 1*, 74fn.
67 *The Middle Way*, "Alan Watts, 1915-73: In Memoriam," 212.
68 M. Furlong, "Alan Watts," 216.
69 D. Harding, "Alan Watts—Sage or Anti-Sage?", 221
70 Unnamed academic quoted in T. Roszak, *The Making of a Counter-culture*, 132.
71 P. Zaleski, "Farewell and Far Out!", 46.
72 A. Watts, *In My Own Way*, 423.

Eastern teachings, even if he often cast these in somewhat unorthodox terms. He wrote more than twenty books, lectured and toured tirelessly, edited journals, made frequent radio broadcasts, television programs and video tapes. He rubbed shoulders with just about all the "names" in American and English Buddhist circles, the Beat writers, leaders of the counter-culture and knew many Eastern savants as well as clerics and scholars from various fields. A random sample of friends and associates: Christmas Humphreys, Ruth Fuller Sasaki, D.T. Suzuki, Aldous Huxley, Sokei-an Sasaki, Gary Snyder, Ananda Coomaraswamy, Krishnamurti, Aelred Graham, Gregory Bateson, Timothy Leary, R.D. Laing, Fritz Perls, Bishop John Robinson, the Zurich Jungians. A quarter of a century after his death most of his books are still in print and, indeed, there is a constant flow of "new" tapes, videos, transcripts of lectures, journal entries and the like. Sales show no sign of abating.

"New Consciousness," New Universalism?

Late in his life Watts enjoyed a Conference ("spiritual bash" might be a more appropriate term!) he attended at a Benedictine monastery in New York, along with "a whole gaggle of gurus"—Hindu swamis, Trappist monks, rabbis, Zen practitioners, Orthodox monks, Buddhist teachers. By Watts' account a great time was had by all. But the episode raises many questions about the kind of freewheeling eclecticism and somewhat sentimental spiritual "hospitality" exemplified by figures such as Watts. We might also ask how qualified such figures are to speak in the name of the *sophia perennis* to which they so often paid at least lip service.

In a caustic but considered essay Whitall Perry has elaborated a traditionalist critique of some of the characteristics shared by many of the teachings of the "prophets" of a "new consciousness." Amongst the people he mentions as representing "the tip of the iceberg" are Aldous Huxley, Gerald Heard, R.C. Zaehner, Teilhard de Chardin, Aurobindo, Gopi Krishna, Krishnamurti and Alan Watts—the list is obviously representative rather than exhaustive.[73] Perry is dealing in this essay with generalities which will apply with varying emphases according to the case at hand but the tendencies to which he takes exception in the work of such people are these:

> ... a patent individualism, a scientific and moralistic humanism, evolutionism, a relativistic "intuitionism," inability to grasp metaphysical and cosmological principles and the realities of the Universal Domain, a mockery (latent or overt) of the sacred, a prodigal dearth of spiritual imagination, no eschatological understanding, a pseudo-mysticism in the form of a "cosmic consciousness."[74]

---

73 W. Perry, "Anti-Theology and the Riddles of Alcyone," 176-192.
74 W. Perry, "Anti-Theology and the Riddles of Alcyone," 186.

For the moment we shall amplify a few of these points with reference to the ideas of Alan Watts and Krishnamurti.

The "patent individualism" of people like Watts and Krishnamurti is attested by their refusal to submit to any traditional doctrine or spiritual discipline. Watts' flirtation with Zen can hardly pass muster while Krishnamurti was an unabashed iconoclast. Instead of conforming themselves and their ideas to an orthodoxy which would take them past the limitations of individualism they remained locked into various intellectual and existential stalemates which stem from the conflict between an aspiration to "selflessness" and the absence of any traditional doctrine or method.

In the case of Watts this is plain enough in his later writings which are marked by an ambivalent attitude to the status of the ego. In a searching study of Watts' work Louis Nordstrom and Richard Pilgrim have demonstrated how his self-professed "spiritual materialism" (his own term) ends, and can only end, in an affirmation of the human ego.[75] No amount of Watts' literary wizardry or his amiable wit could camouflage the fact. What we find in Watts' later work is indeed what Schuon calls "the disordered subjectivism of a personal mysticism."[76] Indeed, Watts seemed happy to concede that he was "a shameless egotist."[77] None of this, perhaps, would much matter were it not for the fact that Watts was often seen as a spokesperson for a kind of mystical rapprochement of the different religions. A good many people would endorse the claim that Watts "has done more perhaps than any other writer to open the eyes of the West to the spiritual significance of Eastern religions and philosophies and to show that Truth is not the monopoly of any one school."[78] Watts indeed affirmed that "the Paths are many but their end is One." Insofar as this principle governed Watts' enterprise we can applaud it but the question remains as to whether he was qualified to understand and interpret traditional doctrines. The traditionalist judgment must be that he was not: his interpretation of traditional doctrines was too idiosyncratic to carry any authority. It should come as no surprise that Watts was a great admirer of Madame Blavatsky, Annie Besant, Gurdjieff and Krishnamurti.[79] The title of his autobiography, *In My Own Way*, is a more fitting epitaph than he realized. It might also be said that Perry's admonitions would apply no less forcefully to a good many of the "pop gurus" adopted by the counter-culture: names such as Idries Shah, Bhagwan Rajneesh and Bubba Free John come readily to mind.

75 L. Nordstrom & R. Pilgrim, "The Wayward Mysticism of Alan Watts," 381-399.
76 F. Schuon, "Nature and Function of the Spiritual Master," 54.
77 D. Sibley, "The Legacy of Alan Watts: A Personal View," 219-220.
78 L. Watts, "Foreword" to A. Watts, *In My Own Way*, vii-viii.
79 See M. Furlong, *Genuine Fake*, 146.

A Note on Drugs, Mysticism and Spirituality

There have, in recent times, been many claims about the relationship between drug-induced changes in consciousness and various religious/spiritual experiences which can be gathered together under the canopy of "mysticism." Indeed, this is a subject on which rivers of ink have been spilt, often to no very good end. Rather than rehearsing the many arguments that have been canvassed and the many controversies which have dogged the debate, I shall here restrict myself to a few general remarks. Certainly it is a subject which no account of the spiritual dimensions of either the Beat movement or the counter-culture can leave out of the reckoning.

Aldous Huxley's *The Doors of Perception* (1954) became the *locus classicus* of what was to become a standard theme in the counter cultural literature, the assimilation of drug-induced changes in consciousness and the mystical experience as understood in the religious literatures of many different cultures. Huxley's essays were followed in the 60s by an efflorescence of books and articles on this subject. *The Psychedelic Experience*, Alan Watts' *The Joyous Cosmology* and Timothy Leary's *The Politics of Ecstasy* were amongst the most widely read. There was also a serious interest in the spiritual and ritual uses of drugs in shamanistic cultures. The books of Carlos Castaneda (*The Teachings of Don Juan, A Separate Reality, Journey to Ixtlan*, and endless sequels), purportedly accounts of the esoteric practices of the Yaqui Indians, were hugely popular. Many commentators noted the striking similarities between the accounts of a unitive, transcendental experience in the vast cross-cultural mystical literature and the kinds of experiences to which hallucinogenic drugs apparently gave rise. There was a good deal of excitable talk about short-cuts to the "White Light" via LSD, peyote, magic mushrooms, mescalin and the like. Nor was the excitement merely theoretical and academic: seekers of one kind and another were eager to experiment with consciousness-changing drugs of every conceivable sort.

In *The Doors of Perception* (1954) Aldous Huxley asserted that the "aspiring mystic" could achieve "the transcendental experience" through chemical aids. He wrote:

> In one way or another, all our experiences are chemically conditioned ... Knowing as he does ... what are the chemical conditions of transcendental experience, the aspiring mystic should turn for technical help to the specialists—in pharmacology, in biochemistry ... [80]

Whitall Perry and others have anatomized the confusions which run rampant through the drug experiences = mysticism literature and there is no point in going over the same ground. Suffice it to note that the formulation above would be worthy of the most unabashed materialist.[81]

---

80 A. Huxley, *The Doors of Perception and Heaven and Hell*, 121-122.
81 See W. Perry, *Challenges to a Secular Society*, 7-16.

There is no doubt that drugs can release certain psychic/mental inhibitions and open "the doors of perception" to dimensions of reality which are inaccessible to the mundane consciousness which, to use a phrase of Chögyam Trungpa's, is ordinarily under the control and surveillance of the "bureaucracy of the ego." There is also no doubt that the shocks administered by drug-induced experiences to a recalcitrant materialism were often therapeutic, and helped to lead many people towards the spiritual teachings and practices enshrined in the various religious traditions. This was all to the good. However, many others, mistakenly believing that drugs themselves could lead to "enlightenment," ended up in a *cul-de-sac*, sometimes with personal consequences both tragic and pathetic. In this respect, the claim that drug-induced experiences were identical or akin to the mystical experience, caused a good deal of mischief. There is much that might be said on this subject but here I make only two points. Firstly, the mystical experience, as described by countless saints and sages through the ages, results in *absolute certitude* about the supra-sensorial Reality to which the experience gives access. (The ways in which this Reality is subsequently described will vary according to the symbolic vocabulary appropriate to the spiritual culture in question, though there is overwhelming unanimity about the nature of the experience itself.) And secondly, the mystical experience-proper leads to a radical and spontaneous *self-transformation* which ineradicably alters the whole trajectory of the life in question. The case of the great Indian sage, Ramana Maharshi, provides a spectacular recent example. Drug-induced experiences are *very rarely* (it would be reckless to say "never") accompanied by these profound and permanent changes in the subject: one has had an "interesting" experience (or "amazing" or "hellish" or "blissful" as the case may be), but one remains more or less the same person. The "enlightenment" in question turns out, in Theodore Roszak's nice phrase, to be a trip into a "counterfeit infinity."

The explanation of this difference is readily to hand in the mystical and religious literature of any of the great traditions: the drug-induced experience is essentially *psychic*, which is to say that it is still contingent, still within the realm of relativities and conditionings, a kind of movie, if you like, projected by the subconscious mind. The mystical experience, on the other hand, is essentially *spiritual*, which is to say that it liberates the "subject" (who actually no longer exists as a subject) not only from the physical limitations of time and space and from psychic constraints, but from the conditioned world (in both its gross and subtle aspects) altogether. The spiritual experience infinitely surpasses the psychic experience (extraordinary though that may be)—hence its incommensurate power which no amount of drug-induced experience could more than adumbrate. This also explains why a good deal of the psychedelic literature often looks rather tawdry when lined up against the genuine article. Neither Tim Leary nor Ken Kesey was ever going to write *The Cloud of Unknowing*! (Tim went on to make a lot of money as a computer spruiker: so much for spiritual self-transformation!)

There remain many vexed and interesting questions about both drugs and the mystical experience which must here be left aside but we shall be better positioned to consider these matters if we do not allow ourselves to be seduced by the facile assimilations made by Huxley *et al*. In conclusion it might be added that mysticism is a subject about which modern psychology has nothing whatsoever to tell us, and anyone who imagines it does has not begun to understand what mysticism is! As Frithjof Schuon has remarked, "The spirit escapes the hold of profane science in an absolute fashion."[82]

Closing Reflections

The Beats and hippies who turned Eastwards, particularly artists, intellectuals and teachers, have had a significant role to play in what Mircea Eliade has called the "deprovincializing" of Western culture in a "crepuscular era."[83] The epoch of self-contained and more or less homogeneous civilizations is, of course, long since gone. As Lyotard remarked of the postmodernist condition, "One listens to reggae, watches a western, eats McDonald's food for lunch and local cuisine for dinner, wears Paris perfume in Tokyo and 'retro' clothes in Hong Kong."[84] He might have added something about mantras, mandalas, *mudras* or maharishis! The cultural fabric itself becomes a Barthesian text, "a tissue of quotations drawn from the innumerable centers of culture."[85] In Ginsberg's case, for instance, it was a matter of a disaffiliated American Jew of Russian background careering around America chanting Hindu mantras, reciting Blake and Whitman, playing an Indian harmonium and Aboriginal song sticks, expounding Tibetan metaphysics, quoting Milarepa, Jewish mystics and the Sixth Patriarch. The possible connections between expressive artistic forms and religious teachings, between aesthetics and metaphysics, were foregrounded by the Beats. As Susan Sontag has remarked,

> Every era has to reinvent the project of "spirituality" for itself ... In the modern era one of the most active metaphors for the spiritual project is "art" ... a particularly adaptable site on which to stage the formal dramas besetting consciousness, each individual work of art being a more or less astute paradigm for regulating or reconciling these contradictions ...[86]

The Beat and counter-cultural involvement in Eastern spirituality was not without precedent, nor was it either ephemeral or trivial and, indeed, it is still bearing fruit. On one level one might suppose that a good deal

82 F. Schuon, "No Activity Without Truth," 37.
83 See M. Eliade, *Autobiography 2*, 152-153, and *The Quest*, 62-63.
84 Jean-François Lyotard quoted in Todd Gitlin, "Style for Style's Sake," 9.
85 R. Barthes, "The Death of the Author" in *Image Music Text*, 146.
86 S. Sontag, "The Aesthetics of Silence" in *A Susan Sontag Reader*, 181.

of the Beat/counter-cultural infatuation with the exotic, the "oriental," the "mystical" and "magical" was indeed of a sentimental and fashionable order. Doubtless, there was a good deal of counterfeit spirituality peddled by false gurus, by charlatans and hucksters, as there is today under the canopy of New Age-ism which often seeks to meld together heterogeneous elements of Western esotericism (particularly eschatological doctrines), modern psychology and Eastern religion into a new syncretism. But, no question, the interest in Eastern spirituality met some deep yearning for a *vision of reality* deeper, richer, more adequate, more attuned to the fullness of human experience, than the impoverished world view offered by a scientifically-grounded humanism. In short, the Beats and the hippies said "no way José!" to the "grand narrative" of the Enlightenment, and turned to other sources for the wellsprings of wisdom and individual/collective well-being: the religious traditions of the East, the beliefs and practices of indigenous cultures, the quasi-mystical experiences apparently offered by drugs, the mythology and mystical literature enshrined in the pre-Renaissance traditions of the West, and the like. As J.J. Clarke has observed,

> As living social phenomena the beat and hippie movements are now part of history, or survive on the margins as vestigial remnants, but in all sorts of ways their legacy lives on, not least in the popularity of Asian philosophies. Though the utopian rhetoric has cooled, and the revolutionary given way to apolitical pragmatism, the quest for personal authenticity and for a new form of spiritual growth has continued to preoccupy later generations, and indeed in many respects the Eastward search for alternatives to home-grown philosophies has if anything gained in depth and seriousness.[87]

The adherence of a rapidly growing and significant portion of the Western intelligentsia—artists, writers, philosophers, social activists prominently—to Eastern religious forms (most notably from the Tibetan and Japanese branches of Buddhism), and the assimilation of Asian modes of spiritual experience and cultural expression into Western forms, is one of the more remarkable cultural metamorphoses of the late 20th century, one as yet barely recognized let alone understood. It is a transformation in which the Beats and hippies played a vital role.

---

87 J.J. Clarke, *Oriental Enlightenment*, 105.

11.

Eastern Teachings, Western Teachers, 1950-2000

A. Hinduism/Vedanta in the West: The Ramakrishna Movement—Yogananda and the Self Realization Fellowship (SRF)—Swami Prabhupada and ISKON (Hare Krishna Movement)—Maharishi Mahesh Yogi and Transcendental Meditation—"Hindu" Pseudo-Cults and the Strange Case of Ananda Marg—Western Appropriations of Tantra—A Sample of Western Gurus with claims to Hindu Affiliations—Reflections on Hinduism in the West **B. Theravada Buddhism in the West:** the Venerable Urgyen Sangharakshita and the Friends of the Western Buddhist Order (FWBO)—*Vipassana* and the Thai Forest Tradition—Western *Vipassana* Teachers (Insight Meditation) **C. Tibetan Buddhism in the West:** The Tibetan Diaspora and American Vajrayana—Western Vajrayana Teachers/Leaders **D. Zen in the West in the Post-War Period:** Japanese Zen Masters—Western Zen Teachers—Scholar-Adepts and Buddhist Studies—A Note on some Key Issues for Western Teachers and Practitioners

---

Transmitting Buddhism to America isn't so simple. You can have your own way some-day, but first learn mine. And don't be in too big a hurry. It's not like passing a foot-ball. (Shunryu Suzuki)[1]

The number of Westerners undertaking some kind of religious training in Asian countries or giving Eastern teachings in the West, if not quite akin to the stars in the sky, is now well beyond counting. In this chapter we shall consider some of the most influential Western exponents of Eastern teachings in the second half of the century. Our attention will be fixed on individuals who have undergone formal training and who are recognized as properly creden-tialed teachers within one of the Oriental traditions. Unhappily, an orthodox transmission is no guarantee that the person in question will remain faithful to the teachings of which they are the privileged heirs and custodians. In the case of Hinduism we shall focus not on Western gurus (many of whom have been quite unable to maintain the traditional role in an alien Western envi-ronment) but on several movements which have met with varying degrees of success.[2]

---

1   Shunryu Suzuki quoted in D. Chadwick, *Crooked Cucumber*, 227.
2   Several figures who might properly have been discussed here will appear in later chapters deal-ing with the impact of Eastern ideas and techniques in such fields as psychology, philosophy, politi-cal activism, environmentalism and the like.

A. Hinduism/Vedanta in the West

The Ramakrishna Movement

The Ramakrishna Order has become a permanent presence in India where it maintains many Vedanta Centers, running hospitals, dispensaries, schools, clinics and orphanages. In the West the Order has also engaged in social work but its focus is on the dissemination of the teachings of Ramakrishna and Vivekananda.[3] Vedanta Societies are to be found throughout the Western world. However, the movement has thrown up very few Western figures who have become widely known as teachers, whilst many of those who have become swamis have broken away from the Order. Sylvia Hellman might serve as a representative example. She was born in Germany in 1911.[4] She emigrated to Canada in 1951 and three years later attended a Self Realization Fellowship meeting during which she apparently saw a vision, not of Yogananda but of Swami Shivananda.[5] In 1955 she traveled to Rishikesh and spent six months with Shivananda receiving some sort of initiation and, later, becoming a *sannyasi* and taking the name Swami Radha. She returned to Canada and established the Shivananda Ashram in Vancouver, later renamed Yashodra Ashram, where Westerners could take courses in hatha yoga, kundalini yoga, the Tibetan Wheel of Life, dream imagery, mantras and the like. She died in 1995.

Yogananda and the Self Realization Fellowship (SRF)

One of the most influential "Hindu" teachers in the West was Swami Yogananda, an Indian who arrived in Boston in 1920.[6] He was soon giving talks with such titles as "Recharging Your Business Battery Out of the Cosmos" and "How Oriental Methods Can Help Occidental Business." In 1925 he established the Self Realization Fellowship in Los Angeles, dedicated to the teaching of *kriya yoga*. He spent the rest of his life in America until his death in 1952. His *Autobiography of a Yogi* (1946) was a mid-century best seller. Yogananda claimed to be not only a *paramahamsa* but an *avatar* in a lineage descended from Babaji through Sankara and Kabir.[7] His teachings are a ragbag of traditional yogic doctrines/practices and half-baked Western ideas about "spiritual evolution," "spiritual psychology" and various other contradictions and neologisms which are the very calling card of neo-yogic movements and of their New Age progeny. His disciples include Sri Daya Mata (Faye Wright, b.c.1914) (Elvis Presley's "favorite yogi"),[8] Roy Eugene

---

3   See P. Vrajaprana, "What Do Hindus Do?"
4   On Sylvia Hellman see A. Rawlinson, *The Book of Enlightened Masters*, 482.
5   Shivananda was a disciple of Ramakrishna and second President of the Ramakrishna Order.
6   On Yogananda see A. Rawlinson, *The Book of Enlightened Masters*, 599-600.
7   A. Rawlinson, *The Book of Enlightened Masters*, 599.
8   A. Rawlinson, *The Book of Enlightened Masters*, 235fn.

Davis[9] (b.c.1930) who eventually broke with the SRF and set up as an independent teacher, Swami Kriyananda[10] (Donald Walters, b.c.1936) who was
ejected from the SRF and went on to establish the Yoga Fellowship in
California (where else?), and Goswami Kriyananda[11] (Melvin Higgins,
b.c.1930) who claims to be carrying "the lineage of Babaji into the New Age."
The history of the SRF is riven with internecine squabbles, schisms, lawsuits
and "revisions" of the canonical text of the movement, *Autobiography of a Yogi*.
One of the breakaways from Yogananda's SRF was the Self-Revelation
Church of Absolute Monism, founded by Swami Premananda in the 40s; one
of the contemporary leaders of this "church" is Srimati Kamala, an American
woman who was made a Swami by Premananda in 1973 and who is still active
as a teacher in Washington DC.[12]

Swami Prabhupada and ISKON (Hare Krishna Movement)
Shrila Prabhupada[13] (Bhaktivedanta Swami) arrived in New York in 1965, a
penniless Bengali *sannyasi*, aged sixty-nine. He set up a store-front temple in
New York's Eastside and started recruiting young Americans. By the time of
his death in 1977 he was the leader of perhaps the most widely spread
Eastern movement in the West, ISKON (International Society for the
Krishna Consciousness), better known as the Hare Krishna Movement. The
chanting devotees of this movement, garbed in ochre robes, were to become
a common sight in the streets of many Western cities. Prabhupada expounded traditional Gaudiya Vaisnavite teachings and practices (sometimes known
as Caitanyaism, after the 15th century saint) and ISKON may be said to be
one of the few *more or less* orthodox Hindu movements which has met with
significant success in the West. It extols a life of devotional service and strict
discipline (the practice of vegetarianism, abstention from intoxicants, gam-
bling and non-procreational sex) and attempts to maintain the *varna-ashrama* of traditional Hinduism—if that actually can be possible beyond the
shores of India.

Before his death Prabhupada appointed eleven American devotees as
gurus: no less than six have subsequently been expelled from the Governing
Body Commission (GBC) which Prabhupada established in 1970 to administer the movement, two for sexual misdemeanors, one for conducting illegit-
imate initiations, one for setting up a rival organization, another for financial mismanagement, and one over a leadership dispute and drug-taking
(this guru subsequently being murdered by one of his own disciples).[14]

9 On Davis see A. Rawlinson, *The Book of Enlightened Masters*, 231-232.
10 On Walters/Kriyananda see A. Rawlinson, *The Book of Enlightened Masters*, 386.
11 On Higgins/Kriyananda see A. Rawlinson, *The Book of Enlightened Masters*, 385.
12 See A. Rawlinson, *The Book of Enlightened Masters*, 348-349.
13 On Prabhupada see T.K. Goswami, "Servant of the Servant" and A. Rawlinson, *The Book of
Enlightened Masters*, 480-482.
14 A. Rawlinson, *The Book of Enlightened Masters*, 322.

Internal strife was at least partially tranquilized in the late 1980s when the GBC was "re-constituted" but it seems unlikely that ISKON will ever recover the popularity it enjoyed in the 1970s. However, its troubled history since the death of its founder only reinforces the conventional Hindu view that the tradition is not for export, that "conversion" to Hinduism is impossible, and that orthodoxy is almost invariably compromised by any attempt at transplantation (leaving aside expatriate Indian communities). These very principles were also enlisted in Brahminical criticisms of ISKON.[15]

One of the most controversial of the eleven Western gurus appointed by Prabhupada was Keith Ham/Swami Kirtanananda[16] (later Bhaktipada) who broke with ISKON and became an independent teacher. He was born in New York in 1937, traveled to India in 1965 in search of a guru but met Prabhupada on his return to New York, became one of his first disciples and founder of New Vrindaban (West Virginia), the first of ISKON's "Vedic villages." He was expelled from the GBC but continued to claim that he was Prabhupada's true successor. In 1990 he was convicted on a conspiracy charge in a murder case and imprisoned.

Maharishi Mahesh Yogi and Transcendental Meditation

In late 1967 and 1968 the face of "Maharishi" Mahesh Yogi appeared on the front covers of many Western magazines—*Life, Look, Newsweek, Time* and *Esquire* were just a few of the publications which projected the image of this Hollywood-style Indian guru, teacher of the Beatles, the Rolling Stones, Mia Farrow, Shirley MacLaine (surprise!) and various other media celebrities. As Jacob Needleman was soon to remark,

> Here was a "classic" guru, delivered by Central Casting: the flowing hair, the white robes, the floral cascades, the gnomelike twinkling eyes and the "Eastern serenity" ... a holy man surrounded by money, matinee idols, public-relations men, private planes and air-conditioned meditation halls.[17]

The meditation techniques which he taught were called "Transcendental Meditation" (TM) and entailed little more than a short period of daily meditation, the recitation of a mantra and the hopeful anticipation of "bliss-consciousness"—a quick fix which soon proved popular not only with counter-cultural youth but with middle-class America. While the Maharishi himself, after his comet-like traversal of the West, retired to India and faded from media view, TM has proved to be a durable commodity. The extent to which it can be regarded as an Eastern teaching is highly problematic.[18] In the

15 See T.K. Goswami, "Servant of the Servant."
16 On Kirtanananda see A. Rawlinson, *The Book of Enlightened Masters*, 186-193.
17 J. Needleman, *The New Religions*, 128.
18 On Maharishi Mahesh Yogi see A. Bancroft, *Twentieth Century Mystics and Sages*, 165-179, and for a much more rigorous assessment, R.P. Coomaraswamy, "The Desacralization of Hinduism for Western Consumption."

1980s and 90s various allegations concerning financial corruption, child molestation and sexual abuse were made against the so-called Maharishi but he continues to build an extensive network of centers in India as well as owning thirty-five five-star hotels![19] In the West his place as pop guru to the glitterati has been filled by his pupil Deepak Chopra, a kind of Dale Carnegie of an ersatz "Eastern" spirituality.

"Hindu" Pseudo-Cults and the Strange Case of Ananda Marg

There have been many quasi-Hindu movements and cults which have appeared in the West, many of them evanescent, some of them quite bizarre. The infamous Ananda Marg is a specimen of some of the more sinister movements which have developed within the chaotic world of Hinduism. The cult was started by a minor Calcutta bureaucrat, Sarkar by name, who evolved an idiosyncratic philosophy which combined a socialist ideology with Kali worship and black magic. It gained a significant following in India and in some Western countries, most notably Australia, and adherents were active in various forms of social work and devotional practice. Its credibility was more or less destroyed following allegations of Sarkar's pedophilia and the involvement of the cult in ritual murders, assassinations and bombings in India and elsewhere (most infamously, the Hilton bombings in Sydney during a meeting of Asian Commonwealth leaders), and the implication of the notorious Charles Sobhraj.[20] Various rumors circulated that the Ananda Marg was a front organization for the CIA, the KGB and East German Intelligence. The Divine Light Mission (DLM) of the "eternal teenager," Guru Maharaj-ji[21] immensely popular in America for a brief moment in the 70s, supplies us with another instance of a heterodox "Hindu" cult which also spawned its own Western breakaways, such as Lifewave, established by one-time DLM adherent, John Yarr ("Ishvara") (b.1947, England).[22]

Western Appropriations of Tantra

Then, too, there are those sects and cults which propose some kind of merging of "Aquarian" impulses with Eastern "tantra." One such is the Church of Tantra on whose website we can find proclamations such as the following:

> We intend to create a neo-tribal post-dysfunctional multi-dimensional sex and spirit, positive loving and juicy generations of gods and goddesses in the flesh. On the Starship Intercourse we greet and part with: ORGASM LONG AND PROSPER![23]

19 See cover story, *The Illustrated Weekly of India,* January 17, 1988, and R.P. Coomaraswamy, "The Desacralization of Hinduism for Western Consumption," 198.

20 See R. Neville & J. Clarke, *The Life and Crimes of Charles Sobhraj.*

21 On Guru Maharaj-ji and DLM see A. Bancroft, *Twentieth Century Mystics and Sages,* 136-147.

22 See A. Rawlinson, *The Book of Enlightened Masters,* 597-598.

23 Quoted in H. Urban, "The Cult of Ecstasy," 268.

Swami Nostradamus Virato explains that "the art of Tantra could be called spiritual hedonism." The Church of Tantra makes sophisticated use of the internet for publicity, recruiting and revenue-raising. As Hugh Urban has remarked

> A growing number of alternative religions, as well as new spins on old traditions, have found remarkably innovative ways to capitalize on the technologies and marketing of modern business and have even flourished within the volatile world of late capitalism ... Tantrism could be said to represent the quintessential religion for late 20th century consumer capitalist society.[24]

Without venturing too far into the surreal landscape of Western exploitations of tantra it is worth considering this phenomenon a little further. Some thirty years ago Jacob Needleman remarked that

> ... the moment one hears the word "Tantrism," various wild and lurid associations spring forth in the Western mind which add up to a pastiche of psychospiritual science fiction and sexual acrobatics that would put to shame even the most imaginative of our contemporary pornographers ... If it is difficult for us to approach even the simplest *asanas* of hatha Yoga without immediately subverting them to the service of bodily vanity ... then how much more bedazzled are we by the mixture of complex breathing exercises, telepathic and psychokinetic phenomena, magic syllables, and dream manipulation—all within the rubric of heightening and prolonging the ecstasy of sexual intercourse—which we have been told make up the discipline of Tantric Yoga.[25]

The tantric schools of both Hinduism and Buddhism have long since attracted the scholarly attention of orientalists (most notably, perhaps, Sir John Woodroffe) and of Indologists and comparative religionists (Eliade and Zimmer among them) for whom tantric sexuality provided the *locus classicus* of the *coincidentia oppositorum.* Its importation into the popular culture of the West constitutes a minor but melodramatic chapter in the story of the counter-culture of the 60s and 70s, best symbolized, perhaps, by Mick Jagger's psychedelic sex film *Tantra* and the *yantras* which adorned Jimi Hendrix's guitars.[26] Since then the most readily apparent appropriations of tantra have been made by various New Age groups. Here is a pretty standard line from "tantric guru" Nik Douglas:

> As the New Age manifested, traditional Tantra was transformed into a Tantra for the masses, a neo-Tantric cult of sensual pleasure with a spiritual

25 J. Needleman, *The New Religions,* 174-175.
26 H. Urban, "The Cult of Ecstasy," 280.
27 Nik Douglas, *Spiritual Sex: Secrets of Tantra from the Ice Age to the New Millennium,* 1997, quoted in H. Urban, "The Cult of Ecstasy," 280-282.

flavor. Because of its radical sexual and social stance, Tantra is well on the way to becoming a pop religion ...[27]

Needless to say, "pop religion" is no animadversion in the New Age lexicon.

A Sample of Western Gurus with claims to Hindu Affiliations

Brief mention must be made of a raft of Western gurus who claim some sort of initiation into one of the branches of the Hindu tradition but who have shown themselves, at best, to be somewhat heterodox and many of whom have concocted eccentric syncretisms which bear only the most tenuous relationship (if any at all) with Hinduism.

Perhaps Swami Muktananda's first Western disciple was Albert Rudolph (b. Brooklyn, 1928) who was initiated at his ashram near Bombay in 1965 and given the name Rudrananda, soon abbreviated to Rudi. Thereafter he regarded himself as an independent teacher:

> I consider myself a Western man and certainly an American product. I deeply believe in my country. I have no allegiance to anything else ... It as if I were an apple tree and went to India, Japan and China to get additional fertilizer.[28]

He was instrumental in establishing the Siddha Yoga Dham of America, an organization devoted to the propagation of Muktananda's teachings. He died in a plane crash in 1973.

Franklin Jones[29] was born on Long Island in 1939. After studying philosophy at Columbia (a well-worn avenue into Eastern teachings), Jones had some contact with Rudi and, in India, with his gurus Swamis Muktananda and Nityananda, the former "authorizing" Jones to teach kundalini yoga. Returning to America but now calling himself a devotee of Shakti, Jones hovered about the Vedanta Temple in Los Angeles until one day, by his own account, he experienced full enlightenment or Re-Awakening, likening his insight into Reality with that of Ramana Maharshi. In 1972 he opened the Shree Hridayam Satsang ashram in Hollywood where he gave talks and organized meditation courses. He does not seem to have been much impressed by the students whom he attracted, describing them as "whores, pimps, street people, criminals, neurotics, loveless and confused and righteous, self-indulgent people of all kinds."[30] He determined that he needed to purify his "guru function" by a return to India where he took on the first of a series of names—Bubba Free John, to be followed by Da Free John, Heart

---

24 H. Urban, "The Cult of Ecstasy," 268. See also T. Bartholomeusz, "Spiritual Wealth and Orientalism."

28 Rudi quoted in A. Rawlinson, *The Book of Enlightened Masters*, 497-498.

29 On Jones see A. Rawlinson, *The Book of Enlightened Masters*, 221-230.

30 Jones quoted in A. Rawlinson, *The Book of Enlightened Masters*, 224-225.

Master Da Love-Ananda, Da Kalki, Avatar Adi Da Samraj, Ruchira Buddha and Master Da! He has since pursued a glitzy and wildly fluctuating career as a "guru" of the "crazy wisdom" kind, making a favorable impression, at least temporarily, on figures such as Alan Watts, Ken Wilber and Georg Feuerstein.[31] He has also been at the center of allegations of many sexual and financial improprieties.

Andrew Cohen,[32] an American born in 1955, was one of those Westerners who moved through a smorgasbord of Eastern teachers—Sufi, Zen, Hindu, Buddhist, Krishnamurti—before spending some time with Poonjaji, an Indian teacher who apparently combined *Advaita* of the type exemplified by Ramana with Krishna worship. Cohen eventually broke from Poonjaji in the early 90s and became an independent teacher, touring the world before a serious car accident. He has published several books, one of his central themes being a variety of spiritual evolutionism which betrays his departure from all orthodox doctrines.

Swami Abhayananda[33] started life in 1928 as Bill Haines. He joined Sri Ramamurti's Ananda Ashram in Monroe (NY) but was expelled in 1966 for taking LSD. He then founded his own ashram at Millbrook, only a stone's throw from Timothy Leary's League for Spiritual Discovery and Art Klep's Neo-American Church. Each of these three short-lived organizations was dedicated to exploring the spiritual possibilities of psychedelic drugs. Abhayananda moved to Arizona where he apparently returned to the traditional teachings of Patanjali. He died in 1985.

Of the many other teachers and gurus who purport to offer teachings somehow connected with Hinduism, mention might also be made of Eugenie Petersen, Jean Klein and Ram Dass. Under her Indian name, Indra Devi, the Russian-born Eugenie Petersen taught yoga in China, India and America after an apprenticeship with Sri Tirumalai Krishnamacharya (1891-1989), a Sanskritist, naturopath and yoga instructor patronized by the Maharajah of Mysore, and the teacher of B.K.S. Iyengar who became one of the most respected yoga teachers in the West.[34] Jean Klein[35] was born of French parents in about 1916 and grew up in Czechoslovakia, Austria and Germany, studying at the University of Berlin before fleeing from the Nazis to France and then Algeria. As a youth he developed an interest in Dostoevsky, Nietzsche, and Gandhi, later, after moving to India in the early 50s, turning to Aurobindo, Krishnamurti, Coomaraswamy and, particularly,

---

31 See, for example, Ken Wilber's commendation of Bubba Free John's writings in *No Boundary*, 160.

32 On Cohen see A. Rawlinson, *The Book of Enlightened Masters*, 212-219.

33 On Abhayananda see A. Rawlinson, *The Book of Enlightened Masters*, 605. Haines/Abhayananda should not be confused with Marie Louise, the Frenchwoman who was one of Vivekananda's earliest Western disciples and who also took the name Abhayananda.

34 See G, Feuerstein, *Sacred Paths*, 33-34.

35 On Klein see A. Rawlinson, *The Book of Enlightened Masters*, 374-378, and S. Bodian (ed), *Timeless Visions*, 175-185.

René Guénon whose *The Symbolism of the Cross* left a deep impression. Somewhere along the line he met an unidentified Indian teacher who versed him in *Advaita* Vedanta which forms the basis of his teachings. He is the author of several books published over the last twenty-five years. The Jean Klein Foundation has its headquarters in Santa Barbara, California. One of the more reputable and durable of the Western teachers whose reputation at least partly rests on his Indian apprenticeship is Ram Dass (Richard Alpert) whose career we sketched in the last chapter.

We may also here take note of another European who became a *sannyasi* but who has eschewed any pretensions to guru status, rather alternating between his roles as a serious Indological scholar and gadfly commentator on the East-West "spiritual circuit" (or, circus, if one prefers). Agehananda Bharati was the name taken by the Czech-born Leopold Fischer who served as an interpreter to the Indian National Army during World War II before resuming Indological studies at Vienna University. He moved to India in 1947 and became a *sannyasi* in 1951. He spent the next decade in India, lecturing at the University of Delhi and Benares Hindu University as well as visiting Japan and Thailand. He moved to America in the early 70s and took up academic appointments at the Far Eastern Institute at the University of Washington and at Syracuse University. He wrote several scholarly works but is best known as the author of *The Ochre Robe* (1962), an account of his early life and his experiences in India. His writings are laced with caustic and amusing commentaries on neo-yogic movements and contemporary "gurus" both in India and the West.[36]

Reflections on Hinduism in the West

As has been intimated several times, Hinduism does not readily lend itself to missionizing and conversion. Like Judaism and Confucianism, and unlike Christianity, Islam and Buddhism, the Hindu tradition, divinely appointed as an integral religious tradition, is addressed to a particular ethnic collectivity. It is not a universal religion. One the other hand,

> Buddhism is something like a Hinduism universalized, just as Christianity and Islam, each in its own way, are a Judaism rendered universal and therefore detached from its particular ethnic environment and thus made accessible to men of all manner of racial origins.[37]

Nonetheless, Hinduism does carry within itself a metaphysic, that of Sankara's *Advaita* Vedanta, which, by very virtue of being a metaphysic must thereby be universal. Furthermore, the Vedanta provides, if one may so put

---

36 For a scathing, and often amusing, attack on the charlatans on the guru circuit both in India and the West see G. Mehta, *Karma Cola*. For a more sober and thoughtful account see A. Storr, *Feet of Clay*.

37 F. Schuon, *In the Tracks of Buddhism*, 20.

it, a straight and steep road into the understanding of the transcendental unity of religions. This all goes hand in hand with its *discouragement* of converts to Hinduism: rather, one should faithfully follow the path laid down by the tradition into which one is born. Until recent times this has ever been the prevailing orthodox attitude, one evinced, for example, by Ramakrishna who was himself living testament to the essential unity of religions. Allusion has also been made to *varna-ashrama*—the caste system, and the differentiation of the four stages of life—which is integral to Hinduism but quite alien in the social climate of the West. It is one thing to give intellectual assent to Vedantic metaphysic but it is quite another to be a practicing Hindu.

It has often been remarked that Hinduism is a remarkably hospitable tradition, finding a place within its ample embrace for a wide diversity of doctrinal forms and spiritual practices. The "downside" of the elasticity of the tradition, if we may so express it, is that it is peculiarly vulnerable to all manner of heterodoxies, especially once it is removed from its normal and protective social context. Schuon contrasts this aspect of Hinduism with the much-maligned "dogmatism" of the Occidental traditions:

> Monotheistic religions, with their invariable dogmatism and formal homogeneity, have a real advantage here in the sense that their very structure opposes the deviation to which *bhakti* is liable. The structure of Hinduism is too primordial not to be terribly vulnerable at such a period as our own. It is almost impossible for contemporary *bhaktas* to remain fully orthodox.[38]

As Louis Renou once remarked, modern-day India is an El Dorado for charlatans. All these things considered, it is not altogether surprising that Western adoptions of Hinduism have been plagued with difficulties. It is also easy to understand how the various corruptions and compromises which entered Hinduism by way of the neo-Hindu "reform" movements, themselves a product of Western colonialism, should be magnified in Western assimilations of Hinduism. And here one is thinking primarily of the application of the evolutionistic pseudo-mythology of the modern West to the spiritual domain itself—evident in varying degree in such disparate figures as Vivekananda, Aurobindo, and Radhakrishnan as well as in many Western Vedanta enthusiasts.

B. Theravada Buddhism in the West

Perhaps the most notable feature of the Theravadin presence in the West has been the apparent indifference of the indigenous *sangha* of South-east Asia (the stronghold of this tradition) to the establishment of institutional beachheads on foreign soil. Since Anagarika Dharmapala's appearance at the Chicago World's Parliament of Religions in 1893, Asian Theravadin teachers

---

38 F. Schuon, *Spiritual Perspectives and Human Facts*, 118fn.

in the West have remained a comparatively rare phenomenon. This has had two consequences: much teaching of Theravadin Buddhism in the West has been done by Western *bhikkus* and by lay figures such as Christmas Humphreys; secondly, efforts to create institutional networks have been initiated almost exclusively by Westerners. Let us survey the "careers" of several Western Theravadins in the second half of the century.

Sangharakshita and the FWBO

Perhaps the most successful attempt to create an ecumenical international Buddhist organization is the Western Buddhist Order (WBO), associated with the Venerable Urgyen Sangharakshita.[39] The Englishman Dennis Lingwood (b.1925) came to Buddhism in the 1940s through his own reading of texts such as the *Diamond Sutra*, his exposure to the Buddhist Society and the direct teaching of U Thittila, a Burmese monk living in England. In 1943 he was drafted for military service and sent to India and Ceylon. He left the army in 1947 and spent a year as an itinerant mendicant, formally entering the *sangha* in India in 1949 as a *shramanera* (novice monk) and receiving full *bhikku* ordination eighteen months later. Over the next fifteen years Sangharakshita, as he was now named, was based at Kalimpong, in the Himalayas, where he set about establishing a Theravadin *sangha*. He established a Vihara, edited the *Maha Bodhi Journal* (started by Dharmapala), launched a new Buddhist magazine, *Stepping Stones*, and set about creating links between the Theravadin and Mahayana branches of the Buddhist tradition. He came under the influence of Anagarika Govinda and was also closely involved in the "Buddhist Untouchables" movement in India, associated with Dr Ambedkar and directed towards the mass conversion of Hindu outcastes. His early life and his Indian experiences are recounted in *The Rainbow Road: From Tooting Broadway to Kalimpong* (1987).

In 1964 Sangharakshita was invited to England to teach at the Hampstead Buddhist Vihara. After some difficulties with other Buddhist teachers at the Vihara, Sangharakshita established his own non-sectarian Buddhist organization, the WBO and an associated infrastructure, Friends of the WBO (FWBO)—this latter term soon being used to signify the movement as a whole. Several hundred Westerners have been ordained through this organization and many thousands have been introduced to Buddhism through its publicity, its teaching program, meditation courses and the like. In the words of David Tracy,

> The Western Buddhists have not merely rendered a live option for many Westerners, but have subtly changed Buddhism itself as radically as the earlier classic shifts from India to Thailand, Tibet, China, and Japan once did.[40]

39 On Sangharakshita see A. Rawlinson, *The Book of Enlightened Masters*, 501-508.
40 David Tracy quoted in J.J. Clarke, *Oriental Enlightenment*, 220-221.

The distinctive features of FWBO include the following: it teaches a "universal" Buddhism and affirms the fundamental unity of all Buddhist schools; the distinction between monastic and lay Buddhists has been abandoned although practitioners are still "ordained" and observe monastic precepts; the order seeks to adapt Eastern Buddhist forms to the needs and exigencies of modern Western societies (including a radical overhaul—or, from another viewpoint, subversion—of traditional sexual morality). The WBO has also established a thriving business enterprise to support its many activities in Windhorse Publications, teaching and the administration of its many centers. Its most significant aim is the creation of a non-denominational Western Buddhism. In one of his many books Sangharakshita writes

> The FWBO is definitely a Buddhist spiritual movement. But it does not confuse Buddhism with any of its Eastern cultural forms. In the same way, the FWBO does not identify itself exclusively with any particular sect or school ... It is just Buddhist. At the same time it does not reject any of the schools or sects ... taking from them whatever it can find that contributes to the spiritual development of the individual in the West.[41]

The organization is based in Birmingham, England, but has branches in many countries, including nine centers in India—in keeping with Olcott and Dharmapala's vision of a Buddhist renaissance in the birthplace of the tradition.

Sangharakshita is the author of many books, including a biography of Dharmapala, poetry, memoirs and writings on the arts as well as expositions of Buddhism. His books on Buddhist teachings are enthusiastic and accessible but often marred by sloppy scholarship and sentimental over-simplifications.[42] He is also victim of a nonsensical spiritual evolutionism, evolutionism of all kinds being one of the shibboleths of the modern West and to be found in all manner of unlikely places![43] A persistent theme in his later writings is the critique of the more conservative aspects of the Theravadin school and the "incredibly exaggerated importance ... attached to social and ecclesiastical observances which have no essential connection with the Dharma whatsoever."[44] Some of the more puerile of Sangharakshita's themes include not only a psychological evolutionism but a jejune attack on theism of all kinds: "it is not enough to deny in private, as an intellectual proposition, that God exists. One must publicly insult him."[45] Hardly the traditional Buddhist position which, as Dr Suzuki frequently reminded us, is neither theistic nor atheistic, but rather, non-theistic.

---

41 Sangharakshita, *New Currents in Western Buddhism*, 63, quoted in A. Rawlinson, *The Book of Enlightened Masters*, 504.

42 See L.S. Cousins' review of Sangharakshita's *The Eternal Legacy*.

43 On Sangharakshita's "spiritual evolutionism" see S. Bell, "Change and Identity in the Friends of the Western Buddhist Order," 101-102.

44 Sangharakshita quoted in A. Rawlinson, *The Book of Enlightened Masters*, 504.

45 Sangharakshita quoted in S. Bell, "Change and Identity in the Friends of the Western Buddhist Order," 102.

The FWBO and Sangharakshita's place in it raise many disputed issues: the very notion of "Western Buddhism" and its relationship to the Buddhist tradition as a whole; the tension between traditional teachings and modernistic Western ideas about "evolution" and change; the place of "charisma" in Buddhist organizations; the interface between Western religious patterns and Eastern transplants and hybrids. After a detailed study of the FWBO and the English *Sangha* (a group associated with Ajahn Chah), Philip Mellor has suggestively argued that

> Buddhist groups in England are "a significant new cultural development" not because they divert western culture into new religious channels, but because they explore the existing channels in new ways. Their significance rests in their ability to create new religious forms within liberal Protestant culture ... creating discourses which are Buddhist but which have at the same time many of the features of Protestant Christian discourse.[46]

Vipassana and the Thai Forest Tradition

Late in the 19th century a strong reform movement revivifying the "forest tradition" developed in South East Asia, particularly in Burma. It affirmed the primacy of meditational practice and was associated with a line of formidable teachers which stretches down to our own times: Ledi Sayadaw (1856-1923), U Narada (1868-1955), U Ba Khin (1899-1971), Mahasi Sayadaw (1904-1982), U Pandita (b.1921), Ajahn Chah (1918-1992), and the Indian teachers Anagarika Munindra and S.N. Goenka (b.1924).[47] From this movement has emerged a form of Theravadin Buddhism which is "teacher-based, lay-oriented and enlightenment-seeking"[48] and which stresses an orthopraxy largely detached from traditional Theravadin doctrines, rituals and cosmology. The central practice is variously called *vipassana*, insight meditation and mindfulness meditation, and derives from the *Sattipatthana Sutta* in the Pali canon, the Buddha's discourse on "the foundations of mindfulness":

> There is, monks, this way that leads only to the purification of beings, to the overcoming of sorrow and distress, to the disappearance of pain and sadness, to the gaining of the right path, to the realization of *Nirvana*:—That is to say the four foundations of mindfulness.[49]

The four foundations are those aspects of experience on which mindful attention must be focused: body, feelings, mind and objects of mind. The awareness which arises out of this kind of mindfulness in turn leads to deep-

---

46 P. Mellor, "Protestant Buddhism?", 90.

47 Details of the lives and teachings of these masters can be found in Andrew Rawlinson's entry on the *vipassana sangha* in *The Book of Enlightened Masters*, and in Jack Kornfield, *Living Buddhist Masters*. (I have been unable to establish dates for several of these figures.)

48 A. Rawlinson, *The Book of Enlightened Masters*, 589.

49 Quoted in S. Batchelor, *The Awakening of the West*, 342.

er understanding of impermanence, suffering and selflessness.

There is by now a very extensive network of Western *vipassana* teachers, what Rawlinson loosely calls the *vipassana sangha*, many of whom trained under the meditation masters mentioned above. Among their many Western students (by now running into the thousands): Nyanaponika Thera,[50] Freda Bedi (who later joined the Tibetan tradition), Ajahn Sumedho, Jack Kornfield, Joseph Goldstein, Ruth Denison, Sharon Salzberg, Jacqueline Mandell, Lawrence Miles (Phra Khantipalo), and, indirectly, Ilse Lederman (Ayya Khema). Most of these figures are still highly active as meditation teachers in the West. Other *vipassana* teachers of some standing in America include James Baraz, Sylvia Borstein, Anna Douglas, John Orr, Jason Siff, Gil Fronsdal.[51] Among the most respected teachers of *vipassana* in Europe in the last few decades we find Christopher Titmuss and Christina Feldman (England), Corrado Pensa (Italy), John Coleman (Italy), Bhikkhu Vimalo (Walter Kulbarz) (Germany), and Fred von Allmen (Switzerland).[52]

Western *Vipassana* Teachers (Insight Meditation)

After service in the navy in Korea, studies at the university of California and two years in the Peace Corps in Borneo, Robert Jackman[53] (b.1934, Seattle) became the first Western disciple of the Thai meditation teacher, Ajahn Chah. Ajahn Chah was an obscure Thai monk in a remote part of Thailand when he first started training Westerners in the 1960s but by the time of his death he had become widely revered by both Asians and Europeans. His funeral, in 1993, was attended by nearly one million people, including the king and queen of his homeland.[54] Jackman/Ajahn Sumedho spent ten years as a forest monk, eventually attaining teaching status and establishing Wat Pah Nanachat, a traditional forest monastery in Thailand for Westerners. He and several fellow-monks traveled to England with Ajahn Chah at the invitation of the English Sangha Trust, and in 1978 established the Chithurst Buddhist Monastery, run on strictly traditional Thai lines. Over the next two decades associated communities, centered on the practice of *vipassana* meditation, have appeared in other parts of the UK, Western Europe, USA and Australasia, part of a much larger network of over eighty monasteries and centers associated with Ajahn Chah.[55] Like Sangharakshita, Ajahn Sumedho has been involved in intra-Buddhist dialogue but has been much more resolute in his commitment to the strict orthodoxies of the forest tradition into

---

50 See Chapter 4.
51 On some of these figures see G. Fronsdal, "Insight Meditation in the United States."
52 On European *vipassana* teachers see S. Batchelor, *The Awakening of the West*, Ch 20.
53 On Jackman/Ajahn Sumedho, see A. Rawlinson, *The Book of Enlightened Masters*, 553-559.
54 See Jack Kornfield's Foreword to Ajahn Chah, *Being Dharma*, x-xiii.
55 See A. Rawlinson, *The Book of Enlightened Masters*, 556.

which he was inducted in Thailand, including the observance of the two hundred and twenty-seven rules laid down for the *sangha* in the *Vinaya*.

Jack Kornfield was also taught by Ajahn Chah and ordained in Thailand in 1970 but later disrobed and returned to lay life. His 1977 book, *Living Buddhist Masters*, introduced a Western audience to the contemporary teachers and teachings of the Forest Tradition. He has been an influential teacher in America and is the author of several popular works, including *The Path with Heart* (1993), drawing on all Buddhist schools as well as western psychology (in which field he holds a doctorate). For many years he worked closely with Joseph Goldstein who practiced with Munindra in India in the late 60s. The two met at Chögyam Trungpa's Naropa Institute (Boulder) in 1974 whither Kornfield had been invited by Trungpa himself and Goldstein by another star attraction in the Naropa constellation, Ram Dass.[56] Their lives up to that point had run on parallel tracks: brought up in liberal, Jewish, East Coast families, well educated and apparently heading for highly successful careers in medicine and academia, both serving in the Peace Corps in Asia and being drawn to *vipassana*, Kornfield in Thailand, Goldstein in India. Together with Sharon Salzberg they founded the Insight Meditation Society in Barre, Massachusetts, where they taught a form of Buddhism "remarkably free of doctrine, dogma, rituals, ceremonies, hierarchies."[57] Their best known collaborative work is *Seeking the Heart of Wisdom* (1987). Kornfield and Goldstein eventually found themselves in serious disagreement about the relationship of Western psychology and Eastern practice: this subject will be explored in our next chapter. Goldstein remained at the IMS while Kornfield moved to California to establish Spirit Rock, the other nerve-center of American *vipassana*.

Women have been extremely prominent as *vipassana* teachers though several have eventually severed their formal ties with Theravada over the question of the status of women.[58] Ruth Denison's[59] extremely colorful life includes childhood imprisonment in Russian labor camps during World War II, emigration to America, marriage to a swami in the Ramakrishna Order, friendships with Krishnamurti and Alan Watts, *vipassana* training with U Ba Khin in Rangoon in the 60s, Zen practice in Japan under Nakagawa Soen, Yasutani and Yamada, and the establishment of her own *vipassana* center in California which caters mainly for women, many of them lesbians.

As a German Jew Ayya Khema (b. Ilse Kussel, Berlin, 1923) was another caught up in the turmoil of World War II, being evacuated first to Scotland and thence to Shanghai only to be subsequently imprisoned by the Japanese.

56 On Kornfield & Goldstein, see their own books, R. Fields, *How the Swans Came to the Lake*, 318-323, and T. Schwartz, *What Really Matters*, 305-337.

57 T. Schwartz, *What Really Matters*, 306.

58 The interactions of Buddhism and feminism will be discussed in Chapter 14.

59 On Denison see L. Friedman, *Meetings with Remarkable Women*, 135-146; A. Rawlinson, *The Book of Enlightened Masters*, 590-591; S. Boucher, *Turning the Wheel*, 177-184.

Her Buddhist training included an early flirtation with Zen, meditation teaching from the Mother in India, and work with Robert Hover (one of U Ba Khin's first Western students). She eventually became an American citizen, married and took the name Lederman, and lived in Los Angeles. Her later adventures included a journey up the Amazon, study in Bolivia and travels in Pakistan before moving to Australia where, with Phra Khantipalo, she established Wat Buddha Dhamma in the Blue Mountains outside Sydney.[60] She was ordained in Sri Lanka in 1979 and founded the International Buddhist Women's Center near Colombo and the Parrappuduwa Nuns' Island at Dodanduwa (a latter-day women's counterpart of the Island Hermitage founded by Nyanatolika Thera in 1911).[61] The Sri Lankan civil war eventually impelled her return to Germany where she had earlier established a meditation center. She died in 1997. Ayya Khema inspired women from all the Buddhist traditions who have sought to revive the practice of women's monasticism in modern times.

Jacqueline Mandell was appointed a *vipassana* teacher by Mahasi Sayadaw and was ordained in both Burma and Thailand as well as undergoing Rinzai training in Japan. She resigned from the Insight Meditation Center in the early 80s and renounced her formal ties with Theravadin Buddhism because of the inferior status traditionally accorded to women. She has continued as an independent meditation teacher and the director of the non-sectarian Pure Heart Buddhist center in Oregon.[62]

Sharon Salzberg practiced with both Goenka and Munindra as well as studying with Kalu Rinpoche, one of the foremost Tibetan meditation teachers. She was one of the founders of the Insight Meditation Society in 1976 but later moved to a monastery in Burma as a disciple of U Pandita, thus taking a very different path from Dennison and Mandell. She has since returned to Massachusetts and to teaching at the IMS.[63]

Insight meditation has grown rapidly in the West, especially in America, since the early 80s. To furnish a few random statistics: by the mid-90s there were at least one hundred residential centers for *vipassana* courses and retreats in the USA; the mailing list for the Spirit Rock Center ran to some 24,000 people; over 2000 people were taking *vipassana* courses at the IMS each year.[64] Part of its appeal undoubtedly derives from the autonomy of

60 On Ayya Khema see her autobiography, *I Give You My Life: the Autobiography of a Western Buddhist Nun* (1998). See also L. Friedman, *Meetings with Remarkable Women*, 264-268; A. Rawlinson, *The Book of Enlightened Masters*, 372-374; A. Bancroft, *Weavers of Wisdom*, 107-116; on Ayya Khema and Khantipalo in Australia see P. Croucher, *Buddhism in Australia*, 90-91.
61 See S. Boucher, "The Nun's Island."
62 On Mandell see L. Friedman, *Meetings with Remarkable Women*, 255-261; A. Rawlinson, *The Book of Enlightened Masters*, 591; D. Morreale, *The Complete Guide to Buddhist America*, 370.
63 On Salzberg see V. Mackenzie, *Why Buddhism?*, 61-91; L. Friedman, *Meetings with Remarkable Women*, 212-226; T. Schwartz, *What Really Matters*, 308.
64 Statistics taken from G. Fronsdal, "Insight Meditation in the United States," 178, and V. Mackenzie, *Why Buddhism?*, 71.

Western teachers and the fact that, shorn of many of its religious connections, *vipassana* has proved adaptable to an urban, secular Western lifestyle. Students were also attracted to *vipassana* by its "intellectual clarity, psychological sophistication, and elegant simplicity."[65]

Many Western practitioners do not regard themselves as Buddhists, seeing *vipassana* meditation as a therapeutic technique for the alleviation of stress, pain management and the promotion of self-understanding. Indeed, the American *vipassana* movement constitutes one site in which Eastern spirituality and Western psychology freely commingle. We might note the suggestive fact that a 1995 edition of *The Inquiring Mind* listed forty-eight teachers conducting retreats around America: half of these teachers were women and a third of them had professional training in psychotherapy.[66]

Many writers have drawn on the insights of *vipassana* teachings and practices without any reference to Buddhism or to religious issues *per se*. Daniel Goleman's best-selling *Emotional Intelligence* (1995) is a case in point. However, most Western *vipassana* teachers are sympathetic and ecumenically inclined with respect to other Western outgrowths of the spiritual-religious traditions of the East, particularly Zen (with which *vipassana* meditation has much in common), Tibetan Buddhism and *Advaita* Vedanta.[67] The creative interactions of these Asian traditions (often more or less completely independent of each other in their homelands) in the American arena is one of the more fascinating phenomena of recent times. As Gil Fronsdal has noted, "because of the numerous autonomous *vipassana* teachers and centers and the absence of any guiding national organization that certifies *vipassana* teachers, the American *vipassana* movement is inherently open, amorphous and arbitrarily defined."[68] Nonetheless, the American *vipassana* movement (as distinct from the practice of *vipassana* by Asian ethnic communities) is loosely clustered around the Insight Meditation Society, Spirit Rock and the magazine *The Inquiring Mind*.

C. Tibetan Buddhism in the West

The Tibetan Diaspora and American Vajrayana

If the Theravadin schools of Buddhism have been somewhat reluctant to dispatch monastic emissaries to the West and to establish permanent institutional structures, the case is quite the opposite with Tibetan Buddhism. Indeed, with the Chinese invasion of Tibet and the subsequent Tibetan diaspora, the West came to be seen as the new frontier for the establishment and preserva-

65 T. Schwartz, *What Really Matters*, 306.
66 G. Fronsdal, "Insight Meditation in the United States," 178.
67 G. Fronsdal, "Insight Meditation in the United States," 176-177.
68 G. Fronsdal, "Insight Meditation in the United States," 165.

tion of the Vajrayana. Since the mid-50s waves of Tibetan monks and teachers have flowed to all parts of the Western world while the Dalai Lama himself has become, along with the Pope, the most widely recognized religious leader in the contemporary world. The four main lineages in the Tibetan tradition—Gelugpa, Sakyapa, Nyingma, Kargyu—have all sunk deep roots in Western soil. The outward signs of a Tibetan presence—monasteries, teaching and retreat centers, publishing organs and magazines, libraries, collections of sacred artworks—are now visible not only in North America but throughout Western Europe, the English-speaking world and in many parts of Latin America. It has proved remarkably successful in Australia where the Dalai Lama's several visits have attracted huge crowds. Here we shall focus attention on the USA which has become the bastion of Tibetan Buddhism in the West. Whilst our attention in this study is primarily on Western engagements with Eastern traditions, rather than with the indigenous leaders of those traditions, it is impossible to detach the growth of Tibetan Buddhism in the West from the remarkable individual rinpoches, tulkus, geshes and lamas who have spearheaded this movement. A good deal has been written elsewhere about these figures but a brief account here is indispensable to our larger story.

The first influential teacher of Tibetan Buddhism to take up permanent residence in the West was probably the Mongolian Gelugpa, Geshe Wangyal. With the Dalai Lama's blessing Wangyal settled in New Jersey in 1955 and opened the first Tibetan monastery in North America, the Lamaist Buddhist Monastery of America. He also taught at Columbia University, his students including Robert Thurman, America's first ordained Tibetan Buddhist monk, and Jeffrey Hopkins. The first representative of the Sakya lineage in America was Deshung Rinpoche who arrived at Seattle's University of Washington in 1961. Initially he was engaged in a purely academic program of studies (including some collaboration with the Mahayanist scholar, Edward Conze)[69] and it was not until some years later that he taught Vajrayana Dharma directly to individual students. His most important contributions were the rigorous training of Western scholars in Tibetan language and philosophy and the creation of an important Tibetan resettlement center in Seattle.[70]

The Nyingma and Kargyu orders, less academically oriented and less ecclesiastical in structure, traditionally emphasized meditation and tantric

---

69 On the somewhat eccentric Conze see his own *Memoirs of a Modern Gnostic* in two volumes: a third was written but its libelous contents have made it a very rare document. There are conflicting accounts as to whether the third volume was ever actually published. Conze's memoirs are lively, idiosyncratic and acerbic. See also C. Humphreys, "Edward Conze, 1904-1979."

70 There are passing references to Geshe Wangyal and Deshung Rinpoche in R. Fields, *How the Swans Came to the Lake* and J. Coleman, *The New Buddhism*, but generally information about them is very scarce in the written sources.

practice rather than study and scholarship. The two most charismatic and influential Tibetan representatives of these traditions were Tarthang Tulku and Chögyam Trungpa. Tarthang (in Needleman's words, "a husky, catlike man")[71] arrived in Berkeley in the late 60s and soon established the Tibetan Nyingma Meditation Center which proved a real magnet to Western seekers.[72] The Center was soon able to set up Dharma Publishing which produced the journal *Crystal Mirror* and a series of lavish and attractive books, including Tarthang's own works and many translations and commentaries from the Tibetan and Sanskrit sources. In recent times the Nyingma Center has opened a large retreat and study center, Odiyan, in Sonoma County, California.

We have already encountered the mercurial and controversial Chögyam Trungpa in an earlier chapter. Despite his alcoholism (probably the cause of his early death), his inveterate womanizing and his somewhat scandalous lifestyle, this chubby and infectiously good-humored Tibetan was one of the most widely respected and well-loved of all Tibetan teachers. As we have already seen, Andrew Rawlinson reckons him to be one of the century's four most influential popularizers of Eastern teachings. Trungpa was a teacher of mesmeric presence and energy, and his dharma community has been one of the most lively and productive of all the Eastern-based movements in the West. It has been suggested that, "Trungpa Rinpoche's *sangha* may represent the most comprehensive attempt to merge the religious worldview of American Vajrayana with all other aspects of American life."[73] Certainly it has been massively successful in developing an extensive infrastructure of study and retreat centers, the major ones being in Colorado and Vermont, schools, bookstores, and publishing houses (Shambhala, one of the most successful of all the popular "Eastern" presses such as Dharma, Wisdom, Snow Lion, Windhorse, Weatherhill, Dawn Horse, Parallax.)[74] At the same time there is no denying Hugh Urban's well-supported claim that "the history of his life and community is a disturbing history of turmoil, emotional violence and scandal."[75]

Kalu Rinpoche, one of the most senior of the Kargyu lamas, was honored across the Tibetan lineages, and the Dalai Lama regarded him as one of the most authoritative teachers of Tibetan Buddhism. He was instructed to teach

71 J. Needleman, *The New Religions*, 172.
72 For some account of Tarthang Tulku and the Nyingma Center see R. Fields, *How the Swans Came to the Lake.*
73 A. Lavine, "Tibetan Buddhism in America," 103. On the Naropa Institute see R. Goss, "Buddhist Studies at Naropa," 215-237.
74 On the Buddhist presses see D. Lopez, *Prisoners of Shangri-La*, 177ff., and C. Prebish, "The Academic Study of Buddhism in the United States," 277-278.
75 H. Urban, "The Cult of Ecstasy," 284. (For one characteristic and dreadful anecdote see the Merwins' account of their humiliation by Trungpa in B. Miles, *Ginsberg*, 284-285.)

in the West by the Karmapa, head of the Kargyu order, and visited the USA several times where some centers were established under his auspices, the most important in Vancouver and Woodstock. He was also a leading dharma teacher in India. Kalu Rinpoche was the first Tibetan to guide Westerners through the three-year retreats which were an integral feature of monastic training in Tibet. He was also closely associated, as were Chögyam Trungpa, Chime Rinpoche and the Karmapa, with the establishment in 1967 of the Samye-Ling Tibetan Center in England, one of the first and most significant of the Kargyu centers in the West.[76]

We can do no more than list some of the other conspicuous Tibetan figures in the Western landscape:[77] the Gelugpa monks, Lama Thubten Yeshe and Thubten Zopa Rinpoche who until 1974 taught many Westerners at Kopan Monastery (near Katmandu), established the Manjusri Institute in Cumbria and the Foundation for the Preservation of the Mahayana Tradition (FPMT) which now has over one hundred centers in twenty-one countries; Lama Chime Rinpoche, a key figure in implanting Tibetan Buddhism in the UK; the lay teacher of *dzog-chen*, Namkhai Norbu Rinpoche, who came to the West by way of an invitation from Giuseppe Tucci and who has established *dzog-chen* centers on each continent; Chogay Trichen and Sakya Trizen, two very senior Sakya monks who have trained many Westerners in India; Dudjom Rinpoche who became head of the Nyingma lineage,[78] wrote a massive scholarly work on the history of the Nyingmas and established an important Nyingma center in the south of France; Dilgo Khyentse, Dudjom's successor and guru to many of the Nyingma lamas in the West today; Geshe Sopa, one of the foremost scholarly authorities on the tradition and leading figure in the prestigious Buddhist Studies program at Wisconsin University. Of the Tibetan teachers who have been most popular in recent years mention should be made of Sogyal Rinpoche, the author of *The Tibetan Book of Living and Dying*, today one of the standard works to which Westerners turn for an introduction to the Vajrayana.

Western Vajrayana Teachers/Leaders

The Tibetan tradition was sustained by an elaborate system of authority and transmission which revolved around *tulkus* (a lama who is recognized as the reincarnation of a previous lama whose office and status he/she has inherited; a tulku may also be an emanation of one or more of the Tibetan "deities"), *rinpoches* (literally "precious one," usually applied to tulkus), and *geshes* (highly trained monastic scholars who have undergone at least seventeen years of formal study). The Tibetan diaspora has posed many new chal-

76 See I. Oliver, *Buddhism in Britain*, 105-108.

77 Brief notes on some of these teachers are provided in the Checklist of Eastern teachers at the end of this work.

78 This position which had not hitherto existed, and was brought about by the Tibetan diaspora.

lenges to the spiritual leaders of Vajrayana, not least the issue of Western reincarnations—of whom several are now recognized, one of the earliest being Catherine Burroughs/Jetsunna Ahkön Lhamo. Burroughs was born and raised in Brooklyn but after an early marriage moved to California where she lived in rural isolation. She apparently spontaneously began practicing Tibetan forms of meditation. Many years later she encountered Penor Rinpoche, a senior Nyingma leader, who identified her as the reincarnation of a 17th century *yogini*, Genyenna Ahkön Lhamo. Jetsunna (as she is now known) presides over an American Vajrayana Center in Poolesville, Maryland. The center, Kunzang Palyul Chöling, includes a school, crèche, teaching center, and wildlife refuge, and its grounds are adorned by no less than twenty-eight stupas.[79]

Another Western tulku is Ngakpa Chogyam[80] (also Ngak' Chang Rinpoche), an Anglo-German Nyingma teacher, born in Hanover in 1952. He was initiated in India in 1978 as a *ngakpa* (one who practices "inner tantra") by Kyabje Khordong Terchen Tulku who recognized him as an incarnation of a Tibetan monk and visionary artist. Ngakpa Chogyam returned to Britain in 1983 where, with his wife (also a lineage holder), he founded Sang-ngak-cho-dzong, a center dedicated to the creation of a lay *ngakpa* tradition. He has been especially interested in the confluence of Tibetan teachings, art and Western psychology, and has written several books.

The question of the transmission of authority in Western Vajrayana is dramatized by the case of Thomas Rich/Osel Tendzin.[81] Thomas Rich, at that time a disciple of Swami Satchitananda, met Trungpa in Boulder in 1971 and soon became his *chela*. Trungpa identified Osel Tendzin (as he was now known) as his "Vajra Regent" although the ceremony, sanctioned by the Karmapa, did not take place until 1976. Amidst much fanfare he eventually assumed leadership of Vajradhatu (the dharma community) when Trungpa died in 1987. Trouble arose late the following year when reports circulated that Osel Tendzin had AIDS and had indulged in unprotected sex with both male and female dharma students. The case caused some turmoil in the community despite initial attempts to keep it under wraps. Tendzin was quietly eased out of his position and urged to go into lengthy retreat in California. He died in 1990. Trungpa's eldest son, Osel Mukpo, took over temporary leadership of Vajradhatu until the twelfth Trungpa, identified in 1992, is deemed old enough to take over.

79 See A. Lavine, "Tibetan Buddhism in America" and M. Sherrill, *The Buddha from Brooklyn*.

80 On Ngakpa Chogyam see A. Rawlinson, *The Book of Enlightened Masters*, 204-207. On Western tulkus see 562-573 of the same source and V. Mackenzie, *Reborn in the West*.

81 See R. Fields, *How the Swans Came to the Lake*, 336-338, 365-366, and A. Rawlinson, *The Book of Enlightened Masters*, 469-472.

82 See L. Friedman, *Meetings with Remarkable Women*, 93-110, and A. Rawlinson, *The Book of Enlightened Masters*, 476-478.

Pema Chodron (Diedre Blomfield-Brown, b.1936, New York)[82] is one of several influential Western women teachers of Vajrayana. Initially a student of Lama Chime in England she encountered Chögyam Trungpa in 1972 and became his disciple, soon taking novice ordination. As full ordination as a nun was not possible in the Kargyu school she underwent a *bhikshuni* ordination in Hong Kong in 1981.[83] Under Trungpa's guidance she established the Gampo Abbey in Nova Scotia in 1983 and became its resident director, with Thrangu Rinpoche as its spiritual director. Pema Chodron is not only a widely respected teacher but is one of the pioneers of a highly significant development within Tibetan Buddhism—the inclusion of women at all levels of the religious and temporal hierarchy. Tsultrim Allione is another woman teacher who is breaking new ground in the Tibetan tradition. A former nun but now a mother she is concerned with the integration of Buddhist practice into the everyday lives of Western women.[84] In *Women of Wisdom* (1982), an exploration of the feminine dimension of the Tibetan tradition, she argued that

> There is a vast untapped resource of female wisdom within so-called worldly life which could enrich our ideas about spirituality tremendously. Probably these resources have remained untapped because those who have defined the spiritual path for the last few thousand years have been men who associated spirituality with a separateness from nature and all that it represents, in terms of birth, death, children, and so on.[85]

Other prominent Western Vajrayana teachers who have been initiated by Tibetan lamas include Lama Denis Teundrop (Denis Eysserie François, b.1949, Paris,), taught by Kalu Rinpoche and the Karmapa, Ngakpa Jampa Thaye (David Scott, b.1952) student and Dharma Regent of Thinley Rinpoche and head of a Kargyu Center in Manchester, the *dzog-chen* teacher and author of the best-selling *Awakening the Buddha Within*, Lama Surya Das, and Lama Ole Nydahl, another student of the Karmapa, the founder of a Tibetan center in Copenhagen (1976), and head of the Karma drub Djiling Association which now administers one hundred and eighty centers throughout the world.[86]

D. Zen in the West in the Post-War Period

In an earlier chapter we traced the arrival in the West of a series of Zen teachers and chartered the growth of Zen in America through figures such as Soyen Shaku, D.T. Suzuki, Nyogen Senzaki, Nakagawa Soen and the emer-

---

83 See L. Friedman, *Meetings with Remarkable Women*, 95.
84 See S. Boucher, *Turning the Wheel*, 69-75.
85 Tsultrim Allione quoted in S. Boucher, *Turning the Wheel*, 70.
86 See A. Rawlinson, *The Book of Enlightened Masters* for material on Lama Denis Teundrop (559-560), David Scott (335-338) and Lama Ole Nydahl (461-463).

gence of Zen centers in California and New York. The post-war growth of Zen in the West has been inextricably connected not only with the pioneers just mentioned but with the following Japanese masters: Harada, Yasutani, Maezumi, and Yamada.[87] To these should be added one of the most remarkable figures who emerged from obscurity in his homeland to become perhaps the most widely recognized Zen teacher in America, Shunryu Suzuki (unrelated to D.T. Suzuki). Lineages and transmissions are particularly important in this tradition so it is appropriate that before turning our attention to some of the foremost Western exemplars and teachers in the post-war period we spend a moment in clarifying the lines through which they have been authorized. The picture is vastly complicated by the fact that many Westerners have trained in both of the principal Japanese schools, Rinzai and Soto, and have received teachings from at least two different masters. The following chart gives a simplified picture of the main transmissions concerning the figures who will be foregrounded in the ensuing discussion.[88]

Japanese Zen Masters

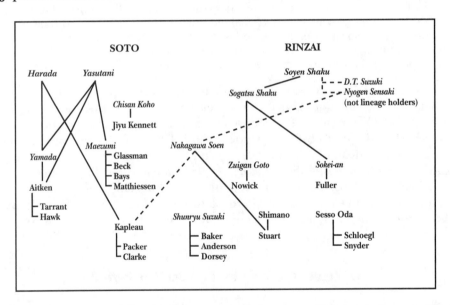

The revitalization of Zen in Japan around the turn of the century was closely associated with Dai'un Harada Roshi (1871-1961), the Abbot of Hosshinji Monastery in northern Japan. In the words of one commentator, he has long

---

87 Most of the information on these figures has been taken from R. Fields, *How the Swans Came to the Lake*.

88 The chart is based on lineage charts in A. Rawlinson, *The Book of Enlightened Masters*, 316, 534; H. Tworkov, *Zen in America*, 253; P. Matthiessen, *Nine-Headed Dragon River*, 262.

been "considered the regenerative force of Soto Zen in this [20th] century."[89] He reanimated the somewhat ossified Soto tradition by several radical innovations including the use of introductory verbalized teachings and the incorporation of *koan* study (formerly more or less restricted to the Rinzai tradition). Among his most accomplished students was Haku'un Yasutani (1885-1973) who spent twenty years at Hosshinji before founding a lay Zen organization near Tokyo. Like Harada, Yasutani broke down some of the sectarian divisions with the Japanese Zen establishment. He toured America in 1962 when Nakagawa Soen was unable to meet his lecturing commitments because of a family illness. Yasutani gave teachings in America each year throughout the 60s. This elderly, gaunt, jug-eared and somewhat raptorial roshi towered over American Zen in the 1960s. Here is Yasutani's description of the meditative mind:

> In *shikan-taza* the mind must be unhurried yet at the same time firmly planted or massively composed, like Mt Fuji ... but it also must be alert, stretched, like a taut bowstring. So *shikan-taza* is a heightened state of concentrated awareness wherein one is neither tense nor hurried, and certainly never slack. It is the mind of someone facing death ... And just as a master swordsman in an emergency unsheathes his sword effortlessly and attacks single-mindedly, just so the *shikan-taza* adept sits without strain, alert and mindful. But do not for one minute imagine that such a sitting can be achieved without long and dedicated practice.[90]

Both Harada and Yasutani were renowned for their fierce commitment to the Zen tradition, their samurai-like severity and their somewhat martial teaching methods, sometimes intimidating to Western neophytes. One of Yasutani's pupils was the ebullient, cigar-smoking hospital administrator Koun Yamada Roshi (1907-1990),[91] a highly colorful lay Zen teacher, significant in our story as the principal teacher of Philip Kapleau, one of the earliest of the post-war Western Zen teachers, and as the *eminence grise* of "Christian Zen." The Japanese monk Hakuyu Taizan Maezumi Roshi (b.1931) joined the Los Angeles Soto Zenshuji temple in 1956. He had trained with both Soto and Rinzai teachers, and was later associated with Yasutani with whom he did *koan* practice.

Shunryu Suzuki, an obscure and humble Soto monk, arrived in San Francisco in 1958 to serve the Japanese-American congregation at the Soto Temple Sokoji. There was little to indicate that he would become one of the most influential of the many remarkable Zen roshis who came west. By the time of his death in 1971 he had established the San Francisco Zen Center and the Zen Mountain Center at Tassajara, taught a generation of

89 H. Tworkov, *Zen in America*, 12.
90 P. Kapleau, *Three Pillars of Zen*, 56-57.
91 See R. Habito, "In Memoriam: Yamada Koun Roshi."

Westerners who were to carry American Zen into the twenty-first century, and written a quiet and modest book, *Zen Mind, Beginner's Mind* (1970), which was wildly successful in captivating many readers hitherto utterly ignorant of Zen. Meeting Suzuki shortly before his death, Jacob Needleman described him this way:

> Short and slight, he appears to be in his early sixties; his head is shaved, and he wears the robes of a priest. One's overwhelming first impression is of openness and warmth. He laughs often, noiselessly—and when I was with him, trying to discuss "profound questions," I found myself laughing with him throughout the interview. Beneath the lightness and the gentleness, however, one feels as well his tremendous rigor; more than one student has described him as "awesome."[92]

Suzuki's life story has been told in an exemplary biography, itself thoroughly imbued with the spirit of Zen, David Chadwick's *Crooked Cucumber: The Life and Zen Teachings of Shunryu Suzuki* (1999). Robert Pirsig quite properly observed, "It is impossible to imagine a better book about Shunryu Suzuki. Its precise picture of Suzuki's values, hopes and problems could make it a major primer of Zen itself."[93]

Whilst the main impulses of Western Zen have originated from the West's encounter with Japan we should also take note of the fact that several important teachers have emerged from the Korean and Vietnamese traditions ("Son" and "Thien" respectively). Among the most influential have been Thich Nhat Hanh (to whom we will return in a later chapter), Dr Thich Thien-an,[94] monk, distinguished scholar and founder of the International Buddhist Meditation Center in Los Angeles, and the Korean Seung-sahn (a.k.a. Soen Sa Nim) who established Zen centers in Los Angeles, Berkeley, Cambridge, New Haven and New York.[95]

Western Zen Teachers
By almost any reckoning the following must be counted in the front rank of Western Zen teachers: Robert Aitken, Philip Kapleau, Bernard Glassman, Maurine Stuart, Jiyu Kennett. To these can be added some other influential figures, several of whom have broken their formal links with Zen Buddhism: Walter Nowick, Toni Packer, Richard Baker, Reb Anderson, Bill Kwong, John Daido Loori, Joko Beck, Bobby Rhodes, Karuna Dharma. (There is also a complex of Christian religious who have been profoundly influenced by Zen, several of them actually receiving transmission. This group will be discussed elsewhere.)

---

92 J. Needleman, *The New Religions*, 49.
93 Back cover of D. Chadwick, *Crooked Cucumber*.
94 See Thich Thien-an, *Zen Philosophy, Zen Practice*.
95 See Mu Soeng, "Korean Buddhism in America: A New Style of Zen," 117-128. See also R. Fields, *How the Swans Came to the Lake*, 346-349.

Robert Aitken[96] was captured on Guam the day after the attack on Pearl Harbor and taken to a detention camp in Japan. There a camp guard, who had been a student of R.H. Blyth, lent him a copy of his teacher's *Zen in English Literature and the Oriental Classics*. Some time later Aitken was to meet the author himself as a fellow-prisoner. Blyth's book, which Aitken "read ten or eleven times straight through,"[97] set him on a Zen path which he has steadfastly followed ever since. Returning to Hawaii after the war Aitken resumed his studies in English literature, eventually spending a semester studying Japanese language and literature at Berkeley. Through the Buddhist scholar Richard Gard, Aitken met Nyogen Senzaki. In 1949 Aitken also met D.T. Suzuki at the second East-West Philosophers' Conference in Hawaii. Somewhat dissatisfied with the *koan* practice he did under Senzaki's guidance Aitken returned to Japan in 1950 to train with Nakagawa Soen Roshi, a Rinzai master. For a time Aitken and his wife lived with the Blyths near Tokyo University. In 1951 Aitken returned to Hawaii and after some years there he returned to California and briefly taught English in Krishnamurti's Happy Valley school at Ojia. He married for a second time in 1957 and honeymooned in Japan where he renewed his ties with Soen Roshi and encountered Yasutani. Returning to Hawaii, and with the permission of Soen, he started conducting small *zazen* groups in his home: this was the modest beginning of his illustrious career as a Zen teacher. For many years Aitken taught at the University of Hawaii. Aitken's wife, Anne (nee Hopkins) (1911-1994) was also a dedicated Zen practitioner, studying under the same masters as her partner, and devoting herself to the establishment and maintenance of the Diamond Sangha which they had founded in Honolulu in 1959.[98] After many years of intermittent study with both Yasutani and Yamada Aitken received dharma transmission from the latter in 1974.

Robert Aitken Roshi is a modest and dignified man of unimpeachable probity who has attracted students by his lively intelligence, quiet humor and total commitment to the teachings and values of a tradition which he exemplifies in his own being. Throughout his adult life he has espoused many political and social causes—campaigns to end the Vietnam War, nuclear testing and arms proliferation, the exploitation of the so-called Third World by multinational capitalism, the despoliation of the environment—and has been a leading figure in breaking down the authoritarian and patriarchal modes within the Zen *sangha*. However, in many respects he is also a rigorous traditionalist, criticizing the kind of "universalized Zen" popularized by D.T. Suzuki, R.H. Blyth and Alan Watts, and insisting on the importance of the lineages maintaining orthodox transmissions.

96   Details on Aitken taken from R. Aitken, *Original Dwelling Place*; H. Tworkov, *Zen in America*, 23-64; A. Rawlinson, *The Book of Enlightened Masters*, 156-58; and R. Fields, *How the Swans Came to the Lake* (see index).
97   R. Aitken, *Original Dwelling Place*, 23.
98   See T.M. Ciolek, "Anne Aitken of the Diamond Sangha."

Amongst Aitken's own dharma-heirs are Father Patrick Hawk, a Catholic priest and head of a retreat center in Amarillo, the Australian teacher and psychotherapist John Tarrant, and the Argentinian Augusto Alcade. Aitken's many writings are marked by a limpid clarity and precision, rigor and penetration not always to be found in the Western literature on Zen. His most important books include *A Zen Wave* (1978), *Taking the Path of Zen* (1982), *The Mind of Clover* (1984) and *Original Dwelling Place: Zen Buddhist Essays* (1996). He has been a creative participant in inter-religious dialogue and with David Steindl-Rast is the author of *The Ground We Share* (1996).

Unlike Aitken, Philip Kapleau[99] spent a long and arduous period of training in Japan. Born in 1912 Kapleau studied law and became a court reporter which led to his appointment as chief reporter for the International Military Tribunal at Nuremberg. He also reported on the war crimes trials in Japan and whilst there contacted D.T. Suzuki under whom he later studied Buddhist philosophy at Columbia University. In 1953 he resigned from his work and went to Japan to undergo Zen training under three different masters: Roshis Nakagawa, Harada, and, principally, Yasutani, to whom he dedicated his first book, *The Three Pillars of Zen* (1965). This book, which includes transcripts of Yasutani's lectures, now translated into a dozen languages and registering sales close on a million, has met with Huston Smith's early expectation that it would "assume a permanent place in the library of Zen literature in Western languages."[100] It was the first book in English to give a detailed account of Zen training. Kapleau's own training in Japan was fraught with difficulties—initial rebuffs from monastic authorities and the usual trials and austerities of monastic life (a meager diet, ill health, the inevitable mental and psychic disturbances)—but he persisted, attaining *kensho* ("seeing one's true nature") in 1958 and ordination as a monk by Yasutani in 1961. In 1965 he returned to America with the master's permission to teach, though not yet with dharma transmission. Yasutani's injunction to the departing Kapleau:

> ... today there are probably not more than ten true masters in all Japan ... This unique teaching must not be lost, it must be transmitted to the West ... It is your destiny to carry it to the West ... Don't quail or quit in spite of the pain and hardships.[101]

In 1966 Kapleau set up the Zen Center in Rochester where teachings and practice were organized around the "three pillars"—*zazen* (meditation),

---

99 Material on Kapleau taken from Kapleau's own books; A. Rawlinson, *The Book of Enlightened Masters*, 354-361; R. Fields, *How the Swans Came to the Lake* (see index).

100 Huston Smith, Foreword to P. Kapleau, *The Three Pillars of Zen*.

101 P. Kapleau, *Three Pillars of Zen*, 237. At about the same time Shunryu Suzuki estimated the number of Zen teachers in Japan who "truly understand Zen" at about twelve. D. Chadwick, *Crooked Cucumber*, 247.

teisho (commentary and instruction from the master) and *dokusan* (individual meeting with the master). Unlike many Western Zen teachers Kapleau has retained much of the ceremonial life of traditional Zen, recognizing the place of time-honored rituals in maintaining the tradition as well as helping to prepare the mind for illumination. Nonetheless, Kapleau also recognized the need for some adaptations and accommodations for Western students for which he sought Yasutani's permission. Kapleau also suggested that the Rochester Center should produce an English translation of the *Heart Sutra*. The roshi, to say the least of it, was not pleased and refused, leading to Kapleau's formal, reluctant and acutely painful break with him in 1967.[102]

Kapleau never received full transmission and has effectively operated as an independent Zen teacher ever since. Despite the fact that he is not, technically, a lineage-holder, Kapleau himself has appointed five dharma-heirs which raises some difficult questions about both the propriety and the efficacy of such "transmissions"[103]—a problem which plagues many Western adoptions of Eastern traditions. Nonetheless, many people would endorse the claim of one of Kapleau's principal students, Albert Low, in his Foreword to Kapleau's *Zen Dawn in the West* (1979):

> ... Roshi Kapleau has tenaciously and unremittingly preserved the spirit of Zen as passed to him from his teachers Harada-roshi and Yasutani-roshi ... He does not tolerate self-indulgence or self-pity, nor does he allow excuses or special pleading. He expects commitment and hard work ... Here is a Westerner, both enlightened and articulate, aware of the doubts, concerns, and hopes of contemporary, technologically oriented people. Such a combination of qualities is rare.[104]

Kapleau has not been afraid to criticize those Zen teachers who have fallen prey to the appetites for sex, money and power, and who have compromised the tradition by the palpable gulf between their ostensible teachings and their own personal behavior. He has also been sharply critical of what has been called Christian Zen (much encouraged by Yasutani's principal dharma-heir, Yamada Roshi). Although Kapleau himself is married and established a lay center at Rochester he has remained committed to the view that a celibate monastic tradition is crucial to the survival of the teachings.[105] Kapleau semi-retired in 1987, leaving the everyday running of the Zen Center to Bodhin Kjolhede, one of his dharma-heirs.

Huston Smith's *The Religions of Man* first piqued Bernard Glassman's interest in Zen Buddhism in 1960 but it was Kapleau's *The Three Pillars of Zen*

---

102 R. Fields, *How the Swans Came to the Lake*, 242.
103 See Bodhin Kjolhede, "Roshi and his teachers, Dharma Transmission, and the Rochester Zen Center Lineage." See also A. Rawlinson, *The Book of Enlightened Masters*, 354-361.
104 Albert Low in P. Kapleau, *Zen Dawn in the West*, xv-xvi.
105 See A. Rawlinson, *The Book of Enlightened Masters*, 361.

that led him into direct practice. Glassman,[106] at that time a space-shuttle designer at McDonnell-Douglas, soon began practicing with Taizan Maezumi at the Zen Center in Los Angeles, attaining *kensho* very early in the training and becoming Maezumi's first dharma-heir. Maezumi recalled his early impressions of Glassman:

> He had a dirty beard! But he also had a flashing light in his eyes, and naïveté in the good sense of the word, open and ready to receive anything he could get. He became an exceptional Zen student because of his devotion to his practice, an ability to hurl himself into whatever he had to do. Very early, he knew how to throw the self away ...[107]

Under Maezumi's instructions, in 1979 Glassman established the Zen Community of New York and was installed as the abbot of Zenshinji Temple. He also set up the Greyston Bakery, modeled on the Tassajara Bakery in San Francisco, a business venture which, somewhat controversially, is also a training ground for Zen students. Glassman has encouraged a non-denominational form of Zen and has enthusiastically generated interactions not only with other Buddhist groups but with Christians and Jews as well. (Glassman himself is of Jewish background.) Furthermore, he has given dharma transmission to the Catholic priest, Father Robert Kennedy and to Rabbi Donald Singer. His business ventures and his embrace of a "can-do," entrepreneurial ethic, his training methods and his ecumenicism have all attracted some flak from within the American Zen community. One of his best-known students, the writer Peter Matthiessen, has characterized him in these terms:

> Tesugen-sensei is the first American Zen master to complete koan study as well as priestly training. He has been recognized as a dharma-holder in formal ceremonies at the great Soto temples of Eihei-ji and Soji-ji in Japan. More important, he is truly enlightened, having experienced two classical *dai kensho* ... he is already a major influence on the future course of American Zen ... He is—and also he is not—plain Bernie Glassman with a passion for pizza, innovative ideas, and mechanical gadgetry of all descriptions.[108]

Maurine Stuart (1922-1990)[109] was a Rinzai Roshi who studied under Nakagawa Soen, Yasutani and Shimano Eido, eventually parting company with Yasutani because his methods were too fierce and with Shimano because of his attitude towards women. Shimano, a protégé of Soen Roshi who had come to America in the late 50s, was caught up in something of a scandal in

---

106 Material on Glassman taken from R. Fields, *How the Swans Came to the Lake* (see index) and P. Matthiessen, *Nine-Headed Dragon River*.

107 P. Matthiessen, *Nine-Headed Dragon River*, 123.

108 P. Matthiessen, *Nine-Headed Dragon River*, 123, 135-136.

109 On Maurine Stuart see H. Tworkov, *Zen in America*, 153-197; S. Boucher, *Turning the Wheel*, 194-202; L. Friedman, *Meetings with Remarkable Women*, 65-92. (Stuart was known for many years under her marred name Freedgood)

the Zen community in 1975 when he was accused of sexual misbehavior with his students.[110] Some time earlier his sexual misadventures as a young monk in Hawaii had caused a rift with Robert Aitken. Nevertheless he continued teaching and it was he who actually ordained Stuart in 1977. Stuart continued studies with Nakagawa Soen who made her a roshi in 1982. In a somewhat informal ceremony Soen, "the ultimate Zen trickster,"[111] apparently made Stuart one of his dharma-heirs but this transmission has a somewhat ambiguous standing within the Zen community and Stuart did not describe herself as a lineage holder. Stuart had been a Canadian concert pianist studying music in Paris in the late 40s when she first came across Zen but didn't take up serious practice until 1965 when she joined the Zen Studies Society of New York, an organization funded by Cornelius Crane to propagate the work of D.T. Suzuki. After moving to Massachusetts Stuart became a close friend of Elsie Mitchell and succeeded her as President of the Cambridge Buddhist Association. She became well known as a creative Zen teacher, often using music as a teaching medium.

One of the most interesting figures in the constellation of Western Zen teachers was Jiyu Kennett (1924-1996).[112] As a young girl living in Sussex she had been moved by Arnold's *The Light of Asia* and a statue of the Buddha which a fellow-student had brought to her "very snooty, very expensive" school. After World War II Peggy Kennett, like Maurine Stuart, became a professional musician and church organist, studying at the Trinity College of Music in London and at Durham University. She developed a close interest in Theravadin Buddhism which she studied under the well-known scholar and teacher, Dr Sadhatissa, joining the Buddhist Society in 1954 and attending Christmas Humphreys' classes on Zen. Through the Society she encountered the Soto abbot, Chisan Koho, who invited her to study at the Dai Hon Zon Sojiji Temple. On her way to Japan Kennett was ordained into the Chinese *sangha* of Malaysia and given the name Jiyu ("true friend"). Like Glassman she reached *kensho* very rapidly and in 1963 became the dharma-heir of Koho Zenji. After the death of her master Kennett moved to America, training Western disciples and founding the Zen Mission Society in San Francisco, the Order of Buddhist Contemplatives of the Soto Zen Church, and two monasteries, Throssel Hole Buddhist Abbey in Northumberland and Shaster Abbey in California.[113] Like all teachers who modify the Japanese tradition to adapt it to the West she came in for some criticism. One of the more controversial aspects of her role was the large number of practi-

---

110 See R. Aitken, *Original Dwelling Place*, 21; A. Rawlinson, *The Book of Enlightened Masters*, 537; H. Tworkov, *Zen in America*, 188-191.

111 H. Tworkov, *Zen in America*, 156.

112 Details on Kennett taken from *The Middle Way*, "In Memoriam: Reverend Master Jiyu-Kennett," A. Rawlinson, *The Book of Enlightened Masters*, 363-371, and S. Boucher, *Turning the Wheel*, 133-144.

113 An account of the abbey can be found in S. Boucher, *Turning the Wheel*, 133-144.

tioners she ordained (approaching one hundred and fifty) and to whom she gave transmission (some ninety-five).[114] She died in 1996 of complications arising from her long-term diabetic condition. Among her writings we find *Selling Water by the River: A Manual of Zen Training* (1972) (later re-titled *Zen is Eternal Life*), and the autobiographical *The Wild White Goose* (1977). Her visionary experiences are recounted in *How to Grow a Lotus Blossom* (1977). Kennett is significant for several reasons: in the late 50s she was one of a very small number of Western women who had entered the somewhat hermetic world of Japanese monasteries (others being Carmen Blacker, Ruth Fuller, Irmgard Schloegl and Gerta Ital); she was ordained in both Rinzai and Soto traditions; she became an abbess of a Japanese temple and trained Western Zen students in Japan; she insisted on celibacy as a pre-condition of the highest form of *kensho*.[115]

*

We should not leave our discussion of American Zen without a cautionary word about the commercial exploitation and trivialization of the tradition. In 1997 *Books in Print* listed some 197 titles beginning with "Zen," most of them in the "Zen in the Art of Golf" and "Zen and Creative Management" vein.[116] A good proportion of these books had little or nothing to do with Zen. Robert Pirsig's *Zen in the Art of Motorcycle Maintenance* is the principal culprit! Although this best-selling book enjoyed some intellectual pretensions and touched on aspects of spirituality, its connection with Zen was extremely tenuous. Since then "Zen" has become an increasingly meaningless buzz-word (as have words like "soul," "spirituality"). Recall Thomas Merton's words on the sentimentality surrounding some Western perceptions of Zen in the 60s:

> Where there is a lot of fuss about "spirituality," "enlightenment" or just "turning on," it is often because there are buzzards hovering around a corpse. This hovering, this circling, this descending, this celebration of victory, are not what is meant by the Study of Zen—even though they may be a highly useful exercise in other contexts. And they enrich the birds of appetite. Zen enriches no one. There is no body to be found. The birds may come and circle for a while in the place where it is thought to be. But they soon go elsewhere. When they are gone, the "nothing," the "nobody" that was there, suddenly appears. That is Zen. It was there all the time but the scavengers missed it, because it was not their kind of prey.[117]

Scholar-Adepts and Buddhist Studies

Since the 60s several significant changes have taken place in Buddhist studies throughout the Western world. These general developments can be

114 Figures taken from A. Rawlinson, *The Book of Enlightened Masters*, 370.
115 L. Friedman, *Meetings with Remarkable Women*, 166.
116 T. Tweed, "Night-Stand Buddhists and Other Creatures," 76.
117 T. Merton, *Zen and the Birds of Appetite*, ix.

traced through their American manifestations. Until the 1960s most academic studies of Buddhism took place under various auspices—philology, comparative religion, Indology and the like. Furthermore, as Charles Prebish has observed, "the founding mothers and founding fathers of Buddhist Studies in the West have had personal religious commitments [if any] entirely separate from Buddhism."[118] Two pivotal changes are easily observed on the American academic scene: Buddhist Studies has emerged as an autonomous discipline; secondly, many of the most eminent scholars in the field are now themselves Buddhist practitioners who have often done extended training under Asian teachers in monastic and other religious institutions in the East. The last few decades have also seen the welcome arrival in the Western academy of distinguished Asian scholars such as Deshung Rinpoche (Washington) and Geshe Sopa (Wisconsin), as well as "practitioner-friendly" institutions of a semi-academic kind among which we find such places as the Naropa and Nyingma Institutes where practice, study and scholarship fertilize each other.[119] These developments have generated some lively debates about disciplinary methodology and about the putative tension between scholarly impartiality and religious commitment—interesting issues which cannot be canvassed here. The principal academic centers for the study of Buddhism are the universities of Hawaii, Harvard, Indiana, Michigan, Wisconsin, Virginia, Columbia, Chicago, Washington.[120] Some of the most conspicuous figures who have been in the vanguard of these changes are Robert Thurman (Columbia), Jeffrey Hopkins (Virginia), and Donald Lopez Jr. (Michigan).[121]

Some Key Issues for Western Teachers and Practitioners

Although somewhat beyond the ambit of the present study it is perhaps worth pausing for a moment to isolate some of the most pressing challenges facing both representatives in the West of the great Eastern religious traditions and communities of Western dharma practitioners. Much has been written about these issues in recent years and interested readers are directed to the works of such contemporary commentators as Jack Kornfield, Rick Fields, Sandy Boucher and Rita Gross. However, it would be misleading to bypass these issues altogether. Rather than offering any commentary on these issues (many of which are touched on elsewhere in this book) I will simply identify them by way of a series of questions, many of which will naturally

---

118 C. Prebish, "The Academic Study of Buddhism in America," 183.

119 See R. Goss, "Buddhist Studies at Naropa."

120 See C. Prebish, "The Academic Study of Buddhism in America," 183-214, and C. Prebish, "Buddhist Studies American Style," 323-330.

121 On these scholar-adepts and the academic institutionalization of dharma studies see D. Lopez, *Prisoners of Shangri-La*, Ch 6. For a recent interview with Robert Thurman see V. Mackenzie, *Why Buddhism?*, 246-260.

arise in any religious community of the kind with which we are presently concerned.

• *Transmission*: Is it important to maintain the meticulously observed conventions and protocols surrounding lineage transmission in the East? How can "credentials" be verified in a mobile, pluralistic and secular Western society quite unlike the Asian worlds of monasteries, ashrams, temple cities and the like?

• *Authority & Governance*: Does the authority to teach derive solely from one's own teacher and the tradition which he/she exemplifies? What of those figures of readily apparent attainment who have had no formal initiation or transmission? Does the authority and status of the teacher depend on the community in which he/she is teaching? Should the finely calibrated hierarchies of status and authority which are a feature of the East be maintained in the West? Is consensus decision-making and democratic procedure appropriate in the spiritual life of a religious community?

• *Teachings*: Is there a "pure" teaching in any tradition? To what extent are both doctrines and practices culturally mediated? How can we distinguish "essential" teachings from disposable cultural accretions and impedimenta? Can/should the teachings and practices of religious traditions, tested over the centuries, assimilate modern "scientific" theories and practices (e.g. psychotherapy) and ideologies (e.g. feminism)?

• *Monastic/Lay*: Should religious traditions which have flourished in the East within a protective monastic environment be adapted to suit the needs of Westerners who are quite unable or unwilling to become monks and nuns? To what extent should accommodations be made? What precisely is the place of vows and precepts? How central to the tradition in question is the ideal of a celibate monastic community?

• *Charismatic leadership and succession*: What happens to movements, groups and institutions which heavily rely on the charismatic leadership of a particular individual after his/her death? (This problem has made itself much more acutely felt in the last two decades with the passing of a whole generation of pioneering Eastern teachers. Considering Buddhism in America alone, the list of highly visible teachers who have died since 1980 includes Chögyam Trungpa, the Gyawal Karmapa, Nakagawa Soen, Lama Thubten Yeshe, Dudjom Rinpoche, Deshung Rinpoche, Dilgo Khyentse Rinpoche.) What are the dangers of Western cults of "hero-worship" of Eastern gurus who become "celebrities" on the "Dharma circuit," often through no fault or wish of their own?

• *Gender & "Feminization"*: Should the patriarchal structures of Eastern religious institutions be dismantled? By whom? How quickly? Should there be religious institutions which cater solely for men or women (or various subgroups, such as lesbians and gays)? Should the whole ethos and "flavor" of Asian traditions be "feminized"? How?

• *Teaching, sexual exploitation and other inappropriate behaviors*: How should Western communities deal with the violations of trust and the betrayal of spiritual ideals evident in the exploitative, anti-social or self-indulgent behavior of teachers and authority-figures, both Eastern and Western? How far can the "crazy wisdom" rationale be taken? What responsibility can be sheeted home to credulous, naïve and willfully ignorant followers? What are the effects of the "conspiracy of silence" which often shrouds these cases? (I make no particular judgments on any individual case but the frequency with which highly respected teachers, both Eastern and Western, have been charged with behavior which would seem to be sharply at odds with their own teachings, must be cause for on-going concern.) Sexual exploitation, the misuse of drugs, personal ambition, financial "irresponsibility" and sybaritic lifestyles seem to be the most widespread problems. Some of the more lurid controversies have accumulated around such powerful figures as Chögyam Trungpa, Osel Tendzin, Sogyal Rinpoche, Anagarika Munindra, Shimano Roshi, Richard Baker Roshi, Maezumi Roshi, Seung-sahn, Swami Muktananda, Bubba Free John and several ISKON gurus.[122] To these could be added a very long list of counterfeit "spiritual teachers" who have exploited their gullible followers sexually—Swami Rama (of biofeedback fame; see next chapter), John Yarr of Lifewave, and Bhagwan Rajneesh being three representatives of the type from whom nothing better could reasonably have been expected.[123] There was also a controversy surrounding the Croydon Center of the FWBO in the late 80s. Almost all of these scandals have involved male teachers but Jetsunna Ahkön Lama has been at the center of allegations of sexual misconduct and an extravagant lifestyle unbecoming to a dharma teacher.[124]

• *Cultural preservation and the "ethnic/American" divide:* what priority should be given to the preservation in the West of unique Asian cultural-religious forms which are gravely imperiled in their own homelands? What is the relationship between the preservation of the tradition and its adaptation to new circumstances and needs? How can the ethnic Asian religious communities and the non-Asian communities best relate to and support each other?

• *Dharma practice, workaday life, families:* for many practitioners the most pressing issues are intimately personal and quite mundane: how can the sometimes conflicting demands of dharma practice, professional work and family life be creatively resolved? How best to integrate spiritual life and everyday lay life?

• *Political and social "engagement."*

• *Intra- and inter-religious relations and dialogue.*

(These last two issues will be taken up in some detail in Chapters 14 and 15.)

---

122 These and other cases are discussed in the following works: R. Fields, *How the Swans Came to the Lake*, Ch 16; S. Boucher, *Turning the Wheel*, Ch 5; P. Kapleau, *Awakening to Zen*, 137-152; J. Coleman, *The New Buddhism*, 139-183; T. Schwartz, *What Really Matters*, 134-137; H. Urban, "The Cult of Ecstasy"; R. Gross, "Helping the Iron Bird Fly." For one response to these and related problems see "Insight Meditation Teachers Code of Ethics" in J. Kornfield, *A Path with Heart*, 340-343.

123 On Bhagwan Rajneesh see H. Urban, "Zorba the Buddha" and "The Cult of Ecstasy" and R.P. Coomaraswamy, "The Desacralization of Hinduism for Western Consumption," 204-206.

124 See J. Coleman, *The New Buddhism*, 171.

III

Eastern Influences

on

Western Thought

12.

The Not-So-Close Encounters of Western Psychology and Eastern Spirituality

---

A. Religion and Psychology: The Goldstein-Kornfield Disagreement—Western Psychology and Religion—A Traditionalist Perspective on Psychologism—The Traditionalist Critique of Jung **B. Eastern Spirituality and Western Psychology:** Erich Fromm and Zen—Existentialism, Herman Hesse, Hubert Benoit—Hans Jacobs on Western Psychotherapy and Hindu Sadhana—Humanistic and Transpersonal Psychology: Ken Wilber and others—Mystical Experience, Meditation and Biofeedback **C. The Lessons of the East**

The intellect does, in fact, harm the soul when it dares to possess itself of the heritage of the Spirit. (Carl Jung)[1]

There is no place to seek the mind;
It is like the footprints of the birds in the sky.
(The Zenrin)[2]

A. Religion and Psychology

The Goldstein-Kornfield Disagreement

As we saw in the previous chapter, two of the most prominent figures in the American *vipassana* movement have been Jack Kornfield and Joseph Goldstein. After their initial collaboration at the Naropa Institute in the early 70s, their joint writings and nearly a decade of closely working together at the Insight Meditation Society, they found themselves in serious disagreement. The issue in question: the relationship of traditional Theravadin teachings and modern Western psychology. More particularly, the question as to whether *vipassana* practice should focus on liberation or on what might be called therapy—the alleviation of psychological stress, the repair of damaged relationships, the promotion of self-esteem and the like. Goldstein articulated what we might deem the traditional attitude:

> For me what's been most important is to aim for the highest liberation of the mind. I see a tendency to let go of that goal and instead become satis-

---

1 C.G. Jung, "Commentary on *The Secret of the Golden Flower*" quoted in C. Ray, "Western Psychology and Buddhist Teachings: Convergences and Divergences," 27.
2 *The Zenrin*, quoted in R. Sohl & A. Carr (eds), *The Gospel According to Zen*, 27.

fied with something less: doing good in the world, having more harmonious relationships, seeking a happier life. That's all beautiful, but in my view, misses the essential point. My teacher U Pandita, who is not at all concerned with pleasing people, likens *vipassana* practice to bitter medicine. Often it doesn't taste good, but it's effective ... Transformation takes practice, effort, and commitment ... As there is less identification with the concept of "I" or "me," there is inherently less feeling of separateness ... Compassion in the world becomes a spontaneous response to the experience of connectedness.[3]

Kornfield, on the other hand, had become somewhat skeptical of the effectiveness of *vipassana* in isolation and came to the view that it could and should engage with personal feelings and experiences, and that it could profitably draw on the insights and techniques of Western psychology. He found U Pandita's mode of teaching (and by implication, Goldstein's as well) too "traditional" and "conservative." Goldstein was not altogether dismissive of the potential benefits of psychotherapeutic approaches but was wary of any compromising of the goal of liberation:

Sometimes people are so stuck psychologically that it's a real obstacle to their ability to pay attention and be mindful [in meditation] and then therapy can help. But unless it's done very skillfully, psychological work can reinforce a sense of self—me, my story, my problems—which I believe is a basic misconception. It might make life more comfortable, but it wouldn't be leading to real freedom. One difference between me and Jack may be in his emphasis on humanistic values versus mine on the values of liberation. Where they conflict, I hold the values of liberation to be the highest. All others are secondary.[4]

In his teachings Kornfield increasingly turned to a psychodynamic approach. In *A Path with Heart* he countered Goldstein's position in this way:

Many people first come to spiritual practice hoping to skip over their sorrows and their wounds, the difficult areas of their lives. They hope to rise above them and enter a spiritual realm full of divine grace, free from all conflict ... [But] as soon as practitioners relax in their discipline, they again encounter all the unfinished business of the body and heart that they had hoped to leave behind ... When we have not completed the basic developmental tasks of our emotional lives or are still quite unconscious in our relation to our parents and families we will find that we are unable to deepen our spiritual practice ...[5]

The particularities of this divergence need not detain us here. It has only been brought into view as an angle of approach to several large questions which will attract our attention in this chapter.

3 T. Schwartz, *What Really Matters*, 329.
4 T. Schwartz, *What Really Matters*, 331.
5 Quoted in T. Schwartz, *What Really Matters*, 332-333.

Western Psychology and Religion

No one needs reminding that the relations between modern psychology and traditional religions have not always been friendly. Freud struck the key note in his insistence that, to state the matter as briefly as possible, religious beliefs were a thinly camouflaged prolongation of childhood pathologies. He identified "three powers which may dispute the basic position of science": art, philosophy and religion, of which, he said, "religion alone is to be taken seriously as an enemy." Philosophy, he suggested, is basically harmless because, despite its ambitious pretensions, it "has no direct influence on the great mass of mankind: it is of interest to only a small number even of top-layer intellectuals and is scarcely intelligible to anyone else." Art "is almost always harmless and beneficent; it does not seek to be anything but an illusion." This leaves religion as "an immense power" and an imposing obstacle to the scientific enlightenment of mankind, the project in which Freud understood himself to be engaged.

> The last contribution to the criticism of the religious *Weltanschauung*, he wrote, was effected by psychoanalysis, by showing how religion originated from the helplessness of children and by tracing its contents to the survival into maturity of the wishes and needs of childhood.[6]

This all sits somewhat uncomfortably with the fact that Freud himself made frequent reference to the insights of the art, philosophy and religion of the past in his own inquiries, and found that they illuminated some of the darkest recesses of the human psyche. His most famous theoretical innovation, after all, took its name from Greek mythology. Perhaps we can defend Freud with the old adage that only small minds are consistent!

Since Freud's time Western psychology has splintered into various schools and movements. At one end of the spectrum we have what might be called "objectivist," "behaviorist" and "empiricist" schools of thought which treat human consciousness as somehow epiphenomenal, or indeed, as irrelevant to the science of psychology. Recall the claim by one of the founders of behaviorist psychology, John Watson:

> Psychology, as the behaviorist views it, is a purely objective, experimental branch of natural science which needs consciousness as little as do the sciences of chemistry and physics.[7]

Here indeed is a science to clip an angel's wings! Of course, even within the domain of the so-called "hard sciences," the whole notion of an objective knowledge, anchored in empirical and verifiable experimentation and observation, has recently been called into the most serious question: one need only mention such developments as the Uncertainty Principle, Chaos Theory and Quantum Physics to signal the tumult into which the tidy assumptions of

---

6 Freud quoted in W. Smith, *Cosmos and Transcendence*, 101-102.
7 Watson quoted in F. Capra, *The Turning Point*, 177.

Newtonian science have been thrown. We are now confronted with the sorry spectacle of the human and social "sciences" clinging to a borrowed episte-mological paradigm which was never appropriate and which is now largely discredited by physicists and the like. Of course, we might want to take the same tack as B.F. Skinner. When it was pointed out to him that Heisenberg's Principle had undermined physical determinism and he was asked whether, in view of the fact that matter did not behave in a predictable fashion, was not psychological determinism rather problematic, he replied that "the mud-dle of physics" was physics' problem, not psychology's. Electrons might be unpredictable, but human beings, apparently, are not![8]

At the other end of the spectrum we have various humanistic, personal-ist and existentialist schools which take the closest interest not in observable behavior but in human consciousness and in the inner world of the experi-encing subject. Some psychologists of this kind would share John Welwood's view that

> Western psychology has so far failed to provide us with a satisfactory under-standing of the full range of human experience ... It appears that we have largely overlooked the central fact of human psychology—our everyday mind, our very real, immediate awareness of being.[9]

The question arises: what is the nature of consciousness? What do we mean by this word? For my own part I would contend that consciousness, inextrica-bly tied up with human subjectivity, is vital, complex, elusive, mysterious. As *The Zenrin* affirms, "There is no place to seek the mind: it is like the foot-prints of the birds in the sky." From another viewpoint we may share Stanislav Grof's contention, in accord with many ancient wisdoms, that "In its furthest reaches, the psyche of each of us is essentially commensurate with all of exis-tence, and ultimately identical with the cosmic creative principle itself."[10] This is a matter for celebration, not a "problem" to be solved by a "science" with pretensions to explaining everything! To borrow a metaphor, trying to pin consciousness to the laboratory bench, or the computer screen for that matter, is like trying to capture the wind in a bag, or a river in a net. And thank goodness for that! Artists, theologians, philosophers, scientists, musi-cians, thinkers of all kinds have grappled with the mystery of consciousness since time immemorial. It is surely absurd to believe that we must now regard all these efforts as only the fumblings and gropings of unsophisticated minds, bereft of the benefits of modern science, and that it is only with the advent of a scientifically-constituted psychology that we can build a true knowledge of human consciousness and behavior. This is a staggering imper-tinence, but one altogether characteristic of the modern mentality. However, I share Grof's conviction that

8   See H. Smith, *Beyond the Post-Modern Mind*, 66fn.
9   Welwood quoted in J.J. Clarke, *Oriental Enlightenment*, 150.
10 S. Grof, *Spiritual Emergency*, 21.

Many open minded scientists and mental health professionals have become aware of the abysmal gap between contemporary [mainstream] psychology, and the great ancient or Oriental spiritual traditions, such as the various forms of yoga, Kashmir Shaivism, Tibetan Vajrayana, Taoism, Zen Buddhism, Sufism, Kabbalah or alchemy. The wealth of profound knowledge about the human psyche and consciousness accumulated within these systems over centuries and often over millennia, has not been adequately acknowledged, explored, and integrated by Western science.[11]

To return to the question: here's a rough working definition of "consciousness": all forms of human awareness, conscious, subconscious or supraconscious, if one may be permitted such a term. This is to say that consciousness includes such modes as not only ratiocination, or what the Romantic poets called "cerebration" (by which they meant conscious mental operations of a more or less rational kind) but all those more subtle and enigmatic modes and states which we signal by such words as imagination, intuition, creativity, dream, fantasy, trance, reverie and the like. Recall these words from one of the 19th century's greatest psychologists, William James:

> Our normal waking consciousness ... is but one special type of consciousness, whilst all about it, parted from it by the flimsiest of screens, there lie potential forms of consciousness entirely different. We may go through life without suspecting their existence; but apply the requisite stimulus, and at a touch they are there in all their completeness ... no account of the universe in its totality can be final which leaves these other forms of consciousness quite disregarded. How to regard them is the question ... At any rate, they forbid our premature closing of accounts with reality.[12]

There are, of course, those who believe that eventually we will be able to reduce all this to the material processes in the brain. To my mind this is ludicrous: it is a reductionism of the crudest and most damaging kind, what Blake called Single Vision. I can do no better than Kathleen Raine's characterization of reductionism as "that mentality which can see in the pearl nothing but the disease of the oyster."

Though modern science has doubtless revealed much material information that was previously unknown it has also supplanted a knowledge which infinitely outreaches it. We see the fruits of this tendency in the complacencies and condescensions of those scientists who like to suppose that we have "outgrown" the "superstitions" of our ancestors. Here is a random example from a prestigious contemporary scientist:

> I myself, like many scientists, believe that the soul is imaginary and that what we call our mind is simply a way of talking about the function of our brains ... Once one has become adjusted to the ideas that we are here because we have evolved from simple chemical compounds by a process of natural selec-

---

11 S. Grof, *The Holotropic Mind*, 21. (We will forgive Grof's indiscretion in claiming Sufism, Kabbalah and alchemy for the Orient!)

12 W. James, *The Varieties of Religious Experience*, 305.

tion, it is remarkable how many of the problems of the modern world take on a completely new light.[13]

This kind of rampant materialism is presently "the reigning orthodoxy among philosophers of the mind."[14] Much academic psychology concerned with the mind has stumbled down the same blind alley.

Many contemporary psychologists are apparently oblivious to the fact that the ancient philosophers and artists of both Orient and Occident were profound psychologists. Indeed, one of the great historical religions might be seen primarily as a psychology, with the proviso that the inquiry is conducted within a religious rather than a profane and secular framework. The words of Christmas Humphreys remain as apposite today as they were in 1951:

> ... in the world of the mind, including that Cinderella of mental science, psychology, the West has more to learn from Buddhism than as yet it knows.[15]

Modern Western psychology exhibits both the strengths and weaknesses of a whole family of so-called sciences which crystallized sometime in the 19th century: we might mention such disciplines as anthropology, sociology and what Carlyle properly called the "Dismal Science" of economics. The encounter of Western psychology and Eastern religion, limited though it has been, can help us to see more clearly what some of the limitations of modern psychology might be, and how these might be at least attenuated. With very broad brush strokes we shall portray the involvement of several modern psychological thinkers with the doctrines and techniques of Eastern spirituality. Later, after some passing remarks about several contemporary thinkers, a few reflections on what Western psychology might profitably derive from the Eastern traditions. However, before that, we must take rather a lengthy detour through the critique of psychologism elaborated by traditionalists, and through their repudiation of some aspects of the work of the century's greatest East-West bridge builder in the psychological domain, Carl Jung.

A Traditionalist Perspective on Psychologism

From the perennialist perspective psychologism is a school of thought, a view of the human condition, built on the sands of a profane science, and as such, another symptom of modernism. Its intrusion into the religious realm has been attended by consequences no less disturbing than those coming in the train of evolutionism. As Coomaraswamy so neatly put it, "While nineteenth century materialism closed the mind of man to what is above him, twentieth century psychology opened it to what is below him."[16]

---

13 F. Crick, *Molecules and Men*, quoted in T. Roszak, *Where the Wasteland Ends*, 188. For an almost identical profession by a scientific popularizer see Carl Sagan, *The Dragons of Eden*, 10.
14 Daniel Dennett quoted in H. Smith, *Beyond the Post-Modern Mind*, 135-136.
15 C. Humphreys, *Buddhism*, 223.
16 Coomaraswamy quoted in W. Perry, *Challenges to a Secular Society*, 13-14.

Psychologism can be described as the assumption that man's nature and behavior are to be explained by psychological mechanisms which can be laid bare by a scientific and empirical psychology. Before we proceed any further an extremely important distinction must be made between modern psychology and traditional pneumatologies with which it shares some superficial similarities. The latter derived from radically different principles, applied different therapies and pursued different ends. Just as it is misleading to talk about modern European philosophy and traditional metaphysics in the same breath and under the same terms, so too with modern psychology and traditional pneumatology. A good deal of confusion would be averted if people would resist such terms as "Buddhist psychology" or "Zen psychotherapy." It would also help clarify the issues at stake if many of the dabblers in this field would abandon the extraordinary notion that the techniques of Western psychology can lead to the "liberation" spoken of in the Eastern traditions.[17] This is to confuse two quite different planes of experience.

Modern psychology can be censured against the backdrop of traditional doctrines in this fashion:

> Psychoanalysis doubly deserves to be called an imposture, firstly because it pretends to have discovered facts which have always been known ... and secondly and chiefly because it attributes to itself functions that in reality are spiritual, and thus in practice puts itself in the place of religion.[18]

In this context we might take note of the fact that many of Freud's apparently revolutionary insights were perfectly well-known not only in the East but in the pre-modern West, and that many of Freud's ideas are actually prefigured in the Kabbalah. Indeed, David Bakan has adduced a good deal of evidence in favor of his claim that Freud's whole project can be read as the secularization of Jewish mysticism.[19]

Psychology of the modern kind defines itself by its inability to distinguish between the psychic plane, the arena in which the more or less accidental subjectivities of the individual ego come into play in the depths of the subconscious, and the infinite realm of the spirit which, in terms of the human individual, is signaled by the capacity for the plenary experience and which is thus marked by an "inward" illimitation and transcendence. The muddling of the psychic realm of the subconscious with the mystical potentialities of the spirit and the boundless reaches of the Intellect has given birth to all manner of confusions. There is indeed a science which reveals the way in which the play of the psyche can communicate universal realities; this is one of the fields of traditional pneumatologies. But—the proviso is crucial—

---

17 On this issue see P. Novak, "C.G. Jung in the Light of Asian Philosophy" and J.M. Reynolds, *Self-Liberation through Seeing with Naked Awareness*, Appendix 1.

18 F. Schuon, "The Psychological Imposture," 98.

19 See Perry's review of David Bakan's book *Sigmund Freud and the Jewish Mystical Tradition* (which I have not seen) in *Challenges to a Secular Society*, 17-38.

such a science cannot flourish outside a properly constituted metaphysic and cosmology. In this context the following passage from Burckhardt deserves the closest attention:

> The connection with the metaphysical order provides spiritual psychology with qualitative criteria such as are wholly lacking in profane psychology, which studies only the dynamic character of phenomena of the psyche and their proximate causes. When modern psychology makes pretensions to a sort of science of the hidden contents of the soul it is still for all that restricted to an individual perspective because it has no real means for distinguishing psychic forms which translate universal realities from forms which appear symbolical but are only vehicles for individual impulsions. Its "collective subconscious" has most assuredly nothing to do with the true source of symbols; at most it is a chaotic depository of psychic residues somewhat like the mud of the ocean bed which retains traces of past epochs.[20]

The confusion of the psychic and the spiritual, which in part stems from the artificial Cartesian dualism of "body" and "mind," was discussed by René Guénon at some length in *The Reign of Quantity*. The confusion, he said,

> appears in two contrary forms: in the first, the spiritual is brought down to the level of the psychic; in the second, the psychic is ... mistaken for the spiritual; of this the most popular example is spiritualism ...[21]

The first form of the confusion thus licenses a degrading reductionism and relativism, often as impertinent as it is inadequate. The "sinister originality" of psychologism lies in its "determination to attribute every reflex and disposition of the soul to mean causes and to exclude spiritual factors."[22] This tendency is often accomplice to a relativism whereby everything becomes

> ... the fruit of a contingent elaboration: Revelation becomes poetry, the Religions are inventions, sages are "thinkers" ... infallibility and inspiration do not exist, error becomes a quantitative and "interesting" contribution to "culture" ... there is ... a denial of every supernatural, or even suprasensory, cause, and by the same token of every principial truth.[23]

Like evolutionism, psychologism attempts to explain the greater in terms of the lesser and excludes all that goes beyond its own limits. In this sense, historicism, relativism and psychologism are all cut from the same cloth:

20 T. Burckhardt, *An Introduction to Sufi Doctrine*, 37. See also S.H. Nasr, *Sufi Essays*, 46ff, and A.K. Coomaraswamy, "On the Indian and Traditional Psychology, or rather Pneumatology" in *Selected Papers 2*, 333-378. What Coomaraswamy said of the individual subconscious can be applied to the psychic realm as a whole: it is "a sink of psychic residues, a sort of garbage pit or compost heap, fitted only for the roots of 'plants,' and far removed from the light that erects them." Cited by Perry, *Treasury of Traditional Wisdom*, 437.
21 R. Guénon, *The Reign of Quantity*, 286. See the chapters "The Misdeeds of Psychoanalysis" and "The Confusion of the Psychic and the Spiritual," 273-290.
22 F. Schuon, "The Psychological Imposture," 99.
23 F. Schuon, *Dimensions of Islam*, 154-155.

> The mentality of today seeks to reduce everything to categories connected with time; a work of art, a thought, a truth have no value in themselves and independently of any historical classification ... everything is considered as an expression of a "period" and not as having possibly a timeless and intrinsic value; and this is entirely in conformity with modern relativism, and with a psychologism ... that destroys essential values. In order to "situate" the doctrine of a scholastic, or even a Prophet, a "psychoanalysis" is prepared—it is needless to emphasize the monstrous impudence implicit in such an attitude—and with wholly mechanical and perfectly unreal logic the "influences" to which this doctrine has been subject are laid bare. There is no hesitation in attributing to saints ... all kind of artificial and even fraudulent conduct; but it is obviously forgotten ... to apply the same principle to oneself, and to explain one's own supposedly "objective" position by psychological considerations: sages are treated as being sick men and one takes oneself for a god ... it is a case of expressing a maximum amount of absurdity with a maximum amount of subtlety.[24]

As Schuon remarks elsewhere, relativism goes about reducing every element of absoluteness to a relativity while making a quite illogical exception in favor of this reduction itself.[25]

Clearly these strictures do not apply with the same force to each and every attempt by scholars to detect and explain historical and psychological factors relating to particular religious phenomena. It is possible, for example, to take these kinds of considerations into account in a sympathetic and sensitive way without falling prey to a reductionist relativism. Nevertheless, Schuon's general point remains valid. It can hardly be denied that a kind of iconoclastic psychologism runs through a good deal of the scholarly literature on religion. A psychologism unrestrained by any values transcending those of a profane science can help to corrode religious forms by infiltrating the religious sphere itself. Schuon notes, by way of an example, the part psychologism has played in discrediting the cult of the Holy Virgin:

> ... only a barbarous mentality that wants to be "adult" at all costs and no longer believes in anything but the trivial could be embarrassed by this cult. The answer to the reproach of "gynecolatry" or the "Oedipus complex" is that, like every other psychoanalytic argument, it by-passes the problem; for the real question is not one of knowing what the psychological factors conditioning an attitude may be but, something very different, namely, what are its results.[26]

The practice of dragging spiritual realities down to the psychological plane can everywhere be seen when religion is reduced to some kind of psychological regimen. Some of the neo-yogic, meditation, "self-realization" and New Age movements are of this kind.

24 F. Schuon, *Light on the Ancient Worlds*, 32-33.
25 F. Schuon, *Logic and Transcendence*, 7.
26 F. Schuon, "The Psychological Imposture," 101.

One of the most insidious and destructive illusions is the belief that depth-psychology ... has the slightest connection with spiritual life, which these teachings persistently falsify by confusing inferior elements [psychic] with superior [spiritual]. We cannot be too wary of all these attempts to reduce the values vehicled by tradition to the level of phenomena supposed to be scientifically controllable. The spirit escapes the hold of profane science in an absolute fashion.

Similarly,

It is not the positive results of experimental science that one is out to deny ... but the absurd claim of science to cover everything possible, the whole of truth, the whole of the real; the quasi-religious claim of totality moreover proves the falseness of the point of departure.[27]

Of course the traditionalists are not alone in unmasking "the misdeeds of psychoanalysis." Thomas Merton, for instance:

Nothing is more repellent than a pseudo-scientific definition of the contemplative experience ... he who attempts such a definition is tempted to proceed psychologically, and there is really no adequate "psychology" of contemplation ... [28]

Lama Govinda, more alert to this danger than some of his colleagues, warns of the "shallow-mindedness" of those who teach a kind of "pseudo-scientific spirituality."[29] Mircea Eliade makes a more general point in writing,

Psychoanalysis justifies its importance by asserting that it forces you to look at and accept reality. But what sort of reality? A reality conditioned by the materialistic and scientific ideology of psychoanalysis, that is, a historical product: we see a thing in which certain scholars and thinkers of the nineteenth century believed.[30]

Psychologistic reductionism, has ramifications on both the practical and the theoretical level: on the one hand we have the notion that psychological techniques and therapies can take the place of authentic spiritual disciplines; on the other, the pretension that psychological science can "explain" religious phenomena. Both of these are related to the first form of the confusion of the psychic and the spiritual. Let us turn briefly to the obverse side, that of falsely elevating the psychic to the spiritual. There is a vast spiritual wasteland here which we cannot presently explore but Whitall Perry identifies some of its inhabitants in writing of those occultist, psychic, spiritualistic and "esoteric" groups who concern themselves with

---

27 F. Schuon, "No Activity Without Truth," 37. See also F. Schuon, *Stations of Wisdom*, 38, and *Light on the Ancient Worlds*, 34ff.

28 T. Merton, *New Seeds of Contemplation*, 6-7.

29 A. Govinda, *Creative Meditation and Multi-Dimensional Consciousness*, 70.

30 M. Eliade, *No Souvenirs*, 269.

spirits, elementals, materializations, etheric states, auric eggs, astral bodies, ids, ods and egos, ectoplasmic apparitions, wraiths and visions, subliminal consciousness and collective unconsciousness, doublings, disassociations, functional disintegrations, communications, obsessions and possessions, psychasthenia, animal magnetism, hypnoidal therapeutics, vibrations, thought-forces, mind-waves and radiations, clairvoyances and audiences and levitations, telepathic dreams, premonitions, death lights, trance writings, Rochester knockings, Buddhic bodies, and sundry other emergences and extravagances of hideous nomenclature ... [31]

—all the while imagining that these are the stuff of the spiritual life. Much of Guénon's work was directed to reasserting the proper distinctions between psychic phenomena and spiritual realities and to sounding a warning about the infernal forces to which the psychic occultists unwittingly expose themselves. As Schuon remarks, "... modern occultism is by and large no more than the study of extrasensory phenomena, one of the most hazardous pursuits by reason of its wholly empirical character and its lack of any doctrinal basis."[32] Without the protective shield of traditional doctrines and disciplines, such as those which guarded the shamans, any forays into these realms are fraught with perils of the gravest kind. In a traditional discipline the psychic can be reintegrated with the spiritual but without the necessary metaphysical framework and religious supports psychism becomes wholly infra-intellectual and anti-spiritual. The traditionalists' critique of psychologism can be more sharply focused by a consideration of their response to the work of Carl Jung.

The Traditionalist Critique of Carl Jung

As we have already seen, Carl Jung was one of the century's most sympathetic commentators on Eastern doctrines and practices. He took a close interest in several key texts of the Chinese and Tibetan traditions. Despite some tension in his work between what might loosely be called the scientific and the mystical, Jung understood that the Eastern traditions enshrined an immense and richly variegated treasury of wisdom and was certainly not given to the preposterous dismissal of Eastern psycho-spiritual disciplines that we find amongst many Western psychologists. Nor did he display any of Freud's deep-seated animus to religion in the name of some kind of "objective" scientific knowledge. Jung's work, inevitably, was attacked from the scientific side as being "symbolistic," "mystical," "occultist" and the like. These kinds of criticisms are of no interest in the present context. Much more disturbing are the charges that have been pressed by exponents of the traditional religious outlook. There are four kinds of criticisms which deserve our

---

31 W. Perry, *Treasury of Traditional Wisdom*, 437.

32 F. Schuon, *Logic and Transcendence*, 1. See also R. Guénon, "Explanation of Spiritist Phenomena," and S.H. Nasr, *Sufi Essays*, 40-41.

attention here. They can be flagged by identifying their targets: pan-psy-chism; the denial of metaphysics; the tyranny of the ego; the subversion of traditional religion.

From a traditionalist perspective the first problem is that Jung's writings often seem to confound the psychic and the spiritual. In Jung's case it is a matter at times of reducing the spiritual to the level of the psychic, and at others of elevating the psychic to the level of the spiritual, or, to put the same point differently, of deifying the unconscious. In *Memories* Jung states that

> All comprehension and all that is comprehended is in itself psychic, and to that extent we are hopelessly cooped up in an exclusively psychic world.[33]

It is difficult to find in Jung's writings a completely unequivocal affirmation of the objective and supra-psychic reality of the *numen,* to borrow a term from Otto, a figure who significantly influenced both Jung and Eliade.[34] In the interview conducted by Mircea Eliade for *Combat,* Jung *does* say this:

> Religious experience is numinous, as Rudolf Otto calls it, and for me, as a psychologist, this experience differs from all others in the way *it transcends the ordinary categories of time, space and causality.*[35]

However, many of his formulations on this subject are ambivalent. It is also undoubtedly true that a great many people, including liberal Christian the-ologians, have used Jung's sometimes confusing ruminations as a theoretical platform for a wholesale psychologizing of religion—Don Cuppitt, to name but one popular exponent of the view that religion needs no metaphysical underpinnings.[36] This is to be guilty of the "psychological imposture," which Schuon castigates in these terms:

> ... the tendency to reduce everything to psychological factors and to call into question not only what is intellectual and spiritual ... but also the human spirit as such, and therewith its capacity of adequation and still more evi-dently, its inward illimitation and transcendence ... Psychoanalysis is at once an endpoint and a cause, as is always the case with profane ideologies, like

---

33 C.G. Jung, *Memories, Dreams, Reflections,* 385.

34 The same kind of ambivalence is evident in most Jungian formulations concerning both the collective unconscious and archetypes. This, for instance, from Marie-Louise von Franz: "Really, it is a modern, scientific expression for an inner experience that has been known to mankind from time immemorial, the experience in which strange and unknown things from our own inner world hap-pen to us, in which influences from within can suddenly alter us, in which we have dreams and ideas which we feel as if we are not doing ourselves, but which appear in us strangely and overwhelming-ly. In earlier times these influences were attributed to a divine fluid (*mana*), or to a god, demon, or 'spirit,' a fitting expression of the feeling that this influence has an objective, quite foreign and autonomous existence, as well as the sense of its being something overpowering, which has the con-scious ego at its mercy"; quoted in G. Wehr, *Jung: A Biography,* 170.

35 C.G. Jung, *C.G Jung Speaking,* 230 (italics mine).

36 See the glib commentary by Cuppitt on Jung's view of religion, quoted in S. Segaller & M. Berger, *Jung: The Wisdom of the Dream,* 179.

materialism and evolutionism, of which it is really a logical and fateful ramification and a natural ally.[37]

Schuon's reference to materialism and evolutionism alert us to these two bugbears (still very much with us, alas!) which occasionally raise their ugly heads in Jung's writings. Even in the autobiography written near the end of his life, Jung is capable of a kind of scientistic gobbledygook which betrays a failure to break free from the stultifying effects of these prejudices. Two examples: "Consciousness is phylogenetically and ontogenetically a secondary phenomenon."[38] (This is a variant on the absurd evolutionist inversion whereby the "flesh" becomes "word".) Likewise in his Introduction to *The Secret of the Golden Flower*, Jung descends into Darwinian hocus-pocus when he suggests that the analogical relationships of symbolic vocabularies and mythological motifs across many different cultures derives from "the identity of cerebral structures beyond all racial differences."[39] Here the psychic domain itself seems to have been reduced to nothing more than an epiphenomenon of a material substrate. This is Jung at his worst, surrendering to a materialistic scientism which he elsewhere deplores.

In *Psychology and Religion* Jung staked out his most characteristic position on metaphysics:

> Psychology treats ... all metaphysical ... assertions as mental phenomena, and regards them as statements about the mind and its structure that derive ultimately from certain unconscious dispositions. It does not consider them to be absolutely valid or even capable of establishing metaphysical truth ... Psychology therefore holds that the mind cannot establish or assert anything beyond itself.[40]

In similar vein, this:

> I am and remain a psychologist. I am not interested in anything that transcends the psychological content of human experience. I do not even ask myself whether such transcendence is possible ... [41]

37 F. Schuon, *Survey of Metaphysics and Esoterism*, 195.
38 C.G. Jung, *Memories, Dreams, Reflections*, 381.
39 From Jung's Introduction to *The Secret of the Golden Flower*, quoted by Burckhardt in "Cosmology and Modern Science," 168. (Burckhardt's essay can also be found in his *Mirror of the Intellect*.) See also P. Sherrard, "An Introduction to the Religious Thought of C.G. Jung"; W. Smith, *Cosmos and Transcendence*, Ch 6; and W. Perry, *The Widening Breach: Evolutionism in the Mirror of Cosmology*, 89. Sherrard argues that Jung's thought can best be understood as an agenda for the displacement of Christianity while Smith highlights some of the contradictions and the "dogmatic relativism" which betrays Jung's confusion of the spiritual with the psychic. Perry notes how Jung inverts the traditional doctrine of Archetypes. On Jung's psychologization of religion see also W. Hanegraaff, *New Age Religion and Western Culture*, 496-512.
40 C. G. Jung, "Psychology and Religion," quoted in P. Novak, "C.G. Jung in the Light of Asian Philosophy," 68.
41 Interview with Eliade for *Combat*, in *C.G. Jung Speaking*, 229.

Jung, to his credit, was not always able to hold fast to this position. In 1946, for example, he was prepared to write that "archetypes ... have a nature that cannot with certainty be designated as psychic," and that the archetype is a "metaphysical" entity not susceptible to any unequivocal (i.e., "scientific") definition.[42] The status of archetypes is a critical issue, particularly if we take the following kind of claim seriously:

> The basis of analytical psychology's significance for the psychology of religion ... lies in C.G. Jung's discovery of how archetypal images, events and experiences, individually and in groups, are the *essential determinants* of the religious life in history and in the present.[43]

From a traditionalist point of view there are two problems: the first is the suggestion, not hard to find in Jung's writings, that the psychic domain contains and exhausts all of supra-material reality, a view we have already designated pan-psychism. But even when Jung retreats from this position, he still insists that the psychic is the only supra-material reality that we can explore and *know*. From the viewpoint of traditional metaphysics this amounts to nothing less than a denial of the Intellect, that faculty by which Absolute Reality can be apprehended, and to which all traditional wisdoms testify.[44]

What of "God"? Jung's position, at least as Aniela Jaffé recalls it, is subtle but clear: "God" and "the unconscious" are inseparable from the point of view of the subject but not identical. One of Jung's most careful formulations on the subject goes like this:

> This is certainly not to say that what we call the unconscious is identical with God or set up in his place. It is simply the medium from which religious experience seems to flow.

So far so good. The problem arises in what follows: "As to what the further cause of such experience may be, the answer to this lies beyond the range of human knowledge."[45] Elsewhere he affirmed that, "the transcendental reality ... [beyond] the world inside and outside ourselves ... is as certain as our own existence."[46] Nevertheless, it *necessarily* remains an unfathomable mystery. In denying the possibility of intellection and of absolute certitude concerning metaphysical realities Jung again falls foul of the traditionalists. Compare Jung's notion that we "are hopelessly cooped up in an exclusively psychic world" and that the cause of religious experience "lies beyond

42 C.G. Jung, "On the Nature of the Psyche," quoted in A. Jaffé, *The Myth of Meaning*, 23.

43 G. Wehr, *Jung: A Biography*, 291 (italics mine). On Jung and archetypes see E. Wasserstrom, *Religion after Religion*, 352, fn21.

44 See P. Novak, "C.G. Jung in the Light of Asian Philosophy," 77. At other points Jung's philosophical position is also reminiscent of a kind of "existentialist" relativism. Thus, "... the sole purpose of human existence is to kindle a light in the darkness of mere being"; *Memories, Dreams, Reflections*, 358.

45 From "The Undiscovered Self," in *Civilization in Transition*, quoted in A. Jaffé, *The Myth of Meaning*, 40.

46 From *Mysterium Coniunctionis*, quoted in A. Jaffé, *The Myth of Meaning*, 42.

human knowledge" with this kind of claim from Frithjof Schuon (who is reaffirming a view that can be found in all traditional metaphysics—those of Plato, Eckhart, Nagajurna and Sankara to cite several conspicuous examples):

> The distinctive mark of man is total intelligence, that is to say an intelligence which is objective and capable of conceiving the absolute ... This objectivity ... would lack any sufficient reason did it not have the capacity to conceive the absolute or infinite ...[47]

Or, even more succinctly,

> The prerogative of the human state is objectivity, the essential content of which is the Absolute. There is no knowledge without objectivity of the intelligence ...[48]

Furthermore,

> This capacity for objectivity and absoluteness is an anticipated and existential refutation of all the ideologies of doubt: if man is able to doubt, this is because certitude exists; likewise the very notion of illusion proves that man has access to reality.[49]

Another stumbling block for traditionalists concerns the relationship of the empirical ego and consciousness. Ananda Coomaraswamy signals the problem when he writes,

> The health envisaged by empirical psychotherapy is a freedom from particular pathogenic conditions; that envisaged by sacred or traditional psychology is *freedom from all conditions and predicaments* ... Furthermore, the pursuit of the greater freedom necessarily entails the attainment of the lesser ...[50]

In other words, Jung sought to rehabilitate the empirical ego rather than to dismantle it. From a traditionalist point of view Jung hoists himself on his own petard when he writes "To us consciousness is inconceivable without an ego ... I cannot imagine a conscious mental state that does not relate to the ego ..."[51] Daniel Goleman elaborates the cardinal point:

> The models of contemporary psychology ... foreclose the acknowledgment or investigation of a mode of being which is the central premise and *summum bonum* of virtually every Eastern psycho-spiritual system. Called variously Enlightenment, Buddhahood ... and so on, there is simply no fully equiv-

---

47 F. Schuon, "To be Man is to Know," 117-118.
48 F. Schuon, *Esoterism as Principle and as Way*, 15ff.
49 F. Schuon, *Logic and Transcendence*, 13.
50 A.K. Coomaraswamy, "On the Indian and Traditional Psychology, or rather, Pneumatology," *Selected Papers 2*, 335 (italics mine). See also T. Burckhardt, "Cosmology and Modern Science," 174-175.
51 From *Psychology and Religion*, quoted by P. Novak, "C.G. Jung in the Light of Asian Philosophy," 82.

alent category in contemporary psychology. The paradigms of traditional Asian psychologies, however, are capable of encompassing the major categories of contemporary psychology as well as this other mode of consciousness.[52]

Fourthly, several traditionalists, most notably Phillip Sherrard, have argued that Jung's covert and perhaps not fully conscious agenda was nothing less than the dethronement of Christianity in all of its traditional and institutional forms, and its replacement by a kind of quasi-religious psychology for which Jung himself was a "prophetic" voice. A variant of this particular kind of argument has been elaborated by Philip Rieff and is adumbrated in the following passage:

> After the failure of the Reformation, and the further fragmentation of Christianity, the search was on for those more purely symbolical authorities to which an educated Christian could transfer his loyalty from the Church. Biblicism gave way to erudition, erudition to historical liberalism, and the latter to a variety of psychological conservatisms, of which Jung's is potentially the most attractive for those not entirely unchurched.[53]

This kind of argument would seem to have some cogency when we recall a few of Jung's many explanations of his own relationship to religion. Take this, for example, from a letter written in 1946:

> I practice science, not apologetics and not philosophy ... My interest is a scientific one ... I proceed from a positive Christianity that is as much Catholic as Protestant, and my concern is to point out in a scientifically responsible way those empirically tangible facts which would at least make plausible the legitimacy of Christian and especially Catholic dogma.[54]

The traditionalist response to this kind of claim is quite implacable. Thus Schuon: "Modern science ... can neither add nor subtract anything in respect of the total truth or of mythological or other symbolism or in respect of the principles and experiences of the spiritual life ..."[55] In the light of these kinds of criticisms it is not hard to see why one traditionalist has suggested that "In the final analysis, what Jung has to offer is a religion for atheists ...,"[56] or why Rieff claims that Jung's thought amounts to "a religion for heretics."[57] In similar vein, Eric Wasserstrom has argued that not only Jung but the whole

---

52 Quoted in P. Novak, "C.G. Jung in the Light of Asian Philosophy", 73. One again sees the problem in Jung's homologizing of the psychosis of the mental patient with the "mythopoeic imagination which has vanished from our rational age"; *Memories, Dreams, Reflections,* 213.

53 P. Rieff, *The Triumph of the Therapeutic,* 110. See also R. Moacanin, *Jung's Psychology and Tibetan Buddhism,* 94.

54 Quoted in G. Wehr, *Jung: A Biography,* 302.

55 F Schuon, "No Activity Without Truth," 36-37.

56 W. Smith, *Cosmos and Transcendence,* 130.

57 P Rieff, *The Triumph of the Therapeutic,* 115.

Eranos group were in search of "religion after religion." In a wonderfully ambiguous phrase, a Dominican admirer of Jung called him "a priest without a surplice."[58] It was meant as a compliment but if we take the lack of a surplice as signifying Jung's detachment from any religious tradition then the epithet carries a different freight. To make the same point differently, a priest without a surplice is no priest at all.

B. Eastern Spirituality and Western Psychology

Before proceeding to a consideration of the encounter of Western psychology and Eastern spirituality we must face the melancholy fact that Western psychology, taken as a whole but especially in its academic aspect, remains astonishingly ignorant of the psycho-spiritual traditions of the East. The exception is the rather small world of Jungian, existentialist and transpersonal psychology. Jung's contribution was to open the doors of an emergent late 19th century "science" to the wealth of psychological insight in the religious traditions of both East and West. As we have just seen, Jung's enterprise was fraught with all manner of ambiguities and anomalies. Nonetheless, it contrasts positively with all those modern schools of psychological thought which treat all religion as pathological and dismiss the whole spiritual dimension.

While Jung's somewhat ambivalent encounter with the East has been the most significant single avenue by which Eastern ideas and themes have flowed into Western psychology there are a good many other engagements of which we must take some note. Earlier in this study we considered some of the intersections of psychology and the study of mythology and made mention of some of the pioneering figures in what can loosely be called the psychology of religious experience—William James, Rudolf Otto, Mircea Eliade. Here we shall dwell briefly on a few developments which signal some intellectual traffic between West and East: Erich Fromm's humanistic appropriation of Zen, existentialist interest in the East, the emergence of transpersonal psychology, and the somewhat curious phenomenon of biofeedback as it has been applied to various yogas.

Erich Fromm and Zen

After his interest in Zen Buddhism was sparked by a meeting with D.T. Suzuki, Erich Fromm participated, in 1957, in a conference on Buddhism and psychoanalysis; it led to a "considerable enlargement and revision" of his ideas, specifically with respect to "the problems of what constitutes the unconscious, of the transformation of the unconscious into consciousness,

---

58 W. Smith, *Cosmos and Transcendence*, 130.
59 J.J. Clarke, *Oriental Enlightenment*, 156.
60 E. Fromm, "Psychoanalysis and Zen" in Erich Fromm, D.T. Suzuki & Richard De Martino, *Zen Buddhism and Psychoanalysis*, 140.

and of the goal of psychoanalytic therapy." Fromm was a humanistic psychologist who married his analytic work to larger social and moral concerns, and whose "emphasis on freedom, responsibility, and the quest for meaning, rather than on the unconscious, set him apart from Freudian orthodoxy."[59] Now, he wrote,

> the knowledge of Zen, and a concern with it, can have a most fertile and clarifying influence on the theory and technique of psychoanalysis ... Zen thought will deepen and widen the horizon of the psychoanalyst.[60]

Like Jung, Fromm believed that modern humankind was suffering from a deep spiritual malaise characterized by widespread ennui and alienation, the symptoms having been diagnosed by thinkers as diverse as Kierkegaard, Marx and Tillich—to whom we might add such exemplary 19th century figures as Nietzsche, Baudelaire and Dostoevsky. For Fromm psychoanalysis was not so much a "cure" for an "illness" but a technique of self-knowledge and self-transformation, one with obvious affinities with Zen which he described as "the art of seeing into the nature of one's being; it is a way from bondage to freedom." Far from being a self-indulgent form of narcissistic navel-gazing, as detractors in the West often portrayed Eastern meditational practices, Zen demanded the most searching confrontation with one's immediate and present condition and "the realization of the relation of myself to the Universe," as Fromm put it.[61] Furthermore, he argued, the Zen path could help us transcend the limitations of rational thought by its emphasis on experiential knowledge, one wherein subject-object dualities are overcome.

Existentialism, Herman Hesse, Hubert Benoit

The reference to experiential knowledge provides us with a link to another school of European thought, much influenced by the emergence of modern Freudian psychology but also occasionally receptive to Eastern influences— existentialism. In our next chapter we shall examine this theme in some detail, particularly in relation to the two Big Hitters of European existentialism, Friedrich Nietzsche and Martin Heidegger. Here, as an example of the confluence of existentialism, Freudian psychology and Eastern interests, we may cite the shadowy figure of Herman Hesse. Like many others who developed a serious interest in Eastern religion and philosophy, Hesse was the son of missionaries who had spent many years in the East; he grew up in a milieu saturated with mementoes of the Orient, some of them lovingly described in several of his autobiographical sketches. Hesse made several visits to the East (not entirely happy experiences) and retained throughout his life an abiding interest in Eastern spirituality and in a synthesis of religious ideas from East

---

61 E. Fromm, "Psychoanalysis and Zen" in Erich Fromm, D.T. Suzuki & Richard De Martino, *Zen Buddhism and Psychoanalysis*, 135.

and West.[62] He was also deeply influenced, like so many European writers of his generation, by the ideas of Freud and Jung—consider, for instance, his fictional exploration of the fragile "self" and the idea of multiple personalities in *Steppenwolf* (1927), a novel in which the European sense of anxiety and cultural dislocation is dramatically rendered. Although Hesse was awarded the Nobel Prize for Literature, largely on the basis of his last novel, *The Glass Bead Game* (1943), the zenith of his acclamation was probably the counter-cultural enthusiasm for his novels *Siddhartha* (1922) and *Journey to the East* (1931) which became obligatory reading for the more serious-minded hippies of the late 60s. In *Siddhartha* Hesse attempted a distillation of what he had learned of Eastern spirituality mingled with what he found most valuable in his own pietistic Protestant background. Many literary histories tell us that *Siddhartha* recounts the life of the Buddha, an error which might be avoided by actually reading the book! Those who have read the novel will remember the charming portrait of the Buddha, but it is only a vignette in the story of the protagonist who shares one of the Awakened One's several names. Also central to Hesse's intellectual and creative projects was the attempt to affirm and demonstrate the underlying unity of all the branches of the human race.

In a psychological context one of the most interesting of those who attempted to weld together existentialist concerns and Eastern ideas was the French psychiatrist Hubert Benoit (1904-1992). His book *The Supreme Doctrine: Psychological Insights in Zen Thought*, published in 1955, drew attention to Buddhism's central concern with the sources of mental suffering. Zen, wrote Benoit, with its emphasis on spontaneity and the non-intellectual process of "emptying out," could lead one into seeing one's own true nature.[63] At this point mention might be made of three other well-known psychologists who developed an interest in Eastern religion and spirituality sufficiently serious to impel extended visits to the sub-continent: the Swiss psychoanalyst Medard Boss, whose psychotherapy was also much influenced by Heidegger; Karen Horney, who spent some time in a Zen monastery in Japan; and the anti-psychiatrist R.D. Laing who practiced with Buddhist meditation teachers in Sri Lanka, Thailand and Japan.[64]

Hans Jacobs on Western Psychotherapy and Hindu *Sadhana*
Hans Jacobs was a former pupil of Jung, and a practicing psychotherapist who traveled to India to study yoga and Hindu metaphysics under properly qualified teachers. He spent over a year there, lecturing for a time at Benares

---

62 See particularly "Childhood of the Magician" (1923) and "Life Story Briefly Told" (1925) in Herman Hesse, *Autobiographical Writings*. See also Ralph Freedman, *Herman Hesse: Pilgrim of Crisis*, 149-156, and Hesse's "Remembrance of India" (1916) in *Autobiographical Writings*.

63 H. Benoit, *Zen and the Psychology of Transformation: The Supreme Doctrine*, rev. ed. (The title was changed for later editions.)

64 J.J. Clarke, *Oriental Enlightenment*, 158.

University, and studying and practicing yoga for several months at Kalimpong and Kedernath. In 1961 he produced one of the earliest and most thoughtful of what was to become a wave of works dealing with the relation of Western psychology to traditional psycho-spiritual disciplines and philosophy, *Western Psychotherapy and Hindu Sadhana*. Generally Jacobs managed to avoid the widespread and intensely irritating assumption that Western psychology was equipped to evaluate or to "confirm" the insights of Eastern traditions. (In much the same vein people are all too ready to talk of the ways in which modern physics "confirms" or "validates" ancient cosmological doctrines, as if these doctrines were hitherto suspect but have now been given the imprimatur of modern science. Rather, one might more properly speak in terms of some modern sciences, despite their limited epistemological base and their often highly flawed conceptual apparatus, becoming dimly and precariously aware of truths which were known to the ancients.) Among the many insights in Jacobs' book we find the following general remark:

> ... one may say, without much exaggeration, that the proper characteristic of Indian philosophy, a detailed exposition of the data and the possibilities of human consciousness, which alone gives man a status of his own ... has up till now been only rather inadequately faced in the Western world.[65]

Jacobs' book offers a judicious consideration of both Freudian and Jungian theory, identifying some of their innovations but also discussing the ways in which the Hindu tradition foreshadows their apparently new insights.

Humanistic and Transpersonal Psychology: Ken Wilber and others
A group of psychologists sometimes loosely gathered under the canopy of "humanistic psychology," prominently Abraham Maslow, Rollo May, Carl Rogers and Fritz Perls, reacted against the mechanistic models of behaviorist psychology and the medical orientation of psychoanalysis. We might characterize this school of thought as assigning more creative agency to the human individual than some other schools of contemporary psychology. Although none of these figures made a sustained study of Eastern doctrines and practices, "the whole flavor of their enterprise, with its emphasis on self-actualization and on the exploration and refinement of consciousness, has an Eastern tang to it."[66] One popular theme, for instance, taken up by both May and Maslow, was the need to overcome the Cartesian mind-body dualism so firm-

65 H. Jacobs, *Western Psychotherapy and Hindu Sadhana*, 18.
66 J.J. Clarke, *Oriental Enlightenment*, 158-159. Likewise John Rowan in his history of humanistic psychology, in 1976: "Humanistic psychology today contains many things which came originally from the East"; quoted in J.J. Clarke, *Oriental Enlightenment*, 159.
67 As Frithjof Capra has remarked, "Transpersonal psychology is concerned, directly or indirectly, with the recognition, understanding and realization of non-ordinary, mystical or 'transpersonal' states of consciousness, and with the psychological conditions that represent barriers to such transpersonal realizations. Its concerns are thus very close to those of the spiritual traditions..."; *The Turning Point*, 405.

ly entrenched in Western thought. Another was the interest in altered states of consciousness, evident in the Gestalt and Transpersonal Psychology of figures such as Claudio Naranjo, Stanislav Grof, Charles Tart and Ken Wilber.[67] Roberto Assagioli's theory of "psycho-synthesis," best displayed perhaps in his late work *Transpersonal Development* (1991), belongs to the same general school. In its affinity with spiritual traditions of both East and West, transpersonal psychology parts company with mainstream psychology which has retained its 19th century hostility to all forms of religion and spirituality as primitive "superstition," "neurosis" or "delusion."

Over the last four decades we note the burgeoning literature on such subjects as near-death experiences, psychedelics, out-of-body experiences and the like, all familiar subjects in the religious literature of the East: one might think, for instance, of the vast mystical literature of the Tibetans of which *The Book of the Dead* is but only one text. As one commentator has observed, "thinkers with interest in transpersonal states of being have generally felt it necessary to look to Eastern thought as a source of conceptual language, theoretical models, and practical guidance."[68]

The leading contemporary figure in this field is Ken Wilber whose work is concerned with a synthesis of scientific and mystical understandings of consciousness, drawn from both East and West. Wilber accepts the perennialist view that at the core of all religious traditions is a single, unifying truth to which mystical experience gives access. To account for the empirical variety of mystical experiences Wilber posits a hierarchy of consciousness, a series of six levels, rising from the uroboric or oceanic consciousness up to the supreme consciousness, that of *Dharmakaya*, beyond all dualities. Different forms of spiritual and psychological practice mesh into different levels of consciousness: many Western psychological approaches, such as that of Freud, only tap into the lower levels of consciousness while the metaphysical and mystical traditions, particularly Vedanta, access the highest reaches.[69] Wilber's work is shot through with the notions of wholeness, integration, unity. He has attempted to integrate the findings and insights of a staggeringly diverse range of sources, ancient and modern, Eastern and Western, scientific and mythological. Admirers such as Tony Schwartz believe Wilber to be "the most comprehensive philosophical thinker of our times" but he has also drawn fire from a wide range of critics. One sympathizes with Jack Crittenden's view that "Most critics have taken umbrage at Wilber's attacks on their particular field, while they condone or concede the brilliance of his attacks on other fields."[70] Wilber cannot be pinned down in any disciplinary field: his work is perhaps best described as a creative synthesis of philosophy,

---

68 J.J. Clarke, *Oriental Enlightenment*, 159.

69 For a sympathetic discussion of Wilber's basic schema see Bede Griffiths, *A New Vision of Reality*, Ch 2; for a critique of Wilber from a traditionalist perspective see J. Segura, "On Ken Wilber's Integration of Science and Religion."

70 J. Crittenden in K. Wilber, *The Eye of the Spirit: An Integral Vision for a World Gone Slightly Mad*, viii.

comparative mysticism, transpersonal psychology, and the new physics. He emerged, in Crittenden's words, as something of a boy wonder, publishing his first book, *The Spectrum of Consciousness* at age twenty-three and turning out a steady stream of arresting and provocative works ever since. Perhaps the most troubling aspect of Wilber's work is his commitment to evolutionistic paradigms, always inappropriate in the spiritual domain. To subscribe to any form of spiritual evolutionism is to fall prey to the preposterous notion that the teachings of the Buddha, of Jesus, of the ancient *rishis*, can be improved upon, as if Truth itself were subject to the contingencies of time. All of this is simply of a piece with the pervasive historicism of the prevailing Western mentality, one which all too often afflicts thinkers who in other respects are quite traditional and orthodox.

One particular debate which impinges on our subject concerns "left-brain" and "right brain" modalities of consciousness, the general argument being that the West has privileged left-brain activities to the neglect of those of the right brain—which is to say that modern European thought has over-valued rationality and verbally-centered mental processes (often associated with "masculinity"), and devalued the intuitive, imaginative, holistic and "feminine" modes and processes which, it is argued, are enhanced in Eastern meditation. The physicist Frithjof Capra states the matter in terms of the traditional Chinese polarities of *yin* and *yang*:

> Our society has consistently favored *yang*, or masculine values and attitudes, and neglected their complementary *yin*, or feminine counterparts. We have favored self assertion over integration, analysis over synthesis, rational knowledge over intuitive wisdom, science over religion, competition over cooperation, expansion over conservation ...[71]

One of the leading figures in this field is Robert Ornstein whose work has remained somewhat controversial since the appearance in 1977 of *The Psychology of Consciousness* whilst other investigators include the Nobel laureate and neurosurgeon, Roger Sperry, and Betty Edwards, author of the best-selling *Drawing on the Right Side of the Brain* (1979).[72]

Throughout the West there are a growing number of psychotherapists, thoroughly trained in at least one of the branches of Western psychology, who have turned eastwards for both theoretical insights and practical therapeutic techniques. There is a mushrooming literature in this field. Jack Kornfield's books stand out but we might also mention the Australian John Tarrant, a Jungian psychotherapist who is also a Zen roshi and the author of the recent and widely-hailed book, *Inside the Dark*, David Brazier, an English psychotherapist, Zen Buddhist and author of *Zen Therapy*, and Maura and Franklin Sills who teach Core-process Psychotherapy, firmly based on

---

71 F. Capra, *The Tao of Physics*, 1991 edition, 15.
72 See T. Schwartz, *What Really Matters*, 159-191, and B. Vinall, *The Resonance of Quality*.

Buddhist principles, at the Karuna Institute in Devon. Akong Rinpoche of Samye Ling has also developed a five-stage system of therapeutic training.[73] We can also see many Oriental traces, often unacknowledged, in the works of pop psychologists such as Louise Hay, Wayne Dyer and John Gray: various techniques of Eastern provenance, such as visualization exercises, the use of mandalas, breathing exercises and yogic postures, have become stock-in-trade. We also find in the contemporary West a great many thinkers and practitioners who are seeking to blend the insights of modern psychology with some of the traditional modes of understanding to be found in the Western heritage—Thomas Moore, Clarissa Pinkola Estés, Robert Sardello, and Jean Shinoda Bolen among them.

Mystical Experience, Meditation and Biofeedback

The study of mystical experience has been taken up in a variety of disciplines—anthropology (particularly through the study of shamanism and other "archaic techniques of ecstasy," to use Eliade's phrase), philosophy (the "cognitive status of the so-called mystical experience" is a staple of philosophy of religion courses), comparative religion, and psychology. The scope of the present work does not allow anything more than a passing glance at this vast and hazardous territory. A large part of the problem derives from the fact—already alluded to in the traditionalist critique of psychologism—that a purely psychological inquiry into mystical experience is doomed from the start as it is based on the false premise that the lesser (an empirical and quantitative psychology) can "explain" the greater (the plenary experience of the mystics). It is also a case of the conflation of the psychic and spiritual planes which constitutes one element of "the psychological imposture." The only psychology of mysticism likely to bear fruitful results is one which develops within the framework of a great religious tradition and which is guided by metaphysical principles—precisely what we find in the traditional "psychologies" and *sacra scientia* of the East (yoga, tantra, alchemy, the theory and practice of the mandala etc.), and precisely what we cannot find in Western psychology so long as it retains its pretensions as an autonomous and profane science—i.e., one which can proceed exclusively through empirical inquiry and analysis, and which is answerable to nothing outside itself.

Since the counter-culture of the 60s meditational practices of one sort and another have become increasingly popular in the West. In the psychological field, more narrowly defined, there has been a growing interest in the use of meditation to promote psychological well-being. Meditation itself has also come under stringent scientific investigation, in respect of both the

---

73 On Akong and Sills see S. Batchelor, *The Awakening of the West*, 364.

physiological and "mental" changes it induces. Elmer and Alyce Green and Dale Walters, drawing on the work of Hans Berger and Joe Kamiya, were among the pioneers of the use of biofeedback to quantify changes in consciousness bought about by meditative states and to demonstrate the linkages between mind and body in the treatment of illness. Their work was based at the Menninger Clinic in Topeka, Kansas, but also included several months in India where they used biofeedback equipment to measure the self-regulatory abilities of Indian yogis. This research included the famous case of the Indian yogi who was buried underground for eight hours, without any air supply and who was apparently able to voluntarily enter a state of deep rest requiring the most minimal levels of oxygen.[74] Back at the Menninger Institute the Greens also conducted experiments and demonstrations with another Indian yogi, "Swami Rama of the Himalayas," about whom Doug Boyd (Alyce Green's son from an earlier marriage) wrote *Swami*.

Biofeedback maps physiological changes in the subject—muscle tension, blood pressure, body temperature, brainwave activity. It also explores the way in which it is possible to bring various physiological processes under voluntary and conscious control and thereby change one's state of consciousness. Biofeedback, in Elmer Green's terms, "provides a bridge between the conscious and unconscious, voluntary and involuntary, cortex and subcortex, and even between reason and intuition."[75] Such work has had some beneficial clinical results (in the control of migraine headaches, the lowering of blood pressure, the alleviation of asthma and insomnia) and also tells us something of the physiological correlates of changes in consciousness. It has also promoted an acceptance of the fact that meditation can lower levels of stress, anxiety, depression and neurosis, and promote feelings of self-worth and authenticity. However, as an "explanation" of meditative states and mystical experiences it remains drastically reductionist and one-dimensional.[76]

C. The Lessons of the East

Some of the figures under discussion have had a part to play in the "deprovincializing" of Western culture, that is to say, in overcoming the limits of our own restrictive Eurocentric assumptions and values at a time when, more than ever before, we need to be open to the lessons of other cultures. The most fertile connections between Eastern spirituality and Western psychology arise out of an interest in consciousness. Andrew Rawlinson usefully articulates four principles which inform most Oriental understandings of the human condition: 1. Human beings are best understood in terms of con-

---

74 T. Schwartz, *What Really Matters*, 141. On the Greens and biofeedback see 117-154.

75 T. Schwartz, *What Really Matters*, 119.

76 Of the myriad books in this field one of the more sober and interesting is *Silent Music*, by William Johnston.

sciousness and its modifications; 2. Consciousness can be transformed by spiritual practices; 3. There are teachers and exemplars who have done this; and 4. They can help others to do the same through some form of transmission. One cannot maintain any vaguely serious interest in Eastern spirituality without being interested in consciousness and in the nature of the "self"— in short, in psychology. Alan Watts, rather recklessly, went so as far as to say this:

> If we look deeply into such ways of life as Buddhism and Taoism, Vedanta and Yoga, we do not find either philosophy or religion as these are understood in the West. We find something more nearly resembling psychotherapy ... The main resemblance between these Eastern ways ... and Western psychotherapy is the concern of both with bringing about changes in consciousness, changes in our own ways of feeling our own existence and our relation to human society and the natural world.[77]

Looking at the large canvas, what might we discern as the theoretical and practical lessons of Eastern teachings? There is a great deal to be learned from Eastern traditions which have, for thousands of years, focused attention on the mysteries of human consciousness and on the problematic nature of the self. As Ramana Maharshi observed, there is one great philosophical, and we might say psychological, question which subsumes all others: "Who am I?" The principal lesson deriving from these traditions would seem to be that the "self" with which most of us identify ourselves, is a psycho-physical construct in a state of permanent change, itself without any permanence, and with no more than an evanescent or fugitive reality. Furthermore, the secret of human happiness, so such traditions teach, ultimately lies not in any rehabilitation or bolstering up of this egoic self, but in liberation from it, more particularly in detachment from what Chögyam Trungpa has called "the bureaucracy of the ego,"[78] a process Hubert Benoit calls "the integral devalorization of the egotistical life."[79] One Western psychologist has recently contrasted, in very general terms, the differing approaches of Western psychology and Buddhism to the problem of the self:

> Western psychology makes much ... of the importance of a coherent self-image and of high self-esteem. It is healthy to have a clear sense of one's own identity and a feeling of autonomy, and to value oneself and one's achievements. Buddhism denies the existence of a self as a distinct entity ... The self is merely a construction, and yet it refers everything to itself and distorts experience. The goal is thus not to try further to enhance the self, but to undermine it.

---

77 A. Watts, *Psychotherapy East and West*, x. See also F. Capra, *The Turning Point*, 167-168. Recall, too, Jung's claim that "... all religions, down to the forms of magical religion of the primitives, are psychotherapies, which treat and heal the sufferings of the soul, and those of the body that come from the soul." C.G. Jung in a 1935 paper on psychotherapy, cited in G. Wehr, *Jung: A Biography*, 293.

78 See Chögyam Trungpa, *Cutting Through Spiritual Materialism*.

79 H. Benoit, *Zen and the Psychology of Transformation*, 26.

She points out that Western models of psychological health often emphasize the importance of predictability and control while Buddhism encourages detachment and an openness where "the task is not to engineer positive outcomes and avoid negative ones, but to transcend all attachments and aversions."[80] Nothing could be further from the mechanistic theories of behaviorist psychology: one need only think of the title of one of the most influential, pernicious and degrading works of our time, *Beyond Freedom and Dignity* by B.F. Skinner.

One might also suggest that at a time when the destructive consequences of Western dualisms, particularly that of subject and object, are becoming ever more apparent, not least in the so-called environmental crisis, there is a great deal to learn from Eastern teachings which "emphasize the basic unity of the universe" and in which

> The highest aim of their followers—whether they are Hindus, Buddhists or Taoists—is to become aware of the unity and mutual interrelation of all things, to transcend the notion of an individual isolated self and to identify themselves with ultimate reality.[81]

Secondly, Eastern traditions, such as Tibetan Buddhism, can provide us with highly sophisticated maps of consciousness, and of states of being, which take account not only of what Freud termed the "subconscious" but also the "supra-conscious," a realm of experience accessible through the individual psyche but by no means bound by it. To cite one example of such a map: the Buddhist Wheel of Life is not only a representation of various post-mortem states but is simultaneously a figuration of various states of consciousness and of the psychic mechanisms which bring them about. Such maps alert us to the limitations of materialistic and mechanistic accounts of consciousness in particular, and of the Cartesian and Newtonian paradigms of scientific inquiry in the West. As Frithjof Capra has observed,

> A science concerned only with quantity and based exclusively on measurement is inherently unable to deal with experience, quality, or values. It will therefore be inadequate for understanding the nature of consciousness, since consciousness is a central aspect of our inner world, and thus, first of all, an experience ... The more scientists insist on quantitative statements, the less they are able to describe the nature of consciousness.[82]

This last observation is critical. Unless we wish to surrender to materialist reductionisms of various ilk then we must accept the very far-reaching implications of Capra's claim that consciousness is simply not amenable to a quantitative analysis. Recall, too, Jung's admonition that, "Overvalued reason has

---

80 C. Ray, "Western Psychology and Buddhist Teachings: Convergences and Divergences," 21.
81 F. Capra, *The Tao of Physics*, 29.
82 F. Capra, *The Turning Point*, 415.

this in common with political absolutism: under its dominion the individual is pauperized."[83]

In this context it must be observed that whilst Western psychology might learn a great deal from Buddhism as a psychological system, the teachings and practices of this tradition amount to something much more. In his autobiography Carl Jung said this: "The decisive question for man is: Is he related to something infinite or not? That is the telling question of his life."[84] One can only say that all Western attempts, especially by those with a tendentious agenda, to reduce Buddhism to one of its elements must be resisted, like all the manifold forms of an inveterate reductionism to which the modern scientific mentality is particularly vulnerable. We must always remember that Buddhism, like all religions, answers Jung's question in the affirmative. In so doing it parts company with all secular and humanistic "psychologies," including warm-and-fuzzy New Ageism which appropriates the term "spirituality" only to empty it of all meaning by wrenching it from its religious context.

On the practical level perhaps the most central lesson of the East is that various techniques of self-inquiry, such as meditation, are therapeutic in the broadest possible sense, which is to say that they are not meant only, or even primarily, for the "mentally ill" or the "maladjusted" individual, but for everyone. Indeed, from a certain perspective, we are *all* "mentally ill" and "maladjusted"! A Western professor of child psychology, asked recently why Westerners, and particularly psychologists, might profitably show some interest in Buddhism, wrote this:

> At its simplest level, the answer for the psychologist lies in the profound effect that Buddhism appears to have upon human behavior, an effect that many of us would accept is highly beneficial in that it promotes psychological health. That is, if by psychological health we mean the ability to live in harmony with oneself and nature, to show tolerance and compassion to one's fellow human beings, to endure hardship and suffering without mental disintegration, to prize non-violence, to care for the welfare of all sentient beings, and to see a meaning and purpose in one's life that allows one to enter old age or to face death with serenity and without fear ... The most obvious reason for psychologists to interest themselves in Buddhism, therefore, is the issue of psychological health (their own as well as their clients'!)[85]

Similarly, Rawlinson writes of a spiritual psychology of the East which, far from being concerned only with some ethereal and "mystical" condition, touches on all aspects of life:

> what it is to be alive, to be born, to have a body, to die; the nature of sickness and suffering, of happiness and love; what it is to be male, female, heterosexual, homosexual; what it is to be a child, a parent; the nature of the

83 C.G. Jung, *Memories, Dreams, Reflections*, 333.
84 C.G. Jung, *Memories, Dreams, Reflections*, 356-357.
85 D. Fontana, "Mind, Senses and Self," 35.

family (and its alternatives ...); how society should be organized and according to what principles; how one should eat, dress and earn one's living; the proper form of the arts ...; the world and its origin; how consciousness works from the most mundane levels to the most rarefied ...[86]

Huston Smith has usefully summarized eight psychological insights which have informed the Indian tradition for at least two millennia and to which the West is only now becoming sensitive. It is worth paraphrasing his catalogue (with a few minor modifications):

• Our consciousness is multi-layered, some levels being difficult of access to everyday awareness.
• The human being is a psycho-physical whole in which there is continuous and subtle interaction between these two aspects.
• In addition to the gross material body there exists a subtle body or sheath, still physical but subtle and invisible.

• With respect to the operations of the mind we must distinguish between rational, critical, analytical thought and deeper, more synthetic, symbolic and intuitive modes.

• The basic emotions are governed not by the superficial mind but by deeper forces.

• What we perceive is not a simple reflection of the external "objective" world "out there" but is, in part, a function or projection of the perceiving organism.

• That life as we normally experience it is dislocated or out of joint (*dukkha*) and that the root cause of this is *tanha*, the drive to maintain a separate egoic existence.[87]

To imagine that we have nothing to learn from this vast body of experience and knowledge, in its myriad forms, is not only insufferably arrogant and provincial, but also, not to put too fine a point on it, obtuse in the extreme. Let us conclude with some hopeful words from the physicist and proponent of the Uncertainty Principle, Werner Heisenberg:

It is probably true quite generally that in the history of human thinking the most fruitful developments frequently take place at those points where two different lines of thought meet. These lines may have their roots in quite different parts of human culture, in different times or different cultural environments or different religious traditions: hence, if they actually meet, that is, if they are at least so much related to each other that real interaction can take place, then one may hope that new and interesting developments may follow.[88]

86 A. Rawlinson, *The Book of Enlightened Masters*, xvii-xviii.
87 See H. Smith, *Essays on World Religion*, 10-11.
88 Heisenberg quoted in F. Capra, *The Tao of Physics*, 6.

13.

Eastern Currents in Western Philosophy and Science

A. Conditions for a Meaningful Comparative Philosophy: S.H. Nasr—The Traditionalist Perspective on Metaphysics and Philosophy **B. Existentialism and the East:** Nietzsche—Heidegger—Buber—Tillich **C. The Intellectual and Spiritual Bankruptcy of Modern Science D. Eastern Influences on New Scientific Paradigms**

The possession of all the sciences, if unaccompanied by the knowledge of the best, will more often than not injure the possessor. (Plato)[1]

European philosophers have been guilty of the insularity which afflicts so many of their counterparts in other disciplines. Many books purporting to give us a history of philosophical thought or some kind of conspectus of philosophical trends within a given period still assume that "philosophy" and "Western philosophy" are synonymous. Eastern philosophical thought is all too often ignored, marginalized or treated as a kind of fumbling proto-philosophy, hopelessly mired in religious superstition. As Wilhelm Halbfass has demonstrated, the dominant trend in Western histories of philosophy has been to disqualify the Orientals altogether. Early exceptions, such as the German Sanskritist Paul Deussen and the Russian orientalist Theodore Stcherbatsky, only confirm the rule.[2] Here is a characteristic 19th century formulation:

> Ancient philosophy is essentially Greek philosophy ... That which the mind of other peoples and especially the Orient has aspired to in a related direction has remained more or less at the stage of primeval phantasies of the peoples. Everywhere, they lack the freedom of thought and the concomitant nobility of thought which tolerates the thralldom of myth for only a certain length of time and only in the infant stage of experience and thought.[3]

These days philosophers might be more cautious in expressing such flagrantly Eurocentric judgments, but the attitudes and values informing this cultural myopia remain alive and well amongst Western intellectuals. Rationalistic, positivist, materialist and pragmatic philosophers have generally, insofar as Eastern thought comes within their purview at all, adopted an altogether predictable and somewhat condescending stance, reserving

1 Plato in W. Perry, *Treasury of Traditional Wisdom*, 731.
2 On Stcherbatsky see P.V. Bapat, *2500 Years of Buddhism*, 343-344.
3 E. Dühring quoted in W. Halbfass, *India and Europe*, 153.

their meager approbations for those aspects of Eastern philosophy which are seen to be "rational," "humanistic," "empirical" and the like. Other influential modern philosophical movements, such as logical positivism and other schools in the analytic movement, have retreated into a rarefied and highly technical domain which has little connection with philosophy's traditional purpose, the study and pursuit of wisdom; indeed, they may be considered as proponents of what a German scholar has called "misosophy"—a hatred of wisdom.[4] They have also taken for granted that mysticism is necessarily antithetical to rationality and thus thrown the Eastern traditions out of the court of philosophy.[5] One might note in passing that African influences on the Western tradition are generally subsumed under the rubric of "Greek philosophy" (as if Hypatia, Augustine, Origen, Cyril and Tertullian were surrogate Greeks—a point made by the African philosopher Innocent Onyewuenyi.)[6]

But the picture is not completely bleak. Over the past two centuries there *have* been some creative philosophical engagements with the thought of the East, and some self-critical recognition of the intellectual parochialism of much Western thought. Although European orientalism has remained, to a large extent, locked in the historico-philological scholarship of the 19th century, since World War II it is no longer unusual to find Anglophone philosophers teaching comparative philosophy—one may mention such names as Charles Moore (the moving force behind the East-West Philosophers' Conferences in Hawaii), Dale Riepe, Arthur Danto, Charles Hartshorne, Robert Nozick, Ninian Smart, and Eliot Deutsch as well as Asian scholars who have worked in Western universities—Chang Chung-yuan, Garma Chang, J.N. Mohanty, J.L. Mehta, Arvind Sharma, Purisottima Bilimoria, to name a few.[7]

Earlier we glanced at the impact of Eastern religious and philosophical thought on German Romanticism, particularly through Schopenhauer, and on American Transcendentalism. In this chapter we will explore the Oriental concerns of several philosophers who can loosely be situated under the canopy of existentialism, that philosophical movement which has shown itself most receptive to Eastern influences. The latter part of the chapter will offer a few general remarks about the impact of Eastern thought on perceptions of Western science.

Over the past fifty years the academic field of comparative philosophy has emerged as one of the intellectual sites where the East-West encounter has produced some interesting results. Certainly the prospects have improved considerably since Thomas Merton, in 1964, wrote the following:

---

4 See S.H. Nasr, *Knowledge and the Sacred*, 43. See also I. Watson, "The Anti-Wisdom of Modern Philosophy."

5 See R. King, *Orientalism and Religion*, 28-34.

6 See R. King, *Orientalism and Religion*, 29.

7 See W. Halbfass, *India and Europe*, 162-163.

There have of course been spurious attempts to bring East and West together. One need not review all the infatuated theosophies of the nineteenth century. Nor need one bother to criticize the laughable syncretisms which have occupied the talents of publicists (more often Eastern than Western) in which Jesus, Buddha, Confucius, Tolstoy, Marx, Nietzsche, and anyone else you like join in the cosmic dance which turns out to be not Shiva's but just anybody's. However, the comparison of Eastern and Western philosophy is, in our time, reaching a certain level of seriousness and this is one small and hopeful sign. The materials for a synthesis of science and wisdom are not lacking.[8]

Tokens of this development include the East-West Philosophers' Conferences in Hawaii and the appearance of journals such as *Philosophy East and West*, and more recently, *Asian Philosophy*. Since the 70s there has also been a steady output of scholarly monographs in this field. A representative sample: Chris Gudmunsen's *Wittgenstein and Buddhism* (1977), Masao Abe's *Zen and Western Thought* (1985), Harold Coward's *Derrida and Indian Philosophy* (1990), and compilations such as *Heidegger and Asian Thought* and *Nietzsche and Asian Thought*, both edited by Graham Parkes, and *Buddhism and Western Philosophy* (1981), edited by Nathan Katz. In such books and in the dozens of disciplinary journals carrying the work of comparative philosophers and religionists one nowadays comes across any number of articles drawing connections and comparisons between the philosophical ideas, schools and movements of East and West: here Nagarjuna is compared to Kant, there Sankara to Eckhart, and over there is an inquiry into the relation between Hume's thought and Buddhism, or perhaps a comparison of the Buddha's teaching of *dukkha* and Kierkegaard's *angst*.[9] Such comparative philosophy also encompasses the impact on Eastern thought of Western philosophers. Scholars like Graham Parkes, for example, have traced the post-war Japanese and Chinese enthusiasm for both Nietzsche and Heidegger.[10] Less common is the analysis and evaluation of Western philosophical constructs in traditional Eastern terms. One of the salutary results of this kind of inquiry is to administer some shock-therapy to the over-valuation of a misperceived "originality" of this or that Western thinker: any scholar thoroughly familiar with Nagarjuna will be less likely to be seduced by claims along the lines of "Kant was the first to show ..."

It is not our present purpose to survey these rapidly proliferating and occasionally fertile inquiries but rather to consider the assumptions which often underlie them. Some thirty years ago Seyyed Hossein Nasr, at that time Dean and Professor of Philosophy at Tehran University, laid down the "conditions for a meaningful comparative philosophy." Before turning to partic-

---

8 T. Merton, *Gandhi on Non-Violence*, 3.

9 Some of the linkages and comparisons have become commonplace: Confucius: Aristotle; Mencius: Aquinas; Sankara: Eckhart, Spinoza, Kant, Bradley; Nagarjuna: Hume, Nietzsche, Heidegger, Wittgenstein, Derrida; Dogen: Heidegger.

10 See G. Parkes, "Nietzsche and East Asian Thought."

ular Western philosophical engagements with the East, it is worth revisiting Nasr's important essay from which, one would have hoped, many more comparativists might have derived considerable profit. We shall reinforce Nasr's argument by reference to some of his predecessors in the exposition of the perennial philosophy.

A. Conditions for a Meaningful Comparative Philosophy

S.H. Nasr

Early in his analysis Nasr states the nature of the problem which bedevils many of the enterprises of those scholars, of both East and West, who attempt some manner of comparative philosophy (referred to henceforth simply as comparativists):

> The Western students of Oriental doctrines have usually tried to reduce these doctrines to "profane" philosophy; and modernized Orientals, often burdened by a half-hidden inferiority complex, have tried to give respectability to these doctrines and to "elevate" them by giving them the honor of being in harmony with the thought of whichever Western philosopher was in vogue. On both sides, usually the relation of the "philosophy" in question to the experience or direct knowledge of the Truth, which is the source of this "philosophy," is forgotten and levels of reality confused.[11]

One of the principal sources of this confusion is a failure to understand the crucial distinction between metaphysics as a *scientia sacra* on one hand, wedded to direct spiritual experience and complementing revealed religious doctrines, and what is usually meant in the modern West by "philosophy," an autonomous and essentially *rational* and *analytical* inquiry into a range of issues and problematics. As Nasr observes,

> What is usually called Oriental philosophy is for the most part the doctrinal aspect of a total spiritual way tied to a method of realization *and is inseparable from the revelation or tradition which has given birth to the way in question.*[12]

Thus there is little common measure between the sapiential doctrines of the East which form part of a total spiritual economy and which draw on the wellsprings of revelation, tradition and direct experience, and those *mental* constructions of Western thinkers which are usually circumscribed by the various alliances of rationalism, materialism, empiricism and humanism which so dominate the "philosophical" thinking of the modern West. As the acidic Agehananda Bharati noted in reference to various Western excursions into comparative philosophy,

11 S.H. Nasr, "Conditions for a Meaningful Comparative Philosophy," 53.
12 S.H. Nasr, "Conditions for a Meaningful Comparative Philosophy," 55 (italics mine).

No effort, however valiant and well-meant, should disabuse us of the fact that nobody from Kant to Heidegger, Rorty and Derrida has been interested in *moksa* while nobody from Nagarjuna to Bhartrhari and Samkara has not.[13]

The only philosophers of the Western tradition who can meaningfully be compared with their Eastern counterparts are those theologians and metaphysicians who were indeed elaborating "the doctrinal aspect of a total spiritual way"—Plato, Plotinus, Eckhart, Aquinas, Bonaventura and the like.[14] On the other hand,

> To speak of rationalistic philosophy and Chinese or Hindu philosophy in the same breath is a contradiction, unless the word philosophy is used in two different senses: first as a wisdom that is wed to spiritual experience, and second as mental construct, completely cut off from it. A lack of awareness of this basic distinction has made a complete sham of many studies of comparative philosophy and has helped to reduce to nil the real significance of Oriental metaphysics. This metaphysics, far from being the object of mental play, has the function of enabling men to transcend the mental plane.[15]

A meaningful comparative philosophy can only proceed on the basis of a proper understanding of the different levels on which metaphysics, theology and philosophy (in the modern sense) are situated.[16] To approach a Sankara, a Nagarjuna, a Chuang-tse, through the categories of a profane and one-dimensional "philosophy," stripped of all reference to the transcendent and what this implies for the human destiny, is to fall prey to that most pernicious of modern prejudices—the notion that the greater can be reduced to and "explained" by the terms of the lesser:

> If a blind man were to develop a philosophy based upon his experience of the world derived from his four senses, surely it would differ from one based upon these four senses as well as upon sight. How much more would a "philosophy" based upon man's rational analysis of sense data differ from one that is the result of the experience of a world which transcends both reason and the sensible world? ... One must always remember the dictum of Aristotle that knowledge depends upon the mode of the knower.[17]

It is not only possible but highly desirable that scholars, equipped with the proper tools and cognizant of the profound differences between any tradi-

---

13 A. Bharati, review of Harold Coward, *Derrida and Indian Philosophy*, 340.

14 In this context it is worth recalling Bertrand Russell's assessment of St Thomas Aquinas in *A History of Western Philosophy* (453-54): "There is little of the true philosophic spirit in Aquinas ... The finding of arguments for a conclusion given in advance is not philosophy but special pleading. I cannot, therefore, feel that he deserves to be put on a level with the best philosophers either of Greece or of modern times." George Steiner was quite right to refer to Russell's history as "a vulgar but representative book" (*Heidegger*, 11).

15 S.H. Nasr, "Conditions for a Meaningful Comparative Philosophy," 55.

16 See K. Oldmeadow, *Traditionalism: Religion in the light of Perennial Philosophy*, Ch 8. (The discussion of the interrelations which follow is largely taken from this chapter.)

17 S.H. Nasr, "Conditions for a Meaningful Comparative Philosophy," 57.

tional civilization and the modern West, should illuminate the similarities and contrasts between the doctrines of the different religious traditions. In the case of comparative studies between traditional doctrines and the ideas of modern thinkers, such a task will necessarily foreground the chasm which separates them. It will also expose the hazards of glib formulations of similarities which exist only at relatively superficial levels. Furthermore,

> Oriental doctrines can fulfill the most fundamental and urgent task of reminding the West of truths that have existed within its own tradition but which have been completely forgotten ... Today it is nearly impossible for Western man to rediscover the whole of his own tradition without the aid of Oriental metaphysics. This is because the sapiential doctrines and the appropriate spiritual techniques ... are hardly accessible in the West, and "philosophy" has become totally divorced from the nature of the spiritual experience.[18]

The Traditionalist Perspective on Metaphysics and Philosophy

Thus far we have been considering the case against profane comparative philosophy as stated in a short but forceful essay by Nasr. To these considerations we can now add an exposition of the traditionalist understanding of the relationship of metaphysics and philosophy, highly pertinent to the subject at hand. As René Guénon observed more than once, metaphysics cannot properly and strictly be defined, for to define is to limit, while the domain of metaphysics is the Real and thus limitless. Consequently, metaphysics "is truly and absolutely unlimited and cannot be confined to any formula or any system."[19] Its subject, in the words of John Tauler, is "that pure knowledge that knows no form or creaturely way."[20] As Nasr observes elsewhere,

> This supreme science of the Real ... is the only science that can distinguish between the Absolute and the relative, appearance and reality ... Moreover, this science exists as the esoteric dimension within every orthodox and integral tradition and is united with a spiritual method derived totally from the tradition in question.[21]

The ultimate reality of metaphysics is the Supreme Identity in which all oppositions and dualities are resolved, those of subject and object, knower and known, being and non-being; thus a Scriptural formulation such as "The things of God knoweth no man, but the Spirit of God."[22] As Coomaraswamy remarks, in traditional civilizations, such as that of India, the philosophy, or

---

18 S.H. Nasr, "Conditions for a Meaningful Comparative Philosophy," 59.
19 R. Guénon, "Oriental Metaphysics," 43-44.
20 Tauler quoted in C.F. Kelley, *Meister Eckhart on Divine Knowledge*, 4.
21 S.H. Nasr, *Man and Nature*, 81-82. See also Coomaraswamy's undated letter to "M," *Selected Letters*, 10: "... traditional Metaphysics is as much a single and invariable science as mathematics."
22 *1 Corinthians* II.11. The Absolute may be called God, the Godhead, *nirguna Brahman*, the *Tao*, and so on, according to the vocabulary at hand. See F. Schuon, *Light on the Ancient Worlds*, 96, fn1.

metaphysics, provided the vision, and religion the way to its effective verification and actualization in direct experience.[23] The estrangement of metaphysics, philosophy and religion only appears in modern times.

Because the metaphysical realm lies "beyond" the phenomenal plane the validity of a metaphysical principle can be neither proved nor disproved by any kind of empirical demonstration, by reference to material realities.[24] The aim of metaphysics is not to prove anything whatsoever but to make doctrines intelligible and to demonstrate their consistency. Metaphysics is concerned with a direct apprehension of reality or, to put it differently, with a recognition of the Absolute and our relationship to it. It thus takes on an imperative character for those capable of metaphysical discernment.

> The requirement for us to recognize the Absolute is itself an absolute one; it concerns man as such and not man under such and such conditions. It is a fundamental aspect of human dignity, and especially of that intelligence which denoted "the state of man hard to obtain," that we accept Truth because it is true and for no other reason.[25]

Metaphysics assumes man's capacity for absolute and certain knowledge:

> The capacity for objectivity and for absoluteness is an anticipated and existential refutation of all the ideologies of doubt: if man is able to doubt this is because certitude exists; likewise the very notion of illusion proves that man has access to reality ... If doubt conformed to the real, human intelligence would be deprived of its sufficient reason and man would be less than an animal, since the intelligence of animals does not experience doubt concerning the reality to which it is proportioned.[26]

Metaphysics, therefore, is immutable and inexorable, and the "infallible standard by which not only religions, but still more 'philosophies' and 'sciences' must be 'corrected' ... and interpreted."[27] Metaphysics can be ignored or forgotten but not refuted "precisely because it is immutable and not related to change *qua* change."[28] Metaphysical principles are true and valid once and for all and not for this particular age or mentality, and could not, in any sense, "evolve." They can be validated directly in the plenary and unitive experience of the mystic. Thus Martin Lings can write of Sufism—and one could say the same of any intrinsically orthodox esotericism—that it

> ... has the right to be inexorable because it is based on certainties and not on opinions. It has the obligation to be inexorable because mysticism is the sole repository of Truth, in the fullest sense, being above all concerned with the Absolute, the Infinite and the Eternal; and "If the salt have lost its savor,

23 A.K. Coomaraswamy, "A Lecture on Comparative Religion" quoted in R. Lipsey, *Coomaraswamy: His Life and Work*, 275. See also "Vedanta and Western Tradition" in *Selected Papers 2*, 6.
24 See R. Guénon, *Oriental Metaphysics*, 53.
25 F. Schuon, *In the Tracks of Buddhism*, 33.
26 F. Schuon, *Logic and Transcendence*, 13. See also F. Schuon, *Esoterism as Principle and as Way*, 15ff.
27 Letter to J.H. Muirhead, August 1935, in A.K. Coomaraswamy, *Selected Letters*, 37.
28 S. H. Nasr, *Sufi Essays*, 86. See also F. Schuon, *Stations of Wisdom*, 42.

wherewith shall it be salted?" Without mysticism, Reality would have no voice in the world. There would be no record of the true hierarchy, and no witness that it is continually being violated.[29]

One might easily substitute the word "metaphysics" for "mysticism" in this passage, the former being the formal and objective aspect of the "subjective" experience. However, this is not to lose sight of the fact that any and every metaphysical doctrine will take it as axiomatic that every formulation is "but error in the face of the Divine Reality itself; a provisional, indispensable, salutary 'error' which, however, contains and communicates the virtuality of the Truth."[30]

In a discussion of Sankara's *Advaita* Vedanta Coomaraswamy exposed some of the crucial differences between metaphysics and modern philosophy:

> The Vedanta is not a "philosophy" in the current sense of the word, but only as the word is used in the phrase *Philosophia Perennis* ... Modern philosophies are closed systems, employing the method of dialectics, and taking for granted that opposites are mutually exclusive. In modern philosophy things are either so or not so; in eternal philosophy this depends upon our point of view. Metaphysics is not a system, but a consistent doctrine; it is not merely concerned with conditioned and quantitative experience but with universal possibility.[31]

Modern European philosophy is dialectical, which is to say analytical and rational in its modes. From a traditionalist point of view it might be said that modern philosophy is anchored in a misunderstanding of the nature and role of reason; indeed, the idolatry of reason could otherwise hardly have arisen. Schuon spotlights some of the strengths and deficiencies of the rational mode in these terms:

> Reason is formal by its nature and formalistic in its operations; it proceeds by "coagulations," by alternatives and by exclusions—or, it can be said, by partial truths. It is not, like pure intellect, formless and fluid "light"; true, it derives its implacability, or its validity in general, from the intellect, but it touches on essences only through drawing conclusions, not by direct vision; it is indispensable for verbal formulations but it does not involve immediate knowledge.[32]

Titus Burckhardt likens reason to "a convex lens which steers the intelligence in a particular direction and onto a limited field."[33] Like any other instru-

---

29 M. Lings, *What is Sufism?*, 93.

30 F. Schuon, *Spiritual Perspectives and Human Facts*, 162-163. Cf. A.K. Coomaraswamy: "... and every belief is a heresy if it be regarded as the truth, and not simply as a signpost of the truth"; from "Sri Ramakrishna and Religious Tolerance" in *Selected Papers 2*, 38. See also F. Schuon, *Sufism, Veil and Quintessence*, 2.

31 A.K. Coomaraswamy, "Vedanta and Western Tradition," *Selected Papers 2*, 6.

32 F. Schuon, *Understanding Islam*, 24. See also F. Schuon, *Stations of Wisdom*, 18ff.

33 T. Burckhardt, *Alchemy*, 36, fn1.

ment it can be abused. Much European philosophy, adrift from its religious moorings, has surrendered to a kind of totalitarian rationalism and in so doing has violated a principle which was respected wherever a metaphysical tradition and a religious framework for the pursuit of wisdom remained intact—the principle of adequation, articulated thus by Aquinas: "It is a sin against intelligence to want to proceed in an identical manner in typically different domains—physical, mathematical, metaphysical—of speculative knowledge."[34] This, it would seem, is precisely what modern philosophers are bent on. No less apposite in this context is Plotinus' well-known maxim "knowing demands the organ fitted to the object."[35] The grotesqueries of modern philosophy spring, in large measure, from an indifference to this principle. The situation is exacerbated further by the fact that many philosophers have been duped by the claims of a totalitarian scientism and thus suffer from a drastically impoverished view of reality and of the avenues by which it might be apprehended.

The place of reason, of logic and dialectic, in metaphysics is altogether more subordinate as the following sample of quotes makes clear. It is worth mobilizing several quotations as this issue is so often misunderstood, with bizarre results. From Schuon:

> In the intellectual order logical proof is only a quite provisional crystallization of intuition, the modes of which ... are incalculable. Metaphysical truths are by no means accepted because they are merely logically clear, but because they are ontologically clear and their logical clarity is only a trace of this imprinted on the mind.[36]

Or again:

> Metaphysics is not held to be true—by those who understand it—because it is expressed in a logical manner, but it can be expressed in a logical manner because it is true, without—obviously—its truth ever being compromised by the possible shortcomings of human reason.[37]

Similarly Guénon:

> ... for metaphysics, the use of rational argument never represents more than a mode of external expression and in no way affects metaphysical knowledge itself, for the latter must always be kept essentially distinct from its formulation ... [38]

Metaphysical discernment proceeds more through contemplative intelligence than through ratiocination. Metaphysical formulations depend more on symbol and on analogy than on logical demonstration, though it is a grave

34 Quoted in S. H. Nasr, *Man and Nature*, 35.
35 Quoted in E.F. Schumacher, *A Guide for the Perplexed*, 49.
36 F. Schuon, *Spiritual Perspectives and Human Facts*, 10.
37 F. Schuon, *Esoterism as Principle and as Way*, 28.
38 R. Guénon quoted in F. Schuon, *Stations of Wisdom*, 29, fn1.

error to suppose that metaphysics has any right to irrationality.[39] What many modern philosophers apparently fail to understand is that thought can become increasingly subtle and complex without approaching any nearer to the truth. An idea can be subdivided into a thousand ramifications, fenced about with every conceivable qualification and supported with the most intricate and rigorous logic but, for all that, remain purely external and quantitative for "no virtuosity of the potter will transform clay into gold."[40] Furthermore,

> ... that a reasoning might simply be the logical and provisional description of an intellectual evidence, and that its function might be the actualization of this evidence, in itself supralogical, apparently never crosses the minds of pure logicians.[41]

Analytical rationality, no matter how useful a tool, will never, in itself, generate metaphysical understanding. Metaphysicians of all ages have said nothing different. Sankara, for instance: "... the pure truth of *Atman* ... can be reached by meditation, contemplation and other spiritual disciplines such as a knower of *Brahman* may prescribe—but never by subtle argument."[42] The Promethean arrogance of much modernist thought, often bred by scientistic ideologies, is revealed in the refusal to acknowledge the boundaries beyond which reason has no competence or utility. This has, of course, prompted some quite ludicrous claims about religion. As Schuon remarks,

> The equating of the supernatural with the irrational is characteristic ... it amounts to claiming that the unknown or the incomprehensible is the same as the absurd. The rationalism of a frog living at the bottom of a well is to deny the existence of mountains: this is logic of a kind but it has nothing to do with reality.[43]

The intelligibility of a metaphysical doctrine may depend upon a measure of faith in the traditional Christian sense of "assent to a credible proposition." As Coomaraswamy observes

> One must believe in order to understand and understand in order to believe. These are not successive, however, but simultaneous acts of the mind. In other words, there can be no knowledge of anything to which the will refuses its consent ...[44]

This mode of apprehension is something quite other than the philosophical thought that

> ... believes it can attain to an absolute contact with Reality by means of analyses, syntheses, arrangements, filtrations and polishings—thought that is

---

39 See F. Schuon, *Esoterism as Principle and as Way*, 28.
40 F. Schuon, *Understanding Islam*, 149.
41 F. Schuon, *Logic and Transcendence*, 37.
42 Swami Prabhavananda & C. Isherwood (eds), *Shankara's Crest Jewel of Discrimination*, 73.
43 F. Schuon, *Logic and Transcendence*, 37.

mundane by the very fact of this ignorance and because it is a vicious circle which not merely provides no escape from illusion, but even reinforces it through the lure of a progressive knowledge which in fact is inexistent.[45]

It is in this context that we can speak of modern philosophy as "the codification of an acquired infirmity."[46] Unlike modern philosophy, metaphysics has nothing to do with personal opinion, originality or creativity—quite the contrary. It is directed towards those realities which lie outside mental perimeters and which are unchanging. The most a metaphysician will ever want to do is to reformulate some timeless truth so that it becomes more intelligible in the prevailing climate.[47] A profane system of thought, on the other hand, is never more than a portrait of the person who creates it, an "involuntary memoir" as Nietzsche put it.[48]

The metaphysician does not seek to invent or discover or prove a new system of thought but rather to crystallize direct apprehensions of Reality insofar as this is possible within the limited resources of human language, making use not only of logic but of symbol and analogy. Furthermore, the science of metaphysics must always proceed in the context of a revealed religion, protected by the tradition in question which also supplies the necessary supports for the full realization or actualization of metaphysical doctrines. The metaphysician seeks not only to formulate immutable principles and doctrines but to live by them, to conform his or her being to the truths they convey. In other words, there is nothing of the "art for art's sake" type of thinking about the pursuit of metaphysics: it engages the whole person or it is as nothing.[49] As Schuon states,

> The moral exigency of metaphysical discernment means that virtue is part of wisdom; a wisdom without virtue is in fact imposture and hypocrisy ... plenary knowledge of Divine Reality presupposes or demands moral conformity to this Reality, as the eye necessarily conforms to light; since the object to be known is the sovereign Good, the knowing subject must correspond to it analogically ... [50]

A point often overlooked: metaphysics does not of necessity find its expression only in verbal forms. Metaphysics can be expressed visually and ritually as well as verbally. The Chinese and Red Indian traditions furnish pre-eminent examples of these possibilities. Moreover,

44 A.K. Coomaraswamy, "Vedanta and Western Tradition," *Selected Papers 2*, 8. See also S.H. Nasr, *Knowledge and the Sacred*, 6.

45 F. Schuon, *Logic and Transcendence*, 34.

46 F. Schuon, *The Transfiguration of Man*, 4.

47 Here we are at the opposite end of the spectrum not only from the philosophical relativists but from those who hold a "personalist" or "existentialist" view of truth.

48 Nietzsche in *Beyond Good and Evil*, taken from *A Nietzsche Reader*, Extract 13. See also F. Schuon, *Logic and Transcendence*, 34 and *The Transfiguration of Man*, 4. (For a striking passage on both the grandeur and the "dementia" of Nietzsche's work see F. Schuon, *To Have a Center*, 15.)

49 See A.K. Coomaraswamy, "Vedanta and Western Tradition," *Selected Papers 2*, 9.

50 F. Schuon, *Roots of the Human Condition*, 86.

... the criterion of metaphysical truth or of its depth lies not in the complexity or difficulty of its expression, having regard to a particular capacity of understanding or style of thinking. Wisdom does not lie in any complication of words but in the profundity of the intention; assuredly the expression may according to the circumstances be subtle and difficult, or equally it may not be so.[51]

One is irresistibly reminded of the Buddha's Flower Sermon.

*

The relationship between metaphysics and theology, and theology and philosophy, demands a similar exposition. However, given that we are here primarily concerned with the practice of comparative philosophy we shall restrict ourselves to two passages from Schuon which go to the heart of the matter. From Schuon's *The Transcendent Unity of Religions*:

... intellectual or metaphysical knowledge transcends the specifically theological point of view, which is itself incomparably superior to the philosophical point of view, since, like metaphysical knowledge, it emanates from God and not from man; but whereas metaphysics proceeds wholly from intellectual intuition, religion proceeds from Revelation ... in the case of intellectual intuition, knowledge is not possessed by the individual insofar as he is an individual, but insofar as in his innermost essence he is not distinct from the Divine Principle ... the theological point of view, because it is based in the minds of believers on a Revelation and not on a knowledge that is accessible to each one of them ... will of necessity confuse the symbol or form with the naked and supraformal Truth while metaphysics ... will be able to make use of the same symbol or form as a means of expression while at the same time being aware of its relativity ... religion translates metaphysical or universal truths into dogmatic language ... What essentially distinguishes the metaphysical from the philosophical proposition is that the former is symbolical and descriptive ... whereas philosophy ... is never anything more than what it expresses. When philosophy uses reason to resolve a doubt, this proves precisely that its starting point is a doubt it is striving to overcome, whereas ... the starting point of a metaphysical formulation is always something intellectually evident or certain, which is communicated to those able to receive it, by symbolical or dialectical means designed to awaken in them the latent knowledge that they bear unconsciously, and it may even be said, eternally within them.[52]

This should be qualified by an observation Schuon makes in a more recent work,

In our first book [from which the preceding passage is taken] ... we adopted the point of view of Ghazali regarding "philosophy": that is to say, bear-

51 F. Schuon, *Understanding Islam*, 111.
52 F. Schuon, *The Transcendent Unity of Religions*, xxviii-xxx.

ing in mind the great impoverishment of modern philosophy, we simplified the problem, as others have done before us, by making "philosophy" synonymous with "rationalism."[53]

We have followed more or less the same procedure here and will only modify it with two brief points. Firstly, the term "philosophy" in itself "has nothing restrictive about it"; the restrictions which we have imposed on it in this discussion have been expedient rather than essential. Schuon has exposed some of the issues raised by both the ancient and modern use of the term in an essay entitled "Tracing the Notion of Philosophy."[54] Secondly, it must also be admitted that our discussion of the relationships of philosophy, theology and metaphysics has been governed by some necessary oversimplifications. From certain points of view the distinctions we have established are neither as clear-cut nor as rigid as our discussion has suggested. As Schuon himself writes,

> In a certain respect, the difference between philosophy, theology and gnosis is total; in another respect, it is relative. It is total when one understands by "philosophy" only rationalism; by "theology," only the explanation of religious teachings; and by "gnosis," only intuitive and intellective, and thus supra-rational, knowledge; but the difference is only relative when one understands by "philosophy" the fact of thinking, by "theology" the fact of speaking dogmatically of God and religious things, and by "gnosis" the fact of presenting pure metaphysics, for then the genres interpenetrate.[55]

It is only in the context of the considerations elaborated above, admittedly at some length, that we can return to the question of East-West comparative philosophy.

In the light of the preceding discussion it will come as no surprise that the scholars and thinkers whose comparative studies have produced the most impressive results are precisely those who have a firm purchase on traditional principles. Of the traditionalists themselves one must particularly mention the works of Ananda Coomaraswamy and Frithjof Schuon. Earlier in this work we have highlighted the role of René Guénon in explicating the metaphysical doctrines of the East in such works as *Man and His Becoming According to the Vedanta*. In the present context, however, he recedes somewhat into the background for several reasons to which some allusion was made earlier. Guénon proceeded on the basis of first principles with comparatively little concern for their historical manifestations and applications. His scholarship was sometimes precarious and he was entirely disdainful of modern thought in all its guises. To undertake comparative philosophy of the kind with which we are here concerned requires some sensitivity to the historical milieu in which traditional doctrines were given expression. Schuon

53 F. Schuon, Sufism, *Veil and Quintessence*, 123, fn10.
54 F. Schuon, Sufism, *Veil and Quintessence*, 115-128. See also F. Schuon, *The Transfiguration of Man*, 3.
55 F. Schuon, *Sufism, Veil and Quintessence*, 125.

and Coomaraswamy were much better equipped to undertake this kind of task. Nasr himself has produced some of the most authoritative works in the field of comparative philosophy but these have been concerned with the Islamic and Christian worlds, and thus fall outside the scope of the present study.

Ananda Coomaraswamy was one of the few scholars of the century who was equally at home in the worlds of Eastern and Western philosophy. Recall his observation that "my indoctrination with the *Philosophia Perennis* is primarily Oriental, secondarily Mediaeval, and thirdly classic."[56] His later work is saturated with references to Plato and Plotinus, Augustine and Aquinas, Eckhart and the Rhineland mystics, to Sankara and Lao-tse and Nagarjuna. Amongst his most profound studies in the field of comparative philosophy we find "The Vedanta and Western Tradition" (1939), "Recollection, Indian and Platonic" (1944), "*Akimcanna*: Self-Naughting" (1940), and "*Atmayajna*: Self-Sacrifice" (1942)—but one can turn to almost any of his later writings to find profound comparative exegeses. He was, of course, keenly interested in the philosophical underpinnings of traditional art, and produced two brilliant comparative works in *The Transformation of Nature in Art* (1934) and *The Christian and Oriental, or True, Philosophy of Art* (1939). Readers familiar with these works will not quarrel with the claim that they offer us a comparative philosophy of the most fruitful kind.

Much of Schuon's vast corpus focuses primarily on the Sufi tradition and on classical and Christian thinkers. Nonetheless, one is likely, at any turn, to come across illuminating references to Eastern metaphysicians and theologians, Sankara and Ramanuja being two to whom Schuon often refers. However, four of his works entail more detailed comparisons of Eastern and Western doctrines: *The Transcendent Unity of Religions* (1953), *Language of the Self* (1959), *In the Tracks of Buddhism* (1967) and *Logic and Transcendence* (1975). The last-mentioned work is also where Schuon confronts the profane philosophies of the modern period most directly.

Many traditionalist works also fall under the umbrella of comparative mysticism, the distinction between "philosophy" and "mysticism" being somewhat fluid in the traditional worlds of the Orient. In the academic domain we might say that comparative mysticism oscillates between philosophy and comparative religion. Impressive work has been done in this arena by several scholars and thinkers some of whom we have already encountered. Rudolf Otto's *Mysticism East and West* (1926), D.T. Suzuki's *Mysticism: Christian and Buddhist* (1957),[57] Toshihiko Izutsu's *A Comparative Study of the Key Philosophical Concepts in Sufism and Taoism* (1967) and Thomas Merton's *Zen and the Birds of Appetite* (1968) are amongst the more commanding works.

---

56 Letter to Artemus Packard, May 1941, A.K. Coomaraswamy, *Selected Letters*, 299.

57 Suzuki was, to some degree, guilty of what Richard King calls the "Buddhification" of Eckhart. See R. King, *Orientalism and Religion*, 157.

B. Existentialism and the East

Nietzsche

Schopenhauer's Eastern interests reverberated through the cultural and intellectual life of Germany in the 19th century, most significantly perhaps in the music of Wagner, the thought of Nietzsche and the scholarship of Paul Deussen. The potent friendship of Nietzsche and Wagner, and their reciprocal influences,[58] are well known but each was also closely acquainted with several prominent Indologists including Deussen, H. Brockhaus and E. Windisch in whose discoveries Nietzsche took a close interest.[59] However, he never made any systematic study of Buddhism or any other Eastern tradition: indeed the very notion of "system" was anathema to a thinker whose thought was often erratic and phosphoric. Comparativists have found some concordance between Nietzschean and Buddhist ideas, most evident in Nietzsche's themes of self-awakening, the eternal return, the over-man (*Übermensch*), "the transvaluation of all values," the meeting of extremes, the poetic and "metaphysical" significance of silence, and the Nietzschean rendering of the Zarathustra myth. It is not difficult to find passages in Nietzsche's writings with Buddhist and deconstructivist resonances and what Coomaraswamy called "characteristic mystic intuitions":[60]

> But everything has become: there are no eternal facts, just as there are no absolute truths.[61]

> What then is truth? A mobile army of metaphors, metonyms, and anthropomorphisms—in short, a sum of human relations, which have been enhanced, transposed, and embellished poetically and rhetorically, and which after long use seem firm, canonical, and obligatory ...[62]

> Every moment beginneth existence, around every "Here" rolleth the ball "There." The middle is everywhere.[63]

> Becoming must appear justified at every instant ... the present must not under any circumstances be justified by a future, nor the past be justified for the sake of the present.[64]

> ... the value of the world lies in our interpretation ... previous interpretations have been perspectival valuations by virtue of which we can survive in life ... the world with which we are concerned is false ...[65]

---

58 See L. Chamberlain, *Nietzsche in Turin*, Ch's 3 & 5.
59 See W. Halbfass, *India and Europe*, 124. On Wagner's Eastern interests see R. Schwab, *The Oriental Renaissance*, 438-444.
60 A.K. Coomaraswamy, *The Dance of Shiva*, 141.
61 From *Human, All Too Human*, in P. Novak, *The Vision of Nietzsche*, 44.
62 From "On Truth and Lie in an Extra Moral Sense" in P. Novak, *The Vision of Nietzsche*, 42.
63 Quoted in A.K. Coomaraswamy, *The Dance of Shiva*, 141.
64 Quoted in A.K. Coomaraswamy, *The Dance of Shiva*, 141.
65 Quoted in M. Abe, *Zen and Western Thought*, 139.

In recent years the apparent convergence of Nagarjuna, Nietzsche and post-modernist deconstructionism has attracted a great deal of interest. Glen Martin, for instance:

> Nagarjuna's dialectical analysis of the common categories by which people understand existence carries radical implications, somewhat comparable to those of Nietzsche's philosophy, in which a deconstructive process ultimately leads to the realization that both everyday existence and the categories by which we comprehend it are self-contradictory and incoherent.[66]

More interesting than these speculations about "concordances" (always suspect for reasons detailed already and to which Martin himself is sensitive) are the more visible Indian presences in Nietzsche's work.

Mervyn Sprung has argued that Nietzsche was not influenced by Indian thought in any significant sense.[67] It is probably true that Nietzsche's core themes and his intellectual trajectory would have remained much the same if he had remained in complete ignorance of Indian thought. Rather, his Oriental excursions allowed some philosophical replenishments. It was also the case that Nietzsche's understanding of both Hinduism and Buddhism was distinctively Schopenhauerian. Wilhelm Halbfass has identified two perspectives in which Indian thought figures in Nietzsche's philosophy. Firstly, his perception of the proud, "life-affirming," powerful and non-moralistic religion of the Aryan elite, nobly expressed in *The Law Book of Manu* which generates a contrast with the sickly, decadent and "egalitarian" "herd-religion" of Christianity which Nietzsche so vehemently berates. In *The Law Book*, which he bought in Turin, Nietzsche found "noble words everywhere, a feeling of completion, an affirmation of life, a triumphant, pleasant feeling about oneself and about life,—the sun shines upon the entire book," even though it rests on the usual "priestly lie." We are not surprised to find Nietzsche endorsing the caste system described in this Hindu Scripture. Secondly, Buddhism, like Christianity, is seen as a nihilistic, life-denying religion but one which is "freer, more aristocratic, and more cultivated."[68] Whilst both Christianity and Buddhism are both "decadence religions" (i.e., they appeal to morality and compassion), Nietzsche's withering contempt for Christianity is replaced by an almost tender nostalgia for a Buddhism which must give way to the great world affirmation and soteriology which Nietzsche himself envisaged. Buddhism, he wrote, expresses "a lovely evening, a perfect sweetness and mildness," free of *ressentiment*, a religion for "late men" who have become "over-spiritual and excessively susceptible to pain."[69] Buddhism is also elevated by its insistence on "self-salvation" and its refusal of theism. In short, Buddhism represents the highest and most refined form of what Nietzsche himself opposes—the denial of the world. Nietzsche took a similar

---

66 G.T. Martin, "Deconstruction and Breakthrough in Nietzsche and Nagarjuna," 91.
67 See M. Sprung, "Nietzsche's Trans-European Eye."
68 Nietzsche quoted in W. Halbfass, *India and Europe*, 126.
69 Nietzsche quoted in W. Halbfass, *India and Europe*, 126.

view of Vedanta (to which he was introduced by his friend Deussen) although he seems to have found it less attractive than Buddhism and wrote much less about it. (He did write in a letter to Deussen that the Vedanta was "the classical expression of the mode of thinking most alien to me.")[70] We also find in Nietzsche an anticipation of an East-West dialogue which might open up entirely new intellectual, even ontological, possibilities:

> I imagine future thinkers in whom European-American indefatigability is combined with the hundredfold-inherited contemplativeness of the Asians: such a combination will bring the riddle of the world to a solution.[71]

In 1884 Nietzsche himself resolved "to think *more orientally*" and the following year, in a letter to his sister, lamented that neither his health nor his finances allowed him to emigrate to Japan.[72]

Joseph O'Leary has suggested that the uncovering of analogies between Asian thought and European philosophy is less useful than a critique of thinkers such as Nietzsche from an Asian perspective. He argues that, in the end, Nietzsche's dalliance with Buddhism and his radical challenges to Western metaphysics "enacts a volcanic crisis of the West rather than any opening to the East."[73] Similarly, Graham Parkes, a leading scholar in the field of comparative philosophy and one alert to the dangers of over-emphasizing convergences, has reminded us that comparative studies provide a way of reflecting upon the Western tradition itself, and that, in Nietzsche's case, a comparison with Eastern thinkers bears directly on the endgame of the Western metaphysical tradition.

Heidegger

In this context another European philosopher irresistibly presents himself, Martin Heidegger, whom Clarke identifies as "the most important 20th-century philosopher to engage with the Orient"[74]—this despite the scanty explicit references to Eastern philosophy in Heidegger's writings:

> Heidegger's radical questioning of the entire Graeco-Christian metaphysical, logocentric tradition, culminating, he claimed, in modern scientistic and technological modes of thinking, with their calculative and objectifying tendencies, invites comparison with Eastern, and especially Chinese and Japanese, modes of thinking. It should not be surprising, therefore, that Heidegger, like so many other critics of the Western tradition, found an affinity with the more meditative and intuitive thinking of Taoism and Zen.[75]

70 16th March, 1883, quoted in J. L. Mehta, "Heidegger and Vedanta," 30.
71 Nietzsche in 1876, quoted in G. Parkes, "Nietzsche and East Asian Thought," 356.
72 G. Parkes, *Composing the Soul*, 358.
73 J.L. O'Leary, review of *Nietzsche and Asian Thought*, 93.
74 J.J. Clarke, *Oriental Enlightenment*, 114.
75 J.J. Clarke, *Oriental Enlightenment*, 115.

Indeed, in the mid-40s, in collaboration with a Chinese scholar, Heidegger embarked on a translation of the *Tao Te Ching*, a project which never came to fruition but which, so testified one of his students, gave his thinking a new slant in a period of extreme personal crisis (the de-Nazification proceedings).[76] In the inter-war period Heidegger also had some personal contacts at Freiburg with several Japanese philosophers of the Kyoto School, including Hajime Tanabe and Keiji Nishitani who later acclaimed Heidegger's work as a possible bridge between Japanese and Western thought.[77] Of D.T. Suzuki's work on Zen Heidegger remarked, "If I have understood Suzuki correctly, this is what I have been trying to say in all my work."[78] This observation has become a very well-worn coin.

As a young man Heidegger had aspired to the priesthood, but the path was blocked by his ill health. He developed a close interest in the apophatic mysticism of Meister Eckhart whose theology of "Divine Nothingness" and resistance to all forms of dualism shared philosophical and metaphysical ground with the intuitions of Eastern sages such as Nagarjuna and Sankara whom Heidegger was to encounter in his later explorations. (This theme was pursued in Suzuki's *Mysticism: Christian and Buddhist* and Otto's *Mysticism East and West*.) Both the Oriental and Occidental mystics were shaping influences in Heidegger's thinking about such pivotal concepts as "being," "time" and "nothingness" and his deconstruction of "metaphysical foundationalism."[79]

Michael Zimmerman identifies several important overlaps of Mahayanist and Heideggerian philosophy: suffering or inauthenticity arises from a mistaken understanding of the self as an entity; the release from the restricted self-understanding of dualistic egocentricism allows people and phenomena to appear as no longer separate and threatening but as profoundly interrelated; both discount the primacy of causality in their account of "reality"; both are more "cosmocentric" than "anthropocentric" although many scholars, both Japanese and European, have argued that Heidegger was never able to completely escape either the anthropocentricism or the metaphysical frame of the Western tradition.[80] Some of Heidegger's key ideas—such as "lettings things be" and his resistance to dualistic anthropocentricism—have been taken up in the deep ecology movement. Arne Naess, generally recognized as one of its leading lights, has drawn on Heidegger as well as Mahayana Buddhism in his attempt to dismantle the ontological man/nature dualism and to promote the idea that there is no "environment"

76 See O. Pöggeler, "West-East Dialogue: Heidegger and Lao-tzu," 51-52, and Paul Shi-yi Hsiao, "Heidegger and Our Translation of the *Tao Te Ching*," 93-103.
77 See G. Parkes, "Nietzsche and East Asian Thought," 366-367; G. Parkes, *Heidegger and Asian Thought*, 9-10; O. Pöggeler, "West-East Dialogue: Heidegger and Lao-tzu," 48.
78 Heidegger quoted in C. Schrag, "Heidegger on Repetition and Historical Understanding," 295.
79 See M. Zimmerman, "Heidegger, Buddhism and Deep Ecology." See also M. Zimmerman, *Eclipse of the Self*, 255-276.
80 See M. Zimmerman, "Heidegger, Buddhism and Deep Ecology," 255-259.

in which "people" move and act—rather, there is a field of inter-related, inter-dependent and constantly changing processes in which there are no ontologically stable entities (an idea to which we will return in a later chapter).[81]

Interesting in Heidegger's thought is his belief that the "Europeanization of the earth" has been brought about by a science and technology whose origins lie in the classical development of philosophy: the metaphysical tradition of the West is the pre-condition of its planetary domination. Halbfass comments,

> Heidegger's thesis concerning the Greek-European origin and essence of "philosophy" and "science" is no longer a self-confident proclamation of the uniqueness of Europe as it was for the historians of the nineteenth century ... It is, rather, a statement concerning a global predicament.[82]

To understand how the predicament of "Europeanization" has arisen we must not only interrogate the ancient Greeks, but enter "the inescapable dialogue with the East Asian world," even though this dialogue always stands in danger of itself being "Europeanized." In this context it is worth considering J.L. Mehta's conclusion to his essay on Heidegger and the Vedanta:

> If the bringing together of "Heidegger" and "Vedanta" is to have any sense it can only lie in enabling us to see that there is more to Vedanta—something that is its very own and yet unfulfilled—than providing those who are in revolt against the establishment (the religious, the Western metaphysical), and in flight from thinking, with a "mystical" alternative; that as a way or path of thinking, not so much as a doctrine, Vedanta may also have some relevance to that other task to which Heidegger points, the task of planetary thinking, in an age of homelessness and of the coming together of East and West in the extremity of fate ...[83]

Graham Parkes usefully asks why Western scholars have been so slow to take up the plea of Hans-Georg Gadamer (the most eminent of Heidegger's many illustrious students) that Heidegger's thought should be illuminated by serious comparative studies, a task begun at the University of Hawaii symposium, "Heidegger and Eastern Thought" in 1969. Parkes isolates several factors which shed some light on the problems attending the whole comparative enterprise: the dismissal of Heidegger as a "muddle-headed obscurantist" by many influential analytic philosophers; the "blatant chauvinism" of the analytic school in their even more peremptory dismissal of "Asian philosophy" as a "contradiction in terms"; the resistance to "poetic" and creative forms of philosophizing, common both to Heidegger (and existentialism in general) and the East, which go well beyond the bounds of logical ratiocina-

---

81 See P.R. Oldmeadow, "Buddhist Yogacara Philosophy and Deep Ecology."
82 W. Halbfass, *India and Europe*, 169.
83 J.L. Mehta, "Heidegger and Vedanta," 42.

tion;[84] the difficulties of fashioning an appropriate vocabulary able to do justice to the philosophical materials of both East and West.[85]

Buber
Martin Buber, the Jewish philosopher-theologian and for some years Professor of Comparative History of Religion at the University of Frankfurt, was another existentialist concerned with "Europeanization" and dialogue, particularly in the context of comparative mysticism. Although his scholarly focus was on Hasidic mysticism (a field in which he exchanged fire with Gershom Scholem) Buber showed an interest in Vedantic non-dualism and Buddhism early in his career, later turning to a deeper engagement with Zen and Taoism where the parabolic story-telling and use of cryptic humor revealed affinities with the Hasidic tradition. He also developed personal friendships with Eastern thinkers such as Rabindranath Tagore. Buber's most significant work on Eastern spirituality is probably the long essay "The Teaching of the Tao" (1911), published as an afterword to his translation, *The Parables of Chuang-tzu*. Although he later rejected the Taoist "mysticism of unity" in favor of his own mature philosophy, articulated in *I and Thou*, Buber regarded this essay "as an indispensable part of my way. I had to go through this encounter with mysticism in general and the Tao, in particular, to reach my own independent thought."[86] He also believed that the West had a great deal to learn from the Taoist teaching of *wu-wei*.[87]

Tillich
Paul Tillich, one of the Christian theologians most influenced by existentialist thought, was also interested in the "dramatic encounter of world religions," particularly the "conversation" between Christianity and Buddhism. He saw these living religions in a relationship of "polar tension," dramatized in the teleological, ontological and ethical oppositions implicit in their respective ideals of "*the kingdom of God*" and "*nirvana*."[88] During his visit to Japan in 1960 Tillich was gripped by an interest in the Zen understanding of *satori* and saw in Zen training elements of spiritual practice which might well be incorporated into Christianity (thus anticipating the emergent "Christian Zen").[89] Tillich is also interesting as an eminent Protestant theologian who abandoned the exclusive claims of Christianity, understanding each religion

84 Something of Heidegger's eclectic pedagogical method can be seen in his choice of texts for a lecture he gave in Bremen in 1960, entitled "Image and Word": a quotation from Augustine's *Confessions*, a Heracleitian fragment, Chuang-tzu's story of the bell-stand, and Paul Klee's Jena lecture on modern art. See O. Pöggeler, "West-East Dialogue: Heidegger and Lao-tzu," 55.

85 See Graham Parkes' Introduction to *Heidegger and Asian Thought*, 5-6.

86 Buber quoted in M. Friedman, "Martin Buber and Asia," 415.

87 Buber's engagement with Asian thought and spirituality is thoroughly and sympathetically discussed in M. Friedman, "Martin Buber and Asia," 411-426.

88 See M. Abe, *Zen and Western Thought*, 173-185.

89 J.J. Clarke, *Oriental Enlightenment*, 143.

as embodying partial accounts of the truth. An inevitable corollary was the jettisoning of the missionary enterprise in favor of conversation, Tillich famously remarking, "Not conversion, but dialogue. It would be a tremendous step forward if Christianity were to accept this."[90]

Other 20th century philosophers with more than a passing interest in Eastern ideas include George Santayana who followed in the footsteps of his predecessors at Harvard, Josiah Royce and William James, the existentialists Karl Jaspers and Maurice Merleau-Ponty, A.N. Whitehead, and F.R.C. Northrop.

C. The Intellectual and Spiritual Bankruptcy of Modern Science

In order to understand something of the role that Eastern wisdom might play in the resurrection of a science attuned to the whole of reality (spiritual and psychic as well as material, subtle as well as gross), it is necessary to take a rapid overview of the processes whereby a wholly profane and one-dimensional science has established its tyrannical reign over the European mind.[91] A decisive shift took place in the European worldview in the 17th century, through what we now think of as the Scientific Revolution: Descartes, Bacon, Copernicus, Galileo and Newton were amongst the seminal figures. The triumph of the scientific outlook inaugurated by such figures was more or less complete by the early 20th century: it provided the basis of the prevailing intellectual orthodoxies amongst the European intelligentsia. Modern science is not simply a disinterested and, as it were, a detached and "objective" mode of inquiry into the material world; it is an aggregate of disciplines anchored in a bed of very specific and culture-bound assumptions about the nature of reality and about the proper means whereby it might be explored, explained and controlled. It is, in fact, impossible to separate the methodologies of modern science from their theoretical base which we can signal by the term "scientism." Perhaps the central plank in the scientistic platform is the assumption that modern science contains within itself the necessary and sufficient means for any inquiry into the material world, and that it can and should be an autonomous and self-validating pursuit, answerable to nothing outside itself. This was a new idea in the history of human thought, radically at odds with the traditional view that the inquiry into the natural world could only proceed within a larger framework provided by philosophy and religion.

Modern science, as it has developed since the Renaissance, is flanked on one side by philosophical rationalism and empiricism which provides its theoretical rationale, and by technology and industry on the other, a field for its applications. It is rational, analytical and empirical in its procedures, materi-

---

90 P. Tillich, *Christianity and the Encounter of World Religions*, 1963, 95, quoted in J.J. Clarke, *Oriental Enlightenment*, 140.

alistic and quantitative in its object, and utilitarian in application. By its very nature modern science is thus unable to apprehend or accommodate any realities of a suprasensorial order. Science (a method of inquiry) becomes scientism (an ideology) when it refuses to acknowledge the limits of its own competence, denies the authority of any sources which lie outside its ambit, and lays claim, at least in principle, to a comprehensive validity as if it could explain no matter what, and as if it were not contradictory to lay claim to totality on an empirical basis. (Witness Stephen Hawking's absurd pretensions to a "theory of everything"!)

Critiques of scientism are much in vogue these days both from within the scientific community and from without. The insecure philosophical foundations of modern science, its epistemological ambiguities, its inability to accommodate its own findings within the Cartesian-Newtonian frame, the consequences of a Faustian pursuit of knowledge and power, the diabolical applications of science in the military industry, the dehumanizing reductionisms of the behavioral sciences—all of these have come under the most severe censure in recent times. Recent "discoveries" by physicists and the paradoxes of quantum theory throw conventional assumptions about time, space and matter into disarray: Heisenberg's Uncertainty Principle and Chaos Theory cuts the ground from under the "objectivity" on which science has so much prided itself; the mechanistic conceptions of a materialistic science, the very language of science, are found to be useless in the face of bewildering phenomena to which European science has until now been blind. Everywhere cracks are appearing in the scientific edifice. Titus Burckhardt, writing from a traditional viewpoint, exposes some of the issues involved here in writing that

> ... modern science displays a certain number of fissures that are due to the fact that the world of phenomena is indefinite and that therefore no science can ever hope to exhaust it; these fissures derive above all from modern science's systematic exclusion of all the non-corporeal dimensions of reality. They manifest themselves right down to the foundations of modern science, and in domains as seemingly "exact" as that of physics; they become gaping cracks when one turns to the disciplines connected with the study of life, not to mention psychology, where an empiricism that is relatively valid in the physical order encroaches in bizarre fashion on a foreign field. These fissures, which do not merely affect the theoretical realm, are far from harmless; on the contrary, in their technical consequences, they constitute so many seeds of catastrophe.[92]

Social commentators have become more alert to the dangers of a totalitarian materialism, an instrumentalist rationality and its attendant technology. We see that rationality has been allowed to become man's definition

---

91 For a decisive treatment of this subject, see *Science and the Myth of Progress*, ed. Mehrdad M. Zarandi.

92 T. Burckhardt, *Mirror of the Intellect*, 25-26.

instead of his tool. We sense that the disfigurement of the environment mirrors our internal state, that the ecological crisis is, at root, a spiritual crisis which no amount of science and technology can, of itself, remedy. We are awakening to the consequences of a science which answers to nothing but itself. In an era of nuclear threat, genetic engineering and unparalleled environmental vandalism Mary Shelley's nightmare vision in *Frankenstein* becomes a paradigm for our times. Commentators like René Guénon, Theodore Roszak, E.F. Schumacher, and Mircea Eliade awaken us to the provincialism of modern science and to the dangers of that Single Vision so fiercely denounced by William Blake.

Though modern science has doubtless revealed much material information that was previously unknown it has also supplanted a knowledge which infinitely outreaches it. As Gai Eaton has observed of the much-vaunted "discoveries" of modern science, "Our ignorance of the few things that matter is as prodigious as our knowledge of trivialities."[93] We see this in the complacencies and condescensions of those scientists who like to suppose that we have "outgrown" the "superstitions" of our ancestors.

It is nowadays a commonplace that many of the ills of our time stem from the rift between "faith" and "science" but few people have suggested any convincing means of reconciling the two. Certainly the effusions and anxious compromises of the liberal theologians and "demythologizers" are of no help, marking little more than a thinly-disguised capitulation of religion to science. However, in the light of traditional metaphysical understandings many of the apparent contradictions between "science" and "religion" simply evaporate. It is not necessary, to say the least, to throw religious beliefs on the scrap-heap because they are "disproved" by modern science; nor is it necessary to gainsay such facts as modern science does uncover—provided always that what science presents as facts are indeed so and not merely precarious hypotheses. Furthermore, there may be some convergences of the new physics and ancient metaphysical truths if their relationship is properly understood. After all, as Huston Smith reminds us, there are certain parallels between science-proper (as distinct from scientism) and religion:

> Both claim that: (1) things are not as they seem; (2) the other than the seeming is a "more"; indeed a stupendous more; (3) this more cannot be known in ordinary ways; (4) it can, however, be known in ways that are appropriate to it; (5) these appropriate ways require cultivation; (6) and they require instruments.[94]

The key to traditional understandings lies in the nature of their symbolism—a mode of knowledge quite inaccessible to the scientific mentality. No one will deny that, from one point of view, the earth is not the center of the solar system; this is no reason for jettisoning the more important truth which

---

93 Cited as an epitaph in *Tomorrow*, 13:3, 1964:191.
94 H. Smith, *Forgotten Truth*, 97-98.

was carried by the symbolism of the geocentric picture of the universe. Another example: it is preferable to believe that God created the world in six days and that heaven lies in the blue skies above the flat surface of the earth than it is to know precisely the distance from one nebula to another whilst forgetting the truth embodied in this symbolism, namely that all phenomena depend on a higher Reality which determines us and gives our human existence meaning and purpose. A materially inaccurate but symbolically rich view is always preferable to the regime of brute fact. In falling under the tyranny of a fragmentary, materialistic and quantitative outlook modern science is irremediably limited by its epistemological base. Of spiritual realities, modern science knows, and can know, absolutely nothing. Schuon:

> There is scarcely a more desperately vain or naïve illusion—far more naïve than Aristotelian astronomy!—than to believe that modern science, in its vertiginous course towards the "infinitely small" and the "infinitely great," will end up by rejoining religious and metaphysical truths and doctrines.[95]

The ways in which the triumph of scientism has contributed to man's dehumanization have been written about a good deal in recent years. It matters not a jot how quick contemporary scientists now are to disown discredited "facts" which stood between man and any true self-awareness—the mechanistic theories of the 17th century for instance—on the grounds that these were, after all, only provisional hypotheses which a more "humane" scientific vision can now abandon. The simple fact is that modern science cannot be "humanized" or "reformed" from within itself because it is built on premises which are both inadequate and inhuman. It is in this context that the wisdom of the East might be helpful in bringing us to a more adequate understanding of the human condition and our place in the tissue of relativities which comprise the visible cosmos.

D. Eastern Influences on New Scientific Paradigms

J.J. Clarke has remarked that "the link between science and Eastern philosophies is, on the face of it, an unlikely one."[96] However, as Clarke goes on to point out, the recent scientific interest in Eastern philosophies has many precedents stretching back at least to the Enlightenment. Buddhism, particularly, has repeatedly been enlisted by both philosophers and scientists in the attack on Western metaphysics and religion. Many Western Buddhists have been only too happy to see Buddhism deployed in this way. Thus Christmas Humphreys in 1951:

> The Buddhist attitude to all phenomena and to all teaching about it has ever been that of the modern scientist. Let all things be examined dispassionate-

95 F. Schuon, *Dimensions of Islam*, 156.
96 J.J. Clarke, *Oriental Enlightenment*, 165.

ly, objectively, assuming nothing, testing all, for such was the Buddha's own injunction to his followers.[97]

Indeed, there is a long line of European thinkers who have wished to "reconcile" a religious outlook exemplified in the Eastern traditions with modern science, by-passing the "illusions," "pitfalls" and "obsolete doctrines" of the Occidental religions. Sir John Woodroffe, Aldous Huxley, Christopher Isherwood and Gerald Heard are just a few who have trimmed their sails to this prevailing fashion. We will here leave aside the question of how far such enthusiasts for Eastern ideas have painted them in the colors of their own liberal-secular-rationalist outlook (an issue touched on elsewhere in this study). We may find their counterparts in the East, sympathetic to modern Western science and eager to assimilate its discoveries into their own indigenous philosophic and scientific traditions: Radhakrishnan, Aurobindo and Tagore might stand as three Indian representatives.[98] Here, however, we must turn our attention specifically to the implication of Eastern thought in the recent constructions of new scientific paradigms.[99]

Frithjof Capra's *The Tao of Physics* (1975) heralded a spate of books which, in one way or another, aligned themselves *with* "Eastern" modes of thought and experience, and *against* the hyper-rationalistic, mechanistic, instrumentalist and masculinist paradigm of the Cartesian-Newtonian science which has dominated the West since the 17th century. Capra was by no means the first to venture into this field. Back in the 30s no less a figure than Carl Jung, through his collaboration with Wolfgang Pauli, had surmised some congruities between an emergent quantum theory and the principles which informed the *I Ching*. Jung's great theme of the marriage of the opposites was also suggestive for those thinkers seeking a more organic and holistic understanding, as was his work *Synchronicity*. At about the same time several physicists were further undermining the epistemological base of an atomistic paradigm and of what Capra calls the "billiard ball theory of the universe" (i.e., the idea that the universe comprises empty space in which discrete objects move about, their relations being governed by the laws of gravity etc.), a theory already teetering in the wake of Einstein's theory of relativity. Over the next few decades the "new physics" developed a whole new repertoire of models, hypotheses and terms—the indeterminacy principle, quantum theory, quarks, photons, bootstrapping, probability waves, wave packets, time-reversal, dark matter, superstring theory, and the like entered scientific discourse. However bewildering all this was to lay people it was clear that the Newtonian model was rapidly crumbling.

---

97 C. Humphreys, *Buddhism*, 223, quoted in J.J. Clarke, *Oriental Enlightenment*, 166.

98 See H.P. Sinha, *Religious Philosophy of Tagore and Radhakrishnan*. For some critical remarks about Aurobindo see Rama P. Coomaraswamy, "The Desacralization of Hinduism for Western Consumption."

99 A consideration of the relation of such paradigms to ecological movements, and the involvement of Western adherents of Eastern religious traditions in "green" politics will be delayed until the next chapter.

Several of the scientists most closely involved in these developments—Niels Bohr, Werner Heisenberg and Erwin Schrödinger—had serious Oriental interests. The Danish physicist related his leading idea of complementarity to the Chinese motif of *yin-yang* and incorporated its symbol into his own coat of arms. He claimed that

> For a parallel to the lesson of atomic theory ... [we must turn] to those kinds of epistemological problems with which already thinkers like the Buddha and Lao Tzu have been confronted, when trying to harmonize our position as spectators and actors in the great drama of existence.[100]

Heisenberg, whose Uncertainty Principle delivered a lethal blow to a naïve materialism,[101] visited India in the 30s and through his friendship with figures such as Rabindranath Tagore and Anagarika Govinda, deepened his understanding of both Hindu and Buddhist cosmology. He posited "a certain relationship between philosophical ideas in the tradition of the Far East and the philosophical substance of quantum theory."[102] Schrödinger re-traced the paths taken by Schopenhauer, Max Müller and Paul Deussen in their Indological inquiries and was an avid reader of Eastern Scriptures. He found in the Vedanta a foundation for a unified vision of reality, one more consonant with new scientific findings than the traditional Judeo-Christian worldview.[103] As is well known, Robert Oppenheimer was a student of Eastern religions and was closely familiar with the *Bhagavad Gita*. In 1954, Oppenheimer wrote.

> The general notions of human understanding ... which are illustrated by discoveries in atomic physics are not in the nature of things wholly unfamiliar, wholly unheard of, or new. Even in our own culture they have a history, and in Buddhist and Hindu thought a more considerable and central place. What we find here is an exemplification, an encouragement, and a refinement of old wisdom.[104]

In the same year as *The Tao of Physics* appeared, Jacob Needleman published *A Sense of the Cosmos*, another book which marked the growing disenchantment of the western intelligentsia with the epistemological foundations of post-medieval science. The book's sub-title signaled its central theme: the encounter of modern science and ancient truth. Needleman (a philosopher, psychologist and comparativist rather than a physicist) rehearsed the theoretical inadequacies and the disastrous effects (psychic, social, environmen-

---

100 Bohr quoted in F. Capra, *The Tao of Physics*, 16.
101 The Uncertainty Principle was nicely defined by Sir Arthur Eddington as "Something unknown is doing we know not what." Eddington quoted on cover of K. Wilber (ed), *Quantum Questions*.
102 F. Capra, *The Tao of Physics*, 17.
103 On Bohr, Heisenberg and Schrödinger see J.J. Clarke, *Oriental Enlightenment*, 167-169. For extracts from the "mystical" writings of such physicists, see K. Wilber (ed), *Quantum Questions*. Schrödinger's reflections on the Vedanta can be found on pages 91-97.
104 Oppenheimer quoted in F. Capra, *The Tao of Physics*, 16.

tal) of the mechanistic, materialist worldview and drew not only on Indian and Chinese sources but on the traditions of Tibet and ancient Egypt as well.

> For several centuries Western civilization has operated under the assumption that man can understand the universe without understanding himself. But having turned the available energy of our minds towards the external world, we now find ourselves more perplexed and anxious than ever in front of a reality that simply will not yield to our hopes and desires ... Now—fitfully and with great uncertainty—it seems we are being called back from the impulse to believe we can stride into nature with our mind pointed outward like an unsheathed sword ... New teachings about man and his place in the cosmos are entering our culture from the Orient and the ancient worlds. These teachings from India, Tibet, China and the Middle East; these ideas from the priests of Pharaonic Egypt and from the mystics and alchemists of antiquity now exist among us like the whisperings of another reality. And the discoveries of science about the organic interconnection of all things from the atomic nucleus to the unfathomed psyche of man to the inconceivable entities of cosmic space, in a like manner invite us to something greater than the search for additional facts and explanations.[105]

Following in the wake of Capra and Needleman came such books (of widely varying degrees of distinction) as Sukie Colegrave's *The Spirit of the Valley* (1979), Gary Zukav's *The Dancing Wu Li Masters* (1980), David Bohm's *Wholeness and the Implicate Order* (1980), Ken Wilber's *The Holographic Paradigm and Other Paradoxes* (1982) and *Quantum Questions: Mystical Writings of the World's Great Physicists* (1984), Bede Griffiths' *A New Vision of Reality* (1989), Rupert Sheldrake's *The Rebirth of Nature* (1994) and John Broomfield's *Other Ways of Knowing* (1997). Many of these books, by now constituting a kind of sub-genre which melded insights from the new physics, transpersonal psychology and archaic mythology as well as the Eastern traditions, rehearse and elaborate themes first introduced to a general audience in Capra's *The Tao of Physics*. Capra himself has since contributed to many conferences, seminars and anthologies concerned with the relationship of science and spirituality. It comes as no surprise that Capra's book (and his work in general) has received a rather frosty reception in the Western scientific establishment.

The Tao of Physics reaffirms the centrality of consciousness and the role of the conscious subject in any unified theory of reality, a theme explored by Carl Jung in his ruminations on Eastern texts and reinforced by Heisenberg's re-iteration of one of the key ideas in Eastern cosmologies: "the same regulating forces, that have created nature in all its forms, are responsible for the structure of our psyche and also for our capacity to think."[106] Following Heisenberg, Capra subverts the mind-body dualism which has been so foundational to modern Western philosophy and science. He

---

105 J. Needleman, *A Sense of the Cosmos*, 1-2.
106 Heisenberg quoted in *Creative Meditation and Multi-Dimensional Consciousness*, 31.

returns repeatedly to traditional Eastern formulations which emphasize the unity of the universe, its integrity as a single, organic whole. Ideas about the "inter-wovenness," "inter-relatedness," "inter-connectedness," "inter-dependence" of all phenomena run through Capra's work which frequently resorts to the mystical literature of the East to polish and enhance the findings of the new sciences. Unlike some of his successors, Capra is not so foolish as to imagine that Eastern mysticism is "verified" or "validated" by modern scientific "discoveries," nor does he advocate any kind of "synthesis" of the two. Rather, he draws on Eastern mystical traditions to create a new climate of understanding, one which will help to heal the disastrous Western breach between "science" and "religion" and, he hopes, make his readers more receptive to a range of values and insights drawn from culturally divergent sources.

Capra's central thesis is encapsulated in his Epilogue where he sums up his findings:

> ... the principal theories and models of modern physics lead to a view of the world which is internally consistent and in perfect harmony with the views of Eastern mysticism ... The mechanistic world view of classical physics is useful for the description of the kind of physical phenomena we encounter in our daily life ... and it has proved extremely successful as a basis for technology ... Beyond the dimensions of our everyday environment, however, the mechanistic concepts lose their validity and have to be replaced by organic concepts which are very similar to those used by the mystics ... What we need ... is not a synthesis but a dynamic interplay between mystical intuition and scientific analysis ...[107]

He goes on to argue that this "dynamic interplay" must be achieved not only in the intellectual and theoretical realm but in a "cultural revolution in the true sense of the word." Our civilization's capacity to survive and grow may well depend, Capra argues, on our ability to absorb some of the *yin* ideal of Eastern mysticism so that we may properly "experience the wholeness of nature and the art of living with it in harmony."[108] In *The Turning Point: Science, Society and the Rising Culture* (1982) Capra confronted the task of envisaging the kind of "cultural revolution" of which Western society stands in such urgent need.

Slowly and haltingly an increasing number of thoughtful people in the West are coming to understand the burden of the observation that, with all the so-called advances of a profane science and the powers of technology, we come to know more and more about less and less. The crucial point, which many of the more prescient Western commentators seem to understand intuitively but which is rarely articulated with any real authority, has been stated thus by Frithjof Schuon:

---

107 F. Capra, *The Tao of Physics*, 320, 321, 324.
108 F. Capra, *The Tao of Physics*, 325.

People no longer sense the fact that the quantitative richness of a knowledge—of any kind of knowledge—necessarily entails an interior impoverishment unless accompanied by a spiritual science able to maintain balance and re-establish unity.[109]

This is one of the lessons of the East of which the West most urgently needs to take heed.

109 F. Schuon, *In the Tracks of Buddhism*, 41.

14.

Orientalism, Ideology and Engagement

A. Orientalism, Fascism and the "Mystic East": Zen and Japanese Nationalism and Militarism—Orientalism, Racial Theory and the Allure of Fascism **B. Gandhi's Legacy C. Thich Nhat Hanh and Engaged Buddhism D. The Meeting of Buddhism and Feminism**

I could not be leading a religious life unless I identified myself with the whole of mankind, and that I could not do unless I took part in politics. The whole gamut of man's activities today constitutes an indivisible whole. You cannot divide social, economic, political and purely religious work into watertight compartments. (Gandhi)[1]

Many people have taken action, but if their state of being is not peaceful or happy, the actions they undertake only sow more troubles and anger and make the situation worse. So instead of saying "Don't just sit there; do something," we should say the opposite, "Don't just do something; sit there." (Thich Nhat Hanh)[2]

The stereotypical image of the "mystic East" and its study as a realm beyond politics has been shattered by various developments in the last few decades: the political analyses and critiques of Orientalism by Edward Said and his successors in the field of post-colonial theory and subaltern studies; the political engagements of globally recognized spiritual leaders such as Mohandas Gandhi, Thich Nhat Hanh and the present Dalai Lama; the dialectic between transformative socio-political ideologies (feminism, environmentalism, pacifism) and Western outgrowths of the Eastern religious traditions; the increasing involvement of religious institutions of both East and West in global political debates and movements combating imperialism, racism, patterns of exploitation, the abuse of human rights, war, terrorism, and ecological calamity. In this chapter we will examine four nodal points at which Eastern "religion" and Western "politics" are inextricably intertwined: the collusion between orientalism and fascism; Western attempts to apply Gandhi's politico-religious ethic; the emergence of "engaged Buddhism" and other attempts to marry Eastern spirituality and radical forms of Western *praxis*; the convergence of Buddhism and feminism.

---

1   Gandhi in T. Merton, *Gandhi on Non-Violence*, 64.
2   Thich Nhat Hanh quoted in T. Schwartz, *What Really Matters*, 305.

A. Orientalism, Fascism and the "Mystic East"

Zen and Japanese Nationalism and Militarism

The most concerted attempt to expose and unravel the obscure relations between orientalism and fascism came from a group of American scholars whose researches were gathered together in *Curators of the Buddha: the Study of Buddhism Under Colonialism* (1995). In six closely argued essays, bristling with the somewhat baroque conceptual and rhetorical apparatus of post-colonial studies, the authors anatomized the growth of Buddhist studies within the context of the ideologies of Empire. For the moment we shall isolate their treatment of one particular strand in a very complex web, the nexus between Orientalism and fascism. Three figures who have loomed large in the present study came under the sternest scrutiny: D.T. Suzuki, Giuseppe Tucci and Carl Jung.

Earlier in this study mention was made of Robert Sharf's critique of D.T. Suzuki's representation of Zen in "The Zen of Japanese Nationalism." In the context of our immediate concerns it is worth returning to this provocative article. Robert Sharf opens with an account of the "conceptually incoherent" and "historically naïve" Western construction of Zen as an iconoclastic and antinomian tradition which, purportedly, nurtures a spiritual awakening into the "eternal present," marked by a liberation from the disabling constraints of cerebration, abstraction and religious dogmatism, and an escape from history. Furthermore, such an unmediated experience, "untainted by cultural accretions," comprises the "ultimate source of all authentic religious teaching" and is thereby "preeminently suited to serve as the foundation for inter-faith dialogue."[3] This image of Zen, Sharf argues, is only thinly connected with historical realities, and is to be at least partially explained by "the activities of an elite of internationally minded Japanese intellectuals and globe-trotting priests, whose missionary zeal was often second to their vexed fascination with Western culture."[4] After tracing changes within a Japanese Buddhist establishment increasingly influenced by Western infiltration in the Meiji period of modernization, Sharf turns his attention to Soyen Shaku's participation in the World's Parliament of Religions and to its aftermath out of which D.T. Suzuki surfaced as the leading spokesman for Zen in the West. Much of Sharf's analysis is given to demonstrating that Suzuki, and other apologists for the "New Buddhism," such as Nishida Kitaro, Nishitani Keiji and Tanabe Hajime, present a Zen jaundiced by the polemics of *nihonjinron*—a narcissistic, racist, nativist and supremacist theory positing a unique Japanese character and spiritual "essence," in contradistinction to both other Asians and Westerners, and one closely connected with the growth of Japanese nationalism. Sharf argues that Suzuki and the Kyoto

3   R. Sharf, "The Zen of Japanese Nationalism," 107.
4   R. Sharf, "The Zen of Japanese Nationalism," 108.

School popularized an idiosyncratic form of Zen which had little standing within the Japanese Zen establishment, which was full of "obfuscations and confusions" as well as "nascent chauvinism and nationalist tendencies."[5] He commends those few Western thinkers who put up some resistance to these "self-appointed representatives" of Zen in the West—Arthur Koestler, Gershom Scholem, Paul Demiéville and R.J. Zwi Zerblowsky among them.

In a postscript to the original article, Sharf discusses Suzuki's participation in the Order of the Star in the East (a Theosophical sub-group associated with the messianic mission of Krishnamurti). Whilst conceding Suzuki's energy, sincerity and commitment to Zen, Sharf again deplores his "profligate apologetics" and upbraids Western scholars for their uncritical acceptance of Suzuki's version of Zen, their apparent suspension of the "hermeneutical suspicion" which attends most of their inquiries.[6]

Sharf's analysis underlines the connections between the "New Buddhism," a re-valorized samurai ethos,[7] a chauvinistic Japanese nationalism (eventually issuing in an oriental form of fascism), the Kyoto School and Suzuki's construction of Zen. Brian Victoria, himself a Soto Zen priest and academic in New Zealand, turns more directly to the collusion of the Japanese Zen establishment in the jingoistic militarism of Japanese fascism. In *Zen at War* (1997) he dispels any ingenuous view that Zen Buddhism could not have been directly implicated in the brutalities of this regime. Victoria's researches into this dark chapter in Buddhist history unveil the processes by which "Buddhism, a religion rooted in universal compassion, could have been transformed into a religion whose leaders, almost to a man, unconditionally pledged their support for Japanese militarism."[8] Victoria charts the incorporation of institutional Buddhism into the Japanese war machine, starting with the Russo-Japanese War of 1905 and fully accomplished by about 1930, and the emergence of "Imperial Way Buddhism" (crossing all the Buddhist sects), which marked "the total and unequivocal subjugation of the Law of the Buddha to the Law of the Sovereign."[9] Among the many functions of Imperial Way Buddhism was the religious justification of Japan's "holy war," waged with savage ferocity in China and Korea, and throughout South-east Asia. In the course of his discussion Victoria also establishes that figures such as Soyen Shaku, D.T. Suzuki, Yamada Mumon, Harada Dai'un and Yasutani Haku'un were significantly implicated in these developments.

Whatever else might be said of the indictment prosecuted by Sharf, Victoria and others, there is no doubt that they have administered a powerful blow to the somewhat sentimentalized picture of Zen popularized by Alan Watts, Christmas Humphreys and others in the West. They have also awakened us to the ever-present dangers of the ideological annexation of reli-

---

5   R. Sharf, "The Zen of Japanese Nationalism," 142.
6   R. Sharf, "The Zen of Japanese Nationalism," 145.
7   On the samurai ethos and its relationship to Zen, see W. King, *Zen and the Way of the Sword*.
8   B. Victoria, *Zen at War*, 192.
9   B. Victoria, *Zen at War*, 79.

gious institutions and teachings. In this context Christian readers may recall the dismay and outrage prompted by the exposure of the Vatican's complicity in the genocidal regime of the Nazis.[10] Graham Parkes, in a lengthy article in *Philosophy East and West*, issues a salutary caution about the whole debate about Zen and fascism, warning that we should not allow ourselves to lapse into a dismissive condemnation of Japanese Zen as a whole:

> ... a recent trend within the North American academy jeopardizes the study of the most accessible area of Japanese philosophy: 20th century thought— and the philosophy of the so-called "Kyoto School" in particular ... I am referring to the current fashion, evident in the work of several figures in Japanese and Buddhist studies, of branding thinkers associated with the Kyoto School, such as Nishida Kitaro, Kuki Shuzo and Nishitani Keiji, as mere fascist or imperialist ideologues, with the implication that their work is philosophically nugatory. The neo-Marxist revisionism that has been sweeping (at least a corner of) the field of Japanology threatens to suppress open discussion of some important ideas—and thereby risks falling, with sad irony, into a "fascism of the left."[11]

Orientalism, Racial Theory and the Allure of Fascism

Let us assemble a few now well-known facts, each of which, in isolation, may seem of little significance but which cumulatively suggest a problematic requiring the attention of anyone interested in our general subject. W.B. Yeats, Ezra Pound and T.S. Eliot (and, to confuse the mix, Richard Wagner and Madame Blavatsky) were not only keen students of the Orient but were all anti-Semitic while Pound, notoriously, espoused the ideology of fascism.[12] Mircea Eliade, Joseph Campbell and Georges Dumézil, the doyen of Indo-European studies, were also anti-Semitic and were susceptible to the anti-modern appeal of extreme right wing political ideologies.[13] A more overt and virulent form of "spiritualized" fascism can be found in the person and work of the Italian orientalist Julius Evola. Martin Heidegger publicly and theatrically aligned himself with the Nazi regime in the early 30s, and became an unabashed propagandist for Hitler's domestic and foreign policies. He was a Nazi informer and betrayed several Jewish friends and colleagues.[14] Carl Jung evinced some enthusiasm for Nazism in its early years,

---

10 See J. Cornwell, *Hitler's Pope*.

11 G. Parkes, "The Putative Fascism of the Kyoto School and the Political Correctness of the Modern Academy," 305.

12 On Pound's anti-Semitism see P. Morrison, "'Jewspapers': Ezra Pound, Post-structuralism and the Figure of the Jew"; on Wagner see Steven Beller, "Herzl, Wagner, and the Ironies of 'True Emancipation.'"

13 On Dumézil's political sympathies see Bruce Lincoln's review article, "Shaping the Past and the Future" in *Death, War and Sacrifice*, 231-243. On Eliade, Campbell and Jung see R. Ellwood, *The Politics of Myth*.

14 See T. Sheehan, "Reading a Life: Heidegger and Hard Times," 84-89, and R. Gibbs, "Reading Heidegger: Destruction, Thinking, Return," 157-172.

discerning in it a hope of a spiritual regeneration of Europe; there are also more than a few traces of anti-Semitism in his writings.[15] (Unlike Heidegger, Jung was later implacably opposed to Nazism.)[16] As George Steiner has observed, the "alpine priesthood" of Eranos was susceptible to a kind of conservative-romantic mysticism which was at least tinged with *"Führer*-politics."[17] Heinrich Harrer was a member of the SS and maintained his links with other Nazis after the War; Karlfried Graf Dürckheim worked for Hitler's government in Japan in the late 30s; Eugen and Gustie Herrigel were members of the Nazi Party. The Nazi administration (1933-1945) had little difficulty in enlisting the services of several eminent orientalists, including Walter Wüst, Ludwig Alsdorf and Erich Frauwallner, in the construction of its nationalist-racist-militaristic discourse.[18] Heinrich Himmler, we are told, was an aficionado of the *Bhagavad Gita*. One of the foremost scholars of Germanic Indology writes,

> In German Indology of the NS [National Socialist] era, a largely nonscholarly mystical nativism deriving ultimately from a mixture of romanticism and protonationalism merged with that objectivism of *Wissenschaft* ... and together they fostered the ultimate "orientalist" project, the legitimation of genocide.[19]

Despite his disclaimer in *To Lhasa and Beyond*—"... if there is anything I intensely dislike, it is just politics, anywhere and at any time"[20]—Giuseppe Tucci, Italy's most illustrious orientalist, supported Mussolini, enjoyed his patronage and became an apologist for the fascist regime. He also nurtured a closer relationship between the fascist regimes of his own country and Japan.

Let us consider two of these figures, Evola and Eliade, in a little more detail. Julius Evola,[21] painter, philosopher, "disciple" of René Guénon, colleague of Mircea Eliade,[22] orientalist and fascist ideologue, translated into Italian *The Protocols of the Elders of Zion*, a poisonous anti-Semitic work whose authors included the racial ideologue of Nazism, Alfred Rosenberg. Evola claimed that this document, whether genuine or not, fitted the facts. In *The Doctrine of Awakening* he elaborated an ideologically charged representation of Buddhism as "Aryan," anti-democratic, aristocratic, esoteric and elitist—a

---

15 For an interesting letter from Gershom Scholem to Aniela Jaffé on Jung's anti-Semitism see E. Wasserstrom, *Religion after Religion*, 262, fn72.

16 See L. Gómez, "Oriental Wisdom and the Cure of Souls," 236, fn20.

17 G. Steiner, "Ecstasies, not Arguments."

18 See S. Pollock, "Deep Orientalism?", 89-96.

19 S. Pollock, "Deep Orientalism?", 96.

20 G. Tucci, *To Lhasa and Beyond*, 11.

21 For a general discussion of Evola's thought, particularly its political dimensions, see F. Farraresi, "Julius Evola: Tradition, Reaction and the Radical Right," and T. Sheehan, "Myth and Violence: The Fascism of Julius Evola and Alain de Benoist."

22 On the relationship between Evola and Eliade see E. Wasserstrom, *Religion after Religion*, 306, fn12.

path fitted to the "spiritual warrior." He refers to "the unity of blood and spirit of the white races who created the greatest civilizations" and claims that the Aryans "stood essentially for an aristocracy opposed, both in mind and body ... to obscure, bastard 'demoniacal' races."[23]

It is worth quoting at some length from an essay Evola wrote in 1957 as it captures several themes pertinent to the discussion at hand.

> ... the Western friends of Buddhism have been almost unanimous in appraising it as a sentimental doctrine of love and universal compassion, a doctrine composed of democracy and tolerance, to be admired also for its freedom from dogma, rites, sacraments: almost a sort of secular religion ... this is a falsification of the message of the Buddha, a deteriorated version suited not to virile men, standing with head erect, but to men lying prostrate in search of escape and spiritual alleviation ... Buddhism ... is above the plane of all that can be defined as "religion." Zen Buddhism could be called the doctrine of the Samurai, i.e., the Japanese nobility who are certainly not noted for their abhorrence of arms and bloodshed ... He who has a knowledge of these dimensions of Buddhism ... what can he think of those who consider that Buddhism is not even a religion but a system of sickly sentimental secular morality, consisting of humanitarianism and indiscriminate love, the pale evanescent wisdom of one who has recognized that the "world is suffering"? ... As to the forms in which Buddhism has become a religion *sui generis*, and worse still, as to those forms in which it is conceived and appreciated as a democratizing humanitarian morality, they should rightly be considered as an unparalleled contamination of the truth.[24]

The Nietzschean echoes reverberating through this passage are audible enough.

Given his influence on the emergence of the history of religions as a reputable academic discipline Mircea Eliade's fascist involvements raise some particularly painful questions. Adriana Berger has assembled the evidence for the prosecution in a disturbing essay, "Mircea Eliade: Romanian Fascism and the History of Religions in the United States."[25] Eliade's early intellectual milieu was pervaded by a potent admixture of German romanticism, Romanian nationalism and Orthodox traditionalism, all stained with an anti-Semitism which became more rabid in the interwar period during which he came to maturity. Anti-Semitism was often intertwined with a rejection of communism, democracy and materialism (all seen as symptoms of a decadent modernity) and with the affirmation of a Romanian identity (racial and political). The myth of Aryan superiority was imbricated with Romania's mythological past ("Dacism," the cult of Zalmoxis, the assimilation of a pagan warrior ethos and Orthodox Christianity) and consolidated by the specter of a Jewish threat to racial "purity." All these elements were on full display in the fascist organization, the Iron Guard, also known as the Legion

---

23 Evola quoted in A. Rawlinson, *The Book of Enlightened Masters*, 449, fn1.
24 J. Evola, "Spiritual Virility in Buddhism," 318, 322, 325, 326.
25 Most of the material immediately following is taken from Berger's article.

of the Archangel Michael, headed by the notorious Captain Codreanu who declared,

> The greatest wrong done to us by Jews ... is neither the grabbing of the Romanian soil ... nor the great number of Jews in our schools, professions, etc., and not even the influence they exercise over our political life—though each of these is a mortal danger for our people. The greatest national peril is the fact that they have deformed, disfigured our Daco-Romanic racial structure ... From among all pests brought to us by the Jewish invasion, this is the most frightening one.[26]

The Iron Guard was "a nationalist and mystico-religious movement of a messianic character, violently opposed to democracy and communism—which were associated with the Jews."[27] Codreanu repeatedly warned of the international threat of the Jews and asserted that "a total solution of this problem could not be reached except through action by all the Christian nations." He applauded Hitler's war against the "Judeo-Masonic hydra" and declared that "We shall crush the Jews under our heels, or else we shall gloriously die ..."[28]

During the 1930s Eliade supported anti-Semitic laws and echoed some of Codreanu's themes in his own writings, including the need for "racial detoxification" (though his references to the Jews were somewhat more oblique). He wrote of "the noble religious ideals" and the "virile vitality" of the Iron Guard and applauded its program of national purification and spiritual regeneration. During the war Eliade served the pro-Nazi Romanian government as press and propaganda attaché in Lisbon. After his forced move to Paris in 1945 Eliade maintained contacts with the followers of the military dictator Antonescu. Whilst he retreated from some of the more extreme racial and nationalist themes to be found in his writings of the 1930s (which have only recently come to light) his work continued to bear the stamp of that peculiar blend of mystico-religious and nationalist elements. There is no evidence that he showed any signs of regret for his earlier fascist enthusiasms and we may share George Steiner's disquiet over the "central silence" about the Holocaust in the voluminous writings of an historian of religions so deeply concerned with the "cultural crisis" of his times.[29]

In the writings of many of the figures mentioned above we can find a romantic exaltation of an ascesis and an aesthetic of violence presented in terms of "creative force," the "samurai ethic," "spiritual virility," the "will to power," "the spirit of Bushido" and the like.[30] They were also heirs to a continental Romanticism central to which, in Theodor Adorno's memorable phrase, was "the agitator's dream, a union of the horrible and the wonder-

---

26 Codreanu quoted in A. Berger, "Mircea Eliade: Romanian Fascism," 59.
27 A. Berger, "Mircea Eliade: Romanian Fascism," 60.
28 Codreanu quoted in A. Berger, "Mircea Eliade: Romanian Fascism," 61.
29 See G. Steiner, "Ecstasies, not Arguments." (This "central silence" is what the poststructuralist critics might call a "structuring absence.")
30 See L. Fader, "Arthur Koestler's Critique of D.T. Suzuki's Interpretation of Zen," 54.

ful, a delirium of annihilation masked as salvation."[31] What are we to make of this disturbing web of connections between Orientalism and ideologies which led to the extermination chambers of Auschwitz? Perhaps Arthur Koestler's preposterous and generally ignorant attack on Zen carried a germ of truth when he claimed that, "By virtue of its anti-rationality and amorality, Zen always held a fascination for a category of people in whom brutishness combines with pseudo-mysticism, from Samurai to Kamikaze to Beatnik"?[32]

It might be argued that any sizable group, such as "orientalists," is likely to attract individuals from across the political spectrum and that we should not be surprised that some of these will inevitably be susceptible to the appeal of extremist ideologies. This demonstrates nothing more than the trite fact that orientalists are "all too human." Certainly we should not expect orientalists to be somehow immune to the political and cultural fashions of the day. It would not be difficult to show that many Western scholars today engaged in the study of Eastern religions are disproportionately liberal-left-ist (admittedly a horribly vague but not entirely empty label) in their politi-cal leanings, or that their inquiries are colored by both theoretical and ideo-logical sympathies which are currently fashionable in various quarters. But such a reading would be to dispose of the problem rather too easily. We must at least pose the question of whether there is some deeper connection between fascism (or more generally movements of the extreme right) and orientalism.

The immediate background to this issue is the growth of racial theory and the intensification of 19th century racist attitudes (of which anti-Semitism was the most pervasive in the European intelligentsia) in a climate which was largely the creation of continental Romanticism. Romanticism itself must be seen as a highly problematic and ambiguous cultural move-ment. As Robert Sayre and Michel Löwy have written,

> But what exactly is Romanticism? An indecipherable enigma ... because it is a *coincidentia oppositorum*: at the same time (or alternately) revolutionary and counter-revolutionary, cosmopolitan and nationalist, realist and fanciful, restorationist and utopian, democratic and aristocratic, republican and monarchist, red and white, mystical and sensual.[33]

Romanticism was not only one avenue through which European intellectuals were exposed to Eastern ideas and values but was also the vehicle for a plethora of theoretical formulations about race, nation and identity. Several streams of thought merged in Romanticism and left their mark on an emer-gent Orientalism: an animus to Judaic theology (easily identified in the writ-ings of Herder, Schlegel, Hegel and Schopenhauer), which was sometimes

31 Adorno quoted in E. Wasserstrom, *Religion after Religion*, 76.
32 A. Koestler, "Neither Lotus nor Robot," *Encounter* 16, February 1960, quoted in L. Fader, "Arthur Koestler's Critique of D.T. Suzuki's Interpretation of Zen," 54.
33 Quoted in E. Wasserstrom, *Religion after Religion*, 76.

an accomplice to anti-Semitism, either mild or virulent; the idealization of an Aryan race which, supposedly, bequeathed civilization the Indo-European family of languages; the nascent "blood and soil" ideology of the Germanic *volk* and the search for national self-definition, cultural identity and national "mission," often associated with an anti-liberal, anti-egalitarian, anti-democratic revolt against modernity; the reinforcement of popular, stereotypical racist images of non-Aryan Indians and the Chinese; the elaboration of quasi-biological and evolutionistic racial theories, such as those of the French diplomat and orientalist J. Arthur de Gobineau (1816-1852) and Richard Wagner's son-in-law, the Englishman Houston Stewart Chamberlain (1855-1926). Gobineau constructed one of the most sinister of the 19th century racial theories. In *Essai sur l'inégalité des races humaines* (1853-55) he posited an inherent inequality of races, a racial purity which could only be preserved by the prevention of miscegenation, and the racial superiority of whites amongst whom the Aryans were "the most noble, the most intelligent and the most dynamic."[34] The National Socialists drew on the ideas of both Gobineau and Chamberlain in constructing the idea of the German-Aryan master race.

Considering this chaotic intellectual and ideological terrain J.J. Clarke, one of the more thoughtful commentators on the phenomena in question, has this to say:

> It is evident that in the late 19th century and early 20th centuries orientalism sometimes became ensnared by and gave succor to the emerging racist discourse. However, the extraordinary web of ideological convergences which characterized European thought at that time, involving *inter alia* race, eugenics, nationalism, naturalism, evolutionism, and occultism, and responding to the "kindling fever" that had taken hold of Europe, became entangled together in what must seem in retrospect to be a series of unlikely and contingent associations. It would be a mistake, then, to ascribe some "essentially" racist taint to orientalism ... Apart from the awkward interwovenness of so many disparate intellectual and cultural strands, we need to keep in mind as well the fact that the intercalation of the languages, histories, and religions of India and Europe, sketched out by a series of orientalists from Jones and Schlegel to Quinet and Max Müller, represented a powerful force for the expansion and enrichment of traditional Western outlooks, laying foundations for an enhancement of inter-cultural understanding, and helping to moderate endemic xenophobic attitudes.[35]

Nonetheless, it should not be forgotten that Gobineau and others turned to the East to "conceptualize redemptive options" with which to combat what they perceived as the degenerate pathologies of a decadent Europe. Analogous considerations, Clarke suggests, apply in the association of orien-

---

34 Gobineau quoted in M. Edwardes, *East-West Passage*, 164-165. See also R. Schwab, *The Oriental Renaissance*, 43ff.

35 J.J. Clarke, *Oriental Enlightenment*, 193.

talism and fascism. Certainly the early-century European sense of both existential and cultural crisis, widespread amongst intellectuals and artists, impelled an adversarial posture towards a mediocre and moribund bourgeois civilization and stimulated the search for spiritual and intellectual sustenance in sources outside the mainstream: "orientalism and fascism were two amongst the many exemplifications of this transformative *angst*."[36] Another was the nostalgia for the *ancien regime* and a repudiation of democratic egalitarianism.[37] Something of the mood of the 30s is caught in Heidegger's *Introduction to Metaphysics* (1935):

> For the darkening of the world, the flight of the gods, the destruction of the earth, the transformation of man into a mass, the hatred and suspicion of everything free and creative, have assumed such proportions throughout the earth that such childish categories as pessimism and optimism have long since become absurd.[38]

For many of the figures mentioned above "the East" came to symbolize a realm uncontaminated by the corruptions of Europe while fascism seemed to hold out the promise of a "spiritual regeneration." Both orientalism and fascism also tapped into subterranean currents of irrationalism which originated in the Romantic rebellion against the Enlightenment and which sometimes manifested themselves in bizarre cults and extremist politics directed towards a cultural *renovatio*.[39]

The point of our considerations must be to recognize the dangers of any scholarship (or religious commitment for that matter) which opportunistically allows itself to be turned to inhumane political ends and which thereby compromises its allegiance to the truth. By the same token we must not baulk at the unpalatable fact that many distinguished scholars, intellectuals and religious leaders allowed themselves to be used for malignant political purposes, both in the East and the West. Far from allowing us to indulge in vacuous moralizing or rhetorical point-scoring, a sharpened awareness of these past complicities should make us all the more sensitive to the ever-present ways in which both intellectual and moral integrity can be compromised and "scholarship" bent to the service of sinister purposes. But let us not surrender to the facile judgments evident in the peremptory dismissal of some of these figures, solely on ideological grounds. The fact that Heidegger was susceptible to the evil conjurations of Nazism certainly raises some deeply troubling questions about his whole intellectual project ... but this hardly justifies catapulting all of his work into the nearest dustbin without further ado! Acknowledging and deploring the anti-Semitism of an Eliade or a T.S. Eliot does not entail a wholesale rejection of their work any more than a recogni-

---

36 J.J. Clarke, *Oriental Enlightenment*, 194.
37 See E. Wasserstrom, *Religion after Religion*, Ch. 2.
38 Heidegger quoted in E. Wasserstrom, *Religion after Religion*, 128.
39 See M. Eliade, "The Occult and the Modern World" in *Occultism, Witchcraft, and Cultural Fashions*.

tion of the same prejudice in Shakespeare means we must burn our copies of his plays.[40] At the same time, a recognition of currents of venomous anti-Semitism, authoritarianism and xenophobic nationalism in Romantic orientalism, often camouflaged by a pseudo-mystical vocabulary, must qualify our enthusiasm for the very real and imposing achievements of figures such as Eliade, Heidegger and Tucci. Their indisputable intellectual feats cannot exculpate them from some degree of complicity in the barbarisms of European fascism—one which must be faced squarely in any assessment of their work and their significance as "cultural heroes."[41]

B. Gandhi's Legacy

Shortly after Gandhi's assassination, early in 1948, a Western commentator pondered his significance for India and the world at large:

> ... the gift of Gandhi to India was something more than a wise, paternal guidance: it was something greater, even, for India, than his historic demonstration of the moral strength of the philosophy of non-violence, which was rather a gift to modern civilization than to India alone ... he embodied the spiritual force of an awakened and concentrated mind, fixed on his chosen objectives. No one could enslave Gandhi. No one could "conquer" Gandhi. Gandhi was a living example of the unconquerable human spirit. He might be imprisoned, but he could not be made unfree. In Gandhi became manifest a quality of manhood which holds the secret of the only future worth striving after for modern man.[42]

Events since these words were written have only gone to confirm the urgent relevance of Gandhi's message for the contemporary world.

Mohandas Gandhi came to symbolize three great 20th century revolutions—against colonialism, against racism and against violence. In India it has been said that "he carried the cave within him," which is to say that he always understood his vocation as a spiritual one which happened to manifest itself within the external domain of politics. It has also been remarked of Gandhi, as it was of Socrates, "he was the one man capable of making us ashamed." Gandhi, essentially, was a *karma-yogin*, a man of deeds as he himself acknowledged when asked for his teaching: "My life is my message." Millions of people, both within his homeland and in the West, came to recognize the moral authority of one whom Rabindranath Tagore had named the Mahatma ("great soul").

---

40 We also need to make carefully nuanced discriminations concerning different forms of anti-Semitism: there is, for example, clearly a gulf between Eliot's comparatively mild anti-Semitism which is peripheral to his work and the fascistic enthusiasms which lie much closer to the heart of Eliade's enterprise.

41 See Nancy Harrowitz's Introduction to *Tainted Greatness*, ed. N. Harrowitz, 1-11.

42 *Manas* editorial, "Gandhi," 309.

Gandhi's biography is well-known: an upbringing in a pious Vaisnavite family in Gujurat; legal training in England where he also aspired to the refinements of the late Victorian gentleman; the apprenticeship in the crucible of South African race politics, lasting two decades; his gradual assumption of the political and moral leadership of the Indian independence movement. Gandhi's religious development was shaped by his mother's piety, a Jain monk who was close to the family, and by his reading of several texts for which he came to feel a kind of filial reverence, particularly the *Bhagavad Gita* which first came to his serious attention through his Theosophical friends in London. He was also deeply influenced by several works which he encountered in England and South Africa: the *New Testament* (especially the Sermon on the Mount),[43] the writings of Thoreau on civil disobedience, Tolstoy on non-violence, Kropotkin on the evils of the state and Ruskin on the abuses of industrialization and the moral dignity of manual labor. It was out of these disparate sources and out of his own experiences that he was to forge a philosophy of political action which, in its clarity and moral austerity, has become an exemplum to people of various kind and color throughout the world.

Gandhi's political campaigns were informed by three principles to which he held fast during the many trials through which he had to pass: *satyagraha* which has been translated as "truth-force" (the power which is born out of a steadfast love of the truth) and which informed a dynamic form of non-violent resistance; *ahimsa*, the principle of non-injuriousness which has been an elevated ethical principle in all the major Indian traditions, Jain and Buddhist as well as Hindu; *brahmacharya*, disciplined self-control and renunciation to develop the resolve and courage indispensable in the practice of both *satyagraha* and *ahimsa*. In Gandhi's own case this self-control took the form of celibacy, vegetarianism, abstention from intoxicants, regular prayer and fasting, as well as his unwavering refusal to hold formal political office and his practice at the spinning wheel.

Something of the nuances of Gandhian *ahimsa* can be sensed in his marvelous commentary on the Hindu tradition of reverencing the cow:

> The central fact of Hinduism ... is "Cow Protection." "Cow Protection" to me is one of the most wonderful phenomena in all human evolution; for it takes the human being beyond his species. The cow to me means the entire subhuman world. Man through the cow is enjoined to realize his identity with all that lives ... Hindus will be judged not by their correct chanting of sacred texts, not by their pilgrimages, not by their most punctilious observance of Caste rules, but by their ability to protect the cow ... "Cow Protection" is the gift of Hinduism to the world; and Hinduism will live so long as there are Hindus to protect the cow.[44]

43 See D. Eck, *Encountering God*, 206.
44 Gandhi quoted in E. Sharpe, "To Hinduism through Gandhi," 61-62.

Gandhi derived these three principles from traditional Indian teachings, inflected by his Western education—evident, for instance, in his elevation of the moral authority ascribed to conscience.

Given the veneration in which Gandhi is held by so many people it is worth pausing to consider several other aspects of his example and outlook. In India and elsewhere Gandhi is remembered not only as the pathfinder of Indian independence but for his tireless campaign on behalf of the "untouchables," that sizable portion of the sub-continent's population who were, literally, out-castes, people without any caste status, usually eking out a marginal existence on the scrap-heaps of Indian society. Unlike most of the neo-Hindu reformers (Rama Mohun Roy, Vivekananda, Dayananda), Gandhi never advocated the abolition of *varna-ashrama* (the four-tiered caste system and the four-staged conception of life) arguing that these divisions were natural (a view he shared with Plato): "*Varnashrama* is in my opinion inherent in human nature, and Hinduism has simply reduced it to a science."[45] However, he did insist that the caste system conferred responsibilities but not privileges and that it should not be used to validate discrimination and social privilege. "The caste divisions," wrote Gandhi "define a man's calling; they do not restrict or regulate social intercourse. The divisions define duties; they confer no privileges."[46] He could find no Scriptural validation for the institution of the *pancamas* (out-castes) whom he re-named "Harijans" (children of God). So fiercely was he committed to the dismantling of this institution that he insisted that India could not achieve real independence so long as it persisted. Gandhi is also interesting as a religious universalist, not of the syncretic kind, but as one who, like Ramakrishna, recognized the inner unity and the essential truths of all the integral traditions. "It is not Hinduism," he wrote, "which I prize most highly, but the religion which transcends Hinduism—the basic truth which underlies all the religions of the world."[47]

In 1949 George Orwell opened his essay on Gandhi thus: "Saints should always be judged guilty until they are proved innocent ..."[48] In an essay full of interesting perceptions and resistances, the following is perhaps the most crucial:

> Of late years it has been the fashion to talk about Gandhi as though he were not only sympathetic to the western left-wing movement, but were even integrally part of it. Anarchists and pacifists, in particular, have claimed him for their own, noticing only that he was opposed to centralism and State violence and ignoring the other-worldly, anti-humanist tendency of his doctrines. But one should, I think, realize that Gandhi's teaching cannot be squared with the belief that Man is the measure of all things ... They make

45 Gandhi quoted in E. Sharpe, "To Hinduism through Gandhi," 61.
46 Gandhi quoted in E. Sharpe, "To Hinduism through Gandhi," 61.
47 Gandhi quoted in J.F.T. Jordens, *Gandhi: Conscience of Hinduism*, 28.
48 G. Orwell, "Reflections on Gandhi," 523.

sense only on the assumption that God exists and that the world of solid objects is an illusion to be escaped from ...[49]

Orwell, who felt an "aesthetic distaste" for Gandhi, also reflected that

> It is difficult to see how Gandhi's methods could be applied in a country where opponents of the regime disappear in the middle of the night and are never heard of again ... Is there a Gandhi in Russia at the moment? And if there is, what is he accomplishing?[50]

But perhaps it was Rudolf Otto who most clearly discerned Gandhi's vocation:

> True, Gandhi impresses us through his profound humanity, and we admire "the human" in him. But he is an Indian, and it is as a great Indian that he is a great person ... We misunderstand Gandhi when we attempt to understand the strong powers and virtues of this man simply in terms of a generalized humanity ... "the great nationalist," "the friend of the people," "a clever politician," "a born leader." He is all these things, but he is so as an Indian sadhu. He is these things as a result of his situation, but if the situation were different, his character as a sadhu would remain the same and would find other ways to express itself.[51]

Lanzo del Vasto furnishes us with one example of a Westerner whose life was transformed by Gandhi. A Sicilian of noble family, del Vasto was born in 1901. Before visiting India he led a somewhat itinerant life and was of no fixed profession though he was an accomplished linguist, artist, poet and *litterateur*. He was a friend of the Gurdjieff disciples, Madame Jeanne de Salzmann and her husband Alexandre, who established small Gurdjieffian groups in Paris which included the esotericist and writer René Daumal, author of *Mount Analogue*, and Luc Dietrich. Del Vasto spent a year in the sub-continent in 1936-37, meeting Ramana Maharshi and spending three months with Gandhi at Wardha. After his return to France he established several communities (known collectively as The Ark) which ran on strictly Gandhian lines which del Vasto summarized as "politics without violence, production without machines, society without exploitation, religion without intolerance."[52] In 1958 he founded the Action Civique Non-violente; its early campaigns were directed against the French internment camps in Algeria and in favor of the right of conscientious objection to military service. Here is an excerpt from del Vasto's book, recounting his first meeting with the Mahatma:

> Dawn already streaks the sky, but our path still twists and turns in the dark countryside. We meet a group of disciples returning from the ashram and

---

49 G. Orwell, "Reflections on Gandhi," 526.
50 G. Orwell, "Reflections on Gandhi," 529.
51 R. Otto, *Autobiographical and Social Essays*, 195-196.
52 L. del Vasto, *Return to the Source*, 9.

greet them by joining our hands against our closed lips. The Mahatma has already spoken to them. We are among the last to arrive. Daylight has come by the time we reach the little close. In the middle of the parched field is a small clay hut, open and so low that it makes no break in the countryside. In the doorway under the slope of the thatched roof, a little, half-naked old man is seated on the ground. It's he! He waves to me—yes, to me!—makes me sit down beside him and smiles to me. He speaks—and speaks of nothing else but me—asking me who I am, what I do and what I want. And no sooner has he asked me than I discover that I am nothing, have never done anything and want nothing except to stay like this in his shadow. Here he is before my eyes, the only man who has shown us a green shoot in the desert of this century. A man who knows the hard law of love, hard and clear like a diamond. The captain of the unarmed, the father of the pariahs, the king who reigns by the divine right of sainthood. He has come to show us the power over this earth of absolute innocence. He has come to prove that it can stop machines, hold its own against guns and defy an empire. He has come into this world to bring us news from beyond, where nothing changes, to teach us the truth we have always known, being Christians. Truth so ill-assorted with us, so strangely contradictory to everything that the world and men had taught us, that we did not know what to do with it. We kept it between the four walls of the church and in the dark of our hearts. He, the Hindu, had come for us to learn what we had always known. While the old man questions me and smiles, I am silent, trying not to weep.[53]

It would be a tedious exercise to catalogue the many political activists and spiritual leaders on whom Gandhi has had a profound affect and any analysis of his influence is well beyond the scope of the present work. However, it is well known that Gandhi's political philosophy has informed non-violent movements in the American civil rights and anti-war campaigns of the 60s, anti-apartheid and black nationalist movements in South Africa, and the resistance to totalitarian regimes in Eastern Europe. Here is a cross-section of public figures who, on their own testimony, found inspiration in Gandhi's example: Thomas Merton, Martin Luther King Jr, Freda Bedi, Daniel Berrigan, Danilo Dolci, Desmond Tutu, Eric Erikson, E.F. Schumacher, Robert Aitken, Jean Klein, Kathleen Raine, Wendell Berry, Vaclav Havel, Arne Naess, Joanna Macy, Ken Jones. In recent times the gospel of non-violence has been taken up by two other Asian renunciates also engaged in some of the most traumatic political struggles of our era, Thich Nhat Hanh and the Dalai Lama.

C. Thich Nhat Hanh and Engaged Buddhism

In 1963 Western television sets carried horrific images of an elderly Vietnamese Buddhist monk in a fiery self-immolation, a protest against the

---

53 L. del Vasto, *Return to the Source*, 100-101. (I have collapsed several paragraphs in reproducing this extract.)

war which had been raging in his homeland, with some intermittent pauses, since the late 40s. In the same year another Vietnamese monk, Thich Nhat Hanh (b.1926), wrote a book called *Engaged Buddhism* and formed the School of Youth for Social Service in Vietnam, a non-aligned organization dedicated to ending the war and to peaceful reconstruction. In 1965 Thich Nhat Hanh wrote a remarkable letter to Martin Luther King to explain the motivation of those Buddhist monks who through their self-immolations had become "lotuses in a sea of fire." These heroic acts, he explained, were neither despairing suicides nor political protests but were aimed solely at

> moving the hearts of the oppressors, and at calling the attention of the world to the suffering endured by the Vietnamese. To burn oneself by fire is to prove that what one is saying is of the utmost importance ... To say something while experiencing this kind of pain is to say it with utmost courage, frankness, determination, and sincerity ... I believe with all my heart that the monks who burned themselves did not aim at the death of the oppressors but only at a change in their policy. Their enemies are not man. They are intolerance, fanaticism, dictatorship, cupidity, hatred and discrimination which lie within the heart of man ... I am sure that since you have been engaged in one of the hardest struggles for equality and human rights, you are among those who understand fully, and who share with all their heart, the indescribable suffering of the Vietnamese people. The world's greatest humanists would not remain silent. You yourself cannot remain silent.[54]

This letter played a decisive role in persuading King to publicly enter the campaign against the Vietnam war; he had previously thought it necessary to keep the anti-war and the civil rights movements quite separate. King subsequently nominated Thich Nhat Hanh for the Nobel Peace Prize of which he would have been one of the most worthy recipients had those awarding the prize had more prescience. (It might be remarked in passing that the awarding of the Nobel Peace Prize to the Dalai Lama restored some of the luster which had been tarnished by some peculiar choices in earlier years—none more so than Richard Nixon and Henry Kissinger, both embroiled in the ruthless and unprincipled war against Thich Nhat Hanh's country.)

Thich Nhat Hanh had spent three years studying comparative religion and lecturing on Buddhism at Columbia University. In 1966 he was invited by the Christian-based organization, Fellowship of Reconciliation, to tour America. He met with political and religious leaders such as Secretary for Defense Robert McNamara, Dr Martin Luther King Jr and Father Thomas Merton. His three-week tour was soon extended to three months, also taking in lectures in Europe and a meeting with the Roman Pontiff. He developed a warm relationship with his fellow-monk and war critic, Thomas Merton, about whom he wrote a poem "Thomas Merton is My Brother." The Trappist

---

54 Thich Nhat Hanh, "In Search of the Enemy of Man," excerpt from a letter to Martin Luther King in *Vietnam: Lotus in the Sea of Fire*, 117-19.

monk was one of the first to recognize his personal stature and the relevance of his message to the Western world. In 1967, Merton introduced Hanh's *Vietnam: The Lotus in the Sea of Fire*:

> Thich Nhat Hanh is a Vietnamese scholar and a poet, a contemplative monk who felt himself obliged to take part in his country's effort to escape destruction in a vicious power struggle between capitalism and communism ... he speaks for his people and for a renewed and "engaged" Buddhism that has taken up the challenge of modern and western civilization in its often disastrous impact upon the East. This new Buddhism is not immersed in an eternal trance. Nor is it engaged in a fanatical self-glorifying quest for political power. It is not remote and withdrawn from the sufferings of ordinary men and their problems in a world of revolutions. It seeks to help them solve these problems. But at the same time it struggles to keep itself independent of massive pressures ... in order to assert certain claims which have never been clearly apprehended or understood in the West.[55]

The Vietnamese monk was the leader of the Buddhist Peace Delegation at the Paris Peace talks and was forced into exile in south-western France where he founded the retreat community of Plum Village, near Sainte Foy la Grande. He was also involved in attempts to rescue and alleviate the plight of the "boat people" who fled Vietnam during the aftermath of three decades of warfare. This "gentle and fearless monk"[56] travels widely in the West and has continued to offer meditation retreats for all manner of people all over the world, one of his most distinctive contributions being his work with Vietnam veterans. Thich Nhat Hanh has become one of the best-known and best-loved of Buddhist teachers as well as the pre-eminent spokesman of "engaged Buddhism." He has proved to be one of the most remarkable of all the Eastern teachers who have made such an impact in the West over the last half-century. In some respects he, along with the Dalai Lama, might be seen as one of Gandhi's principal successors in the revolution against violence. Rick Fields suggests that during the 80s Thich Nhat Hanh and the Dalai Lama, "both celibate monks firmly rooted in the monastic tradition," became "the most visible and influential teachers for American Buddhists."[57]

Thich Nhat Hanh is the author of some seventy-five books, two of his recurrent themes being the relationship between "inner/individual" and "outer/global" peace and the necessity of inter-religious dialogue and moral solidarity in the face of the world's most pressing problems. He stresses the dangers of rigid polarizations such as that between the inner and outer worlds, between spiritual practice and social activism:

> In the past we may have made the primary mistake in distinguishing between the inner world of our mind and the world outside. These are not

---

55 T. Merton, Foreword to Thich Nhat Hanh, *Vietnam: Lotus in the Sea of Fire*, 5.
56 R. Fields, *How the Swans Came to the Lake*, 358.
57 R. Fields, *How the Swans Came to the Lake*, 376.

two separate worlds but belong to the same reality. If we are able to see deeply into our mind we can simultaneously see deeply into the world.[58]

One of his most widely read books is *Being Peace* (1987), a collection of his talks in which he stresses the vital necessity of living out *within oneself* the social and moral ideals informing a pursuit of peace in the wider world. In 1986 he founded the Parallax Press, based in California and dedicated to the dissemination of engaged Buddhist writings.

The term "engaged Buddhism" (dating back to movements in Vietnam in the 1930s) soon started circulating in Western circles. Its initial signification—the politically engaged, non-aligned, non-violent coalition of Buddhists in Vietnam seeking to end the war—was soon broadened to a more general movement, galvanized by Thich Nhat Hanh's example, to identify a form of Buddhism which sought to apply its ancient principles directly to the most pressing socio-economic and political problems of the day. Over the decades since Thich Nhat Hanh brought the term into Western currency its exponents have come to recognize that "engaged Buddhism" is nothing new and have re-valorized earlier and often hidden impulses of this sort within a tradition which has been constructed as "quietist," "other-worldly," "escapist," "passive" and the like. As Stephen Batchelor has written,

> Engaged Buddhism in Asia is merely the renewal of a dimension that had either lain dormant or been suppressed during the colonial period. Likewise, in the West today, as the alienated and disaffected generations of the second half of the 20th century outgrow their romantic fascination with Buddhism, it is no surprise to find a growing concern among them for social, cultural and political issues.[59]

Batchelor sensibly observes that it matters little whether we label this "engaged Buddhism" or simply recognize that the Buddhist insight "into the selfless and interconnected nature of life" issues in compassionate activity in the world. One of the institutional rallying points for engaged Buddhism has been the Buddhist Peace Fellowship, formed in the late 1970s by Robert Aitken and other members of the Diamond Sangha of Hawaii. Western Buddhists are now prominent throughout most of the Western world as peace campaigners, environmentalists, prison and hospice workers, pastoral counselors, educators, and in the resistance to the more destructive aspects of "globalization." They are disproving the claim made in one of R.C. Zaehner's several shallow books that Buddhism is "steeped in pessimism and passive mysticism" which, while it may briefly satisfy some individuals, "cannot be integrated into modern society."[60]

---

58 Thich Nhat Hanh quoted in S. Boucher, *Turning the Wheel*, 264.

59 S. Batchelor, *The Awakening of the West*, 360-361. The question of whether there is, in fact, an indigenous Asian tradition of engaged Buddhism is a contested one: see, for example, W. King, "Engaged Buddhism," 18-20.

60 R.C. Zaehner, *Matter and Spirit*, quoted in J.J. Clarke, *Oriental Enlightenment*, 200.

Over thirty years ago Thomas Merton, writing about the work of the still little-known Thich Nhat Hanh, pondered the relationship of spiritual practice and political activism in the context of Vietnamese Buddhism. Merton's reflections remain as germane today as they did three decades ago:

> Can there be a Buddhist humanism in a society where a half-dead, half-ossified traditionalism identifies "Buddhism" with a decaying social structure? There is only one answer: a radical renewal of the Buddhist experiential grasp of reality within the framework and context of a bitter, agonizing social struggle and in terms that are comprehensible to those who are most deeply involved in that struggle. This formula applies not only to Buddhism but to every religion that seeks to find its real place in the world of today.[61]

Philip Kapleau articulated the contemporary agenda of "engaged Buddhism" in the West in this way:

> A major task for Buddhism in the West ... is to ally itself with religious and other concerned organizations to forestall the potential catastrophes facing the human race: nuclear holocaust, irreversible pollution of the world's environment, and the continuing large-scale destruction of non-renewable resources. We also need to lend our physical and moral support to those who are fighting hunger, poverty, and oppression everywhere in the world.[62]

Implicit in this formulation is what Kenneth Kraft identifies as the touchstone of engaged Buddhism: a vision of interdependence in which the universe is experienced as an organic whole, each "part" affecting every other.[63] This theme, of course, is not new. It was given a powerful reformulation in the Romantic movement, especially in the work of William Blake. However, engaged Buddhism seeks to draw out of its own rich tradition principles, insights and practical methods whereby a compassionate and creative vision of interconnectedness can be brought to bear on the perplexities and problems of our own time. One of its key themes is embodied in the title of a recent collection of essays, *Inner Peace, World Peace*—which is to say that a lasting transformation of oppressive structures and patterns of exploitation can only be achieved through the self-transformation of individuals. Ultimately all of our problems are located in samsaric greed, hatred and delusion which can only flourish in the soil of egoism. The counter-cultural slogan "the personal is the political" is given a new depth and a richer resonance in this Buddhist context. A deeper understanding of the "path of compassion" is attained with the full understanding of the Mahayanist ideal of the Bodhisattva, within the framework of the metaphysical doctrine of *sunyata* (voidness). Speaking of this ideal Frithjof Schuon observes that

---

61 T. Merton, *Mystics and Zen Masters*, 287.
62 Kapleau quoted in K. Kraft, "Engaged Buddhism: An Introduction," xii.
63 K. Kraft, "Engaged Buddhism: An Introduction," xii.

> It first declares that Compassion is a dimension of Knowledge, then adds that one's "neighbor" is non-real and that charity must therefore be exercised "quietly when the occasion arises" and without slipping into the dualist and objectivist illusion, for, as it says, there is no one whom our charity could concern, nor is there a charity which could be "ours."[64]

It is precisely this principle which informed D.T. Suzuki's reply when, at a conference on Zen he was asked, "What about society, what about others?" After a pause, Suzuki replied, "But there are no others."[65]

It is interesting to note that it is Zen, in many respects one of the most conservative traditions and the one most rigorously focused on the individual attainment of *satori*, which has produced a preponderance of Western "engaged Buddhists"—Robert Aitken, Ken Jones, Gary Snyder, Roshi Glassman, Peter Matthiessen among them. Pondering the possible factors at work here Winston King suggests, "It is perhaps that Zen has less doctrinal fixity and the possibility of more freedom of action, and hence can more readily adapt to new conditions once it escapes its Japanese institutional shell."[66] The Tibetan Vajrayana, in which the ideal of the Bodhisattva is so central and in which the interplay of compassion (*karuna*) and wisdom (*prajna*) is foregrounded, has also proved most amenable to Western interpretations of engaged Buddhism.[67] In addition to those already mentioned, Westerners who have been prominent in the "engaged Buddhism" movement include Robert Thurman, Jack Kornfield, Christopher Titmus, and Joanna Macy. It should also be noted that Taoism and Hinduism, as well as Buddhism,

> have all in various ways been drawn into a number of central moral and social debates as stimulants rather than as tranquilizers, and as catalysts in the formulation of new social and political norms rather than as paths of retreat from contemporary problems.[68]

Kenneth Kraft identifies some of the issues with which engaged Buddhists have recently wrestled: the dangers of trivialization and inappropriate partisanship when traditional teachings are harnessed to specific social and political goals; the philosophical basis of non-violence and the circumstances under which it may be inappropriate; the relationship between engaged Buddhism and secular movements such as Marxist communism which might share some common immediate goals but which are philosophically incompatible.[69]

One issue which has generated a good deal of confusion amongst Westerners is the apparent tension between the ideal of "altruistic" engage-

---

64 F. Schuon, *In the Tracks of Buddhism*, 130.
65 B. Pennington, *Thomas Merton, Brother Monk*, 133.
66 W. King, "Engaged Buddhism," 29.
67 See P.R. Oldmeadow, "Buddhist Yogacara Philosophy and Deep Ecology."
68 J.J. Clarke, *Oriental Enlightenment*, 202-203.
69 K. Kraft, "Engaged Buddhism: An Introduction," xvii.

ment, expressed in terms of a social and political activism, and the apparently "non-altruistic" contemplative spirituality of monks and other recluses. Like so many other "problems" this one is misconceived, firstly because it predicates an impossibility—a spirituality devoid of charity or compassion—and, secondly, because it confuses the levels of worldly contingencies and of Knowledge unqualified. The pursuit of this Knowledge, supremely exemplified by the Buddha Himself, cannot but benefit the surrounding world. To posit any antagonism between the (relative) ideal of compassionate activity in this world and the (absolute) ideal of Enlightenment would be to tear asunder the Bodhisattva and the Buddha! All of this is beautifully and precisely expressed in Frithjof Schuon's meditation on the Bodhisattva ideal of the Mahayana:

> There are, in effect, four realities to be envisaged: *Samsara, Nirvana,* the Bodhisattva and the Buddha: the latter may be described, in his capacity of Tathagata as "*Samsara* entered into *Nirvana,*" while the Bodhisattva is on the contrary and in principle "*Nirvana* present in *Samsara.*" Equally it has been said that the Buddha represents the contemplative aspect and the Bodhisattva the dynamic aspect of Nirvana, or that the former is turned towards the Absolute and the latter towards contingency. The Buddha is a ray coming forth from the Center and returning to it, and the Bodhisattva is a circle projecting the Center into the periphery; the Buddha illumines or saves by his radiance like the sun lighting and warming up its own planetary system; while the Bodhisattva ... traces as it were a spiraling converging course through *Samsara,* using the very current of becoming as a means of drawing behind him the unnumbered myriads of beings till, sooner or later, they can be bought to the Center where the wheel of existence itself does not turn and where alone felicity is to be found.[70]

Our discussion of engaged Buddhism has been concerned primarily with the American scene. However, it is well to remember not only that such developments may be easily discerned in other parts of the Western world, but that engaged Buddhism is Asian in provenance and that it is also flourishing in South and Southeastern Asia where many Buddhists, both individually and collectively, are at the coal-face of movements for social change, popular empowerment and political liberation.[71]

D. The Meeting of Buddhism and Feminism

In *Oriental Enlightenment* J.J. Clarke introduces his discussion of the relationship of feminism and Eastern traditions with these words:

70 F. Schuon, *In the Tracks of Buddhism,* 144-145.
71 See C. Queen & S. King, *Engaged Buddhism: Buddhist Liberation Movements in Asia* and B.E. Findly, *Women's Buddhism, Buddhism's Women.*

On the face of it, feminist concerns may seem remote from the wisdom traditions of the East which are deeply embedded in traditionally patriarchal societies. Furthermore, there is a growing body of literature in recent years that has drawn attention to the relationship between imperial rule and gender politics, and has attempted to demonstrate the complicity of orientalism in oppressive gender discourse. In spite of this, however, there are many signs of a developing recognition of the relevance of oriental traditions to issues about gender, and a belief that the feminist agenda can be illuminated by oriental ideas. These latter are drawn on explicitly to help uncover the shortcomings of Western social and moral ideas and practices, such as a patriarchal, rule-based deontological conception of morality; and to help articulate techniques of self-awareness and self-criticism which can be especially important for feminist praxis.[72]

The point at which these developments are most clearly taking place is in the meeting of Buddhism and feminism in America. Some years ago Gary Snyder suggested that

> the single most revolutionary aspect of Buddhist practice in the United States is the fact that women are participating in it ... From the beginning, women essentially had been excluded. But in America, fully fifty per cent of the followers everywhere are women. What that will do to some of the inherited teaching methods and attitudes is going to be quite interesting.[73]

Since that time American Buddhism has witnessed the emergence of women teachers, scholars and activists who are indeed transforming the structures and attitudes of which Snyder spoke. In the pages of the present study we have already met with many of these figures—Toni Packer, Maurine Stuart, Sharon Salzburg, Jiyu Kennett, Joko Beck, Christina Feldman, Ayya Khema, Pema Chodron and Ruth Denison, to name only some. Many of these teachers have written and spoken about the issues which they, as women, have confronted in their own spiritual journeys whilst some have also contributed to the theorization of such subjects as women and Buddhism. Many of these teachers are reluctant to describe themselves as feminists, even though they may share many of the attitudes, values and perspectives which are commonly understood as "feminist." This reluctance would seem to derive not from any equivocation but from a "disinclination to polarize, exclude, proclaim enemies, or solidify around any fixed idea."[74]

Conferences, workshops and retreats directed towards women's issues are now commonplace throughout the Western world, as are women's retreat centers and monasteries. There has also been a steady growth in the literature devoted to the exploration of gender, much of it informed by feminist concerns both theoretical and practical. There has been a growing

72 J. J. Clarke, *Oriental Enlightenment*, 203-204.
73 G. Snyder, *The Real Work*, 106.
74 L. Friedman, *Meetings with Remarkable Women*, 26.

recognition of the pioneering efforts of those women earlier in this century who helped to break down some of the seemingly impenetrable barriers to female participation within the patriarchal traditions of the East and who often worked in more or less complete isolation from other Western women, and without the supportive milieu provided to their successors by the feminist movement. One might mention as illustrative examples Miriam Salanave's little-known three months of training in a Rinzai Zen monastery in Japan in 1929,[75] or the scholarly work of Isaline Horner in *Women Under Primitive Buddhism* (1930), as well as the breakthroughs achieved by women such as Alexandra David-Neel, Ruth Fuller Sasaki, Nancy Wilson Ross and Elsie Mitchell.[76]

Some scholars have re-read the tradition from a feminist perspective to recuperate its often hidden or buried "feminine" dimension, just as feminist theologians such as Rosemary Ruether have done with the Occidental traditions, while others are seeking to inflect traditional teachings in ways which make them more accessible and relevant to contemporary women. Many women practitioners, often bringing the theoretical insights of feminism into play, have also been in the vanguard of on-going debates about sexual exploitation and the abuse of power by (usually male) teachers. Within the American Buddhist community male teachers have reacted in various ways, sometimes resisting, sometimes welcoming the ways in which feminism is changing American Buddhism. Amongst the established male teachers Roshi Robert Aitken has been one of the most sympathetic and creative, making the Diamond Sangha in Hawaii one of the dharma communities which is pioneering these changes. Women writers, poets, painters and the like are also seeking to bring Buddhist principles and insights to bear on their creative work. Earlier we touched on the work of such writers as Diane di Prima, Joanne Kyger, and Lenore Kandel to whom we can now add other figures such as Natalie Goldberg.[77]

Another closely-related development is the growing attention directed towards the issues and problems faced by gay and lesbian practitioners. American Buddhist communities, largely made up of well-educated, liberal-minded people, have been much more accepting of gay and lesbian members than many other religious communities. Jose Ignacio Cabezon, a scholar of contemporary Buddhism, has observed that

> To my knowledge no North American Buddhist institution has ever marginalized its lay homosexual community, nor have any ever impeded the full participation of lay homosexual men and women by, for example, requiring their abstinence. To my knowledge, no gay Westerner has ever been denied Buddhist ordination because of his or her sexual orientation.[78]

75 See A. Rawlinson, *The Book of Enlightened Masters*, 500.
76 On Ross and Mitchell see S. Boucher, *Turning the Wheel*, 184-191.
77 See N. Goldberg, *Long Quiet Highway: Waking Up in America* (1994).
78 Jose Ignacio Cabezon quoted in J. Coleman, *The New Buddhism*, 165-166.

Nonetheless, many questions remain about traditional Buddhist perceptions of and attitudes to sexuality, and about the role that American Buddhism can play in promoting acceptance and respect for sexual difference. Recent times have seen the establishment of groups such as the Gay Buddhist Fellowship and Dharma Sisters, explicitly avowing a gay or lesbian orientation. Buddhist communities have also been especially responsive to the needs of AIDS sufferers, most famously through the Hartford Street Zen Center and the Maitri Hospice in San Francisco, under the leadership of former junkie, drag queen and hooker Issan Dorsey. Dorsey was a student of Shunryu Suzuki in the early 70s and eventually took ordination from Roshi Richard Baker, shortly before his AIDS-related death in 1990.[79]

Signpost works of recent years include *Women in Buddhism* by Diana Paul (1979), Leonore Friedman's anthology of interviews, *Meetings with Remarkable Women* (1987), Sandy Boucher's *Turning the Wheel: American Women Creating the New Buddhism* (1988), and perhaps most significantly, *Buddhism After Patriarchy* (1993) by Rita Gross. In the late 80s Leonore Friedman perceived the changes brought about by the "feminization" of Buddhism in these terms:

> The trend seems to be toward more open, fluid, feminist structures and away from rigid, patriarchal ones; toward democratic consensus processes and away from hierarchy and authoritarianism, toward secular communities of great diversity, centered on practice in the world, in families, in relationships, and concerned with the traditional female values of caring and nurturance.[80]

She expressed the view that the interpenetration of Buddhism and feminism was "wholly natural, wholly auspicious," given their shared premium on direct experience, their positive valuation of intuition and the common theme of the interconnectedness of all beings.[81] Jack Kornfield also wrote of the changes which attended the "reintroduction of the feminine: ... a return to the heart, the validation of feelings and emotion, receptivity, and connection to the earth."[82] Many Buddhist women (and men also) endorse one of the central themes of Rosemary Radford Ruether's early feminist critique of patriarchal religion: spiritual traditions which over-emphasize an other-worldly ideal tend to become misogynistic and ensnared in sexual polarizations. This theme is taken up by Rita Gross, the pre-eminent scholar-adept in the field of the "mutual transformation" of Buddhism and feminism.

Rita Gross is a historian of religions at the University of Wisconsin and also teaches at the Naropa Institute in Boulder, Colorado.[83] She is an editor

---

79 On Dorsey see A. Rawlinson, *The Book of Enlightened Masters*, 245.
80 L. Friedman, *Meetings with Remarkable Women*, 25.
81 L. Friedman, *Meetings with Remarkable Women*, 26.
82 Kornfield quoted in L. Friedman, *Meetings with Remarkable Women*, 32.
83 On Gross' biography see S. Boucher, *Turning the Wheel*, 52-59.

of *Buddhist-Christian Studies,* one of the principal forums for inter-religious dialogue and discussion. Her personal journey has taken her through the strict and dogmatic Lutheranism in which she was raised, through Judaism, to Tantric Buddhism and the Vajradhatu community founded by Chögyam Trungpa. Her principal interests are the encounter of Buddhism and feminism, and inter-religious dialogue.[84] In the "auspicious coincidence of Buddhism and feminism" she finds three central affinities: both are anchored in personal experience rather than theory; the "allegiance to experience before theory" encourages its adherents to "go against the grain at any cost"; both are deeply concerned with the nature of consciousness and the workings of the mind.[85]

In *Buddhism After Patriarchy* Gross argues for feminism both as an academic method, replete with its own theoretical perspectives and conceptual apparatus with which to critique patriarchy, and as a social vision which can enhance the lives not only of men and women but of all living beings and of the entire eco-system. As a historian of religions Gross argues for a move away from an androcentric paradigm which assumes that the males in a religious tradition are normative, takes for granted "the generic masculine habit of thought, language and research," and which deals with women only in relation to men. Gross' agenda for the transformation of Buddhism identifies three far-reaching changes: the embrace of a life- and world-affirming spirituality which would blur the traditional sacred/profane distinctions; the acceptance of an androgynic "two-sex" model of humanity which accepts the co-humanity of women and men[86] and which institutionalizes gender equality;[87] and the re-envisioning of the *sangha* nourished by "the feminist values of community, nurturance, communication, relationship and friendship."[88]

Gross is no less interested in the ways in which Buddhism can transform feminism, believing that "Buddha-dharma simply goes far deeper than feminism in laying bare the basic human situation."[89] Buddhist teachings can deepen the feminist understanding of suffering and qualify the simplistic assumption that human pain arises only out of patriarchy and faulty social organization. Buddhist meditational practice Gross sees as a powerful method by which feminist anger and aggression can be transmuted and harnessed to more enlightened social purposes.[90] Meditation can also give birth to more "gentleness and humor, some spaciousness in the intelligence"[91] and break down the hard protective shell of rigid ideology.

84 On the latter subject see, for instance, R. Gross, "This Buddhist's View of Jesus."
85 R. Gross, "Buddhism and Feminism I," 47-49.
86 R. Gross, *Buddhism After Patriarchy,* 222.
87 R. Gross, *Buddhism After Patriarchy,* 128.
88 R. Gross, *Buddhism After Patriarchy,* 265.
89 R. Gross, "Buddhism and Feminism I," 51.
90 See S. Boucher, *Turning the Wheel,* 52-59.
91 R. Gross, "Buddhism and Feminism I," 54.

Sandy Boucher interviewed all manner of women involved in Buddhist teaching and practice for her book *Turning the Wheel*. In the second edition of 1993 Boucher summed up the goals and aspirations of many dharma practitioners:

> As we move toward the twenty-first century, we as women involved in Buddhist practice must support women teachers, become teachers, and insist on the accountability of teachers to their students. We must seek a truer account of women's past involvement in Buddhism, demanding that women be visible in the texts and rituals. We must become more aware of our Asian Buddhist sisters, laywomen and monastics, support them, and learn from them. Psychology, feminism, peacemaking, efforts to honor and protect our environment, all complement our practice of Buddhist meditation, encourage compassionate action, and interweave with our study of Buddhist lore.[92]

Before leaving this subject it should be noted that feminism has exerted its presence in other Western dharma communities and amongst students of Eastern traditions. The Hindu tradition is well-stocked with doctrinal, mythological and ritual elements which command the attention of feminists while Taoism, with its valorization of the "valley spirit," the "mysterious Feminine," has also proved to be a fertile source of materials for those working to redress the imbalance of hyper-rationalist and over-masculinized Western conceptions of gender, sexuality, spirituality and nature.[93] The *yin-yang* motif in Chinese thought has frequently been appropriated by feminists and others seeking to dismantle some of the rigid dichotomies that afflict Western thought at almost every turn.[94] We should also note recent attempts to examine the ramifications of race and ethnicity as well as gender in the Western assimilation of Eastern traditions.[95]

*

In this chapter we have been concerned with some of the political issues arising out of the encounter of Eastern traditions and modern Western culture, and with the more general relationship of "politics," "religion" and "spirituality." Two of the figures, one Indian and one American, who have considered these issues most deeply and most creatively, are Mahatma Gandhi and Thomas Merton. It is fitting that we should conclude with the Trappist monk's meditation on Gandhi's significance for the world as a whole, one which can be endorsed by practitioners of all religious traditions:

> One of the great lessons of Gandhi's life remains this: through the spiritual traditions of the West he, an Indian, discovered his Indian heritage and with

92 See S. Boucher, *Turning the Wheel*, 361.
93 See S. Colegrave, *Uniting Heaven and Earth*.
94 See J.C. Cooper, *Yin & Tang: the Union of Opposites*.
95 See, for example, J. Willis, "Diversity and Race: New *Koans* for American Buddhism" and R. Fields, "Divided Dharma: White Buddhists, Ethnic Buddhists, and Racism."

it his own "right mind." And in his fidelity to his own heritage and its spiritual sanity, he was able to show [people] of the West and of the whole world a way to recover their own "right mind" in their own tradition, thus manifesting the fact that there are certain indisputable and essential values—religious, ethical, ascetic, spiritual and philosophical ... It was the spiritual consciousness of a people that awakened in the spirit of one person. But the message of the Indian spirit, of Indian wisdom, was not for India alone. It was for the entire world. Hence Gandhi's message was valid for India and for himself in so far as it represented the awakening of a new world. The Indian mind that was awakening in Gandhi was inclusive not exclusive. It was at once Indian and universal. It was not a mind of hate, of intolerance, of accusation, of rejection, of division. It was a mind of love, of understanding, of infinite capaciousness.[96]

96 T. Merton, *Gandhi on Non-Violence*, 4-5.

IV

Notes

on

Inter-religious Re-visionings

15.

"The Translucence of the Eternal": Towards a Cross-cultural Religious Understanding of the Natural Order

---

Traditional Cosmogonies and Cosmological Principles—The Nature of *Maya* and the Putative "World-Denial" of the East—The Sacred and Profane, and the Human Situation—The Symbolism of Natural Forms and the Cosmological Sciences—Beauty: Divine Rays—The Western Desacralization of Nature

---

Thou art the fire,
Thou art the sun,
Thou art the air,
Thou art the moon,
Thou art the starry firmament,
Thou art Brahman Supreme:
Thou art the waters,
The creator of all!

Thou art woman, thou art man,
Thou art the youth, thou art the maiden,
thou art the old man tottering with his staff;
Thou facest everywhere.
Thou art the dark butterfly,
thou art the green parrot with red eyes,
Thou art the thunder cloud, the seasons, the seas.
Without beginning art thou, beyond time, beyond space.
Thou art he from whom sprang the three worlds.
                    (Svetasvatara Upanishad)[1]

For the sage each flower is metaphysically a proof of the Infinite.
(Frithjof Schuon)[2]

As we have seen, the theme of the inter-relatedness of all phenomena is integral to "engaged Buddhism," as indeed it is to the new physics. One of the arenas in which this idea is on prominent display, often enhanced by reference to Eastern traditions, is what is loosely called environmentalism. Not only Buddhism but Hinduism, Taoism and Confucianism have all been seen

---

1   *Svetasvatara Upanishad* IV.2-4.
2   F. Schuon, *Spiritual Perspectives and Human Facts*, 10.

to have a contribution to make, particularly in the development of "ecoso-phy" or "eco-spirituality"—a philosophy of nature which surpasses materialis-tic and humanistic concerns and reaches towards a holistic understanding which entails a more sensitive and creative way of "being in the world," and which might be better equipped to lighten the way out of our present predicaments. Wayne Teasdale has gone so far as to say that

> Eco-spirituality, or creation-centered spirituality, is the most important development in [the 20th] century, ranking in significance to the discovery of the printing press and the Copernican Revolution ... for with it emerges the realization of the earth and the universe as the heart or focus of our intellectual, moral, aesthetic, practical and spiritual lives ... the pantheis-tic intuition and experience will be perennially relevant, inspiring afresh future generations for as long as man inhabits this planet.[3]

Rather than isolating each of the Eastern religions and examining their potential contributions to an emergent ecosophy we will here discuss the broader issue of what role a cross-cultural *religious* understanding of the nat-ural order might play. Wilfred Cantwell Smith, a scholar and bridge-builder of some eminence, has argued that, "Our new task is to interpret intellectu-ally the cosmic significance of human life *generically*" within the context of a "single religious history of mankind" in which the different traditions are, so to speak, strands within a single rope.[4] Our discussion here is conducted in the spirit of Smith's clarion call. We will make some reference to Eastern themes and motifs which have been heavily accented in ecosophical dis-course. Our purpose is to identify some of the central *principles* which must inform a properly constituted trans-religious understanding of the whole cos-mos. This will also allow us to incorporate archaic mythological traditions and primal religions, another primary source for those looking beyond the recent European past for deeper modes of understanding and for planetary solutions. However, it should be stated quite unequivocally at the outset that this enterprise could never produce the foundation for some sort of univer-sal "religion" or any other such sentimentality. Rather, its purpose must be to re-awaken a sense of the "eco-spirituality" which already exists within each religious tradition, and to heighten our awareness of those principles and values which we share despite the necessary diversity of religious forms. To believe that there is a necessary conflict between these forms and the imper-atives of a new planetary consciousness is to misunderstand the case altogeth-er and, worse, to imagine that "religion" is something which humankind can construct out of its own resources.

Seyyed Hossein Nasr opens his book, *Religion and the Order of Nature* (1996), with these words:

---

3 W. Teasdale, "Nature Mysticism," 230.
4 W. C. Smith, *Towards a World Theology*, 86-87, quoted in P. Novak, "Universal Theology," 183.

> The Earth is bleeding from wounds inflicted upon it by a humanity no
> longer in harmony with Heaven and therefore in constant strife with the ter-
> restrial environment.[5]

That we are now in a state of "constant strife" is widely recognized but the
root cause of this condition—the scission between man and God—is rarely
understood. We witness a flood of writings on the "ecological crisis," often
well-intentioned and enlivened by partial insights, but fundamentally confused because of an ignorance of timeless metaphysical and cosmological
principles. As William Blake pithily remarked, "A fool sees not the same tree
that a wise man sees." The modern mentality characteristically looks for solutions to our most urgent problems in the wrong places; more often than not
the proposed remedies aggravate the malady. Various responses to the so-
called environmental crisis are of this type. As Nasr has observed,

> most Western intellectuals think about environmental issues as if everyone
> were an agnostic following a secular philosophy cultivated at Oxford,
> Cambridge or Harvard and so they seek to develop a rationalist environ-
> mental ethics based upon agnosticism, as if this would have any major effect
> whatsoever upon the environmental crisis ... the very strong prejudice
> against religious ethics ... is itself one of the greatest impediments to the
> solution of the environmental crisis itself. This fact cannot be doubted in
> any way.[6]

Hardly anyone is now foolish enough to deny that there is something fundamentally wrong with our way of "being in the world." The evidence is too
overwhelming for even the most sanguine apostles of "progress" to ignore.
However, as Nasr notes, much of the debate about the "environment" (itself
a rather problematical term) continues to be conducted in terms derived
from the secular-scientific-rationalist-humanist world-view bequeathed to us
by that series of upheavals which sabotaged the medieval outlook—the
Renaissance and Reformation, the Scientific Revolution, the Enlightenment.
It is a sign of the times that a book as muddled as E.O. Wilson's *Consilience*
should have been so widely heralded.[7] We have recently seen a plethora of
articles and essays devoted to questions such as "How ecological is
Buddhism?" Much of this literature is misconceived, firstly because it
assumes (with an impertinence that is characteristically modern) that an ecological science, of a more or less purely materialistic kind and of recent
Western provenance, provides us with a platform from which to "evaluate"
the environmentalist "credentials" of ancient wisdoms such as Buddhism,
and secondly, because it is riddled with scientistic assumptions (of which evolutionism in both its biological and cultural guises is the most conspicuous)
which immediately disqualify it from any understanding of what the Eastern
conceptions might actually comprise. To make the same point slightly differ-

5 S.H. Nasr, *Religion and the Order of Nature*, 3.
6 S.H. Nasr, *The Spiritual and Religious Dimensions of the Environmental Crisis*, 7, 9.

ently: bringing a Eurocentric, post-Enlightenment, "scientific" mentality to bear on traditional metaphysical and cosmological doctrines is unlikely to shed much light on the "environmental" problem which is itself largely a product of the very mentality in question. What is needed is, rather, a re-assessment of the paradigms and procedures of a materialistic science in the light of a wisdom which far surpasses it.

Nor does it much advance our cause to point out, as many scholars have recently done, that the environmental record of many Asian countries is quite deplorable. It is increasingly clear that not only have air and water pollution, acid rain, deforestation, desertification, and the extinction of species reached terrible proportions in many countries, but that many of these processes are the culmination of centuries of exploitation and neglect. For centuries a holistic and benevolent understanding of "nature" and its thoughtless and rapacious exploitation have co-existed. Environmental delinquency cannot simplistically be pinned on to the already lengthy catalogue of ills introduced by the West although it is no doubt true that Western industrial technologies have often accelerated the despoliation of nature. It is also palpably true that these processes cannot be arrested without recourse to modern science and technology.[8]

All this notwithstanding, it is perfectly evident to those with eyes to see and ears to hear that the desecration (one uses the word advisedly) of nature cannot be remedied without recourse to the principles which governed traditional understandings of the natural order, from both East and West, and from the primal cultures of non-literate peoples. These might offer some hope where modern scientism has so spectacularly failed. This intuition informs the work of some of the more perspicacious of recent participants in the ecological debate, amongst whom we may include several thinkers deeply influenced by Eastern cosmologies—Huston Smith, Gary Snyder, E.F. Schumacher, Arne Naess, Joanna Macy, Edward Goldsmith.[9] However, it is those thinkers who have most fully and thoroughly understood the cosmological sciences *within* a properly constituted *metaphysical* framework and through the *religious* forms of particular traditions—René Guénon, Frithjof Schuon, Titus Burckhardt, Seyyed Hossein Nasr—who can fully fathom the issues at stake here. Of living writers, Seyyed Hossein Nasr has written on this subject with peerless authority and no one seriously interested in this subject can afford to ignore his three major works in this field: *Man and Nature* (1968), *Knowledge and the Sacred* (1981), and *Religion and the Order of Nature* (1996).

None of what follows should be construed as an attack on science proper: we are concerned with the inadequacies of a *scientistic* epistemology,

7 For a compelling critique of Wilson's *Consilience* see W. Berry, *Life is a Miracle*.
8 See P. Novak, "Tao How?"
9 Two others prominent in this debate, Thomas Berry and Matthew Fox, have apparently taken no more than a superficial interest in Eastern cosmology.

ontology and world view, not with scientific discoveries as such. Nor does the following attempt to synthesize a cross-cultural and religious understanding of the natural order amount to a denial of the role that scientific inquiry can and should play in finding a way out of the environmental catastrophe in which we find ourselves—but assuredly, it cannot do this on its own. One of the lessons which the Western scientific establishment is so loath to learn is that a Promethean science, rooted in materialistic assumptions and procedures, can only exacerbate the problem.[10] It will only be when our scientific endeavors are harnessed to the service of the principles and values enshrined in tradition that there may be some small hope that the headlong rush towards wholesale ecological ruination might yet be turned around.

Traditional Cosmogonies and Cosmological Principles
The first question which might present itself in any inquiry into religious perspectives on nature is this: how does this or that religion in particular, or how do religions in general, envisage the origin, the source of the universe? Generally speaking we can say that the different religions, from both East and West, and from both primal and literate cultures, account for the beginnings of the universe through a mythological account, a cosmogony. In the Judeo-Christian tradition we find it in the *Genesis* story. While the narrative details vary, this is not essentially different from, let us say, the mythical accounts of the *Vedas*, or of the Aboriginal Dreaming. We have already noted how "myth" has acquired a negative and pejorative meaning—a naïve and childish fabrication or simply a story which is untrue. We must return to earlier outlooks if we are to understand religious myths (from wherever they come) aright, not as the fumbling attempts by ignorant "primitives" to explain natural phenomena, but rather as allegorical or symbolic narratives which articulate, in dramatic form, a world-view whose elements will necessarily include a *metaphysic* (an account of the Real; the metacosmic), a *cosmology* (an account of the visible world, in the heavens and here on earth; the macrocosmic) and an *anthropology* (an account of the human situation; the microcosmic). In combating the impudent reductionisms of the anthropologists Ananda Coomaraswamy reminds us that,

> Myth is the penultimate truth, of which all experience is the temporal reflection. The mythical narrative is of timeless and placeless validity, true nowhere and everywhere ... Myth embodies the nearest approach to absolute truth that can be stated in words ...[11]

Cosmogonies can be located on a spectrum one end of which might be labeled *creationist/theistic* and the other *emanationist/monistic*: the former kind

---

10 It should be acknowledged that there are an increasing number of individual scientists who have indeed learned this lesson.

11 A.K. Coomaraswamy, *Hinduism and Buddhism*, 6 & 33, fn21.

envisages the universe as a creation of a divine power or deity while the latter conceives of the universe as a spatio-temporal manifestation of an ultimate, spiritual reality. The Abrahamic monotheisms are of the former type, while Platonism and most Oriental cosmogonies represent the latter. In the *Mundaka Upanishad*, for instance, we are told that,

> As a spider sends forth and draws in its threads, as herbs grow on the earth, as hair grows on the head and the body of a living person, so from the Imperishable arises here the universe.[12]

Traditional cosmogonies necessarily deal with the relationship of spiritual and material realities, one which lies at the heart of all religious understandings of nature. Religions posit the existence of two "worlds," one spiritual, immutable and absolute, the other material, mutable and relative, usually with an intermediary realm (which might variously be referred to as ethereal, subtle, astral and the like). Cosmogonies affirm the primacy of the spiritual: the material world derives from a divine creativity, or, at least, from a divine plenitude. Schuon states the relationship between God and man, in the vocabulary of monotheism, this way:

> That we are conformed to God—made in His image—this is certain; otherwise we should not exist. That we are contrary to God, this is also certain; otherwise we should not be different from God. Without analogy to God we should be nothing. Without opposition to God we should be God. The separation between man and God is at the same time absolute and relative ... The separation is absolute because God alone is real and no continuity is possible between nothingness and Reality; but the separation is relative—or rather "not absolute"—because nothing is outside God. In a sense it might be said that the separation is absolute as from man to God and relative as from God to man.[13]

In the religious context it is axiomatic that the material world did not and could not create itself; it is suspended, so to speak, within a reality which is immaterial and which is beyond time and space; the material world has no independent or autonomous existence. Consider a few quotes (one could easily assemble hundreds of such passages from all over the globe):

> There is something obscure which is complete
> before heaven and earth arose;
> tranquil, quiet, standing alone without change,

---

12 *Mundaka Upanishad* I.i.7. Of the major religious traditions the one which has least to say about the origins of the universe is Buddhism which is generally suspicious of metaphysical speculation and eschews what the Buddha called the Indeterminate Questions, which is to say questions which are either unanswerable, at least in terms accessible to the ordinary human mentality, or which are distractions from the business at hand. Sometimes it is said by Buddhists that the universe "always was"; this, perhaps, is to be understood as being *upaya*—a kind of sufficient expedient, so to speak. However, from a metaphysical viewpoint, the *Prajna-Paramita* states, "the belief in the unity or eternity of matter is incomprehensible ..."; quoted in W. Perry, *The Widening Breach: Evolutionism in the Mirror of Cosmology*, 44.

13 F. Schuon, *Spiritual Perspectives and Human Facts*, 160-161.

moving around without peril.
It could be the Mother of everything.
I don't know its name,
and call it Tao. (*Tao Te Ching*)[14]

The Imperishable is the Real. As sparks fly upward from a blazing fire, so from the depths of the Imperishable arise all things. To the depths of the Imperishable they again descend. Self-luminous is that Being, and formless. He dwells within all and without all ... From him are born breath, mind, the organs of sense, ether, air, fire, water and the earth, and he binds all these together. (*Mundaka Upanishad*)[15]

This world, with all its stars, elements, and creatures, is come out of the invisible world; it has not the smallest thing or the smallest quality of anything but what is come forth from thence. (William Law)[16]

Cosmogonies tell of the coming into being of the *cosmos*, a living, organic unity displaying beauty, harmony, meaning, intelligibility, as against the chaotic, inert, and meaningless universe of modern science. Joseph Campbell has argued that it was the ancient Mesopotamians who first articulated the idea of a vast cosmic *order*, and calls this "discovery" "the most important and far reaching cultural mutation ... in the history of the human race."[17] Whether one accepts this claim or is content to believe that a sense of cosmic order is actually part of the human birthright and thus without any historical origin, it remains true that a sense of cosmic harmony, evident to primordial man in the regular movements of the heavenly bodies, has been an integral part of all mythological and religious traditions. Furthermore, each tradition, in its own spiritual vocabulary and with regards to the whole spiritual economy which it enshrines, has insisted that the individual human subject must attune him/herself to an eternal order of which the visible cosmos is an expression. As one contemporary historian of philosophy has put it:

> On the traditional view, the notion of a subject coming to self-presence and clarity in the absence of any cosmic order, or in ignorance of and unrelated to the cosmic order, is utterly senseless.[18]

Yes, quite so! *Kosmos*, in its original Greek and in archaic times meant Great Man as well as "world": in the light of various cosmogonies, particularly the Greek and the Indian, this fact is pregnant with significance. In the *Vedas* we have but one of many accounts of the universe being created out of *Purusa*, a cosmic man, Primordial Man, a Divine Archetypal figure.

14 *Tao Te Ching* XXV.
15 *Mundaka Upanishad* II.i.1-4.
16 *Selected Mystical Writings*, quoted in W. Perry, *Treasury of Traditional Wisdom*, 26.
17 J. Campbell, *The Mythic Image*, quoted in P. Novak, "Universal Theology," 85.
18 Charles Taylor quoted in P. Novak, "Universal Theology," 86.

One of the most beautiful expressions of the idea of an underlying harmony in the universe is to be found in the Taoist tradition and in the symbol of the *Tao* itself wherein we see the forces of *yin* and *yang* intertwined, these being the two fundamental energies out of which the fabric of the material universe is woven. In Hinduism the harmony, order and intelligibility of the universe is signaled by the Vedic term *rta* which we find in the earliest Scriptures. Later the idea of *rta* is subsumed within the concept of *dharma* which has many fields of application, both social and cosmic. We also find a sense of this underlying order and harmony in the writings of the great Romantic poets. From Wordsworth's "Lines Composed Above Tintern Abbey," for instance:

And I have felt
A presence that disturbs me with joy
Of elevated thoughts: a sense sublime
Of something far more deeply interfused,
Whose dwelling is the light of setting suns,
And the round ocean and the living air,
And the blue sky, and in the mind of man;
A motion and a spirit, that impels
All thinking things, all objects of all thought,
And rolls through all things. Therefore am I still
A lover of meadows and the woods,
And mountains; and of all that we behold
From this green earth; of all the mighty world
Of eye, and ear,—both what they half create,
And what perceive; well pleased to recognize
In nature and the language of sense,
The anchor of my purest thoughts, the nurse,
The guide, the guardian of my heart, and soul
Of all my moral being.

The harmony, intelligibility and beneficent influence on humankind of the natural order, and the attunement of the sage to natural rhythms, are particularly strong leitmotifs in Taoism but are to be found in many Eastern Scriptures. By the same token, humans are enjoined to play their part in the maintenance of the cosmic order, largely through their ritual life. This idea, everywhere to be found in the archaic worlds, makes no sense from a materialistic point of view which now determines the prevailing outlook—one completely impervious to the fact that, in Nasr's memorable phrase, "nature is hungry for our prayers."[19]

Religious doctrines (which might be expressed in any number of forms, not necessarily verbal) about the relationship of the spiritual and material worlds necessarily deal with the *transcendence* and *immanence* of the Absolute (whether this be envisaged in theistic, monistic, panentheistic or apophatic

19 S.H. Nasr, *The Spiritual and Religious Dimensions of the Environmental Crisis*, 13.

terms—God, Allah, *Brahman, Tao, Wakan-Tanka, nirvana,* or whatever): the "interplay" of these two "dimensions" varies from religion to religion but both are always present. Whatever accent a particular spiritual economy might place on these aspects of the Real the underlying principle is always the same and might best be summed up by an old Rabbinical dictum: "The universe is not the dwelling place of God; God is the dwelling place of the universe."[20] In the light of these kinds of formulations we can also dispense with the sharp dualistic separation of the "two worlds": the world of phenomena is held together by a numinous spiritual presence—indeed, without it the world of "matter" would vanish instantly and completely. Eternity is ever-present within (so to speak) the phenomenal world. The mystic Jan van Ruysbroeck referred to this inner reality as

> beyond Time; that is, without before or after, in an Eternal Now ... the home and beginning of all life and all becoming. And so all creatures are therein, beyond themselves, one being and one Life ... as in their eternal origin.[21]

That such a passage has strong Eastern resonances should surprise no one.

At this point it is as well to dispel a misunderstanding which bedevils many discussions of the beliefs of non-literate peoples, one signaled by the term "pantheism," i.e. the worship of the natural order as coterminous with "God." This, we are sometimes told (usually by anthropologists) was the practice of this or that "primitive" people. In reality, pantheism, if ever it existed as anything other than an anthropological fiction, could never have been more than a degenerate form of what is properly called "panentheism,"[22] which is to say a belief in the overwhelming presence of the spiritual within the natural world—a quite different matter from the "pantheistic" fallacy that the natural world is somehow identical to (and thus exhausts) "God." Black Elk, the revered holy man of the Oglala, clearly articulated the panentheistic principle in the inimitable idiom of the Plains Indians:

> We should understand that all things are the work of the Great Spirit. We should know that He is within all things; the trees, the grasses, the rivers, the mountains, all the four-legged animals and the winged peoples; *and even more important we should understand that He is also above all these things and peoples.*[23]

There are those who seek to develop an "eco-spirituality" which actually amounts to no more than a kind of secular pantheism, if one may allow such a term—a view of the natural order which retains some sort of "religiosity," surrendering to the view that it is possible to have an immanent "sacred"

---

20 Quoted in S. Radhakrishnan, *Selected Writings on Philosophy, Religion and Culture,* 146.

21 Ruysbroeck quoted in P. Sherrard, *Christianity: Lineaments of a Sacred Tradition,* 208.

22 The term was coined by the German philosopher Karl C.F. Krause (1781-1832); see W. Teasdale, "Nature Mysticism," 228.

23 J.E. Brown, *The Sacred Pipe,* xx (italics mine).

while dispensing with the transcendent, as if there could be a circle with no center.[24] Like all such concoctions this kind of naturism is a form of idolatry. As Philip Sherrard has so plainly put it, "an agnostic and materialistic science of nature is a contradiction in terms ... its findings will necessarily correspond to the living reality of nature as little as a corpse corresponds to the living reality of a human being ..."[25] Equally absurd is the notion of a "secular scientific spirituality" which has recently been proposed.[26]

Maya and the Putative "World-Denial" of the East

Another tenacious misunderstanding, often promulgated by the early orientalists, is the notion that the Eastern traditions, particularly Hinduism and Buddhism, are "world-denying"—i.e., they hold the view that the world of material phenomena (*maya*) is completely illusory and without any positive value. This is to understand only one aspect of the doctrine of *maya* and its relation to the absolute (*Brahman*). We shall counter this misunderstanding by a brief discussion of the positive aspect of *maya*, as understood in the *Advaita* Vedanta of Sankara (supposedly one of the seed-beds of "world-denial"). *Maya* is indeed "cosmic illusion" but

> ... she is also divine play. She is the great theophany, the unveiling of God "In Himself and by Himself" as the Sufis would say. *Maya* may be likened to a magic fabric woven from a warp that veils and a weft that unveils; she is the quasi-incomprehensible intermediary between the finite and the Infinite—at least from our point of view as creatures—and as such she has all the multi-colored ambiguity appropriate to her part-cosmic, part-divine nature.[27]

Thus,

> ... the term *maya* combines the meanings of "productive power" and "universal illusion"; it is the inexhaustible play of manifestations, deployments, combinations and reverberations, a play with which *Atma* clothes itself even as the ocean clothes itself with a mantle of foam ever renewed and never the same.[28]

Maya has also been called the principle of "self-expression" of Isvara (the Lord of the universe). In this context:

> Creation is expression. It is not a making of something out of nothing. It is not making so much as becoming. It is the self-projection of the Supreme.

---

24 For a specimen see N. Hettinger, "Ecospirituality: First Thoughts."

25 P. Sherrard, *Christianity: Lineaments of a Sacred Tradition*, 219.

26 See, for example, Holmes Rolston III, "Secular Scientific Spirituality."

27 F. Schuon, *Light on the Ancient Worlds*, 89. See also A. Lakhani, "What Thirst is For" in *Sacred Web*, 4, 13-14.

28 F. Schuon, *Logic and Transcendence*, 89fn.

Everything exists in the secret abode of the Supreme. The primary reality contains within itself the source of its own motion and change.[29]

In the *Brahma-Sutra Bhasya* Sankara says:

The activity of the Lord ... may be supposed to be mere sport [*lila*] proceeding from his own nature, without reference to any purpose.[30]

This recalls Krsna's words in the *Bhagavad Gita.*

There is naught in the three worlds that I have need to do, nor anything I have not gotten that I might get, yet I participate in action.[31]

This idea of the playfulness of the Creator Lord is found in the *Rg Veda*, the *Upanishads* and the *Gita* though the word *lila* as such is not always used.[32] The notion conveys that Isvara's creation answers to no compelling necessity or constraint but arises out of an inherent exuberance or joy. It is spontaneous, purposeless, without responsibility or moral consequence—in short, like play.

Ramakrishna was fond of recounting the following story which contains something of this idea of the playfulness of Isvara. (The anecdote is perfumed with the scents of Hindu spirituality.)

Once there came a *sadhu* here [Ramakrishna would relate] who had a beautiful glow on his face. He just sat and smiled. Twice a day, once in the morning and once in the evening, he'd come out of his room and look around. He'd look at the trees, the bushes, the sky and Ganges and he'd raise his arms and dance, beside himself with joy. Or he'd roll on the ground, laughing and exclaiming "Bravo! What fun! How wonderful it is, this *maya.* What an illusion God has conjured up!" This was his way of doing worship.[33]

It may be noted in passing that the idea of God's playfulness is by no means peculiar to the Hindu tradition. This formulation from Meister Eckhart, for instance, is in no way at odds with Sankara's: "There has always been this play going on in the Father-nature ... sport and players are the same."[34] Or this, from Boehme: "The creation is the same sport out of himself."[35]

The *maya*-world is "illusory," but not in the sense that it is a mirage or a fantasy, but in that its "reality" is only relative: it has no independence, no autonomy, no existence outside the Divine Principle Itself. It is an ever changing and fugitive tissue of relativities, one which both veils and disclos-

---

29 S. Radhakrishnan, *Selected Writings*, 141.

30 Sankara, *Brahma-Sutra Bhasya* II.i.33, quoted in E. Deutsch, *Advaita Vedanta*, 38. For the context see Swami Gambhirananda's translation, 361.

31 *Bhagavad Gita* 3.xxii-xxv. See A.K. Coomaraswamy, "Lila" in *Selected Papers 2*, 150.

32 A.K. Coomaraswamy, "Lila" in *Selected Papers 2*, 151. See also "Play and Seriousness" in the same volume, 156-158.

33 C. Isherwood, *Ramakrishna and His Disciples*, 103.

34 A.K. Coomaraswamy, "Lila" in *Selected Papers 2*, 148.

35 A.K. Coomaraswamy, "Lila" in *Selected Papers 2*, 148.

es the Absolute. The sages of the East, in all traditions, have never been seduced by the idea that the material universe is a self-existing entity, which is to say that they have ever understood that there is no such thing as "pure matter." Their understanding of the cosmos derives from *all* the sources of knowledge—mystical intuition and the revealed Scriptures *as well as* the instruments of the mind and the senses. Modern science (from whence the modern West derives its understanding of the universe), on the other hand, is

> ... a totalitarian rationalism that eliminates both Revelation and Intellect, and at the same time a totalitarian materialism that ignores the metaphysical relativity—and therewith the impermanence—of matter and the world. It does not know that the supra-sensible, situated as it is beyond space and time, is the concrete principle of the world, and consequently that it is also at the origin of that contingent and changeable coagulation we call "matter." A science that is called "exact" is in fact an "intelligence without wisdom," just as post-scholastic philosophy is inversely a "wisdom without intelligence."[36]

Without pursuing the matter here we can note that the charge of "world-denial" directed particularly against Buddhism rests on a very partial understanding of *samsara* to the neglect of its complement, *dharma*, by which is meant not simply the teachings of the Awakened One (its most familiar sense, at least to Westerners) but a pre-existent and eternal order to which these teachings testified and of which they are one expression.[37]

The Sacred and the Profane, and the Human Situation

A category without which we cannot proceed very far in the study of religion is the sacred. There are many ways of defining it. Here is one from a discussion of Sacred Books by Frithjof Schuon:

> That is sacred which in the first place is attached to the transcendent order, secondly possesses the character of absolute certainty, and thirdly, eludes the comprehension of the ordinary human mind ... The sacred is the presence of the center in the periphery ... The sacred introduces a quality of the absolute into relativities and confers on perishable things a texture of eternity.[38]

Of course, the category can apply to all manner of things: events, texts, buildings, images, rituals. In the context of our present concerns we might isolate two applications of this category or principle: to space and time, and to life itself. The traditional mind, especially in primal societies, perceives and experiences space and time as "sacred" and "profane," which is to say that

---

36 F. Schuon, *Light on the Ancient Worlds*, 117.
37 On this crucial point see P. Novak, "Universal Theology," 87-88.
38 F. Schuon, *Understanding Islam*, 48.

they are not uniform and homogeneous as they are for the scientific mind, but are *qualitatively* differentiated. A good deal of ceremonial life is concerned with entry into or, better, *participation in* sacred time and space.[39] Through ritual one enters into sacred time, into real time, the "once upon a time," *illo tempore*, a time radically different from any "horizontal" temporal duration. Likewise with sacred places, remembering that a natural site can be *made* sacred through various rituals and practices, or it can be recognized as sacred—a place where the membrane, so to speak, between the worlds of matter and spirit are especially permeable. Rivers, mountains, particular types of trees and places related to the mythological events are sites of this sort. The sacredness of Mt Kailas or Uluru, for instance, is not *conferred* but *apprehended*.

The sanctity of life itself is expressed in different ways in the various religious vocabularies. In the Judeo-Christian tradition this principle or theme begins in the affirmation in *Genesis* that man is made in the image of God, that the human being carries an indelible imprint of the divine. Thence we have what might be called the principle of the spiritual equality of all human beings no matter what their station in life or their natural attributes and shortcomings—"all equal before God," as the Christian formulation has it. The Judeo-Christian tradition has primarily affirmed the sanctity of human life, sometimes to the neglect or abuse of other life forms. One of the lessons of the great Eastern and primal religions is the principle of the moral solidarity, if one may so express it, of all living forms: in Hinduism, Buddhism and Jainism this is embodied in the traditional Indian value of *ahimsa* (non-injuriousness). William Blake affirmed the same notion in his famous words, "all that lives is holy."

The principle of the sanctity of life, and what I have termed the moral solidarity of living forms should not blind us to the fact that all traditional wisdoms affirm, in their different ways, that the human being is especially privileged. The human is an axial or amphibious being who lives in both the material and spiritual worlds in a way which is not quite true of other living beings, and is thus a bridge between them. Seyyed Hossein Nasr reminds us that,

> Man's central position in the world is not due to his cleverness or inventive genius but because of the possibility of attaining sanctity and becoming a channel of grace for the world around him ... the very grandeur of the human condition is precisely that he has the possibility of reaching a state "higher than the angels" and at the same time of denying God.[40]

This religious understanding is, of course, quite incompatible with the notion that man is simply another biological organism. By the same measure,

---

39 One of the most useful expositions of archaic understandings of sacred and profane time and space is to be found in M. Eliade, *The Sacred and the Profane*.

40 S.H. Nasr, *Ideals and Realities of Islam*, 24-25.

it is utterly at odds with that most seductive and elegant (and certainly one of the most pernicious) of scientistic hypotheses, Darwinian evolutionism. As Blake so well understood, "Man is either the ark of God or a phantom of the earth and of the water." As "the ark of God" man is the guardian and custodian of the natural order, the pontifex, the caliph, in Qur'anic terms "the viceregent of God on earth."[41]

The peculiar position of the human being can also be illuminated by recourse to the traditional cosmological principle of the microcosm/macrocosm, expressed most succinctly in the Hermetic maxim, "as above, so below." In brief, man is not only in the universe but the universe is in man: "there is nothing in heaven or earth that is not also in man" (Paracelsus).[42] The Buddha put it this way: "In truth I say to you that within this fathom-high body ... lies the world and the rising of the world and the ceasing of the world."[43] Others have rendered the same truth poetically. Recall the beautiful lines of Thomas Traherne:

> You never enjoy the world aright, till the Sea
> itself floweth in your veins, till you are
> clothed with the heavens, and crowned with
> the stars: and perceive yourself to be the sole
> heir of the whole world, and more than so,
> because men are in it who are every one sole
> heirs as well as you.[44]

Similarly, from Blake:

> To see a world in a grain of sand,
> And Heaven in a wild flower,
> Hold infinity in the palm of your hand,
> And Eternity in an hour.[45]

One of the keys to this principle resides in the traditional understanding of consciousness as infinite, as surpassing the temporal and spatial limits of the ever-changing world of appearances.

The Symbolism of Natural Forms and the Cosmological Sciences
An adequate comprehension of the natural order must be informed by the doctrine of archetypes and the attendant understanding of symbolism.[46] In former times the doctrine of archetypes was espoused the world over. No integral tradition has been able to do without it though the language in

---

41 See Jean-Louis Michon, "The Vocation of Man According to the Koran." See also K. Cragg, *The Mind of the Qur'an*.
42 Quoted in T.C. McLuhan, *Cathedrals of the Spirit*, 270.
43 Quoted in H. Smith, *Forgotten Truth*, 60.
44 "Centuries of Meditations."
45 "Auguries of Innocence."
46 Considering the popularity of Jung's ideas about "archetypes" it is as well to make it clear that

which it is clothed may speak not of archetypes but of "essences," "universals," "lights," "Divine Ideas" and so on. Plato gave the doctrine its most definitive European expression but there is nothing peculiarly Occidental about it as such. It lies at the root of all traditional theories of art. By way of introduction, let us consider the following sample of suggestive quotations:

> Yonder world is in the likeness of this world, this world is the likeness of that. (*Aitereya Brahmana*)[47]

> A form is made in the resigned will according to the platform or model of eternity, as it was known in God's eternal wisdom before the times of this world. (Jacob Boehme)

> All forms of being in this corporeal world are images of pure Lights, which exist in the spiritual world. (Suhrawardi)

> The Sages have been taught of God that this natural world is only an image and a copy of a heavenly and spiritual pattern; that the very existence of this world is based upon the reality of its celestial archetypes. (Michael Sendivogius)

> Things in every instance involve universals ... If there were no universals we could not speak of things as things. (Kung-sun Lung)[48]

> Crazy Horse dreamed and went out into the world where there is nothing but the spirits of things. That is the real world that is behind this one, and everything we see here is something like a shadow from that world. (Black Elk)[49]

Formulations of this kind could be multiplied more or less indefinitely but their burden is clear enough. Meister Eckhart provided a concise statement of the doctrine in writing "Form is revelation of essence."[50] Everything that exists, whatever its modality, necessarily participates in universal principles which are uncreated and in immutable essences contained, in Guénon's words, in "the permanent actuality of the Divine Intellect." Consequently, all phenomena, no matter how ephemeral or contingent, "translate" or "represent" these principles in their own fashion at their own level of existence. Without participation in the immutable, they would "purely and simply be nothing."[51] The doctrine of archetypes also implies the multiple states of being and a hierarchic structure of the cosmos. As Abu Bakr Siraj Ed-Din writes:

---

these do not constitute any kind of metaphysical doctrine but a precarious hypothesis about certain psychic phenomena.

47 Trans. A.K. Coomaraswamy, quoted in W. Perry, *The Widening Breach*, 21.

48 The four quotations immediately above are taken from W. Perry, *Treasury of Traditional Wisdom*, 671, 673, 672 & 670 respectively.

49 In J. Neihardt, *Black Elk Speaks*, 67.

50 Meister Eckhart quoted in W. Perry, *Treasury of Traditional Wisdom*, 673.

51 René Guénon, *Autorité spirituelle et pouvoir temporel*, quoted in W. Perry, *Treasury of Traditional Wisdom*, 302.

... if a world did not cast down shadows from above, the worlds below it would vanish altogether, since each world in creation is no more than a tissue of shadows entirely dependent on the archetypes in the world above.[52]

The analogies between the archetypes or "Divine Ideas" and the transitory material forms of this world, "this changing and ephemeral multiplicity" as Guénon calls it, give to phenomena certain *qualitative* significances which render them symbolic expressions of higher realities. The same idea is implicit in Mircea Eliade's claim that *homo religiosus* is also, necessarily, *homo symbolicus*.[53]

The traditional understanding of both nature and sacred art is predicated upon a very precise understanding of the nature of symbolism. A symbol may generally be defined as a reality of a lower order which participates analogically in a reality of a higher order of being. Therefore, a properly constituted symbolism rests on the inherent and objective qualities of phenomena and their relationship to spiritual realities. It follows that the science of symbolism is a rigorous discipline which can only proceed through a discernment of the qualitative significances of substances, colors, forms, spatial relationships and so on. This is crucial. Schuon:

> ... we are not here dealing with subjective appreciations, for the cosmic qualities are ordered both in relation to being and according to a hierarchy which is more real than the individual; they are, then, independent of our tastes ... [54]

So important is this principle that it deserves re-stating, this time in Nasr's words:

> The symbol is not based on man-made conventions. It is an aspect of the ontological reality of things and as such is independent of man's perception of it. The symbol is the revelation of a higher order of reality in a lower order through which man can be led back to the higher realm. To understand symbols is to accept the hierarchic structure of the Universe and the multiple states of being.[55]

Symbolic significances cannot be invented or imputed. Traditional symbolism, then, is an objective language which is conceived not according to the impulses of individual or collective "taste" but in conformity with the nature of things. It will take account not only of "sensible beauty" but "the spiritual foundations of this beauty."[56] Because of its precision and objectivity a traditional symbolism may be called a "calculus" or "algebra" for the expression of universal ideas: "the function of every symbol is to break the

---

52 Abu Bakr Siraj Ed-Din, *The Book of Certainty*, 50. This book gives an account of the doctrine of archetypes and of the multiple states of being from a Sufic perspective. See also R. Guénon, *The Multiple States of Being*.
53 See M. Eliade, "Methodological Remarks on the Study of Religious Symbolism," 95.
54 F. Schuon, *Gnosis: Divine Wisdom*, 110.
55 S.H. Nasr, *Sufi Essays*, 88. See also M. Pallis, *A Buddhist Spectrum*, 144-163.

shell of forgetfulness that screens the knowledge immanent in the Intellect."[57] The conception of symbolism as an objective language is axial in Coomaraswamy's mature work, much of which was directed towards reawakening a proper understanding of the symbolic vocabulary of the traditional arts of Asia. A characteristic formulation:

> Symbolism is a language and a precise form of thought; a hieratic and a metaphysical language and not a language determined by somatic or psychological categories. Its foundation is in analogical correspondences ... symbolism is a calculus in the same sense that an adequate analogy is a proof.[58]

The study of traditional symbols, therefore, demands methods no less rigorous or sensitive than those of the philologist. Nothing could be more ill-conceived than a subjective interpretation of traditional symbols which are no more amenable to guess-work than is an archaic language. As Coomaraswamy points out, the study of such symbolisms is no easy business, not only because the same symbol may be deployed in different senses but because we are no longer familiar with the metaphysical burden which it once carried.[59]

The science of symbolism is a kind of objective analogue of the gift of "seeing God everywhere," that is, an awareness of the transparency of phenomena and of the transcendent dimension which is present in every cosmic situation.[60] Ramakrishna, who could fall into ecstasy at the sight of a lion, a bird, a dancing girl, exemplified this gift though in his case, Schuon adds, it was not a matter of deciphering the symbolism but of "tasting the essences."[61] Eliade, approaching the whole question from a different angle, has noted how, for *homo religiosus*, everything in nature is capable of revealing itself as a "cosmic sacrality," as a hierophany. He also observes that for our secular age the cosmos has become "opaque, inert, mute; it transmits no message, it holds no cipher."[62]

In "Frost at Midnight" Coleridge, addresses these lines to his baby son:

> But *thou*, my babe! shalt wander like a breeze
> By lakes and sandy shores, beneath the crags

56 F. Schuon, "Foundations of an Integral Aesthetics," 130. See also B. Keeble, "Tradition, Intelligence and the Artist," 240-241.

57 F. Schuon, *Esoterism as Principle and as Way*, 11. See also F. Schuon, *Spiritual Perspectives and Human Facts*, 40.

58 A.K. Coomaraswamy, "The Nature of Buddhist Art" in *Selected Papers 1*, 174-175. See also Coomaraswamy's undated letter to an anonymous recipient and to Robert Ulich, July 1942, in *Selected Letters*, 210-212 & 214-215.

59 A.K. Coomaraswamy, "The Iconography of Durer's 'Knots' and Leonardo's 'Concatenation,'" *The Art Quarterly*, 7:2, 1944, quoted in W. Perry, *Treasury of Traditional Wisdom*, 305. One of the clearest expositions of the guiding principles of traditional symbolism can be found in A. Snodgrass, *The Symbolism of the Stupa*, 1-10.

60 See F. Schuon, *Gnosis: Divine Wisdom*, 106-121, and S.H. Nasr, *Man and Nature*, 131.

61 F. Schuon, "Foundations of an Integral Aesthetics," 135fn. See also C. Isherwood, *Ramakrishna and His Disciples*, 61ff.

62 M. Eliade, *The Sacred and the Profane*, 12 & 178.

Of ancient mountain, and beneath the clouds,
Which image in their bulk both lakes and shores
And mountain crags: so shalt thou see and hear
The lovely shapes and sounds intelligible
of that eternal language, which thy God
Utters, who from eternity doth teach
Himself in all, and all things in himself.

The idea of the natural order (the *"Liber mundi,"* "the Book of Creation") as not only sacred but as a *symbolic language* strikes the modern mind as somewhat strange, perhaps as "poetic fancy." In reality it is the modern outlook which is idiosyncratic. The traditional mind perceives the natural world as a teaching about the Divine Order. Bede Griffiths, whose own spiritual trajectory was much influenced by the Romantic poets, put the matter this way:

> Always it has been understood that our life in this world, as Keats said, is a "perpetual allegory": everything has meaning only in reference to something beyond. We are, as Plato saw it, like men in a cave who see reality reflected on the walls of the cave ... We only begin to awake to reality when we realize that the material world, the world of space and time, as it appears to our senses, is nothing but a sign and a symbol of a mystery which infinitely transcends it.[63]

This kind of symbolism is an altogether different matter from arbitrary sign systems and artificial representational vocabularies with which the postmodernist theorists and semioticians are so besotted. Only when we understand the revelatory aspect of natural phenomena, their metaphysical transparency, can we fully appreciate the import of a claim such as this:

> Wild Nature is at one with holy poverty and also with spiritual childlikeness; she is an open book containing an inexhaustible teaching of truth and beauty. It is in the midst of his own artifices that man most easily becomes corrupted, it is they who make him covetous and impious; close to virgin Nature, who knows neither agitation nor falsehood, he had the hope of remaining contemplative like Nature herself.[64]

Or this, from the great 13th century Zen sage, Dogen:

> They passed eons living alone in the mountains and forests; only then did they unite with the Way and use mountains and rivers for words, raise the wind and rain for a tongue, and explain the great void.[65]

Nature, then, is a *teaching*, a primordial Scripture. To "read" this Scripture, to take it to heart, is "to see God everywhere," to be aware of Divine transcen-

---

65 From Dogen's *Shobogenzo*, quoted in *Dharma Gaia: A Harvest of Essays on Buddhism and Ecology*, ed. Alan H. Badiner, xiii.

63 B. Griffiths, *The Golden String*, 181.

64 F. Schuon, *Light on the Ancient Worlds*, 84.

dence and immanence, to see "the translucence of the Eternal through and in the temporal" (Coleridge).[66] Here are a few formulations which signal the same principle.

> The invisible things of him from the creation of the world are clearly seen, being understood by the things that are made. (St Paul)[67]

> If we look at the world ... with the eyes of the spirit we shall discover that the simplest material object ... is a symbol, a glyph of a higher reality and a deeper relationship of universal and individual forces ... (Lama Anagarika Govinda)[68]

> Stones, plants, animals, the earth, the sky, the stars, the elements, in fact everything in the universe reveals to us the knowledge, power and the will of its Originator. (Al-Ghazali)[69]

> The creatures are, as it were, traces of God's passing, wherein he reveals his might, power, wisdom and other divine qualities. (St John of the Cross)[70]

> The great, gashed, half-naked mountain is another of God's saints. There is no other like him. He is alone in his own character; nothing else in the world ever did or ever will imitate God in quite the same way. That is his sanctity. (Thomas Merton)[71]

> ... through the grandeur and beauty of the creatures we may, by analogy, contemplate their Author. (*Wisdom* 13.1.5)

It is in the primal cultures (so often patronized as "primitive" and "pre-literate"), such as those of the Australian Aborigines, the African Bushmen and the American Indians, that we find the most highly developed sense of the transparency of natural phenomena and the most profound understanding of the "eternal language." As Joseph Epes Brown has remarked of the Sioux experience, "each form in the world around them bears such a host of precise values and meanings that taken all together they constitute what one would call their 'doctrine'."[72]

66 Coleridge quoted in K. Raine, *Defending Ancient Springs*, 109.

67 *Romans* I.20.

68 A. Govinda, *Creative Meditation*, 102.

69 Al-Ghazali quoted in *Cathedrals of the Spirit*, 107. For a study of the symbolism of animals within one particular spiritual economy see J.E. Brown, *Animals of the Soul: Sacred Animals of the Oglala Sioux*.

70 *The Spiritual Canticle* V.iii, quoted in E. Hamilton, *The Voice of the Spirit: The Spirituality of St John of the Cross*, 89. Compare with the well-known *hadith qudsi* (in which God Himself speaks): "I was a hidden treasure, I wanted to be known and I created the creatures"; or with St. Thomas Aquinas: "Each creature is a witness to God's power and omnipotence; and its beauty is a witness to the divine wisdom ... Every creature participates in some way in the likeness of the Divine Essence." Aquinas quoted in M. Fox, *The Coming of the Cosmic Christ*, 75.

71 T. Merton, *New Seeds of Contemplation*, 31.

72 J.E. Brown, *The Spiritual Legacy of the American Indians*, 37. Two works, comparatively free of the evolutionist and modernistic prejudices which color much of the anthropological literature, might be recommended as introductions to the Bushmen and Aboriginal cultures: Laurens van der Post, *The Heart of the Hunter* and James Cowan, *Mysteries of the Dreaming*.

In the traditional world the natural order was never understood or studied as an autonomous and independent reality; on the contrary, the natural order was only to be understood within a larger context, drawing on theology and metaphysics as well as the cosmological sciences themselves. The material world was (and is) only intelligible through recourse to axiomatic principles which could not, and can not, be derived from empirical inquiry but from revelation, esoteric knowledge, gnosis, metaphysics:

> The knowledge of the whole universe does not lie within the competence of science but of metaphysics. Moreover, the principles of metaphysics remain independent of the sciences and cannot in any way be disproved by them.[73]

No one has stated the crucial principle here better than Sankara, who taught that the world of *maya* (the world of time-space relativities) is "not inexplicable, it is only not self-explanatory."[74] To describe the futility of a purely materialistic science (such as we now have in the West), Sankara compares it to an attempt to explain night and day without reference to the Sun. In other words, the study of the natural world is not primarily an empirical business, although it does, of course, have an empirical dimension: *matter does not exist independently and its nature cannot be understood in purely material terms.* This principle makes a complete nonsense of claims such as the following (one altogether characteristic of the modern mentality): "Religion must—if it is to have any respectability—fit with our best scientific account of the nature of reality."[75] As we are told in the *Prajna-Paramita Sutra,* "Belief in the eternity or unity of matter is incomprehensible; and only common, worldly-minded people, for purely materialistic reasons, covet this hypothesis."[76] This is the great dividing line between the sacred sciences of the traditional worlds and the Faustian science of our own time.

Beauty: Divine Rays

A few words on Beauty which we find everywhere in the natural order as well as in the human form itself, and in sacred art. Firstly, in the traditional world, there is the intimate nexus between Truth, Goodness and Beauty.[77] The inter-relationships of the three are more or less inexhaustible and there is no end to what might be said on this subject. Here we shall establish only a few general points, taking the nature of Beauty as our point of departure. Marsilio Ficino, the Renaissance Platonist, defined Beauty as "that ray which parting from the visage of God, penetrates into all things."[78] Beauty, in most traditional canons, has this divine quality. Beauty is a manifestation of the

---

73 S.H. Nasr, *Man and Nature*, 35.
74 See my article, "Sankara's Doctrine of Maya."
75 N. Hettinger, "Ecospirituality," 95, fn1.
76 Quoted in W. Perry, *The Widening Breach*, 44.
77 See Lord Northbourne, "A Note on Truth, Goodness and Beauty."
78 Quoted in R.J. Clements, *Michelangelo's Theory of Art*, 5.

Infinite on a finite plane and so introduces something of the Absolute into the world of relativities. Its sacred character "confers on perishable things a texture of eternity."[79] Schuon:

> The archetype of Beauty, or its Divine model, is the superabundance and equilibrium of the Divine qualities, and at the same time the overflowing of the existential potentialities in pure Being ... Thus beauty always manifests a reality of love, of deployment, of illimitation, of equilibrium, of beatitude, of generosity.[80]

It is distinct but not separate from Truth and Virtue. As Aquinas affirmed, Beauty relates to the cognitive faculty and is thus connected with wisdom.[81] The rapport between Beauty and Virtue allows one to say that they are but two faces of the one reality: "goodness is internal beauty, and beauty is external goodness" or, similarly, "virtue is the beauty of the soul as beauty is the virtue of forms."[82] To put it another way, and Oscar Wilde notwithstanding, there are no beautiful vices just as there are no ugly virtues. The inter-relationships of Beauty, Truth and Goodness explain why, in the Oriental traditions, every *avatara* embodies a perfection of Beauty. It is said of the Buddhas that they save not only by their doctrine but by their superhuman Beauty.[83]

Schuon gathers together some of these principles in the following passage:

> ... the earthly function of beauty is to actualize in the intelligent creature the Platonic recollection of the archetypes ... there is a distinguo to make, in the sensing of the beautiful, between the aesthetic sensation and the corresponding beauty of soul, namely such and such a virtue. Beyond every question of "sensible consolation" the message of beauty is both intellectual and moral: intellectual because it communicates to us, in the world of accidentality, aspects of Substance, without for all that having to address itself to abstract thought; and moral, because it reminds us of what we must love, and consequently be.[84]

Beauty, whether natural or man-made, can be either an open or a closed door: when it is identified only with its earthly support it leaves man vulnerable to idolatry and to mere aestheticism; it brings us closer to God when "we perceive in it the vibrations of Beatitude and Infinity, which emanate from Divine Beauty."[85]

79 F. Schuon, *Understanding Islam*, 48.

80 F. Schuon, *Logic and Transcendence*, 241.

81 See A.K. Coomaraswamy, "The Mediaeval Theory of Beauty" in *Selected Papers 1*, 211-20, and two essays, "Beauty and Truth" and "Why Exhibit Works of Art?" in *Christian and Oriental Philosophy of Art*, 7-22 (esp. 16-18 & 102-109).

82 F. Schuon, *Logic and Transcendence*, 245-246. See also F. Schuon, *Esoterism as Principle and as Way*, 95.

83 As Schuon notes, the name "Shunyamurti"—manifestation of the void—applied to a Buddha, is full of significance; *Spiritual Perspectives and Human Facts*, 25fn. See also F. Schuon, *In the Tracks of Buddhism*, 121.

84 F. Schuon, "Foundations of an Integral Aesthetics," 131-132.

The Western Desacralization of Nature

Western attitudes to nature, before the onslaughts of a materialistic scientism, had been influenced by archaic pagan ideas (derived principally from Greece and from Northern Europe), Platonism and Islam, and, pre-eminently, the Judeo-Christian tradition. Many contemporary environmentalists point the finger at the so-called "dominion ethic" apparently sanctioned by the *Genesis* account. One of the most influential arguments of this type was advanced by the historian Lynn White Jr. in 1967; he wrote of "orthodox Christian arrogance toward nature" as the root cause of the ecological crisis and accused Christianity of being "the most anthropocentric religion the world has seen."[86] There is no escaping the fact that Christian institutions have for centuries been accomplices in an appalling environmental vandalism and one understands the reasons why many environmentalists resort to a clutch of clichés about the destructive influence of Christianity. Like all clichés, those bandied about by anti-religious propagandists in the environmental debate have some truth in them. However, if we look a little more closely we will find that the story is rather more complicated than is often supposed.[87] Here I can do no more than offer a few fragmentary remarks.

Like all cosmogonies, the *Genesis* myth deals with the relationship of the spiritual and the material. The natural world is affirmed as God's handiwork. Throughout both Testaments of the Bible we are reminded that "All things were made by him; and without him was not anything made that was made."[88] Furthermore, we are to understand the Creation itself as both a psalm of praise to its Creator and as a revelation of the divine qualities. As one contemporary Christian commentator put it, "Creation is nothing less than a manifestation of God's hidden Being."[89] In the *Psalms* we have many affirmations of this kind: "The heavens declare the glory of God; and the firmament sheweth his handiwork." We find many similar passages in the *Koran*: "The seven heavens, and the earth, and all that is therein, magnify Him, and there is naught but magnifieth his praise; only ye understand not their worship,"[90] and "All that is in the heavens and the earth glorifieth Allah."[91] In fact we can find like passages in many of the great Scriptures from around the globe: thus in the *Bhagavad Gita*, to choose one example, the universe is celebrated as the raiment of Krishna who contains within himself all the worlds of time and space.[92]

---

85 F. Schuon, "Foundations of an Integral Aesthetics," 135.

86 See N. Hettinger, "Ecospirituality," 85.

87 See Wendell Berry's essay "Christianity and the Survival of Creation" in *Sex, Economy, Freedom & Community*, 92-116.

88 *John* I.3.

89 P. Sherrard, *Human Image: World Image*, 152.

90 *Qur'an* XVII.44.

91 *Qur'an* LVII.2.

92 Goethe had something of the sort in mind when he wrote, "Nature is the living, visible garment of God"; quoted in Victor Gollancz, *From Darkness to Light*, 246.

In the *Genesis* account, the world of nature is *not* man's to do with as he pleases but rather a gift from God, one saturated with divine qualities, to be used for those purposes which sustain life and which give human existence in particular, dignity, purpose and meaning. That this stewardship ethic could degenerate into a sanction for wholesale exploitation and ruination is actually a criminal betrayal of the lessons of *Genesis*. How did this come about? The cooperative factors at work in the Western desacralization of nature are complex but we may here mention a few of the more salient: Christianity's emergence in a world of decadent pagan idolatry which necessitated a somewhat imbalanced emphasis on God's transcendence and on "other-worldliness"; the consequent neglect of those sacred sciences which might later have formed a bulwark against the ravages of a materialistic science; the unholy alliance of an anti-traditional Protestantism with the emergent ideologies of a new and profane world-view.[93]

Today many thoughtful Christians are well aware of the abuses stemming from the dominion ethic and to a lesser degree from the ideal of stewardship, and are re-thinking their understanding of traditional Christian doctrines in an effort to develop an ecologically aware theology. Among the best known are the one-time Dominican and now Episcopalian Matthew Fox, the former Passionist Thomas Berry, the Kentucky farmer and writer Wendell Berry, and the eco-feminist theologian, Rosemary Radford Ruether. Other Christian thinkers who have promoted a more reverential attitude to the whole of the natural order include Bede Griffiths, David Steindl-Rast and, most profoundly, the late Philip Sherrard whose *The Rape of Man and Nature* (1987) has been largely neglected, no doubt because of its allegiance to traditional metaphysical and cosmological principles, particularly as expressed in the Orthodox branch of Christianity. Wendell Berry's essay "Christianity and the Survival of Creation" also deserves to be much more widely known. Berry not only explores ways of redressing several imbalanced dualisms which have dominated Western thinking (spirit/nature; soul/body; human/nonhuman; worship/work) but is one of the few contemporary writers with some understanding of the need to restore the religious dimension of work.[94]

In the post-medieval European world, various other ideas about and understandings of nature have appeared: nature as *chaos, disorder, wild-ness*, in contrast to civilization, a threatening space which lay outside the social order (this motif has some pagan antecedents, especially in the Teutonic-Scandinavian religions rather than the Mediterranean and classical); nature

---

93 The most authoritative analysis of this process is to be found in Nasr's *Man and Nature*. There is also much interesting material on the emergence of a mechanistic and masculinist science in Mary Midgley's *Science as Salvation*.

94 On this subject see also R. Sworder, *Mining, Metallurgy and the Meaning of Life* and M. Hallpike (ed), *Work as Worship*.

as *matter* and as a *mechanistic system* governed by various physical laws amenable to investigation by an autonomous, secular and materialistic science (the legacy of the Scientific Revolution, of Newton, Bacon, Locke, Copernicus, Galileo, *et al.*); as *raw material*, an inexhaustible quarry to be plundered and, simultaneously, as "enemy" to be subdued, "tamed" or, even more ludicrously, "conquered" (industrialism, which provided a new field of applications for the "discoveries" of science); as an *Edenic paradise* peopled by "noble savages" (the romantic naturism of Rousseau and his many descendants); as uplifting *spectacle* (Wordsworth); as the *Darwinian jungle*, "red in tooth and claw"; as an *amenity*, a "resource" to be "managed" and protected for human recreation, tourism and the like; as *Gaia*, a single living organism ("deep ecology"); and as "*Wilderness*" (a quasi-religious secularism, if one might so put it, which absolutizes "Nature" under a certain guise and thus becomes a form of idolatry—which is nothing other than the mistaking of the symbol for its higher referent).

None of the post-medieval understandings *in themselves* offer any very real hope of providing a way out of our predicament. Clearly some contemporary developments and movements ("deep ecology," "eco-feminism," the new physics) yield some insights and can be helpful in dismantling the modern mind-set which has brought us to the current situation. But too often these well-intentioned gropings towards a more holistic understanding are bereft of any properly-constituted metaphysical and cosmological framework.[95] This is evident, for instance, in the fact that for all their radical aspirations the proponents of "a new ecological awareness" often fall prey to the materialistic and evolutionist assumptions which are at the root of the problem which they are trying to address. It must also be said that those who are properly skeptical about the pretensions of scientism are also often vulnerable to a kind of sentimental and warmed-over pantheism—sometimes on display in the gushings of New Agers. Nor will the problem be solved by some appeal to moral conscience and catch-calls about reduced consumption and the like, necessary though these doubtless are. No, what is required is a reanimation of the principles and understandings which governed traditional cosmologies. The key is to be found in the word "sacramental"—and the catechistic formula is altogether precise and apposite: "an outward and visible sign of an inner and invisible grace." In Wordsworth's words, the world is indeed "appareled in celestial light." Nasr stated the case perfectly plainly three decades ago but it is only now that a significant number of people are beginning to understand his message:

> If the terrestrial sphere has fallen into the danger of disorder and chaos, it is precisely because Western man has tried for several centuries to remain a purely terrestrial being and has sought to cut off his terrestrial world from

95 For a recent anthology of writings which do locate this debate in the appropriate framework, see *Seeing God Everywhere*, ed. Barry McDonald.

any reality that transcends it. The profanation of nature through its so-called conquest and the development of a purely secular science of nature would not otherwise have been possible ... Present ecological considerations can overcome some of the barriers that separative and compartmentalized studies of nature have brought about but they cannot solve the profounder problems which involve man himself ... *The spiritual revolt of man against heaven has polluted the earth, and no attempt to rectify the situation on earth can ever be fully successful without the revolt against heaven coming to an end.* For it is only the light of heaven cast upon the earth through the presence of seers and contemplatives living within the framework of the authentic religious traditions of humanity that preserves the harmony and beauty of nature and in fact maintains the cosmic equilibrium. Until this truth is understood all attempts to re-establish peace with nature will end in failure, although they can have partial success in preventing a particular tragedy from occurring here or there.[96]

One might schematize the contrast between traditional and modern world-views, and their respective "attitudes" to nature this way:

Traditional Cultures	Modern "Civilization"
mythological cosmogonies	the geological/historical "record"
spiritual worldview; primacy of the spiritual	scientific worldview; primacy of the material
qualitative, synthetic and holistic sacred sciences	quantitative, analytic and fragmentary sciences
natural forms symbolic and transparent	natural forms mute and opaque
religious culture	secular culture
reciprocal & cooperative relationship with nature	exploitative & combative relationship with nature
ecological and "natural" economies	industrial and artificial economies
sacramental worldview	profane worldview

Like all such schemas, this vastly oversimplifies the case—but it can perhaps serve as a signpost to those modes of understanding and of "being in the world" which we need to reawaken in the modern West. Before any such healing process can proceed (a healing of ourselves, of the earth, of our "relationship" with the whole cosmos and with what lies beyond it) we must accept that, at root, the "environmental crisis" is actually the symptom of a spiritual malaise. To return to health we must get to the seat of the disease rather than merely palliating the symptoms. As a contemporary Sufi has so well expressed it:

The state of the outer world does not merely correspond to the general state of men's souls; it also in a sense depends on that state, since man himself is

the pontiff of the outer world. Thus the corruption of man must necessarily affect the whole ... [97]

In this context we might also feel the force of Emerson's claim that, "the
views of nature held by any people determine all their institutions."[98]

In this severely circumscribed discussion we are not able to detail the
ways in which we might escape the tyrannical grip of a profane scientism and
its various accomplices (industrialism, consumerism, "development," "economic growth" and other such shibboleths) and so begin to free ourselves
and our world from the catastrophic consequences of a collective blindness
and a quite monstrous *hubris* (the two, of course, being intimately related).
We must relinquish our Luciferian ideas about "conquering" nature, and
allow Mother Nature not only to heal herself but to heal us: only then can we
hear the "timeless message of Nature" which "constitutes a spiritual viaticum
of the first importance."[99] As Kenneth Cragg has so properly observed,

> ... nature is the first ground and constant test of the authentically religious
> temper—the temper which does not sacralize things in themselves nor dese-
> crate them in soul-less using and consuming. Between the pagan and the
> secular, with their contrasted bondage and arrogance, lies the reverent
> ground of a right hallowing where things are well seen as being for men
> under God, seen for their poetry, mystery, order and serviceability in the
> cognizance of man, and for their quality in the glory of God.[100]

What can be said, in brief and in conclusion, is that the way forward must
also be a way back. Let us never forget the truth of Black Elk's words:

> Peace comes within the souls of men when they realize their relationship,
> their oneness, with the universe and all its powers, and when they realize
> that at the center of the Universe dwells *Wakan-Tanka* [the Great Spirit] and
> that this center is really everywhere, it is within each of us.[101]

All those concerned about the current ecological crisis would do well also to
ponder the implications of the following passage from Schuon:

> This dethronement of Nature, or this scission between man and the earth—
> a reflection of the scission between man and God—has borne such bitter
> fruits that it should not be difficult to admit that, in these days, the timeless
> message of Nature constitutes a spiritual viaticum of the first importance ...
> It is not a matter of projecting a supersaturated and disillusioned individu-
> alism into a desecrated Nature—this would be a worldliness like any other—

97   Abu Bakr Siraj Ed-Din, *The Book of Certainty*, 33.
98   Quoted in T.C. McLuhan, *Cathedrals of the Spirit*, 223.
99   F. Schuon, *The Feathered Sun*, 13.
100 K. Cragg, *The Mind of the Qur'an*, 148. Recall, too, Einstein's remark that, "The most beautiful emotion that we can have is the mysterious. It is the fundamental emotion that stands at the cradle of all true art and all true science. Whoever does not have it and can no longer wonder, no longer
marvel, is as good as dead, and his eyes are dim." Einstein quoted in B. Vinall, *The Resonance of Quality*,
110.
101 J.E. Brown, *The Sacred Pipe*, 115.

but, on the contrary, of rediscovering in Nature, on the basis of the traditional outlook, the divine substance which is inherent in it; in other words, to "see God everywhere"... [102]

*

The Upanishadic psalm with which we opened this chapter finds its echo in a visionary hymn by the 12th century German mystic Hildegard of Bingen. It will provide a fitting close.

I am the supreme fiery force
That kindles every spark of life;
What I have breathed on will never die,
I order the cycle of things in being;
Hovering round in sublime flight,
Wisdom lends it rhythmic beauty.

I am divine fiery life
Blazing over the full-ripened grain;
I gleam in the reflection of the waters,
I burn in the sun and moon and stars.
In the breeze I have secret life
Animating all things and lending them cohesion.

I am life in all its abundance,
For I was not released from the rock of ages
Nor did I bud from a branch
Nor spring from man's begetting:
In me is the root of life.
Spirit is the root which buds in the word
And God is the intelligible spirit.[103]

102 F. Schuon, *The Feathered Sun*, 13.
103 I have taken this from S.H. Nasr, *Religion and the Order of Nature*, 59.

16.

Dialogue, Pluralism and the Inner Unity of Religions

The Collision of Religions in the Contemporary World—The Western Pursuit of Inter-religious Understanding—Religious Dialogue and Spiritual Practice—The Case of Christian Zen—Jesuits in Japan—The Traditionalist Perspective on the Formal Diversity and Inner Unity of Religions—Religion, Revelation and Orthodoxy—The Exoteric and Esoteric Domains—The Limits of Religious Exclusivism—A Note on the Exposure of Esoteric Doctrines—Traditionalism, Interfaith Encounters and Comparative Religion

I am seated in the hearts of all. (Bhagavad Gita 15.15)

The Collision of Religions in the Contemporary World

It is now a commonplace that we are living in an unprecedented situation in which the different religious traditions are everywhere impinging on each other. There has always been some intercourse in ideas and influences between the great religious civilizations. Nevertheless, each civilization formerly exhibited a spiritual homogeneity untroubled, for the most part, by the problem of religious pluralism. For the vast majority of believers in a traditional civilization the question of the inter-relationship of the religions was one which was either of peripheral concern or one of which they remained unaware. Martin Lings:

> Needless to say our ancestors were aware of the existence of other religions besides their own; but dazzled and penetrated as they were by the great light shining directly above them, the sight of more remote and—for them— more obliquely shining lights on the horizons could raise no positive interest nor did it create problems. Today, however those horizons are no longer remote; and amidst the great evil which results from all that has contributed to bring them near, some good has also inevitably stolen its way in.[1]

Over the last century all manner of changes have made for a "smaller" world, for "the global village"—the spread of new technologies of transport and communication, the unprecedented migrations of peoples, international economic and political developments which pay no heed to national and cultural boundaries, the emergence of various dangers which now threaten humankind as a whole. For some time now it has been impossible to ignore the presence of religious cultures and traditions different from our own. The

---

1   M. Lings, *Ancient Beliefs and Modern Superstitions*, 70.

question of the relationship of the religions one to another and the imperatives of mutual understanding take on a new urgency both for the comparative religionist and theologian, and indeed, for all those concerned with fos-
tering a harmonious world community. This problem has especially disturbed some Christian thinkers conscious of the excesses and brutalities to
which an aggressive Christian exclusivism has sometimes given rise. Klaus
Klostermaier, Cantwell Smith, Bede Griffiths, Thomas Merton and Diana Eck
are amongst some of the better-known Christian writers who have recently
pondered this question. Furthermore, in an age of rampant secularism and
skepticism the need for some kind of inter-religious kinship makes itself ever
more acutely felt. It may be that in the West we are in a period of what historian William McLoughlin has called an "awakening":

> Awakenings—the most vital and yet most mysterious of all folk arts—are
> periods of cultural revitalization that begin in a general crisis of beliefs and
> values and extend over a period of a generation or so, during which time a
> profound reorientation in beliefs and values takes place.[2]

Between the Chicago Parliament of 1893 and our own day there have
been many initiatives aimed at promoting mutual understanding between
the adherents of different religious traditions. Many such attempts have
taken place under the rubric of inter-religious dialogue. A good many
attempts to create international cross-religious institutions have come and
gone in the intervening century while individuals continue to search for
common ground where the suspicions and antagonisms of the past might be
dissipated. Many of the individual figures that we have met in this study have
avowed the aim of inter-religious understanding and global harmony. There
is no doubt that much of the ignorance and prejudice of past eras has been
dispelled and that we in the West are now much better situated to appreciate
traditions other than our own. Despite the resurgence of various forms of
religious fundamentalism and a hardening of exclusivist attitudes in some
quarters we may rest assured that amongst religious folk in the West, particularly amongst the well-educated, there has been a growing acceptance of
the validity of the Eastern traditions and more widespread attitudes of
respect and openness. Amongst scholars and theologians, clergy and religious, and many serious-minded Christians and Jews, an awareness of Eastern
traditions has penetrated quite deeply—one might say that the psyche of
contemporary Christianity has been profoundly and irreversibly affected by
the presence of the East. One sign among many is the revision of the Roman
Church's posture during Vatican II, evident in the decree *Nostra Aetate*. The
comparative religionist Geoffrey Parrinder echoes many other thinkers when
he suggests that the encounter with the East is "one of the most significant
events of modern times," amounting to another Reformation within the

2   McLoughlin quoted in R.E. Wentz, "The Prospective Eye of Inter-religious Dialogue," 8.

Christian world.[3] Nonetheless, the question must be asked whether we are very much closer to finding a philosophical/theological/metaphysical basis for inter-religious harmony, one that can take us past high-minded intent, neighborly good will and the demolition of the more gross forms of mutual ignorance, prejudice and suspicion. In this chapter we shall identify some of the developments which have promoted deeper inter-religious understanding and momentarily focus on a few representative initiatives of recent years before turning to the traditionalist perspective on religious pluralism wherein may be found a basis for an inter-religious exegesis.

Our discussion will primarily concern the responses to the Eastern traditions of Christian thinkers and practitioners, sensitive to the issue of religious pluralism, who wish to engage in creative dialogue and for whom the new Eastern presence in the West presents itself as a challenge and an opportunity rather than as a threat to be repulsed. Whilst many Asian scholars and practitioners have studied in the West it is generally the case that most of the initiatives in inter-religious dialogue have come from the Christian side. This may be related to the keener sense in this tradition of some deficiency which might be remedied by creative intercourse with Eastern traditions. Inter-religious dialogue may also be felt, perhaps subconsciously, as a kind of atonement for the historical ignominies of missionizing triumphalism and Western colonialism, and as a counter to the evangelical excesses of current day fundamentalists.[4] More positively it may derive from certain dynamic, outward-looking and frontier-seeking tendencies in Christianity and the Western *mythos* generally.[5] On the other side, the comparative reticence of Easterners in sponsoring inter-religious dialogue may stem from a post-colonial wariness of the colonizing and universalizing tendencies in Western thought whilst many Asian adherents feel no dissatisfaction with their own tradition such as might impel initiatives in this direction. Also of some significance is the fact that many of the Asians who *are* enthusiastic proponents of dialogue have themselves been exposed to Western education. Of course, these are somewhat facile generalities to which one can find many exceptions. Certainly, many prominent Asian religious leaders and scholars—D.T. Suzuki, the Dalai Lama and Thich Nhat Hanh are conspicuous examples— have readily engaged in serious inter-religious dialogue.

We cannot here consider the significant resistances and reactions *against* the Eastern religions within the Christian churches (nor in the other Occidental religions). However, mention might be made of the re-affirmations of Christian exclusivism by theologians such as Karl Barth, Hendrik Kraemer and Pope John-Paul II. We might also note the imperviousness to any Oriental influences of shield-beating evangelical movements which are

---

3   G. Parrinder, *The Christian Debate: Light from the East*, 12, 22 quoted in J.J. Clarke, *Oriental Enlightenment*, 130.
4   See H. Coward, "Hinduism's Sensitizing of Christianity," 77.
5   See R.E. Wentz, "The Prospective Eye of Inter-religious Dialogue."

thriving in many Western countries. In this chapter we must also leave aside the alarming tensions and hostilities generated by reactionary and fundamentalist theologies and aggressive religious and quasi-religious xenophobic movements in both East and West—one might mention the extreme "religious right" in America, and the growth of militant politico-religious movements in the Middle East, the sub-continent and the Far East.[6] Today, under the spectcr of international terrorism and against the background of the smoldering problems in the Middle East and Asia, we are confronted with apocalyptic scenarios envisaging "the clash of civilizations," of new "holy wars" and "crusades," of the violent confrontation of militant "fundamentalists" and the forces of "modernity." Whilst these movements lie outside our immediate concern it would be foolish to discuss moves towards greater inter-religious understanding and harmony without acknowledging that there are potent, volatile and ominous forces pulling in the opposite direction.

The Western Pursuit of Inter-religious Understanding

We can distinguish several distinct, sometimes overlapping 20th century movements which, in various ways, have been directed towards the general goal of promoting inter-religious understanding and which can be associated with many of the figures discussed earlier in this study. A brief catalogue:

(1) the growth of *comparative religion* as a discipline amongst whose practitioners one frequently finds an allegiance to the development of a "true cosmopolitanism," a "global culture" or a "planetary humanism" which re-visions the world community, leaving behind the religious and cultural provincialism of the past, and which provides a frame in which the different religious traditions may find new modes of creative co-existence and mutual enrichment. Thus, for instance, Mircea Eliade: "The history of religions can play an essential role in this effort toward a planetization of culture; it can contribute to the elaboration of a universal type of culture."[7] (Mircea Eliade, Joachim Wach, Joseph Kitagawa, Ninian Smart, Wilfred Cantwell Smith, Klaus Klostermaier, W.T. Oxtoby, Arvind Sharma).

(2) the emergence within the general field of comparative religion of *comparative mysticism* (and comparative esotericism) as the arena in which the formal and institutionalized differences of the various religions may be at least partially reconciled, sometimes under the aegis of the perennial philosophy. (Rudolf Otto, D.T. Suzuki, Frithjof Schuon, W.T. Stace, Aldous Huxley, William Johnston).

(3) the development of *comparative philosophy* (East-West Philosophy Conferences, Radhakrishnan, John Hick), *comparative theology* (Dumoulin,

6   See K. Armstrong, *The Battle for God*. On recent tensions between the West and the Islamic world see R. Blackhirst & K. Oldmeadow, "Shadows and Strife."
7   M. Eliade, *The Quest*, 69.

Karl Rahner, Hans Kung, Paul Knitter, John Cobb), and *comparative psychology* (William James, C.G. Jung, Eranos, Ken Wilber) to compare and contrast and/or synthesize Eastern and Western understandings within a particular theoretical framework or field of practice.

(4) the development of *supra-religious universalist movements* which seek to synthesize or syncretize elements from many different religions and which claim to offer a new global "super-religion" or "spiritual way" which subsumes the religious differences of the past, and which often draws on "esoteric" doctrines from different traditions (Theosophy, neo-Hindu Vedanta, Bahai, some forms of "ecosophy"); a sub-set of this group are the "esotericists" who construct systems purporting to meld esoteric religion and modern science (Blavatsky, Gurdjieff, Rudolf Steiner), iconoclasts who lay claim to some sort of "spiritual" teaching (Krishnamurti) and eclectic free-for-all "gurus" (Rajneesh)—but whether any of these types should come under the umbrella of "inter-religious understanding" is, to say the least, highly doubtful!

(5) the various attempts to establish *international and trans-religious institutions and forums* such as the World Parliament of Religions, Francis Younghusband's World Congress of Faiths, Otto's "Religiöser Menschhietsbund," and the like, as well as organizations with more modest aims, such as the Fellowship of Reconciliation or the International Association for Religious Freedom.

(6) the cultivation of *inter-faith religious dialogue*, usually about matters of doctrine and spiritual practice but often also encompassing cross-religious responses to problems such as social injustice, political oppression or ecological calamity, conducted by religious adherents who remain faithful to their own tradition but who wish to share their ideas and experiences and to learn from participants of other religious faiths. (Paul Tillich, Klaus Klostermaier, Thomas Merton, Raimundo Pannikar, Diana Eck, David Steindl-Rast, Thomas Keating.)

(7) *existential engagements in a bi-traditional spiritual practice* which is firmly anchored in a particular tradition (usually Christianity) but which self-consciously and reflexively incorporates teachings and disciplines from another tradition in an effort to revitalize or reform a spiritual life which has in some respects atrophied (Bede Griffiths, Henri Le Saux, "Christian Zen," Pascaline Coff), and *inter-religious encounters aimed at mutual transformation.* (John Cobb, Ruben Habito, Frederick Streng.)

(8) *the traditionalist exposition of the "religio perennis"* and the explication of the metaphysical basis from which both the inner unity and the outer diversity of the religious traditions derive. (René Guénon, Ananda Coomaraswamy, Frithjof Schuon, Titus Burckhardt, Seyyed Hossein Nasr, Marco Pallis.)

Much of this study has been concerned with developments which come under (1) to (5) above. This chapter is especially concerned with developments in (6) and (7) before we turn to (8) and Ananda Coomaraswamy's claim that

> ... the only possible ground upon which an effective *entente* of East and West can be accomplished is that of the purely intellectual (i.e., metaphysical) wisdom that is one and the same at all times and for all men, and is independent of all environmental idiosyncrasy.[8]

Religious Dialogue and Spiritual Practice

The 20th century has witnessed myriad attempts at inter-religious dialogue of the kind outlined under (6) above. Here Roshi Robert Aitken and Brother David Steindl-Rast converse about "the ground we share,"[9] there the Dalai Lama participates in the John Main Seminar and ponders the Christian Gospels[10] while Thich Nhat Hanh considers the parallels between the founding figures of the Christian and Buddhist traditions.[11] A group of forty Japanese priests and monks spend several weeks in Benedictine and Trappist monasteries in Germany.[12] Elsewhere Christians and Muslims and Hindus meet to talk, to pray, to meditate together, and here is a dialogue on Judaism and Confucianism.[13] And so it goes. There is now what might loosely be called a "dialogue industry" which operates both within academia and religious institutions. In the pages of journals such as *Buddhist-Christian Studies, Dialogue & Alliance, Studies in Formative Spirituality, Ching Feng, Hindu-Christian Studies Bulletin, Inter-Religious Bulletin* and *Studies in Inter-religious Dialogue* (the list is by no means exhaustive!) one may encounter a veritable blizzard of writings on the subject. One comes across accounts of countless symposia, workshops, seminars, conferences and retreats devoted to inter-religious themes. Through these publications one can also keep abreast of the endlessly proliferating books in the field. Rather than skeltering through this maze we will isolate one small episode from the larger story and use it to illustrate the kinds of developments which are taking place throughout the world.

In 1984 representatives of all the major religions gathered at St Benedict's Monastery in Snowmass, Colorado, to "meditate together in silence and share their personal spiritual journeys"[14] as well as deliberating on those elements of belief and practice which their traditions shared. Out of this gathering and subsequent meetings emerged a list of points of agree-

---

8 A.K. Coomaraswamy, "The Pertinence of Philosophy," 160. Cf.: "I am in fullest agreement about the necessity of recognizing a common basis of understanding, but see no basis ... other than that of the *philosophia perennis* ..." Letter to H.G.D. Finlayson, December 1942, *Selected Letters*, 285-286.

9 R. Aitken & D. Steindl-Rast, *The Ground We Share*.

10 The Dalai Lama, *The Good Heart*.

11 Thich Nhat Hanh, *Living Buddha, Living Christ* (1995).

12 See J. van Bragt, "An East-West Spiritual Exchange."

13 See, for example, exchanges between Eugene B. Borowitz and Masao Abe in *Buddhist-Christian Studies*, 13, 1993.

14 T. Keating, "Meditative Technologies," 115.

ment. It is worth considering this list as an example of the kinds of conver-gences which can be discerned by adherents working together in a spirit of cooperative fellowship and dialogue. The Snowmass meeting proved less vaporous than many attempts at dialogue and produced the following list of elements common to all the major religions:

- The world religions bear witness to the experience of Ultimate Reality to which they give various names ...
- Ultimate Reality cannot be limited by any name or concept.
- Ultimate Reality is the ground of infinite potentiality and actuality.
- Faith is opening, accepting and responding to Ultimate Reality ...
- The potential for human wholeness—or in other frames of reference, enlightenment, salvation, transformation, blessedness, nirvana—is present in every human person.
- Ultimate Reality may be experienced not only through religious prac-tices but through nature, art, human relationships and service to oth-ers.
- As long as the human condition is experienced as separate from Ultimate Reality, it is subject to ignorance and illusion, weakness and suffering.
- Disciplined practice is essential to the spiritual life ... Humility, grati-tude and a sense of humor are indispensable in the spiritual life.[15]

A point made by one of the participants, Father Thomas Keating, was that each of the people in this dialogue were long-standing practitioners with a thorough grasp of their own tradition. Furthermore, they were able to dis-cuss creatively their differences as well as points of agreement. They were also alert to the dangers of any facile admixing of spiritual doctrines and practices such as would compromise the integrity of the distinct religious tra-ditions. Keating makes the interesting observation that the open ventilation of their differences created even stronger bonds than the discovery of simi-larities. He also suggests that this kind of dialogue can only usefully proceed in an atmosphere of trust where people are able to speak from the heart, and to share their spiritual *experience* rather than engaging in academic debate about doctrinal divergences.

Meetings of this kind, large and small, have been taking place all over the globe for many decades now and signal the search not only for some sort of inter-religious theological and philosophical understanding but for moral solidarity. The religious representatives at Snowmass were acutely conscious

15 These points were later expanded and others added. See T. Keating, "Meditative Technologies," 115-116.

of the "violence, injustice and persecution" to which religious sectarianism and bigotry have given rise and affirmed the obligation of the world religions to play a decisive role in the cause of world peace:

> ... the world religions will have to give the witness of mutual respect and understanding to the world community if political, ethnic, and nationalistic divisions are to be overcome or at least held in check.

They stressed that such an agenda would not be served by any attempt to blur the differences between the traditions:

> While emphasizing our common values and uniting in social action, however, the world religions must at the same time accept their diversity and cherish the integrity of each other's traditional spiritual paths. Genuine dialogue on this level is the catalyst that would facilitate harmony and cooperation on all the other levels of ever-increasing global interaction.[16]

People of good will must surely applaud such initiatives towards dialogue which can only result in greater mutual understanding and the formation of a common front against those many forces in the modern world which count against the spiritual life as well as against the attainment of a more peaceful international order. Such initiatives also throw into sharper relief those impulses and attitudes within the religious traditions which obstruct the possibilities of creative dialogue. Of these the most tenacious is a blind clinging to the belief that one's own tradition is the *exclusive* custodian of the Truth and provides the only path to salvation/enlightenment/transformation. This kind of exoteric exclusivism constitutes a very partial view but is not altogether unjustified, often arising out of a fierce commitment to the Truth as it has been revealed by the limited lights at one's disposal. It is to be preferred to a sentimental "tolerance" which actually holds fast to nothing whatsoever and which can easily cloak an insolent condescension on one side or, worse, an impious indifference to each and every religion on the other. "Tolerance" can often signify nothing more than a vacuum of any firmly-held beliefs or pieties. Recall Joachim Wach's observation that, "There is something pathetic about the modern historian of religion who uses strong words only to convince us that he has no strong convictions."[17] Nonetheless, global circumstances are now such that an obstinate commitment to any rigid exotericism will, in the end, amount to a kind of suicide.

Klaus Klostermaier has borrowed Niels Bohr's principle of complementarity to argue against three earlier models of religious pluralism (fundamentalist exclusivism, an irenic universalism, and fulfillment theory) and suggested four principles which, we can reasonably surmise, would be widely accepted by many contemporary participants in inter-religious dialogue:

16 T. Keating, "Meditative Technologies," 122-123.
17 J. Wach, *The Comparative Study of Religion*, 8.

1. The acknowledgement of real paradox in the relation between different traditions, e.g., the categories of one tradition cannot explain the other, and vice versa. 2. The acceptance of true mutuality between religious traditions ... [i.e., each can illuminate the other]. 3. The firm refusal to reduce one religion to another ... 4. The admission of the fragmentary and "incomplete" nature of each tradition ...[18]

This is but one of many recent models and is cited only to indicate the general movement away from Christian exclusivism in what might be called the international dialogue community. That Christian scholars and dialogists have abandoned the condescending models of earlier times (of which "anonymous Christianity" and "fulfillment theory" were the least offensive!) is heartening. The kind of inter-religious dialogue exemplified by the Snowmass gathering is also certainly to be welcomed. As Thomas Merton pointed out,

> ... genuine ecumenism requires the communication and sharing, not only of information about doctrines which are totally and irrevocably divergent, but also of religious intuitions and truths which may turn out to have something in common ... Ecumenism seeks the inner and ultimate spiritual "ground" which underlies all articulated differences. A genuinely fruitful dialogue cannot be content with a polite diplomatic interest in other religions and their beliefs. It seeks a deeper level ...[19]

However, of itself, this kind of dialogue cannot neutralize the negative effects of exoteric dogmatisms on whose survival the religious traditions actually, and somewhat paradoxically, depend. Later in this chapter I will argue in favor of the traditionalist perspective on religious pluralism which provides the only entirely stable base for inter-religious encounters, at least on the esoteric level. But first we must pay some attention to the developments signaled by (7) and which might be approached from any number of angles.

In the pages of this work we have met with several figures who have attempted to marry the spiritual practices of different religions whilst remaining true to the tradition to which they belong by birthright and upbringing. In Chapter 9, for example, we traced the spiritual explorations of several Catholic monks who immersed themselves in the world of Hindu spirituality. For Jules Monchanin the confrontation with Hinduism precipitated a personal crisis arising out of the tension between a recognition of the spiritual riches of Hinduism and a simultaneous inability to surrender a belief in Christian exclusivism. Henri Le Saux/Swami Abhishiktananda, fortified by his mystical experiences at Arunachala, was able to go much further in achieving some sort of rapprochement of Benedictine spirituality and the *Advaita* Vedanta into which he was initiated by his guru and whose truths were attested by his own spiritual illumination. Nonetheless, the nature of

18 K. Klostermaier, "All Religions Are Incomplete," 74.
19 T. Merton, *Mystics and Zen Masters*, 204.

the proper relationship of the two traditions remained somewhat problematic for him. Bede Griffiths, on the other hand, rather than seeking any sort of synthesis of Hinduism and Christianity, strived to assimilate Hindu insights and practices into what remained an essentially Christian praxis. Both Abhishiktananda and Griffiths believed that the ideal of the spiritual renunciate (*sannyasi, sadhu,* monk, nun, recluse) was the most fertile meeting ground for the traditions of East and West, a view shared by Thomas Merton.

These particular cases bear on the more general issue of the extent to which doctrines and methods belonging to one tradition can be synthesized with those of another, or transplanted from one spiritual and cultural milieu into a foreign terrain. These questions are sharpened by another development of recent decades, the emergence of what has come to be known as "Christian Zen" which furnishes us with a kind of inter-religious interaction which goes further than the sort of enterprise achieved at Snowmass; it leads to an existential engagement with alien spiritual practices.

The Case of Christian Zen

Eastern meditational practices, especially of the Zen tradition, have proved to be an attractive and practical instrument for the renewal of a Christian contemplative and mystical tradition which has often been obscured by more dogmatic and institutional structures. As Father Patrick Hawk, himself a Catholic priest and a Zen teacher, has written of those Christians who have wanted to return contemplation to the center of spiritual practice,

> Some of these pioneers realized that traditional Christianity does not have a systematic teaching on contemplation, and have discovered that the techniques of Zen meditation provide a definite way of practice. At the same time, they have discovered that the teaching of the Buddha and later masters not only does not contradict, but enriches, their insight into Christian teaching. Above all, they have come to appreciate the vital necessity of having the guidance of an authentic teacher.[20]

There are several Christian figures prominent in this movement who might have come on stage earlier in this study but who must now make cameo appearances: Fathers Hugo Enomiya-Lassalle, Heinrich Dumoulin, Aelred Graham, and William Johnston.

Jesuits in Japan

Hugo Enomiya-Lassalle and Heinrich Dumoulin

Hugo Lassalle was a German Jesuit who, two years after his ordination in 1927, went to Japan where, apart from occasional visits to his homeland, he spent the rest of his life. He became a Japanese citizen and took on an extra

---

20 P. Hawk, "Authority 1: The Role of the Teacher in Buddhist/Christian Formation," 24.

Japanese surname. Enomiya-Lassalle studied and undertook *koan* training with Roshis Harada, Yasutani and Yamada Roshi, and was authorized by the last-mentioned as a roshi, thus becoming the first Christian priest to undergo the full and arduous training and to be recognized within the Zen tradition as a teacher. He practiced Zen, while remaining a Christian, for fifty years and taught Zen in Europe and Japan for two decades. He was also the author of several pioneering works which familiarized the West with the whole notion of "Christian Zen." These included *Zen: Way to Enlightenment* (1964), *Zen Meditation for Christians* (1974) and *Living the New Consciousness* (1984). We are told that he was assiduous in his *koan* practice even as he approached his ninetieth year.[21] He died in 1990.

Heinrich Dumoulin is a Jesuit theologian who has been professor of philosophy and history of religion at Sophia University, Tokyo, since 1946. He has traveled extensively throughout Asia, Europe and the USA, and published many works on Japanese religions and on inter-religious subjects. Among his best-known works are *A History of Zen Buddhism* (1963) (later revised as the two-volume *Zen Buddhism: A History*), *Christianity Meets Buddhism* (1974), *Buddhism in the Modern World* (1976), and *Zen Buddhism in the Twentieth Century* (1992).[22]

Born in the Rhineland in 1905, Dumoulin studied in Holland and France and at the University of Berlin, completing his doctorate in 1929 and being ordained in 1933. After a brief period in England he left for Japan in 1935 where his regional superior was Father Hugo Lassalle. After mastering the Japanese language Dumoulin pursued further studies in the field of oriental religions, focusing first on the Shinto tradition but eventually turning to Buddhism. He established himself as an authority on Zen and a prominent leader of Christian-Buddhist dialogue, particularly under the auspices of the Institute of Oriental Religions at Sophia University. It was Dumoulin who finalized the passage on Buddhism in *Nostra Aetate*. In *Christianity Meets Buddhism* Dumoulin suggested that Zen meditation could help counter the frantic achievement ethic of the West which disturbs the "inner balance of stillness and motion"[23] that is a condition of the spiritual life. Dumoulin has always resisted any kind of syncretism, as his colleague James W. Heisig writes, "As a Christian he has always felt it his duty to inspire respect for Buddhism among his fellow believers and to open them to a wider understanding of the unfathomable, inscrutable ways of the divine providence that guides the Buddhist and Christian faiths alike."[24]

---

21 R. Habito, "Yamada Koun Roshi (1907-1989)," 234.

22 For a full bibliography up to 1984 see Special Issue of *Japanese Journal of Religious Studies* 12:2-3, 1985, 263-271.

23 H. Dumoulin, *Christianity Meets Buddhism*, 12-13.

24 James W. Heisig, Introduction to Dumoulin Issue of *Japanese Journal of Religious Studies*, 115.

Aelred Graham

Although Dumoulin and Lasalle were studying Zen many years before, it was Aelred Graham's book *Zen Catholicism: A Suggestion* (1963) which first brought the encounter of Christianity and Zen to the attention of many Westerners. Something of the flavor and intention of this book is captured in its Introduction:

> This book has no message. In its original draft, it bore the title Zen Catholicism?—but I have allowed myself to be persuaded that the tentative note, the interrogative mood, emerge with sufficient clarity from the subtitle. A question, not a proposal or a thesis, is here conveyed ... The questions to be discussed are whether what is essential to Buddhism, with its Zen emphasis (i.e., meditation), does not have its counterpart in Catholicism; whether Catholics might not be helped, by the Zen insight, to realize more fully their own spiritual inheritance; and whether Zennists need to be as exotic as they are.[25]

Like Bede Griffiths, Graham was an English Benedictine monk. He entered Ampleforth Abbey in Yorkshire in 1930, telling us in his most autobiographical work that, "I entered on a way of life in which, despite periods of difficulty, I was never to experience a seriously unhappy moment."[26] He studied theology with the Dominicans at Blackfriars, Oxford, and was ordained to the priesthood in the late 30s. In 1951 he moved to Rhode Island to become Prior of the Priory (later Abbey) of St Gregory the Great in Portsmouth. During his American years he developed a close friendship with Thomas Merton, sharing his interest in Oriental religions and in inter-religious dialogue. Graham spent some time in Japan in the 50s where he developed a keen interest in Zen and in the late 60s traveled extensively in Asia, meeting such figures as John Blofeld, Phra Khantipalo (in Bangkok), Dr T.R.V. Murti (Benaras Hindu University), Dr Radhakrishnan, and Dr Venkatarama Raghavan (University of Madras), Swami Muktananda, Krishnamurti, the Gyalwa Karmapa and the Dalai Lama ("one of the most memorable encounters of my life").[27] He also spent a month in Iran where he learnt a good deal about Sufism through Seyyed Hossein Nasr. Many of his experiences in dialogue are recounted in *The End of Religion: Autobiographical Explorations* (1971) and *Conversations: Christian and Buddhist—Encounters in Japan* (1971).

Graham's sensibility might be described as one shaped by Eckhart, Thomism and the contemporary Catholic philosopher Jacques Maritain, the German philosophical tradition, the various existentialisms of Heiddeger, Sartre, Husserl and Tillich, the work of "de-mythologizers" such as Rudolf Bultmann, and the more liberal and outward-looking ethos of the Latin church as it moved away from its monolithic triumphalism and evinced a new sensitivity towards other religious views and values. He was also impatient

25 A. Graham, *Zen Catholicism*, xi.
26 A. Graham, *The End of Religion*, 51.
27 A. Graham, *The End of Religion*, 186.

with what he saw as the hyper-bureaucratized structures of the Church as well as some of its mustier attitudes. He was critical of the approach taken by many Catholics to other religions:

> One knows from experience how strong is the urge to operate in any religious investigation with the whole panoply of Catholic assumptions, forgetful that some of them, to say the least, may be open to question. This state of affairs appears conspicuously when Catholics well equipped in terms of scholarship are dealing with the religions of India and the Far East. The approach is frequently sympathetic and appreciative but rarely is there any attempt to view, say, Hinduism or Buddhism on their own terms. Implicitly, the point of interest is where and how they can finally be assimilated by the Church. The superiority complex of Western Christianity—made up, it may prove to be, of cultural and political rather than intrinsically religious elements—has still to be resolved.[28]

It is perhaps not altogether surprising that a man of these interests and proclivities should be attracted to Zen. In *The End of Religion* he writes of the existential quest for "authenticity" which he applied to his own theology: "the authentic person ... must act in 'obedience to the voice of being'; that is, the existence in which his own life situation is immersed..."[29] He was fond of Tillich's apophthegm that "religion is not a special function of man's spiritual life, but it is the dimension of depth in all of its functions."[30] His encounter with other religions was never an academic, or even primarily a theological matter, but a way of deepening his own spiritual practice:

> When we reach a certain level of religious understanding, the light we seek is not what confirms us in our present position but something that leads us beyond it ... So it was with my own interest in Buddhism ... [31]

Although *Zen Catholicism* has been surpassed in both originality and depth by some of Graham's successors it remains a fresh and charming work. Graham deserves recognition as a pioneering popularizer of "Christian Zen" and as a thoughtful participant in dialogue at a time when many of his contemporaries were still victim to triumphalist and exclusivist prejudices. To Coleridge's observation that "He who begins by loving Christianity better than truth will proceed by loving his own sect of church better than Christianity, and end by loving himself better than all" he added: "Might we not take that as a pointer to a wider ecumenism than most Western Christians, understandably enough, are yet ready to consider?"[32] He would no doubt have been pleased by developments in "wider ecumenism" over the last three decades.

28 A. Graham, *The End of Religion*, 12.
29 A. Graham, *The End of Religion*, 10.
30 A. Graham, *The End of Religion*, 60.
31 A. Graham, *The End of Religion*, 58.
32 A. Graham, *The End of Religion*, 102.

William Johnston
William Johnston continues the line of Lassalle and Dumoulin as a Jesuit scholar based at Sophia University. Johnston was born in Belfast in 1925 and went to Japan in 1951, eventually succeeding Dumoulin as the Director of the Institute of Oriental Religions. He has written extensively on the mystical theology of Christianity, Buddhism, and the science of meditation techniques, but his central subject has been the encounter of Christianity and Zen, particularly as it has developed in Japan. Johnston has traveled and lectured in many different countries and is the author of several lively and accessible works, including *The Still Point: Reflections on Zen and Christian Mysticism* (1970), *Christian Zen* (1971), *Silent Music* (1974), *The Inner Eye of Love* (1978) and *The Mirror Mind* (1981). The first two of these works were in the vanguard of Christian-Zen dialogue and are marked by a blend of personal reminiscences and anecdotes, a lightly-worn learning and a serious engagement with both the existential and theological issues raised by inter-religious dialogue. Johnston believes that if Western Christianity can develop the humility necessary to make her receptive to Oriental wisdom, particularly Buddhism, the encounter with the East could be no less epochal than the early Christian encounter with the Greeks.[33] Johnston would no doubt endorse Merton's claim that

> It is absolutely essential to introduce into our study of the humanities a dimension of wisdom oriented to contemplation as well as wise action. For this, it is no longer sufficient merely to go back over the Christian and European cultural tradition. The horizons of the world are no longer confined to Europe and America. We have to gain new spiritual perspectives, and on this our spiritual, and even our physical survival may depend.[34]

As Johnston remarks in one of his works, East-West dialogue "will be a miserable affair if the Western religions do not rethink their theology in the light of mystical experience,"[35] a task to which the Oriental traditions can make the most profound contribution.[36]

Johnston belongs in the company of such other Christian figures as Thomas Merton, Bede Griffiths, Beatrice Bruteau and Diana Eck whose writings grow out of the existential encounter with other religions and for whom dialogue is not primarily a matter of the intellectual discernment of doctrinal affinities and divergences but of the sharing of *spiritual experience*, the immediate enrichment of *religious practice* and the re-vivification of a vital *Christian mysticism*. Their work constitutes, amongst other things, a summons to a deeper and more mystical spiritual life.

33 W. Johnston, *The Still Point*, xiv, 193.
34 T. Merton, *Mystics and Zen Masters*, 80.
35 W. Johnston, *The Inner Eye of Love*, 10.
36 On Johnston's approach to inter-religious dialogue see So Yuen-tai, "William Johnston's Contemplation Approach to Buddhist-Christian Dialogue," 83-105.

Others
In the post-World War II period twenty-two non-Japanese completed *koan* training with Yamada Koun Roshi and became authorized Zen teachers, most of them Catholic religious and including Father Niklaus Brantschen (Switzerland), Sister Ludwigis (Germany), Sister Elaine MacInnes (Canada), Father Willigis Jäger (Germany), Father Samy (India), as well as lay folk such as Reuben Habito (Philippines/USA), Brigitte D'Ortschy (Germany), and Victor Low (Germany). Jiyu Kennett ordained the Protestant cleric James Ford while Father Patrick Hawk was one of Robert Aitken's dharma-heirs.[37] Father Robert Kennedy is one of Bernard Glassman's dharma-heirs and the author of *Zen Spirit, Christian Spirit: The Place of Zen in Christian Life* (1995). As well as these Christians who have been formally recognized within the Zen tradition there are many more who have found their own bearings in the Christian tradition only after a radical encounter with Zen. One may mention such figures as Donald Mitchell, John Dykstra Eusden and John Healey.[38]

Not surprisingly, the Christian Zen movement has generated some controversy. Yasutani Roshi and Philip Kapleau Roshi have both criticized "Christian Zen" as a contradiction in terms and have argued that Christian theism is a significant obstacle to enlightenment—a view shared by Christmas Humphreys.[39] Kapleau also believes that the sanctioning of Catholic monks and nuns, Protestant ministers and rabbis as Zen teachers poses "a threat to the integrity of Zen, and in many ways the most bizarre."[40] Father Patrick Hawk, on the other hand, has argued that neither Zen nor Christianity need be compromised as long as there is no attempt at syncretism on the doctrinal and intellectual level where they are "irreconcilably contrary."

> Only if each body of teaching is respected and preserved can the encounter between Christian contemplatives and Zen Buddhists, and between Christian contemplation and Zen within each individual, be mutually enriching. It is like becoming ambidextrous. Right is right and left is left; but at the same time and all the time, there is only one person. The real integration of traditions is not in doctrines or ecumenical meetings or action; it is something which takes place in the souls of individuals struggling on their own spiritual paths.[41]

The Traditionalist Perspective on Formal Diversity and Inner Unity
The contemporary global situation offers the major religious traditions little cause for complacency. Despite the efforts of religious adherents to preserve

---

37 On these various Christian teachers of Zen see A. Rawlinson, *The Book of Enlightened Masters*, 258, and R. Habito, "Yamada Koun Roshi (1907-1989)."
38 See S. Postal, "Zen Mind/Christian Mind."
39 See W. Johnston, *The Still Point*, 189-190.
40 Interview with Kapleau in *Tricycle*, quoted in A. Rawlinson, *The Book of Enlightened Masters*, 360.
41 P. Hawk, "Authority 1: The Role of the Teacher in Buddhist/Christian Formation," 28.

their spiritual heritages and the enormous energy and good will dedicated to inter-religious understanding and solidarity, the traditions face four alarming possibilities which arise out of the inexorable and sinister processes of modernization and globalization, each disastrous for humankind's spiritual welfare: intensifying conflicts such as those envisaged in Samuel Huntington's "clash of civilizations" scenario and in which religious and political factors become disastrously entangled; internecine theological and/or political strife within religious traditions; the disappearance of the religions under the onslaughts of modernity (secularism, humanism, materialism, nihilism etc.); the dilution of the religions into some sentimental, "universal" pseudo-religion centered on nothing but fuzzy platitudes and an ersatz "spirituality." If these malignant possibilities are to be averted we need a proper understanding of what Frithjof Schuon has called "the transcendent unity of religions," an understanding which would allow us to fathom a characteristic mystical formulation such as the following from Rumi,

> I am neither Christian nor Jew nor Parsi nor Muslim. I am neither of the East nor of the West, neither of the land nor sea ... I have put aside duality and have seen that the two worlds are one. I seek the One, I know the One, I see the One, I invoke the One. He is the First, he is the Last, he is the Outward, he is the Inward.

Such an understanding can help us through the many impasses and conundrums growing out of inter-religious dialogue. Crucial to any recognition of this unity is the ability to discern the distinction between the exoteric and esoteric dimensions of the great religious traditions, and thus to forestall the terrible excesses of religious literalism. Recall this portentous passage from Frithjof Schuon's *The Transcendent Unity of Religions* (1953), one which takes on a new resonance in the present:

> The exoteric viewpoint is, in fact, doomed to end by negating itself once it is no longer vivified by the presence within it of the esoterism of which it is both the outward radiation and the veil. So it is that religion, according to the measure in which it denies metaphysical and initiatory realities and becomes crystallized in literalistic dogmatism, inevitably engenders unbelief; the atrophy that overtakes dogmas when they are deprived of their internal dimension recoils upon them from outside, in the form of heretical and atheistic negations.[42]

At a time when the outward and readily exaggerated incompatibility of divergent religious forms is used to exploit all manner of anti-religious prejudices the clarification of the underlying unity of the religions is a task which can only be achieved through a *trans-religious* understanding. The open confrontation of different exotericisms, the vandalism visited on traditional civilizations everywhere, and the tyranny of secular and profane ideologies all

---

42 F. Schuon, *The Transcendent Unity of Religions*, 1975 edition, 9.

play a part in determining the peculiar circumstances in which the most exigent needs of the age can only be answered by recourse to traditional esotericisms. There is perhaps some small hope that in this climate and given a properly constituted metaphysical framework in which to affirm the "profound and eternal solidarity of all spiritual forms" the different religions might yet "present a singular front against the floodtide of materialism and pseudo-spiritualism."[43]

The philosophical question of the inter-relationship of the religions and the moral concern for greater mutual understanding are, in fact, all of a piece. We can distinguish but not separate questions about *unity* and *harmony*; too often both comparative religionists and those engaged in dialogue have failed to see that the achievement of the latter depends on a metaphysical resolution of the former question.

Religion, Revelation and Orthodoxy

The traditionalist understanding of the nature of religion, and thus of the inter-relationships of the religious traditions, depends on four key principles. These are the necessary diversity of multiple Revelations and thus of the religious forms which derive from those Divine dispensations; the principle of orthodoxy which ensures that each integral religious tradition furnishes its adherents with an adequate metaphysical doctrine and an effective spiritual method; the distinction between the outer, exoteric and the inner, esoteric domains of religion; and, fourthly, the transcendent or metaphysical unity of religions which surpasses but in no way invalidates their formal diversity.

There is a good deal of talk these days about the traditional religions being "played out," "inadequate to the problems of the age," "irrelevant to contemporary concerns" and so on. "New solutions" are needed, "appropriate to the times." From the traditionalist viewpoint,

> Nothing is more misleading than to pretend, as is so glibly done in our day, that the religions have compromised themselves hopelessly in the course of the centuries or that they are now played out. If one knows what a religion really consists of, one also knows that the religions cannot compromise themselves and they are independent of human doings ... The fact that a man may exploit a religion in order to bolster up national or private interests in no wise affects religion as such ... as for an exhausting of the religions, one might speak of this if all men had by now become saints or Buddhas.[44]

Schuon's view of religion turns on the axiomatic notion of multiple and diverse Revelations. Humankind is neither a monolithic psychic entity nor an amorphous agglomerate but is divided into several distinct branches, each with its own peculiar traits, psychological and otherwise, which determine its receptivity to truth and shape its apprehensions of reality. Needless to say

43 F. Schuon, *Gnosis: Divine Wisdom*, 12.
44 F. Schuon, "No Activity Without Truth," 11.

there is no question here of any kind of racialism or ethnocentrism which attributes a superiority or inferiority to this or that ethnic collectivity. Nor, however, is there any sentimental prejudice in favor of the idea that the world's peoples are only "superficially" and "accidentally" different: "We observe the existence, on earth, of diverse races, whose differences are 'valid' since there are no 'false' as opposed to 'true' races."[45] Each branch of humanity exhibits a psychic and spiritual homogeneity which may transcend barriers of geography and biology. An example: that shamanism should extend through parts of Northern Europe, Siberia, Mongolia, Tibet and the Amerindian cultures betokens a certain spiritual temperament shared by the peoples in question, one quite independent of physical similarities and leaving aside the question of "borrowings" and "influences."[46]

To the diverse human collectivities are addressed Revelations which are determined in their formal aspects by the needs and receptivities at hand. Thus,

> ... what determines the differences among forms of Truth is the difference among human receptacles. For thousands of years already humanity has been divided into several fundamentally different branches, which constitute so many complete humanities, more or less closed in on themselves; the existence of spiritual receptacles so different and so original demands differentiated refractions of the one Truth.[47]

In a sense the Revelations are communicated in different divine languages. Just as we should baulk at the idea of "true" and "false" languages, so we need to see the necessity and the validity of multiple Revelations.[48] (This is not to suggest that all "religions" which claim to derive from a "Revelation" do so in fact, nor that there is no such thing as a pseudo-religion.) The principle of multiple Revelations is not accessible to all mentalities and its implications must remain anathema to the majority of believers. This is in the nature of things. However, as each religion proceeds from a Revelation, it is, in Seyyed Hossein Nasr's words, both

> ... *the* religion and *a* religion, *the* religion inasmuch as it contains within itself the Truth and the means of attaining the Truth, *a* religion since it emphasizes a particular aspect of Truth in conformity with the spiritual and psychological needs of the humanity for whom it is destined.[49]

45 F. Schuon, *Gnosis: Divine Wisdom*, 32.
46 See F. Schuon, *Light on the Ancient Worlds*, 72.
47 See F. Schuon, *Gnosis: Divine Wisdom*, 29. For some mapping of these branches and some account of their differences see Schuon's essay "The Meaning of Race" in *Language of the Self*, 173-200. This essay should be read in conjunction with "Principle of Distinction in the Social Order" in the same volume. These essays can also be found in F. Schuon, *Castes and Races*, the latter essay appearing under the title "The Meaning of Caste."
48 The comparison of religions and languages is a common one. For some examples see M. Müller, "Chips from a German Workshop," 88-89; and R. Z. Werblowsky, "Universal Religion and Universalist Religion," 10-11.
49 See S.H. Nasr, *Ideals and Realities of Islam*, 15.

Further potential ambiguities are dispelled by the principle of ortho-doxy:

> In order to be orthodox a religion must possess a mythological or doctrinal symbolism establishing the essential distinction between the Real and the illusory, or the Absolute and the relative ... and must offer a way that serves both the perfection of concentration on the Real and also its continuity. In other words a religion is orthodox on condition that it offers a sufficient, if not always exhaustive, idea of the Absolute and the relative, and therewith an idea of their reciprocal relationships ... [50]

Schuon re-states the same principle in writing,

> For a religion to be considered intrinsically orthodox—an extrinsic ortho-doxy hangs upon formal elements which cannot apply literally outside their own perspective—it must rest upon a fully adequate doctrine ... then it must extol and actualize a spirituality that is equal to this doctrine and thereby include sanctity within its ambit both as concept and reality; this means it must be of Divine and not philosophical origin and thus be charged with a sacramental or theurgic presence ... [51]

In other words each religion is sufficient unto itself and contains all that is necessary for man's sanctification and salvation. Nevertheless, it remains lim-ited by definition. The recognition and reconciliation of these two apparent-ly antagonistic principles is crucial to the traditionalist perspective. Schuon states the matter this way:

> A religion is a form, and so also a limit, which "contains" the Limitless, to speak in paradox; every form is fragmentary because of its necessary exclu-sion of other formal possibilities; the fact that these forms—when they are complete, that is to say when they are perfectly "themselves"—each in their own way represent totality does not prevent them from being fragmentary in respect of their particularization and their reciprocal exclusion.[52]

The key to the inter-relationships of the religious traditions is to be found in the relationship of the exoteric and esoteric aspects of religion.

The Exoteric and Esoteric Domains

We are accustomed to drawing sharp dividing lines between the religious tra-ditions. The differences here are, of course, palpably real and Schuon has no wish to blur the distinctions. We shall not find in the work of the traditional-ists any Procrustean attempt to find a unity on a plane where it does not exist nor an insipid universalism which posits a unity of no matter what elements as long as they lay some claim to being "religious" or "spiritual." However, this

---

50 F. Schuon, *Light on the Ancient Worlds*, 138.
51 F. Schuon, *Islam and the Perennial Philosophy*, 14.
52 See F. Schuon, *Understanding Islam*, 144. See also F. Schuon, *Dimensions of Islam*, 136.

notwithstanding, Schuon draws another kind of dividing line which in some senses is much more fundamental: that between the exoteric and esoteric.

In discriminating between the exoteric and the esoteric we are, in a sense, speaking of "form" and "spirit." Exotericism rests on a necessary formalism:

> Exotericism never goes beyond the "letter." It puts its accent on the Law, not on any realization, and so puts it on action and merit. It is essentially a "belief" in a "letter," or a dogma envisaged in its formal exclusiveness, and an obedience to a ritual and moral Law. And, further, exotericism never goes beyond the individual; it is centered on heaven rather than on God, and this amounts to saying that this difference has for it no meaning.[53]

It follows that exotericism must thereby embody certain inevitable and in a sense therapeutic limits or "errors" which from a fuller perspective can be seen in both their positive and negative aspects. Religion, in its formal aspect, is made up of what the Buddhists call *upaya*, "skillful means" which answer the necessities of the case, what Schuon calls "saving mirages" and "celestial stratagems."[54] The limiting definitions of exoteric formalism are "comparable to descriptions of an object of which only the form and not the colors can be seen."[55] Partial truths which might be inadequate in a sapiential perspective may be altogether proper on the formal exoteric plane:

> The formal homogeneity of a religion requires not only truth but also errors—though these are only in form—just as the world requires evil and as Divinity implies the mystery of creation by virtue of its infinity ... The religions are "mythologies" which, as such, are founded on real aspects of the Divine and on sacred facts, and thus on realities but only on aspects. Now this limitation is at the same time inevitable and fully efficacious.[56]

A specific example of an exoteric dogma might help to reinforce some of the points under discussion. In discussing the Christian dogmas about heaven and hell, Schuon has this to say:

> We are made for the Absolute, which embraces all things and from which none can escape; this truth is marvelously well presented in the monotheistic religions in the alternative between the two "eternities" beyond the grave ... the alternative may be insufficient from the point of view of total Truth, but it is psychologically realistic and mystically efficacious; many lives have been squandered away and lost for the single reason that a belief in hell and in paradise is missing.[57]

53 F. Schuon, *Light on the Ancient Worlds*, 76.
54 F. Schuon, *Survey of Metaphysics and Esoterism*, 185fn2. See also F. Schuon, *The Transfiguration of Man*, 8: "In religious exoterisms, efficacy at times takes the place of truth, and rightly so, given the nature of the men to whom they are addressed."
55 F. Schuon, *Understanding Islam*, 80.
56 F. Schuon, *Spiritual Perspectives and Human Facts*, 70.
57 F. Schuon *Light on the Ancient Worlds*, 22.

The statements of a formal exotericism can thus be seen as intimations of Truth, as metaphors and symbols, as bridges to the formless Reality.[58] In other words the forms of exotericism represent certain accommodations which are necessary to bring various truths within the purview of the average mentality. As such they are adequate to the collective needs in question. For the normal believer the exoteric domain is the only domain.

However, if "exotericism consists in identifying transcendent realities with dogmatic forms" then esotericism is concerned "in a more or less direct manner with these same realities."[59] Esotericism is concerned with the apprehension of Reality as such, not Reality as understood in such and such a perspective and "under the veil of different religious formulations."[60] While exotericism sees "essence" or "universal truth" as a function of particular forms, esotericism sees the forms as a function of "essence." To put it another way, exotericism particularizes the universal, esotericism universalizes the particular:

> What characterizes esoterism to the very extent that it is absolute, is that on contact with a dogmatic system, it universalizes the symbol or religious concept on the one hand, and interiorizes it on the other; the particular or the limited is recognized as the manifestation of the principial and the transcendent, and this in its turn reveals itself as immanent.[61]

Esotericism is "situated" on the plane of mystical experience, of intellection and realization, of gnosis, a plane on which the question of orthodoxy cannot arise, operative as it is only on the formal plane:

> If the purest esotericism includes the whole truth—and that is the very reason for its existence—the question of "orthodoxy" in the religious sense clearly cannot arise: direct knowledge of the mysteries could not be "Moslem" or "Christian" just as the sight of a mountain is the sight of a mountain and not something else.[62]

Nevertheless, the two realms, exoteric and esoteric, are continually meeting and interpenetrating, not only because there is such a thing as a "relative esotericism" but because "the underlying truth is one, and also because man is one."[63] Furthermore, even if esotericism transcends forms, it has need of doctrinal, ritual, moral and aesthetic supports on the path to realization.[64] Herein lies the point of Schuon's tireless advocacy of orthodoxy: "Orthodoxy includes and guarantees incalculable values which man could not possibly

58 F. Schuon, *Understanding Islam*, 110.
59 F. Schuon, *Logic and Transcendence*, 144. See also F. Schuon, *Esoterism as Principle and as Way*, 37.
60 F. Schuon, *Esoterism as Principle and as Way*, 19.
61 F. Schuon, *Esoterism as Principle and as Way*, 19.
62 F. Schuon, *Understanding Islam*, 139. See also F. Schuon, *Sufism, Veil and Quintessence*, 112.
63 F. Schuon, *Esoterism as Principle and as Way*, 16.
64 F. Schuon, *Esoterism as Principle and as Way*, 29.

draw out of himself."[65]

It is not surprising that the exoteric elements in a religious tradition should be preserved and protected by custodians whose attitude to esotericism will be, at best, somewhat ambivalent, at worst openly hostile. In addressing itself to the defense of the *credo* and of the forms which appear as guarantors of truth the exoteric "resistance" to esotericism is entirely positive. But sometimes the exoteric defendants of orthodoxy overstep themselves and in so doing beget results that are both destructive and counterproductive, especially when a religious tradition is endangered by a preponderantly exoteric outlook. How much of post-medieval Christian history bears witness to this truth! Recall the theological and ecclesiastical ostracisms that have befallen some of the mystics and metaphysicians seeking to preserve the esoteric dimension within Christianity.

The supra-human origin of a religious tradition in a Revelation, an adequate doctrine concerning the Absolute and the relative, the saving power of the spiritual method, the esoteric convergence on the unitive Truth: all these point to the inner unity of all integral traditions which are, in a sense, variations on one theme. However, there remain certain puzzling questions which might stand in the way of an understanding of the principial unity which the *religio perennis* discloses.

The Limits of Religious Exclusivism

One frequently comes across formulations such as the following:

> It is sometimes asserted that all religions are equally true. But this would seem to be simply sloppy thinking, since the various religions hold views of reality which are sharply different if not contradictory.[66]

This kind of either/or thinking, characteristic of much that nowadays passes for philosophy, is in the same vein as a dogmatism which

> reveals itself not only by its inability to conceive the inward or implicit illimitability of a symbol, but also by its inability to recognize, when faced with two apparently contradictory truths, the inward connection that they apparently affirm, a connection that makes of them complementary aspects of one and the same truth.[67]

It is precisely this kind of incapacity which must be overcome if the transcendent unity of the religions is to be understood. As Schuon remarks,

---

65 F. Schuon, *Spiritual Perspectives and Human Facts*, 113. See also F. Schuon, *Islam and the Perennial Philosophy*, 5.

66 O. Thomas quoted in H. Smith, Introduction to the revised edition of F. Schuon, *The Transcendent Unity of Religions*, xiiifn.

67 F. Schuon, *The Transcendent Unity of Religions*, 3. See also S.H. Nasr, *Knowledge and the Sacred*, 281.

A religion is not limited by what it includes but by what it excludes; this exclusion cannot impair the religion's deepest contents—every religion is intrinsically a totality—but it takes its revenge all the more surely on the intermediary plane ... the arena of theological speculations and fervors ... extrinsic contradictions can hide an intrinsic compatibility or identity, which amounts to saying that each of the contradictory theses contains a truth and thereby an aspect of the whole truth and a way of access to this totality.[68]

Examples of "contradictory" truths which effectively express complementary aspects of a single reality can be found not only across the traditions but within them. One might instance, by way of illustration, the Biblical or Koranic affirmations regarding predestination and free will.[69]

From an esoteric viewpoint the exclusivist claims of one or another religion have no absolute validity. It is true that "the arguments of every intrinsically orthodox religion are absolutely convincing if one puts oneself in the intended setting."[70] It is also true that orthodox theological dogmatisms are entitled to a kind of "defensive reflex" which makes for claims to exclusivism. However,

the exoteric claim to the exclusive possession of a unique truth, or of Truth without epithet, is ... an error purely and simply; in reality, every expressed truth necessarily assumes a form, that of its expression, and it is metaphysically impossible that any form should possess a unique value to the exclusion of other forms; for a form, by definition, cannot be unique and exclusive, that is to say it cannot be the only possible expression of what it expresses.[71]

The argument that the different religions cannot all be repositories of the truth because of their formal differences and antagonisms rests on a failure to understand this principle. The lesson to be drawn from the multiplicity of religious forms is quite different:

The diversity of religions, far from proving the falseness of all the doctrines concerning the supernatural, shows on the contrary the supra-formal character of revelation and the formal character of ordinary human understanding: the essence of revelation—or enlightenment—is one, but human nature requires diversity.[72]

Schuon has deployed several images to clarify the relationship of the religions to each other. He likens them to geometric forms. Just as it would be absurd to imagine that spatial extensions and relationships could only be expressed by one form, so it is absurd to assert that there could be only one doctrine giving an account of the Absolute. However, just as each geometric

68 F. Schuon, *Islam and the Perennial Philosophy*, 46.
69 F. Schuon, *The Transcendent Unity of Religions*, 4.
70 F. Schuon, *Spiritual Perspectives and Human Facts*, 14.
71 F. Schuon, *The Transcendent Unity of Religions*, 17.
72 F. Schuon, "No Activity Without Truth," 4. See also M. Pallis, *A Buddhist Spectrum*, 157.

form has some necessary and sufficient reason for its existence, so too with the religions. To affirm that the Truth informing all religious traditions is one and that they essentially all vehicle the same message in different forms is not to preclude qualitative discriminations concerning particular aspects of this or that tradition. Schuon extends the geometric analogy:

> The differentiated forms are irreplaceable, otherwise they would not exist, and they are in no sense various kinds of imperfect circles; the cross is infinitely nearer the perfection of the point ... than are the oval or the trapezoid, for example. Analogous considerations apply to traditional doctrines, as concerns their differences of form and their efficacy in equating the contingent to the Absolute.[73]

A Note on the Exposure of Esoteric Doctrines

We live in anomalous times. Nowhere is this more graphically demonstrated than in the fact that in the most irreligious and impious period in human history the esoteric wisdoms preserved by the religious traditions are more widely and easily accessible than ever before. Sapiential truths which previously had remained extrinsically inexpressible and which had been protected by those few capable of understanding them are now on public display, as it were. The traditionalists themselves have played a significant role in bringing esoteric wisdoms within the purview of a greater number of people. This calls for some explanation.

The erosion of the protective barriers which previously enclosed traditions has, in part, been caused by historical factors which, in a sense, are "accidental." One might cite the exposure of the Upanishadic Scriptures as a case in point. Here certain historical factors, such as the introduction into India of cheap printing presses, combined with a degree of imprudence on the part of some of the "reformers" of Hinduism to subvert the esoteric status of these Scriptures which became available to anyone and everyone. There are also innumerable cases where a garbled version of half-understood secret doctrines has been thoughtlessly and carelessly put into public circulation. The Biblical verse "For there is nothing covered, that shall not be revealed ..." has sometimes been taken as a license for all manner of excesses in the popularizing of esoteric doctrines. The warnings about false prophets might often be more to the point.

In the case of the traditionalists the unveiling of some esoteric teachings has been considered and prudent. What sorts of factors have allowed this development? Firstly, there are certain cosmic and cyclic conditions now obtaining which make for an unprecedented situation. In discussing the fact that what was once hid in the darkness is now being brought into the light, Schuon writes,

---

73 F. Schuon *Light on the Ancient Worlds*, 139.

there is indeed something abnormal in this, but it lies, not in the fact of the exposition of these truths, but in the general conditions of our age, which marks the end of a great cyclic period of terrestrial humanity—the end of a maha-yuga according to Hindu cosmology—and so must recapitulate or manifest again in one way or another everything that is included in the cycle, in conformity with the adage "extremes meet"; thus things that are in themselves abnormal may become necessary by reason of the conditions just referred to.[74]

Secondly, from a more expedient point of view,

... it must be admitted that the spiritual confusion of our times has reached such a pitch that the harm that might in principle befall certain people from contact with the truths in question is compensated by the advantages that others will derive from the self-same truths.[75]

Schuon reminds us of the Kabbalistic adage that "it is better to divulge Wisdom than to forget it."[76] And thirdly there is the fact already mentioned: esoteric doctrines have, in recent times, been so frequently "plagiarized and deformed" that those who are in a position to speak with authority on these matters are obliged to give some account of what "true esoterism is and what it is not."[77]

From another perspective it can be said that the preservation, indeed the very survival, of the formal exotericisms may depend on the revivifying effects of an esotericism more widely understood:

exoterism is a precarious thing by reason of its limits or its exclusions: there arrives a moment in history when all kinds of experiences oblige it to modify its claims to exclusiveness, and it is then driven to a choice: escape from these limitations by the upward path, in esoterism, or by the downward path, in a worldly and suicidal liberalism.[78]

The hazards and ambiguities attending the exposure of esoteric doctrines to an audience in many respects ill-equipped to understand them have posed the same problems for representatives of traditional esotericisms the world over. Joseph Epes Brown writes of the disclosure of traditional Lakota wisdom, to choose one example, in terms very similar to those used by Schuon:

... in these days those few old wise men still living among them say that at the approach of the end of a cycle, when men everywhere have become unfit to understand and still more to realize the truths revealed to them at the origin ... it is then permissible and even desirable to bring this knowledge out

74 F. Schuon, *The Transcendent Unity of Religions*, xxxi.
75 F. Schuon, *The Transcendent Unity of Religions*, xxxi.
76 F. Schuon, *The Transfiguration of Man*, 10.
77 F. Schuon, *The Transfiguration of Man*, 10.
78 F. Schuon, *Esoterism as Principle and as Way*, 19.

into the light of day, for by its own nature truth protects itself against being profaned and in this way it is possible it may reach those qualified to penetrate it deeply.[79]

It is no accident that the few remaining holy men amongst the American Indians and traditionalists like Schuon should see this matter in the same terms.

Traditionalism, Interfaith Encounters and Comparative Religion

From a traditionalist viewpoint, the vexed issues of ecumenism, dialogue and the inter-relationship of the religions are all strands in the same web. It should be noted, firstly, that the recognition of the proper status of traditions other than one's own depends on various contingent circumstances and does not in itself constitute a spiritual necessity. In some respects a religious intolerance is preferable to the kind of tolerance which holds fast to nothing: "... the Christian saint who fights the Moslems is closer to Islamic sanctity than the philosopher who accepts everything and practices nothing."[80] "Tolerance" is no substitute for a properly constituted understanding of the inner unity of formally divergent and sometimes antagonistic religious traditions. As Coomaraswamy remarked, "the very implications of the phrase 'religious tolerance' are to be avoided: diversity of faith is not a matter for 'toleration,' but of divine appointment."[81] Certainly a well-intentioned tolerance is preferable to an atheistic hostility or a materialistic skepticism about religion; to say as much is to say very little! Nevertheless, tolerance as nothing more than a vague and undemanding sentimentality is, from a traditionalist vantage point, not a firm foundation on which to construct any comparative study. Secondly, traditional orthodoxy is the prerequisite of any creative intercourse between the traditions themselves. To imagine that dialogue can usefully proceed without firm formal commitments is to throw the arena open to any and every kind of opinion and to let loose a kind of anarchy which can only exacerbate the problem. Thirdly, the "problem" of religious pluralism and the relationship of the religions to each other can only be decisively resolved by resort to traditional esotericisms and by the application of trans-religious metaphysical principles. As Seyyed Hossein Nasr has pointed out, "Ecumenism if correctly understood must be an esoteric activity if it is to avoid becoming the instrument for simple relativization and further secularization."[82]

---

79 J.E. Brown *The Sacred Pipe* (University of Oklahoma Press, 1953 edition), xii. (This passage was omitted from the Penguin edition.) See also Schuon's "Human Premises of a Religious Dilemma" in *Sufism, Veil and Quintessence*, 97-113.

80 F. Schuon, *Logic and Transcendence*, 182. See also S.H. Nasr, *Knowledge and the Sacred*, 291 & 307, fn28.

81 A.K. Coomaraswamy, "Sri Ramakrishna and Religious Tolerance," *Selected Papers 2*, 42.

82 S.H. Nasr, *Knowledge and the Sacred*, 282.

A proper understanding of the exoteric-esoteric relationship would put an end to all the artificial and quite implausible means by which attempts have been made to reconcile formal divergences. As Marco Pallis, starting from a Buddhist perspective, has suggested,

> *Dharma* and the *dharmas*, unitive suchness and the suchness of diversified existence: here is to be found the basis of an inter-religious exegesis which does not seek a remedy for historical conflicts by explaining away formal or doctrinal factors such as in reality translate differences of spiritual genius. Far from minimizing the importance of these differences in the name of a facile and eventually spurious ecumenical friendliness, they will be cherished for the positive message they severally carry and as necessities that have arisen out of the differentiation of mankind itself.[83]

The outlook informing this passage depends on a recognition of the exoteric-esoteric relationship and a subordination (*not* an annihilation) of exoteric dogmatism to the metaphysical principles preserved by traditional esotericisms. The "pious extravagances"[84] of the champions of exoteric exclusivism, perhaps altogether appropriate in former times, must now give way to a deeper understanding of both the formal diversity and the inner unity of all integral traditions. Unhappily, the guardians of religious dogmas, sensing the changed circumstances in which we live, often turn in the wrong direction. Schuon:

> ... if exoterism, the religion of literalism and exclusive dogmatism, has difficulty in admitting the existence and legitimacy of the esoteric dimension ... this is understandable on various grounds. However, in the cyclic period in which we live, the situation of the world is such that exclusive dogmatism ... is hard put to hold its own, and whether it likes it or not, has need of certain esoteric elements ... Unhappily the wrong choice is made; the way out of certain deadlocks is sought, not with the help of esoterism, but by resorting to the falsest and most pernicious of philosophical and scientific ideologies, and for the universality of the spirit, the reality of which is confusedly noted, there is substituted a so-called "ecumenism" which consists of nothing but platitudes and sentimentality and accepts everything without discrimination.[85]

For many scholars concerned with the inter-relationship of the religions the central dilemma has been this: any "theoretical" solution to the problem of conflicting truth claims demands a conceptual platform which *both* encompasses *and* transcends any specific theological position; it must go beyond the premises of any *particular* theological outlook but at the same time not compromise the theological position to which one might adhere. Traditionalism shows the way out of this impasse. It neither insists on nor

83 M. Pallis, *A Buddhist Spectrum*, 109-110.
84 The phrase is from Schuon's essay "Deficiencies in the World of Faith," *Survey of Metaphysics and Esoterism*, 125.
85 F. Schuon, *Logic and Transcendence*, 4.

precludes any particular religious commitment. Once the necessity of orthodoxy is accepted, and the principles which govern the relationship of the exoteric and the esoteric are understood, then one can remain fully committed to a particular tradition while recognizing the limits of the outlook in question. Traditionalism requires neither a betrayal of one's own tradition nor a wishy-washy hospitality to anything and everything. The observation made by an early reviewer of Schuon's *Transcendent Unity of Religions* might be applied to traditionalism as a whole. It presents "a very concrete and specific philosophy of religion for an ecumenical age ... It opens [the] way for discovering a basis for coexistence for the different creeds."[86]

Traditionalism addresses itself to the inner meaning of religion through an elucidation of immutable metaphysical and cosmological principles and through a penetration of the forms preserved in each religious tradition. The sources of the traditionalist vision are Revelation, tradition, intellection, realization. It is neither a vestigial pseudo-scientific methodology nor a subjectively-determined "hermeneutic" but a *theoria* which bridges the *phenomena* and the *noumena* of religion; it takes us "from the forms to the essences wherein resides the truth of all religions and where alone a religion can be really understood ..."[87] It provides an all-embracing context for the study of religion and the means whereby not only empirical but philosophical and metaphysical questions can be both properly formulated and decisively answered. It would be sanguine in the extreme to imagine that comparative religion as a discipline will harness itself to a traditionalist agenda. Nor, by the same token, can traditionalism itself ever be primarily an academic discipline. Nevertheless, there remain considerable possibilities for the discipline of religious studies to assimilate something of the traditionalist outlook or, at least, to accept it as one of the perspectives from which religion can be studied.

The argument that traditionalism is too normative to be allowed to shape academic studies is no argument at all. As currently practiced by many of its exponents comparative religion is quite clearly normative anyway. As soon as we are prepared, for instance, to talk of "sympathy," of "mutual understanding," of "world community," and so on, we have entered a normative realm. It is time scholars ceased to be embarrassed by this fact and stopped sheltering behind the tattered banner of a pseudo-scientific methodology which forbids any engagement with the most interesting, the most profound and the most urgent questions which naturally stem from any serious study of religion. The question is not whether the study of religion will be influenced by certain norms—it will be so influenced whether we admit it or not—but to what kind of norms we are prepared to give our allegiances. The time has come to nail our colors to the mast in arguing for approaches to religion

---

86 F.H. Heinemann in *The Journal of Theological Studies* 6, 1955, 340.
87 S.H. Nasr, *Sufi Essays*, 38.

which do justice to the traditional principle of adequation, and which will help rescue the discipline from the ignominious plight of being nothing more than another undistinguished member of a disreputable family of pseudo-sciences.

The discipline of religious studies will never have any integrity so long as it is pursued as a self-sufficient, self-validating end in itself. As Klaus Klostermaier has so acutely observed,

> The study of religions can no longer afford the luxury of creating pseudo-problems of its own, of indulging in academic hobbies, or of acting as if religion or the study of it were ends in themselves. The one thing that might be worse than the confusion and uncertainty in the area of religious studies would be the development of a methodology of religious studies, by scholars of religious studies, for the sake of religious studies: playing a game by rules invented by the players for the sake of the game alone.[88]

To this reflection we might add another, this time from René Guénon:

> The passion for research taken as an end in itself [is] ... "mental restlessness" without end and without issue ... this substitution of research for knowledge is simply giving up the proper object of intelligence ... [89]

If this is not to be the fate of the discipline then, at the very least, there must be a much more radical debate about philosophical, theological and metaphysical questions generated within the discipline. E.O. James many years ago observed that "The study of religion ... demands both a historical and a scientific approach and a theological and philosophical evaluation if ... its foundations are to be well and truly laid."[90] A serious consideration of the works of the traditionalists and of the whole traditionalist perspective would, at least, open the way for a fruitful reconvergence of philosophy, theology, comparative religion and metaphysics.

Those who accept the traditionalist position can reap a richer harvest. The explication of the *sophia perennis* and its application to contingent phenomena show the way to an outlook invulnerable to the whim and fancy of ever-changing intellectual fashions and armors one against the debilitating effects of scientism and its sinister cargo of reductionisms. It annihilates that "neutrality" which is indifferent to the claims of religion itself and removes those "optical illusions" to which the modern world is victim. For those who see religions as something infinitely more than mere "cultural phenomena," who believe them to be the vehicles of the most profound and precious truths to which we must not immunize ourselves, who wish to do justice to

---

88 K. Klostermaier, "From Phenomenology to Meta-Science: Reflections on the Study of Religion," 563.

89 R. Guénon, *Orient et Occident* quoted in W. Perry, *Treasury of Traditional Wisdom*, 732.

90 E.O. James, quoted in E.J. Sharpe, "Some Problems of Method in the Study of Religion," 12.

both the external forms and the inner meanings of religion, who cleave to their own tradition but who wish to recognize all integral religions as pathways to God, whose pursuit of religious studies is governed by something far more deep-seated than mental curiosity—for such people traditionalism can open up whole new vistas of understanding. Ultimately, for those prepared to pay the proper price, it can lead to that "light that is neither of the East nor the West."[91]

A rediscovery of the immutable nature of man and a renewed understanding of the *sophia perennis* must be the governing purpose of the most serious comparative study of religion. It is, in Seyyed Hossein Nasr's words, a "noble end ... whose achievement the truly contemplative and intellectual elite are urgently summoned to by the very situation of man in the contemporary world."[92] The principles on which the undertaking can be based and the framework within which it can be pursued have been reconstructed by Guénon, Coomaraswamy, Schuon and the other traditionalists. Their work is there for those who seek a vision of religion and the religions adequate to the needs of the age. In their work, too, is to be found the ultimate significance of the convergence of the traditions of East and West. Not for the first time in this study I will turn for a final word to the writer who, in recent times, has done more than anyone else to elucidate the proper inter-relationships of all the integral religious traditions.

> *If we can grasp the transcendent nature of the human being, we thereby grasp the nature of revelation, of religion, of tradition; we understand their possibility, their necessity, their truth. And in understanding religion, not only in a particular form or according to some verbal specification, but also in its formless essence, we understand the religions ... the meaning of their plurality and diversity; this is the plane of gnosis, of the religio perennis, whereon the extrinsic antinomies of dogmas are explained and resolved.* (Frithjof Schuon)[93]

---

91 From the *Qur'an*, quoted by S.H. Nasr, "Conditions for a Meaningful Comparative Philosophy," 61.

92 S.H. Nasr, "Conditions for a Meaningful Comparative Philosophy," 61.

93 F. Schuon, *Light on the Ancient Worlds*, 142.

Appendix

A Checklist of Eastern Teachers in the West

(listed chronologically by birth date, when known)

Hinduism

• *Swami Vivekananda* (1863-1902): principal disciple of Ramakrishna (along with Swami Brahmananda), founder of the Ramakrishna Order and Mission. Addressed the World's Parliament of Religions in Chicago 1893 and toured extensively in the West. Championed Vedanta as the basis of a universal religion.

• *Sri Aurobindo Ghose* (1872-1950): philosopher and teacher, educated in England, whose Integral Yoga sought to synthesize ascetical, scientific and artistic ideals. Popular with Indian and Western intellectuals.

• *Sri Ramana Maharshi* (1879-1950): universally revered *Advaitin* saint and sage of Arunachala in southern India. Attracted devotees of all kinds through his extraordinary *darsan.*

• *Swami Ramdas* (1884-1963): wandering *sadhu* who traveled the length of India repeating the sacred *Ram-mantram.* Later established an ashram and instructed disciples in japa-yoga.

• *Swami Shivananda* (1887-1963): former doctor, teacher and founder of the Divine Light Mission, established 1939; based at Rishikesh. Guru of many Indian teachers in the West.

• *Swami Prabhavananda* (1893-1976): disciple of Swami Brahmananda. Sent by the Ramakrishna Order to San Francisco in 1923. Founder and head of the Vedanta Society of Southern California from 1930 to 1976. A prolific author and associated with the emergence of "Californian Vedanta."

• *Swami Yogananda* (1893-1952): founder of the Self Realization Fellowship and author of the best-selling *Autobiography of a Yogi.*

• *Swami Nikhilananda* (1895-1973): a disciple of Sarada Devi and founder of the New York Ramakrishna-Vivekananda Center in 1933. Translator of the *Gospel of Ramakrishna.* Later involved with the Eranos group and showed some interest in Jungian psychology.

• *Prabhupada Bhaktivedanta* (c.1896-1977): teacher of Gaudiya Vaisnavism. Arrived in New York in 1965 and soon established ISKON (International Society for Krishna Consciousness) which was one of the most rapidly growing Eastern movements of the 1970s.

• *Swami Muktananda* (1908-1983): came to America in 1970 and was one of the most popular gurus with "counter-cultural" Americans. Founded the network of Siddha Yoga Centers (now numbering something upwards of 350).

• *Anandamayi-ma* (Nirmala Sundari) (1896-1982): born in Bangladesh region of India. Attracted many devotees through her powerful presence and was revered as a divine figure. Like Ramana Maharshi, her teaching was a function of her presence rather than of verbalized doctrines. Major centers at Benares, Vrindaban and Mumbai.

• *Swami Chinmayananda* (1916-1993): Former journalist and Indian nationalist, disciple of Shivananda, teacher of *Advaita* Vedanta and karma yoga, and author of thirty-odd books.

• *Maharishi Mahesh Yogi* (1911-): Has obscured his origins but probably from Allahabad. Started teaching Transcendental Meditation in London in 1959 and became something of a "pop guru" associated with media celebrities in the late 60s. Founder of the International Transcendental Meditation Society. Has attracted a good deal of controversy in the last twenty years.

Theravadin Buddhism & *Vipassana* Meditation

• *Ledi Sayadaw* (1856-1923): Burmese monk, reformer who reinstated *vipassana* as the central practice of Buddhism for *sangha* and lay people alike.

• *U Ba Khin* (1899-1971): civil servant and lay meditation teacher.

• *Mahasi Sayadaw* (1904-1982): student of Mingun Jetawan Sayadaw; became a very popular meditation teacher in Burma. His approach was rather more open to external influences than that of most of the other Burmese *vipassana* masters.

• *Ajahn Chah* (1918-1992): Thai forest tradition; many of his students now teachers in the West. Established the only Theravadin monastery in the West entirely populated by Westerners, in England.

• *Sayadaw U Pandita* (1921-): Student of Mahasi Sayadaw and helped him establish centers in Sri Lanka. Has taught *vipassana* courses in USA, UK, Australia, India and Nepal.

• *S.N. Goenka* (1924-): Burmese-Indian teacher of *vipassana* meditation. Student of U Ba Khin. Moved to India in 1969. Based at Igatpuri near Mumbai. His ten-day retreats were very popular in the 70s—one of the main access points to Buddhism for Westerners (along with Kopan, Dharamsala and Bodhgaya). Industrialist and layman, Hindu by upbringing. Teaches to people of all religions; *vipassana* somewhat detached from specifically Buddhist-religious framework. *Vipassana* centers, inspired by Goenka's teachings have been established in Nepal, Australia, New Zealand, England, France and the USA. It has been estimated that something in the order of 19,000 people have done retreats under Goenka in different parts of the world.

• *Anagarika Munindra*: Born Chittagong, Bangladesh. One-time superintendent of the Mahabodhi Temple in Bodhgaya. He began teaching *vipassana* meditation at the Mahasi Thathana Meditation Center in Rangoon, Burma after receiving training there in the early 1960s. Since then he has traveled widely and has students in several western countries as well as India.

Zen Buddhism

• *Soyen Shaku* (1859-1919): Rinzai monk and abbot. Spent a period in Ceylon in the late 1880s and was probably the first Zen priest to visit and teach in the West. Delegate at the World's Parliament of Religions in 1893 and teacher of many later Zen Masters and of Daisetz T. Suzuki.
• *Nyogen Senzaki* (1876-1958): disciple of Soyen Shaku and the first Japanese Zen teacher to take up permanent residence in America in 1905. Became a prominent Zen teacher in Los Angeles.
• *Haku'un Yasutani* (1885-1973): Soto Zen Master, student of Dai'un Harada Roshi, visited America frequently in the 60s and trained many Western Zen teachers.
• *Shunryu Suzuki* (1904-1971): Soto Zen monk, founder of the San Francisco and Tassajara Zen Centers, author of *Zen Mind, Beginner's Mind*. One of the most widely respected of all Zen teachers.
• *Nakagawa Soen* (1907-1984): initiate of both Rinzai and Soto Zen traditions, teacher who came to America at the invitation of Nyogen Senzaki; married to Ruth Fuller Everett (who took Soen's family name, Sasaki).
• *Yamada Koun* (1907-1990): Student of both Harada and Yasutani. Ebullient lay Zen teacher and hospital administrator. Principal teacher of Philip Kapleau. Sympathetic to the development of "Christian Zen."
• *Thich Nhat Hanh* (1926-): Vietnamese Zen Buddhist who came to prominence as peace activist during the Vietnam War. Founder of Plum Village, a retreat community in southwestern France. A highly influential teacher, author and participant in inter-religious dialogue.
• *Dr Thich Thien-an* (d.1980): Vietnamese Rinzai Zen teacher and distinguished scholar who went to America in 1967. Founder of the International Buddhist Meditation Center in Los Angeles.
• *Seung Sahn* (aka *Soen Sa Nim*) (1927-): Korean teacher who arrived in USA in 1972 and established Zen centers in Los Angeles, Berkeley, Cambridge, New Haven, and New York.
• *Hakuyu Taizan Maezumi* (1931-): Trained in both Soto and Rinzai traditions, moved to Los Angeles in 1956 and became a prominent teacher of Western Zen practitioners.

Tibetan Buddhism

• *Kalu Rinpoche* (1905-1989): one of the most senior of the Kargyu lamas but widely respected across the Tibetan lineages. Teacher of the Dalai Lama and the 16th Karmapa. One of the first to guide Westerners through three-year retreats. Instructed to teach in the West by the Karmapa. Mainly taught in India but visited USA several times where many centers were established under his auspices. Regarded by the Dalai Lama as one of the most authoritative of all Tibetan teachers.

• *Dudjom Rinpoche* (c.1905-1987): became head of the Nyingma lineage (a position which had not hitherto existed, bought about by the Tibetan diaspora). Great scholar and meditation master who wrote a large work on the history of the Nyingmas. He and Dilgo Khyentse were gurus to most of the Nyingma lamas in the West today. Founded an important Nyingma center at Dordogne in the south of France.

• *Geshe Wangyal* (c.1905?-1984?): a Mongolian Gelugpa who was one of the first lamas to teach in the West after arriving in New Jersey in 1955. Established the first Tibetan monastery in America open to non-Tibetans. Stressed a scholarly understanding of the tradition and was highly significant as a teacher, along with Geshe Sopa, of such figures as Robert Thurman and Jeffrey Hopkins who became leading Tibetologists.

• *Dilgo Khyentse Rinpoche* (1910-1991): One of the last of the great Tibetan teachers who completed his training in Tibet. Succeeded Dudjom as head of the Nyingmas. Lived in Bodnath near Katmandu.

• *Deshung Rinpoche* (c.1910?-1982): a great scholar within the Sakya tradition. Worked with scholars such as Turrell Wylie, Agehananda Bharati, E. Gene Smith and Edward Conze at the University of Washington in the Inner Asian Program. Began teaching in the West in the mid-70s.

• *Chogye Trichen Rinpoche* (1920-): one of the most senior Sakya lamas and head of the Tsarpa branch of this lineage. Resides in Dharamsala, heads two monastic centers in Nepal and teaches in the West intermittently. He transmits the central teaching of *Lam-dre* of the Sakya tradition. Has spent most of his adult life in retreat. One of the last living lamas who was trained entirely in Tibet and the foremost authority on the Kalachakra.

• *The Sixteenth Gyalwa Karmapa* (Rangjung Rigpe Dorje) (1924-1981): head of the Kargyu school of Tibetan Buddhism and one of the first religious leaders to leave Tibet. Founded the large Kargyu monastery at Rumtek, Sikkim. Close association with Chögyam Trungpa who first invited the Karmapa to America in 1974.

• *Karma Thinley Rinpoche* (1931-): master of the Kargyu and Sakya traditions. Fled Tibet with the Karmapa in 1959 and started teaching Westerners in the late 60s before moving to Canada in 1971. Teaches at his centers in Nepal, Canada, the USA, New Zealand and the UK.

• *Lama Yeshe* (1935-1984): Gelugpa teacher who left Tibet in 1959. One of the earliest teachers of Westerners in the West. The month-long meditation courses, which he established in 1969 at Kopan monastery near Katmandu, were hugely popular with Westerners. Established first Tibetan Buddhist organization in Australia, believing that Australia had a particular role to play in the preservation of Tibetan Buddhism.

• *Tarthang Tulku*: fled Tibet in 1959 to Bhutan and India before going to Sikkim to study with Dzongsar Khyentse. Published many important Tibetan texts in India before going to USA in 1969 where he founded the Nyingma Institute in San Francisco and Dharma Publishing.

• *The Fourteenth Dalai Lama* (Tenzin Gyatso) (1935-): the spiritual and temporal leader of Tibet since 1951. Head of the government-in-exile based at Dharamsala. Recipient of the 1989 Nobel Peace Prize and a globally recognized religious leader. He is the author of many books.

• *Namkhai Norbu*: (1938-): trained in several lineages, early training in Sakya. Lay teacher of *Dzog-chen*. Not aligned with any particular sect. Left Tibet at a young age and went to Sikkim where he met Giuseppe Tucci. Based in Italy where he was a Professor of Tibetan and Mongolian Language and Literature at Naples University. His *Dzog-chen* community has a center in each continent.

• *Chögyam Trungpa* (1939-1987): began monastic training at an early age after being identified as the eleventh Trungpa. Studied at Oxford in the 1960s and founded the Samye-Ling Meditation Center in Dumfrieshire, Scotland before moving to the USA where he was a charismatic and influential teacher. Founder of the Naropa Institute in Boulder, Colorado. Author of many best-selling books on Tibetan meditational practice. Attracted considerable controversy.

• *Sakya Trizin* (Kunga Tegchen Palbar Samphel Wanggi Gyalpo) (1945-): Installed as the "holder of the Sakya throne" in Lhasa in 1951, and leader of the Sakya school. Arrived in India in 1959 and soon founded the Ghoom monastery in Darjeeling. Taught at the Tibetan university at Sarnath. Established the headquarters of the Sakyas near Dehru Dun in northern India. Has traveled and taught extensively in the West. Now based at Dolma Phodrang in Rajpur.

• *Lama Zopa Rinpoche* (1946-): Gelugpa, disciple of Lama Yeshe with whom he founded the Fellowship for the Preservation of Mahayana Tradition which has become a worldwide organization with branches in many Western countries. Its headquarters are in Bodhgaya.

• *Sogyal Rinpoche*: Trained by one of the most significant lamas of the century, Jamyung Khyentse, who was "the holder of all lineages in all traditions" and by Dudjom Rinpoche. Highly active in the *ras-med* movement, an ecumenical enterprise which encouraged closer linkages between the different Tibetan traditions. Nyingma teacher of *Dzog-chen*, founder of Rigpa, an international organization with major centers in USA, London and France. Author of the best-selling *The Tibetan Book of Living and Dying*.

Sources

In the case of multiple entries by a single author items are ordered chronologically within each of the following sub-sections: books, journal articles, reviews, contributions to multi-author works, co-authored items, works edited. Publication dates refer to the editions consulted. Occasionally the original date of publication has been indicated immediately following the title, within brackets. When an article is cited from a book edited by a different author only limited details are provided: the full details can be found under the editor's name. All journal volume and issue numbers have been standardized. Website addresses have only been provided where there might be some difficulty in tracing the site through the name of the journal, author or organization in question.

Abdel-Malek, Anouar, "Orientalism in Crisis," *Diogenes*, 44, Winter 1963, 104-112 (reprinted in A. Macfie, *Orientalism: A Reader*, 47-56).

Abe, Masao, *A Zen Life: D.T. Suzuki Remembered*, New York: Weatherhill, 1986 (includes tributes from Christmas Humphreys, Thomas Merton, Erich Fromm, Alan Watts, Philip Kapleau, Gary Snyder, Robert Aitken, and many others).

Abe, Masao (ed), *Zen and Western Thought*, Honolulu: Hawaii University, 1985.

Abe, Stanley K., "Inside the Wonder House: Buddhist Art and the West" in *Curators of the Buddha*, ed. D. Lopez, 63-106.

Abelsen, Peter, "Schopenhauer and Buddhism," *Philosophy East and West*, 43, 1993, 255-278.

Abhishiktananda, *Prayer*, London: SPCK, 1967.

— *Towards the Renewal of the Indian Church*, Ernakulam: KCM, 1970.

— *Guru and Disciple*, London: SPCK, 1974.

— *The Further Shore*, Delhi: ISPCK, 1975.

— *Hindu-Christian Meeting Point*, Delhi: ISPCK, 1976, rev.ed.

— *The Secret of Arunachala*, Delhi: ISPCK, 1978.

— *The Eyes of Light*, Denville: Dimension Books, 1983.

— *Saccidananda: A Christian Experience of Advaita*, Delhi: ISPCK, 1984, rev.ed.

Abu Bakr Siraj Ed-Din, *The Book of Certainty*, New York: Samuel Weiser, 1974.

Adyar Library Bulletin, "Annie Besant: A Tribute," *The Adyar Library Bulletin*, 57, 1993, ix-xiii.

Ahmad, Aijaz, "Between Orientalism and Historicism," *Studies in History*, 7:1, NS, 1991, 135-163.

Aitken, Robert, *Original Dwelling Place: Zen Buddhist Essays*, Washington DC: Counterpoint, 1996.

— "The Christian-Buddhist Life of Dwight Goddard," *Christian-Buddhist Studies*, 16:3, 1996, 3-10.

— "Gandhi, Dogen and Deep Ecology," in *The Path of Compassion: Writings on Socially Engaged Buddhism*, ed. F. Eppsteiner, 86-92.

Aitken, Robert & David Steindl-Rast, *The Ground We Share*, Boston: Shambhala, 1996.

Akong Tulku Rinpoche, *Taming the Tiger: Tibetan Teachings for Improving Daily Life*, London: Rider, 1994.

Alles, Gregory D., "Rudolf Otto and the Politics of Utopia," *Religion*, 21, 1991, 235-256.

Almond, Philip, *Rudolf Otto: An Introduction to His Philosophical Theology*, Chapel Hill:

University of North Carolina, 1984.
— *The British Discovery of Buddhism*, Cambridge: Cambridge University, 1988.
— "Towards an Understanding of the New Age," *Australian Religion Studies Review*, 6:2, 1-6.
— "Rudolf Otto and Buddhism" in *Aspects of Religion: Essays in Honor of Ninian Smart*, ed. P. Masefield & D. Wiebe, 59-72.
Alpert, Richard, Timothy Leary & Ralph Metzner, *The Psychedelic Experience*, New York: Citadel, 1995.
Angel, Leonard, *Enlightenment East and West*, Albany: SUNY, 1994.
Appleyard, Bryan, *Understanding the Present: Science and the Soul of Modern Man*, London: Picador, 1992.
Aris, Michael & Aung San Suu Kyi (eds), *Tibetan Studies in Honour of Hugh Richardson*, Warminster: Aris & Phillips, 1979.
Armstrong, Karen, *The Battle for God*, New York: Knopf, 2000.
Austin, R.W.J., Review of 1974 edition of Marco Pallis, *Peaks and Lamas* in *Studies in Comparative Religion*, 9:4, 1975, 253-254.
Badiner, Alan H., *Dharma Gaia: A Harvest of Essays on Buddhism and Ecology*, Berkeley: Parallax Press, 1990.
Bancroft, Anne, *Twentieth Century Mystics & Sages*, London: Heinemann, 1976.
— *Weavers of Wisdom: Women Mystics of the Twentieth Century*, London: Arkana/Penguin, 1989.
Bando, Shojun, "In Memory of Professor Blyth," *The Eastern Buddhist*, NS, 1:1, September 1965, 134-137.
— "D.T. Suzuki's Life in La Salle," *The Eastern Buddhist*, NS, 2:1, August 1967.
Bapat, P.V., *2500 Years of Buddhism*, New Delhi: Ministry of Information & Broadcasting, Government of India, 1956.
Barnhart, Michael G., "Ideas of Nature in an Asian Context," *Philosophy East and West*, 47:3, July 1997, 417-432.
Barthes, Roland, *Image Music Text*, selected & trans. Stephen Heath, London: Fontana, 1977.
Barrett, T.H., "Arthur Waley, D.T. Suzuki and Hu Shih: New Light on the 'Zen and History' Controversy," *Buddhist Studies Review*, 6:2, 116-119.
Baistrocchi, Marco, "The Last Pillars of Wisdom" in *Ananda Coomaraswamy: Remembering and Remembering Again and Again*, ed. S.D.R. Singam, 350-359.
Bartholomeusz, Tessa, "Spiritual Wealth and Orientalism," *Journal of Ecumenical Studies*, 35:1, Winter 1988, 19-32.
Batchelor, Stephen, *The Awakening of the West*, Berkeley: Parallax, 1994.
Baumann, Martin, "The Dharma Has Come West: A Survey of Recent Studies and Sources," *Journal of Buddhist Ethics* (website).
Baumer-Despeigne, Odette, "The Spiritual Journey of Henri Le Saux-Abhishiktananda," *Cistercian Studies*, 18, 1983, 310-329.
— "A Way of Initiation" in *The Other Half of My Soul: Bede Griffiths and the Hindu-Christian Dialogue*, ed. B. Bruteau, 42-63.
Beck, Charlotte Joko, *Everyday Zen: Love and Work*, San Francisco: Harper & Row, 1989.
Beckingham, C. F., Review of Edward Said's *Orientalism* in *Bulletin of the School of Oriental and African Studies*, 42, 1979, 38-40.
Behdad, Ali, *Belated Travelers*, Cork: Cork University, 1994.
Bell, Sandra, "Change and Identity in the Friends of the Western Buddhist Order," *Scottish Journal of Religious Studies*, 17:2, Autumn 1996, 87-107.
Beller, Steven, "Herzl, Wagner, and the Ironies of 'True Emancipation,'" in *Tainted Greatness*, ed. N. Harrowitz, 127-156.
Benavides, Gustavo, "Giuseppe Tucci, or Buddhology in the Age of Fascism," in *Curators of the Buddha*, ed. D. Lopez, 161-196.

Bendle, Mervyn, "Traditionalism in Australia," *Australian Religious Studies Review*, 14:1, Autumn 2001, 5-18.

Benoit, Hubert, *Zen and the Psychology of Transformation: The Supreme Doctrine*, New York: Inner Traditions, 1990.

Benz, Ernst, "Buddhism in the Western World" in *Buddhism in the Modern World*, ed. H. Dumoulin, 305-322.

Berger, Adriana, "Mircea Eliade: Romanian Fascism and the History of Religions in the United States" in *Tainted Greatness*, ed. N. Harrowitz, 51-74.

Berkson, Mark, "Buddhist-Christian Dialogue: Promises and Pitfalls," *Buddhist-Christian Studies*, 19.1, 1999, 181-186.

Bernis, Ursula, "Tibet in the Shadow of Our Imagination," *Parabola*, 22:3, August 1997, 83-88.

Berrigan, Daniel & Thich Nhat Hanh, *The Raft is Not the Shore: Conversations Toward a Buddhist/Christian Awareness*, Boston: Beacon Press, 1975.

Bernstein, Jeremy, "The Road to Lhasa," *The New York Review of Books*, June 12th, 1997 (website).

Berry, Wendell, *What are People For?*, San Francisco: North Point Press, 1991.

— *Sex, Economy, Freedom and Community*, New York: Pantheon, 1993.

— *Life is a Miracle: An Essay Against Modern Superstition*, Washington DC: Counterpoint, 2000.

Besserman, Perle & Manfred Steger, *Crazy Clouds: Zen Radicals, Rebels and Reformers*, Boston: Shambhala, 1991.

Bevir, Mark, "The West Turns Eastwards: Madame Blavatsky and the Transformation of the Occult Tradition," *Journal of the American Academy of Religion*, 62:3, 1994, 747-765.

Bharati, Agehananda, *The Ochre Robe: An Autobiography*, New York: Doubleday, 1970.

— "Fictitious Tibet: The Origins and Persistence of Rampaism," *Tibet Society Bulletin*, 7, 1994 (website).

— Review of Harold Coward's *Derrida and Indian Philosophy* in *Philosophy East and West*, 42:2, April 1992, 339-343.

Bishop, Peter, *Tibet in Its Place*, Bedford Park: Charles Strong Trust, 1983.

— *The Myth of Shangri-La: Tibet, Travel Writing and the Western Creation of Sacred Landscape*, London: Athlone, 1989.

Blacker, Carmen, *The Catalpa Bow: A Study of Shamanistic Practices in Japan*, London: Allen & Unwin, 1975.

— "Some Reminiscences of Zen Training in Japan" in *The Nature of Religious Man: Tradition and Experience*, ed. D.B. Fry, 104-118.

— "Intent of Courtesy" in *Madly Singing in the Mountains: An Appreciation and Anthology of Arthur Waley*, ed. I. Morris, 21-28.

Blackhirst, Rodney & Kenneth Oldmeadow, "Shadows and Strife: Reflections on the Confrontation of Islam and the West," *Sacred Web*, 8, December 2001, 121-136.

Blavatsky, H.P., *The Secret Doctrine* (3 vols) (1888), London: Theosophical Publicity Society, 1893-1895.

— *Isis Unveiled* (1877), Pasadena: Theosophical University Press, 1972.

Blofeld, John, *The Wheel of Life*, Berkeley: Shambhala, 1972.

— *The Secret and the Sublime: Taoist Mysteries and Magic*, New York: E.P. Dutton, 1973.

— *The Tantric Mysticism of Tibet*, New York: Causeway Books, 1974.

— *Beyond the Gods: Taoist and Buddhist Mysticism*, New York: E.P. Dutton, 1974.

— *Bodhisattva of Compassion: The Mystical Tradition of Kuan Yin*, Boulder: Shambhala, 1978.

— *Taoism: the Road to Immortality*, Boston: Shambhala, 1981.

— "A Farewell Letter," *The Middle Way*, 62:3, November 1987, 151-155.

Blume, Harvey, "Allen Ginsberg: Anxious Dreams of Eliot" (interview), *The Boston Book Review Interview* 1995 (website).

Blyth, R.H., *Haiku*, Tokyo: Hokusaido, 1949-1952.
— *Zen in English Literature and Oriental Classics*, New York: Dutton, 1960.
Bodian, Stephen (ed), *Timeless Visions, Healing Voices: Conversations with Men and Women of the Spirit*, Freedom, California: Crossing Press, 1991.
Borella, Jean, "René Guénon and the Traditionalist School" in *Modern Esoteric Spirituality*, ed. A. Faivre & J. Needleman, 330-358.
Borowitz, Eugene, "Buddhism and Judaism: Some Further Considerations," *Buddhist-Christian Studies*, 13, 1993, 223-227.
Borup, Jørn, "Zen and the Art of Inverting Orientalism," *NIASnytt*, Nordic Newsletter of Asian Studies, No 4, December 1995 (website).
Boucher, Sandy, *Turning the Wheel: American Women Creating the New Buddhism*, Boston: Beacon, 1993.
— "The Nuns' Island," *Tricycle* 1:2, Winter 1991 (website).
Bradbury, Malcolm (ed), *Forster: A Collection of Critical Essays*, Englewood Cliffs: Prentice-Hall, 1966.
Brazier, David, *Zen Therapy*, London: Constable, 1995.
Breckenridge, Carol A. & Peter van der Veer (eds), *Orientalism and the Postcolonial Predicament*, Philadelphia: University of Pennsylvania, 1993.
Broomfield, John, *Other Ways of Knowing*, Rochester: Inner Traditions, 1997.
Brown, Joseph Epes, *The Sacred Pipe*, Norman: University of Oklahoma, 1953.
— *The Spiritual Legacy of the American Indians*, New York: Crossroad, 1972.
— *Animals of the Soul*, Rockport: Element, 1993.
Brown, Richard, "Nietzsche and the *Bhagavad Gita*: Elective or Ironic Affinities?" in *Nietzsche and the Divine*, ed. J. Lippitt & J. Urpeth, 162-180.
Brunton, Paul, *A Message from Arunachala* (1936), London: Rider, 1969.
— *The Secret Path* (1934), London: Rider, 1969.
— *A Hermit in the Himalayas* (1937), London: Rider, 1980.
— *A Search in Secret India* (1934), York Beach: Samuel Weiser, 1985.
Bruteau, Beatrice, *What We can Learn from the East*, New York: Crossroad, 1995.
— (ed), *The Other Half of My Soul: Bede Griffiths and the Hindu-Christian Dialogue*, Wheaton: Quest, 1994.
Buchanan, James, "The Total Hermeneutics of Mircea Eliade," *Religious Studies Review*, 9:1, January 1983, 22-24.
Buddhist Society, *The Buddhist Directory*, London: The Buddhist Society, 1994, 6th ed.
Buddhist Studies Review, "Giuseppe Tucci" (Obituary), *Buddhist Studies Review*, 1:2, 1983-84, 157-163.
— "Agehananda Bharati (1923-1991)" (Obituary), *Buddhist Studies Review*, 8:1-2, 1991, 157-158.
— "K.S. von Dürckheim (24.10.1896-28.12.1988)" (Obituary), *Buddhist Studies Review*, 7:1-2, 1990, 98.
Bull, Geoffrey T., *When Iron Gates Yield*, London: Hodder & Stoughton, 1955.
Burckhardt, Titus, *Sacred Art in East and West*, Bedfont: Perennial Books, 1967.
— *Mirror of the Intellect: Essays on Traditional Science and Sacred Art*, ed. William Stoddart, Cambridge: Quinta Essentia, 1987.
— "Cosmology and Modern Science" in *The Sword of Gnosis*, ed. J. Needleman, 122-178.
Burroughs, William, *The Letters of William S. Burroughs 1945-1959*, ed. Oliver Harris, London: Picador, 1993.
Cabezon, Jose Ignacio (ed), *Buddhism, Sexuality and Gender*, Albany: SUNY, 1992.
Callicott, J. Baird & Roger T. Ames (eds), *Nature in Asian Traditions of Thought: Essays in Environmental Philosophy*, Albany: SUNY, 1989.
Campbell, Eileen & J.H. Brennan, *Dictionary of Mind, Body and Spirit*, London: Aquarian Press, 1994
Campbell, Joseph, *The Hero with a Thousand Faces* (1949) Bollingen Series, Princeton:

Princeton University, 1968, rev. ed.
— *The Masks of God*, 4 vols., New York: Viking, 1959-1968.
— *The Mythic Image*, Bollingen Series, Princeton: Princeton University, 1974.
— *Baksheesh and Brahman: Indian Journals 1954-1955*, ed. R. & S. Larsen & A. Van Couvering, San Francisco: Harper Collins, 1995.
— (ed), *Spiritual Disciplines: Papers from the Eranos Yearbooks*, Bollingen Series, Princeton: Princeton University, 1960.
Campbell, Joseph & Michael Toms, *An Open Life: Joseph Campbell in Conversation with Michael Toms*, ed. Betty Flowers, New York: Larson, 1988.
Campbell, June, *Traveler in Space: in Search of Female Identity in Tibetan Buddhism*, London: Athlone, 1996.
Canadian Broadcasting Corporation, "Interview with Allen Ginsberg," http://www.myna .com/~davidck/giinsb~1.htm.
Capps, Walter H. (ed), *Seeing with a Native Eye*, New York: Harper & Row, 1975.
Capra, Frithjof, *The Tao of Physics*, London: Fontana, 1976.
— *The Turning Point: Science, Society and the Rising Culture*, London: Fontana, 1983.
— & David Steindl-Rast, *Belonging to the Universe: Explorations on the Frontiers of Science and Spirituality*, San Francisco: Harper, 1992.
Carlson, Jeffrey, "Pretending to be Buddhist and Christian: Thich Nhat Hanh and the Two Truths of Religious Identity," *Buddhist-Christian Studies*, 20, 2000, 115-125.
Carmody, Denise L., *Women and World Religions*, Englewood Cliffs, Prentice-Hall, 1997.
Carola, Trevor, "The Wild Mind of Gary Snyder," *Shambhala Sun* (website).
Case, Margaret (ed), *Heinrich Zimmer: Coming into His Own*, Princeton: Princeton University, 1994.
Casewit, Fatima Jane, "Islamic Cosmological Concepts of Femininity and the Modern Feminist Movement," *Sacred Web*, 7, 2001, 81-92.
Cash, William, "The Nazi who Climbed a Mountain and Came Down a Hollywood Film Star," *The Age* (Melbourne), October 18, 1997, News Extra 8 (reproduced from *The Spectator*).
Casteneda, Carlos, *Journey to Ixtlan*, Harmondsworth: Penguin, 1972.
Chacornac, Paul, *The Simple Life of René Guénon* (1958), tr. Bernard Bethell, Perth: privately published, 1991.
Chadwick, David, *Crooked Cucumber: The Life and Zen Teaching of Shunryu Suzuki*, London: Thorsons, 1999.
Chah, Ajahn, *Being Dharma: the Essence of the Buddha's Teaching*, Foreword by Jack Kornfield, Boston: Shambhala, 2001.
Chakoo, B.L., *Aldous Huxley and Eastern Wisdom*, Delhi: Atma Ram, 1981.
Chamberlain, Lesley, *Nietzsche in Turin: the End of the Future*, London: Quartet Books, 1997.
Chan, W.T. "The Unity of East and West" in *Radhakrishnan: Comparative Studies in Philosophy Presented in Honor of His Sixtieth Birthday*, ed. W.R. Inge *et al*, 104-117.
Chandran, K. Narayana, "The Pining Gods and Sages in Emerson's 'Brahma,'" *English Language Notes*, 27:1, 55-57.
Chapman, Spencer, *Lhasa, the Holy City*, London: Readers Union/Chatto & Windus, 1940.
Chapple, Gerald, "Heinrich Zimmer and Henry R. Zimmer: The Translator Translated," in *Heinrich Zimmer: Coming into His Own*, ed. Margaret Case, 61-86.
Charlesworth, Max, "Ecumenism Between the World Religions," *Sophia* (Melbourne), 34:1, 1995, 140-160.
Charters, Anne, *Kerouac: a Biography*, London: Pan Books, 1978.
— (ed), *The Portable Beat Reader*, New York: Penguin, 1992.
Chatterjee, Partha, *Nationalist Thought and the Colonial World: A Derivative Discourse*, London: Zed Books, 1986.
Chen, E., "Taoism and Ecology," *Dialogue and Alliance*, 9:2, Fall 1995.
Ching, Julia, *Confucianism and Christianity: A Comparative Study*, Tokyo: Kodansha, 1977.

Chittick, William, *The Works of Seyyed Hossein Nasr Through His Fortieth Birthday*, Research Monograph No 6, Middle East Center, Salt Lake City: University of Utah, 1977.

Chowka, Peter Barry, "The *East West* Interview" (April 1977), reproduced in Gary Snyder, *The Real Work: Interviews and Talks 1964-1979*, ed. Wm. Scott McLean, New York: New Directions, 1980, 92-137.

— "This is Allen Ginsberg?", the 1976 *New Age* Interview, http://members.aol.com/pbchowka/ginsberg76.html.

Ciolek, T. Matthew, "Anne Aitken (1911-1994) of the Diamond Sangha," zenbuddhism -l@coombs.anu.edu.au.

Clarke, J.J., *Jung and Eastern Thought*, London: Routledge, 1994.

— *Oriental Enlightenment: The Encounter Between Asian and Western Thought*, London: Routledge, 1997.

Clasper, Paul, "Christian Faith and Asia," *Ching Feng*, 20:2, 1977, 89-97.

— "Christian Faith, Asian Wisdom Traditions and the Newly Emerging Paradigm Shift," *Ching Feng*, 26:4, December 1983, 195-207.

Claxton, Guy (ed), *Beyond Therapy: The Impact of Eastern Religions on Psychological Theory and Practice*, Sturminster Newton (Dorset): Prism, 1996.

Clements, R.J., *Michelangelo's Theory of Art*, New York: New York University, 1971.

Clews, Frederick, "The Consolation of Theosophy," *The New York Review of Books*, September 19th, 1996 (website).

Clifford, James, *The Predicament of Culture*, Cambridge, Massachusetts: Harvard University, 1988.

Clooney, Francis, "No Other Name? A Survey of Christian Attitudes Toward the World Religions," *Religious Studies Review*, 15:3, July 1989, 198-203.

Cobb, Jr, John B., *Beyond Dialogue: Toward a Mutual Transformation of Christianity and Buddhism*, Philadelphia: Fortress Press, 1982.

— "Christianity and Eastern Wisdom," *Japanese Journal of Religious Studies*, 5:4, December 1978, 285-298.

Coff, Pacaline, "Existential Breakthrough" in *The Other Half of My Soul: Bede Griffiths and the Hindu-Christian Dialogue*, ed. B. Bruteau, 98-111.

Cohen, J.M., "Dr Waley's Translations," in *Madly Singing in the Mountains: An Appreciation and Anthology of Arthur Waley*, ed I. Morris, 29-36.

Colasuonno, Nicholas, "The Pilgrim Missionary," *Studies in Formative Spirituality*, 13:3, November 1992, 273-288.

Colegrave, Sukie, *Uniting Heaven and Earth*, Los Angeles; Jeremy P. Tarcher, 1979 (previously published as *The Spirit of the Valley*).

Coleman, James W., *The New Buddhism: The Western Transformation of an Ancient Tradition*, New York: Oxford University, 2001.

Conner, James, "The Monk as a Bridge between East and West," in *The Other Half of My Soul: Bede Griffiths and the Hindu-Christian Dialogue*, ed. B. Bruteau, 80-97.

Conner, Tarcisius, "Monk of Renewal" in *Thomas Merton, Monk*, ed. P. Hart, 173-194.

Conze, Edward, *Buddhism: Its Essence and Development*, New York: Harper & Row, 1959.

— *Thirty Years of Buddhist Studies*, London: Cassirer, 1967.

— *The Memoirs of a Modern Gnostic*, 2 volumes, Sherbourne: The Samzidat Publishing Co, 1979.

— "A Personal Tribute" (to D.T. Suzuki), *The Eastern Buddhist*, NS, 2:1, August 1967, 84-85.

Coomaraswamy, Ananda, *Hinduism and Buddhism*, New York: Philosophical Library, 1945.

— *Figures of Speech or Figures of Thought: Collected Essays on the Traditional or "Normal" View of Art*, London: Luzac, 1946.

— *Time and Eternity*, Ascona: Artibus Asiae, 1947.

— *Christian and Oriental Philosophy of Art*, New York: Dover, 1956.

— *The Transformation of Nature in Art*, New York: Dover, 1956.

— *The Dance of Shiva and Other Essays*, New York: Noonday, 1957.

— *Coomaraswamy 1: Selected Papers, Traditional Art and Symbolism*, ed. Roger Lipsey, Princeton: Bollingen Series, Princeton University, 1977.

— *Coomaraswamy 2: Selected Papers, Metaphysics*, ed. Roger Lipsey, Princeton: Bollingen Series, Princeton University, 1977.

— *The Bugbear of Literacy*, London: Perennial Books, 1979.

— *Sources of Wisdom*, Colombo: Ministry of Cultural Affairs, 1981.

— *What is Civilization? and Other Essays*, Ipswich: Golgonooza, 1989.

— *Spiritual Authority and Temporal Power in the Indian Theory of Government*, New York: Oxford University, 1994.

— "The Pertinence of Philosophy" in *Contemporary Indian Philosophy*, ed. S. Radhakrishnan & J.H. Muirhead, London: Allen & Unwin, 1952, rev. ed.

— "The Influence of Greek on Indian Art" (1908), reprinted in *Studies in Comparative Religion*, 8:1, Winter 1974, 42-50.

— "The Bugbear of Democracy, Freedom and Equality," *Studies in Comparative Religion*, 11:3, 1977, 133-158.

Coomaraswamy, Rama P., "Who Speaks for the East?", *Studies in Comparative Religion*, 11:2, Spring 1977, 85-91.

— "The Desacralization of Hinduism for Western Consumption," *Sophia: The Journal for Traditional Studies*, 4:2, Winter 1998, 194-219.

— Review of M. Eliade, *No Souvenirs*, in *Studies in Comparative Religion* 12:1-2, 1978, 123.

— & Alvin Moore Jr (eds), *Selected Letters of Ananda Coomaraswamy*, New Delhi: Indira Gandhi National Center, 1988.

Cooper, Jean, *Taoism, the Way of the Mystic*, Wellingborough: Aquarian Press, 1972.

— *Yin & Yang: the Taoist Harmony of Opposites*, Wellingborough: Aquarian Press, 1981.

Coreless, Roger, "Coming out in the Sangha: Queer Community in American Buddhism" in *The Faces of American Buddhism*, ed. C. Prebish and K. Tanaka, 253-265.

Cornwell, John, *Hitler's Pope: the Secret History of Pius XII*, New York: Viking, 1999.

Cousins, L.S., Review of Sangharakshita's *The Eternal Legacy* in *Studies in Comparative Religion*, 17:1-2, (no date, early 1980s), 118-120.

Cowan, James, *Mysteries of the Dreaming*, Lindfield (NSW): Unity, 1989.

Coward, Harold, *Hindu-Christian Dialogue: Perspectives and Encounters*, Maryknoll, NY: Orbis, 1989.

— "Hinduism's Sensitizing of Christianity to its own Sources," *Dialogue & Alliance*, 7:2, Fall-Winter 1993, 77-85.

— "Joseph Campbell and Eastern Religions: The Influence of India," in *Paths to the Power of Myth: Joseph Campbell and the Study of Religion*, ed. Daniel C. Noel, 47-67.

— (ed), *Jung and Eastern Thought*, Albany: SUNY, 1985.

Cragg, Kenneth, *The Mind of the Quran*, London: Allen & Unwin, 1973.

Crawford, Alan, "Ananda Coomaraswamy and C.R. Ashbee," in *Ananda Coomaraswamy, Remembering and Remembering Again and Again*, ed. S.D.R. Singam, 239-243.

Crittenden, Jack, "What is the Meaning of 'Integral'?" in K. Wilber, *Eye of the Spirit*, vii-xii.

Cronin, Richard, "The Indian English Novel: *Kim* and *Midnight's Children*," *Modern Fiction Studies*, 33:2, Summer 1987, 201-213.

Cross, Stephen, "*Ex Oriente Lux*: How the *Upanishads* Came to Europe," *Temenos Academy Review*, 2, Spring, 1999, 106-129.

Crouch, James, *A Bibliography of Ananda Kentish Coomaraswamy*, New Delhi: Manohar, 2002.

Croucher, Paul, *Buddhism in Australia, 1848-1988*, Kensington: University of New South Wales, 1989.

Curtin, Deane, "Dogen, Deep Ecology and the Ecological Self," *Environmental Ethics*, 16:2, Summer 1994.

— "A State of Mind Like Water: Ecosophy and the Buddhist Traditions," *Inquiry*, 39:2, 1996, 239-253.

Cusack, Carol & Peter Oldmeadow (eds), *This Immense Panorama*, Sydney: University of Sydney, 2001.

— (eds), *The End of Religions? Religion in an Age of Globalization*, Sydney: University of Sydney, 2001.

Cush, Denise, "British Buddhism and the New Age," *Journal of Contemporary Religion*, 11:2, 1996, 195-208.

Cutsinger, James, *Advice to the Serious Seeker: Meditations on the Teachings of Frithjof Schuon*, Albany: SUNY, 1996.

— "On Earth as It Is in Heaven: A Metaphysical Cosmogony," *Dialogue & Alliance*, 4:4, Winter 1990-91, 45-68.

Dallmayr, Fred, *Beyond Orientalism*, Albany: SUNY, 1996.

Daniélou, Alain, *The Gods of India* (original title *Hindu Polytheism*, 1964), New York: Inner Traditions, 1985.

— *The Way to the Labyrinth: Memories of East and West*, New York: New Directions, 1987.

— *Gods of Love and Ecstasy: The Traditions of Shiva and Dionysius*, Rochester: Inner Traditions, 1992.

Danner, Victor, "The Inner and Outer Man" in Y. Ibish & P.L. Wilson (eds) *Traditional Modes of Contemplation and Action*, 407-415.

Das, G.K., "E.M. Forster and Hindu Mythology" in *E.M. Forster: Centenary Revaluations*, ed. J.S. Harz & R.K. Martin, Toronto: University of Toronto, 1982.

Dass, Ram, *Be Here Now*, San Francisco: Lama Foundation, 1972.

— *The Only Dance There Is*, New York: Anchor, 1973.

— *Miracle of Love: Stories about Neem Karoli Baba*, New York: Dutton, 1979.

— & Stephen Levine, *Grist for the Mill*, Santa Cruz: Unity Press, 1977.

David-Neel, Alexandra, *Magic and Mystery in Tibet* (1931), New York: University Books, 1956.

— *Initiates and Initiations in Tibet* (1931), New York: University Books, 1959.

— *My Journey to Lhasa* (1927), London: Virago, 1983.

Davies, Paul, "Esoteric Dimensions of Deep Ecology," *Sacred Web*, 6, 2000, 31-45.

De Jong, J.W., *A Brief History of Buddhist Studies in Europe and America*, Delhi: Sri Satguru Publications, 1987.

Del Vasto, Lanza, *Return to the Source*, New York: Touchstone, 1971.

De Silva, Padmasiri, *Tangles and Webs: Comparative Studies in Existentialism, Psychoanalysis and Buddhism*, Colombo: Lake House Investments, 1976.

Desjardins, Arnaud, *The Message of the Tibetans*, London: Stuart & Watkins, 1969.

Deutsch, Eliot, *Advaita Vedanta: a Philosophical Reconstruction*, Honolulu: University of Hawaii, 1973.

Dinnage, Rosemary, *Annie Besant*, Harmondsworth: Penguin, 1986.

Dixon, Bernard (ed), *Journeys in Belief*, London: Allen & Unwin, 1968.

Doniger, Wendy, "The King and the Corpse: Zimmer's Legacy to Mythologists and Indologists" in *Heinrich Zimmer: Coming into His Own*, ed. Margaret Case, 49-60.

— "Origins of Myth-Making Man" in *Paths to the Power of Myth*, ed. D. Noel, 181-186.

Doty, William G., "Dancing to the Music of the Spheres: The Religion in Joseph Campbell's 'Non-Religious' Mythography," in *Paths to the Power of Myth*, ed. D. C. Noel, 3-12.

Douglas, James W., *Resistance and Contemplation: The Way of Liberation*, New York: Delta, 1972.

Dresser, Marianne (ed), *Buddhist Women on the Edge: Contemporary Perspectives from the Western Frontier*, Berkeley: North Atlantic Books, 1996.

Du Boulay, Shirley, *Beyond the Darkness: A Biography of Bede Griffiths*, London: Rider, 1998.

Sources

Dumoulin, Heinrich, *Christianity Meets Buddhism*, tr. John Maraldo, La Salle: Open Court, 1974.
— *Zen Buddhism: A History*, 2 vols, New York: Macmillan, 1988 & 1990.
— *Zen Buddhism in the 20th Century*, New York: Weatherhill, 1992.
— "Meetings with Daisetz Suzuki," *The Eastern Buddhist*, NS, 2:1, August 1967, 153-156.
— (ed), *Buddhism in the Modern World*, London: Collier Macmillan, 1976.
Dunbar, Scott, "The Place of Inter-religious Dialogue in the Academic Study of Religion," *Journal of Ecumenical Studies*, 35:3-4, Summer-Fall 1998, 455-469.
Dürckheim, Karlfried, *The Japanese Cult of Tranquility*, London: Rider, 1960.
— *Hara: the Vital Center of Man*, London: Allen & Unwin, 1985.
— *The Way of Self-Transformation*, London: Allen & Unwin, 1988.
Eastern Buddhist, Memorial Issue on D.T. Suzuki, *The Eastern Buddhist*, NS, 2:1, August 1967.
Eaton, Gai, *The Richest Vein*, London: Faber & Faber, 1949.
— *King of the Castle: Choice and Responsibility in the Modern World*, London: Bodley Head, 1977.
Eck, Diana, *Encountering God: A Spiritual Journey from Bozeman to Banaras*, Boston: Beacon, 1993.
— & Devaki Jain, *Speaking of Faith: Cross-cultural Perspectives on Women, Religion and Social Change*, London: Women's Press, 1986.
Eden, P.M., "Alan Watts—An Appreciation," *The Middle Way*, 58:4, Feb 1984, 217.
Edwardes, Michael, *East-West Passage: The Travel of Ideas and Inventions between Asia and the Western World*, London: Cassell, 1971.
Eliade, Mircea, *Patterns in Comparative Religion*, New York: Sheed & Ward, 1958.
— *Yoga: Immortality and Freedom* (1948), Bollingen Series, New York: Routledge Kegan Paul, 1959.
— *The Sacred and the Profane*, New York: Harcourt Brace Jovanovich, 1959.
— *Myths, Dreams and Memories*, New York: Harper & Row, 1960.
— *Shamanism: Archaic Techniques of Ecstasy*, Bollingen Series, Princeton: Princeton University, 1964.
— *The Quest: History and Meaning in Religion*, Chicago: University of Chicago, 1969.
— *Myth and Reality*, New York: Harper Colophon, 1975.
— *Occultism, Witchcraft and Cultural Fashions*, Chicago: University of Chicago, 1976.
— *A History of Religious Ideas*, 3 vols, Chicago: University of Chicago, 1978, 1982, 1985.
— *Ordeal by Labyrinth: Conversations with Claude-Henri Rocquet*, Chicago: University of Chicago, 1982.
— *Symbolism, the Sacred and the Arts*, ed. Diana Apostolos-Cappadona, New York: Crossroad, 1988.
— *Autobiography Vol. 1 1907-1937: Journey East, Journey West*, New York: Harper & Row, 1981; *Vol. 2 1937-1960: Exile's Odyssey*, Chicago: University of Chicago, 1988.
— *Journal, Vols 1-4*, Chicago: University of Chicago, 1990. (Vol. 2 also published under the title *No Souvenirs*, New York: Harper & Row, 1977).
— "Encounters at Ascona" in *Spiritual Disciplines: Papers from the Eranos Yearbooks*, ed. J. Campbell, xvii-xxi.
— "Methodological Remarks on the Study of Religious Symbolism" in *The History of Religions: Essays in Methodology*, ed. M. Eliade & J. Kitagawa, 86-107.
— "Giuseppe Tucci (1895-1984)," *History of Religions*, 24:2, November 1984, 157-159.
— "Cultural Fashions and the History of Religions" in *The History of Religions: Essays on the Problem of Understanding*, ed. J. Kitagawa, Chicago: University of Chicago, 1967, 21-38.
— (editor-in-chief), *The Encyclopedia of Religion*, New York: Simon & Schuster/ Macmillan, 1995.
Eliot. T.S., *Notes towards the Definition of Culture* (1948), London: Faber & Faber, 1962.

Elliott, William, *Tying Rocks to Clouds: Meetings and Conversations with Wise and Spiritual People*, Wheaton: Quest, 1995.

Ellwood, Robert, *The Politics of Myth: A Study of C.G. Jung, Mircea Eliade and Joseph Campbell*, Albany: SUNY, 1999.

— "Buddhism," sub-section "Buddhism in the West" in *The Encyclopedia of Religion*, *Vol. 2*, ed. M. Eliade, 436-439.

Emerson, Ralph W., *Selected Writings of Ralph Waldo Emerson*, ed. William Gilman, New York: New American Library, 1965.

Emilsen, William W., "The Legacy of John Copley Winslow, (1882-1974)," *The International Bulletin of Missionary Research*, 21:1, January 1997, 26-29.

Enomiya-Lassalle, Hugo, *Zen Meditation for Christians*, La Salle: Open Court, 1974.

Epstein, Lawrence & Richard F. Sherburne (eds), *Reflections on Tibetan Culture: Essays in Memory of Turrell V. Wylie*, Lewiston: Edwin Mellen, 1990.

Eppsteiner, Fred (ed), *The Path of Compassion: Writings on Socially Engaged Buddhism*, Berkeley: Parallax Press, 1988.

Études Traditionnelles, Special Issue of *Études Traditionnelles: Le Sort de l'Occident*, November, 1951.

Eusden, John D., *Zen & Christian: The Journey Between*, New York: Crossroad, 1981.

Evans-Wentz, W.Y., *The Tibetan Book of the Dead* (1927), Oxford: Oxford University Press, 3rd ed, 1960.

— *Tibetan Yoga and Secret Doctrines* (1935), Oxford: Oxford University Press, 1967.

— *The Tibetan Book of the Great Liberation*, Oxford: Oxford University Press, 1967.

Evola, Julius, *The Doctrine of Awakening*, London: Luzac, 1951.

— "Spiritual Virility in Buddhism," *East and West*, 7, 1957, 319-326.

Faas, Ekbert, *Towards a New American Poetics: Essays and Interviews*, Santa Barbara: Black Sparrow, 1978.

Fader, Larry, "Arthur Koestler's Critique of D.T. Suzuki's Interpretation of Zen," *The Eastern Buddhist*, NS, 13:2, 1980, 46-72.

— "Zen in the West: Historical and Philosophical Implications of the 1893 Chicago World's Parliament of Religions," *The Eastern Buddhist*, NS, 15:1, Spring 1982, 122-145.

Faivre, Antoine, *Access to Western Esotericism*, Albany: SUNY, 1994.

— "Theosophy" in *The Encyclopedia of Religion, Vol. 14*, ed. M. Eliade, 465-469.

— & Jacob Needleman (eds), *Modern Esoteric Spirituality*, New York: Crossroad, 1995.

Farraresi, F., "Julius Evola: Tradition, Reaction and the Radical Right," *The European Journal of Sociology*, 28, 107-151.

Fernando, Ranjit (ed), *The Unanimous Tradition*, Colombo: Sri Lanka Institute of Traditional Studies, 1991.

Ferrando, Guido, "Emerson and the East" in *Vedanta for Modern Man*, ed. C. Isherwood, 351-356.

Ferris, Timothy, "Past Present" (on R.H. Blyth), *The Nation*, 250:17, April 30, 1990, 609.

Feuerstein, Georg, *Sacred Paths: Essays on Wisdom, Love and Mystical Realization*, Burdett (NY): Paul Brunton Foundation/Larsons, 1991.

Fields, Rick, *How the Swans Came to the Lake*, Boston: Shambhala, 1992, 3rd ed.

— "Divided Dharma: White Buddhists, Ethnic Buddhists, and Racism" in *The Faces of American Buddhism*, ed. C. Prebish & K. Tanaka, 196-206.

Findly, Ellison Banks, *Women's Buddhism, Buddhism's Women*, Boston: Wisdom, 2000.

Finley, James, *Thomas Merton's Palace of Nowhere*, Notre Dame: Ave Maria, 1978.

Fontana, David, "Mind, Senses and Self" in *Beyond Therapy: The Impact of Eastern Religions on Psychological Theory and Practice*, ed. G. Claxton, 31-48.

Forman, Charles W., "The Growth of the Study of the Expansion of Christianity," *Religious Studies Review*, 13:1, January 1987, 30-33.

Foster, Barbara & Michael, *The Secret Lives of Alexandra David-Neel*, Woodstock: Overlook Press, 1998.

Forster, E.M., *A Passage to India* (1924), Harmondsworth: Penguin, 1936.

Fox, Matthew, *The Coming of the Cosmic Christ*, Melbourne: Collins Dove, 1988.

— *Confessions: The Making of a Post-Denominational Priest*, San Francisco: HarperSanFrancisco, 1996.

— & Bede Griffiths, "Spirituality for a New Era: A Dialogue," in *The Other Half of My Soul: Bede Griffiths and the Hindu-Christian Dialogue*, ed. B. Bruteau, 314-335.

— *et al, Creation Spirituality and the Dreamtime*, Newtown (Australia): Millennium Books, 1991.

Foxe, Barbara, *Long Journey Home: A Biography of Margaret Noble*, London: Rider, 1975.

France, Peter, *Hermits: The Insights of Solitude*, London: Pimlico, 1996.

Freedman, Ralph, *Herman Hesse: Pilgrim of Crisis*, London: Jonathan Cape, 1979.

Freeman, Dom Laurence, "Bede Griffiths," *Vedanta for East and West*, 254, November-December 1993, 275-282.

French, Patrick, *Younghusband: The Last Great Imperial Adventurer*, London: HarperCollins, 1994.

Friedman, Lenore, *Meetings with Remarkable Women: Buddhist Teachers in America*, Boston: Shambhala, 1987.

Friedman, Maurice, *Martin Buber: The Life of Dialogue*, New York: Harper & Row, 1960.

— "Martin Buber and Asia," *Philosophy East and West*, 26:4 October 1976, 411-426.

Fromm, Erich, D.T. Suzuki & R. De Martino, *Zen Buddhism and Psychoanalysis*, London: Souvenir Press, 1974.

Fromm, Erich, "Memories of Dr. D. T. Suzuki," *The Eastern Buddhist*, NS, 2:1, August 1967, 86-89.

Fronsdal, Gil, "Insight Meditation in the United States" in *The Faces of Buddhism in America*, ed. C.S. Prebish & K. Tanaka, 164-180.

Fry, D.B. (ed), *The Nature of Religious Man: Tradition and Experience*, London: Octagon, 1982.

Furlong, Monica, *Merton: A Biography*, London: Collins, 1980.

— *Genuine Fake: A Biography of Alan Watts*, London: Heinemann, 1986.

— "Alan Watts," *The Middle Way*, 58:4, Feb 1984, 213-216.

Gabrieli, Francesco, "Apology for Orientalism," *Diogenes*, 50, Summer 1965, 128-136 (reprinted in A. Macfie, *Orientalism: A Reader*, 79-85).

Gandhi, Leela, *Post-colonialism*, Lindfield, NSW: Allen & Unwin, 1998.

Gare, Arran E., "Understanding Oriental Cultures," *Philosophy East and West*, 45:3, July 1995, 309-328.

Gibbs, Robert, "Reading Heidegger: Destruction, Thinking, Return" in *Tainted Greatness*, ed. N. Harrowitz, 157-172.

Gill, Eric, *Autobiography*, London: Jonathan Cape, 1940.

Ginsberg, Allen, *Indian Journals March 1962 - May 1963*, San Francisco: Dave Haselwood Books & City Lights Books, 1970.

— "Meditation and Poetics" in *Spiritual Quests: The Art and Craft of Religious Writing*, ed. William Zinsser, 143-165.

— "The Vomit of a Mad Tyger," *Shambhala Sun*, July 1995 (website).

— Excerpt from *Disembodied Poetics: Annals of the Jack Kerouac School*, http://www.naropa.edu/ginsbuddhist2.html.

Gitlin, Todd, "Style for Style's Sake" in *The Weekend Australian*, January 21-22, 1989, Weekender, 9.

Glazer, Steven (ed), *The Heart of Learning: Spirituality in Education*, New York: Putnam, 1999.

Gnoli, Gheraldo, "Mircea Eliade 1907-1986," *East and West*, 36:1-3, September 1986, 281-296.

Goddard, Seth, "The Beats and Boom: A Conversation with Allen Ginsberg" (website).

Godwin, Joscelyn, *The Theosophical Enlightenment*, Albany: SUNY, 1994.

— "Facing the Traditionalists: An Approach to René Guénon and his Successors," *Gnosis*, 7, Spring 1988, 23-27.

Goel, Sita Ram (ed), *Catholic Ashrams: Adopting and Adapting Hindu Dharma*, New Delhi: Voice of India, 1988.

Goldberg, Natalie, *Long Quiet Highway: Waking Up in America*, New York: Bantam, 1994.

Goldsmith, Edward, *The Way: An Ecological World-View*, Foxhole, Dartington: Themis Books, 1996, rev. ed.

Goldsmith, Jeffrey, "Allen Ginsberg Interviewed by Jeffrey Goldsmith," http://www.sirius .com/ginsberg_0995.html.

Goldstein, Joseph, *The Experience of Insight: A Natural Unfolding*, Santa Cruz: Unity Press, 1976.

— & Kornfield, Jack, *Seeking the Heart of Wisdom: the Path of Insight Meditation*, Boston: Shambhala, 1987.

Gollancz, Victor (ed), *From Darkness to Light*, London: Victor Gollancz, 1956.

Gómez, Luis O., "Oriental Wisdom and the Cure of Souls: Jung and the Indian East," in *Curators of the Buddha*, ed. D. Lopez, 197-250.

Goodman, Russell B., "East-West Philosophy in Nineteenth-Century America: Emerson and Hinduism," *Journal of the History of Ideas*, 51:4, 1990, 625-645.

Goss, Robert E., "Buddhist Studies at Naropa: Sectarian or Academic?" in *American Buddhism: Methods and Findings of Recent Scholarship*, ed. D. Williams & C. Queen, 215-237.

Goswami, Tamal Krishna, "Servant of the Servant: A.C. Bhaktivedanta Swami Prabhupada, Founder-acharya of the International Society for Krishna Consciousness," *Dialogue and Alliance*, 13:1, 1999, 5-17.

Goswamy, B.N., "Ananda Coomaraswamy as a Historian of Rajput Painting," in S.D.R. Singam, *Ananda Coomaraswamy, Remembering and Remembering Again and Again*, 75-83.

Gottlieb, Roger S. (ed), *This Sacred Earth: Religion, Nature, Environment*, New York: Routledge, 1996.

Govinda, Anagarika, *Foundations of Tibetan Mysticism*, London: Rider, 1969.

— *The Way of the White Clouds*, Boulder: Shambhala, 1970.

— *Creative Meditation and Multi-Dimensional Consciousness*, Wheaton: Quest, 1976.

— *A Living Buddhism for the West*, Boston: Shambhala, 1990.

— *Insights of a Himalayan Pilgrim*, Berkeley: Dharma, 1991.

Graham, Aelred, *Zen Catholicism*, New York: Harcourt, Brace & World, 1963.

— *Conversations: Christian and Buddhist—Encounters in Japan*, New York: Harcourt, Brace & World, 1968.

— *The End of Religion: Autobiographical Explorations*, New York: Harcourt Brace Jovanovich, 1971.

— "On Meditation," *Studies in Comparative Religion*, 1:1, Winter 1967, 6-12.

Green, Elmer & Alyce, *Beyond Biofeedback*, Fort Wayne: Knoll, 1977.

Greenstidel, Sister Christine, "Memories of Swami Vivekananda" in *Vedanta for Modern Man*, ed. C. Isherwood, 156-175.

Griffin, John Howard, *A Hidden Wholeness: the Visual World of Thomas Merton*, Boston: Houghton Mifflin, 1977.

Griffiths, Bede, *The Golden String: An Autobiography*, London: Collins, 1964.

— *Return to the Center*, London: Collins, 1976.

— *The Marriage of East and West*, London: Collins, 1982.

— *The Cosmic Revelation: The Hindu Way to God*, Springfield: Templegate, 1983.

— *Christ in India: Essays towards a Hindu-Christian Dialogue*, Springfield: Templegate, 1984.

— *A New Vision of Reality: Western Science, Eastern Mysticism and Christian Faith*, London: HarperCollins, 1992.

— *The River of Compassion: A Christian Commentary on the Bhagavad Gita*, New York: Continuum, 1995.

— *A Human Search: Bede Griffiths Reflects on His Life*, ed. John Swindells, Blackburn (Australia): HarperCollins Religious, 1997.

Grof, Stanislav, *The Holotropic Mind*, San Francisco: Harper Collins, 1993.

— & C. Grof (eds), *Spiritual Emergency: When Personal Transformation becomes Crisis*, New York: G.P. Putnam, 1998.

Gross, Rita, *Buddhism After Patriarchy: A Feminist History, Analysis and Reconstruction of Buddhism*, Albany: SUNY, 1993.

— "Buddhism and Feminism: Toward their Mutual Transformation," Parts I & II, *The Eastern Buddhist*, 91:1, Spring 1986, 44-58, and 91:2, Autumn 1986, 62-74.

— "Religious Pluralism: Some implications for Judaism," *Journal of Ecumenical Studies*, 26:1, Winter 1989, 29ff.

— "Towards a Buddhist Environmental Ethic," *Journal of the American Academy of Religion*, 65:2, Summer 1997.

— "Helping the Iron Bird Fly: Western Buddhist Women and Issues of Authority in the Late 1990s," in *The Faces of Buddhism in America*, ed. C. Prebish & K. Tanaka, 238-252.

— "This Buddhist's View of Jesus," *Buddhist-Christian Studies*, 19.1, 1999, 62-75.

Gudmunsen, Chris, *Wittgenstein and Buddhism*, London: Macmillan, 1977.

Guénon, René, *Introduction to the Study of Hindu Doctrines*, London: Luzac, 1945.

— *The Crisis of the Modern World*, London: Luzac, 1975.

— *Man and His Becoming According to the Vedanta*, New Delhi: Oriental Books Reprint Co., 1981.

— *The Great Triad*, Cambridge: Quinta Essentia, 1991.

— *East and West*, Ghent: Sophia Perennis et Universalis, 1995.

— *The Reign of Quantity & the Signs of the Times*, Ghent: Sophia Perennis et Universalis, 1995.

— *Fundamental Symbols: The Universal Language of Sacred Science*, Cambridge: Quinta Essentia, 1995.

— "Explanation of Spiritist Phenomena," *Tomorrow*, 14:1, 1966.

— "Taoism and Confucianism," *Studies in Comparative Religion*, 6:4, Autumn 1972, 239-250.

— "Oriental Metaphysics," in *The Sword of Gnosis*, ed. J. Needleman, 40-56.

Guibaut, André, *Tibetan Venture*, London: Readers Union/John Murray, 1949.

Guignon, Charles (ed), *The Cambridge Companion to Heidegger*, Cambridge: Cambridge University, 1993.

Gustin, Marilyn, "Tribute to Huston Smith as a Teacher," in *Fragments of Infinity*, ed. A. Sharma, 11-13.

Gyatso, Tenzin (the Dalai Lama), *The Good Heart*, ed. Robert Kiely, London: Rider, 1996.

Haberman, D.L., "The Transformation of Ronald Nixon," *Religion*, 23, 1993, 217-227.

Habito, Ruben, *Total Liberation: Zen Spirituality and the Social Dimension*, Maryknoll NY: Orbis, 1989.

— "In Memoriam: Yamada Koun Roshi, 1907-1989," *Buddhist-Christian Studies*, 10, 1990, 19-25.

Hakutani, Yoshinobu, "Emerson, Whitman, and Zen Buddhism," *The Midwest Quarterly*, 31:4, Summer 1990, 433-448.

Halbfass, Wilhelm, *India and Europe: An Essay in Philosophical Understanding*, Delhi: Motilal Banarsidass, 1990.

Hall, A. Ripley, "The Keeper of the Indian Collection: An Appreciation of Ananda Kentish Coomaraswamy," in *Ananda Coomaraswamy, Remembering and Remembering Again and Again*, ed. S.D.R. Singam, 106-124.

Halliday, Fred, "Orientalism and Its Critics," *British Journal of Middle Eastern Studies*, 20:2, 1993, 145-163.

Hallisey, Charles, "Roads Taken and Not Taken in the Study of Theravada Buddhism" in *Curators of the Buddha*, ed. D. Lopez, 31-61.

Hallpike, Michael (ed), *Work as Worship*, Templestowe (Victoria, Australia): Chinmaya Mission South, 1991.

467

Halper, Jon, *Gary Snyder: Dimensions of a Life*, San Francisco: Sierra Club Books, 1991.

Hamilton, Elizabeth, *The Voice of the Spirit: The Spirituality of St John of the Cross*, London: Dartman, Todd & Longman, 1976.

Hanh, Thich Nhat, *Vietnam: The Lotus in the Sea of Fire*, London: SCM, 1967.

— *Being Peace*, ed. Arnold Kotler, Berkeley: Parallax, 1987.

— *Living Buddha, Living Christ*, New York: Riverhead Books, 1995.

Hanegraaff, Wouter J., *New Age Religion and Western Culture: Esotericism in the Mirror of Secular Thought*, Albany: SUNY, 1998.

Hanson, A.S., "The Buddhism of T.S. Eliot," *The Middle Way*, 46:1, May 1971, 29-33.

Harding, Douglas, "Alan Watts—Sage or Anti-Sage?", *The Middle Way*, 58:4, Feb 1984, 221-223.

Hardy, Jean, *A Psychology with Soul: Psychosynthesis in Evolutionary Context*, London: Routledge and Kegan Paul, 1987.

Harrer, Heinrich, *Seven Years in Tibet*, London: Rupert Hart-Davis, 1952.

Harris, Ian, "Buddhist Environmental Ethics and Detraditionalization: The Case of Eco-Buddhism," *Religion*, 25, 1995, 199-211.

Harrowitz, Nancy (ed), *Tainted Greatness: Antisemitism and Cultural Heroes*, Philadelphia: Temple University, 1994.

Hart, Patrick Brother (ed), *Thomas Merton, Monk*, New York: Doubleday, 1976 (includes tributes and essays by John Eudes Bamberger, Jean Leclercq, Thérèse Lentfoehr, and David Steindl-Rast).

Hart, William, *The Art of Living: Vipassana Meditation as taught by S.N. Goenka*, San Francisco, 1987.

Harvey, Andrew, *A Journey to Ladakh*, London: Jonathan Cape, 1983.

Harz, Judith Scherer & Robert K. Martin (eds), *E.M. Forster: Centenary Revaluations*, Toronto: University of Toronto, 1982.

Hastings, James (ed), *Encyclopaedia of Religion and Ethics*, Edinburgh: T.&T. Clark, 1913.

Hawk, Patrick, "Authority (1): the Role of the Teacher in Buddhist/Christian Formation," *Studies in Formative Spirituality*, 14:1, February 1993, 23-29.

Hawkes, David, "From the Chinese," in *Madly Singing in the Mountains: An Appreciation and Anthology of Arthur Waley*, ed. I. Morris, 45-51.

Hearn, Lafcadio, *The Buddhist Writings of Lafcadio Hearn*, Intro. Kenneth Rexroth, Santa Barbara: Ross-Erickson, 1977.

— *Gleanings in Buddha-fields*, Rutland: C.E. Tuttle, 1971.

Heiman, Betty, "Indian Art and Its Transcendence," *Ananda Coomaraswamy, Remembering and Remembering Again and Again*, ed. S.D.R. Singam, 24-26.

Heinemann, F.H., Review of F. Schuon's *The Transcendent Unity of Religions* in *Journal of Theological Studies*, 6, 1955, 338-340.

Heisenberg, Werner, *Physics and Philosophy*, New York: Harper & Row, 1962.

Heisig, James & John Maraldo, *Rude Awakenings: Zen, the Kyoto School and the Question of Nationalism*, Honolulu: University of Hawaii, 1995.

— Introduction to Special Henri Dumoulin Issue of *Japanese Journal of Religious Studies*, 12:2-3, 1985, 109-117.

Herrigel, Eugen, *Zen in the Art of Archery*, New York: Vintage, 1971.

— *The Method of Zen*, New York: Vintage, 1974.

Herrigel, Gustie, *Zen in the Art of Flower Arrangement*, London: Routledge & Kegan Paul, 1958.

Herman, A.L., "A.K.C. and the Pertinence of Philosophy" in *Ananda Coomaraswamy: Remembering and Remembering Again and Again*, ed. S.D.R. Singam, 84-93.

Herman, Jonathan R., *I and Tao: Martin Buber's Encounter with Chuang Tzu*, Albany: SUNY, 1996.

Hesse, Herman, *Siddhartha*, New York: Bantam Books, 1971.

— *Autobiographical Writings*, ed. Theodore Ziolkowski, London: Picador, 1975.

— *My Belief,* ed. Theodore Ziolkowski, St. Albans: Triad/Panther, 1978.

Hettinger, Ned, "Ecospirituality: First Thoughts," *Dialogue & Alliance,* 9:2, Fall-Winter 1995, 81-98.

Hick, John (ed), *Truth and Dialogue: the Relationship of the World Religions,* London: Sheldon, 1974.

— & Paul Knitter (eds), *The Myth of Christian Uniqueness,* London: SCM, 1988.

— & Lamont C. Hempel, *Gandhi's Significance for Today,* London: Macmillan, 1989.

Hilton, James, *Lost Horizon* (1933), London: Pan, 1947.

Hinduism Today, "Jewish-Hindu Dialogue," *Hinduism Today,* Issue 94-07 (website).

Hodder, Alan D., "*Ex Oriente Lux*: Thoreau's Ecstasies and the Hindu Texts," *The Harvard Theological Review,* 86:4, 1993, 403-438.

Hoffman, Daniel (ed), *Harvard Guide to Contemporary American Writing,* Cambridge, Massachusetts: Belknap Press, 1979, 519.

Holmes, Charles M., *Aldous Huxley and the Way to Reality,* Bloomington: Indiana University, 1970.

Homans, Peter, "Jung, C.G." in *The Encyclopedia of Religion, Vol. 8,* ed. M. Eliade, 210-213.

Hoover, Thomas, *Zen Culture,* New York: Random House, 1977.

Houghton, Frank, *Amy Carmichael of Dohnavur,* London: Hodder & Stoughton, 1974.

Hourani, A. "The Road to Morocco," *New York Review of Books,* March 8th, 1979.

Hsiao, Paul Shih-yi, "Heidegger and Our Translation of the *Tao Te Ching*" in *Heidegger and Asian Thought,* ed. G. Parkes, 93-103.

Hultkrantz, Åke, "Some Critical Reflections on the Ecology of Religions," *Temenos,* 21, 1985, 83-90.

Humphreys, Christmas, *Buddhism,* Harmondsworth: Penguin, 1951.

— *A Western Approach to Zen,* London: Allen & Unwin, 1971.

— *Exploring Buddhism,* London: Allen & Unwin, 1974.

— *Both Sides of the Circle,* London: Allen & Unwin, 1978.

— "Ananda Metteya," *The Middle Way,* 47:3, November 1972, 133-136.

— "The Buddhist Society: A Brief History," *The Middle Way,* 49:3, November 1974, 8-12.

— "Dr. Edward Conze, 1904-1979" (Obituary), *The Middle Way,* 54:4, February 1980, 229-231.

Huxley, Aldous, *The Perennial Philosophy* (1944), New York: Harper & Row, 1970.

— *Island,* London: Chatto & Windus, 1962.

— *The Doors of Perception, and Heaven and Hell,* Harmondsworth: Penguin, 1959.

Ibish, Yusuf & Peter Lamborn Wilson (eds), *Traditional Modes of Contemplation and Action,* Tehran: Imperial Academy of Philosophy, 1977.

Ichiro, Hori *et al., Japanese Religion: A Survey,* Tokyo: Kodansha, 1981.

Inden, Ronald, *Imagining India,* Oxford: Blackwell, 1990.

— "Orientalist Constructions of India," *Modern Asian Studies* 20:3, 1986, 401-446.

Inge, W.R. *et al., Radhakrishnan: Comparative Studies in Philosophy Presented in Honor of His Sixtieth Birthday,* London: Allen & Unwin, 1951.

Ingram, Paul O., "Two Western Models of Inter-religious Dialogue," *Journal of Ecumenical Studies,* 26:1, Winter 1989, 8-28.

— "Reflections on Buddhist-Christian Dialogue and the Liberation of Women," *Buddhist-Christian Studies,* 17, 1997, 49-60.

Ingram, Paul O. & Frederick Streng (eds), *Buddhist-Christian Dialogue: Mutual Renewal and Transformation,* Honolulu: University of Hawaii, 1986.

Isherwood, Christopher, *A Meeting by the River,* New York: Avon Books, 1965.

— *Ramakrishna and His Disciples* (1965), Calcutta: Advaita Ashrama, 1974.

— *My Guru and His Disciple,* London: Methuen, 1981.

— *Diaries, Volume 1: 1939-1960,* ed. Katherine Bucknall, New York: HarperCollins, 1997.

— "What Vedanta Means to Me" in *Journeys in Belief,* ed. Bernard Dixon, 125-138.

— (ed), *Vedanta for Modern Man* (1945) New York: New American Library, 1972.

— (ed), *Vedanta for the Western World* (1948), London: Allen & Unwin, 1963.

Isichei, Elizabeth, "Passages to India: Western Images of Western Spirituality in the Ancient and Medieval World," *Dialogue & Alliance*, 5:2, Summer 1991, 66-67.

Ital, Gerta, *The Monks, the Master and I*, Wellingborough: Crucible, 1981.

— *On the Road to Satori: A Woman's Experience of Enlightenment*, Shaftesbury: Element, 1990.

Ives, Christopher, *Zen Awakening and Society*, Honolulu: University of Hawaii, 1992.

Iyer, Pico, "Lost Horizons," *New York Review of Books*, January 15th, 1998 (website).

Izutsu, Toshihiko, *Sufism and Taoism: A Comparative Study of Key Philosophical Concepts*, Berkeley: University of California, 1983.

Jackson, Carl T., *The Oriental Religions and American Thought: Nineteenth-Century Explorations*, Westport: Greenwood Press, 1981.

— *Vedanta for the West: the Ramakrishna Movement in the United States*, Bloomington: Indiana University, 1994.

— "The Meeting of East and West: The Case of Paul Carus," *Journal of the History of Ideas*, 29:1, 1968, 73-92.

Jacobs, Hans, *Western Psychotherapy and Hindu Sadhana*, London: Allen & Unwin, 1961.

Jaffé, Aniela, *The Myth of Meaning*, tr. R. F. C. Hull, Penguin, Baltimore, 1975.

— *From the Life and Work of C.G. Jung*, tr. R.F.C. Hull, London: Hodder & Stoughton, 1972.

James, William, *The Varieties of Religious Experience*, London: Fontana, 1961.

Jochim, Christian, "The Contemporary Confucian-Christian Encounter: Inter-religious or Intra-religious Dialogue?", *Journal of Ecumenical Studies*, 32:1, Winter 1995, 35-62.

Johnston, William, *The Still Point: Reflections on Zen and Christian Mysticism*, New York: Harper & Row, 1970.

— *Christian Zen*, New York: Harper Colophon, 1971.

— *Silent Music: The Science of Meditation*, London: Collins, 1974.

— *The Mirror Mind: Spirituality and Transformation*, London: Fount/Collins, 1981.

— *The Inner Eye of Love: Mysticism and Religion*, London: Fount/Collins, 1981.

— "Buddhists and Christians Meet," *The Eastern Buddhist*, NS, 3:1, June 1970, 139-146.

Jones, Ken, *The Social Face of Buddhism: An Approach to Social and Political Activism*, London: Wisdom Books, 1989.

Jordens, J.F.T., *Gandhi: Conscience of Hinduism and Scourge of Orthodoxy*, Canberra: Australian National University, 1991.

Jung, Carl G., *Collected Works, V11, Psychology and Religion: West and East* London: Routledge, 1969, 2nd ed.

— *Psychology and the East*, London: Routledge & Kegan Paul, 1978

— *Memories, Dreams, Reflections*, ed. Aniela Jaffé, Fontana, London, 1983.

— *C. G. Jung Speaking: Interviews and Encounters*, ed. W. McGuire & R. F. C. Hull, London: Thames & Hudson, 1978.

— "Psychological Commentary" on *The Tibetan Book of the Dead*, ed. W.Y. Evans-Wentz, London: OUP, 1960 (also in *Collected Works*, V11, 509-526).

— "Psychological Commentary" on *The Tibetan Book of the Great Liberation*, ed. W.Y. Evans-Wentz, *Collected Works*, V11, 475-508.

— "Foreword" to D. T. Suzuki, *An Introduction to Zen Buddhism* (1927), New York: Grove Press, 1964 (also in *Collected Works*, V11, 538-557.)

— "The Holy Men of India" (Introduction to Heinrich Zimmer's *Der Weg zum Selbst: Lehre und Leben des indischen Heiligen Shri Ramana Maharsi aus Tiruvannamalai*, Zurich, 1944) in *Collected Works*, V11, 576-586.)

— "Foreword" to Richard Wilhelm's translation of the *I Ching* in *Collected Works*, V11, 589-608.

— "Commentary on *The Secret of the Golden Flower*," in *Collected Works*, V13, 1-56.

— "Richard Wilhelm: In Memoriam," *Collected Works, V15*, 53-62.

Kamaliah, K.C., "Ananda Coomaraswamy's Assessment of Dravidian Civilization and Culture," in *Ananda Coomaraswamy, Remembering and Remembering Again and Again*, ed. S.D.R. Singam, 43-52.

Kapleau, Philip, *The Three Pillars of Zen*, New York: Anchor/Doubleday, 1980, rev. ed.

— *Zen Dawn in the West*, London: Rider, 1980.

— *Awakening to Zen: The Teachings of Roshi Philip Kapleau*, Moorebank (NSW, Australia): Bantam, 1997.

Kapstein, Matthew, "Schopenhauer's *Shakti*," in *Heinrich Zimmer: Coming into His Own*, ed. M. Case, 105-118.

Kasbekar, Veena P., "The Experience of OM in Hesse's *Siddhartha* and Forster's *A Passage to India*," *Scottish Journal of Religious Studies*, 13:2, Autumn 1992, 84-90.

Katz, Eric, A. Light & D. Rothenberg (eds), *Beneath the Surface: Critical Essays in the Philosophy of Deep Ecology*, Cambridge, Massachusetts: MIT, 2000.

Katz, Nathan (ed), *Buddhist and Western Philosophy*, Atlantic Highlands, NJ: Humanities Press, 1981.

— (ed), *Buddhist and Western Psychology*, Boulder: Prajna Press, 1983.

Kaza, Stephanie & Kenneth Kraft (eds), *Dharma Rain: Sources of a Buddhist Environmentalism*, Boston: Shambhala, 2000.

Kazantzakis, Nikos, *Travels in China and Japan*, Oxford: Bruno Cassirer, 1964.

Keating, Thomas, "Meditative Technologies: Theological Ecumenicism" in *The Other Half of My Soul*, ed. B. Bruteau, 112-125.

Keeble, Brian, "Tradition, Intelligence and the Artist," *Studies in Comparative Religion*, 11:4, 1977, 235-250.

Kelly, Bernard, "Notes on the Light of the Eastern Religions" in *Religion of the Heart*, ed. S.H. Nasr & W. Stoddart, 155-176.

Kelley, C.F., *Meister Eckhart on Divine Knowledge*, New Haven: Yale University, 1977.

Kelly, Peter, *Buddha in a Bookshop: Harold Stewart and the Traditionalists—the Story of Australian Interest in Asian Religions before 1960*, Melbourne: privately published, c.1995.

Kennedy, Robert E., *Zen Spirit, Christian Spirit: the Place of Zen in Christian Life*, New York: Continuum, 1995.

Kerouac, Jack, *Mexico City Blues*, New York: Grove Press, 1990.

— *On the Road*, New York: Penguin, 1991.

— *The Dharma Bums*, New York: Penguin, 1991.

— *The Scripture of the Golden Eternity*, San Francisco: City Lights Books, 1994.

— *Desolation Angels*, New York: Riverhead Books, 1995.

Khema, Ayya, *I Give You My Life: The Autobiography of a Western Buddhist Nun*, Boston: Shambhala, 1998.

King, Richard, *Orientalism and Religion: Postcolonial Theory, India and "the mystic East,"* London: Routledge, 1999.

King, Winston L., *Zen and the Way of the Sword: Arming the Samurai Psyche*, New York: Oxford University, 1993.

— "Engaged Buddhism: Past, Present, Future," *The Eastern Buddhist*, NS, 27:2, Autumn 1994, 14-29.

Kipling, Rudyard, *Kim* (1901), London: Macmillan, 1927.

Kitagawa, Joseph, *Religions of the East*, Philadelphia: Westminster, 1960.

— *Religion in Japanese History*, New York: Columbia University, 1966.

— *On Understanding Japanese Religion*, Princeton: Princeton University, 1987.

— *The Quest for Human Unity: A Religious History*, Minneapolis: Fortress Press, 1990.

— "Daisetz Teitaro Suzuki (1870-1966)," *History of Religions*, 6:3, Feb. 1967, 265-269.

— "Mircea Eliade" in *The Encyclopedia of Religion, Vol. 5*, ed. M. Eliade, 84-90.

— (ed), *The History of Religions: Essays on the Problem of Understanding*, Chicago: University of Chicago, 1967.

— & Mircea Eliade (eds), *The History of Religions: Essays in Methodology*, Chicago: University of Chicago, 1959.

Kjolhede, Bodhin, "Roshi [Kapleau] and his Teachers, Dharma Transmission, and the Rochester Zen Center Lineage," *Zen Bow*, 17:4 & 18:1, Fall 1995, Winter 1996.

Klostermaier, Klaus, *In the Paradise of Krishna*, Philadelphia: Westminster Press, 1969.

— *A Survey of Hinduism*, Albany: SUNY, 1989.

— "From Phenomenology to Meta-Science: Reflections on the Study of Religion," *Studies in Religion* 6:4, 1976-1977, 551-564.

— "All Religions are equal—Complementarity as Theoretical Model to Guide the *Praxis* of Inter-religious Dialogue," *Dialogue & Alliance*, 7:2, Fall-Winter 1993, 60-76.

— "Bhakti, Ahimsa and Ecology," *Journal of Dharma*, 16:3, July 1991, 246-254.

— "Ecology and Religion: Christian and Hindu Paradigms," *Hindu-Christian Studies Bulletin*, 6, 1993.

— "The Hermeneutic Center," *Journal of Ecumenical Studies*, 34:2, Spring 1997, 159-170.

Koestler, Arthur, *The Lotus and the Robot*, London: Hutchinson, 1960.

Kopf, David, "Hermeneutics versus History," *Journal of Asian Studies*, 39:3, 1980, 495-506.

Kornfield, Jack, *Living Buddhist Masters*, Santa Cruz: Unity Press, 1977.

— *A Path with Heart*, New York: Bantam, 1993.

— "American Buddhism" in *The Complete Guide to Buddhist America*, ed. D. Morreale, Boston: Shambhala, 1998, xxi-xxx.

— Foreword to Ajahn Chah, *Being Dharma*, ix-xiii.

Kotler, Arnold (ed), *Engaged Buddhist Reader: Ten Years of Engaged Buddhist Publishing*, Berkeley: Parallax Press, 1996.

Kraft, Kenneth, "Engaged Buddhism: An Introduction" in *The Path of Compassion*, ed. F. Eppsteiner, xi-xviii.

— (ed), *Inner Peace, World Peace: Essays on Buddhism and Non-Violence*, Albany: SUNY, 1992.

Kunz, Dora, "Besant, Annie" in *The Encyclopedia of Religion, Vol. 2*, ed. M. Eliade, 117-118.

Lachs, Stuart, "Coming Down from the Zen Clouds," http://www.mandala.hr/5/6slachs .html.

Lai, Pan-chiu, "Christian Ecological Theology in Dialogue with Confucianism," *Cheng Fing*, 41:3-4, September-December 1998, 309-335.

Lake, David, Review of M. Eliade's *No Souvenirs, Studies in Comparative Religion*, 12:3-4, Summer-Autumn 1978, 243-245.

Lakhani, Ali, "What Thirst is For" (Editorial), *Sacred Web*, 4, 1999, 13-16.

Lannoy, Richard, *The Speaking Tree*, London: Oxford University, 1974.

Larsen, Robin & Stephen, and Antony Van Couvering, Editors' Foreword to J. Campbell, *Baksheesh and Brahman: Indian Journals 1954-1955*, vi-xvi.

Laurant, Jean-Pierre, *Le Sens Caché Selon René Guénon*, Lausanne: L'Age D'Homme, 1975.

— "Le problème de René Guénon," *Revue de l'histoire des religions*, 179:1, 1971.

Lavine, Amy, "Tibetan Buddhism in America: The Development of American Vajrayana" in *The Faces of Buddhism in America*, ed. C. Prebish & K. Tanaka, 99-116.

Leach, Edmund, "Sermons from a Man on a Ladder," *New York Review of Books*, October 20, 1966.

Lederman, Arthur & P. Bjaaland, review of John Blofeld's *Wheel of Life* in *The Eastern Buddhist*, NS, 6:2, October 73, 154-156.

Lee, Chwen Jiuan A. & Thomas G. Hand, *A Taste of Water: Christianity through Taoist-Buddhist Eyes*, New York: Paulist Press, 1990.

Lee, Peer H. K. (ed), *Confucian-Christian Encounters in Historical and Contemporary Perspective*, Lewiston, NY: Edwin Mellen, 1991.

Leet, Ann, "Buddhism and T.S. Eliot," *The Middle Way*, 47.4, February 1973, 168-172.

Lewis, Bernard, "The Question of Orientalism," in *Orientalism: A Reader*, ed. A. Macfie, 249-270.

Leyland, Winston (ed), *Queer Dharma: Voices of Gay Buddhists*, San Francisco: Gay Sunshine, 1998.

Lincoln, Bruce, *Death, War and Sacrifice: Studies in Ideology and Practice*, Chicago: University of Chicago, 1991.

Linda, Mary F., "Zimmer and Coomaraswamy: Visions and Visualizations," in *Heinrich Zimmer: Coming into His Own*, ed. M. Case, 119-142.

Lings, Martin, *Ancient Beliefs and Modern Superstitions*, London: Allen & Unwin, 1980.

— *A Sufi Saint of the Twentieth Century*, Berkeley: University of California, 1971.

Lippitt, John & Urpeth, Jim (eds), *Nietzsche and the Divine*, Manchester: Clinamen Press, 2000.

Lipsey, Roger, *Coomaraswamy: His Life and Work*, Bollingen Series, Princeton: Princeton University, 1977.

Long, Charles, "The Dreams of Joseph Campbell: Joseph Campbell's *The Mythic Image*" in *Paths to the Power of Myth*, ed. D. Noel, 157-180.

Loomba, Ania, *Colonialism/Postcolonialism*, London: Routledge, 1998.

Lopez Jr, Donald S., *Prisoners of Shangri-La*, Chicago: University of Chicago, 1998.

— "Foreigners at the Lama's Feet" in *Curators of the Buddha*, ed. D. Lopez, 251-295.

— "New Age Orientalism: The Case of Tibet," *Tricycle: The Buddhist Review*, 3:3, 1994.

— (ed), *Curators of the Buddha: The Study of Buddhism Under Colonialism*, Chicago: University of Chicago, 1995.

— & Steven Rockefeller (eds) *The Christ and the Boddhisattva*, Albany: SUNY, 1987.

Loy, David R., "Is Zen Buddhism?", *The Eastern Buddhist*, NS, 28:2, Autumn 1995, 273-286.

Lowe, Lisa. *Critical Terrains: French and British Orientalisms*, Ithaca: Cornell University, 1991.

Luke, Helen, "Bede Griffiths at Apple Farm: A Personal Memory" in *The Other Half of My Soul: Bede Griffiths and the Hindu-Christian Dialogue*, ed. B. Bruteau, 36-40.

Lund, Søren, "The Christian Mission and Colonialism," *Temenos*, 17, 1981, 116-123.

Lutyens, Mary, *The Life and Death of Krishnamurti*, London: John Murray, 1990.

Mabbett, Ian, "Nagarjuna and Deconstruction," *Philosophy East and West*, 45:2, April 1995, 203-225.

Macaulay, Thomas B., *Letters of Lord Macaulay*, London: Longman, 1876.

Macfie, A.L. (ed), *Orientalism: A Reader*, Edinburgh: Edinburgh University, 2000.

MacInnes, Elaine, *Teaching Zen to Christians*, Wheaton: Theosophical Publishing House, 1993.

Mackenzie, John, *Orientalism: History, Theory and the Arts*, Manchester: Manchester University, 1995.

Mackenzie, Vicki, *Reborn in the West: the Reincarnation Masters*, London, 1995.

— *Why Buddhism? Westerners in Search of Wisdom*, Sydney: Allen & Unwin, 2001.

Macy, Joanna, *World as Lover, World as Self*, London: Rider, 1993.

Maezumi, Hakuyu Taizan & Bernard Tetsugen Glassman, *The Hazy Moon of Enlightenment*, Los Angeles: Center Publications, 1977.

Magee, Bryan, *The Philosophy of Schopenhauer*, Oxford: Oxford University, 1983.

Magnus, Bernd & Katherine M. Higgins (eds), *The Cambridge Companion to Nietzsche*, Cambridge: Cambridge University, 1996.

Mailer, Norman, *The Armies of the Night*, New York: New American Library, 1968.

MANAS, "Editorial: M.K. Gandhi" (2-25-48) in *The MANAS Reader*, New York: Grosman, 1971, 310-311.

Manavath, Xavier, "Summary of Books Relevant to Spiritual Formation and the Hindu-Christian Dialogue," *Studies in Formative Spirituality*, 11:3, November 1990, 425-438.

Manganaro, Marc, *Myth, Rhetoric, and the Voice of Authority: A Critique of Frazer, Eliot, Frye, & Campbell*, New Haven: Yale University, 1992.

Mariani, Fosco, *Secret Tibet*, London: Hutchinson, 1952.

Martin, Glen T. "Deconstruction and Breakthrough in Nietzsche and Nagarjuna," in *Nietzsche and Asian Thought*, ed. G. Parkes, 91-111.

Masefield, Peter & Donald Wiebe (eds), *Aspects of Religion: Essays in Honor of Ninian Smart*, New York: Peter Lang, 1994.

Masson, Jeffery, *My Father's Guru*, Reading: Addison-Wesley, 1993.

Mataji, Sister Vandana, *Gurus, Ashrams and Christians*, Delhi: ISPCK, 1988.

— *Christian Ashrams: A Movement with a Future?*, Delhi: ISPCK, 1993.

— "Spiritual Formation in Ashrams in Contemporary India," *Studies in Formative Spirituality*, 11:3, November 1990, 355-379.

Mathur, Rakesh, "Shiv Sharan: Not Your Typical French Hindu," *Hinduism Today*, 17:10, October 1955 (website).

Matthiessen, Peter, *The Snow Leopard*, London: Chatto & Windus, 1979.

— *Nine-Headed Dragon River: Zen Journals 1969-1982*, London: Collins Harvill, 1986.

Maugham, Somerset, *The Razor's Edge*, London: Heinemann, 1949.

— *Points of View*, London: Heinemann, 1958.

McCarthy, Harold E., "T.S. Eliot and Buddhism," *Philosophy East and West*, 2:1, 1952, 31-55.

McDonald, Barry (ed), *Seeing God Everywhere: Essays on Nature and the Sacred*, Bloomington: World Wisdom, 2003.

McGuire, William, "Zimmer and the Mellens" in *Heinrich Zimmer: Coming into His Own*, ed. M. Case, 31-42.

McLuhan, T.C., *Cathedrals of the Spirit: The Message of Sacred Places*, Toronto: Harper Collins, 1996.

Mehta, Gita, *Karma Cola*, London: Minerva, 1990.

Mehta, J.L., "Heidegger and Vedanta" in *Heidegger and Asian Thought*, ed. G. Parkes, 15-45.

Mellor, Philip, "Protestant Buddhism? The Cultural Translation of Buddhism in England," *Religion*, 21, 1991, 73-92.

Melman, Billie, *Women's Orients*, London: Macmillan, 1992.

Merchant, Carolyn, *The Death of Nature: Women, Ecology, and the Scientific Revolution*, New York: 1980.

Merkur, Dan, "Transpersonal Psychology: Models of Spiritual Awakening," *Religious Studies Review*, 23:2, April 1997, 141-147.

Merquior, J.G., *Foucault*, London: Fontana, 1985.

Merton, Thomas, *The Silent Life*, New York: Farrar, Straus & Giroux, 1957.

— *Disputed Questions*, New York: Farrar, Straus & Giroux, 1960.

— *New Seeds of Contemplation*, New York: New Directions, 1961.

— *The Way of Chuang Tzu*, New York: New Directions, 1965.

— *Gandhi on Non-Violence*, New York: New Directions, 1965.

— *Raids on the Unspeakable*, New York: New Directions, 1966.

— *Mystics and Zen Masters*, New York: Farrar, Straus & Giroux, 1967.

— *Conjectures of a Guilty Bystander*, New York: Doubleday, 1968.

— *Zen and the Birds of Appetite*, New York: New Directions, 1968.

— *The Asian Journal of Thomas Merton*, ed. Naomi Burton, Patrick Hart & James Laughlin, New York: New Directions, 1972.

— *The Seven Storey Mountain*, San Diego: Harcourt Brace & Jovanovich, 1976.

— *Thomas Merton on Zen*, ed. Irmgard Schloegl, London: Sheldon Press, 1976.

— *Thoughts on the East*, ed. George Woodcock, New York: New Directions, 1995.

— "The Man and His Work" (on D.T. Suzuki), *The Eastern Buddhist*, NS, 2:1, August 1967, 3-9.

— Foreword to Thich Nhat Hanh, *Vietnam: The Lotus in the Sea of Fire*, 5-8.

Michon, Jean-Louis, "The Vocation of Man According to the Koran" in *Fragments of Infinity: Essays in Religion and Philosophy*, ed. A. Sharma, 135-152.

Middleton, Ruth, *Alexandra David-Neel: Portrait of an Adventurer*, Boston: Shambhala, 1989.

Middle Way, Memorial Issue on Christmas Humphreys, *The Middle Way*, 58:3, August 1983.

— "Alan Watts, 1915-73: In Memoriam," *The Middle Way*, 58:4, February 1984, 210-212.

— "Ayya Khema (1923-1997)," *The Middle Way*, 72:4, February 1998, 241-242.

— "In Memoriam: Reverend Master Jiyu Kennett, 1924-1996," *The Middle Way*, 72:2, August 1997, 111-112.

Midgley, Mary, *Science as Salvation: A Modern Myth and its Meaning*, London: Routledge, 1992.

— *Utopias, Dolphins and Computers: Problems of Philosophical Plumbing*, London: Routledge, 1996.

Migot, André, *Tibetan Marches*, London: Hart-Davis, 1955.

Milcinski, M., "The Notion of the Feminine in Asian Philosophical Traditions," *Asian Philosophy*, 7:3, 1997.

Miles, Barry, *Ginsberg: A Biography*, New York: Harper Perennial, 1989.

Miller, David, "Comparativism in a World of Difference: The Legacy of Joseph Campbell to the Postmodern History of Religions" in *Common Era: Best New Writings on Religion*, ed. S. Scholl, 168-177.

Miller, Luree, *On Top of the World: Five Women Explorers in Tibet*, Seattle: The Mountaineers, 1984.

Mitchell, Donald W., "A Bibliographical Review of Books on Spirituality in the Buddhist-Christian Dialogue," *Studies in Formative Spirituality*, 14:1, February 1993, 139-143.

Mitchell, Elsie, *Sun Buddhas Moon Buddhas: A Zen Quest*, New York: Weatherhill, 1973.

Moacanin, Radmila, *Jung's Psychology and Tibetan Buddhism*, Boston: Wisdom Publications, 1986.

Monchanin, Jules & Henri le Saux, *A Benedictine Ashram*, Douglas: Times Press, 1964, rev. ed.

Moore, Jr, Alvin, "Nature, Man and God," *Sacred Web*, 2, 1998, 51-64.

Moore, Charles A., " Suzuki: The Man and the Scholar," *The Eastern Buddhist*, NS, 2:1, August 1967, 10-18.

Moore, Jim, "Public Heart: An Interview with Allen Ginsberg," http://www.bookwire.com/hmr/REVIEW/moore.html.

Moore-Gilbert, Bart, *Postcolonial Theory: Contexts, Practices, Politics*, London: Verso, 1998.

Morgan, Kenneth, *Reaching for the Moon: On Asian Religious Paths*, Chambersberg, Pennsylvania: Anima, 1990.

Morreale, Don (ed), *The Complete Guide to Buddhist America*, Boston: Shambhala, 1998, rev.ed.

Morris, Ivan, "The Genius of Arthur Waley" in *Madly Singing in the Mountains: An Appreciation and Anthology of Arthur Waley*, ed. I. Morris, 67-87.

— (ed), *Madly Singing in the Mountains: An Appreciation and Anthology of Arthur Waley*, London: Allen & Unwin, 1970.

Morris, Stephen, "Beyond Christianity: Transcendentalism and Zen," *The Eastern Buddhist*, NS, 24:2, Autumn 1991, 33-68.

Morrison, Paul, "'Jewspapers': Ezra Pound, Poststructuralism, and the Figure of the Jew," in *Tainted Greatness*, ed. N. Harrowitz, 211-236.

Mott, Michael, *The Seven Mountains of Thomas Merton*, London: Sheldon Press, 1984.

Mullen, Kenneth, "Ananda Metteya: Buddhist Pioneer," *The Middle Way*, 65:2, August 1990, 91-94.

Müller, Max, "Plea for a Science of Religion" from *Chips from a German Workshop*, in *Classical Approaches to the Study of Religion*, ed. J. Waardenburg, 86-88.

Naipal, V.S., *An Area of Darkness*, London: Reprint Society, 1966.

Nagarajan, S., "Emerson and *Advaita*: Some Comparisons and Contrasts," *American Transcendental Quarterly*, 3:4, 1989, 325-336.

Nakamura, Hajime, *Ways of Thinking of Eastern Peoples: India, China, Tibet, Japan*, Delhi: Motilal Banarsidass, 1991.

Nanjivako, Bhikkhu, "The Technicalization of Buddhism: Fascism and Buddhism in Italy: Giuseppe Tucci and Julius Evola," Parts I & II, *Buddhist Studies Review*, 6:1 & 2, 1989, 27-39, 102-115.

Naravarne, V.S., "Ananda Coomaraswamy: A Critical Appreciation" in *Ananda Coomaraswamy, Remembering and Remembering Again and Again*, ed. S.D.R. Singam, 204-209.

Nasr, Seyyed Hossein, *Ideals and Realities of Islam*, London: Allen & Unwin, 1966.

— *Man and Nature: The Spiritual Crisis of Modern Man*, London: Allen & Unwin, 1968.

— *Sufi Essays*, London: Allen & Unwin, 1972.

— *Islamic Science: An Illustrated History*, London: World of Islam Festival, 1976.

— *Knowledge and the Sacred*, New York: Crossroad, 1981.

— *Religion and the Order of Nature*, New York: Oxford University, 1996.

— *The Spiritual and Religious Dimensions of the Environmental Crisis*, London: Temenos Academy, 1999.

— "Conditions for a Meaningful Comparative Philosophy," *Philosophy East and West*, 22:1, 1972, 53-61.

— "Homage to Huston Smith on His Eightieth Birthday," *Sophia: the Journal of Traditional Studies*, 3:2, Winter 1997, 5-8.

— "The Biography of Frithjof Schuon" in *Religion of the Heart*, ed. S.H. Nasr & W. Stoddart, 1-6.

— & W. Stoddart (eds), *Religion of the Heart* (Essays Presented to Frithjof Schuon on His Eightieth Birthday), Washington DC: Foundation of Traditional Studies, 1991.

— & K. O'Brien (eds), *In Quest of the Sacred: the Modern World in the Light of Tradition*, Washington DC: Foundation of Traditional Studies, 1994.

Nattier, Jan, "Buddhist Studies in the Post-Colonial Age," (review article on *Curators of the Buddha*, ed. D. Lopez) in *Journal of the American Academy of Religion*, 1997, 469-485.

Needham, Joseph, *Within the Four Seas: The Dialogue of East and West*, London: Allen & Unwin, 1969.

— *Science in Traditional China: A Comparative Perspective*, Cambridge: Harvard University, 1981.

— "Femininity in Chinese Thought and Christian Theology," *Ching Feng*, 23:2, 1980, 57-70.

— & Ronan, C.E., *The Shorter Science and Civilization in China: An Abridgement of Joseph Needham's Original Text*, 2 vols, Cambridge: Cambridge University, 1978.

Needleman, Jacob, *The New Religions*, New York: Pocket Books, 1972.

— *A Sense of the Cosmos*, New York: Doubleday, 1975.

— (ed), *The Sword of Gnosis*, Baltimore: Penguin Books, 1974.

— & A.K. Bierman & James Gould (eds), *Religion for a New Generation*, New York: Macmillan, 1977.

Neihardt, John, *Black Elk Speaks*, London: Abacus, 1974.

Neil, Stephen, *A History of Christian Missions*, Harmondsworth: Penguin, 1964.

— *Bhakti: Hindu and Christian*, Madras: Christian Literature Society, 1974.

— "Missions: Christian Missions" in *The Encyclopedia of Religion, Vol. 9*, ed. M. Eliade, 572-579.

Nette, Herbert, "An Epitaph for Heinrich Zimmer," in *Heinrich Zimmer: Coming into His Own*, ed. M. Case, 21-30.

Neville, Richard & Julie Clarke, *The Life and Crimes of Charles Sobhraj*, London: Pan, 1980.

Nietzsche, Friedrich, *A Nietzsche Reader*, ed. R.J. Hollingdale, Harmondsworth: Penguin 1977.

Nizet, Gérard, "Dr. Hubert Benoit" (Obituary), *The Middle Way*, 67:4, February 1993, 201-202.

Noel, Daniel C. (ed), *Paths to the Power of Myth: Joseph Campbell and the Study of Religion*, New York: Crossroad, 1990.

Norbu, Namkhai, *The Crystal and the Way of Light: Sutra, Tantra and Dzogchen*, ed. John Shane, London: Penguin/Arkana, 1986.

Nordstrom, Louis & Richard Pilgrim, "The Wayward Mysticism of Alan Watts," *Philosophy East and West*, 30:3, 1980, 381-399.

Northbourne, Lord, "A Note on Truth, Goodness and Beauty," *Studies in Comparative Religion*, 7:2, Spring 1973, 107-112.

Norgay, Tenzing, *Man of Everest: the Autobiography of Tenzing* (as told to James Ramsey Ullman), London: Harrap, 1955.

Nouwen, Henri, *Pray to Live: Thomas Merton, Contemplative Critic*, Notre Dame: Fides/Claretian, 1972.

Novak, Philip, *The Vision of Nietzsche*, Rockport: Element, 1996.

— "C.G. Jung in the Light of Asian Psychology," *Religious Traditions* 14, 1991, 66-87.

— "Tao How? Asian Religions and the Problem of Environmental Degradation," *ReVision*, 16:2, Fall 1993, 77-82.

— "Universal Theology and the Idea of Cosmic Order," *Dialogue & Alliance*, 6:1, Spring 1992, 82-92.

— "The Chun-tzu" (on Huston Smith) in *Fragments of Infinity*, ed. A. Sharma, 8-10.

O'Flaherty, Wendy Doniger, *Women, Androgynes and Other Mythical Beasts*, Chicago: Chicago University, 1980.

Oldmeadow, Harry, *Mircea Eliade and Carl Jung: "Priests without Surplices"?*, Department of Arts, La Trobe University Bendigo, 1995 (Studies in Western Traditions: Occasional Papers, 1).

— "Sankara's Doctrine of Maya," *Asian Philosophy*, 2:2, 1992, 131-146.

— "'Delivering the Last Blade of Grass': Aspects of the Bodhisattva Ideal in the Mahayana," *Asian Philosophy*, 7:3, November 1997, 131-146.

— "To a Buddhist Beat: Allen Ginsberg on Politics, Poetics and Spirituality," *Beyond the Divide* (Bendigo), 2:1, Winter 1999.

Oldmeadow, Kenneth ("Harry"), *Traditionalism: Religion in the light of the Perennial Philosophy*, Colombo: Sri Lanka Institute of Traditional Studies, 2000.

— "'The Translucence of the Eternal': Religious Understandings of the Natural Order," *Sacred Web*, 2, 1998, 11-32.

— "'Signposts to the Suprasensible': Notes on Frithjof Schuon's Understanding of 'Nature,'" *Sacred Web*, 6, 2000, 47-58.

— "The Religious Tradition of the Australian Aborigines" in *Fragments of Infinity*, ed. A. Sharma, 168-197.

— "Biographical Sketch" (of René Guénon) in R. Guénon, *The Reign of Quantity and the Signs of the Times*, (1995 edition), vi-xxxvii.

Oldmeadow, Peter, *Zen: An Ancient Path to Enlightenment for Modern Times*, Sydney: Lansdowne, 2001.

— "Buddhist Yogacara Philosophy and Deep Ecology" in *This Immense Panorama*, ed. C. Cusack and P. Oldmeadow.

— "Tibetan Buddhism and Globalization" in *The End of Religions?*, ed. C. Cusack & P. Oldmeadow, 266-279.

O'Leary, Joseph, review of *Heidegger and Asian Thought*, ed. G. Parkes, in *Japanese Journal of Religious Studies*, 15:4, 311-313.

— Review of *Nietzsche and Asian Thought*, ed. G. Parkes, in *Japanese Journal of Religious Studies*, 19:1,192, 90-94.

Oliver, Ian P., *Buddhism in Britain*, London: Rider, 1979.

O'Neill, William, *Coming Apart: An Informal History of America in the Sixties*, Chicago: Quadrangle Books, 1971.

Organ, Troy Wilson, *Western Approaches to Eastern Philosophy*, Athens: Ohio University, 1975.

Orwell, George, "Reflections on Gandhi" (1949), *The Collected Essays, Journalism and Letters of George Orwell, Vol 4: In Front of Your Nose, 1945-1950*, ed. Sonia Orwell & Ian Angus, Harmondsworth: Penguin, 1980, 523-531.

Otto, Rudolf, *India's Religion of Grace and Christianity Compared and Contrasted*, New York: Macmillan, 1930.

— *The Original Gita: the Song of the Supreme Exalted One*, London: Allen & Unwin, 1939.

— *Mysticism East and West: A Comparative Analysis of the Nature of Mysticism*, (1932), New York: Meridian Books, 1957.

— *The Idea of the Holy*, London: Oxford University, 1958.

— *Autobiographical and Social Essays*, ed. Gregory D. Alles, Berlin: Mouton de Gruyter, 1996.

— "Professor Rudolf Otto on Zen Buddhism," *The Eastern Buddhist* 3:2, July-September 1924, 117-125.

— "Buddhism and Christianity—Compared and Contrasted," ed. & tr. Philip Almond, in *Buddhist-Christian Studies* 4, 1984, 87-101.

Paden, William, *Religious Worlds*, Boston: Beacon, 1988.

— *Interpreting the Sacred*, Boston: Beacon, 1992.

Paine, Jeffery, *Father India*, New York: HarperCollins, 1998.

Palakeel, Thomas, "Thomas Merton and Bede Griffiths," *North Dakota Quarterly*, 62:4, 1994, 141-152.

Pallis, Marco, *Peaks and Lamas*, London: Readers Union/Cassell, 1948.

— *The Way and the Mountain*, London: Peter Owen, 1960.

— *A Buddhist Spectrum*, London: Allen & Unwin, 1980.

— "Thomas Merton 1915-1968," *Studies in Comparative Religion*, 3:3, 1969, 138-146.

— Review of Jacob Needleman (ed), *The New Religions* in *Studies in Comparative Religion* 5:3, 1971, 189-190.

— "A Fateful Meeting of Minds: A.K. Coomaraswamy and René Guénon," *Studies in Comparative Religion*, 12:2-4, 1978, 175-188.

Pannikar, Raimon, "A Tribute" (to Bede Griffiths) in *The Other Half of My Soul: Bede Griffiths and the Hindu-Christian Dialogue*, ed. B. Bruteau, 30-33.

Parkes, Graham, *Composing the Soul: Reaches of Nietzsche's Psychology*, Chicago: University of Chicago, 1994.

— "The Putative Fascism of the Kyoto School and the Political Correctness of the Modern Academy," *Philosophy East and West*, 47:3, July 1997, 305-336.

— "Nietzsche and East Asian Thought: Influences, Impacts, and Resonances" in *The Cambridge Companion to Nietzsche*, ed. B. Magnus & K.M. Higgins, 356-383.

— "Nature and the Human Redivinized: Mahayana Buddhist Themes in *Thus Spake Zarathustra*," in *Nietzsche and the Divine*, ed. J. Lippitt & J. Urpeth, 181-199.

— (ed), *Heidegger and Eastern Thought*, Honolulu: Hawaii University, 1987.

— (ed), *Nietzsche and Asian Thought*, Honolulu: Hawaii University, 1991.

Parks, Mercedes Gallagher, *Introduction to Keyserling: An Account of the Man and His Work*, London: Jonathan Cape, 1934.

Parry, Benita, "Passage to More than India" in *Forster: A Collection of Critical Essays*, ed. M. Bradbury, 160-174.

Patterson, George, *Tibetan Journey*, London: Readers Book Club, 1956.

Paul, Diana, *Women in Buddhism: Images of the Feminine in the Mahayana Tradition*, Berkeley: University of California, 1985, 2nd ed.

Pennington, Basil M., *Thomas Merton, Brother Monk: The Quest for True Freedom*, New York: Continuum, 1997.

Perl, J. & Tuck, A., "The Hidden Advantage of Tradition: On the Significance of T.S. Eliot's Indic Studies," *Philosophy East and West*, 35:2, April 1985, 115-131.

Perry, Barbara, *Frithjof Schuon: Metaphysician and Artist*, Bloomington: World Wisdom Books, 1981.

Perry, Whitall, *The Widening Breach: Evolutionism in the Mirror of Cosmology*, Cambridge: Quinta Essentia, 1995.

— *Challenges to a Secular Society*, Washington DC: Foundation of Traditional Studies, 1996.

— "Drug-Induced Mysticism: The Mescalin Hypothesis," *Tomorrow*, 12:3, 1964, 192-198.

— "The Revolt Against Moses, A New Look at Psychoanalysis," *Tomorrow*, 14:2, 1966, 103-119.

— "Anti-Theology and the Riddles of Alcyone," *Studies in Comparative Religion* 6:3, 1972, 176-192.

— "The Bollingen Coomaraswamy Papers and Biography," *Studies in Comparative Religion*, 11:4, 1977.

— "Coomaraswamy: the Man, Myth and History," *Studies in Comparative Religion* 11:3, 1977, 159-165.

— "The Man and His Witness," (on A.K. Coomaraswamy) in *Ananda Coomaraswamy: Remembering and Remembering Again and Again*, ed. S.D.R. Singam, 3-7.

— "The Revival of Interest in Tradition" in *The Unanimous Tradition*, ed. R. Fernando, 3-16.

— Review of *The Secret of the Golden Flower* (with an Introduction by C. G. Jung) in *Studies in Comparative Religion*, 7:3, 1973, 187-192.

— Review of Christopher Evans' *Cults of Unreason* in *Studies in Comparative Religion*, 9:3, 1975, 183-187.

— Review of Frithjof Schuon's *Logic and Transcendence* in *Studies in Comparative Religion*, 9:4, Autumn 1975, 250-253.

— (ed), *A Treasury of Traditional Wisdom*, London: Allen & Unwin, 1971.

Petech, Luciano, "Giuseppe Tucci," *The Journal of the International Association of Buddhist Studies* 7, 1984, 137-142.

Phillips, John, "The Vedanta Movement in England," *Vedanta*, 271, September-October 1996, 216-222.

Phillips, K.J., "Hindu Avatars, Moslem Martyrs, and Primitive Dying Gods in E.M. Forster's *A Passage to India*," *Journal of Modern Literature*, 15:1, Summer 1988, 121-140.

Pickering, Carole, "Murray T. Titus: Missionary and Islamic Scholar," *International Bulletin of Missionary Research*, 19:3, July 1995, 118-120.

Pöggeler, Otto, "West-East Dialogue: Heidegger and Lao-tzu" in *Heidegger and Eastern Thought*, ed. G. Parkes, 47-78.

Pollock, Sheldon, "Indology, Power and the Case of Germany" in *Orientalism: A Reader*, ed. A. Macfie, 302-323.

— "Deep Orientalism? Notes on Sanskrit and Power Beyond the Raj" in *Orientalism and the Postcolonial Predicament*, ed. C. Breckenridge & P. van der Veer, 76-133.

Possamaï, Adam, "The Aquarian Utopia of the New Age," *Beyond the Divide* (Bendigo), 2:1, Winter 1999, 68-79.

Postal, Susan, "Zen Mind/Christian Mind: Practice across Traditions," *Buddhist-Christian Studies*, 14, 1994, 209-213.

Powers, J. & D. Curtin, "Mothering: Moral Cultivation in Buddhist and Feminist Ethics," *Philosophy East and West*, 15:2, 1994.

Prabhavananda, Swami & Christopher Isherwood (eds), *Shankara's Crest Jewel of Discrimination*, New York: Mentor, New York, 1970.

Prebish, Charles S., "Buddhist Studies American Style: A Shot in the Dark," *Religious Studies Review*, 9:4, October 1983, 323-330.

— "The Academic Study of Buddhism in the United States: A Current Analysis," *Religion*, 24, 1994, 271-278.

— "The Academic Study of Buddhism in America: A Silent Sangha," in *American Buddhism: Methods and Findings of Recent Scholarship*, ed. D. Williams & C. Queen, 183-214.

479

Prebish, Charles & Kenneth Tanaka (eds), *The Faces of Buddhism in America*, Berkeley: University of California, 1998.

Prothero, Stephen, *The White Buddhist: The Asian Odyssey of Henry Steel Olcott*, Bloomington: Indiana University, 1996.

— "Theosophy's Sinner/Saint: Recent Books on Madame Blavatsky," *Religious Studies Review*, 23:3, July 1997, 256-262.

Queen, Christopher & Sallie King, *Engaged Buddhism: Buddhist Liberation Movements in Asia*, Albany: SUNY, 1996.

Quinn, Jr, William W., *The Only Tradition*, Albany: SUNY, 1997.

Radhakrishnan, Sarvepalli, *Eastern Religions and Western Thought*, New York: Oxford University, 1959.

— *Selected Writings on Philosophy, Religion and Culture*, ed. Robert A. McDermott, New York: E.P. Dutton, 1970.

— *The Hindu View of Life*, London: Allen & Unwin, 1974.

Raine, Kathleen, *Defending Ancient Springs*, Ipswich: Golgonooza, 1985.

— *India Seen Afar*, New York: George Brazilier, 1991.

Rajan, Jesu, *Bede Griffiths and Sannyasa*, Bangalore: Asian Trading Co, 1989.

Rajan, Jesu & Judson Trapnell, Bede Griffiths Bibliography in *The Other Half of My Soul: Bede Griffiths and the Hindu-Christian Dialogue*, ed. B. Bruteau, 380-395.

Ralston, Helen, *Christian Ashrams: A New Religious Movement in Contemporary India*, Lewiston (NY): Edwin Mellen, 1987.

Randhava, M.S., "Rediscovery of Kangra Painting" in *Ananda Coomaraswamy, Remembering and Remembering Again and Again*, ed. S.D.R. Singam, 201-204.

Ranganathan, A., "Ananda Coomaraswamy: Confluence of East and West" in *Ananda Coomaraswamy, Remembering and Remembering Again and Again*, ed. S.D.R. Singam, 53-58.

Ravindran, Sankaran, *W.B. Yeats and Indian Tradition*, Delhi: Konark, 1990.

Rawlinson, Andrew, *The Book of Enlightened Masters: Western Teachers in Eastern Traditions*, Chicago: Open Court, 1997.

— "The Transmission of Theravada Buddhism to the West" in *Aspects of Religion: Essays in Honor of Ninian Smart*, ed. P. Masefield & D. Wiebe, 357-388.

Ray, Colette, "Western Psychology and Buddhist Teachings: Convergences and Divergences" in *Beyond Therapy*, ed. G. Claxton, 17-30.

Raymond, Lizelle, *To Live Within*, Baltimore: Penguin Books, 1973.

RBW, "Lama Anagarika Govinda (17.5.1898-14.1.1985) and the Arya Maitreya Mandala," *Buddhist Studies Review*, 2:1, 1985, 79-86.

Redington, James, "The Hindu-Christian Dialogue and the Interior Dialogue," *Theological Studies*, 44, 1983, 587-603.

Reynolds, John (trans. & ed.), *Self-Liberation through Seeing with Naked Awareness*, Barrytown: Station Hill, 1989.

Reynolds, P.L., *René Guénon: His Life and Work* (unpublished paper).

Rieff, Philip, *The Triumph of the Therapeutic*, Harmondsworth: Penguin 1973.

Riepe, Dale, *Indian Philosophy and Its Impact on American Thought*, Springfield: Charles C. Thomas, 1970.

Rocher, Rosane, "British Orientalism in the Eighteenth Century: The Dialectics of Knowledge and Government," in *Orientalism and the Postcolonial Predicament*, ed. C. Breckenridge & P. van der Veer, 215-249.

Rockmore, Tom & Joseph Margolis (eds), *The Heidegger Case: On Philosophy and Politics*, Philadelphia: Temple University, 1992.

Rodinson, Maxime, "The Western Image and Western Studies of Islam" in *The Legacy of Islam*, ed. J. Schacht & C. Bosworth, 9-62.

Rolland, Romain, *Life of Ramakrishna*, Calcutta: Advaita Ashrama, 1929.

— *Mahatma Gandhi: The Man who became One with Universal Being*, New York: Century & Co, 1924.

Rollmann, Hans, "Rudolf Otto and India," *Religious Studies Review*, 5:3, July 1979, 199-203.

Rolston III, Holmes, "Can the East Help the West to Value Nature?", *Philosophy East and West*, 37:2, 1987,172-190.

— "Secular Scientific Spirituality" in *Spirituality and the Secular Quest*, ed. P.H. Van Ness, New York: Crossroad, 1996, 387-413.

Ross, Nancy Wilson, *Three Ways of Asian Wisdom*, New York: Simon & Schuster, 1966.

Roszak, Theodore, *The Making of a Counter-culture*, London: Faber & Faber, 1970.

— *Where the Wasteland Ends*, New York: Doubleday, 1972.

— (ed), *Sources*, New York: Harper & Row, 1972.

Royster, James E., "Abhishiktananda: Hindu-Christian Monk," *Studies in Formative Spirituality*, 9:3. November 1988, 309-328.

Rudy, John G., "Engaging the Void: Emerson's Essay on Experience and the Zen Experience of Self-Emptying," *The Eastern Buddhist*, NS, 26:1, Spring 1993, 101-125.

Ruether, Rosemary Radford, *Gaia & God*, San Francisco: HarperSanFrancisco, 1992.

Russell, Bertrand, *A History of Western Philosophy* (1946), London: Unwin, 1989.

Sadik, Jalal al-'Azm, "Orientalism and Orientalism in Reverse" in *Orientalism: A Reader*, ed. A. Macfie, 217-238.

Sadler, A.W., "The Vintage Alan Watts," *The Eastern Buddhist*, NS, 7:1, May 1974, 143-150.

Sagan, Carl, *The Dragons of Eden*, New York: Ballantine Books, 1978.

Said, Edward, *Orientalism*, London: Penguin, 1978.

— *The World, the Text and the Critic*, Cambridge, Massachusetts: Harvard University, 1983.

— *Culture and Imperialism*, New York: Vintage, 1993.

— "Orientalism Reconsidered" (1986) in *Orientalism: A Reader*, ed. A. Macfie, 345-361.

Sangharakshita, *The Rainbow Road: From Tooting Broadway to Kalimpong: Memoirs of an English Buddhist*, Birmingham, Windhorse, 1997.

Sandler, Florence & Darrell Reeck, "The Masks of Joseph Campbell," *Religion*, 11, 1981, 1-20.

Sardar, Ziauddin, *Orientalism*, Buckingham: Open University, 1999.

Schact, Joseph & C.E. Bosworth (eds), *The Legacy of Islam*, Oxford: Oxford University Press, 1974.

Schloegl, Irmgard, (Myokyo-ni), *The Zen Way*, London: Sheldon Press, 1977.

— *Gentling the Bull*, London: Zen Center, 1987.

— "My Memory of Ruth Fuller Sasaki," *The Eastern Buddhist*, NS, 2:2, November 1969, 129-130.

— (ed), *Wisdom of the Zen Masters*, New York: New Directions, 1975.

Scholl, Steven (ed), *Common Era: Best New Writings on Religion*, Oregon: White Cloud, 1995.

Schrag, C., "Heidegger on Repetition and Historical Understanding," *Philosophy East and West*, 20:3, 1970.

Schumacher, E.F., *Small is Beautiful*, London: Sphere, 1974.

— *A Guide for the Perplexed*, London: Jonathan Cape, 1977.

Schumacher, Michael, *Dharma Lion: A Critical Biography of Allen Ginsberg*, New York: St Martin's Press, 1992.

Schuon, Frithjof, *Language of the Self*, Madras: Ganesh, 1959.

— *Stations of Wisdom*, London: Perennial Books (no date given); reprint of John Murray edition, London, 1961.

— *Light on the Ancient Worlds*, London: Perennial Books, 1966.

— *Spiritual Perspectives and Human Facts*, London: Perennial Books, 1967.

— *In the Tracks of Buddhism*, London: Allen & Unwin, 1968.

— *Dimensions of Islam*, London: Allen & Unwin, 1969.

— *The Transcendent Unity of Religions*, New York: Harper & Row, 1975 (also published by Quest: Wheaton, 1984 & 1993).

— *Logic and Transcendence*, New York: Harper & Row, 1975.

— *Understanding Islam*, London: Allen & Unwin, 1976.

— *Islam and the Perennial Philosophy*, London: World of Islam Festival, 1976.

— *Gnosis: Divine Wisdom*, London: Perennial Books, 1979.

— *Esoterism as Principle and as Way*, London: Perennial Books, 1981.

— *Sufism, Veil and Quintessence*, Bloomington: World Wisdom Books, 1981.

— *Castes and Races*, London: Perennial Books, 1982.

— *Survey of Metaphysics and Esoterism*, Bloomington: World Wisdom Books, 1986.

— *The Essential Writings of Frithjof Schuon*, ed. S.H. Nasr, New York: Amity House, 1986.

— *To Have a Center*, Bloomington: World Wisdom Books, 1990.

— *The Feathered Sun*, Bloomington: World Wisdom Books, 1990.

— *Roots of the Human Condition*, Bloomington: World Wisdom Books, 1991.

— *The Transfiguration of Man*, Bloomington: World Wisdom Books, 1995.

— *The Eye of the Heart*, Bloomington: World Wisdom Books, 1997.

— "The Psychological Imposture," *Tomorrow*, 14:2, 1966, 98-101.

— "Nature and Function of the Spiritual Master," *Studies in Comparative Religion* 1:2, 1967.

— "Foundations of an Integral Aesthetics," *Studies in Comparative Religion*, 10:3, 1976, 130-135.

— "The Problem of Sexuality," *Studies in Comparative Religion*, 11:1, Winter 1977, 2-17.

— "To be Man is to Know," *Studies in Comparative Religion* 13:1-2 1979, 117-118.

— "No Activity Without Truth," in *The Sword of Gnosis*, ed. J. Needleman, 27-39.

Scorer, R. & A. Veraik, *Spacious Skies*, London: David and Charles Newton-Abbot, 1984.

Schwab, Raymond, *The Oriental Renaissance: Europe's Discovery of India and the East, 1660-1880*, New York: Columbia University, 1984,

Schwartz, Tony, *What Really Matters: Searching for Wisdom in America*, New York: Bantam Books, 1995.

Segal, Robert A., "Joseph Campbell on Jews and Judaism," *Religion*, 22, 1992, 151-170.

— "Joseph Campbell the Perennial Philosopher: An Analysis of His Universalism" in *Paths to the Power of Myth: Joseph Campbell and the Study of Religion*, ed. D.C. Noel, 81-94.

— (ed) *Hero Myths*, Oxford: Blackwell, 2000.

Segaller, S. & Berger, M., *Jung: The Wisdom of the Dream*, Peribo: Chatswood (NSW), 1989.

Segura, José, "On Ken Wilber's Integration of Science and Religion," *Sacred Web*, 5, 2000, 71-83.

Sellon, Emily B. & Renée Weber, "Theosophy and the Theosophical Society" in *Modern Esoteric Spirituality*, ed. A. Faivre & J. Needleman, 311-329.

Shannon, William H., *Thomas Merton's Dark Path: The Inner Experience of a Contemplative*, New York: Farrar, Straus & Giroux, 1981.

— *Silent Lamp: The Thomas Merton Story*, New York: Crossroad, 1992.

Sharf, Robert, "The Zen of Japanese Nationalism" in *Curators of the Buddha*, ed. D. Lopez, 107-160.

Sharma, Arvind, "The Meaning and Goals of Inter-religious Dialogue," *Journal of Dharma*, 8:3, July-September 1983, 225-247.

— "Pearls on a String," in *Fragments of Infinity*, ed. A. Sharma, 3-7.

— (ed) *Fragments of Infinity: Essays in Religion and Philosophy*, a *festschrift* in Honor of Huston Smith, Bridport: Prism, 1991.

— & Katherine Young (eds), *Women in World Religions*, Albany: SUNY, 1987.

Sharpe, Eric J., *Not to Destroy But to Fulfill: The Contribution of J.N. Farquhar to Protestant Missionary Thought in India before 1914*, Upsalla: Gleerup, 1965.

— *Comparative Religion*, London: Duckworth, 1975.

— *Faith Meets Faith: Some Christian Attitudes to Hinduism in the Nineteenth and Twentieth Centuries*, London: SCM, 1977.

— *The Universal Gita: Western Images of the Bhagavadgita*, London: Duckworth, 1985.

— "Some Problems of Method in the Study of Religion," *Religion* 1:1, 1971.

— "The 'Johannine' Approach to the Question of Religious Plurality," *Ching Feng*, 22:3-4, 1980, 117-127.

— "The Legacy of Lars Peter Larsen," *The International Bulletin of Missionary Research*, 18:3, July 1994, 119-125.

— "The Legacy of Amy Carmichael," *The International Bulletin of Missionary Research*, 20:3, 1996, 121-125.

— "The Goals of Inter-religious Dialogue" in *Truth and Dialogue: the Relationship of the World Religions*, ed. John Hick, 77-95.

— "To Hinduism through Gandhi" in *The Wisdom of the East*, Sydney: ABC, 1979, 52-63.

Shaw, D.W.D., *The Dissuaders*, London: SCM, 1978.

Sheehan, Thomas, "Reading a Life: Heidegger and Hard Times" in *The Cambridge Companion to Heidegger*, ed. C. Guignon, 70-96.

— "Myth and Violence: the Fascism of Julius Evola and Alain de Benoist," *Social Research*, 48:1, 45-73.

Sheldrake, Rupert, *The Rebirth of Nature*, Rochester: Park Street Press, 1994.

— "Mysticism and the New Science" in *The Other Half of My Soul: Bede Griffiths and the Hindu-Christian Dialogue*, ed. B. Bruteau, 336-355.

Sherburne, Richard, "A Christian-Buddhist Dialog? Some Notes on Desideri's Tibetan Manuscripts" in *Reflections on Tibetan Culture: Essays in Memory of Turrell V. Wylie*, ed. L. Epstein & R.F. Sherburne, 295-305.

Sherrard, Philip, *The Rape of Man and Nature*, Colombo: Sri Lanka Institute of Traditional Studies, 1987.

— *Human Image: World Image*, Cambridge: Golgonooza Press, 1992.

— *Christianity: Lineaments of a Sacred Tradition*, Brookline: Holy Cross Orthodox Press, 1998.

— "An Introduction to the Religious Thought of C. G. Jung," *Studies in Comparative Religion*, 3:1, 1969, 33-49.

— "The Sexual Relationship in Christian Thought," *Studies in Comparative Religion*, 5:3, Summer 1971, 151-172.

Sherrill, Martha, *The Buddha from Brooklyn*, New York: Random House, 2000.

Shewring, Walter, "Ananda Coomaraswamy and Eric Gill" in *Ananda Coomaraswamy, Remembering and Remembering Again and Again*, ed. S.D.R. Singam, 89-90.

Shiro, Naito, "Yeats and Zen Buddhism," *The Eastern Buddhist*, NS, 5:2, October 1972, 171-178.

Shoji, Yamada, "The Myth of Zen in the Art of Archery," *Japanese Journal of Religious Studies*, 28:1-2, 2001, 1-29.

Sibley, Dennis, "The Legacy of Alan Watts: A Personal View," *The Middle Way*, 58:4, Feb 1984, 219-220.

Silberman, Steve, "How Beat Happened," http://www.ezone.org:1080/ez/e2/articles/digaman.html.

Singam, S.D.R. (ed), *Ananda Coomaraswamy: Remembering and Remembering Again and Again*, Kuala Lumpur: privately published, 1974.

Sinha, Harendra Prasad, *Religious Philosophy of Tagore and Radhakrishnan: A Comparative and Analytical Study*, Delhi: Motilal Banarsidass, 1993.

Smart, Ninian, *A Dialogue of Religions*, Westport: Greenwood Press, 1981.

— *Beyond Ideology: Religion and the Future of Western Civilization*, London: Collins, 1981.

— *Religious Pluralism and Truth: Essays on Cross-cultural Philosophy of Religion*, ed. Thomas Dean, New York: SUNY, 1995.

— "Rudolf Otto and Religious Experience" in *Philosophers and Religious Truth*, ed. N. Smart, 109-138.

— (ed) *Philosophers and Religious Truth*, New York: Macmillan, 1970.

— & B.S. Murthy (eds), *East-West Encounters in Philosophy and Religion*, London: Sangram Books, 1997.

Smith, Joel R., "Religious Diversity, Hindu-Christian Dialogue, and Bede Griffiths,"

Proceedings of the Eighth International Symposium on Asian Studies, Hong Kong: Asian Research Service, 1986, 1413-1429.

Smith, Huston, *The Religions of Man*, New York: Harper, 1958 (revised and expanded as *The World's Religions: Our Great Wisdom Traditions*, San Francisco: Harper, 1991).

— *Forgotten Truth: the Primordial Tradition*, New York: Harper & Row, 1977.

— *Beyond the Post-Modern Mind*, Wheaton: Theosophical Publishing House, 1982.

— *Essays on World Religion*, ed. M. Darrol Bryant, New York: Paragon House, 1992 (includes a bibliography of Smith's work).

— *Why Religion Matters*, San Francisco: HarperSanFrancisco, 2001.

— "D.T. Suzuki: Some Memories," *The Eastern Buddhist*, NS, 2:1, August 1967, 150-152.

— Introduction to the second Quest edition of Frithjof Schuon, *The Transcendent Unity of Religions*, ix-xxvii.

— "Frithjof Schuon's *The Transcendent Unity of Religions*: Pro," *Journal of the American Academy of Religion*, 154:4, 1976, 721-724.

— "The Ambiguity of Matter," *Sophia: the Journal of Traditional Studies*, 5:1, Summer 1999, 17-34.

— Dialogue with Rabbi Zamna Schacter-Shalomi in *The Heart of Learning: Spirituality in Education*, ed. Steven Glazer, New York: Putnam, 1999, 217-231.

— Review of Marco Pallis' *A Buddhist Spectrum* in *The Eastern Buddhist*, NS, 15:2, Autumn, 1982, 145.

— & David Ray Griffin, *Primordial Truth and Postmodern Theology*, Albany: SUNY, 1989.

Smith, W. Cantwell, *Towards a World Theology*, Philadelphia: Westminster, 1981.

— "Comparative Religion: Whither—and Why?" in *The History of Religions: Essays in Methodology*, ed. M. Eliade & J. Kitagawa, 31-58.

Smith, Wolfgang, *Cosmos and Transcendence: Breaking Through the Barrier of Scientist Belief*, La Salle: Sherwood Sugden & Co, 1984.

Smyth, Stuart J., "Gauging Missionary Successes and Failures," *Asia Journal of Theology*, 15:1, April 2001, 105-114.

Snellgrove, David, "An Appreciation of Hugh Richardson" in *Tibet Studies in Honor of Hugh Richardson*, ed. M. Aris & Aung San Suu Kyi, vii-xv.

Snellgrove, David & H. Richardson, *A Cultural History of Tibet*, Boston: Shambhala, 1995.

Snelling, John, *The Sacred Mountain: Travelers and Pilgrims at Mount Kailas in Western Tibet, and the Great Universal Symbol of the Sacred Mountain*, London: East West Publications, 1983.

Snodgrass, Adrian, *The Matrix and Diamond World Mandalas in Shingon Buddhism* (2 vols), New Delhi: P.K.Goel/Aditya Prakashan, 1988.

— *Architecture, Time and Eternity: Studies in the Stellar and Temporal Symbolism of Traditional Buildings* (2 vols), New Delhi: P.K.Goel/Aditya Prakashan, 1990.

— *The Symbolism of the Stupa*, Delhi: Motilal Banarsidass, 1992.

Snyder, Gary, *The Real Work: Interviews and Talks, 1964-1979*, ed. Wm. Scott McLean, New York: New Directions, 1980.

— *Passage Through India*, San Francisco: Grey Fox Press, 1983.

— *Turtle Island*, Boston: Shambhala, 1993.

— *A Place in Space: Ethics, Aesthetics and Watersheds*, Washington DC: Counterpoint, 1995.

— *The Gary Snyder Reader: Prose, Poetry, and Translations, 1952-1998*, Washington DC: Counterpoint, 1999 (Foreword by Jim Dodge, xv-xx).

— "Epitaph for Alan Watts," *The Eastern Buddhist*, NS, 7:1, May 1974, 142.

Söderblom, Nathan, "Holiness" in *Encyclopaedia of Religion and Ethics, Vol. 6*, ed. J. Hastings.

Sogyal, Rinpoche, *The Tibetan Book of Living and Dying*, London: Rider, 1992.

Sohl, Robert & Audrey Carr, (eds), *The Gospel According to Zen*, New York: New American Library, 1970.

Sontag, Susan, *A Susan Sontag Reader*, ed. Elizabeth Hardwick, Harmondsworth: Penguin, 1983.

Sophia, Special Issue, "In Memory: Frithjof Schuon," *Sophia: The Journal of Traditional Studies*, 4:2, Winter 1988.

Spender, Stephen, *T.S. Eliot*, New York: Viking, 1976.

Spiegelman, J. Marvin & A.U. Vasavada, *Hinduism and Jungian Psychology*, Phoenix: Falcon Press, 1987.

Spink, Katherine, *A Sense of the Sacred: A Biography of Bede Griffiths*, Blackburn (Victoria): Collins Dove, 1988.

Sprung, Mervyn, "Nietzsche's Trans-European Eye" in *Nietzsche and Asian Thought*, ed. G. Parkes, 76-90.

Stackhouse, Max L., "Missions: Missionary Activity," *The Encyclopedia of Religions, Vol. 9*, ed. M. Eliade, 563-570.

Steiner, George, *In Bluebeard's Castle*, New Haven: Yale University, 1971.

— *Heidegger*, Glasgow: Fontana/Collins, 1978.

— "Ecstasies, Not Arguments," Review of Eliade's *Journals* in *Times Literary Supplement*, 4565, 28 September-4 October, 1990.

Stevens, John, *Lust for Enlightenment: Buddhism and Sex*, Boston: Shambhala, 1990.

Stewart, Harold, *A Net of Fireflies*, Rutland: C.E. Tuttle, 1960.

— *By the Old Walls of Kyoto: A Year's Cycle of Landscape Poems and Prose Commentaries*, New York: Weatherhill, 1981.

Stoddart, William, "Right Hand of Truth" in the Titus Burckhardt Memorial Issue of *Studies in Comparative Religion*, 16:1 & 2, Winter-Spring 1984, 3-8.

Storr, Anthony, *Feet of Clay: A Study of Gurus*, London, HarperCollins, 1996.

Streng, Frederick J., "Mutual Transformation: An Answer to a Religious Question," *Buddhist-Christian Studies*, 13, 1993, 121-126.

Strenski, Ivan, *Four Theories of Myth in Twentieth-Century History*, Iowa City: Iowa University, 1987.

Stuart, J.M.D., "Sri Ramana Maharshi and Abhishiktananda," *Vidjajyoti*, April 1980, 167-176.

Suleri, Sara, *The Rhetoric of English India*, Chicago: University of Chicago, 1992.

Surya Das, Lama, *Awakening the Buddha Within*, New York: Broadway Books, 1998.

Suyin, Han, *Lhasa, the Open City*, London: Jonathan Cape, 1976.

Suzuki, D.T., *Essays in Zen Buddhism*, (third series), ed. Christmas Humphreys, London, 1970.

— *Mysticism: Christian and Buddhist*, London: Allen & Unwin, 1979.

— *Essays in Zen Buddhism*, (first series) (1927), New York: Grove Press, 1986.

— *The Buddha of Infinite Light*, Boston: Shambhala, 1997 (original title *Shin Buddhism*).

— "Reginald Horace Blyth (1898-1964)," *The Eastern Buddhist*, NS, 1:1, September 1965, 133-134.

Suzuki, Shunryu, *Zen Mind, Beginner's Mind*, San Francisco: Weatherhill, 1970.

Sworder, Roger, *Mining, Metallurgy and the Meaning of Life*, Quakers Hill (NSW): Quakers Hill Press, 1995.

Taber, John, Review of Wilhelm Halbfass' *India and Europe* in *Philosophy East and West*, 41, April 1991, 229-240.

Tähtinen, Uto, *Ahimsa: Non-violence in the Indian Tradition*, London: Rider, 1976.

Tarnas, Richard, *The Passion of the Western Mind*, London: Pimlico, 1991.

Tarrant, John, *The Light Inside the Dark: Zen, Soul and the Spiritual Life*, New York: Harper Collins, 1998.

Tart, Charles T. (ed), *Transpersonal Psychologies*, New York: Harper & Row, 1975.

Tate, Allen (ed), *T.S. Eliot: The Man and His Work*, Harmondsworth: Penguin, 1971.

Teasdale, Wayne, "Nature Mysticism as the Basis of Eco-spirituality," *Studies in Formative Spirituality*, 12:2, May 1991, 215-231.

— "*Sannyasa*: the Primordial Tradition of Renunciation—A Radical Monastic Proposal," *Cistercian Studies Quarterly*, 31:1, 1996, 75-93.

— "Bede Griffiths as Visionary Guide," in *The Other Half of My Soul: Bede Griffiths and the Hindu-Christian Dialogue*, ed. B. Bruteau, 2-25.

— "Christianity and the Eastern Traditions: the Possibility of Mutual Growth" in *The Other Half of My Soul*, ed. B. Bruteau, 126-163.

Thien-an, Thich, *Zen Philosophy, Zen Practice*, Berkeley: Dharma/College of Oriental Studies, 1975.

Thoreau, Henry David, *The Portable Thoreau*, ed. Carl Bode, New York: Viking, 1964.

Thurman, Robert, "Seeking the Religious Roots of Pluralism," *Journal of Ecumenical Studies*, 34:3, Summer 1997, 394-398.

— & Tad Wise, *Circling the Sacred Mountain: A Spiritual Adventure Through the Himalayas*, New York: Doubleday, 2000.

Thurston, Bonnie Bowman, "The Conquered Self: Emptiness and God in a Buddhist-Christian Dialogue," *Japanese Journal of Religious Studies*, 12:4, December 1985, 343-353.

— "Self and the Word: Two Directions of the Spiritual Life," *Cistercian Studies*, 18:2, Summer 1983, 149-155.

— "Thomas Merton: Pioneer of Buddhist-Christian Dialogue," *The Catholic World*, 233:129, May 1, 1990, 126-128.

Tibawi, A.L., *English Speaking Orientalists*, London: Luzac, 1964 (reprinted in *Orientalism: A Reader*, ed. A. Macfie, 57-78).

Tillich, Paul, *Christianity and the Encounter with World Religions*, New York: Columbia University, 1965.

Tischler, Henry, Interview with Henry Tischler, "Allen Ginsberg—Journals Mid-Fifties: 1954-1958," http://www.authorsspeak.com/ginsberg.

— "San Francisco Says Goodbye to a Bard," *San Francisco Chronicle*, Monday April 21, 1997, A1.

— http://www.tricycle.com/ginsberg.html.

— "Writings about Allen Ginsberg," http://www.charm.net/~brooklyn/Biblio/GinsbergBiblio.html.

Toms, Michael (ed), *Buddhism in the West*, Carlsbad, California: Hay House, 1998.

Tonkinson, Carole (ed), *Big Sky Mind: Buddhism and the Beat Generation*, New York: Riverhead, 1995.

Tourniac, J., *Propos René Guénon*, Paris: 1973.

Tracy, David, *Dialogue with the Other: The Inter-religious Dialogue*, Louvain: Peters, 1990.

Trapnell, Judson B., *Bede Griffiths: A Life in Dialogue*, Albany: SUNY, 2001.

— "Bede Griffiths, Mystical Knowing, and the Unity of Religions," *Philosophy and Theology*, 7:4, Summer 1993, 355-379.

— "Two Models of Christian Dialogue with Hinduism. 1. Bede Griffiths and Abhishiktananda," *Vidyajyoti*, 60, 1996, 101-110.

— "Multireligious Experience and the Study of Mysticism" in *The Other Half of My Soul: Bede Griffiths and the Hindu-Christian Dialogue*, ed. B. Bruteau, 198-223.

Tricycle, "Ancestors: R.H. Blyth" (website).

Trungpa, Chögyam, *Cutting Through Spiritual Materialism*, Berkeley: Shambhala, 1973.

— *Born in Tibet*, Boston: Shambhala, 1995.

Tucci, Giuseppe, *The Theory and Practice of the Mandala*, Rider: London, 1961.

— *Tibet, Land of Snows*, London: Paul Elek, 1967.

— *The Religions of Tibet*, Berkeley: University of California, 1980.

— *To Lhasa and Beyond*, Ithaca: Snow Lion Books, 1983.

— "A Propos East and West: Considerations of an Historian," *East and West*, 8, 1958, 343-349.

Tucker, Mary Evelyn, "Confucianism and Christianity: Resources for an Ecological Spirituality," *Ching Feng*, 34:2, June 1991, 94-100.

— & John A. Grim (eds), *Worldviews and Ecology*, Bucknell University Press, 1994.

Turner, B.S., *Marx and the End of Orientalism*, London: Allen & Unwin, 1979.

Turner, Harold & Peter McKenzie, *Commentary on "The Idea of the Holy": A Guide for Students*, Aberdeen: Aberdeen Peoples Press, no date.

Tweed, Thomas, *The American Encounter with Buddhism, 1844-1912*, Bloomington: Indiana University, 1992.

— "Night-Stand Buddhists and Other Creatures: Sympathizers, Adherents, and the Study of Religion," in *American Buddhism: Methods and Findings of Recent Scholarship*, ed. D. Williams & C. Queen, 71-90.

Tworkov, Helen, *Zen in America*, New York: Kodansha International, 1994.

Urban, Hugh B., "Zorba the Buddha: Capitalism, Charisma and the Cult of Bhagwan Shree Rajneesh," *Religion*, 26, 1996, 161-182.

— "The Cult of Ecstasy: Tantrism, the New Age and the Spiritual Logic of Late Capitalism," *History of Religions*, 39:3, February 2000, 268-304.

Valsan, Michel, "Notes on the Shaikh al-'Alawi, 1869-1934," *Studies in Comparative Religion*, 5:3, Summer 1971, 145-150.

Van Bragt, Jan, "An East-West Spiritual Exchange: An Unusual Happening in the Religious World of 1979," *The Eastern Buddhist*, NS, 12:1, 1980, 141-150.

Van der Post, Laurens, *The Heart of the Hunter*, Harmondsworth: Penguin, 1965.

Van der Wetering, Janwillem, *The Empty Mirror*, Boston: Houghton Mifflin, 1973.

— *A Glimpse of Nothingness*, London: Routledge & Kegan Paul, 1974.

Van Ness, Peter H. (ed), *Spirituality and the Secular Quest*, New York: Crossroad, 1996.

Vasquez, Juan A., "A Metaphysics of Culture," in *Ananda Coomaraswamy, Remembering and Remembering Again and Again*, ed. S.D.R. Singam, 225-237.

Vattakuzhy, Emmanuel, *Indian Christian Sannyasa and Swami Abhishiktananda*, Bangalore: Theological Publications in India, 1981.

Verhoeven, Martin J., "Americanizing the Buddha: Paul Carus and the Transformation of Asian Thought" in *The Faces of Buddhism in America*, ed. C. Prebish & K. Tanaka, 196-206.

Versluis, Arthur, *American Transcendentalism and Asian Religions*, New York: Oxford University, 1993.

Victoria, Brian, *Zen at War*, New York: Weatherhill, 1997.

Vidyatmananda, Swami, "A Holy Man of Europe: Swami Atulananda," *Vedanta for East and West*, Issue 238, March-April 1991, 32-48.

Vinall, Bruce, *The Resonance of Quality: Paintings as Maps of Consciousness*, unpublished PhD thesis, La Trobe University Bendigo, 2002.

Vinson, James (ed), *Novelists and Prose Writers*, New York: St. Martin's Press, 1979.

Vrajaprana, Pravrajika, "What Do Hindus Do?—the Role of the Vedanta Societies in North America," *Cross Currents*, 47:1, 1997, 69-85.

— (ed), *Living Wisdom: Vedanta in the West*, Hollywood: Vedanta Press, 1994.

Waardenburg, Jacques (ed), *Classical Approaches to the Study of Religion, Vol.1: Introduction and Anthology*, The Hague: Mouton, 1973.

Wach, Joachim, *Types of Religious Experience*, Chicago: University of Chicago, 1951.

— *The Comparative Study of Religion*, New York: Columbia University, 1958.

Waddell, L. Austine, *Lhasa and Its Mysteries*, New York: Dover, 1905.

Waley, Alison, *A Half of Two Lives*, Weidenfeld & Nicholson, London, 1982.

Waley, Arthur, *Three Ways of Thought in Ancient China* (1939), New York: Doubleday, 1983.

— "Zen Buddhism and Its Relation to Art" from *An Introduction to the Study of Chinese Painting*, London: Ernest Benn, 1923, 226-234 (reprint London: Luzac, 1959).

Ward, B., "Christianity and the Modern Eclipse of Nature: Two Perspectives," *Journal of the American Academy of Religion*, 63:4, Winter 1995, 823-843.

Wasserstrom, Steven, *Religion After Religion: Gershom Scholem, Mircea Eliade and Henry Corbin at Eranos*, Princeton: Princeton University, 1999.

Waterfield, Robin, *René Guénon and the Future of the West*, London: Crucible, 1987.

— "Baron Julius Evola and the Gnostic Tradition," *Gnosis*, 14, Winter 1989-90, 18-20.

487

Journeys East

Watson, Ian, "The Anti-Wisdom of Modern Philosophy: A Passing Note," *Studies in Comparative Religion*, 6:4, Autumn 1972, 221-224.

Watts, Alan, *Behold the Spirit*, New York: Pantheon Books, 1947.

— *Beat Zen, Square Zen, and Zen*, San Francisco: City Lights Books, 1959.

— *The Way of Zen*, Harmondsworth: Penguin, 1962.

— *The Joyous Cosmology*, New York: Vintage, 1965.

— *Does It Matter*, New York: Vintage, 1971

— *In My Own Way*, New York: Vintage, 1972.

— *This is It, and Other Essays on Zen and Spiritual Experience*, New York: Vintage, 1973.

— *Psychotherapy East and West* (1961), Harmondsworth: Penguin, 1973.

— *The Book on the Taboo Against Knowing Who You Are*, London: Sphere, 1973.

— *The Early Writings of Alan Watts*, ed. John Snelling, Mark Watts & Dennis Sibley, Berkeley: Celestial Books, 1987.

— & Al Chung-liang Huang, *Tao, The Watercourse Way*, New York: Pantheon, 1975.

Weber, J.G., *In Quest of the Absolute: The Life and Work of Jules Monchanin*, Introduction by Bede Griffiths, Kalamazoo: Cistercian Publications, 1977.

Wehr, Gerhard, *Jung: A Biography*, Boston: Shambhala, 1988.

— "C.G. Jung and Christian Esotericism," in *Modern Esoteric Spirituality*, ed. A. Faivre & J. Needleman, 381-399.

— "The Life and Work of Karlfried Graf Dürckheim," http://tedn.hypermart.net/trans3.htm.

Weil, Andrew, *The Natural Mind*, Harmondsworth: Penguin, 1975.

Welbon, G.R., "Zimmer, Heinrich" in *The Encyclopedia of Religion, Vol. 15*, ed. M. Eliade, 568-569.

Welwood, John (ed), *Awakening the Heart: East/West Approaches to Psychotherapy and the Healing Relationship*, Boulder: Shambhala, 1983.

Wentz, Richard E., "The Prospective Eye of Inter-religious Dialogue," *Japanese Journal of Religious Studies*, 14:1, 3-15.

Werblowsky, R.J. Zwi, "Universal Religion and Universalist Religion," *International Journal for Philosophy of Religion*, 2:1, 1971.

— "The Western Perception of China 1700-1900," *Dialogue & Alliance*, 4:2, Summer 1990, 60-70.

White, Jr, Lynn, "The Historical Roots of Our Ecologic Crisis," *Science*, 155: 3767, 10th March, 1967. (This essay can be found in various places, including *Religion for a New Generation*, ed. J. Needleman *et al.*, 231-239.)

Wiggins, James B., "Reflections on an Unforgettable Colleague: Huston Smith," in *Fragments of Infinity*, ed. A. Sharma, 14-18.

Wilber, Ken, *The Holographic Paradigm and Other Paradoxes*, Boulder: Shambhala, 1982.

— *No Boundary: Eastern and Western Approaches to Personal Growth*, Boston: Shambhala, 1985.

— *The Eye of the Spirit: An Integral Vision for a World Gone Slightly Mad*, Boston: Shambhala, 1997.

— (ed), *Quantum Questions: Mystical Writings of the World's Great Physicists*, Boston: Shambhala, 1984.

Wilby, Sorrell, *Tibet, a Woman's Lone Trek across a Mysterious Land*, Melbourne: Macmillan, 1988.

Wilde, Oscar, "The Decay of Lying" in *The Complete Works of Oscar Wilde*, ed. Vyvyan Holland, London: Collins, 1966, 970-992.

Williams, Duncan R. & Christopher S. Queen (eds), *American Buddhism: Methods and Findings of Recent Scholarship*, Richmond (Surrey): Curzon, 1999.

Williams, Raymond, *Culture and Society*, London: Hogarth Press, 1990, rev. ed.

Willis, Janice D. (ed), *Feminine Ground: Essays on Women and Tibet*, Ithaca: Snow Lion, 1995.

— "Diversity and Race: New *Koans* for American Buddhism" in *Women's Buddhism, Buddhism's Women*, ed. Ellison Banks Findly, 303-316.

Willy, Margaret, "Somerset Maugham" in *Novelists and Prose Writers*, ed. James Vinson, New York: St. Martin's Press, 1979, 822-826.

Wilson, Bruce M., "'From Mirror After Mirror': Yeats and Eastern Thought," *Comparative Literature*, 34:1, 1982, 28-46.

Wilson, E.O., *Consilience: The Unity of Knowledge*, New York: Knopf, 1998.

Wilson, Peter Lamborn, Review of Joseph Needham's *Science and Civilization in China, Vol. 5*, in *Studies in Comparative Religion*, 9:3, Summer 1975, 187-191.

Windshuttle, Keith, *The Killing of History*, New York: Free Press, 1996.

Winkler, Ken, *Pilgrim of the Clear Light: The Biography of Dr. Walter Y. Evans-Wentz*, Berkeley: Dawnfire, 1981.

— *A Thousand Journeys: the Biography of Lama Anagarika Govinda*, Shaftesbury: Element, 1990.

Woodcock, George, *Thomas Merton, Monk and Poet*, Vancouver: Douglas & McIntyre, 1978.

— *Gandhi*, London: Fontana, 1972.

Wynn, Mark, "Primal Religions and the Sacred Significance of Nature," *Sophia* (Melbourne), 36:2, September-October 1997, 88-110.

Yuen-tai, So, "William Johnston's Contemplation Approach to Buddhist-Christian Dialogue," *Ching Feng*, 42:1-2, March-June 1999, 83-105.

Zaehner, R.C., *Matter and Spirit: Their Convergence in Eastern Religions, Marx and Teilhard de Chardin*, New York: Harper & Row, 1963.

Zaleski, Philip, "Farewell and Far Out!" (Review of Alan Watts, *Zen and the Beat Way*), *New York Times Book Review*, September 14, 1997, 46.

— Review of Monica Furlong's *Genuine Fake*, http://socrates.cs.man.ac.uk/reviews/watts-amiss.html.

Zarandi, Mehrdad M. (ed), *Science and the Myth of Progress*, Bloomington: World Wisdom, 2004.

Zhang, Longzi, "The Myth of the Other: China in the Eyes of the West," *Critical Inquiry*, 15:1, 1988, 108-131.

Zimmer, Heinrich, *Myths and Symbols in Indian Art and Civilization*, ed. J. Campbell, Bollingen Series, Princeton: Princeton University, 1946.

— *The King and the Corpse: Tales of the Soul's Conquest of Evil*, ed. J. Campbell, Bollingen Series, Princeton: Princeton University, 1948.

— *Philosophies of India*, ed. J. Campbell, Bollingen Series, Princeton: Princeton University, 1951.

— *The Art of Indian Asia: Its Mythology and Transformations* (2 vols), ed. J. Campbell, Bollingen Series, Princeton: Princeton University, 1955.

— *Artistic Form and Yoga in the Sacred Images of India*, Princeton: Princeton University, 1984.

— "On the Significance of Indian Tantric Yoga" in *Spiritual Disciplines: Papers from the Eranos Yearbooks, Vol. 4*, ed. J. Campbell, Bollingen Series, Princeton: Princeton University, 1960.

— "The Impress of Dr. Jung on My Profession," in *Heinrich Zimmer: Coming into His Own*, ed. M. Case, 43-48.

Zimmerman, Michael E., *Eclipse of the Self: The Development of Heidegger's Concept of Authenticity*, Athens: Ohio University, 1982.

— "Heidegger, Buddhism and Deep Ecology" in *The Cambridge Companion to Heidegger*, ed. C.B. Guignon, 240-269.

Zinsser, William (ed), *Spiritual Quests: The Art and Craft of Religious Writing*, Boston: Houghton Mifflin, 1988.

Ziolkowski, Eric J., "The Literary Bearing of Chicago's World's Parliament of Religions," *The Eastern Buddhist*, NS, 26:1, Spring 1993, 10-25.

Zukav, Gary, *The Dancing Wu Li Masters*, New York: Bantam Books, 1980.

Acknowledgments

The following people have been helpful in ways too numerous and varied to catalogue here. They may each be assured of my gratitude. All the usual provisos ("all errors are mine" etc.) apply.

Mervyn Bendle
Cecil Bethell
Rod Blackhirst
Stuart Brain
Brian Coman
James Crouch
Loris Ferguson
Andrea Francis
Gerry Gill
Paul Goble
Peter Kelly
Susana Marin
Clinton Minnaar
Mary-Kathryne Nason
Seyyed Hossein Nasr
John Paraskevopoulos
John Reiss
Tim Scott
Huston Smith
William Stoddart
Roger Sworder
Arthur Versluis
Stephen Williams
Louise Wilson

I particularly acknowledge Ranjit Fernando who has given me every encouragement and support in the task of bringing the traditionalist exposition of the *sophia perennis* to a wider audience. I am more deeply indebted than I can say to Barry McDonald and Michael Fitzgerald at World Wisdom. To these names must be added those of three generations of my family to whom this book is dedicated: Rose, Misha, Joshua, Danni, Diana, Russell, Pamela, Wendy and Peter.

Biographical Notes

HARRY OLDMEADOW was born in Melbourne, Australia in 1947. His parents were Christian missionaries in India where he spent nine years of his childhood and developed an early interest in the civilizations of the East. He studied history, politics, and literature at the Australian National University, obtaining a First Class Honors degree in history. In 1971 a Commonwealth Overseas Research Scholarship led to further studies at Oxford University, followed by extensive travel in Europe and North Africa. In 1980 he completed a Masters dissertation on the work of the renowned author Frithjof Schuon and the other principal traditionalist writers. This study was awarded the University of Sydney Medal for excellence in research and was eventually published under the title *Traditionalism: Religion in the light of the Perennial Philosophy.*

Dr. Oldmeadow is currently the Coordinator of Philosophy and Religious Studies at La Trobe University, Bendigo, Australia. His intellectual interests include not only the traditionalist school of thinkers but the mystical and esoteric dimensions of the major religious traditions, especially Christianity, Hinduism, and Buddhism. He also has an abiding interest in the primal traditions of the American Plains Indians and the Aborigines of Australia. Over the last decade he has published extensively in such journals as *Sacred Web, Sophia,* and *Asian Philosophy.* He currently resides with his wife and younger son on a small property outside Bendigo.

HUSTON SMITH is Thomas J. Watson Professor of Religion and Distinguished Adjunct Professor Emeritus, Syracuse University. He is widely regarded as the most accessible contemporary authority on the history of religions and is a leading figure in the field of comparative religion. His best-selling work *The World's Religions* (formerly *The Religions of Man*) has sold over two million copies. His many books include *Forgotten Truth: The Common Vision of the World's Religions, Beyond the Post-Modern Mind,* and *Why Religion Matters: The Fate of the Human Spirit in an Age of Disbelief.* His discovery of Tibetan multiphonic chanting was lauded as "an important landmark in the study of music," and his film documentaries on Hinduism, Tibetan Buddhism, and Sufism have won numerous international awards. In 1996 Bill Moyers hosted a five-part PBS television series entitled *The Wisdom of Faith with Huston Smith.*

Index of Persons

For a glossary of all key foreign words used in books published by World Wisdom, including metaphysical terms in English, consult: www.DictionaryofSpiritualTerms.org.
This on-line Dictionary of Spiritual Terms provides extensive definitions, examples and related terms in other languages.

Titles in the Perennial Philosophy series by World Wisdom

A Buddhist Spectrum by Marco Pallis, 2003

The Essential Ananda K. Coomaraswamy, edited by Rama P. Coomaraswamy, 2004

The Essential Titus Burckhardt: Reflections on Sacred Art, Faiths, and Civilizations, edited by William Stoddart, 2003

Every Branch in Me: Essays on the Meaning of Man, edited by Barry McDonald, 2002

Islam, Fundamentalism, and the Betrayal of Tradition: Essays by Western Muslim Scholars, edited by Joseph E. B. Lumbard, 2004

Journeys East: 20th Century Western Encounters with Eastern Religious Traditions by Harry Oldmeadow, 2004

Living in Amida's Universal Vow: Essays in Shin Buddhism, edited by Alfred Bloom, 2004

Paths to the Heart: Sufism and the Christian East, edited by James S. Cutsinger, 2002

Returning to the Essential: Selected Writings of Jean Biès, translated by Deborah Weiss-Dutilh, 2004

Science and the Myth of Progress, edited by Mehrdad M. Zarandi, 2003

Seeing God Everywhere: Essays on Nature and the Sacred, edited by Barry McDonald, 2003